THE ULTIMATE
THAI
AND ASIAN COOKBOOK

THE ULTIMATE
THAI
AND ASIAN COOKBOOK

All the traditions, ingredients and techniques, with over
300 spicy and aromatic recipes illustrated step-by-step

Deh-Ta Hsiung, Becky Johnson and Sallie Morris

LORENZ BOOKS

This edition is published by Lorenz Books, an imprint of Anness Publishing Ltd,
Hermes House, 88–89 Blackfriars Road, London SE1 8HA; tel. 020 7401 2077; fax 020 7633 9499
www.lorenzbooks.com; www.annesspublishing.com

If you like the images in this book and would like to investigate using them for publishing, promotions or
advertising, please visit our website www.practicalpictures.com for more information.

UK agent: The Manning Partnership Ltd; tel. 01225 478444; fax 01225 478440;
sales@manning-partnership.co.uk
UK distributor: Grantham Book Services Ltd; tel. 01476 541080; fax 01476 541061;
orders@gbs.tbs-ltd.co.uk
North American agent/distributor: National Book Network; tel. 301 459 3366; fax 301 429 5746;
www.nbnbooks.com
Australian agent/distributor: Pan Macmillan Australia; tel. 1300 135 113; fax 1300 135 103;
customer.service@macmillan.com.au
New Zealand agent/distributor: David Bateman Ltd; tel. (09) 415 7664; fax (09) 415 8892

Publisher: Joanna Lorenz
Editorial Director: Judith Simons
Project Editor: Felicity Forster
Text: Judy Bastyra and Deh-Ta Hsiung (ingredients), Becky Johnson (recipes) and Sallie Morris (recipes)
Additional recipes: Mridula Baljekar, Jane Bamforth, Jenni Fleetwood, Yasuko Fukuoka,
Christine Ingram, Kathy Man and Kate Whiteman
Photography: Janine Hosegood (ingredients) and Nicki Dowey (recipes)
Food for photography: Annabel Ford (ingredients) and Becky Johnson (recipes)
Additional photography (recipes): Craig Robertson, Dave King and William Lingwood
Copy Editor: Molly Perham
Designer: Nigel Partridge
Jacket design: Chloë Steers
Editorial Readers: Richard McGinlay and Jay Thundercliffe
Production Controller: Ben Worley

ETHICAL TRADING POLICY
Because of our ongoing ecological investment programme, you, as our customer, can have the pleasure
and reassurance of knowing that a tree is being cultivated on your behalf to naturally replace the materials
used to make the book you are holding. For further information about this scheme, go to
www.annesspublishing.com/trees

Previously published in two separate volumes, *The Practical Encyclopedia of Asian Cooking* and *Thai Food*

NOTES
Bracketed terms are intended for American readers.

For all recipes, quantities are given in both metric and imperial measures
and, where appropriate, measures are also given in standard cups and spoons.
Follow one set, but not a mixture, because they are not interchangeable.

Standard spoon and cup measures are level.
1 tsp = 5ml, 1 tbsp = 15ml, 1 cup = 250ml/8fl oz

Australian standard tablespoons are 20ml. Australian readers should use
3 tsp in place of 1 tbsp for measuring small quantities of gelatine, flour, salt, etc.

Medium (US large) eggs are used unless otherwise stated.

CONTENTS

INTRODUCTION

The food of Thailand and South-east Asia is a joy to the senses, combining the refreshing aroma of lemon grass and kaffir lime leaves with the pungency of brilliant red chillies and the magical flavours of coconut milk and fresh basil. The curries of the region follow this tradition for flavourings, and are very different from their Indian counterparts: Indian curries are traditionally slow-cooked for a rich, creamy taste, while Thai and South-east Asian dishes are famously quick and easy to prepare.

Exotic cuisines are increasingly popular in the West, and enthusiastic cooks are keen to reproduce them in their own kitchens. This book, with its extensive and wide-ranging collection of recipes from Thailand, China, through Japan and Korea, down to the South-east Asian islands of Malaysia, Indonesia and the Philippines, will appease the appetite for new gastronomic discoveries.

FOOD STALLS

Wherever you go in the Far East, you will inevitably come across the noisy and energetic food vendors who prepare and cook their dishes on the side of the street, on the rivers and waterways, and in markets. Street food is part of the way of life, and is eaten and enjoyed by everyone, regardless of social standing and income.

Navigating the streets and walkways of most Asian cities is an exhilarating journey for the senses. Street vendors advertise their produce loudly, banging spoons against metal pots, ringing bells, striking gongs, shouting the names of the strange and exotic-sounding delicacies while their woks and cooking vessels emit the heady aromas of a variety of spices and sauces. Their produce is appealing because of the speed of preparation, the freshness of the ingredients and the low cost.

Above: A Thai street hawker prepares a snack for a customer over the brazier in his hahp – a bamboo pole with a basket balanced at each end.

SNACKING

Asians are keen snackers, and tasty morsels can be found on virtually every street. Freshly sliced fruit including sweet pineapple, tart green mango and crispy guava is a popular snack that can be bought coated in sugar, salt or dried crushed chilli flakes.

In Thailand *Khao poot* (corn) is a very common snack. It is often cooked in a giant aluminium steamer, and the buyer can choose to have it on the cob or dunked in salty water and the kernels sliced off and eaten separately. The steamed cobs can also be cooked over a brazier. *Salapao*, which are steamed rice flour dumplings stuffed with pork or a sweetened bean paste, are also very popular. Vendors who specialize in *salapao* often also make *khanom jip*, a steamed snack made from minced (ground) pork or shrimp wrapped in wonton skins. *Salapao* vendors are frequently seen roaring down the streets on motorbikes with sidecars filled with piles of the small, white puffy snacks.

Sushi is a national favourite in Japan. The most famous, called *nigiri*, are hand-moulded fingers of vinegared rice with slices of raw fish on top. They are sold from street stalls everywhere. *Yakitori* are Japanese-style kebabs, made with chicken. Skewered food makes a popular snack throughout the whole region.

China is famous for its *dim sum* (literally, "to please the heart"), which originated in Canton but are now popular all over the country.

In Vietnam and the Philippines bread rolls called *ensaimadas* are a popular snack. They come with sweet and savoury fillings, including cheese.

Samosas and spring rolls are sold by street vendors all over Asia. These and other pastry "parcels" may be filled with vegetables, shellfish or meat and flavoured with fresh herbs and spices.

Many of these tasty snacks can be prepared in the Western kitchen. They make ideal party food and will be certain to impress your guests.

Below: Glass-sided carts filled with wedges of freshly prepared fruit are a common sight throughout Asia.

PREPARATION AND PRESENTATION

From the vastness of China to the island states of Indonesia and the Philippines, food is prepared with pleasure and keen attention to detail. Each of the countries in this broad sweep has its own unique style of cooking, coloured by climate, local crops, cultural mores and the impact of historical events such as invasion or war, but there are common threads, too. Throughout the region, the emphasis is always on serving food that is as fresh as possible. Presentation is paramount, particularly in Japan and Thailand, and the sharing of food is so fundamental to the faith of each culture that honoured guests are precisely that.

Rice is the staple food of the whole of this region, cultivated in South-east Asia for over five thousand years. Eaten at every meal, including breakfast, it is the basis of both sweet and savoury snack foods, as well as being a source for both wine and vinegar.

Fish forms an important part of the diet. Every country, with the exception of Laos, has miles of coastline, as well as rivers, lakes and ponds, all of which yield plentiful supplies of fish. The Asian preoccupation with the freshest possible food, be it animal or vegetable, can be a little disconcerting for the Western visitor. Before enjoying the famous Hong Kong dish Drunken

Above: A selection of skewered snacks are displayed on banana leaves, ready to be cooked over a brazier.

Prawns, for instance, the diner must first watch as the live prawns (shrimp) are marinated in Shao Xing rice wine, then cooked in fragrant stock.

At the other end of the spectrum, salted and cured fish is a valuable source of food throughout the area, but particularly in South-east Asia. All sorts of fish and shellfish are prepared in this way, either in brine or by being dried in the sun. Dried fish and shellfish also furnish the raw material for fish sauce and shrimp paste, essential ingredients that go under various names, and contribute a subtle but unique signature to so many dishes.

Even more important is soy sauce, which was imported by the Chinese thousands of years ago. Tofu is another soybean product that was originally peculiar to the region, but is now widely used in the Western world, as are noodles, another valuable food.

As well as having many ingredients in common, South-east Asian countries share a similar approach to food. All prepare, cook and serve their daily meals according to the long-established principle called fan-cai. The "fan" is the main part of the meal, usually rice or

another form of grain, while the "cai" includes the supplementary dishes such as fish, meat, poultry and vegetables. These elements must be balanced in every meal, as must the ingredients in each supplementary dish, so that aromas, colours, textures and tastes are in perfect harmony.

Harmony dictates that all the dishes be served together, buffet style, rather than as separate courses. Guests begin by taking a portion of rice, and then one of the supplementary dishes on offer, relishing it on its own before taking another portion of rice and a second choice. Soup is served at the same time as other dishes, and is enjoyed throughout the meal.

Harmony extends to presentation, too, an art which reaches its apogee in Japan, where food is valued as much for its aesthetic appearance as for its flavour. In Thailand, too, food is beautifully served. Thai girls learn the

Above: A variety of crops and grains are grown on the terraced fields on river banks in southern China.

Below: A chef preparing a variety of fresh fish, meats, vegetables and herbs at a roadside food stall in Hong Kong.

art of fruit carving from a young age, and fruit (and vegetables) are cut into fabulous shapes of birds, flowers and butterflies. They are, of course, fortunate in having such wonderful raw materials. Visit the floating market in Bangkok – or, indeed, any market in this part of the world – and you will marvel at the array of vegetables and fruit on offer, many of them relatively unknown in the West until recently, when South-east Asia became such a sought-after travel destination.

REGIONAL DIVERSITY

The food culture of South-east Asia varies widely across the region, with each country following its own traditions for spice blends, flavourings and cooking styles. However, there are also many similarities, largely because of the trade in ingredients, and the influences of climate, geography and religion.

Thailand

Buddhism is the religion of Thailand, so fish, shellfish and vegetables constitute the main part of the Thai diet. However, despite Buddhist law, there is also an extensive range of meat-based recipes.

Below: Fresh red chillies, which are used in many South-east Asian dishes, being sold at a market in Myanmar.

Salads are central to a Thai meal, and there are many varieties made, some of which use exotic fruits such as mangoes, pineapple and papaya, as well as raw vegetables. A small quantity of shredded meat, such as pork, is sometimes added, perhaps with a few prawns (shrimp). Thai salad dressings are a delicious blend of fish sauce, brown sugar and lime juice.

Coconut plays a very important role in Thai cooking. Coconut milk, flavoured with ginger, lemon grass, pungent local

Above: Planting rice in a paddy field in the Mekong Delta, Vietnam. Two crops are harvested each year.

chillies and basil leaves, forms the basis of most Thai curries. Many desserts are also made using coconut milk and palm sugar. Whatever the dish, there is always a fine balance and complexity of flavour, texture and colour. Thai people regard food as a celebration, and it is considered bad luck to eat alone.

Burma

As in Thailand, Buddhism forbids the taking of another life for reasons of personal gratification, but in practice most people eat a fair amount of meat, and fish is even more popular. *Mohingha* (Burmese fish stew) is flavoured with Indian spices, and is almost the national dish. Burmese food has noticeable Indian and Chinese influences. Spices from India are often sold in the local street markets, although the country's cuisine generally has more subtle flavours than its Indian counterpart. Rice is the staple food, but noodles, a Chinese contribution, are also very popular. The use of groundnut (peanut) oil and coconut suggests an Indian influence, whereas sesame oil, which is also used as a cooking medium, is a distinctly Chinese ingredient.

Vietnam

Lying virtually next door to Thailand, Vietnam has a cuisine that is in a class of its own. The country was ruled by the French for nearly 80 years, and a French culinary influence can still be detected. The most prominent influence, however, is that of the Chinese, who occupied Vietnam for nearly a thousand years.

Vietnamese food is light and delicate, and the use of fat is limited. Generally speaking, the Vietnamese prefer spicy food, with a well-balanced flavour and a clean taste. As in other South-east Asian and Far Eastern countries, rice and noodles are the staples. Plenty of fresh fruit and vegetables are eaten, with small quantities of meat, and fish and shellfish feature high on the menu.

China

A vast country, China has many different regional styles of cooking. The cuisine of the north is light and elegant, with Peking Duck being the best-known speciality. Cantonese cuisine in the south is based on abundant fresh vegetables, fish and shellfish. Stir-frying was perfected here, and Canton is the home of *dim sum*.

Eastern China is famous for noodles and dumplings. The southern provinces are known as the "Land of Fish and Rice", although their cuisine also

Above: Mushrooms grow in abundance across Japan, and are an essential part of everyday cooking.

includes many duck and pork dishes. The cuisine of Szechuan in the west of China is known for its superb balance of spices and aromatic flavourings. What all the classic dishes of the regional cuisines share is a harmonious balance of flavours, colours and textures and a long tradition of excellence.

Japan

In Japan, rice is so important that the word for cooked rice, *gohan* or *meshi*, also means "meal". Japanese cuisine is largely fish- and vegetable-based, and if meat is included it is used sparingly and often cooked with vegetables. The regional foods and dishes vary greatly from Hokkaido, the northern island, to Kyushu, in the south. Most seafood – crabs, oysters, squid, salmon, trout, herring, cod and konbu – comes from Hokkaido. It is also the only place in Japan where sheep are reared. Ramen was developed in Sapporo, the capital.

The north of Honshu island is Japan's rice belt, and this region also produces *sansai* (mountain vegetables) and the *maitake* mushroom. Tokyo and the surrounding area, Kanto, no longer produce agricultural fare but are culinary centres for regional foods and dishes. In Kansai, which includes Osaka and Kyoto, specialities include udon and beef dishes. In the two southern islands of Shikoku and Kyushu fresh fish and shellfish are abundant. Various citrus fruits are produced, and Kyushu is the largest shiitake producer in Japan.

Below: A typical, bustling fruit and vegetable market in Ameyokocho Street, in the Ueno district of Tokyo.

Malaysia

The culinary heritage of Malaysia reaches back for at least six centuries, when the country began to attract traders and travellers from India and Arabia, followed by the Chinese and Portuguese. Many Chinese people settled in the country, and a style of cuisine was created that had Chinese influences but flavours that were essentially local. Southern India also had an impact on Malaysian cooking, as Indian workers from the south were hired to work in the rubber plantations. There are striking resemblances between southern Indian and Malaysian cooking, with only minor differences, such as the use of lime leaves in Malaysian cooking and curry leaves in south Indian.

The tremendous variety in Malaysian cuisine is also partly a result of the range of religious beliefs within this country. For example, no pork is eaten among the Muslim community, although pork is a particular favourite of the Chinese. The Hindus from India will not eat beef, whereas the local Malay population has excellent beef-based recipes. Dishes such as rendang and sambal, which suggest an Indonesia

Below: A diner in Tokyo's Ginza district with decorations of red lanterns.

influence, exist side-by-side with biryanis and samosas, which are unmistakeably Indian.

Indonesia

Comprising 13,000 islands spread along the Indian Ocean, Indonesia is a lush, green fertile land with steamy tropical heat and snow-capped mountain peaks. For over two thousand years,

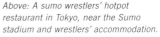

Above: A sumo wrestlers' hotpot restaurant in Tokyo, near the Sumo stadium and wrestlers' accommodation.

waves of foreign traders and merchants entered the islands, and Hindu, Muslim, and Buddhist kingdoms have all been established and destroyed. Arab traders arrived in the 15th century, and they were followed by Portuguese, Dutch, English and Spanish. With such diverse cultural influences, Indonesian cuisine emerged as one of the most varied and interesting in South-east Asia.

In no other South-east Asian country does rice play such a major role as in Indonesia. It is eaten twice a day with numerous types of curry. On the island of Bali, Hindus eat rice with fish curries, Muslims eat it with beef and chicken, and the Chinese eat it with almost any meat, including duck. The famous Indonesian style of serving a meal, known as *nasi gerai* (loosely translated as "the rice table"), was even popular with the Dutch. *Nasi goreng* (fried rice) is one of the best-known dishes. Beef rendang, with the pungency of chillies and ginger, the warmth of cumin and the sweet, mellow flavour of coconut milk, is one of Indonesia's most endearing dishes.

The Philippines

Like that of its neighbours, Filipino cooking is a harmonious blend of the cuisine of many countries and cultures. There are notable similarities with other South-east Asian countries, in terms of the way that ingredients are grown, prepared and cooked. Traders arrived from many neighbouring countries, including China, Malaysia, Japan and Indonesia, but the strongest influence came from the Spanish, who arrived in the 16th century. Dishes such as *bombonese arroz* (rice fritters), *arroz caldo* (rice with chicken) and *puchero* (a mixed meat soup) are among the more popular Spanish-influenced dishes still eaten today.

Chinese influence was also strong, and this is clearly evident from the endless variety of noodle-based dishes. Rice is the staple food, however, and

Above: The colourful floating market in Bangkok, Thailand, sells a wonderful selection of fresh fruits and vegetables.

is eaten daily with almost every meal. The everyday diet of Filipinos is based on a simple dish of rice, stir-fried with meat, fish and vegetables. *Adobo*, a Filipino spicy stew made with pork, chicken or even fish and shellfish, is a real speciality of the island.

Visitors to Vietnam and Thailand learned to enjoy – and distinguish between – cuisines of those countries and, when they returned home, they wanted to be able to continue eating the meals that had been so much a part of their holiday. In major cities the world over, it is now possible to enjoy authentic Thai, Vietnamese, Indonesian, Malayan and even Filipino food, and it is only a matter of time before lesser-known cuisines are equally well represented.

Home cooks are eager to experiment with this quick, healthy and sensual style of cooking too. Ingredients such as lemon grass and galangal are now readily available in many supermarkets. There's never been a better time to discover or extend your repertoire of recipes from the Far East.

Below: Asia is a vast region, from China, through Japan and Korea, down to the South-east Asian islands of Malaysia, Indonesia and the Philippines.

EXPERIMENTING AT HOME

Tourism is one of the major reasons why Thai and South-east Asian food has become so popular in Europe, America, Australia and elsewhere. Travellers discovered that Chinese food was not a single cuisine, but many, ranging from Peking cooking in the north, to the hot and spicy Sichuan-style in the west and Cantonese in the south. They found that Japan, too, is rich in regional specialities.

INGREDIENTS

This section of the book gives detailed information about all the different ingredients used

in Asian cuisine, from daily staples, such as rice and noodles, to unusual fruit and

vegetables, aromatic herbs and spices, and spicy sauces and pastes. It also includes

suggestions for equipment and utensils and an overview of Asian cooking techniques.

RICE

Rice is the staple grain of the whole of Asia, which is well over half the world's population. It is true that wheat is also grown in northern China and India, but its consumption is rather small in comparison with rice.

Throughout Asia, the importance of rice is underlined by the fact that in Chinese and other Asian languages, there is no single word for rice, but many. The crop, grain, raw rice and cooked rice are all referred to by different terms, and the Chinese character *fan* for cooked rice has acquired a much wider meaning in colloquial speech; it is also synonymous with nourishment and good health. When friends meet, instead of asking "How do you do?" they will often greet each other with the words: "Have you eaten rice?" An affirmative answer indicates that all is well.

Another common Chinese word with more than one meaning is *fan-wan* (rice-bowl). Aside from the obvious, this also means a job or livelihood; so the expression "to lose one's rice bowl" or "to have one's rice bowl broken", suggests that one has been given the sack; similarly, someone described as having an "iron rice-bowl" has probably got a job for life. Paradoxically, the expression *fan-tong,* which means a rice bucket (something that holds a large amount of cooked rice) has become a derogatory expression to describe a person who lacks refinement (a big eater of plain rice).

Rice has been cultivated in southern Asia for over five thousand years. There are more than forty thousand different strains grown in China alone. Since rice requires a wet and warm climate for its cultivation, some 90 per cent of the world production of rice is grown (and consumed) in the monsoon regions of Asia. A small amount of rice is cultivated on dry land in northern China, but because of the cold climate, only one crop can be grown each year, whereas two crops per annum is the norm in the temperate south.

Above: Thai fragrant rice has a delicate, fragrant scent.

Freshly harvested rice has a special aroma, and is eagerly sought after in China and Japan, the rice from the autumn harvest (usually in November) being reckoned to taste the best.

TYPES OF RICE

Broadly speaking, rice can be classified as being either *Oryza sativa indica* or *Oryza sativa japonica.* Varieties of both types are cultivated in Asia. Long grained indica *(xian)* rices – of which there are many strains – are the most common. Long grain white rice has had its husk, bran and germ removed, taking most of the nutrients with them and leaving a bland-flavoured rice that is light and fluffy when cooked. Long grain brown rice has had only its outer husk removed, leaving the bran and germ intact, which gives it a chewy, nutty flavour. It takes longer to cook than white rice but contains more fibre, vitamins and minerals.

Patna rice gets its name from Patna in India. At one time, most of the long grain rice sold in Europe came from Patna, and the term was used loosely to mean any long grain rice. The custom

Below: Patna rice is one of the many types of long grain rice.

persists in parts of America, but elsewhere Patna is used to describe a variety of long grain rice from the Bihar region of India.

Basmati rice is a slender long grain rice that is grown in northern India, in the Punjab, in parts of Pakistan and in the foothills of the Himalayas. After harvesting it is aged for a year, which gives it a characteristic flavour and a light, fluffy texture. The grains are long and slender, and become even longer during cooking. Widely used in Indian cooking, basmati rice has a cooling effect on hot and spicy curries.

Thai fragrant rice has a delicate but distinctive scent of jasmine, and is particularly highly prized.

Short-grained japonica *(geng)* rices are less fragrant, but tend to taste slightly sweeter than indicas. This type of rice is cultivated in northern China, Japan, Korea and surrounding areas. The rices are higher in amylopectin than long grains, and are therefore more starchy. The grains cling together when cooked, which makes them ideal for sushi and similar Japanese dishes.

Glutinous rice – also known as sweet or waxy rice – is even more sticky than Japanese short grain rice. This endears it to South-east Asian cooks, as the cooked rice can be shaped or rolled, and is very easy to pick up with chopsticks. White glutinous rice, with its fat, opaque grains, is the most common type, but there is also a black glutinous rice, which retains the husk and has a nutty flavour. A pinkish-red glutinous rice is cultivated on the banks of the Yangtze River, and a purple black variety has recently been developed. Glutinous rice has a high sugar content, and is used in Japan for making *senbei* (rice crackers) and *mochi* (rice cakes), as well as sweet rice wine.

Right: Short-grained japonica rice is ideal for sushi because, when cooked, the grains stick together.

Above: Basmati rice is considered by many people to be the prince of rice. There are various grades of basmati, but it is impossible to differentiate between them except by trying various brands to discover the best fragrance and taste.

Culinary uses

It is impossible to think of Asian food without rice. Rice is served in one form or another at every meal, including breakfast. Although wheat – in the form of dumplings or noodles – is eaten more often than rice in some parts of Asia, such as northern China, Asians everywhere regard rice as their staple food, with wheaten foods as mere supplements. In some languages the phrase for eating rice is the same as that for eating food.

The most common way of serving rice throughout Asia is simply boiled or steamed; fried rice does not normally form part of an everyday meal, but is either served as a snack on its own, or reserved for a special occasion such as a banquet. Unlike the India pilau, the Italian risotto or the Spanish paella, Asian fried rice dishes are never based upon raw rice, but always use ready cooked rice (either boiled or steamed). For the finest results, the rice should be cold and firm, rather than soft.

The universal breakfast in all Asian countries is a creamy, moist rice dish, which is known as congee or rice pudding. Considered to be highly nutritious, it is often given to babies and people with digestive problems as well as the elderly. Coconut milk is used instead of water in many South-east Asian countries, but because it usually takes over an hour to make a smooth, creamy congee, many Japanese cooks (and some Chinese) cheat by simply adding hot water to cold cooked rice.

Below: Black and white glutinous rice

others, and the amount of liquid required varies, too. The general rule is to use double the amount of water by volume to dry rice. However, if the rice has been washed or soaked first, less water will be needed otherwise, when cooked, the rice will be soft and sticky, instead of firm and fluffy.

Asian cooks often add a teaspoon of vegetable oil to the water to prevent the rice from sticking to the bottom of the pan. Whether to add salt or not is a matter of choice. It is usually added when cooking regular long grain rice, but not for Thai fragrant rice. The width, depth and material of the pan used will also make a difference to the result. One of the best ways of cooking perfect boiled rice is in an electric rice-cooker, while some cooks get very good results in the microwave.

Storage

Raw rice should not be kept for too long, or the grains will lose their fragrance. Keep the rice in an airtight container in a dry, cool place, away from strong light, and use it within 3–4 months of purchasing.

Preparation and cooking techniques

There can never be a definitive recipe for cooking plain rice, because each type requires individual treatment.

Some benefit from being rinsed in cold water first, while others should be soaked before use. Some types of rice need to be cooked for longer than

---

Plain boiled rice

Use long grain Patna or basmati rice; or better still, try Thai fragrant rice. Allow 50g/2oz/generous ¼ cup raw rice per person.

1 Put the dry rice in a strainer and rinse it under cold running water.

2 Tip into a large pan, then pour in enough cold water to come 2cm/¾in above the surface of rice. (In Asia the traditional way of measuring this is with the help of the index finger. When the tip of the finger is touching the surface of the rice, the water level should just reach the first joint.)

3 Add a pinch of salt, and, if you like, about 5ml/1 tsp vegetable oil, stir once and bring to the boil.

4 Stir once more, reduce the heat to the lowest possible setting and cover the pan with a tight-fitting lid.

5 Cook for 12–15 minutes, then turn off the heat and leave the rice to stand, tightly covered, for about 10 minutes. Fluff up the rice with a fork before serving.

FLOURS

Popular thickening agents in Asian cooking are cornflour (cornstarch), tapioca flour and potato flour. Mung bean flour, water chestnut flour, lotus root and arrowroot are used for clear sauces, and chickpea flour for batters. Rice flour is a thickener, and is used for rice papers, dumplings and cakes.

Cornflour/cornstarch

This fine white powder, made from corn (maize) is a useful thickening agent for sauces, soups and casseroles.

Rice flour

More finely milled than ground rice, this is also known as rice powder. The texture is similar to that of cornflour. Rice flour is used for thickening sauces, and to make rice papers and the dough for dumplings. It is often used to make sticky Asian cakes and sweets, but because rice flour does not contain gluten, the cakes made with it are rather flat. Rice flour can be combined with wheat flour to make bread, but this produces a crumbly loaf.

Chick-pea flour

This very fine flour is also called gram flour, or besan. Mainly used in India, where it originated, it also plays a role in Malayan cooking, thanks to Indian immigrants who introduced it.

Wheat flour

Ground from the whole grain, this may be wholemeal or white. Hard, or strong wheat flour is high in gluten, which makes it ideal for adding to rice flour to make bread.

Soya flour
This is a finely-ground, high-protein flour made from the soya bean. It is used as a thickener in a wide range of sauces and soups, and is often mixed with other flours such as wheat flour to make bread and pastries. It adds a pleasant nutty flavour.

Left: Japanese rice flour

Far left: Japanese wheat flour

Below: Chickpea flour

Left: Thai rice flour

Right: Cornflour

Left: Japanese soya flour

NOODLES

MANDARIN: *MIAN (TIAO)*; CANTONESE: *MEIN*;
THAI: *GUEYTEOW*

Whether Marco Polo actually introduced noodles from China to Italy is a debatable point, but we do know that noodles made from wheat flour appeared in China as early as the first century BC, around the time of the Roman Empire. Noodles rapidly became a popular food, not only in China, but throughout the whole of Asia.

Up to the end of the last century, when modern machinery was first imported from Europe, noodles were always made by hand, and even today, certain types of noodle are still hand-made, most notably, the "hand-pulled" or "drawn" noodles made by chefs in northern China. It takes more than ten years to master the technique, so is beyond the reach of ordinary mortals.

Noodles form an important part of the daily diet in the Far East, ranking second only to rice as a staple food. Unlike rice and steamed buns, however, which are usually served plain to be eaten with cooked dishes, noodles are

usually cooked with other ingredients. For this reason, noodle dishes are seldom served as accompaniments, but are eaten on their own as light meals or snacks. In Vietnam, rice noodle soup is the standard breakfast. In Japan there are restaurants that specialize in noodle dishes such as noodles served solo with dipping sauces; bowls of steaming noodle soup; and noodles cooked with slivered vegetables and seaweed.

Left: Four types of Japanese Udon noodles

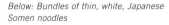

Below: Bundles of thin, white, Japanese Somen noodles

Thailand has its noodle stalls, noodle boats and even noodle meals on wheels available from vendors with ingenious mobile shops mounted on their bicycles. In Asia, you need never be far from a noodle seller.

WHEAT NOODLES

Asian noodles are made from a variety of flour pastes, including wheat, rice, mung bean, buckwheat, seaweed, corn and even devil's tongue, which is a plant related to the arum lily. Some noodles are plain, others are enriched with egg. Dried wheat noodles, with or without eggs, are often called "longevity noodles" because of their association with long life.

Below: Plain Chinese (top) and Thai noodles (bottom)

Right: Fresh egg noodles

Plain noodles

Made from strong white bread flour and water, these can be flat or round and come in various thicknesses. In Japan, they are known as **Udon** and are available fresh, pre-cooked or dried. **Somen** are thin, delicate, white Japanese noodles. They are sold in bundles, held in place by a paper band.

Egg noodles These are far more common than plain wheat noodles. In China they come in various thicknesses and are sold fresh or dried. **Ramen** are the Japanese equivalent and are usually sold in coils or blocks. Very fine egg noodles, which resemble vermicelli, are called **Yi noodles** in China, after the family that originally made them. They are popular in Hakka-style cooking.

Shrimp noodles These seasoned egg noodles are flavoured with fresh shrimp and/or shrimp roe. They are usually sold dried, in coils of various widths.

Instant noodles Packets of pre-cooked egg noodles are a familiar sight in the West. Flavourings include chicken, prawn (shrimp) and beef.

Preparation and cooking techniques

Noodles are very easy to prepare. Some types benefit from being soaked before being cooked, so see individual recipes for advice, read the instructions on the packet or seek advice from someone in the store where you bought them. Both dried and fresh noodles have to be cooked in boiling water before use. How long for depends on the type of noodle, the thickness of the strips, and whether (as is usual) the noodles will be cooked again in a soup or sauce. Dried noodles generally require about 3 minutes' cooking, while fresh ones will often be ready in less than a minute, and may need to be rinsed under cold water to prevent them from overcooking.

After the initial cooking, noodles are then usually prepared and served in one of the following ways:

Noodles in soup Most popular in China, Korea, Japan, Vietnam, Burma and Singapore, this usually consists of noodles served in bowls of clear broth with pieces of cooked meat, poultry, seafood and/or vegetables, sometimes with a sharp sauce on the side.

Braised noodles *(lao mein)* The difference between this and noodles in soup is that braised noodles are first cooked in a broth, then served with a thickened sauce.

Fried noodles *(chow mein)* This has to be one of the most popular Chinese dishes in the West (and in South-east Asia, but not so much in north China or Japan). The two basic types of fried noodles are dry-fried (crisp) or soft-fried. Generally speaking, only the fine vermicelli-type of noodles are used for dry-frying; the thicker round or flat noodles are more suitable for soft-frying.

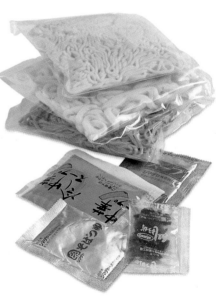

Left: Blocks of dried Japanese Ramen noodles

Above: Instant noodles come in a variety of flavourings.

RICE NOODLES

CHINESE: *MIFEN;* VIETNAMESE:
LAI FAN

Wheat noodles must
have preceded rice
noodles by
several
centuries,
since there
were no written
records of their
existence until
well into the Han
Dynasty in the
third century AD. Not surprisingly,
rice noodles are very popular in
southern China and South-east Asia
where not much wheat is grown.

Unlike most other noodles, which are
made from flour of one type or another,
rice noodles are made from whole
grains of rice, which are soaked and
then ground with water into a paste.
This paste is drained through a sieve to
form a dough, which is divided into two.
One half is cooked in boiling water for

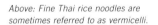

*Above: Fine Thai rice noodles are
sometimes referred to as vermicelli.*

15 minutes, before it is kneaded with
the raw half to make a firm dough. The
dough is then put through a press,
which cuts it into various shapes and
sizes. The finished strands are
blanched in water, drained and rinsed
before being sold as fresh noodles, or
dried in the sun before packaging.

Types of rice noodles

Although they are known by different
names, the rice noodles sold in
southern China, Thailand and Vietnam
are all similar. Like wheat noodles, they
come in various widths, from the very
thin strands known as rice
vermicelli or *lai fan* (*sen mee*
in Thailand) to rice sticks,
which start at around
2mm/$\frac{1}{16}$in and can be as
wide as 1cm/$\frac{1}{2}$in, as in
the case of *ho fun,* a
special variety from south
China reputedly made with
river water rather than tap
water. In Thailand it is possible
to buy a rice noodle enriched
with egg. Called *ba mee,* it is
sold in nests. A wide range
of dried rice noodles is
available in Asian or
Chinese stores, and
fresh ones can
occasionally be
found in the chiller cabinets.

*Below: Thin and thick Chinese rice
noodles or sticks*

Preparation and cooking techniques

Because all rice noodles are pre-
cooked, they need only be soaked in
hot water for a few minutes to soften
them before use. If they are soaked for
too long, they will go soggy and lose the
texture that is part of their appeal.

Below: Japanese rice noodles

Preparing rice noodles
Rice noodles need only to be
soaked in hot water for a few
minutes to soften them.

Add the noodles to a large bowl of
water that has been recently
boiled and leave for 5–10 minutes,
or until softened, stirring
occasionally to separate the
strands as they soften.

MUNG BEAN (CELLOPHANE) NOODLES

CHINESE: *FENSI;* VIETNAMESE: *BUN;*
JAPANESE: *HARUSAME*

Also known as transparent noodles, bean thread vermicelli or glass noodles, these very fine, rather brittle strands are made from green mung beans, which are the same beans as those used for sprouting. Although very thin, the strands are firm and resilient, and they stay that way when cooked, never becoming soggy, which doubtless contributes to their popularity.

Preparing cellophane noodles

Cellophane noodles are never served on their own, but always used as an ingredient in a dish. Soak them in hot or warm water for 10–15 minutes to soften them.

When they are soft, use a pair of scissors or a sharp knife to chop the noodles into shorter strands for easier handling.

Left: Cellophane noodles

Cellophane noodles are almost tasteless unless cooked with other strongly flavoured foods and seasonings, but they have a fantastic texture. They are not served solo, but are always used as an ingredient in a dish, most notably in vegetarian cooking and in hot pots, as well as in Vietnamese spring rolls. They are only available dried. In Japan, cellophane noodles are called *harusame,* which means "spring rain".

BUCKWHEAT NOODLES

JAPANESE: *SOBA*

The best-known buckwheat noodles are the Japanese soba, which are usually sold dried in bundles of fine strands. Soba are much darker in colour than wheat noodles. There is also a dark green variety called cha-soba (tea soba), which is made of buckwheat and green tea. Korean cooks use buckwheat noodles, too, preferring a very thin variety.

Unusual noodles

Shirataki This popular Japanese noodle (*above left*) is made from a starch derived from the tubers of the devil's tongue plant, which is related to the arum lily.
Bijon Made from corn, these noodles (*above right*) are made in South-east Asia.
Canton These Chinese wheat noodes are sometimes enriched with eggs (*above top*).

Storage

Packets of fresh noodles normally carry a use-by date, and must be stored in the refrigerator. Dried noodles will keep for many months if kept sealed in the original packet, or in airtight containers in a cool, dry place, but again, the packets have an expiry date.

Below: Soba noodles

PANCAKES AND WRAPPERS

PANCAKES

CHINESE: *BING*

The pancakes of Asia are quite different from their counterparts in the West. For a start, they are almost always made from plain dough, rather than a batter, and they are more often than not served with savoury fillings rather than sweet.

There are two types of pancakes in China, either thin or thick. Thin pancakes *(bobing)* are also known as mandarin or duck pancakes, because they are used as wrappers for serving the famous Peking duck. They are also served with other savoury dishes, most notably the very popular *mu-shu* or *moo-soo* pork, which consists of scrambled egg with pork and wood ears

(dried black fungus). Making pancakes demands considerable dexterity, so many cooks prefer to buy them frozen from the Chinese supermarket.

Thick pancakes are made with lard and flavoured with savoury ingredients such as spring onions (scallions) and rock salt. In northern China, they are eaten as a snack, or as part of a main meal, rather like the Indian paratha. Both thin and thick pancakes are sometimes served as a dessert, with a filling of sweetened bean paste.

NONYA SPRING ROLL PANCAKES

These are the exception to the rule that most pancakes in the East are made from dough. Typical of the Singaporean style of cooking known as Nonya, they

are made from an egg, flour and cornflour batter and are traditionally served with a wide selection of fillings.

Reheating Chinese pancakes

1 Stack the pancakes, interleaving them with squares of baking parchment.

2 Carefully wrap the stacked pancakes in foil, folding over the sides of the foil so that the pancakes are completely sealed.

3 Put the foil parcel in a steamer and cover. Place the steamer on a trivet in a wok of simmering water. Steam for 3–5 minutes until the pancakes are hot.

Above: Thick pancakes are eaten as a savoury snack, or filled with sweet bean paste and served as a dessert.

Below: Thin pancakes are used as wrappers, notably for Peking duck, or served with savoury dishes.

SPRING ROLL WRAPPERS

MANDARIN: *CHUNJUAN PI;* CANTONESE:
SHUEN GUEN PIE

Spring rolls are called egg rolls in the USA, and pancake rolls in many other parts of the world. They must be one of the most popular Chinese snacks everywhere, including China itself. While the fillings may vary from region to region, or even between different restaurants and fast food stalls, the wrappers are always more or less the same. They are made from a simple flour and water dough, except in Vietnam, where wrappers are made from rice flour, water and salt.

There are three different sizes of ready-made spring roll wrappers available from the freezers of Asian stores: small, medium and large. They are all wafer-thin. The smallest wrappers, which are about 12cm/4½ in square, are used for making dainty, cocktail-style rolls. The standard-size

wrappers measure 21–23cm/8½–9in square, and usually come in packets of 20 sheets. The largest, 30cm/12in square, are too big for general use, so they are usually cut in half or into strips for making samosas and similar snacks.

Above: Small and medium-size spring roll wrappers. Any unused wrappers can be returned to the freezer.

Preparing spring rolls

Use medium-size spring roll wrappers, which you will find in the freezer cabinet in Asian or Chinese stores. They should be thawed before use. For a filling, use ingredients such as beansprouts, bamboo shoots, water chestnuts and dried mushrooms, with chopped prawns (shrimp) or finely minced (ground) pork. When the rolls are prepared, deep-fry them a few at a time in hot oil for 2–3 minutes, or until golden and crisp.

2 Spoon the spring roll filling diagonally across the wrapper.

4 Brush the edges with cornflour (cornstarch) and water paste.

1 Peel off the top spring roll wrapper. Cover the rest to keep them moist.

3 Fold over the nearest corner of the wrapper to cover the filling.

5 Fold the edges towards the middle, then roll up in to a neat parcel.

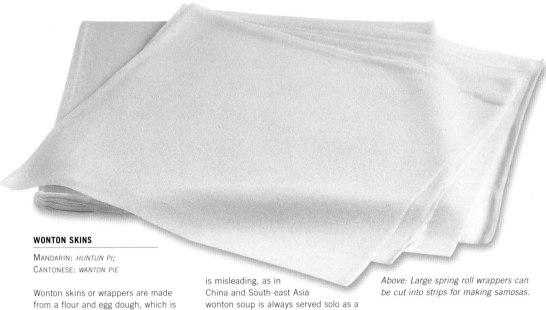

WONTON SKINS

MANDARIN: *HUNTUN PI;*
CANTONESE: *WANTON PIE*

Wonton skins or wrappers are made from a flour and egg dough, which is rolled out to a smooth, flat thin sheet, as when making egg noodles. The sheet is usually cut into small squares, although round wonton wrappers are also available. Ready-made wonton skins are stacked in piles of 25 or 50, wrapped and sold fresh or frozen in Asian or Chinese stores.

Unlike spring roll wrappers, which have to be carefully peeled off sheet by sheet before use, fresh wonton skins are dusted with flour before being packed, This keeps each one separate from the others and so they are very easy to use. Frozen wrappers must, however, be thawed thoroughly before use, or they will tend to stick together. Any unused skins can be re-frozen, but should be carefully wrapped in foil so that they do not dry out in the freezer.

There are several ways of using wonton skins. They can be deep-fried and served with a dip, filled and boiled, steamed or deep-fried, or simply poached in a clear broth. On most Chinese restaurant menus in the West, this last option is listed under soups, which is misleading, as in China and South-east Asia wonton soup is always served solo as a snack, never as a separate soup course as part of a meal.

Above: Large spring roll wrappers can be cut into strips for making samosas.

Below: Wonton skins can be square or round and come in a variety of sizes.

Preparing wontons

Place the filling in the centre of the wonton skin and dampen the edges. Press the edges of the wonton skin together to create a little purse shape, sealing the filling completely.

RICE PAPERS

VIETNAMESE: *BANH TRANG*

The rice paper used in Vietnamese (and Thai) cooking is quite different from the rice paper that is used for writing and painting in China and Japan, nor does it bear any resemblance to the sheets of rice paper British cooks use as pan liners when baking macaroons. Made from rice flour, water and salt, it is a round, tissue-thin "crepe", dried on bamboo mats in the sun, which results in the familiar crosshatch pattern being embedded on each sheet.

Rice paper is used for wrapping Vietnamese spring rolls and small pieces of meat and fish to be eaten in the hand. The sheets are rather dry and brittle, so must be softened by soaking in warm water for a few seconds before use. Alternatively, they can be placed on damp dish towels and brushed with water until they are sufficiently pliable to be used. Spring rolls are usually deep-fried, but this is not always the case. Vietnamese cooks also make a fresh version. Cooked pork, prawns (shrimp), beansprouts and vermicelli are wrapped in rice paper, which has been dipped in cold water until it is pliable and transparent. The filling can clearly be seen through the wrappers, and the rolls look very pretty.

Storage

Packaged and sold in 15cm/6in, 25cm/10in and 30cm/12in rounds, rice papers will keep for months in a cool, dry place, provided the packets are tightly sealed. When buying, look for sheets that are of an even thickness, with a clear, whitish colour. Broken pieces are a sign of bad handling, and are quite useless for wrapping, so avoid any packets look as if they have been knocked about.

Below: Rice papers are dried on bamboo mats, which give them their familiar cross-hatch pattern.

DUMPLINGS

MANDARIN: *JIAO ZI/BAO ZI;* CANTONESE:
DIM SUM

Dumplings are very popular in China, and there is a wide variety of different shapes and sizes, with fillings ranging from pork and vegetables to mushrooms and bamboo shoots. Some enclose the filling in a very thin dough skin *(jiao zi)* while others use a dough made from a glutinous rice flour. There are also steamed buns *(bao zi)* filled with meat or a sweet bean paste.

The best way to experience the diversity and delicious flavours of dumplings is to indulge in dim sum, that wonderful procession of tasty morsels that the Cantonese have elevated to an art form. Although dumplings originated in northern China, it was in Canton that the practice developed of enjoying these snacks with tea at breakfast or lunch time.

Dim sum literally means "dot on the heart" and indicates a snack or refreshment, not a full blown meal. Although the range of dishes available on a dim sum menu now embraces other specialities (spring rolls, wontons and spare ribs, for instance), dumplings remain the essential items.

Below: Grilled dumplings or "pot stickers" and chilli sauce.

What is more, unlike the majority of dim sum, which are so complicated to make that they can only be prepared by a highly skilled chef, dumplings are comparatively simple to make at home. Both *jiao zi* and *bao zi* are available ready-made from Asian or Chinese stores – the former are sold uncooked and frozen, and the latter are ready-cooked and sold chilled.

Preparation and cooking techniques

Frozen *jiao zi* dumplings should be cooked straight from the freezer. There are three different ways of cooking and serving them.

Poaching

The most common way of cooking dumplings in China is to poach them in boiling water for 4–5 minutes – longer if cooking from frozen.

The dumplings are added to boiling water. When the water boils again, a cupful of cold water is added to the pan and the water is brought to the boil again. This is repeated twice more, by which time the dumplings will be ready. They are traditionally served hot with a vinegar and soy sauce dip, chilli sauce or chilli oil.

Cooking dumplings

1 To poach dumplings, drop them into boiling water. When the water boils again, add a cupful of cold water. Repeat twice more, cooking the dumplings for 4–5 minutes.

2 To steam dumplings, place them on a bed of lettuce or spinach leaves on the base of a bamboo steamer, cover with the lid and cook for 8–10 minutes.

3 To "grill" dumplings, fry in a shallow frying pan until they are brown, then add a little water, cover with a bamboo steamer lid, and cook until the water has completely evaporated.

Above: Plain steamed buns and sweet buns filled with bean paste.

Steaming

The best way to do this is by using a bamboo basket as a steamer. The dumplings are placed on a bed of lettuce or spinach leaves on the rack of the steamer, which is then covered. The dumplings are served hot with a dip.

Grilling/broiling

This description is a bit misleading, because the dumplings are not grilled (broiled) in the conventional sense but cooked in a frying pan. They are first shallow-fried, then a small amount of boiling water is added to the pan and they are steamed under cover until all the liquid has evaporated. When cooked by this method, the dumplings are crispy on the base, soft on top and juicy inside. They are often called by their popular name, which is "pot stickers".

PEKING DUMPLINGS

These crescent-shaped dumplings are filled with minced (ground) pork, greens and spring onions (scallions) and seasoned with salt, sugar, soy sauce, rice wine and sesame oil. In northern China they are eaten for breakfast on New Year's Day, but are often served all year round as snacks or part of a meal.

STEAMED BUNS

Steamed buns are to Asia what baked bread is to the West, and *bao* (filled buns) are the Chinese fast food equivalent of hot dogs, hamburgers and sandwiches. There are two main types of steamed buns, either plain or filled. The plain, unfilled buns made from leavened dough are treated in much the same way as plain boiled rice and are intended to be eaten with cooked food. Then there are filled buns *(bao zi)*. The name literally means "wraps" and these can be savoury or sweet. The sweet ones usually contain either a lotus seed paste or a sweet bean paste filling and are usually eaten cold. Savoury *bao zi* come with a wide range of fillings, the most common being pork, and a very popular type is filled with Cantonese *char siu* (honey-roasted pork). These are available ready-made, and are best eaten hot.

Also available ready-made, but uncooked, are what are known as Shanghai dumplings. These are little round dumplings, much smaller than *char siu bao*, and each consisting of minced pork wrapped in a thin skin of unleavened dough.

Prawn crackers

Also called shrimp chips, prawn crackers are made from fresh prawns (shrimp), starch, salt and sugar. They are very popular as cocktail snacks, and some restaurants serve them while you wait for your order to arrive. The raw crackers are grey in colour. The small Chinese ones are not much bigger than a thumbnail, while those used in Indonesia are much larger, about 15cm/6in long and 5cm/2in wide. Indonesian prawn crackers are more difficult to find in the West. Once deep-fried, both types puff up to four or five times the original size, and become almost snow white. Ready-cooked crackers are also available. They are sold in sealed packets, but do not keep well once exposed to the air, so eat them as soon as possible after opening.

VEGETABLES

CHINESE LEAVES/CHINESE CABBAGE

MANDARIN: *DA BAICAI; HUANG YA BAI;*
CANTONESE: *SHAO CHOI; WONG NGA BAK*

There are almost as many names for this member of the brassica family as there are ways of cooking it. In the West, it is generally called Chinese leaves, but it is also known as Chinese cabbage, Napa cabbage (mainly in the USA) or celery cabbage. The alternative Chinese name translates as "yellow-sprouting-white", a description of the crinkled leaves, and the Cantonese call it Peking or Tianjin cabbage in honour of its northern origin.

It is a cool season vegetable, most abundant from November through to April, but available all year round. There are three common varieties which all look similar, but differ in length, width and tightness of leaf.

Aroma and flavour

Chinese leaves have a delicate sweet aroma with a mild cabbage flavour that disappears completely when the vegetable is cooked. The white stalk has a crunchy texture, and it remains succulent even after long cooking.

Culinary uses

This is a very versatile vegetable and it can be used in stir-fries, stews, soups or salads. It will absorb the flavours of any other ingredients with which it is cooked – be they fish or shellfish, poultry, meat or vegetables – and yet retain its own characteristic flavour and texture. In Asian or Chinese restaurants, braised Chinese leaves are often served as a flavoursome base for roasted meats or duck.

Preparation and cooking techniques

Discard the outer layer of leaves and trim off the root, then slice off as much you need. Should you wish to wash the leaves (and this is not strictly necessary unless you are using them in a salad), do so before cutting them, otherwise you will wash away much of the vitamins. If you stir-fry Chinese leaves in hot oil, the stalks often develop dark scorch marks. Restaurant chefs blanch the vegetable in boiling stock, which enhances the flavour, before frying.

Storage

Chinese leaves can be stored for a long time without losing their resilience. Keep in the salad compartment of the refrigerator and they will stay fresh for up to 10–12 days. Don't worry if there are tiny black specks on the leaves as this is quite normal and will not do any harm.

Left: Chinese leaves have a crunchy texture and a delicate aroma. The mild cabbage flavour disappears when the vegetable is cooked.

Preparing Chinese leaves

1 Discard any damaged outer leaves and trim off the root.

2 It is not usually necessary to wash the leaves, simply cut the head of Chinese leaves crossways into thin shreds.

3 You may prefer to wash the leaves, before using in a salad, for instance. Separate the leaves, then wash under cold running water. Shake off any excess water before shredding.

Right: Dark green bok choy tastes similar to spinach. The white stems can be cooked and eaten separately.

BOK CHOY/PAK-CHOI

MANDARIN: *XIAO BAICAI;*
CANTONESE: *BOK CHOI*

Another member of the brassica family, bok choy goes by lots of different names. In the West it is sometimes known as *pak-choi*, horse's ear (from the shape of the leaves) or Chinese white cabbage. In Cantonese, the name means simply white vegetable, which is a bit of a misnomer, as the glossy leaves that are a distinctive feature of this vegetable are dark green. The stalks, however, are pale, and range from light green to ivory white. Bok choy is a perennial, and several varieties are available throughout the year.

Aroma and flavour

Although bok choy is less delicate and does not taste as sweet as Chinese leaves, it has a distinctive flavour, which is a sort of cross between a mild cabbage and spinach.

Culinary uses

Bok choy and Chinese leaves are interchangeable in most dishes, even though their colour and flavour are different. Bok choy can be used in soups and stir-fries, and is delicious when quickly braised, but should not be subjected to prolonged stewing.

Preparation and cooking techniques

Bok choy is prepared in much the same way as Chinese leaves, except that the stems are as important (some would say more important) than the leaves. It is a good idea to separate leaves and stems for cooking, as the latter take slightly longer. Baby bok choy can be cooked whole or in halves or quarters. Only when very young and tender can bok choy be eaten raw.

Storage

Bok choy is completely different from Chinese leaves when it comes to storage. Try to use it as soon as you buy it, because the leaves will start to wilt, and the outer leaves will turn yellow, after 2–3 days, much sooner than lettuce and spinach.

Below: Bright green choi sum is easy to prepare.

CHOI SUM

MANDARIN: *YOU CAIXIN;*
CANTONESE: *CHOI SUM*

Choi sum is a Cantonese word, meaning "cabbage heart". A member of the brassica family, it is related to oilseed rape. It has bright green leaves and thin, pale green stalks that are slightly grooved. The bright yellow flowers at the centre are responsible for its common name of Chinese flowering cabbage.

Aroma and flavour

Choi sum has a pleasant aroma with a mild taste, and remains crisp and tender if correctly cooked.

Culinary uses

A very popular green vegetable, choi sum can be used for soups or stir-fries, either solo or with other ingredients.

Preparation and cooking techniques

Little preparation is required, just wash and shake off excess water before cutting the leaves to the required size. Most restaurant chefs leave the stalks whole, simply blanching them in stock for a minute or two before draining them and serving with oyster sauce.

Preparing choi sum

Choi sum is easy to prepare. You can chop leaves and stalks into large pieces before cooking, but they are more often left whole.

Wash choi sum under cold running water, then shake off the excess water and separate the stalks before use.

Storage

Choi sum can be kept in the salad compartment of a refrigerator for 3–4 days if bought fresh, but should ideally be used as quickly as possible.

Right: Every part of Chinese broccoli is edible.

MUSTARD GREENS

MANDARIN: *GAICAI;* CANTONESE: *GAI CHOI*

Although this vegetable is related to choi sum it looks and tastes completely different. In shape, it resembles a cos or romaine lettuce. Unlike many Asian vegetables, which were relatively unknown outside their country of origin until recently, mustard greens have long been cultivated in Europe. However, the dark green, slightly puckered leaves were always thrown away; only the seeds were prized. It took the Chinese to introduce us to their delicious flavour. Mustard greens are most abundant during the winter and spring, especially from Asian groceries, but also from specialist producers and farm stores.

Aroma and flavour

Although mustard greens look a bit like lettuces, there the resemblance ends. The leaves have a robust, often fiery flavour. They can taste quite bitter.

Culinary uses

Very young leaves can be eaten raw in salads; mature leaves are best stir-fried or simmered in soups. In China, most of the crop is salted and preserved.

Preparation and cooking techniques

Before being stir-fried, mustard greens benefit from being blanched in lightly salted boiling water or stock; this preserves the green colour of the leaves and also gets rid of some of the bitter taste.

Storage

Provided that they are fresh when you buy them, mustard greens will keep for a few days if stored in the salad compartment of a refrigerator.

CHINESE BROCCOLI

CHINESE: *GAILAN*

Chinese broccoli has more in common with purple sprouting broccoli than the plump, tight heads of Calabrese broccoli familiar to Western shoppers. The Chinese version has long, slender stems, loose leaves and can be recognized by the tiny white or yellow flowers in the centre.

Aroma and flavour

As its Chinese name *gailan* (mustard orchid) implies, Chinese broccoli belongs to the same family as mustard greens, but is more robust, both in terms of texture and of taste. There is a definite cabbage flavour.

Culinary uses

Every part of this beautiful vegetable is edible – the flower, leaves and stalk – and each has its own individual flavour and texture. Chinese broccoli is often served on its own as a side dish, but it can also be combined with other ingredients that have contrasting colours, flavours and textures.

Preparation and cooking techniques

Discard the tough outer leaves, then peel off any tough skin from the stalks. Leave each stalk whole if it is to be served on its own, or cut into two to three short sections if it is to be cooked with other ingredients. Before stir-frying it is usual to blanch the vegetable briefly in salted boiling water or in stock, which will enhance the flavour.

Storage

Chinese broccoli will keep for only 2–3 days even if it is very fresh when bought; after that the leaves will start to wilt and go yellow, and the stalks are liable to become tough.

AUBERGINE/EGGPLANT

<small>MANDARIN: *QIEZI;* CANTONESE: *NGAI GWA*</small>

There are numerous varieties of this wonderfully versatile vegetable, which is technically a fruit. Although it belongs to the same family as peppers and tomatoes, which originated in America, the aubergine (eggplant) is native to tropical Asia, where it has been cultivated for more than 2,000 years.

The most common type in Asia – the Asian or Japanese aubergine – is tubular rather than ovoid in shape and is usually straight or slightly curved. As a rule, Asian aubergines tend to be much smaller and more slender than western varieties, and some are tiny.

Below: Purple and green aubergines from Thailand

Right: Thai baby aubergines

In Thailand, there are aubergines that are not much bigger than peas. Aubergines come in a wide range of colours, from black through purple, orange and green to the white egg-shaped vegetables that inspired the vegetable's American name of eggplant.

Aroma and flavour

Whatever its shape, size or colour, the aubergine has a unique flavour that is almost impossible to describe. Some object to its smoky, subtly bitter taste, others prize it for the same reason.

Culinary uses

Aubergine absorbs the flavours of other ingredients like a sponge, and therefore benefits from being cooked with strongly flavoured foods and seasonings. It can be stir-fried, deep-fried, stuffed and baked, braised, steamed, or served cold, but seldom eaten raw except in Thailand, where strips of very young aubergine are served like crudités, with spicy dips.

Preparation and cooking techniques

Wash and remove the stalk, then cut into slices, strips or chunks. It is seldom necessary to peel an aubergine, and the smooth skin not only adds a beautiful colour, but also provides the dish with an interesting texture and flavour.

Some recipes advise layering aubergine slices with salt before cooking. This is not essential if the vegetables are young and tender, but in older specimens this is done to reduce bitterness and to prevent the slices from absorbing excessive amounts of oil during cooking. If you do salt an aubergine, be sure to rinse and dry it thoroughly afterwards.

Another method that stops the aubergine from drawing up too much oil, but which has the advantage of retaining the succulent texture, is to dry-fry the strips or slices over a medium heat for 4–5 minutes before cooking them in hot oil.

Storage

Aubergines from various parts of the world are available all year round. Select small- to medium-size firm aubergines with a uniformly smooth skin that is free from blemishes. Large specimens with a shrivelled skin are overmature and are likely to be bitter and rather tough.

When bought in prime condition, aubergines will keep for 3–4 days in the salad compartment of the refrigerator.

CHAYOTE

CANTONESE: *FAT SAU GWA*

There are several names for this pear-shaped marrow, vegetable pear being one, and custard marrow being another. In the Caribbean they know it as christophine, but in other parts of the world it is *choko, shu-shu* or *chinchayote.* The Chinese call it "Buddha's fist", because it resembles hands clasped in prayer, with the fingers folded inside.

Aroma and flavour

Chayote has a smooth, pale green skin with a subtle aroma. The taste is delicate, and the texture is fairly firm, not unlike that of courgette (zucchini).

Culinary uses

Because of the religious connotations of its shape, chayote is often used as an offering during Buddhist festivals. It can be eaten raw or cooked, and in Asia is usually stir-fried or simmered in soups.

Preparation and cooking techniques

Wash but do not peel the vegetable, cut it open and remove the stone from the centre, then cut into thin slices or strips. Since chayote has a mild taste, Asian cooks often cook it with strong seasonings such as garlic, ginger, onion and/or chillies.

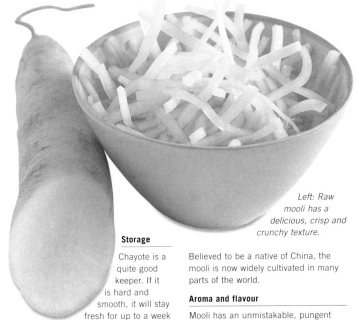

Left: Raw mooli has a delicious, crisp and crunchy texture.

Storage

Chayote is a quite good keeper. If it is hard and smooth, it will stay fresh for up to a week if stored in the salad compartment of the refrigerator.

MOOLI/DAIKON

MANDARIN: *LUOBO;* CANTONESE: *LOH BAK;* VIETNAMESE: *LOBAC;* MALAY: *LAPHUG*

This large, thin cylindrical vegetable looks rather like a carrot, but with a smooth, white skin. A member of the radish family, it is sometimes known as the oriental radish.

Believed to be a native of China, the mooli is now widely cultivated in many parts of the world.

Aroma and flavour

Mooli has an unmistakable, pungent smell of radish. The texture is crisp and crunchy and it tastes quite mild, with a juicy, sweet flavour similar to turnip.

Culinary uses

Mooli can be eaten raw or cooked. Both the Chinese and the Japanese also pickle it. Cantonese cooks use it to make a stiff pudding with rice flour, which is often served as part of the dim sum selection in a restaurant. At home, mooli is usually braised with meat such as pork or beef, but it is also delicious in a stir-fry. Add it for the last few minutes of cooking so that the slices stay crisp and juicy.

Preparation and cooking techniques

Like carrots, mooli should be scraped or peeled, then cut into slices or chunks before cooking. The beauty of this vegetable is that it withstands long cooking without disintegrating, and absorbs the flavours of other ingredients, but also tastes good raw.

Storage

Buy mooli with firm, unblemished skin. Stored in a cool, dark place or in the salad compartment of the refrigerator, it should keep for 3–4 days.

Above: Chayote can be eaten raw, stir-fried or cooked in soups.

BITTER MELON

MANDARIN: *KUGUA*; CANTONESE: *FOO GWA*

Also called "bitter gourd", this warty-skinned vegetable originated in Southeast Asia, and is popular in Indonesia, the Philippines and Thailand, where it is used as the basis for a delicious curry. The plant resembles a wild grape vine, and is grown in the West mainly as an ornament, for its attractive foliage and strange-looking fruit.

Aroma and flavour

As the name implies, the flesh of this vegetable tastes quite bitter, especially when it is green and immature, but it has a rather sweet and fragrant smell. The flavour mellows somewhat as the vegetable ripens and turns first pale green and then yellow-orange (when it is past its prime).

Culinary uses

Bitterness may be an acquired taste, but it has a cooling effect in a hot climate, and is highly regarded in Asia. The flesh readily absorbs other flavours and its bitter tang can provide a wonderful accent in a dish.

Preparation and cooking

Since the odd-looking skin is a special feature of this vegetable, it is never peeled. Just wash it, slice it in half lengthways, remove and discard the seeds, then cut into slices or chunks. Blanch these in lightly salted boiling water for about 2 minutes to remove excess bitterness, then drain before stir-frying or adding to soups.

Right: In China and Thailand winter melon is made into a soup and served in the shell.

Storage

Firm, green bitter melon will keep for 3–4 days (and should be allowed to ripen a little before use), but a soft yellowish one should be used within a day or two.

WINTER MELON

CHINESE: *DONG GUA*

This is one of the largest vegetables grown in Asia, or anywhere else. They can grow to 25cm/10in in diameter, and weigh more than 25kg/55lb. Thankfully for the cook, there are small ones, and the larger melons are normally sliced and sold in sections.

Above: Despite its name, bitter melon has a sweet smell.

Aroma and flavour

Winter melon has a delicate smell and tastes rather like courgette (zucchini).

Culinary uses

Despite its name, winter melon is really a warm season vegetable, and since more than 90 per cent of it is water, it is popular in hot weather as it is juicy yet not too filling. It is always cooked before being eaten.

Preparation and cooking

Winter melon is prepared in much the same way as pumpkin. The rind must be cut off and the seeds and coarse fibres at the centre scooped out before the flesh is cut into thin strips or wedges. It tastes good in stir-fries or soups. Winter melon readily absorbs other flavours, and is often cooked with strongly-flavoured ingredients such as dried shrimps, ham and dried mushrooms.

Storage

A whole winter melon will keep for days if not weeks, but if it has been sliced open, it should be eaten as soon as possible as the exposed surface will deteriorate rapidly.

ONIONS

MANDARIN: *YANG CONG;* CANTONESE: *YUN TS'UNG*

The common onion so widely used in the West is known as "foreign onion" in Asia, where shallots and spring onions are generally preferred. They come in a wide variety of sizes and colours from huge golden-skinned globes to smaller, milder red and white onions.

Aroma and flavour

There is no mistaking the strong aroma and flavour of the onion. It is used as a flavouring ingredient throughout Asia, but is seldom served on its own as a side vegetable.

Culinary uses

The onion is a very versatile vegetable. It can be eaten fried, boiled, steamed or raw, and it is an essential component of a great number of sauces and dishes, such as curries and stews. Fried onions are a popular garnish, especially in South-east Asia.

Preparation and cooking techniques

Peel the onions and remove the papery skin, then slice and chop as required. A good tip for avoiding irritation to the eyes when cutting an onion is to leave the root in place until the last minute, and, when the root is exposed, to press it down on the surface of the chopping board rather than expose it to the air.

Storage

If you buy firm onions with smooth, unmarked skins, and store them in a cool, dry place, they will keep for several weeks. If any show signs of sprouting, use them immediately.

SHALLOTS

MANDARIN: *FEN CONG;* CANTONESE: *TS'UNG TAU;* THAI: *HOM DAENG*

Although they belong to the same family as garlic, leeks, chives and onions – and look suspiciously like baby onions – shallots are very much their own vegetable. Sometimes called bunching onions, they have bulbs that multiply to produce clusters joined at the root end.

Aroma and flavour

Shallots tend to be sweeter and much milder than large onions. Some Thai varieties are sweet enough to be used in desserts.

Above: Small red onions

Culinary uses

Indispensable in South-east Asian kitchens, shallots are far more popular than both regular onions and spring onions (scallions) for everyday use. Ground with garlic, ginger and other aromatics, shallots form the standard marinade and are also an essential ingredient in curry pastes and satay sauce. Dried shallots *(hanh huong)* are a popular alternative in Vietnam.

Preparation and cooking techniques

Trim the shallots, peel off the skin, then prise the bulbs apart. Leave these whole for braising, or chop as required. Thinly-sliced shallot rings are sometimes dry-fried until crisp, then used as a garnish.

Storage

Shallots will keep for several months in a cool, dry place.

SPRING ONIONS/SCALLIONS

MANDARIN: *QING CONG;* CANTONESE: *TS'UNG;* JAPANESE: *NEGI*

Spring onions, known as green onions or scallions in the West, have been cultivated in China and Japan since time immemorial. The leaves are tubular, and are always sold with the small white onion bulb attached. Japanese spring onions are larger than the European variety and have blue-green stems.

Above: Small and large onions

Aroma and flavour

Spring onions have a more subtle smell than onions and the taste can vary from fairly mild to really pungent. Smaller bulbs generally have a milder flavour.

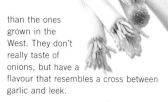

Left: Spring onions

How to make spring onion curls

1 Trim off most of the green leaves from the spring onion bulbs to leave a 7.5cm/3in length.

2 Finely shred the spring onions to within about 1cm/½ in of the root end.

3 Place the shredded spring onions in a bowl of iced water and chill for 15–20 minutes or until the shredded ends have curled.

Culinary uses

In Asia, spring onions are served as a vegetable as well as being used as a flavouring agent. The vegetable forms a yin-yang pair when used in combination with ginger. Spring onions are yin, and ginger is yang.

Preparation and cooking techniques

Trim off the roots from the bulbs and discard any wilted outer leaves, then separate the green and white parts, and cut these into short lengths or shreds. Recipes sometimes stipulate that only the white parts are used. If spring onion green is used in a recipe, it is usually added at the last moment (the white part takes longer to cook) or is simply used raw, as a garnish.

Storage

It is best not to keep spring onions in a plastic bag, but instead store them loose in the salad drawer of the refrigerator to allow them to "breathe". That way they should stay fresh for up to 4–5 days if bought in prime condition.

CHINESE CHIVES

MANDARIN: *JIUCAI;* CANTONESE: *GAU CHOI*

Although they belong to the same family, Chinese chives are quite different from the Western variety, both in their appearance and taste. Two species are available: one has long, flat green leaves like a small, thin leek, the other has long, tubular stalks with a single bud at the tip.

Aroma and flavour

Chinese chives have a much stronger aroma than the ones grown in the West. They don't really taste of onions, but have a flavour that resembles a cross between garlic and leek.

Culinary uses

Chinese chives are seldom used as a garnish, but are either served as a vegetable in their own right, or used as an ingredient in cooked dishes, especially with seafood or meat. A very popular Chinese vegetarian dish features chopped chives cooked with scrambled eggs and tofu. This is not only colourful, but tastes delicious.

Preparation and cooking techniques

Chinese chives are always sold as leaves only, without the bulb. Uniformly dark green leaves are good, and any that are turning yellow should be discarded. Wash well, drain, then chop or slice into short sections. Cantonese cooks often blanch chives in boiling water or stock for a minute or two before stir-frying.

Storage

Fresh chives kept in an airtight box in the refrigerator will keep for 4–5 days.

Right: Chinese chives

POTATOES AND SWEET POTATOES

MANDARIN: *PENSHU;* CANTONESE: *FAN SHUE*

Although potatoes and sweet potatoes are unrelated, this was not appreciated when they first reached Asia, and they were both given the same Chinese name. In northern China white potatoes are a staple food, although not as important as noodles; in southern China they are far less significant. Sweet potatoes are popular in the Philippines.

Aroma and flavour

Several varieties of both regular potatoes and sweet potatoes are grown in the East, so tubers vary in size, shape and colour, as well as in taste and texture. The sweet potatoes have a red skin and flesh that varies from pale white to yellow-orange in colour.

Culinary uses

Where potatoes are used, they generally form part of a braised dish, or are served as a side dish or snack. Potato flour is a popular thickener.

Preparation and cooking techniques

Both regular potatoes and sweet potatoes are prepared in the same way: after peeling, they are sliced or diced, then stir-fried or braised with seasonings or spices. Thai cooks make a very sweet dessert based on deep-fried sweet potatoes.

Above: Potatoes and sweet potatoes

Storage

Potatoes should always be stored in a cool, dark, dry place. Because of their high sugar content, sweet potatoes do not keep well.

TAROES

MANDARIN: *YUTOU;* CANTONESE: *WOO TAU*

These tubers grow in tropical areas and are widely used throughout South-east Asia. There are two basic varieties: the big, barrel-shaped one with the hairy brown skin is the most common, but there is also a smaller variety which is known in the West as eddo or dasheen. The flesh is white, with purple flecks.

Aroma and flavour

Cooked taro has a subtle flavour that has been described as resembling floury water chestnuts.

Culinary uses

Taroes can be substituted for potatoes in most dishes. They take up a great deal of liquid, so are good in stews. Asian cooks often include taro when cooking belly pork or duck as it absorbs the excess fat.

Above: A barrel-shaped taro

Preparation and cooking techniques

It is essential to cook taroes as there are toxins just below the skin. These are eliminated when the vegetable is boiled. Peel the vegetables thickly, wearing gloves, or cook them in their jackets.

Storage

Store in a cool, dark, dry place. Taroes have a thick skin, so they keep well.

YAMS

MANDARIN: *SHANYAO;* CANTONESE: *SA GOT*

Yams are believed to have originated in China, but are now grown in all tropical regions. The Chinese yam has fine whiskers and the flesh is creamy white.

Aroma and flavour

Yams do not have a pronounced flavour, but are mildly sweet and quite juicy.

Culinary uses

Like taroes, yams can be used instead of potatoes. Asian cooks often use them as a substitute for bamboo shoots.

Preparation and cooking techniques

Peel yams thickly, removing both the outer skin and the layer underneath. Like taroes, they contain a toxin that is eliminated when boiled. Slice or dice the flesh and put into salted water.

Storage

As for taroes.

LOTUS ROOT

MANDARIN: *LIAN OU;* CANTONESE: *LEEN NGAU*

Lotus root, also known as *renkon,* is used throughout Asia and is particularly popular in China and Japan. Raw lotus root looks like a string of fat sausages covered in black mud. Clean, peel and slice it, however, and a beautiful pattern emerges in each cross-section, the result of narrow channels that run through the root. Fresh lotus roots can sometimes be purchased from Asian stores. Canned lotus root is readily available, and dried slices are popular for serving in soups.

Aroma and flavour

The root has very little aroma, but the flavour is mild and subtly sweet. It has a wonderful crunchy texture.

Culinary uses

Apart from the root being used as a vegetable, the seeds of the lotus are eaten as a delicate fruit when fresh, or used as a dessert in dried form. They can also be puréed and blended with sugar to make a filling for cakes and buns. Dried lotus leaves are used for wrapping food in a number of famous Asian dishes.

Preparation and cooking techniques

Fresh lotus roots must be scrubbed. Chop them into sections, discarding the tough "necks" between, then peel off the outer skin. The sliced flesh is usually

Above: Lotus root and seeds

sliced or cut into large chunks, but whole roots can also be stuffed. Japanese cooks often soak the slices in water acidulated with rice vinegar for 5 minutes before boiling them. They cook quickly and make a pretty garnish. Dried lotus roots are sold sliced, and should be soaked in water for 1–2 hours before using in soups or stews. Canned lotus roots are ready for use.

Storage

Fresh lotus root should keep for about 4 days if bought in good condition. Select firm and unblemished roots. If the surface is punctured, dirt will have penetrated inside, which makes the roots difficult to clean. Dried roots will keep almost indefinitely if stored in a dry, cool place.

DRIED LILY BUDS

MANDARIN: *HUANG HUA; JINZHEN*
CANTONESE: *GUM JUM*

Also known in Chinese as "yellow flower" or "golden needles", these dried buds of the tiger lily are popular throughout China and South-east Asia.

Aroma and flavour

Tiger lily has a unique fragrance, which intensifies when the buds are dried. They have a mild sweet taste and a pleasant crunchy texture.

Culinary uses

In Chinese cooking, dried lily buds are often combined with dried black fungus to create an interesting contrast in colour, flavour and texture. The buds are also a popular ingredient in Buddhist vegetarian cooking.

Preparation and cooking techniques

Dried lily buds must be soaked in warm water for 30 minutes or so, then drained and rinsed in cold water until clean. Once the hard ends have been snipped off, the buds can be used whole, or cut in half.

Storage

Dried lily buds keep almost indefinitely if stored in an airtight jar, away from strong light, heat or moisture.

Below: Lily buds are never used fresh, but always dried.

the canned ones, but need more preparation. They must be soaked in water for 2–3 hours before use.

Storage

Fresh shoots will keep for up to a week in winter, but only 2–3 days in summer. Unused shoots from a can will keep in the refrigerator for several days if stored in a jar of fresh water that is changed daily. Dried shoots will keep almost indefinitely in a cool, dry place.

BEANSPROUTS

MANDARIN: *DOUYA;*
CANTONESE: *DAU NGA CHOI*

Several types of bean can be sprouted, but the ones most often used in Asian cooking are the small "green" sprouts from mung beans and the larger "yellow" or soya bean sprouts. The fresh sprouts are widely available in supermarkets, health food shops and markets, or you can sprout the beans at home. Avoid canned beansprouts, which are limp and tasteless.

BAMBOO SHOOTS

MANDARIN: *ZHUSUN;* CANTONESE: *CHUK SUN;*
JAPANESE: *TAKENOKO*

Bamboo is one of the most important plants of eastern Asia, and several species are grown, of varying sizes. The shoots used as a vegetable are dug just before they come above ground. Fresh bamboo shoots are difficult to come by outside Asia, but canned shoots are readily available. Vietnamese cooks are fond of pickled bamboo shoots.

Aroma and flavour

The aroma of bamboo shoots is quite delicate. Lovers of this vegetable – and they are legion – claim that the mild sweet flavour changes subtly with the seasons. Therefore winter bamboo shoots are more highly prized.

Culinary uses

In China, where bamboo shoots have been eaten for well over a thousand years, they are regarded as the queen of all vegetables. The shoots not only taste delicious of themselves, but also complement the flavours of other ingredients with which they are cooked.

Above: Chunks of raw bamboo shoot and canned slices

Preparation and cooking techniques

If you are lucky enough to locate fresh bamboo shoots, it is vital to parboil them before cooking, as they contain an acid that is highly toxic. Remove the base and the hard outer leaves, then cut the core into large chunks. Boil these in salted water for 20–30 minutes, then drain, rinse in clean water and drain again. Cut into slices, shreds or cubes for further cooking. Canned bamboo shoots are ready cooked, so they just need to be rinsed and drained before using them. Dried bamboo shoots have been dried in the sun, so they are tastier than

Right: Mung bean sprouts (in bowl) and soya bean sprouts

Aroma and flavour

Soya bean sprouts have a stronger flavour than mung bean sprouts, but both are relatively delicate, with a pleasant crunchy texture.

Culinary uses

Stir-frying, with or without meat, is the most popular way of cooking beansprouts. Mung bean sprouts can be eaten raw in salads, while soya bean sprouts are often used in soups.

Preparation and cooking techniques

Wash the beansprouts in cold water to remove the husks and tiny roots. Some restaurants actually top and tail each individual shoot, which turns this humble vegetable into a luxury dish. Since the sprouts are largely composed of water, overcooking will render them limp and fibrous, and the characteristic crisp texture will be lost.

Storage

To preserve their lily-white translucence, keep beansprouts in water in a covered box in the refrigerator. They will stay fresh for 2–3 days.

WATER CHESTNUTS

MANDARIN: *BIQI;* CANTONESE: *MA TAI*

Water chestnuts are popular throughout Asia, cropping up in Chinese, Japanese, Korean and South-east Asian recipes. The name is slightly misleading as they do grow in water (and are actually cultivated in paddy fields) but they certainly aren't nuts. Instead, they are corms, which are about the size of walnuts. There are several varieties, but the Chinese type, which are dark brown and look a bit like small daffodil bulbs, are the most widely available outside Asia. They have a soft skin which, because they grow in water, tends to be covered in dried dirt. Fresh water chestnuts are superior to canned.

Aroma and flavour

The best thing about water chestnuts is their texture. The snow-white flesh is crunchy and juicy, and stays that way,

no matter how long they are cooked for. This, coupled with their pleasantly sweet taste, makes them irresistible.

Culinary uses

Water chestnuts can be eaten raw in both savoury and fruit salads. In many Asian countries they are eaten as a snack food, in much the same way as peanuts are eaten in the West. Cooked water chestnuts taste wonderful in stir-fries or braised dishes. The flesh is also made into a flour, which is used both as a thickening agent and in cakes.

Preparation and cooking techniques

Fresh water chestnuts are not very appealing, especially as they are usually covered in dried mud, but once they are washed and peeled, they do not look very different from the canned variety. Water chestnuts can be left whole, sliced or diced, and are sometimes minced with fish or meat.

Storage

Fresh, unpeeled water chestnuts will keep well if stored in a paper bag in the vegetable crisper in the refrigerator. Once peeled, however, they must be kept in water in a covered container in the refrigerator and should be used within a week.

Horned water chestnuts
This nut is often confused with the vegetable of the same name, but they look entirely different. Horned water chestnuts (*ling gok*), which have been eaten in China for hundreds of years, have a hard, shiny black shell with two distinctive, sharp horns. The nuts measure about 5cm/2in from tip to tip, and the shells, which are extremely difficult to crack, enclose ivory coloured flesh that is starchy and sweet tasting. The nuts are never eaten raw, but can be steamed or boiled and served like a vegetable, added to soups or braised in stews.

Horned water chestnuts can be bought in Asian and Chinese stores and will keep fresh for several weeks in the refrigerator. However, once shelled the flesh, which should be white and unblemished, needs to be used within a day or two as it quickly becomes rancid.

Below: Canned water chestnuts (in bowl) and fresh water chestnut corms, which look a little like small daffodil bulbs.

MANGETOUTS

MANDARIN: *XUEDOU*; CANTONESE: *HOH LAN DAU*

Also known as snow peas, mangetouts must be one of the best known and best loved of all Asian vegetables, yet its Cantonese name, meaning Dutch bean, suggests that at some point in its long history it was perceived as being of Western origin. The French name – *mangetout* – means "eat all" and is an apt description, for the vegetable is valued for its pods, not the peas, which never mature. Sugar snap peas are similar, but have slightly plumper pods.

Aroma and flavour

Freshly picked mangetouts have a fresh aroma, but this vanishes quite quickly. The flavour is slightly sweet. The best way to appreciate these delicate, tender pods is to stir-fry them, when they will prove perfect partners for prawns (shrimp), scallops and other shellfish.

Preparation and cooking techniques

Mangetouts need very little by way of preparation. Simply wash, then top and tail the pods. It should not be necessary to string them if the pods are young and tender. Leave whole if small; snap in half if large. Stir-fry on their own, or with other vegetables such as carrots, spring onions and baby corn cobs, in hot oil over high heat for a short time, and do not use too much seasoning.

Storage

Young, crisp and unblemished mangetouts with thin skins will keep fresh for up to 4–5 days in the salad compartment of the refrigerator.

SNAKE BEANS/GREEN BEANS

MANDARIN: *DOUJIAO* CANTONESE: *DAU GOK*

Also called yard-long beans, asparagus beans or Thai beans, these resemble French beans but are much longer. There are two

Above: Snake beans are also known as yard-long beans.

varieties: a pale green type, and a darker green one that is considered to be better. Thinner beans are best.

Aroma and flavour

These exceptionally long beans smell and taste rather like their French cousins, but the flavour is not identical. When young they are slightly sweeter and more tender, but the mature beans can be tough, and may need slightly longer cooking than French beans.

Culinary uses

Snake beans are usually stir-fried, either on their own or with other ingredients, or served cold as a salad after blanching. They are also delicious blanched and tossed in sesame oil.

Preparation and cooking techniques

Having washed the beans, cut them into 5cm/2in lengths. They go particularly well with shredded pork, chicken or prawns (shrimp), and should only be lightly seasoned. In Sichuan, they are used for a dish called *kan shao* (dry-frying), with strongly flavoured seasonings such as garlic, ginger or chillies.

Storage

Try to use snake beans within about 3 days of purchase before they turn yellow and become stringy.

Right: Mangetouts (top) and sugar snap peas

LUFFA

MANDARIN: *SIGUA;*
CANTONESE: *SZE GWA*

Also known as angled luffa, silk gourd, silk squash or Chinese okra, this vegetable looks like a long, skinny courgette or a very large okra pod. The most common variety is ridged down its length and is dark green in colour. Although not so common, smooth luffa is larger and the shape is more cylindrical, with a slightly thicker base. It is much heavier than ridged luffa, and is lighter in colour.

Aroma and flavour

Luffa has a mild, delicate taste, very similar to that of cucumber and the two are interchangeable in most cooked dishes.

Culinary uses

Used mostly in stir-fries and soups, luffa goes well with foods that will not overwhelm its delicate flavour, such as chicken breast, fish and seafood. It is also a popular ingredient in all kinds of vegetable dishes.

Preparation and cooking techniques

If the luffa is young, all you need to do is wash and slice it. Luffas seldom need peeling, but sometimes the ridges toughen as the vegetable ripens, in

Above: A whole luffa and slices

which case remove the ridges but leave the skin between, so that the luffa is striped green and white. If the skin is very tough, it is best to peel it completely. Like cucumber, luffa should not be overcooked, but unlike cucumber, it is never eaten raw.

Above: Crunchy-textured baby corn cobs make a colourful addition to stir-fries.

Storage

Keep fresh luffa in the vegetable compartment of the refrigerator, but do not store it for too long as within two or three days of purchase it will start to go limp.

BABY CORN COBS

MANDARIN: *YUMI SUN;*
CANTONESE: *YOOK MY SON*

Baby corn cobs are available both fresh and canned. The canned ones can be quite large, and are not as tender and delicate as the smaller, fresh cobs.

Aroma and flavour

Baby corn has a lovely sweet fragrance and flavour, as well as an irresistible crunchy texture.

Culinary uses

The baby cobs can be used in salads, stir-fries and soups. In stir-fries, they add colour as well as flavour, and are good combined with carrots, (bell) peppers, broccoli and mangetouts (snow peas).

Preparation and cooking techniques

Wash the cobs. Large ones can be halved lengthways or sliced in thick diagonal chunks, but small ones are best left whole. Asian cooks blanch them in lightly salted water for 1 minute before stir-frying. Drain and rinse canned cobs before use. Do not overcook them.

Storage

Fresh baby corn cobs will keep for up to a week in the salad compartment of the refrigerator, but they are best eaten soon after purchase.

FRESH AND DRIED MUSHROOMS

SHIITAKE

MANDARIN: *XIANG GU*; CANTONESE: *HUNG GWO*; JAPANESE: *SHIITAKE*

Fresh shiitake mushrooms used to be a rarity in the West, but are now cultivated and are freely available in supermarkets. They resemble large, brown button mushrooms in appearance, but are actually a type of fungus that grows on hardwood logs in their native Japan. Shiitake mushrooms are frequently dried (see Dried Black Mushrooms, overleaf) and are also available in cans.

Aroma and flavour

These meaty mushrooms taste slightly acidic, and have a decidedly slippery texture. They contain twice as much protein as button mushrooms. When shiitake are dried the flavour intensifies.

Culinary uses

Although small mushrooms can be eaten raw, cooking brings out their flavour. They are used in soups, stir-fries and braised dishes. They are a popular ingredient in vegetarian dishes, and go well with noodles and rice. They are good combined with less strongly flavoured food.

Below: Fresh and dried shiitake mushrooms

Preparation and cooking techniques

The stems of fresh shiitake mushrooms are usually removed before cooking. Whole or sliced caps can be sautéed, used in stir-fries, cooked in braised dishes or added to soups. Because of their robust texture, shiitake need longer cooking than button (white) mushrooms, but they should not be cooked for too long or they may begin to toughen. To serve shiitake mushrooms in a salad, boil

Left: Oyster mushrooms

them briefly in water or stock, then cool them slightly and toss in a French dressing before serving.

Storage

Store fresh shiitake mushrooms in a paper bag in the refrigerator. Eat within three days of purchase.

OYSTER MUSHROOMS

MANDARIN: *BAOYU GU*; CANTONESE: *HOWYOO GWO*; JAPANESE: *SHIMEJI*

In the wild, oyster mushrooms grow in clumps on rotting wood. The caps, gills and stems are all the same colour, which can be pearl grey, pink or yellow. Once thought of exclusively as wild mushrooms, they are now grown commercially and are widely available in Western supermarkets.

Aroma and flavour

The flavour is fairly mild, with a slight suggestion of seafood.

Culinary uses

Oyster mushrooms are popular in soups and stir-fries, and they are also used in noodle and rice dishes.

Preparation and cooking techniques

Oyster mushrooms seldom need trimming. Large ones should be torn, rather than cut into pieces. The soft texture becomes rubbery if they are overcooked, so always add them to cooked dishes at the last moment.

Storage

Buy oyster mushrooms that smell and look fresh, avoiding any with damp, slimy patches and those that have discoloured. Store in a paper bag in vegetable compartment of the refrigerator, and use as soon as possible after purchase. They do not keep for more than 2–3 days.

ENOKI MUSHROOMS

MANDARIN: *JINZHEN GU;* CANTONESE: *GUM JUM GWO;* JAPANESE: *ENO ITAKE*

Also called *enokitaki,* these are slender and exceedingly delicate mushrooms with long thin stems and tiny white caps. The Chinese name – "golden needle mushrooms" – is the same as that given to the dried tiger lily buds which they resemble. Fresh enoki mushrooms are popular in both China and Japan. Avoid canned ones.

Aroma and flavour

Enoki mushrooms have a delicate sweet and almost fruity flavour, and a deliciously crisp texture.

Culinary uses

The delicate flavour of enoki mushrooms is best appreciated if they are added raw to salads or lightly cooked and used as a garnish for soups or hot dishes.

Preparation and cooking techniques

The mushrooms are harvested in clumps, attached to a spongy root base which is cut off before use. The

Below: Sliced straw mushrooms, showing their attractive "umbrella" pattern.

mushrooms are then ready for use. They rapidly toughen if overcooked, so are usually added to soups or braised dishes shortly before serving. They are good in stir-fried dishes, too, but should not be cooked for longer than 1 minute.

Storage

If bought fresh, enoki mushrooms will keep for 4–5 days in the salad compartment of a refrigerator. Avoid any that have damp, slimy patches and those that have discoloured.

Above: Enoki mushrooms have pretty, tiny caps on elegant long stalks.

STRAW MUSHROOMS

MANDARIN: *CAOGU;* CANTONESE: *TSO GWO*

These small, grey-brown mushrooms are grown on beds of rice straw, hence the name. A native of China, they were introduced to South-east Asia by Chinese immigrants.

Aroma and flavour

Fresh straw mushrooms are not readily available in the West, but dried ones can sometimes be found in Asian or Chinese stores. Straw mushrooms have an even stronger aroma than Chinese dried black mushrooms. Canned straw mushrooms are widely available in Asian stores; they have a delicate, silky surface with a subtle, sweet taste and an unusual slippery texture.

Culinary uses

Because they have an almost neutral flavour, straw mushrooms can be combined with all sorts of ingredients in stir-fries, braised dishes and soups. They are an essential ingredient in many Chinese dishes, and they are also used for making mushroom soy sauce.

Preparation and cooking techniques

Canned straw mushrooms must be drained and thoroughly rinsed before use. They are usually cut in half lengthways. This not only reveals the rather attractive "umbrella" pattern, but

it also makes them much easier to pick up with chopsticks. Like all mushrooms, straw mushrooms must not be overcooked, especially the canned ones, as they have been cooked already.

Storage

Fresh straw mushrooms are difficult to store, which explains why they are not often seen outside Asia. Dried ones can be stored almost indefinitely, though they may lose some of their flavour.

DRIED BLACK MUSHROOMS/ FRAGRANT MUSHROOMS

Dried black mushrooms are widely used throughout Asia, and are exported around the world. Although they are frequently labelled as "Chinese", to distinguish them from other dried mushrooms, and have come to be widely known as such, the majority of dried black mushrooms sold in Asian stores actually come from Japan, which produces and exports far more dried black mushrooms than does China.

Aroma and flavour

There are generally three different grades of dried black mushrooms, with caps that range in colour from dark grey, to brown-black or tan. The cheapest of these has quite thin caps, may be sold with or without stalks, and may well be labelled "fragrant mushrooms", which is the generic term for shiitake mushrooms. Next come the "winter mushrooms" which have thicker caps and taste more fleshy. The most expensive type are called "flower mushrooms". These are the best of the winter mushrooms. The caps are so thick that they crack, revealing the flower pattern that earned them their name. All three have a dusky aroma with a fragrant flavour, which is much intensified by the drying process.

Above: Dried black mushrooms are also known as fragrant mushrooms and are the dried form of shiitake mushrooms.

Culinary uses

These mushrooms are wonderfully versatile as they can be stir-fried, braised, steamed and used in soups. They form an important part of the vegetarians' diet, and are an ideal partner for bamboo shoots, as they offer a harmonious contrast in colour, aroma, flavour and texture. For non-vegetarians, they can be cooked with seafood, poultry and meat, and, of course, other vegetables.

Preparation and cooking techniques

Dried mushrooms must be soaked in water under cover until supple, before use. The best way is to soak in cold water for several hours or overnight, depending on the thickness of the caps. When time is short, they can be soaked in warm water for 30 minutes, but should not be soaked in hot water, as much of the fragrance will be lost. Do not discard the soaking water; it will enrich the flavour of the dish.

After soaking the mushrooms squeeze them dry and discard the stalks, if any. Small mushrooms can be left whole, but larger ones should be halved, quartered or coarsely chopped. The thinner dried mushrooms are usually either thinly sliced or shredded, but thicker ones, particularly the pretty "flower mushrooms" are generally left whole to show off their attractive shape.

Storage

Dried black mushrooms should keep for a very long time (over a year) if stored in a dry, dark and cool place.

Using dried mushrooms

Dried mushrooms have a rich, intense flavour and are a useful store-cupboard stand-by for adding to Asian dishes. Once they have been reconstituted they can be stir-fried, braised, steamed and used in soups. Dried mushrooms often require longer cooking than fresh ones.

To reconstitute dried mushrooms, soak them in boiling water for 20–30 minutes, depending on the variety and size of mushroom, until tender. Drain and rinse well to remove any grit and dirt.

WOOD EARS

MANDARIN: *MU'ER;* CANTONESE: *WAN YEE;*
VIETNAMESE: *MOC NHI*

Also known as cloud ears, tree
mushrooms or simply dried black
fungus, these are widely used in
China, Thailand and Vietnam. The
dried fungi are thin and brittle, and
look like pieces of charred paper.

Aroma and flavour

There is a slightly smoky smell when
wood ears are first removed from the
packet, but this disappears once they
have been soaked. They are almost
tasteless, but have an intriguing
texture, which is slippery yet crisp.

Culinary Uses

Wood ears are used in stir-frying,
braising and soups; the fungus is
traditionally paired with dried tiger lily in
several Chinese dishes, including the
popular hot-and-sour soup.

Preparation and cooking techniques

The fungus expands to six or eight
times its volume after soaking, so
use plenty of water in a

*Right: Wood ears are
also known as cloud
ears, tree mushrooms or
dried black fungus*

large bowl. As a guide, a piece of
dried fungus that would fit in a
tablespoon would require at least
250ml/8fl oz/1 cup water. Cover the
bowl and leave the fungus to soak for
about 30 minutes, then drain, rinse well
and drain again. Discard any hard roots
and sandy bits. Do not cut the fungus
into small pieces, just separate the
larger clumps into individual
"ears" in order to
preserve the pretty
wavy shape.

Storage

Dried fungus will
keep almost
indefinitely if stored
in a dry, cool place;
once soaked, it
should be kept in
clean water
in a covered
bowl in the
refrigerator.
It will keep
for 2–3
days.

*Left: Silver ears,
or dried white
fungus*

SILVER EARS

MANDARIN: *YINER;* CANTONESE: *PAK
MOOK YEE*

Also known as dried white fungus, this
earned its Chinese name of "silver ear"
partly because of its rarity, and partly
because of the high price it fetches on
account of its medicinal value. It is
regarded as being an excellent tonic,
and is also used for the relief of
insomnia and lung and liver diseases.

Aroma and flavour

Silver ears do not belong to the same
genus as wood ears. Although the
texture is similar, white fungus has a
sweeter flavour.

Culinary uses

While wood ears are regarded as
everyday ingredients, silver ears are
reserved for special occasions. Besides
being cooked with other vegetables
in vegetarian dishes, silver ears are
often cooked and then served on their
own, as one of the many dishes that
comprise a banquet.

Preparation, cooking techniques
and storage

Dried silver ears should be prepared,
cooked and stored in the same way as
dried wood ears.

SEAWEED

KOMBU

CHINESE: *HAIDAI;* JAPANESE: *KOMBU*

Several types of seaweed are used in Asian cooking, especially in Japan and Korea. The most common variety is the giant seaweed known as kelp in English. It is only available in dried form in the West, usually labelled with the Japanese name of kombu or konbu.

Aroma and flavour

Kombu is full of vitamins and minerals, and is particularly rich in iodine. It has a strong "sea" flavour and a crunchy texture.

Culinary uses

This type of seaweed is mainly used in soups in China, but is served poached or stewed as a vegetable in Japan, as well as being used to flavour the fish stock known as dashi.

Left: Kombu has a strong sea flavour.

Dashi

This stock, based on kombu and dried bonito flakes, is the basis of most Japanese soups; it can also be used instead of water in any dish that requires a delicately flavoured stock.

MAKES 800ML/27FL OZ/3½ CUPS

10cm/4in square of kombu
900ml/1½ pints/3¾ cups water
40g/1½ oz katsuobushi (dried
    bonito flakes)

2 Place the pan over a medium heat. Just before the water boils, lift out the seaweed (shred and use for soup).

1 Wipe the kombu with a damp cloth; cut it into 3–4 strips and put in a pan. Pour over the water, making sure that the seaweed is submerged, and soak for an hour.

3 Stir in the bonito flakes, bring to the boil, remove from the heat and leave to stand until the flakes have sunk to the bottom of the pan. Strain through a muslin-lined strainer.

Preparation and cooking techniques

Kombu has a pale powdery covering that contributes to its flavour, so do not wash it off; just wipe the seaweed with a damp cloth, then cut it into pieces of the required size. Soak these in cold water for 45–50 minutes. Both the seaweed and soaking water are used.

Storage

Kombu keeps for a long time if stored in a dry, cool place away from strong light.

NORI

JAPANESE: *NORI*

This is the wafer-thin, dried seaweed that is mainly used as a wrapping for sushi. It is sold in sheets that are dark green to black in colour, and almost transparent in places. The sheet should be grilled lightly on one side for making sushi, or on both sides until crisp if it is to be crumbled and used as a topping. Ready-toasted sheets known as yaki-nori are available from Asian stores. These are seasoned with ingredients such as soy sauce, salt and sesame oil. Ao-nori is dried seaweed that is crumbled so finely it looks like powder.

WAKAME

JAPANESE: *WAKAME*

This young dark-coloured seaweed has a delicate flavour and soft but crisp texture. It is available shredded, fresh (vacuum-packed) or dried, and is used in soups and salads. Dried wakame should be soaked in tepid water for 10–15 minutes until it softens and the fronds turn green. At this stage it should be drained, blanched in boiling water for about 1 minute, then refreshed under cold water and drained again. Use as directed in recipes or cool and chop to use in a salad.

HIJIK

JAPANESE: *HIJIK*

This Japanese seaweed – sometimes called hijiki – is similar to wakame. It is available dried and finely shredded, and should be reconstituted as for wakame.

AGAR-AGAR

CHINESE: *DONGFEN; YANGCAI;*
JAPANESE: *KANTEN*

This is the gelatinous substance obtained from the seaweed known as "rock-flower vegetable" in Chinese. Available from Asian stores as long dried strips or as a fine white powder sold in tubs, it is a very popular setting agent, especially for vegetarians seeking an alternative to gelatine.

Aroma and flavour

Agar-agar has no aroma or flavour, but will absorb the seasonings with which it is prepared for serving.

Culinary uses

Asian cooks sometimes use soaked strips of agar-agar in a salad, just as they would any other form of seaweed, but it is more often used as a setting agent, usually to make sweet jellies.

Right: Agar-agar is sold in thick and thin strips and as a powder that is used as a setting agent.

Above: Wakame (in bowl), hijik (on top) and nori seaweeds

Preparation and cooking techniques

To use agar-agar in a salad, soften the strips in lukewarm water for about 20–25 minutes, then drain and dry them on some kitchen paper. Separate the strips and cut them into short lengths. Combine the agar-agar with the other salad ingredients, add a dressing and toss to mix.

To use agar-agar to set a jelly, dissolve it slowly in water over a very low heat, which may take up to 10 minutes. Heat some milk and sugar, with a flavouring such as almond essence, in a separate pan, then mix with the agar-agar solution. Leave the mixture to cool, then chill for 3–4 hours until set. Agar-agar varies in strength, so check the packaging to

see how much you should use. As a guide, 5ml/1 tsp powder will set 300ml/½ pint/1¼ cups of liquid.

Storage

Agar-agar, both in strips and in the powdered form, will keep almost indefinitely if stored in a cool, dry place.

FRUIT

DURIAN

CHINESE: *LIU LIAN*; THAI: *THURIAN*

This tropical fruit originated in Malaysia or Borneo, and is very popular in South-east Asia. Round or oval, it has a dull green shell-like skin covered with pointed spines that turn yellow as the fruit ripens. A typical durian weighs about 2kg/4½lb, but they can grow even larger, up to 4.5kg/10lb.

Aroma and flavour

Durian has a very unpleasant smell, often likened to the stench of raw sewage. The ripe flesh, however, is as delicious as the odour is awful: sweet and creamy, with a hint of strawberries.

Culinary uses

The fruit is eaten raw, and the seeds are often roasted and eaten like nuts.

Preparation

Each fruit consists of three, four or five segments. Using a sharp knife, slit the hard shell of the durian at the segment

Below: A durian and its large seeds

Right: Mangosteen can be eaten on its own or added to a fruit salad.

joints, then press the segments out. Take care not to let the juice drip on to your clothes, as it stains. The soft, creamy flesh can be eaten with a spoon, or puréed, either for serving as a dessert or as an accompaniment to a curry. Some Asian cooks soak the durian segments in coconut milk for 10–12 hours before eating them, as they claim this eliminates the unpleasant smell.

Storage

This is not recommended, as the smell will soon pervade your home, however carefully you store the fruit. When buying, look for perfect, undamaged specimens, and get them home as quickly as possible. Don't attempt to take them on public transport; most carriers ban them!

MANGOSTEEN

CHINESE: *SANZHU GUO*; THAI: *MANG KHUT*

The only thing mangosteens and mangoes share in common, aside from being tropical fruits, is the first five letters of their names. Mangosteens are small, apple-shaped fruits with leathery brown skin that turns purple as they ripen. The flesh looks similar to that of a lychee, but tastes completely different. They are native to South-east Asia and are cultivated in Thailand.

Aroma and flavour

The tough skin surrounds delicious white flesh, which is divided into segments, each with a large seed. The pearly white flesh is fresh and fragrant. Some say it tastes like grapefruit.

Culinary uses

Mangosteens are always eaten raw, but the related kokum, which has a pleasant sour taste, is used as a souring agent in Indian cooking.

Preparation

Cut the fruit in half and remove the segments, taking care not to include any of the dark pink pith. Serve the segments solo or in a fruit salad.

Storage

Mangosteens keep well. If not over-ripe when bought, they should remain in good condition for up to 8–10 days.

LYCHEES

MANDARIN: *LIZHI;* CANTONESE: *LA-EE-TZEE;* THAI: *LIN-CHI*

Indigenous to subtropical areas of southern China and Thailand, lychees grow in clusters on small trees. The ripe fruit is about the size of a small plum, with a beautiful, scaly red skin or "shell". Once this is removed, the pearly white fruit, which surrounds a large inedible seed, is revealed. Fresh lychees are seasonal. When they are not available, canned fruit can be used instead, but it lacks the subtlety of the fresh fruit. Choose the ones in natural juice rather than syrup.

Aroma and flavour

Peeled lychees have a delicious perfume. The flesh has a wonderful, clean taste, somewhat like a grape, but much more scented.

Culinary uses

Lychees and their close relatives, longans, "dragon's eyes", are said to boost fertility. In some parts of China it is traditional, when a young person

reaches puberty, to celebrate the event with a meal composed of a young cockerel cooked with dried lychees or longans. On most occasions, however, lychees are eaten fresh, and are good for cleansing the palate after a rich meal. They are also used in fruit salads and for making sorbets.

Preparation

Lychees are very easy to prepare. The brittle skin parts readily, and you can either eat the fruit as is, nibbling the flesh off the stones (pits), or the fruit can be stoned and sliced before being added to a fruit salad or similar dessert.

Storage

Store lychees in the refrigerator, as they taste best chilled. They will stay fresh for up to a week.

Above: Canned and fresh rambutans

RAMBUTANS

CANTONESE: *HONG MAO TANG;* THAI: *NGO*

These small tropical fruits originated in Malaysia, but they are also grown in the Philippines and Thailand. They belong to the same family as lychees and longans, and they have a similar taste and texture, but look

very different. The reddish-brown skins are covered with fine green-tipped hairs. Inside, the flesh is white, and hides an oblong seed.

Aroma and flavour

Rambutans are not as strongly scented as lychees. The delicate flesh tastes a little sharper.

Culinary uses

Rambutans are usually eaten in the hand, served on the bottom half of the shell, with the top half cut off to expose the flesh. They are used in fruit salads, but are seldom cooked.

Preparation

Make a cut around the equator of the rambutan, then remove half or all the skin. The flesh tends to stick to the seed, so they are more difficult to stone than lychees.

Storage

Like lychees, rambutans are best stored in the refrigerator, where they will keep for at least a week.

Right: Canned and fresh lychees

MANGOES

CHINESE: *MANG GUO;* THAI: *MA-MUANG*

One of the world's favourite fruits, mangoes originated in India and are now widely cultivated throughout South-east Asia, as well as in other tropical and sub-tropical countries. There are thousands of different varieties. Most are oval in shape, with green, gold or red skin and succulent orange flesh, which can be quite fibrous, although modern varieties are usually smooth and velvety. Canned and dried mangoes are also available.

Aroma and flavour

The aroma of a ripe mango is quite unique. Some people say it reminds them of a pine wood in springtime. The juicy flesh is highly scented and tastes deliciously sweet.

Culinary uses

Apart from being eaten fresh as a fruit, mangoes are used extensively for making chutneys and pickles. Asian cooks also use them in savoury dishes,

Above: A selection of some of the many different varieties of mangoes

and when stir-frying a rich meat such as duck, will often add mango instead of pineapple. Mango ice cream is legendary, and Thai cooks make a wonderful dessert from glutinous rice, coconut milk and mangoes.

Preparation

To prepare a mango for eating, first cut off both sides of the fruit, on either side of the stone (pit), then scoop the flesh out of the skin with a spoon. After that, strip the skin off the remaining central part and suck the stone clean. This may sound rather messy, but in Asia it is the traditional way of eating a mango. If you are fastidious, you can always peel the mango first, slice the fruit off the stone and then slice it neatly. Finally – and this appeals to children – you can cut two large slices from either side of the stone, cross hatch the flesh on the skin, then press the skin down so that the pieces of mango pop up to make a mango "hedgehog".

Storage

Mangoes are usually picked just before they are ripe, and then they are packed in straw and shipped by air to the West. Fruit that is bought when it is still firm can be ripened at home. One of the easiest ways of doing this is to wrap the mango in newspaper, lay it in a box and cover with more newspaper. Colour is not necessarily an indication of ripeness, but touch is. Ripe fruit will just yield when lightly pressed. Eat mangoes as soon as they are ripe.

Preparing mangoes

Mangoes can be difficult to prepare because they have a large, flat stone that is slighty off-centre, and they are very juicy.

1 Cut off both sides of the fruit in thick slices, keeping as close to the central stone as possible.

2 Scoop the flesh out of the skin using a small spoon. Peel the skin off the remaining central part and slice the fruit off the stone.

PAPAYAS

MANDARIN: *FAN MUGUA;* CANTONESE: *MUK GWA;* THAI: *MALAKO*

Papayas – or paw paws as they are sometimes known – are native to tropical America. It was not until 1600 that they were introduced into Asia, but they rapidly became extremely popular so that today they are one of the most common and most important fruits in all tropical and sub-tropical countries.

Papayas can be small and round, but are more often pear-shaped. When ripe, the skin turns from green to yellow, and the flesh, which can be deep salmon pink or glorious orange, becomes soft and juicy. The small grey seeds are not usually eaten, although Asian cooks use them as a garnish.

Aroma and flavour

The flavour of a ripe papaya is sweet and delicately perfumed. It can be sickly, but this can be counteracted by lemon or lime juice. The flesh of underripe papaya is pale green, and nowhere near as sweet.

Culinary uses

In South-east Asia, papaya is eaten both as a fruit and a vegetable. When ripe, the flesh is usually eaten as it is, sometimes with a squeeze of citrus, but it is also used in fruit salads and other desserts. Papayas that are not too ripe can be added to soups, curries or seafood dishes. Unripe green papayas are served raw in vegetable salads, especially in Thailand, and can also be made into pickles. Papaya contains an enzyme called papain, which is an excellent tenderizer. Both the juice and skins are used to tenderize meat.

Preparation and cooking techniques

Slice lengthways in half and scoop out the seeds. To serve papayas raw as a table fruit, slice in wedges, sprinkle with lemon or lime juice, and either cut the flesh off the skin, slicing it into bitesize chunks,

Right: Papayas are one of the most popular tropical fruits.

or provide spoons for scooping. To serve papaya raw in a salad, peel slightly unripe fruit, shred the flesh and combine it with carrots and lettuce or cucumber, then toss with a spicy dressing. Thai cooks often add dried shrimps, which give a salty tang.

Storage

Green papayas are not often available outside their country of origin but, if located, can be kept in a refrigerator for up to a week. In the West, ripe fruit is much easier to come by. Look for fruit that is yellow all over, and which has a delicate perfume. If the fruit is not quite ripe, check the skin around the stem end and only buy if this is yellow. If it is green, the fruit will never ripen. Fruit that is almost ripe will soften if kept at room temperature for a few days, but should not be left for too long.

Dragon fruit
These brightly coloured fruits are widely grown in Vietnam. They come in pink and yellow varieties. The pink ones are about 10cm/ 4in long, and are covered with pointed, green-tipped scales. The yellow ones are smaller and look more like prickly pears. The flesh is sweet and refreshing, and is best eaten chilled, sprinkled with a little lemon juice.

Nuts and Seeds

PEANUTS

Chinese: *HUASHENG MI*

Also known as groundnuts or monkey nuts, peanuts are thought to have originated in South America, and were introduced into Asia in the 16th century. Today, peanuts are an important world crop, being rich both in oil (40–50 per cent) and protein (about 30 per cent).

Aroma and flavour

Raw peanuts don't have much of a smell, but once cooked – they are usually roasted – they have a powerful, unmistakable aroma, a crunchy texture and a distinctive flavour.

Culinary uses

Peanuts play an important role in Asian cuisine. The smaller ones are used for making oil, while the larger, less oily nuts are widely eaten, both as a snack food and as ingredients in salads and main courses. In Indonesian and Malayan cooking, roasted peanuts, pounded to a paste, are the basis for satay sauce, as well as for a salad dressing in the classic gado-gado salad.

Preparation and cooking techniques

Strictly speaking, the peanut is not a nut, but a legume. Its outer shell is the dried fibrous pod of the plant, and contains the seeds or "nuts", which in turn are coated with a thin layer of reddish skin. This skin has to be removed before the nut can be used as a food, and the easiest way to do that is to roast or fry the peanuts, then, when they are cool enough to handle, rub off the brittle skins with your fingers. When the nuts are processed commercially, a fan is used for winnowing, or the nuts are left outside to allow the wind to do the job.

Storage

Raw peanuts in their shells will keep for many months if stored properly. Shelled peanuts will only keep for 7–10 days, even if stored in an airtight container.

GINKGO NUTS

Chinese: *BAIGUO*; Japanese: *GINGKO BILOBA*

The ginkgo tree is native to China, and has been grown for many centuries in Japan, where it is called the maidenhair tree.

Aroma and flavour

Ginkgo nuts resemble lotus seeds in appearance and taste, but have a smoother and firmer texture and are somewhat less sweet.

Culinary uses

Ginkgo nuts play an important role in vegetarian cooking in Asia, particularly in China and Japan. They feature in the popular Buddha's delight (a vegetarian casserole) and are used in several Japanese vegetable and rice dishes. When cooked, ginkgo nuts have a viscous texture.

Left: Canned ginkgo nuts

Preparation and cooking techniques

These nuts do not travel well. The flesh inside the shells tends to dry up or rot after a time, so only dried and canned ginkgo nuts are available in the West. Dried nuts need soaking in water for several hours. Drain before adding to stir-fries, casseroles and soups.

Storage

Any unused soaked or canned ginkgo nuts can be stored in fresh water in the refrigerator for 2–3 days.

ALMONDS

Mandarin: *XINGREN*; Cantonese: *HANG YAHN*

These nuts come from the kernel of a fruit closely related to the apricot, but the fruit of the ripe almond is leathery, dusky green and quite inedible.

Aroma and flavour

Almonds have a unique aroma quite unlike that of any other nut. There are bitter and sweet varieties, both with a pleasant, crunchy texture.

Culinary uses

In Asia, sweet almonds are mostly used as garnishes and in desserts and cakes. Bitter almonds contain prussic acid. They must not be eaten raw, but their essence is distilled and used as a flavouring for sweet dishes.

Above: Raw and shelled peanuts

Above: Shelled almonds

Preparation and cooking techniques

Whole kernels should be soaked to remove the thin red skin. This is seldom necessary in the West, however, as shelled almonds are readily available, whole, sliced, as thin slivers or ground.

Storage

Almonds have a high fat content, so they become rancid if stored for too long. Keep unopened packets in a sealed container in a cool, dry place, and use within 2–3 months. Nuts bought loose, or in packets that have been opened, should be used as soon as possible.

SESAME SEEDS

CHINESE: *ZHIMA*

The sesame plant probably originated in Africa, but has been cultivated in India and China since ancient times. Today, it is grown all over the world in tropical and sub-tropical countries. Sesame seeds are small, flat and pear-shaped. They are usually white, but can be cream to brown, red or black.

Aroma and flavour

Raw sesame seeds have little aroma and are almost tasteless until they have been roasted or dry-fried, when their nutty aroma becomes very pronounced and their flavour is heightened.

Culinary uses

Sesame seeds are about 50 per cent oil, and processed sesame oil is used in oriental cooking for flavouring. The seeds are used in a number of popular Chinese dishes, most notably in Chinese honeyed apples and bang-bang chicken. They also feature in Singaporean, Malayan Indonesian and Japanese cooking, and are often toasted then sprinkled over salads and other dishes just before serving.

Preparation and cooking techniques

Sesame seeds are frequently roasted before being used. Place them in a wok or pan over a medium heat. They burn readily, so shake the pan constantly to keep them moving and do not leave them unattended at any time. If ground seeds are required, this can be done in a mortar with a pestle, or, as in Korea, between two flat plates. Japanese cooks use a device rather like a pepper mill, which grinds the roasted sesame seeds as finely or as coarsely as needed. The finely ground seeds are called *irigoma*.

Storage

The high oil content means that sesame seeds do not keep well. Store them in a cool, dry place and observe the "use by" dates on packets.

Above: White and black sesame seeds

Other nuts

Candle nuts Native to Indonesia, these nuts are similar to macadamia nuts, which can be used as a substitute. In Asia, the pounded nuts are used as a thickener. They are slightly toxic when raw, and should always be cooked.

Cashew nuts Both raw and roasted cashews are used in Asian cooking.

Chestnuts These have a robust flavour and meaty texture, which makes them a popular addition to a variety of vegetarian dishes. They are particularly delicious stir-fried with bok choy or other leafy vegetables.

Above: From left, cashew nuts, candle nuts and chestnuts

TOFU AND GLUTEN

TOFU

MANDARIN: *DOUFU;* CANTONESE: *DAU FOO;*
JAPANESE: *TOFU*

Made from soya beans, tofu (also commonly known as beancurd) is one of China's major contributions to the world as a cheap source of protein. Highly nutritious and low in fat and sugar, it is a much healthier food than either meat or fish, at a fraction of the cost.

The soya bean plant is a legume that has been cultivated in China for thousands of years. A number of bean by-products constitute an important element in the Chinese diet. Soy sauce is one of them, and tofu is another, as well as miso, the fermented soya bean paste that is essential to Japanese cooking. Written records indicate that fermented bean sauces were in use well over 2,000 years ago, but no one knows precisely when tofu was invented. All we know for certain is that it was introduced to Japan during the Tang dynasty in the 8th century AD, along with Buddhism.

The process of making tofu is not unlike making cheese, only much less time-consuming. The soya beans are soaked, husked, then pounded with water to make soya milk. This mixture is then filtered, boiled and finally curdled with gypsum.

There are two basic types of fresh tofu widely available in the West: soft or silken tofu (called *kinu* in Japan); and a firm type, which Japanese cooks know as *momen*. Both are creamy-white in colour and are either packed in water or sold in vacuum packs. The firm type is usually sold in cakes measuring about 7.5cm/3in square and 2.5cm/1in thick. Also available, but only from Asian stores, are marinated tofu, deep-fried tofu and pressed tofu.

Aroma and flavour

The quality of fresh tofu is largely dependent upon the water used to make it. Good quality tofu should smell fresh with a faint, pleasant "beany" aroma. On its own, it is quite bland, but the beauty of tofu is that its soft, porous texture will absorb the flavour of any other ingredient with which it is cooked.

Culinary uses

The nutritional value of tofu cannot be stressed too highly. As a vegetable protein, it contains the eight essential amino acids plus vitamins A and B. It is free from cholesterol, and is regarded as an excellent food for anyone with heart disease or high blood pressure. In addition, it is very easy to digest, so is an ideal food for infants, invalids and the elderly.

Tofu is very versatile and, depending upon the texture, it can be cooked by almost every conceivable method, and used with a vast array of ingredients, both sweet and savoury.

Preparation and cooking techniques

Soft or silken tofu is mainly steamed or added to soups, since its light and delicate texture means that it will disintegrate if handled roughly. It makes a refreshing sweet dessert and is also used to make "ice cream".

Firm tofu is the most common type, and also the most popular for everyday use. Although it has been lightly pressed, and is more robust than silken tofu, it still needs to be handled with care. Having been cut to the required size and shape – cubes, strips, slices or triangles – the pieces are usually blanched in boiling water or briefly shallow-fried in oil. This hardens them and prevents them from disintegrating when stir-fried or braised. Yaki tofu is a variety has been lightly grilled (broiled) on both sides.

Because tofu is bland, it is important to cook it with strongly flavoured seasonings such as garlic, ginger, spring onions (scallions), chillies, soy sauce, oyster sauce, shrimp paste, fermented

Above: Clockwise from top, deep-fried tofu, silken tofu, and cubes of fresh tofu. All these types of tofu absorb the flavours of the other ingredients with which they are cooked.

black beans, salted yellow beans, or sesame oil. Although its primary purpose is as a vegetarian ingredient, tofu also tastes very good with meat. It is often cooked with either pork or beef, but seldom with chicken. It goes well with fish and shellfish, too. One of the most popular tofu dishes is the world-famous *ma po doufu* from Sichuan, in which cubed tofu is first blanched, then braised with minced (ground) beef, garlic, spring onions, leeks, salt, Sichuan pepper, rice wine, chilli bean paste, fermented black beans and sesame oil.

Left: Pressed tofu

Storage

Buy tofu from an oriental store, if possible. Fresh tofu submerged in water in a plastic box will keep for several days in the refrigerator. Vacuum-packed fresh tofu bought from health food stores and supermarkets will keep for slightly longer, but is unlikely to taste quite as good. Tofu is also available as a powder mix. This has a long shelf life, so is a useful store-cupboard item.

DEEP-FRIED TOFU

MANDARIN: *YOUZHA DOUFU*; CANTONESE: *DAU FOO POK*; JAPANESE: *ABURAGE*

This is fresh, firm tofu that has been cut into cubes, squares or triangles, then deep-fried until light brown. Deep-fried tofu has an interesting texture. It puffs up during cooking, and underneath the crispy brown skin the flesh is white and soft. It sucks up seasonings and the flavours of other ingredients like a sponge.

Culinary uses

Deep-fried tofy can be used in the same way as fresh tofu in soups, stir-fries, braised dishes or casseroles. As it has been fried in vegetable oil, it is suitable for vegetarian cooking. Non-vegetarians stuff the larger squares or triangles of tofu with minced (ground) pork,

chicken, fish and prawns (shrimp), then braise them in a sauce. The Japanese version of deep-fried tofu, known as *aburage*, is a popular addition to a wonderful hotpot called *oden*, which is sold from street stalls during the winter.

Preparation and cooking techniques

Unlike fresh tofu, which is very delicate, deep-fried tofu can be handled fairly roughly without disintegrating. Even though the crisp crust is porous, it is best to chop up the larger pieces a little to allow the seasonings to penetrate more easily.

Storage

Cakes of deep-fried tofu are sold in plastic bags from the chiller or freezer in Asian stores. They usually have a "use by" date stamped on them, and will keep for much longer than uncooked fresh tofu. They can be frozen for up to a year or more.

PRESSED TOFU

MANDARIN: *DOUFU GAN*; CANTONESE: *DAU FOO GONN*

Pressed tofu is fresh tofu that has been compressed until almost all the liquid has been squeezed out, leaving a solid block with a smooth texture. It is usually marinated in soy sauce and seasoned

with five-spice powder, so is pale brown on the surface, but white inside.

Culinary uses

Pressed tofu is cut into thin slices, cubes or fine shreds, then stir-fried with meat and vegetables. It offers a contrast in both texture and flavour when it is combined with other ingredients.

Storage

Pressed tofu is sold in vacuum-packed plastic bags in Asian stores, and will normally keep for several weeks if stored in the refrigerator. Check the "use-by" date on the packet. Do not freeze, as this would alter the texture of the tofu.

DRIED TOFU SKINS

MANDARIN: *FUZHU*; CANTONESE: *FOO PI*; JAPANESE: *YUBA*

Dried tofu skins are made from soya milk. The process is simple, but requires considerable skill: a large pan of soya milk is gently brought to the boil, the thin layer of skin that forms on the surface is skimmed off with a stick in a single swoop, and this is hung up. When it dries, it forms a flat sheet. Dried tofu sticks are made by rolling the skin up while still warm, then leaving the sticks to dry.

Culinary uses

Fermented tofu is either served on its own with rice congee at breakfast, or used as a seasoning in marinating and cooking.

Storage

Fermented tofu is available in cans and jars from Asian stores. Once opened, store the contents in the refrigerator.

Below: Fermented tofu

Above: Dried beancurd skins have no discernible flavour or aroma.

FERMENTED TOFU

MANDARIN: *DOUFU NAI;* CANTONESE: *FOO YU;* THAI: *TAO-HOO-YEE*

This is made by fermenting fresh tofu on beds of rice straw, then drying the curd in the sun before marinating it with salt, alcohol and spices. Finally, it is stored in brine in sealed earthenware urns and left to mature for at least six months before being packaged and sold.

Aroma and flavour

Fermented tofu is definitely an acquired taste. It is no coincidence that it is sometimes referred to as Chinese cheese, because it smells very strong indeed, and the flavour is pretty powerful, too. There are two types of fermented tofu that are available in the West: the red type is coloured on the surface only, and the white one can be quite hot and spicy.

Aroma and flavour

Like fresh tofu, dried beancurd skins have neither aroma nor flavour until they are cooked, when they will absorb the flavour of seasonings and any other ingredients.

Culinary uses

The flat skins are used in soups, stir-fries and casseroles, and are sometimes used as wrappers for spring rolls. The sticks are used in vegetarian dishes, and are also cooked with meat in braised dishes and casseroles.

Preparation

Dried beancurd skins need soaking before use: the sheets only require an hour or two, but the sticks need to be soaked for several hours or overnight.

Storage

Dried beancurd sheets and beancurd sticks will keep for a very long time. Store them in their packet or in a sealed plastic bag in a cool and dry place.

Above: Tempeh has a firmer texture than tofu.

TEMPEH

INDONESIAN: *TEMPEH*

This Indonesian speciality is made by fermenting cooked soya beans with a cultured starter.

Aroma and flavour

Tempeh is similar to tofu but has a nuttier, more savoury flavour.

Culinary uses

It can be used in the same way as firm tofu and also benefits from marinating. Its firm texture means that it can be used as a meat replacement.

Storage

Tempeh is available chilled or frozen. Chilled tempeh can be stored in the refrigerator for up to a week. Frozen tempeh can be left in the freezer for 1 month, Defrost before use.

MISO

JAPANESE: *KOME MISO, MUGO MISO AND HACHO MISO*

This thick paste is made from a mixture of cooked soya beans, rice, wheat or barley, salt and water. Miso is left to ferment for up to 3 years.

Aroma and flavour

There are three main types: kome, or white miso, is the lightest and sweetest; medium-strength mugi miso, which has a mellow flavour and is preferred for everyday use; and hacho miso, which is a dark chocolate colour, and has a thick texture and a strong flavour.

Culinary uses

Miso can be used to add a savoury flavour to soups, stocks, stir-fries and noodle dishes, and is a staple food in Asia.

Storage

Miso keeps very well and can be stored for several months, but it should be kept in the refrigerator once it has been opened.

Left: Hacho miso

Gluten

MANDARIN: *MIANJIN;* CANTONESE: *MING GUN;* JAPANESE: *FU*

Also known as "mock meat", gluten is another source of vegetarian protein. It is made from a mixture of wheat flour, salt and water, from which all the starch has been washed out. What remains is a sponge-like gluten. Its Chinese name literally means "muscle or sinew of flour".

Like tofu, gluten has no aroma nor flavour of its own, but it has a much firmer texture, and can be shaped, coloured and flavoured to resemble meat, poultry or fish.

Unlike tofu, which is often cooked with meat and fish, gluten is regarded as a pure Buddhist ingredient, and as such, no non-vegetarian item may be mixed with it. This does not prevent accomplished Asian cooks from using a bit of sleight of hand, however, and gluten is often used with tofu to produce dishes such as "mock chicken", "mock abalone", "vegetarian duck" or "Buddhist pork" – which are all said to look and taste very much like the real thing.

Although gluten can be made at home, the task is too time-consuming to contemplate. Flavoured and cooked gluten is available in cans from Asian stores. It only needs to be reheated before being served.

Once opened, it will keep in the refrigerator for up to a week.

DRIED FISH AND SHELLFISH

SALTED FISH

MANDARIN: *YAN YU;* CANTONESE: *GON HAHM YU*

Many different types of fish, both freshwater and saltwater, are salted and cured for general use in South-east Asia. They range from tiny whitebait to large croakers, and they are generally preserved in salt or brine, although some are dried in the sun. In Japan, sun-dried young sardines, known as *niboshi*, are eaten as snacks, and are also used for making stock.

Aroma and flavour

To say that salted fish is an acquired taste is an understatement. It smells so pungent and has such a strong flavour that some people may find it positively disagreeable. It is, however, very popular throughout South-east Asia.

Culinary use

Salted fish has two basic functions. It is either eaten on its own with rice, or used as a seasoning for vegetables and meat in steamed dishes, casseroles or soups.

Preparation and cooking techniques

Soak the salted fish in water before use, to remove the excess salt. Large fish are usually sold without the heads.

Storage

Preserved fish in brine is seldom seen in the West, but salted and dried fish are both available from Asian stores. Salted and dried fish will keep almost indefinitely if stored in a cool, dry place.

Left: Dried anchovies

Above: Bonito flakes or shavings (top) and powder

DRIED ANCHOVIES

MALAY: *IKAN BILIS*

Dried anchovies, which are known as *ikan bilis*, are a Malayan speciality. For some unknown reason, anchovies are seldom eaten fresh in South-east Asia, they are either used for making fish sauce, or are salted and dried. Fishing for anchovies is a huge industry in Malaysia. Having located the schools of fish with the aid of electronic fish finders and echo sounding equipment, the fishermen haul in their catch and immediately boil the fish in salted water for about 5 minutes. Back on shore, the fish are dried, graded and packed.

Aroma and flavour

Dried anchovies have an overpowering aroma and a very strong flavour.

Culinary uses

Dried anchovies can be used as a flavouring, as an ingredient in a composite dish, or as a snack food. A favourite Malayan recipe involves steaming and filleting the fish, then serving them with a sauce made from preserved black beans that is flavoured with fresh chillies and lime juice and sweetened to taste with sugar. Dried anchovies are also often deep fried until they are crunchy and served either at parties as a snack to eat with drinks, or as an appetizer. They also make a tasty accompaniment to spicy curries and chicken rendang.

Storage

Dried anchovies will keep for a very long time if stored in a dry and cool place, but make sure that their container is airtight, or you will attract all the neighbourhood cats.

BONITO FLAKES

JAPANESE: *KATSUOBUSHI*

Bonito is the name given to several different kinds of fish in different parts of the world. For instance, the Atlantic bonito is a relative of mackerel, and is known as Spanish mackerel in Europe, while the Pacific bonito is a small tuna, much used in Japanese cooking.

Aroma and flavour

The Pacific bonito has a much stronger flavour than regular tuna, particularly when it is dried.

Culinary uses

In Japan, where dried bonito is widely used, the flakes come in various thicknesses. Fine shavings are one of the main ingredients in the basic stock known as *dashi*, and are also used as a topping or garnish. Powdered bonito flakes are used as a seasoning.

Storage

Dried bonito flakes will keep almost indefinitely if stored in an airtight jar.

DRIED SHRIMPS

MANDARIN: *XIAMI*; CANTONESE: *HA MY*; THAI: *GUNG HAENG*

Dried shrimps are popular throughout Asia, especially in China and Thailand.

They are pale pink in colour, having been boiled before being spread out in the sun to dry. There are several different sizes, from tiny shrimps not much bigger than grains of rice (hence the Chinese name, "sea rice") to large ones, which are still less than 1cm/½in long. The larger ones are usually sold shelled and headless, while the tiny ones are sold whole, heads and all.

Aroma and flavour

Dried shrimps have a very strong smell, so strong that it can be detected through the cellophane bags in which they are sold. The smell dissipates with cooking. The flavour is sharp and salty.

Culinary uses

Because of their strong taste, dried shrimps are usually used as a seasoning rather than as an independent ingredient. They are often used as a garnish in salads and also feature in the popular "eight-treasure stuffing", when they are combined with dried mushrooms, bamboo shoots, glutinous rice and other ingredients.

Preparation and cooking techniques

Dried shrimps must be soaked for an hour or so before use, either in water or rice wine. The soaking liquid is saved and often added to the dish during cooking.

Storage

Dried shrimps keep well in airtight containers if they are stored in a dry, cool place. Their colour is a good indication of freshness as older shrimps tend to fade. Any shrimps that look grey, or

Left: Dried shrimps

start to turn grey while being stored, will be past their prime. Stored dried shrimps may become a bit moist. If this happens, spread them on baking sheets and dry them briefly in a hot oven.

DRIED SCALLOPS

MANDARIN: *GANBEI*; CANTONESE: *GONG YU CHU*

Another oriental delicacy, dried scallops are very expensive because the most sought-after varieties are so scarce. The Chinese variety known as *conpoy*, for instance, is only found in the inland sea called Po Hai, and then only during a short summer season. The best scallops are round and golden, with a delicate, sweet flavour. Japan produces fine dried scallops, including the variety *aomori*.

Aroma and flavour

Before being dried, scallops are cooked in their shells in boiling water. The flesh is then removed and cleaned. Dried scallops have quite a distinct aroma with a highly concentrated flavour.

Culinary uses

Dried scallops are seldom used on their own, but are combined with other ingredients in soups and stuffings.

Above: Dried scallops

Above: Dried squid has a subtle fishy aroma, but a strong flavour.

Preparing dried squid

1 Soak the dried squid in warm water for 30 minutes or so, then drain and wash in fresh water.

2 Score the squid on the inside in a criss-cross fashion, then cut it into small pieces.

Dried and fresh scallops are sometimes used in the same dish. Dried scallops are the classic garnish for crispy seaweed, but when this dish is served in Chinese restaurants overseas, ground fried fish is often used as a substitute.

Preparation and cooking techniques

The scallops must be soaked in boiling water for at least an hour before use, then drained.

Storage

For some inexplicable reason, dried scallops seem to be available only in large boxes in the West. Should you acquire any, transfer them to jars, close

the lids tightly and store them in a cool, dry place. They will keep indefinitely.

DRIED SQUID

MANDARIN: *YOUYU*; CANTONESE: *YOW YU*

In inland China and other parts of Asia that are far from the coast, where fresh seafood was for a long time unobtainable, dried squid and cuttlefish have always been regarded as delicacies.

Aroma and flavour

Dried squid is pale brown in colour and has a subtle fishy aroma, but a very strong taste. Some people find the

texture rather tough when compared to fresh squid, but others like the chewiness of the dried version.

Culinary uses

In Asia, dried squid is mainly used in soups or meat stews. The stronger texture and flavour provides an interesting contrast to fresh squid, and the two are often stir-fried together in a popular dish that is known as "two-coloured squid-flowers".

Preparation and cooking techiques

Before using them for cooking, dried squid must be soaked in warm water for at least 30 minutes, then drained and cleaned in fresh water. If the dried squid is to be stir-fried, it is the normal practice to score the inside of the flesh in a criss-cross pattern, then cut it into small pieces. Cooking causes the cuts to open up so that each piece of squid resembles an ear of corn, which is how they came to be called "squid flowers".

Storage

Dried squid will keep almost indefinitely if they are wrapped tightly and stored in a dry, cool place.

FISH MAW

CHINESE: *YU DU*

Fish maw is the swim bladders or stomachs of certain types of large fish and eels, which have been dried in the sun for several days, then deep-fried. It is considered a delicacy in both China and Thailand.

Aroma and flavour

Fish maw has little aroma, nor does it have a distinctive flavour.

Culinary uses

Fish maw is mainly valued for its texture, which is slippery.

Preparation and cooking techniques

The maws must be soaked in a large bowl of cold water for 24 hours before use. They will float at first, so will need to be kept submerged with the aid of a plate or dish. As they absorb the water, the maws will swell to four times the original size and slowly sink to the bottom of the bowl. Before use, drain but do not dry the maws, then slice or cube them as required.

Above: Fish maw

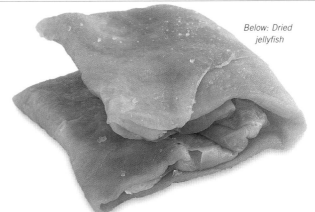

Below: Dried jellyfish

Dried jellyfish
Sheets of dried edible jellyfish are sold in plastic bags in some Chinese stores. This Chinese delicacy is valued for its crunchy yet elastic texture. To prepare, soak the sheets in cold water for several hours, changing the water frequently, and squeezing the jellyfish each time to get rid of as much of the fishy smell as possible. Drain, give the jellyfish sheets a final squeeze to remove the excess water, then cut them into strips. Strips of dried jellyfish are often added to a stir-fry, but they must be tossed in at the last moment; if they are over-cooked, they will become rubbery.

Left: Dried sea cucumber, which is actually a type of sea slug and not a vegetable at all.

Dried sea cucumber Sold as *iriko*, *trepang* or *bêche-de-mer*, this is not a vegetable, but a marine animal, also known as a sea slug. Before use, dried sea cucumber must be soaked in cold water for at least 24 hours, during which time it will double in bulk and become quite gelatinous. It is mainly used in soups, stews and braised dishes.

PRESERVED MEATS AND EGGS

CHINESE SAUSAGES/ WIND-DRIED SAUSAGES

MANDARIN: *XIANG CHANG*; CANTONESE: *LOP CHONG*

Although these are always described as Chinese sausages, wind-dried sausages are made throughout South-east Asia, and are widely available in the West. There are basically two types: a pink and white sausage, which is made from pork and pork fat, and a darker sausage, in which the pork is mixed with duck liver. The sausages are about 15cm/6in long and about 2cm/¾in wide, and are sold in pairs, tied together with string.

Aroma and flavour

The dried sausages do not have any aroma, but as soon as they are cooked, they become really fragrant and taste deliciously sweet.

Culinary uses

Chinese sausages are very versatile. They can be eaten on their own, combined with milder meats such as chicken, or used as the main ingredient in a vegetable dish.

Preparation and cooking techniques

Unlike salami, Chinese sausages must be cooked before eating them. The best way of cooking them is to cut them diagonally into thin slices, then steam them on top of rice for 10 minutes or so. Alternatively, the whole sausage can be steamed for 10 minutes, then skinned and sliced before adding to dishes such as fried rice.

Storage

As the sausages are cured and contain preservatives, they will keep for several months in the refrigerator, and almost indefinitely in the freezer.

Right: Chinese sausages are popular throughout South-east Asia.

Above: Pork crackling

PORK CRACKLING

MANDARIN: *SAI YUDU*; CANTONESE: *JA YUHK PEI*

Also known as chicaron, pork crackling is made from pork rind that has been deep-fried, forming crisp puffy crackers. It is served as a crunchy contrast alongside curries, or sliced in salads.

Aroma and flavour

The deep-fried rind has a meaty aroma with a subtle flavour. It has a very interesting firm yet spongy texture that absorbs other strongly flavoured ingredients.

Wind-dried belly pork

This is a Chinese speciality, found principally in Hunan province but available all over China. It must be cooked before eating. Wind-dried belly pork can be bought in Asian stores.

Culinary uses

Pork crackling is used in soups, stews, hot pots and casseroles.

Preparation

Pork crackling is simply sliced if it is to be used as a crunchy topping for salads, otherwise it needs to be soaked before use, partly to soften it and partly to rid it of excess fat. It is usually soaked in hot water for about 35 minutes before being drained and chopped.

Storage

Pork crackling should keep for several months if well wrapped and stored in a cool, dry place. It will become rancid if kept for too long.

PRESERVED EGGS

MANDARIN: *YANDAN; PIDAN;* CANTONESE:
HAHAM DON; PEI DON

In China, and among the Chinese communities throughout South-east Asia, preserved eggs are a very popular delicacy. There are two main types, and both use duck eggs. This is partly because duck eggs are bigger and have a stronger flavour than hen's eggs, but also because the yolk of a duck egg contains more fat than a hen's egg. The more common type, much favoured in southern China, is the salted duck egg. The other, which has more universal appeal, is the famous thousand-year-old egg.

Both types of preserved egg are made by a similar method; it is the materials used in the process that are different. Basically, salted eggs are made by coating raw duck eggs in a salt and mud paste, then rolling them in rice husks until they are completely covered. At this stage the eggs are packed into an earthenware urn, which is tightly sealed and stored in a cool, dark place for 30–40 days. Thousand-year-old eggs are nothing like as old as their name suggests. They are raw duck eggs that have been covered with a mixture of wood ash and slaked lime and left for up to a hundred days. By the time they are used, the egg whites will have turned to pale brown jelly and the yolks will be creamy and tinged green.

Aroma and flavour

The two types of preserved egg smell and taste quite different. As might be expected, the former are quite salty. Thousand-year-old eggs taste milder, but still have a definite aroma and flavour.

Above: The solid whites and yolks of thousand-year-old eggs are eaten raw. The eggs only require peeling.

Culinary uses

Salted eggs must be cooked. They are often eaten on their own, or used as part of the filling in cakes for festivals. Thousand-year-old eggs need no cooking. Sliced and seasoned with soy sauce and sesame oil, they are often served as an appetizer, or chopped and added to congee and eaten at breakfast time. They can also be used in a delicious omelette, with pork and fresh hen's eggs.

Preparation and cooking techniques

Both types of egg must have their outer coating removed and then they should be thoroughly washed. Salted eggs can then be boiled or steamed before removing the shells. The whites and yolks of thousand-year-old eggs will have solidified, so all that is required is to carefully remove the shell before cutting the eggs into quarters or eighths for serving.

Storage

Since these eggs are preserved, they should keep for a long time in the refrigerator. The salted eggs will keep for about a month, and the thousand-year-old eggs will keep for 4–6 months.

Left: Throughout Asia thousand-year-old eggs (front) and salted duck eggs (back) are a very popular delicacy.

POULTRY

CHICKEN

The chicken is a descendant of a South-east Asian jungle fowl that was domesticated over 4,500 years ago. Today chicken features in almost every cuisine. Its universal popularity is due to the fact that the flesh combines happily with a huge variety of different ingredients. Nowhere is this more amply illustrated than in Asia, where it is used in soups, salads, stir-fries, curries, roasts and braised dishes. Every part of the bird is utilized, including the liver,

gizzard, heart and even the feet, which are used to make a delicious stew in South-east Asia.

Preparation and cooking techniques

Chicken can be cooked whole, jointed, or taken off the bone and chopped or cut into thin strips – this is the usual practice if the meat is to be stir-fried. In China, chicken breasts on the bone are sometimes cut into as many as 20 pieces before being stir-fried. The ability of the Chinese to pick up these

Game birds

Small game birds are eaten in China and South-east Asia, but most are caught in the wild. Only quail and pigeon are farmed.

tiny pieces of chicken with chopsticks and to remove the meat from the bone in the mouth is a marvel of dexterity.

Serving meats and other foods in manageable morsels is the norm in Asia, where knives are viewed as weapons, and therefore inappropriate for such enjoyable communal activities as meals. Chopsticks are widely used, except in Thailand, where it is more common to find a spoon and fork at each table setting.

In Japan, chicken is the most important meat on the menu, second only to fish in terms of popularity. Chicken breast is the favourite cut, largely because it cooks so quickly and remains beautifully tender in dishes such as the famous *yakitori* or *teriyaki*. Skinless, boneless chicken breasts are readily available in Japan, unlike in the rest of Asia, where it is more usual for cooks to buy chickens whole, as portions are regarded as wasteful, or simply as too expensive.

Throughout the East, frugality is a virtue, so one chicken might be used in three dishes: the breasts sliced in strips for a stir-fry; the rest of the meat braised in a red cooked dish or a curry; and the carcass used to make stock.

The skill that is exhibited by oriental cooks with the simplest equipment is testament to their creative love of food. Using a cleaver and a small sharp knife, a chicken can be chopped into appropriate portions in no time at all.

DUCK

Ducks symbolize happiness and fidelity, which doubtless contributes to their popularity in the Chinese cuisine. Duck is central to celebratory meals, and is served in countless imaginative ways. At Chinese New Year, for instance, duck is an essential part of every banquet.

How to joint a chicken

This method will give you eight good-sized portions of chicken.

1 Place the chicken breast side up on a chopping board. Ease one of the legs away from the body, and using a sharp knife make an incision to reveal the ball of the thighbone as you pull the leg further away from the body. When the thigh socket is visible, cut through the bone to release the drumstick and thigh in one piece. Repeat with the other leg.

2 Trim off the end of the leg bone, then locate the knee joint and cut the leg portion in half at this joint. Repeat with the other chicken leg.

3 Cut through the breastbone so that the carcass is in two halves. Cut and separate each breast and wing from the backbone.

4 Cut both of the wing and breast pieces into two portions.

COOK'S TIPS

• Use the backbone to make stock, adding onion, celery and a piece of bruised root ginger if appropriate.
• If more pieces of chicken are required, say for stir-fries, the portions can be further divided. Deft Asian cooks will cut the breast and wing portions into as many as ten pieces, the legs into four pieces and the thighs into six pieces.

Right: In Asia, every part of the chicken is used – even the feet.

Duck is also popular in Vietnam,Thailand and Indonesia, but is seldom served in Japan.

Preparation and cooking techniques

The most famous duck dish has to be Peking duck. The classic way of making this universally popular restaurant dish involves hanging the prepared birds in a windy place to dry before roasting them in a special oven. At one time only the skin was eaten, but it is now more usual to eat the succulent meat as well. This is wrapped in a Mandarin pancake which has been spread with a little plum sauce and sprinkled with a few pieces of shredded spring onion (scallion) and slivers of cucumber. This dish is so popular that is now possible to buy packets of Peking duck, with all the trimmings, in the West.

The Chinese technique for preparing duck for roasting involves pricking the skin lightly all over with a fork, placing the bird on a trivet in the sink, then pouring a kettle of freshly boiled water over the top. The bird is then drained well, and the cavity wiped with kitchen paper, before being suspended from duck hooks or butcher's hooks and left to dry overnight. Once the bird is dry, the skin is sprinkled with a little salt. The bird is then placed on a trivet in a roasting pan and roasted in a hot oven until the skin is quite crisp and golden brown and the bird is fully cooked.

If the duck is to be jointed the same procedure can be used as for chicken.

COOK'S TIP

To make duck sauce to serve with Peking duck, heat 30ml/2 tbsp sesame oil in a small pan. Add 90ml/ 6 tbsp yellow bean sauce and 30ml/2 tbsp soft light brown sugar and stir until smooth. Leave to cool before serving.

Right: An oven-ready duck

MEAT

PORK

This is as popular as chicken in China and in other parts of Asia with large Chinese communities. Like chicken, it blends happily with a wide range of ingredients, from vegetables to shellfish, and is equally at home with salted and pickled foods.

Wherever there are Muslim communities, however, pork is off limits and either beef or lamb is served instead. This is the case throughout Malaysia, the only exception being the Nonya style of cooking. This came about because of the intermarriage of Chinese merchant men with Malayan women who then started to cook pork

dishes for their husbands. Nonya cooking is popular in Singapore, the west coast of Malaysia around Malacca and on the island of Penang.

Pork seldom features in Indonesian cuisine, except where cooked by members of the Chinese communities on the thousands of islands of the archipelago. Bali is an exception. The population of this island are mainly Hindu and therefore pork is permissible and widely used.

Throughout Asia, therefore, the choice of meat is greatly influenced by religious beliefs and habits. Almost all Chinese except those who have converted to Islam love pork. Thais find the smell of lamb and mutton offensive; and Indians would never touch beef, because for them the cow is sacred. Poultry has none of these taboos.

Preparation and cooking techniques

For stir-frying, fillet, lean leg or belly are the preferred cuts, along with the meaty parts of chops or spare ribs. The meat is cut into thin shreds so that it responds to really quick cooking over high heat, which is economical in the use of fuel.

For casseroles and braised dishes shoulder, spare ribs or belly pork might be used, and the meat is often cooked for so long that it forms a luscious jelly-like mixture.

OTHER MEATS

Beef has only relatively recently been eaten in China and Asia, because cattle were considered beasts of burden and highly valued as such. The buffalo, too, has always been used widely, mainly in the paddy fields to plough the land prior to planting by hand. Beef and lamb are traditionally eaten only in the north of China and in places such as Malaysia where there are Muslim communities. However, because of the proximity of Beijing to the northern provinces and the number of Chinese Muslim restaurants in the capital, lamb and beef are becoming increasingly popular there, too.

Lamb is cooked in the famous Mongolian hotpot, while beef is used in many different types of recipes, mainly as a substitute for pork. It is generally thinly sliced and used for dishes where a quick method of cooking such as stir-frying is required. Because it has a stronger flavour than pork, it works best in dishes that contain aromatic flavouring ingredients, such as garlic and onions.

Above: Lean leg steaks, fillet and spare ribs are the preferred cuts of pork.

FISH

There is an old Thai saying that suggests that all is well when "there is fish in the water and rice in the field". The main source of protein in the Thai diet is fish, which is hardly surprising when you take a look at the map and see the immense coastline in addition to the rivers, canals, lakes and flooded paddy fields. Along these waterways local people catch their daily supply of fish using simple fishing poles or nets. The fish is steamed, grilled with local spices or herbs, served in soups or curries, or added to salads or omelettes.

The Cantonese word for fish is "yu" which sounds the same as the word for abundance or bounty. A whole fish is traditionally served at the Chinese New Year banquet as a symbol of hope that the family will enjoy a plentiful supply of food during the coming year. Serving a fish whole, as opposed to cutting it into portions, has great appeal in Asia, as the fish is aesthetically pleasing and complete. Also, by cooking the fish whole the juices are retained and the prized morsel that is the fish cheek can be served to the guest of honour.

Fish – nature's bounty – is exploited and enjoyed all over the East. With a coastline of over three thousand miles China has an abundant and varied supply of saltwater fish, some of which are familiar to Westerners, such as bass and sea bass, halibut, mackerel, sea bream, sole, plaice, tuna, cod, salmon, sardines and herring. China also has majestic rivers and lakes, which are a source of freshwater fish, including the ubiquitous carp.

Indonesia, the Philippines and Japan are all island nations, so it is not surprising that fish plays an important role in their cuisines. This is especially so in Japan, where an early moratorium on meat eating was one of the factors

Above: Freshwater carp, mackerel and grey mullet

that led to the Japanese expertise in preparing this popular food. Sashimi – very fresh fish that is finely sliced and served raw – is a delectable treat that is now appreciated well beyond the shores of the country that invented it. Trout, mackerel, tuna, salmon and herring are popular in Japan, as well as more exotic varieties, such as parrot fish or pomfret.

The most important requirement when buying and preparing is that it be as fresh as possible. This goes for all of Asia, but particularly Japan.

Buying fish

When buying fresh fish, the following indicators should be considered:
• The eyes of the fish should be bright and clear, not sunken.

• Gills should be clean and bright red/coral in colour.
• The skin should be firm and fresh with a sheen and, when held, the fish should feel almost springy, as if it could swim away at any moment.
• Freshness can also be detected in the smell. It is difficult to disguise the odour of a fish that is past its prime.

Cooking fish

Steaming and simmering in clear stock are typical Asian cooking methods, along with deep-frying, pan-frying, stir-frying and braising.

Steaming Choose a very fresh whole fish. It should not be too large (about 675g/1½ lb). Rub the skin with salt and scatter the fish with shredded fresh ginger root. Pour over a mixture of Chinese rice wine, soy sauce and sugar, then steam immediately over rapidly boiling water. For the best results remove the fish from the steamer when the fish is almost, but not absolutely cooked. The flesh should have just begun to flake when tested with the tip of a sharp knife, but should still be beautifully moist. Serve with the cooking juices poured over.

Clear simmering This method is usually reserved for larger fish (about 1.5kg/3lb). Use a fish kettle, if you have one. Pour in 1.75 litres/3 pints/7½ cups water and add salt to taste. Slice a 4cm/1½in piece of fresh ginger root and add to the kettle. Bring the water to the boil. Meanwhile slip a wide strip of foil under the fish to act as a strap. Lift the fish into the kettle, placing it on the trivet. Allow the water to return to the

Right: Snapper, parrot fish and pomfret

boil, then lower the heat and simmer for about 4 minutes. Lower the heat again, until the water barely bubbles, and cook the fish for 6–8 minutes. Lift the fish out of the fish kettle and let it drain before transferring it to a heatproof serving dish. Heat 75ml/5 tbsp groundnut oil and pour this over the hot fish to complete the cooking. This is a finish also used in Vietnamese cuisine, but they would scatter the fish with shredded spring onion (scallion) before pouring over the hot oil.

Frying Fish can be stir-fried, deep fried or pan-fried, and whichever method is used, the fish is always cooked quickly to retain its shape and flavour.

Braising Used for whole fish, which is first fried in garlic and ginger oil. Soy sauce, Chinese mushrooms and other flavourings are added, then the pan is covered tightly and the fish is cooked very briefly.

TYPES OF FISH

Carp A freshwater fish that is believed to have originated in Asia thousands of years ago. It is extensively farmed and thrives in ponds, lakes and flooded paddy fields. There are several varieties. Ask the fishmonger to remove the large scales and strong dorsal fins. The flesh is meaty and moist. Bake carp whole. Like grey mullet, it needs a stuffing with a distinctive flavour.

Cod A handsome fish with greenish bronze skin dappled with yellow, cod can vary in size from 1kg/2¼lb to 30kg/66lb. When properly cooked the flesh is moist and will break into large flakes. It is ideal for grilling (broiling), baking or frying, and is excellent in fish curries, but only add the cubes of pearly white fish at the very end of cooking so that they keep their shape.

Grey mullet This fish has dark stripes along the back, lots of thick scales and a heavy head. The flesh is soft and rather coarse but responds well to distinctive flavours. Try it baked, with a stuffing of minced (ground) pork and prawns (shrimp) with fresh root ginger and spring onion or chopped Chinese mushrooms, or moisten it with fish sauce and steam it.

Halibut This is a rather chunky flatfish and can reach an enormous size. It has a brownish skin on one side and is pearly white underneath with two eyes on the bridge of the snout. The smaller type, called a chicken halibut, weighs under 1.5kg/3lb and is ideal for poaching or baking.

Mackerel Mackerel and bonito are from the same family. The fish is easy to recognize by the dark blue markings which run part of the way down to a silvery green side and pale underbelly. The inside of the mouth is black. Mackerel is an oily fish, with soft, pinkish flesh, and is ideal for grilling and poaching with miso. Serve mackerel with wedges of lemon or lime. It is also excellent in a *laksa* or a Thai fish soup.

Parrot fish Either blue or brightly coloured, these are striking to look at and delicious to eat.

Plaice Easy to recognize, this flatfish has dark brown skin with orange spots and a white underside. The flesh is soft and moist. Cook plaice whole, either deep-fried or poached. If filleted, make a stock from the bones with bruised ginger, onion and seasoning.

Pomfret Held in high regard by Malay and Thai cooks, the pomfret is a fisherman's dream as it is very easy to net. So easy that at one stage these fish were almost fished out. A type of flatfish, pomfret is silver grey with a pearly white underside. The ideal way to preserve the delicate flavour of this fish is to steam it with a few simple flavourings, such as ginger, spring onion (scallion), light soy sauce and seasoning. It is good grilled (broiled) and fried, too.

Salmon Often called the king of fish, the finest wild salmon makes delicious sashimi. Farmed salmon makes a very reasonable and good buy for a vast array of cooked dishes. The skin on a salmon's back is steely blue going down to a silver body. The flesh is oily, an attractive shade of pink, and firm. It is best either clear simmered or poached in a fish kettle or wrapped in foil and baked. Cutlets can be cooked on a barbecue and served with Thai salad or used to make a Filipino dish, escabeche.

Sea bass The family of sea bass also includes the groupers (sometimes called garoupas). Sea bass is silver in colour with a dark back and white underbelly. The flesh is delicate in flavour and holds its shape when cooked. The fish can be grilled, steamed, baked or barbecued whole, or cut into fillets or steaks before being cooked. It is expensive but worth it.

Sea bream Look for the gilt head with a gold spot on each cheek and squat compact body. Sea bream must be scaled before being cooked. The flesh is rather coarse but remains moist if not overcooked. Slash each side two or three times so that the thicker part of the fish will cook more evenly. Sea bream is best baked whole in an oiled or buttered foil parcel with ginger, spring onion and seasoning. It is good served with a sweet and sour sauce.

Above: Tuna steaks and and salmon cutlets

Snapper The red snapper is perhaps the best known but there other colours, too, such as grey, silver and even a silver-spotted grey. The red colour is quite distinctive. The fish has large eyes and very strong dorsal fins which should be removed before cooking. The flesh is moist and well flavoured. Small to medium snappers are good for steaming or baking whole.

Sole Another member of the flatfish family, sole has rough brown skin on top and a long lozenge-shaped body. The flesh has superb texture and a delicate flavour. Sole is best grilled or fried whole. It can be sold filleted, in which case ask for the bones to make stock for a fish soup.

Squid Asian cooks are fond of squid. In the West, this cephalopod usually comes ready cleaned, but if you should you come across squid in the unprepared state here is what to do: Pull the tentacles out from the body sac. Squeeze the tentacle in the centre gently to remove the hard central bone or "beak". Trim the tentacles from the head and set aside. Using fingers pull the quill and innards from the body cavity and discard. Pull off the mottled outer skin, it should come away quite easily. Wash the squid well inside and out. It is now ready for stuffing. When it is two thirds full, pop the tentacles back into the top of the sac. Secure the tentacles and the top of the squid body with a cocktail stick.

If the squid are to be stir-fried, further preparation will be necessary: Slit the sac from top to bottom and turn it inside out. Flatten it on a board and score the inside surface lightly with a knife, pressing just hard enough to make a criss-cross pattern. Cut lengthways into ribbons. These will curl when cooked.

Tuna These enormous fish are the big brothers of the mackerel family. Tuna swim enormous distances at speed and this causes the muscles to fill with blood, which explains the deep red colour of the fresh fish. The skipjack and the albacore are much sought after by the Japanese for making **sashimi** and **sushi.** When grilling or cooking tuna on a barbecue, marinate the fish first and then baste it to keep it moist throughout the cooking. It is also good pan-fried.

SHELLFISH

Asian cooks have access to a wonderful assortment of shellfish, not only from the ocean, but also – in the case of crabs and shrimps – from freshwater lakes, rivers and canals. In Asia it is considered essential that shellfish be as fresh as possible when cooked. This isn't always possible for the Western cook, who often has no option but to resort to using good quality frozen shellfish. In this case, the shellfish should be thawed slowly, and dried before being cooked. The cooking period should be kept to a minimum to preserve the delicate flavour and texture of the shellfish. In Asia, favoured cooking methods for shellfish are steaming, deep-frying and stir-frying, but they are also used in soups, and made into dishes such as crab cakes.

Abalone This large shellfish has a particularly pretty shell, lined with what looks like mother-of-pearl. The flesh of abalone can be tough, and it is usually beaten to tenderize it before cooking. Frozen abalone is available from some Asian markets, and it is also possible to buy canned abalone. This is yellow brown in colour and has a savoury flavour. The texture tends to be rubbery, so canned abalone is seldom served solo, but is usually combined

Above: Mussels and clams

with other ingredients. The can juices can be used in soups and sauces. Dried abalone is an expensive and much sought-after delicacy.

Clams There are many different types of clam. In Japan, the giant clam and the round clam are both used for making sushi, and in China clams with black bean sauce are a favourite treat. When buying clams, check that none of the shells are broken. Wash them well in running water, then leave in salt water before steaming for 7–8 minutes or until the shells open. Serve clams simply, with a dipping

Above: Canned abalone

Mussels and Clams in Coconut Cream

Mussels and clams can be steamed, but here they are cooked Thai-style in coconut cream and flavoured with lemon grass, kaffir lime leaves and Thai green curry paste.

SERVES 4–6

1.75 kg/4 – 4¹/₂lb mussels
450g/1lb baby clams
120ml/4fl oz/¹/₂ cup dry white wine
1 bunch spring onions (scallions), chopped
2 lemon grass stalks, chopped
6 kaffir lime leaves, chopped
10ml/2 tsp Thai green curry paste
200ml/7fl oz/scant 1 cup coconut cream
30ml/2 tbsp chopped fresh coriander (cilantro)
salt and ground black pepper

1 Scrub the mussels, pull off the beards and remove any barnacles. Discard any mussels that are broken or which do not close when tapped sharply. Wash the clams thoroughly.

2 Put the wine in a large pan with the spring onions, lemon grass, lime leaves and curry paste. Simmer gently until the wine has almost evaporated. Add the mussels and clams to the pan, cover tightly and steam the shellfish over a high heat for about 6 minutes, until they open.

3 Using a slotted spoon, transfer the mussels and clams to a heated serving bowl and keep hot. Discard any shellfish that remain closed. Strain the cooking liquid into a clean pan and simmer to reduce to about 250ml/8fl oz/1 cup.

4 Stir in the coconut cream and coriander, with salt and pepper to taste. Heat through. Pour the sauce over the mussels and clams.

is often pan-fried or cooked in a pot of rice where it releases a delicious, delicate flavour.

Lobster This luxury shellfish is usually served as a restaurant dish. To cook a live lobster, put it in a pan of ice cold water, cover the pan tightly and bring the water to the boil. The shell will turn bright red and the flesh will be tender and succulent when the lobster is cooked. If you buy a ready-cooked lobster the tail should spring back into a curl when pulled out straight. One of the best ways of eating lobster is with a dip of soy sauce with grated ginger.

Scallops Prized for their tender, sweet flesh, scallops are popular throughout Asia. The delicate flesh needs the briefest possible cooking. An excellent way of cooking scallops is to marinate them in a mixture of Chinese rice wine, sugar and soy sauce for 30 minutes, then steam them with the marinade and some slivers of ginger and spring onion (scallion).

Above: Lobster and scallops

Below: Blue swimming crabs

sauce based on hoisin sauce, plum sauce or soy sauce with ginger. Clams are also very good in soups.

Mussels Another shellfish that is widely used in oriental cooking. Farmed mussels are now readily available and have the advantage that they are usually relatively free of barnacles. They are generally sold in quantities of 1kg/2¼lb, sufficient for a main course for two or three people. Look for good-size specimens with glossy shells. Discard any that are not closed, or which fail to shut when tapped. Use the back of a short stout knife to scrape away any barnacles, pull away the hairy "beards", then wash the shellfish thoroughly. The best way to cook mussels is to steam them in a small amount of flavoured liquor in a large lidded pan for 3–4 minutes until the shells open. Use finely chopped fresh root ginger, lemon grass, torn lime leaves and some fish sauce to add flavouring to the mussels.

Crabs are eaten with great relish all over the East. There are many different species which are exclusive to Asia. Travellers to Thailand and Hong Kong will doubtless have seen – and enjoyed – blue swimming crabs. This species obligingly moults its shell so that the crab can be eaten whole. The meat

Fantail or phoenix prawns/shrimp
This way of serving prawns (shrimp) comes from China. The cooked prawns, with their bright red tails, are supposed to resemble the legendary phoenix, which is a symbol of dignity and good luck. Large prawns are used.

1 Remove the heads from the prawns and peel away most of the body shell. Leave a little of the shell to keep the tail intact.

2 Make a tiny incision in the back of each prawn and remove the black intestinal cord.

3 Hold the prepared prawns by the tails and dip lightly in seasoned cornflour (cornstarch), and then in a frothy batter before cooking them in hot oil until the tails, which are free from batter, turn red.

Left: Cooked prawns

Shrimps and prawns Both shrimps and prawns can be caught in either fresh water or the sea. The names tend to be used indiscriminately in Asia. Shrimps can be small or large and the same holds good for prawns. Buy fresh raw shellfish where possible, choosing specimens that are a translucent grey colour tinged with blue. If using frozen shrimps and prawns, it is preferable to buy raw shellfish, thaw them slowly and dry them well before using. Further preparation will depend upon the chosen recipe. The shells may be left on or removed, or the shrimps or prawns may be shelled, with the tails left intact.

Left: Raw prawns

Butterfly prawns/shrimp
Prawns (shrimp) prepared this way cook quickly and curl attractively.

1 Remove the heads and body shells of the prawns, but leave the tails intact. Pull out the intestinal cords with tweezers.

2 Make a cut through the belly of each prawn.

3 Gently open out the two halves of the prawn so that they will look like butterfly wings.

HERBS, SPICES AND AROMATICS

Above: Garlic

GARLIC

MANDARIN: *SUAN*; CANTONESE: *SUEN*;
THAI: *KRATIAM*

Garlic is a member of the lily family, which is the same genus as leeks and onions. It is believed to have originated in Asia, and is mentioned in Chinese texts that date back over 3,000 years. The ancient Egyptians valued it for food and also accorded it a ceremonial significance. Garlic's curative qualities are well documented, and in many cultures it is used to ward off evil.

Aroma and flavour

There are several varieties of garlic, from tiny heads to the aptly named elephant garlic. The colour of the skin varies from white through to pink and purple, and the flavour can be anywhere from mild to extremely pungent. The most common variety in the Far East has a purple skin, a distinctive aroma and a fairly strong flavour with a hint of sweetness. In South-east Asia, cooks use a miniature variety of garlic. There are only four to six cloves in each bulb, and both the aroma and the flavour are much more concentrated. Thai cooks favour small garlic bulbs whose cloves have such thin skins that it is seldom necessary to remove them for cooking. The cloves are simply smashed with a cleaver, then added to the pan, where the skins dissolve to become part of the dish.

Culinary uses

Garlic forms a trinity of flavours with spring onion and ginger in thousands of dishes in Chinese cooking, particulary in Beijing and Sichuan. It is a basic ingredient in much of Asia, including Korea, but is less popular in Japan, where it is used mainly for medicinal purposes. Vietnamese cooks use a great deal of garlic, and in Thailand a mixture of crushed garlic, coriander (cilantro) root and pepper is the foundation of many dishes. Garlic is an essential ingredient in the famous Thai curry pastes, too. Throughout Asia, garlic is also used to flavour oil for frying, partly because of the aromatic flavour it imparts, and also because it cuts down on the "oiliness".

Raw garlic is often used in dips, marinades and dressings.

Preparation and cooking techniques

Except in a few rare instances, when whole cloves of garlic are roasted or packed inside a chicken, garlic is always peeled before use. One of the easiest ways of doing this is to place it on a chopping board and crush it with the flat blade of a Chinese cleaver. The skin will separate from the flesh, and can easily be removed before the garlic is crushed completely, again with the flat of the blade. Although both cleaver and board will need to be washed afterwards, this is a lot easier than using a garlic press.

For whole cloves of garlic, or slices, just cut off the root end of the clove and remove the peel with your fingers.

If the garlic is to be used in a spice mix, as is often the case in South-east Asia, put the whole clove in a mortar and give it a blow with a pestle to release the skin. This can then be removed and the garlic crushed with the other ingredients. Recipes indicate whether garlic is to be sliced, chopped or crushed, but as a general rule, crushed garlic is used for overall flavour, the amount determining the intensity. Slices are used for accent, and are sometimes added early in the cooking process, and then removed once they have imparted a subtle flavour to the dish.

Apart from buying whole cloves of garlic, Asian cooks appreciate the convenience of minced garlic in jars. Dried garlic is also available, either as granules or flakes. Flakes need to be reconstituted in water before stir-frying, but can be added directly to braised dishes with plenty of liquid. Garlic purée is available in tubes in the West but is not widely used in Asia.

Storage

Look for firm, plump garlic bulbs with clear, papery skins. Avoid any that are beginning to sprout. Garlic bulbs (also called heads) keep well if stored in a cool, dry place. If it is too warm, the cloves will dry out and become powdery.

Making garlic oil

1 Heat 120ml/4fl oz/½ cup oil in a small pan. Add 30ml/2 tbsp crushed garlic.

2 Cook gently for about 5 minutes until the garlic is pale gold, stirring occasionally. Do not let it burn or the oil will taste bitter. Cool, strain and use as required.

GINGER

MANDARIN: *JIANG*; CANTONESE: *GEUNG*; THAI: *KHING*; JAPANESE: *SHOGA*

Ginger is believed to be indigenous to the tropical jungles of South-east Asia, and was introduced into China by way of India more than two thousand years ago. The portion of the plant popularly called root ginger is actually a rhizome or underground stem. The colour ranges from pale pink (when very young) to a golden beige, with a dry, papery skin. Ginger is highly valued throughout Asia, not only as an aromatic, but also for its medicinal properties. It is believed to aid digestion, check coughs and quell nausea.

Aroma and flavour

Fresh root ginger (green ginger) has a refreshing scent, reminiscent of citrus, and a pleasant, sharp flavour. Young ginger is tender and mild enough to be stir-fried as a vegetable, while older roots become fibrous and more pungent. Root ginger is available dried, but tastes quite different from fresh. It is used mainly as a pickling spice and Asian cooks would not consider it an acceptable substitute for the fresh root. Ground ginger tastes different again; in Asia its use is limited to mixing with other ground spices such as when making curry powder.

Culinary uses

Root ginger is an indispensable ingredient in Eastern cooking. In China, it is usually paired with spring onions (scallions) to create a yin-yang balance in a wide variety of dishes; the cool spring onion providing the yin and the hot ginger the yang. Together they complement (and sometimes tame) the dominant flavours of certain meats and

Above: Fresh root ginger, ground ginger and bottled ginger paste

seafood. Ginger is also used on its own to cut the oily flavour of some cooking oils and marinades. In Thailand, sticks of young ginger are often served as dippers with a spicy sauce, while Indonesians make a wonderful sambal by grinding chillies, shallots and garlic with ginger, and stirring in sugar, salt and rice vinegar. Pickled ginger also plays an important role in Asian cooking. It can be served solo as a side dish, or combined with other ingredients such as beef or duck. One of the most popular items on a Chinese restaurant menu is duck with pineapple and pickled ginger. Chinese pickled ginger is packed in sweetened rice vinegar, and is quite hot. Japanese pickled ginger has a more delicate flavour. The pale pink type called gari is always served with sushi or sashimi to refresh the palate between mouthfuls.

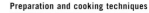

Root ginger is usually peeled before being used. The thin, tough skin is quite easy to scrape or cut away, and the flesh is then thinly sliced, grated, shredded or finely chopped. When the ginger is intended purely for use as a flavouring, and is discarded after cooking, it should be bruised using the flat blade of a knife or cleaver.

Storage

It used to be difficult to get really fresh, juicy root ginger in the shops, but it is now readily available. Look for firm pieces with smooth skin. If bought really fresh, root ginger will keep well for up to two weeks in a cool, dry place, away from strong light. Root ginger can also be frozen. It can be grated straight from the freezer and will thaw on contact with hot food.

Below: Japanese pink, pickled ginger is also known as gari.

Preparing root ginger

1 Thinly peel the skin using a sharp knife or vegetable peeler.

2 Grate the peeled root finely.

3 Alternatively, cut thin slices of ginger into matchstick strips, or coarsely chop the strips.

4 Bruise the root for use in dishes where the ginger will be removed.

GALANGAL

CHINESE: *LIANG JIANG;* THAI: *KHAA;* VIETNAMESE: *CU GIENG*

Like root ginger, galangal is a rhizome that grows underneath the ground. The finger-like protruberances of galangal tend to be thinner and paler in colour, but the two look similar and are used in much the same way. Fresh galangal used to be virtually unobtainable in the West (although it was widely used in medieval Europe), but is now almost as easy to come by as ginger. There are two types. Greater galangal, also known as *lengkuas,* is a native of Indonesia, while lesser galangal originated in southern China. It is not as widely used as its larger relation, but is popular in Thailand, where it is known as *krachai.*

Laos powder is dried galangal that has been ground. Although it does not taste the same as fresh galangal, South-east Asian cooks appreciate its convenience and you will find it in many South-east Asian recipes. As a guide, 5ml/1 tsp of laos powder is equivalent to 1cm/½in fresh galangal, which has been peeled and chopped.

Aroma and flavour

Greater galangal has a pine-like aroma with a correspondingly sharp flavour; lesser galangal is more pungent and the flavour has been likened to a cross between ginger and black pepper. The rhizome is usually used fresh, but is also dried and powdered.

Culinary uses

Galangal is an essential flavouring agent in South-east Asian cooking, particularly in seafood and meat dishes. It is often pounded with shallots, garlic and chillies to make a spice paste for dips or curries. In Thailand, slices of galangal are added to soups, with shreds of lemon grass and lime leaves, while Vietnamese cooks add it to a peanut and lime sauce used to dress meat and vegetable salads.

Preparation and cooking techniques

Fresh galangal should always be peeled. It is usually thinly sliced or cut into matchsticks for cooking. Because it is harder than ginger, you will need to slice it before attempting to crush it, and slices or shreds need to be cooked for somewhat longer than ginger if they are to be tender.

Storage

Fresh galangal will keep for up to 2 weeks if stored in a cool, dry place. It can be stored in the refrigerator, but it must be well wrapped in greaseproof paper to keep it moist.

Right: Fresh and dried galangal

CHILLIES

MANDARIN: *LAJIAO;* CANTONESE: *LAT JIU;*
THAI: *PRIK*

Chillies are native to tropical America. Christopher Columbus introduced them to Europe, having come across them in Mexico while searching for peppercorns. Their fame spread rapidly, and soon they were being cultivated in Africa, India and the Far East, where they rapidly became an integral part of the cuisine. There is, however, a wild variety grown in China's Sichuan province known as "Towards Sky Cannon" or "Peacock's Eye Chilli" (*Capsicum sinense*) which appears to be native to China. Hot chillies and sweet (bell) peppers belong to the same genus, capsicum. There are scores of varieties, but the ones most commonly used in Asia are the Indian *kalyanpur, kovilpatt* and *kesanakurru* chillies, the Japanese *honka* or *hontaka,* the Korean chilli and the family of Thai chillies, which includes the fiery bird's eye. Like sweet peppers, many chillies start out green and ripen to red, while others change from yellow to

Below: Green chillies

Below: The same type of chilli can come in various colours.

Right: Red chillies

red and finally to brown or even black, so what might appear to be a basket of assorted chillies could turn out to be the same type of chilli in varying degrees of ripeness. In size, they range from tiny pods not much bigger than a pea to 30cm/12in monsters. Although Asian cooks tend to use them fresh, chillies are also available dried.

Aroma and flavour

Although heat is the quality most closely associated with chillies, flavour is important too, and aficionados use terms such as sweet, smoky and piquant to describe their favourite types. The degree of heat varies from

> ### Chilli paste
> Ready-made chilli paste is sold in jars, however, it is easy to make at home. Simply halve and seed fresh chillies, then place them in the bowl of a food processor and purée to make a smooth paste. A chopped onion can be added to the processor to add bulk to the paste. Store small amounts of the paste in the fridge for up to 1 week, or spoon into small containers, cover and freeze for up to 6 months. *Sambal oelek,* an Indonesian chilli sauce, is made in a similar way, but first the chillies are blanched.

Left: Medium red chillies

blisteringly hot. Chillies grown in hot climes also tend to be hotter than those grown in cooler conditions.

very mild to positively explosive, but can be moderated somewhat if the seeds and pithy membrane (where most of the heat resides) are removed. The shape and colour give no sure indication of the hotness, for instance, some large green chillies are very mild, while others are

Culinary uses

That chillies and other spicy foods are perfect for hot climates is a bit of a paradox, but because they encourage blood to rush to the surface of the

skin, they actually promote cooling. In many Asian countries, they are eaten out of hand, as snacks, and cooks seeking to determine the strength of a chilli before buying will often do so by nibbling a sample from a market stall. Chillies are used fresh, in sauces and salads, and are essential ingredients in Indonesian sambals. They also find their way into a huge variety of cooked dishes, including stocks, soups, braised dishes and stir-fries, either with

Above: Neither the colour nor the size of chillies gives a sure indication of their hotness as some green chillies are hotter than red ones, and some large chillies are hotter than small ones.

or without the seeds. Where just a hint of heat is required, chillies are sometimes added whole to a dish, then removed again just before serving.

Thailand is one of the world's major producers of fresh chillies, so it is not surprising that Thai cooks have developed some of the most exciting and innovative chilli recipes. A favourite way of serving whole chillies is with a pork and prawn stuffing. The chillies are steamed, then fried.

In Chinese cooking, hot chillies are used not to paralyse the tongue but to stimulate the palate. The regional cuisines of Hunan, Jiangxi, Guizhou and Yunnan all feature chillies, although not as strongly as does the province of Sichuan, which is famous for its spicy food. Even in Sichuan, however, chillies are used with discretion and at least a third of Sichuan dishes do not contain any chillies at all. Even the Cantonese use chillies in some of their dishes, and chilli sauce and chilli oil are popular condiments on Cantonese tables.

Preparing fresh chillies

1 Remove the stalks, then slice the chillies lengthways.

2 Scrape out the pith and seeds from the chillies, then slice, shred or chop the flesh as required. The seeds can be either discarded or added to the dish, depending on the amount of heat that is required.

Preparing dried chillies

1 Remove the stems and seeds and snap each chilli into 2–3 pieces.

2 Put these in a deep bowl, pour over hot water to cover and leave to stand for 30 minutes. Drain, reserving the soaking water if it can usefully be added to the dish, and use the pieces of chilli as they are, or chop them more finely.

Making chilli flowers

Thai cooks are famous for their beautiful presentation, and often garnish platters with chilli flowers. These are quite simple to make.

1 Holding each chilli in turn by the stem, slit it in half lengthways.

2 Keeping the stem end of the chilli intact, cut it lengthways into fine strips.

3 Put the prepared chillies in a large bowl of iced water, cover and chill for several hours.

4 The cut chilli strips will curl back to resemble the petals of a flower. Drain well on kitchen paper and use as a garnish. Small chillies may be very hot, so don't be tempted to eat the flowers.

Right: Dried chillies

Using dried chillies

Dry roasting heightens the flavour of dried chillies. Heat a heavy-based frying pan without adding oil. Press the chillies on to the surface of the pan to roast them, but don't allow them to burn, or their flavour will become bitter. Once the chillies are roasted, remove them from the pan and leave to cool, then crush or grind in a mortar with a pestle before adding to dishes.

Preparation and cooking techniques

Chillies must be handled with care. They contain capsaicin, an oily substance which causes intense irritation to sensitive skin. Get capsaicin on your hands, or worse, transfer it to your eyes by rubbing, and you will experience considerable pain. It is therefore very important to wash your hands immediately after handling chillies, and to use plenty of soap, as the oil does not dissolve in water alone. Some cooks prefer to wear latex gloves when preparing chillies, and some become extremely adept at using a knife and fork, and avoid touching the chillies at all, but whichever method you use, remember that it is also essential to wash cutting boards and implements.

Storage

Look for firm, unblemished fruit, avoiding any chillies that are soft or bruised. Some types look wrinkled even in their prime, so do not let this put you off fruit that otherwise appears to be in good condition. The best way to store chillies is to wrap them in kitchen paper, place them in a plastic bag and keep them in the salad compartment of the refrigerator. They will keep well for a week or more, but it is a good idea to check them occasionally and discard any that begin to show signs of softening. If you intend to use them solely for cooking, they can be frozen. There is no need to blanch them if you plan to use them fairly quickly. To dry your own chillies, thread them on a string, hang them in a warm place for a week or two until they are dry, then crush them in a mortar with a pestle.

Below: Pickled chillies are available in jars. They are mainly used as a relish.

LEMON GRASS

MANDARIN: *NINGMENG CAO;*
CANTONESE: *XIANG MAO;*
MALAY: *SERAI;* THAI: *TAKRAI;*
VIETNAMESE: *XA*

Few ingredients have seized the Western imagination quite so dramatically as has lemon grass in recent years. At one time this scented grass was little known outside South-east Asia; today it is to be found in nearly every supermarket. Lemon grass is a perennial tufted plant with a bulbous base. It grows in dense clumps in tropical and subtropical countries and is commercially cultivated on a grand scale. The cut stems are about 20cm/8in long, and look a little like fat spring onions or very skinny leeks.

Aroma and flavour

It is only when the stems are cut that the distinctive citrus aroma can be fully appreciated. This is matched by the clean, intense lemon flavour, which has a hint of ginger but none of the acidity associated with lemon or grapefruit.

Below: Dried lemon grass

Left: Lemon grass

Lemon rind is sometimes suggested as a substitute, but it lacks the intensity and liveliness of fresh lemon grass, and will give disappointing results. Ground dried lemon grass, also known as serai powder, can be used instead of fresh. As a guide, about 5ml/1 tsp powder is equivalent to 1 fresh stalk. Whole and dried chopped stalks are also available in jars from Asian stores and larger supermarkets, as are jars of lemon grass paste.

Culinary uses

Lemon grass is widely used throughout South-east Asia, in soups, sauces, stir-fries, curries, salads, pickles and marinades. It is a perfect partner for coconut milk, especially in fish, seafood and chicken dishes. Thai cooks often start a stir-fry by adding a few rings of lemon grass and perhaps a little grated or chopped fresh root ginger or galangal to the oil. This not only flavours the oil, but also fills the room with a glorious aroma. A favourite Vietnamese dish consists of sea bream coated in a lemon grass paste, which is left to stand until the flavour penetrates the fish, and then fried.

Preparation and cooking techniques

There are two main ways of using lemon grass. The stalk can be bruised, then cooked slowly in a soup or stew until it releases all its flavour and is removed, or the tender portions of the lemon grass (usually the lower 5cm/2in of the bulbous end of the stem) can be sliced or finely chopped,

Above: Lemon grass paste

then stir-fried or used in a salad or braised dish. Often one stalk will serve both purposes, the tougher top end is used for background flavouring while the tender portion forms the focal point of a dish. For basting food that is to be grilled or barbecued, the upper portion of the lemon grass stalk can be used. The fibrous end is flattened with a cleaver or pestle to make a brush.

Storage

Store lemon grass stalks in a paper bag in the vegetable compartment of the refrigerator. They will keep for 2–3 weeks.

Making a lemon grass brush
Instead of discarding the dry stalk, make it into a basting brush.

Trim off the bottom 5cm/2in of the lemon grass stalk to use in a recipe, then flatten the cut end of the remaining stalk using a cleaver or pestle to produce a fibrous brush.

KAFFIR LIMES

THAI: *BAI MAKRUT;* INDONESIAN: *DAUN JERAK;*
VIETNAMESE: *CHANH SAC;* MALAYSIAN: *LIMAU
PURUT;* BURMESE: *SHAUK-NU*

These fruit are not true limes, but
belong to a subspecies of the citrus
family. Native to South-east Asia, they
have dark green knobbly skins, quite
unlike those of their cousins, the
smooth-skinned limes or lemons.
The fruit is not edible. The rind is
sometimes used in cooking, but it is the
leaves that are most highly prized. Kaffir
limes yield very little juice, and what
there is is very sour. Thai and Malaysian
cooks occasionally use it to heighten
the flavour of dishes with a citrus base.
Vietnamese women use the juice as a
hair rinse.

Japanese citron peel

In Japan, very thin slices of
citron peel *(yuzu)* are used
to garnish soups. The
ground peel is used to
flavour miso.

Aroma and flavour

The scented bouquet
is unmistakably
citrus, and the full
lemon flavour is
released when the
leaves are torn
or shredded.

Culinary uses

Kaffir lime leaves are
synonymous with Thai cooking,
and are also used in Indonesia,
Malaysia, Burma and Vietnam. The
leaves are torn or finely shredded
and used in soups (especially hot and
sour soups) and curries. The
finely grated rind
is sometimes
added to fish or
chicken dishes.

Storage

Fresh kaffir limes and leaves are
obtainable in Asian stores. They will
keep for several days, or can be frozen.
Freeze-dried kaffir lime leaves are also
available. These are used in much the
same way as bay leaves, and do not
need to be soaked in water first.
Stored in a sealed container in a
cool, dry place, the dried leaves
will keep their flavour for only
a few months.

ORANGE OR TANGERINE PEEL

MANDARIN: *CHEN PI;*
CANTONESE: *CHAN PEI*

Both oranges and tangerines
originated in China, where they
were held in high regard for
centuries before traders
introduced them to the
West. The sun-dried
peel of both these
citrus fruits is
used as a spice,
particularly in
the cooking
of Sichuan
and Hunan.

Left: Dried orange peel

*Above: Kaffir
limes and
kaffir lime leaves*

Aroma and flavour

The dried peel is dark brown and brittle,
but retains a strong citrus fragrance.
When it is used in cooking, it imparts
a tangy flavour to the food.

Culinary uses

Originally, dried citrus peels were mainly
used medicinally. Today, they are a
popular seasoning and are often
combined with star anise and cinnamon
when braising meat or poultry.

Preparation and cooking techniques

In braised dishes, pieces of dried peel
are used in much the same way as star
anise, and are discarded after cooking.
When peel is used in a stir-fry, however,
it is first soaked in water until soft, and
the pith is scraped off before the peel is
shredded or sliced.

Storage

Orange and tangerine peel are sold in
plastic bags in stores. Once opened, the
bags should be resealed and kept in a
cool, dry, dark place. The peel will keep
for many months.

Left: Dried curry leaves

CURRY LEAVES

INDONESIAN: *DAUN KARI;* THAI: *BAI KAREE;* BURMESE: *PINDOSIN*

These are the shiny green leaves of a hardwood tree that is indigenous to India. They are widely used in Indian cooking, especially in South India and Sri Lanka, and were introduced into Malaysia by Tamil immigrants. The spear-shaped leaves grow on a thin stem. They are slightly serrated, with a pale underside, and are not unlike small bay leaves.

Aroma and flavour

Curry leaves have an intriguing warm fragrance, with just a hint of sweet, green pepper or tangerine. The full flavour is released when the leaves are bruised. When added to curries or braised dishes, they impart a distinctive flavour. Dried curry leaves come a very poor second to fresh, and rapidly lose their fragrance.

Culinary uses

The leaves are used whole or torn in Indian, Malay and Indonesian curries. Fried in ghee, with mustard seeds, they make a good addition to dhals.

Preparation and cooking techniques

Rinse the leaves and then strip from the stems. Use the leaves whole or chopped as directed in recipes.

Storage

Fresh curry leaves can be bought from stores selling Indian and Gujerati produce. They will keep for several days in the refrigerator, but should be closely wrapped to prevent their distinctive flavour from being transferred to other items. Alternatively – and this is more convenient – open freeze the leaves, then transfer them to a plastic box. Dried leaves do not have much taste, unless you can locate the vacuum-packed variety, which have better colour and flavour.

MINT

CHINESE: *PAK HOM HO;* INDONESIAN: *DAUN PUDINA;* THAI: *BAI SARANAI;* VIETNAMESE: *HUNG QUE*

Mint originated in the Mediterranean region, but it spread rapidly throughout the world. There are many types grown in Asia, but the most commonly used is a tropical variety of spearmint, which has grey-green oval leaves.

Aroma and flavour

Mint has a fresh, stimulating aroma. The Asian variety is much more strongly flavoured than most European types, and is slightly sweet tasting, imparting a cool aftertaste.

Culinary uses

Mint is an essential ingredient in Vietnamese cooking, and it was they who introduced it to the Thais. Its fresh flavour is enjoyed in many salads, and in the delicious rice paper rolls that go by the name of *goi cuon.* Thai cooks like to add a handful of mint leaves just before serving some of their soups and highly spiced dishes. As it has such a dominant flavour, mint is seldom used with other herbs.

Preparation

Wash the leaves on the stem under cold water, shake off the excess moisture and pat dry using kitchen paper.

Storage

Wrap loosely in kitchen paper and keep in the vegetable compartment of the refrigerator, or stand the stems in a jug of cold water covered with a plastic bag and keep in the door of the refrigerator.

Below: Mint

BASIL

THAI: *BAI HORAPA* (SWEET BASIL), *BAI KRAPOW* (HOLY BASIL), *BAI MANGLAK* (HAIRY OR LEMON-SCENTED BASIL); INDONESIAN: *INDRING*; JAPANESE: *MEBOKI*

Basil is one of the oldest herbs known to man. It is an annual and is believed to have originated in India. Hindus hold it sacred and often plant it around their holy places.

In India, however, it is not used in cooking as much as it is in the rest of Asia. In Vietnam, Laos and Cambodia it is an important ingredient, but it is in Thailand that basil is most widely used, and it is the varieties of basil favoured by the Thais that you will find most frequently in oriental shops in the West. *Horapa* (sweet basil) comes closest to the Mediterranean varieties with which we are most familiar. It has shiny green leaves and the stems are sometimes purple. *Krapow,* commonly known as holy basil, is another sweet basil, but with narrower leaves that tend to be dull rather than shiny. The leaves have serrated red or purple edges. Thais also use a lemon-scented basil – sometimes called hairy basil – but this does not travel well and is seldom seen outside Thailand. If you cannot obtain Asian basil when cooking an Eastern dish, any European variety can be used instead, but the flavour will not be the same, and you should use a little more than the amount recommended. Basil is best used fresh, but freeze-dried leaves are also available from larger supermarkets.

Aroma and flavour

Of the Asian basils, *horapa* has a faint aniseed flavour, while holy basil is more pungent. Hairy basil has a lemon scent and is slightly peppery.

Above: Sweet basil

Below: Thai basil

Culinary uses

Sweet basil leaves are added to curries or salads both as an ingredient and also as a garnish. They impart a fresh spicy flavour. Holy basil leaves only release their full flavour when cooked and are therefore frequently used in stir-fries.

Preparation

Strip the leaves from the stem and either tear them into pieces or add them whole to the other ingredients. Avoid chopping basil leaves.

Storage

Wrap bunches of basil loosely in kitchen paper and keep them in the salad compartment of the refrigerator. Alternatively,

stand in a jug of water covered with a plastic bag. Keep in the refrigerator and change the water every day.

SHISO

JAPANESE: *SHISO* (GREEN), *AKA SHISO* (RED); KOREAN: *KKAENNIP*

Also known as *perilla* or the beefsteak plant, this annual herb is grown in China, Korea, Laos and Vietnam and is very well known in Japan, where it is also called *oba*. The leaves can be green or reddish-purple. When crushed, they release a pungent aroma, similar to that of mint. Japanese cooks use shiso in tempura and when making *umeboshi* (pickled plums). In the presence of an acid, the red-leafed variety dyes ginger red.

Above: Shiso

CORIANDER/CILANTRO

MANDARIN: *XIANGCAI;* CANTONESE: *YUAN SUI;*
BURMESE: *NAN NAN BIN;* THAI: *PAK CHEE*

Also known as Chinese parsley – and
familiar to Americans as cilantro –
coriander is one of the oldest known
herbs in the world, and also one of
the most popular. Although a native
of southern Europe, fresh coriander
has become an indispensable
ingredient throughout Asia and
the Middle East, as well as
in Latin America.

Aroma and flavour

Coriander takes its name from
the Greek *koris,* meaning a bug. The
leaves of the plant are supposed to give
off a smell similar to that of a room
infested with bed bugs, yet the Chinese,
displaying a wicked sense of humour,
call coriander "fragrant leaves". When
dry-fried, the seeds smell rather like
burnt orange, while the ground seeds
impart a warm, spicy aroma to food.

Culinary uses

Asian cooks use every part of the plant:
the stems are used for flavouring; the
leaves in stir-fries, soups and noodle
dishes; and as a garnish, the seeds for
spice pastes and
in curries. Ground
coriander is widely used, often in
combination with ground cumin.
In Thailand, the roots are
used, too. This can
present problems for
the Western cook,
because the thin roots
are usually removed
before the coriander
reaches the market. One
answer is to grow your
own, but if this is
impractical, use the bottom
portion of the stem as
a substitute.

*Above: Coriander –
Asian cooks use the
roots as well as the leaves
and stems.*

Below: Ground coriander

Preparation and cooking techniques

Try not to chop fresh
coriander too finely, or
the beauty of the
serrated leaves will be
lost. Never overcook
the leaves or they will
become limp and
unpalatable; either
use them raw as a
garnish, or add them
to a dish at the very
last moment.
     If a recipe
calls for ground
coriander, it is

Left: Coriander seeds

preferable to dry-fry and grind the
seeds yourself, as the aroma and
flavour will be more pronounced than
when ready-ground coriander is used.

Storage

Fresh coriander will not keep for more
than a couple of days unless stood in
a jug of cold water and covered with a
plastic bag, in which case it will stay
fresh for a little longer. Coriander roots
are seldom available, but if you do
locate a supply, the cleaned roots can
be frozen.
     Dried coriander seeds keep well, but
the ready-ground powder rapidly loses
its aroma and flavour. Buy small
quantities so that you can replenish
your supplies regularly.

*Right:
Ground
and fresh
turmeric*

TURMERIC

BURMESE: *HSANWEN;* MANDARIN: *WONG
GEUNG;* CANTONESE: *YU CHIN;*
JAPANESE: *UKON*

Turmeric comes from the ginger family
but does not have the characteristic
"heat" associated with fresh ginger. The
plant, a rhizome, is indigenous to hot,
humid, hilly areas of South-east Asia
from Vietnam to Southern India.
Frequently referred to as "Indian
saffron", it shares with saffron the
capacity to tint foods yellow, but is
nowhere near as subtle as the much
more expensive spice. The bright yellow
colour, which can clearly be seen when
the rhizome is sliced, is also used as a
dye of silks and cottons, including the
fabric used to make robes for Buddhist
monks. When mixed to a paste,
turmeric is sometimes smeared on the
cheeks to protect the skin from the sun.
The world's largest producer of turmeric
is India, but Indonesia and China also
grow significant quantities of this spice.

The bulk of the turmeric crop is used
for domestic consumption or ground
and sold as powder.

Aroma and flavour

Fresh turmeric is sometimes available
from Asian stores. When cut it has a
peppery aroma with a hint of wood in
the background. It imparts a warm,
slightly musky flavour and a rich colour
to any food with which it is cooked. The
dried spice has similar properties.

Culinary uses

Ground turmeric is an essential
ingredient in curry powders, being
responsible for the characteristic yellow
colour. It is also used in the preparation
of some blends of mustard powder and
is the spice that gives piccalilli its lurid
colour. That famous Anglo-Indian
breakfast dish – kedgeree – contains
turmeric, and it is also used in pilau
rice, dhals and vegetable dishes.
Turmeric has a natural affinity with fish,
and is often used in Malayan recipes.

Preparation and cooking methods

Using a sharp knife, slice off the skin,
then slice, grate or chop the flesh. It
can be ground with other ingredients to
make a curry paste. Some people like
to wear gloves when preparing fresh
turmeric as it can stain the skin.
Ground dried turmeric is easy to use
as it needs no preparation.

Storage

Fresh turmeric will keep for up to
2 weeks, if stored in a cool, dry place
away from strong light. It can be stored
in the refrigerator, but must be well
wrapped to keep it moist. Like all
ground spices, ground turmeric will lose
its potency on keeping, so buy only
small quantities and keep the powder in
an airtight container in a cupboard away
from strong light. The only time whole
pieces of dried turmeric are likely to be
called for is in the preparation of some
pickles. Do not attempt to grind the
whole dried spice to make powder; the
rhizomes are too hard.

Preparing fresh turmeric

1 Using a sharp knife, scrape off
the skin.

2 Grate the flesh using a standard
box grater, or slice or chop,
depending on the recipe.

*Above: Star-shaped
star anise*

STAR ANISE

MANDARIN: *PAK KOK;* CANTONESE: *BOAT GOK;*
INDONESIAN: *BUNGA LAWANG;* THAI: *POY
KAK BUA*

Star anise is the unusual star-shaped
fruit of an evergreen tree native to
South-west China and Vietnam. The
tree has yellow flowers that resemble
narcissus. These give way to the star-
like fruits, which are harvested before
they ripen. The points of the star
contain amber seeds. Both the seeds
and the husk are used for the ground
spice. In China, one point, the name
given to one section of the star, is often
chewed after a meal as a digestive.

Aroma and flavour

Star anise both smells and tastes like
liquorice. The flavour can also be
detected in the alcoholic drinks pastis
and anisette.

Culinary uses

The aromatic flavour of star anise
complements rich meats. Star
anise is very popular in Chinese
cuisine, especially with pork and
duck, and it is used to flavour
beef soups in Vietnam. It is also
sometimes used in sweet
dishes, such as fruit salads.
Ground star anise is one of the
main ingredients of five spice powder.

Preparation and cooking methods

Star anise can be added whole, and
looks so attractive that it is often left
in a dish when serving, even though it
no longer fulfils any culinary function.
When a small quantity is required, the
spice can be broken and just one or two
points or segments added. It is possible
to grind star anise at home, but it
should be used sparingly as it has a
quite powerful flavour.

Storage

As a whole spice star anise has a long
shelf life. Buy the ground spice in small
quantities from a shop with a high
turnover of stock, and store in a cool,
dry place, away from direct light, to
retain the maximum aroma and flavour.

*Below: The best cloves are plump
and unbroken.*

CLOVES

MANDARIN: *TING HSIANG;* CANTONESE;
DING HEUNG; JAPANESE: *CHOJI;*
THAI: *KAAN PLOO*

Cloves are the unopened
flower buds of a tree which is
a member of the myrtle family.
They originated in the Spice
Islands in Indonesia and were taken
to the Seychelles and Mauritius early
in the 18th century. The biggest
producer now is Zanzibar where the
fresh pink buds are picked twice a year.
They are then dried on palm leaf mats
or over a gentle heat when they turn the
familiar reddish brown. The name clove
is derived from the Latin *clavus,*
meaning a nail.

Aroma and flavour

Cloves have an intense fragrance and
an aromatic flavour that can be fiery.
They are slightly astringent.

Culinary uses

In Asia, cloves are mainly used in
savoury dishes, and their warm
aromatic flavour complements rich
meats. Thai cooks use cloves to cut the
rich flavour of duck, and also use them
with tomatoes, salty vegetables and in
ham or pork dishes. Ground cloves are
an essential ingredient in many spice
mixtures, including the famous Chinese
five spice powder. They are also one of
the ingredients in Worcestershire sauce.

Preparation

Cloves need no preparation. When
purchasing, look for plump cloves.

Storage

Whole cloves have a long shelf life if
kept in a cool place. Ground cloves
should be bought in small
quantities and stored in an
airtight jar away from
strong light, so that the
spice retains its colour and
flavour. To make a small
amount of ground cloves,
crush the central bud at
the top of the clove and
use immediately.

Above: Cinnamon sticks and ground cinnamon

CASSIA

CHINESE: *KUEI;* JAPANESE: *KEIHI;* THAI: *OB CHOEY*

Cassia is sometimes known as Chinese cinnamon. Like cinnamon, it comes from the bark of a tree which is related to laurel, but whereas cinnamon is native to Sri Lanka, cassia comes from Burma, and is also cultivated in China, Indo-China and Indonesia. It is harvested in much the same way as cinnamon, but the bark is not as fine, so although it curls, it will not form the fine quills we associate with cinnamon.

Aroma and flavour

Cassia smells rather like cinnamon, but is more pungent.

Culinary uses

Chinese cooks make much use of cassia. It is one of the constituents of five spice powder and is also an important ingredient in the elaborate spiced stock known as *lu* which is used throughout China for simmering foods. When this stock is first made, it is very strongly flavoured, and is generally used for cooking beef, pot-roast style. The stock is not served with the beef, but is saved to be used again, perhaps with poultry. It may well be boiled up a third time, to simmer

CINNAMON

INDONESIAN: *KAYU MANIS PADANG;* THAI: *OB CHUEY*

The best quality cinnamon is grown in Sri Lanka but it also flourishes elsewhere in Asia, particularly on the coastal strip of South India and Burma. The spice is actually the bark of a bushy tree that is a member of the laurel family. After three years, the branches are cut off and a long incision is made in the bark, so that this can be lifted off. The operation is carried out during the rainy season, when the humidity speeds the peeling process. The bark is then dried in the sun and hand rolled to produce the familiar quills or sticks. Ground cinnamon is also produced.

Aroma and flavour

Cinnamon has a delightfully exotic bouquet, sweet and fragrant, thanks to an essential oil, oil of cinnamon, which is used medicinally. The flavour is warm and aromatic.

Culinary uses

Cinnamon has universal appeal as a flavouring both in sweet and savoury dishes and in a multitude of cakes and breads. In Asia, the sticks are used in spicy meat dishes, often with star anise, with which cinnamon has an affinity. Indonesian cooks use cinnamon in their famous spiced beef and coconut milk stew known as rendang.

Preparation

Add the whole or broken cinnamon stick as directed in the recipe. The sticks are very hard and it is difficult to grind them at home, so it is preferable to buy ready-ground cinnamon.

Storage

Cinnamon sticks have a long shelf life, and will keep for a year or more in an airtight container. Buy ground cinnamon in small quantities from a store with a high turnover of stock and store it in an airtight container away from both heat and strong light.

Below: Ground cassia and cassia bark

fish or shellfish. In some homes, a pan of *lu* will be kept going for months. Cracked cassia quills and cassia buds (which look like cloves) are used in the East to give a warm aromatic flavour to pickles, curries and spiced meat dishes.

Preparation and cooking methods

Cassia is quite tough. Break the pieces as required with the end of a rolling pin or put them in a mortar and use a stout pestle to shatter them. Where ground cassia is required, it is best to buy it in that form.

Storage

As for cinnamon.

CUMIN

CHINESE: *KUMING*; JAPANESE: *KUMIN*; THAI: *YEERAA*

Cumin has been cultivated since earliest times. It is believed to have originated in the Eastern Mediterranean, but is now widely cultivated, especially in China, India, Indonesia and Japan. The plant is a member of the parsley family, but only the seeds (whole or ground) are used in cooking.

Above: Small green and large black cardamom pods

Aroma and flavour

Cumin has a sweet spicy aroma and the flavour is pungent and slightly bitter.

Culinary uses

Cumin is often partnered with whole or ground coriander seeds. Indian cooks are particularly partial to cumin, and it was they who introduced the spice to Singapore, Malaysia and Indonesia.

Preparation

To bring out their full flavour, the seeds are often dry-fried. They are then used whole or ground in a spice mill or in a mortar using a pestle.

Storage

Buy the whole spice in small quantities. Store in a cool place away from bright light. For best results dry-fry and grind the whole spice as

and when required. You can buy ready ground cumin from supermarkets, but it loses its flavour rapidly.

CARDAMOM

BURMESE: *PHALAZEE*; JAPANESE: *KARUDAMON*; THAI: *LUK KRAVAN*

A native of South India, cardamom is a tall herbaceous perennial belonging to the ginger family. It is largely grown for its pods, although Thai cooks sometimes use the leaves for flavouring. The pods are either added whole to spicy dishes, or opened so that the tiny dark seeds can be extracted. The most familiar pods are pale green, and there are also white pods, which are simply bleached green ones. Black cardamoms, which come from Vietnam and India, are large and coarse, and taste quite different. Cardamom pods are harvested by hand, and this makes them more costly than most other spices.

Aroma and flavour

Cardamoms are sweet, pungent and highly aromatic. They have a pleasantly warm flavour, with hints of lemon and eucalyptus. When chewed after a meal, the pods are said to aid digestion as well as sweeten the breath.

Culinary uses

Indian cooks use cardamom to flavour curries, pilaus and desserts, so it is not surprising that the spice is popular wherever there are Indian communities.

Preparation

The pods can be used whole or bruised and dry-fried to enhance the flavour. If just the seeds are required, discard the outer husks. For ground cardamom, grind the seeds in a mortar using a pestle.

Storage

Buy the whole pods and store in an airtight jar in a cool dry place. Grind seeds as required.

Above: Cumin seeds and ground cumin

FENNEL SEEDS

MANDARIN: *WOOI HEUNG;* CANTONESE: *HUI XIANG;* THAI: *YIRA*

Although native to the Mediterranean, this member of the parsley family is widely grown in India and Japan. The ridged seeds are sage green in colour.

Aroma and flavour

Sweet, warm and aromatic, fennel seeds have a distinct anise flavour.

Culinary uses

Fennel seeds are a constituent in many spice mixtures, especially those that are intended to be used with fish or shellfish. Ground fennel is one of the constituents of Chinese five spice powder.

Preparation

Dry-fry before grinding to release the full flavour of the spice.

Storage

Buy small quantities of seeds at a time and store in an airtight jar away from strong light.

Above: Fennel seeds

Chinese five spice powder

Close your eyes as you enter a Chinese supermarket or store and the distinctive aroma of Chinese five spice power seems to dominate. This reddish brown spice mixture is classically composed of equal quantities of Sichuan peppercorns, cassia or cinnamon, cloves, fennel seeds and star anise. Blends vary, however, and ginger, galangal, black cardamom and liquorice can be included. Ginger gives the spice blend a sweeter flavour, and this version is used in desserts. Five spice powder is very popular in China, and is particularly complementary when used with duck, pork, red cooked meats (cooked in soy sauce) and barbecued meats such as spare ribs. Make your own powder by grinding equal amounts of the five spices with a mortar and pestle, or buy the ready ground powder in small quantities and store in an airtight jar away from strong light. A five spice paste is now available in small jars from many of the larger supermarkets.

Japanese seven spice powder

Seven spice powder, which is also known as *shichimi-togarashi*, seven flavour seasoning or seven taste powder, is a delicious condiment that the Japanese like to shake on to food at the table much as we would use salt and pepper. It is especially popular as a seasoning for soups and noodles and other dishes such as sukiyaki and tempura. *Shichimi* is made from a combination of the following ingredients: ground chilli, hemp seed, poppy seed, rape seed, *sansho* (the Japanese name for Sichuan pepper-corns), black and

Right: Chinese five spice powder (top) and Japanese seven spice powder (bottom) can be bought ready-ground from supermarkets and Asian stores.

white sesame seeds, and dried ground tangerine peel. In some mixes ground nori (seaweed) is added. It would be usual to buy this mixture ready prepared. Blends of this spice mixture vary, from mild to very sharp.

PEPPER

MANDARIN: *HU-CHIAO;* CANTONESE: *WOO JIU;*
INDONESIAN: *MERICA;* THAI: *PRIK THAI;*
VIETNAMESE: *HAT-TRIEU*

Often referred to as the king of spices, pepper has an ancient and illustrious past. Known and valued in India for over two thousand years, it was introduced into Europe in the 4th century BC. Demand rapidly grew, but transporting the spice across Asia by the caravan routes was costly, and the monopoly meant that the prices remained astronomically high. Even in Roman times there was outrage that the spices were sold at one hundred times their original cost.

It was the demand for pepper that inspired the search for sailing routes to the East which changed the course of history. When the Portuguese explorer Vasco da Gama opened up the sea route to India in the 15th century, Lisbon became the spice capital of the world, but still the prices stayed high. Even today pepper is the most important spice on world markets, both in terms of value and volume.

Pepper is a perennial climbing vine indigenous to the Malabar coast of India where it is said that the best pepper is still produced. It grows best near the equator and is cultivated intensively in Sarawak and Thailand, as well as in tropical Africa and Brazil. In the Malayan state of Sarawak the vines are trained up long ironwood frames or round tree trunks. The vines have to be controlled to prevent them from climbing too high, which would make harvesting difficult. The leaves are long, green and pointed, and white flowers blossom on the catkins or "spikes".

The plant starts fruiting three to five years after planting, and the harvest continues every three years thereafter for forty years, which is the life of the plant. When the berries are harvested they are still unripe and green. In Sarawak they are dried on mats in the sun, and are raked frequently until the skin shrivels and the berries darken to become the familiar black peppercorns. Another method is to immerse the berries in boiling water, drain them well, and then dry them in kilns.

White peppercorns are husked ripe berries. The berries are picked when they are red or orange. They are soaked in running water for several days, and then they are trampled underfoot to loosen the husks. Finally the pepper berries are transferred to rattan baskets, where they are washed and the husks and stalks removed by hand to leave the white peppercorns. These are then left to dry on mats in the sun for several weeks, or kiln-dried.

Green peppercorns

These are simply unripe berries. They are sold on the stem in some Thai supermarkets, and are a popular ingredient in that country. They can be used fresh, but are also dried, pickled or canned. Those that are bottled or canned need to be rinsed and drained, then added whole or crushed as the recipe dictates. Freeze-dried green peppercorns can be ground in a peppermill. Green peppercorns have a less complex flavour than white or black peppercorns but are still quite fiery.

Above: Fresh green peppercorns are sometimes sold on the stem in Thai supermarkets.

Aroma and flavour

Black peppercorns have an earthy aroma, which is particularly noticeable when they are crushed. The flavour is hot and pungent. White peppercorns are slightly milder.

Culinary uses

Pepper is the one spice which is used before, during and after cooking. Its value as a seasoning is legendary, for it not only has its own flavour, but has the ability to enhance the flavour of other ingredients in a dish.

Preparation

Use a peppermill and grind fresh black pepper as it is required. White peppercorns are less pungent and are used where flecks of black might spoil the appearance of a dish, such as a light-coloured sauce.

Storage

Buy whole peppercorns. Store in a cool place in an airtight container. They keep for a long time.

*Right:
Black and
white peppercorns*

SICHUAN/SZECHUAN PEPPER

MANDARIN: *FAA JIU*; CANTONESE: *HU CHIAO*;
JAPANESE: *SANSHO*

To call this "pepper" is misleading. This spice actually comes from the prickly ash tree, which is native to the Sichuan province in China, but also grows elsewhere in Asia. Unusually, it is the seed pods themselves, not the seeds they contain, that are used for the spice. The tiny reddish brown pods or husks are harvested when ripe, the bitter black seeds are removed and discarded, and the pods – Sichuan peppercorns – are either added whole to stewed dishes or dried and ground as a seasoning spice.

The prickly ash also grows in Japan, where the ripened pods are called *mizansho* or Japanese peppercorns. When ground, the spice is known as *konazansho* or *sansho*. The wood of the prickly ash is sometimes used to make mortar and pestle sets, which are much sought after by Japanese cooks who claim they impart a subtle flavour when used to grind ingredients.

Left: Sichuan peppercorns

Aroma and flavour

Not as pungent as true pepper, Sichuan peppercorns have a warm aroma with a hint of citrus. The full flavour is released when they are dry-fried.

Culinary uses

Sichuan peppercorns are immensely popular in Chinese cuisine. They are excellent in duck, pork and chicken dishes. The ground peppercorns are used in both Chinese five spice powder and Japanese seven spice powder.

Preparation

The dried seed pods should be picked over carefully to remove any debris. Dry-fry the seed pods to heighten their flavour, then use as directed in recipes.

Storage

Although it is possible to buy ground Sichuan pepper, it is better to buy the peppercorns whole and grind them after dry-frying. Keep them in an airtight jar.

Wasabi

Sometimes described as horseradish mustard, this has much in common with both, although it is related to neither. Wasabi is a Japanese seasoning, derived from a slow-growing plant that is found near mountain streams. The peeled root reveals vivid green flesh. This is very finely grated, preferably on sharkskin, and then dried or powdered. When mixed to a cream with soy sauce or water, it makes an extremely hot condiment, which is traditionally served with sushi and sashimi.

Above: A tube of ready-made apple-green wasabi paste

Right: Wasabi powder is mixed to a paste with a little water or soy sauce.

MUSTARD

MALAY: *BIJI SAVI*

Mustard is one of the oldest spices known to man and has been cultivated as a crop for thousands of years. Both white *(alba)* and black *(nigra)* mustard seeds are indigenous to the Mediterranean region, while brown mustard seeds *(juncea)* are native to India. The word mustard

Below: Brown, black and white mustard seeds

Dry-frying mustard seeds

Mustard seeds have almost no smell until they are heated, so before adding them to dishes, they should be dry-fried to heighten their aroma.

1 Heat a little sunflower oil in a deep, wide pan. Add the seeds and shake the pan over the heat, stirring occasionally, until they start to change colour.

2 Have a pan lid ready to prevent the mustard seeds from popping out of the pan.

comes from the Latin *mustum* or *must*, the newly pressed grape juice that Romans mixed with the ground seeds to make what was aptly described as *mustum ardens* (the burning paste).

In Asia, the mustard plant is valued as much for its dark green leaves, which are called mustard greens and are a popular vegetable, as for its seeds. Mustard powders and pastes are not as widely used as they are in Europe or America.

Aroma and flavour

Mustard seeds have no aroma in their raw state. When they are roasted, however, they develop a rich, nutty smell. Mustard's famous hot taste comes from an enzyme in the seeds, which is only activated when they are crushed and mixed with warm water. Brown mustard seeds, which have largely replaced the black seeds, are not as intensely pungent. White mustard seeds, which are actually a pale honey colour, are slightly larger than the other two varieties and a little milder.

Culinary uses

Throughout Asia, mustard seeds are used for pickling and seasoning. The whole seeds are often used in vegetable and dhal dishes, especially in countries such as Malaysia.

Preparation and cooking techniques

Mustard seeds are frequently roasted or fried before being used to bring out their flavour. A southern Indian technique involves spooning the seeds into hot ghee or oil, with a few curry leaves for extra flavour. A lid is placed over the pan to contain the seeds, which soon begin to splutter and pop. The seeds and oil are then poured, still sizzling, on to hot vegetable dishes, soups, stews or dhal as a flavoursome topping. Mustard oil is occasionally used for frying the seeds.

Mustard powder is used as a condiment. When it is mixed with warm water, milk or beer, a chemical reaction begins which allows the mustard to achieve its maximum potency. It takes about 15 minutes for the full flavour to develop. Boiling water or vinegar would inhibit the action of the enzyme responsible for the process, so should not be used.

Storage

Mustard seeds keep well. Store them in an airtight jar in a cool place.

Left: Tamarind block

may suggest using vinegar or lemon juice instead, but the results will not compare with using the real thing.

Preparation

Compressed tamarind This comes in a solid block and looks rather like a packet of dried dates. To prepare it, tear off a piece that is roughly equivalent to 15ml/1 tbsp and soak it in 150ml/¼ pint/⅔ cup warm water for about 10 minutes. Swirl the tamarind around with your fingers so that the pulp is released from the seeds. Using a nylon sieve, strain the juice into a jug. Discard the contents of the sieve and use the

TAMARIND

CHINESE: *ASAM KOH;* INDONESIAN: *ASAM JAVA;* THAI: *MAK KHAM;* BURMESE: *MA-GYI-THI*

The handsome tamarind tree, commonly called the "date of India", is believed to be a native of East Africa but is now cultivated in India, Southeast Asia and the West Indies. The brown fruit pods are 15–20cm/6–8in long. Inside, the seeds are surrounded by a sticky brown pulp. This does not look very prepossessing, but is one of the treasures of the East. It has a high tartaric acid content, and is widely used as a souring agent.

dried tamarind have been around for a while, but it is now also possible to buy jars of fresh tamarind and cartons of tamarind concentrate and paste. There is no substitute for tamarind. Some recipes

Aroma and flavour

Tamarind doesn't have much of an aroma, but the flavour is wonderful. It is tart and sour without being bitter, and fruity and refreshing.

Culinary uses

Tamarind is used in many curries, chutneys and dhals, and is an essential ingredient of Thai hot and sour soups. It is also one of the ingredients in Worcestershire sauce. Tamarind is available in a variety of forms. Blocks of compressed tamarind and slices of

Above, from top: Tamarind paste, tamarind pods and dried tamarind slices

Stir-fried Prawns/Shrimp with Tamarind

Tamarind is used in many Thai dishes to give a characteristic sour, tangy flavour. Preparing fresh tamarind pods for cooking is a laborious process. The Thais usually use compressed blocks of tamarind paste, which is simply soaked in warm water and then strained.

SERVES 4–6

50g/2oz compressed tamarind
150ml/¼ pint/⅔ cup boiling
  water
30ml/2 tbsp vegetable oil
30ml/2 tbsp chopped onion
30ml/2 tbsp palm sugar
30ml/2 tbsp chicken stock
15ml/1 tbsp fish sauce
6 dried red chillies, fried
450g/1lb raw shelled prawns
  (shrimp)
15ml/1 tbsp fried chopped garlic
30ml/2 tbsp fried sliced shallots
chopped and shredded spring
  onions (scallions), to garnish

1 Put the tamarind in a bowl, pour over the boiling water and stir well to break up any lumps. Leave for 10 minutes. Meanwhile, heat the oil in a wok. Add the chopped onion and stir-fry until golden brown.

2 Strain the tamarind juice, pushing as much of the juice through as possible. Measure 90ml/6 tbsp of the juice. Add to the wok along with the sugar, chicken stock, fish sauce and dried chillies. Stir well until the sugar dissolves.

3 Bring to the boil over a medium-high heat, then add the prawns, garlic and shallots, and stir-fry about 3–4 minutes, or until the prawns are only just cooked. Sprinkle over the spring onions and serve immediately.

liquid as required. Any leftover liquid can be stored in the refrigerator and used for another recipe.

Tamarind slices These look a little like dried apple slices. Place them in a small bowl, then pour over enough warm water to cover and leave to soak for about 30 minutes to extract the flavour, squeeze the tamarind slices with your fingers, then strain the juice.

Tamarind concentrate or paste Mix 15ml/1 tbsp with 60–90ml/4–6 tbsp warm water. Stir until dissolved, then use as required.

Storage

Compressed tamarind and tamarind slices will keep perfectly well in a cool dry place. Jars labelled fresh tamarind, or tamarind concentrate or paste must be kept in the refrigerator once opened, and used within one or two months.

CURRY POWDERS AND PASTES

CURRY POWDERS

The word curry evolved from the Tamil word *kari*, meaning any food cooked in a sauce. There is little doubt that curry powder, a ready-made blend of spices, was an early convenience food, prepared for merchants, sailors and military men who had served in the East and wished to bring these exotic flavours home. In India, the spices would have been prepared in the kitchen on a daily basis.

Over the decades and centuries these spice and curry mixtures have changed and developed, as have our tastes, so that today our supermarket shelves carry a wealth of different spice mixtures from all parts of the globe.

For enthusiastic cooks it is fun and a creative challenge to make up your own curry powder. Keep experimenting until you find the balance of spicing which suits you and your family. Of course, it is perfectly possible to mix ground spices, but it is more satisfying (and more satisfactory in terms of flavour) to start with whole spices where possible.

Left: Curry powder

Dry-frying

Many whole spices benefit from being dry-fried before they are ground. This not only makes sure that no surface moisture remains, but also heightens and develops the flavour. Use a heavy pan, shaking it constantly so the spices do not scorch. Purists dry-fry spices separately, but they can be heated together as long as you watch them closely. All spices react differently to heat, so here are some guidelines:

Coriander seeds often provide the dominant flavour, especially in powders from Southern India and Singapore.

Shake the pan to keep the seeds on the move, and remove them from the heat when they give off a mild, sweet, orangey perfume.

Dried Chillies can be roasted in a cool oven, but it is better to sear them in a heavy pan, where you can keep an eye on them. Place the pan over a medium heat for 2–3 minutes, until the chillies soften and puff up. Do not let them burn, or the flavour will be ruined.

Cumin seeds should be dry-fried in a pan, and will be ready for grinding when the seeds have a nutty smell.

Black peppercorns need gentle dry-frying, just to heighten the flavour.

Fenugreek needs to be watched carefully as it will become bitter if it is dry-fried for too long. It is ready when it turns brownish yellow.

Curry leaves can be dry-fried over a cool to medium heat when fresh. Grind or pound them, using a mortar and pestle, to release their characteristic flavour, then mix them with the other spices. This works well if you are making a curry powder or paste that is to be used immediately, but if it is to be kept, make up the powder, then add the whole fresh or frozen leaves just before you are ready to use it. Remove the leaves before serving the curry. Avoid using dried curry leaves if possible, as they will have lost most of their flavour.

Right: Curry spices

Simple curry powder

This Malayan Chinese spice mixture is good for poultry, especially chicken, and robust fish curries.

MAKES ABOUT 60ML/4 TBSP

2 dried red chillies
6 whole cloves
1 small cinnamon stick
5ml/1 tsp coriander seeds
5ml/1 tsp fennel seeds
10ml/2 tsp Sichuan peppercorns
2.5ml/½ tsp grated nutmeg
5ml/1 tsp ground star anise
5ml/1 tsp ground turmeric

COOK'S TIPS

• If you prefer a very hot and punchy spice mixture, then add some or all of the chilli seeds and dry-fry with the other spices.
• Ensure that you wash your hands, and the chopping board and other utensils very thoroughly after preparing chillies.
• If your skin is particularly sensitive, then you should wear rubber gloves while you are preparing the chillies.

1 Remove the seeds from the dried chillies using the point of a knife, and discard any stems.

2 Put the chillies, cloves, cinnamon, coriander, fennel seeds and Sichuan peppercorns in a heavy frying pan. Dry-fry the spices, tossing them frequently until they give off a rich, spicy aroma.

3 Grind the spices to a smooth powder in a mortar, using a pestle. Alternatively, use a spice grinder, or an electric coffee grinder that is reserved for blending spices.

4 Add the grated nutmeg, star anise and turmeric. Use immediately or store in an airtight jar away from strong light.

CURRY PASTES

On market stalls throughout South-east Asia are mounds of pounded wet spices: lemon grass, chilli, ginger, garlic, galangal, shallots and tamarind. After purchasing meat, chicken or fish all the cook has to do is to call on the spice seller. He or she will ask a few questions: "What sort of curry is it to be? Hot or mild? How many servings?" Having ascertained the answers and perhaps exchanged a few more pleasantries (the buying of spices is a serious yet sociable affair) the appropriate quantities of each spice will be scooped on to a banana leaf and folded into a neat cone, ready to be taken home.

We may not be able to buy our ingredients in such colourful surroundings, but supermarkets stock some very good ready-made pastes, or you can make your own. By experimenting, you will find the balance of flavours you like, and can then make up one or more of your favourite mixtures in bulk.

If you grind wet spices a lot, you may wish to invest in a traditional, large oriental mortar with a rough, pitted or ridged bowl, which helps to "hold" the ingredients while they are being pounded with the pestle.

Alternatively, for speed, you can use a food processor or blender instead of a mortar and pestle. Store any surplus curry paste in plastic tubs in the freezer.

Above: Thai curry pastes

Malay spice paste for chicken rendang

This is a fairly pungent spice paste. It can be made milder by leaving out some of the chillies.

MAKES ABOUT 350G/12OZ

6 fresh red chillies, seeded
   and sliced
12 shallots, roughly chopped
4 garlic cloves
2.5cm/1in piece fresh turmeric
   root, peeled and sliced or 5ml/
   1 tsp ground turmeric
10 macadamia nuts
2.5cm/1in cube of shrimp paste,
   prepared
3 lemon grass stalks

1 Place the chillies, shallots, garlic, turmeric, nuts and shrimp paste in a food processor.

2 Trim the root end from the lemon grass and slice the lower 5cm/2in of the stalk into thin slices using a sharp knife.

3 Add the lemon grass to the remaining ingredients in the food processor and process them to a fine paste, scraping down the side of the bowl once or twice during processing.

COOK'S TIP
Use the curry paste immediately or spoon into a glass jar, seal it tightly and store in the refrigerator for up to 3 or 4 days. Alternatively, transfer the paste to a plastic tub and store in the freezer.

Thai mussaman curry paste

This hot and spicy paste is used to make the Thai version of a Muslim curry, which is traditionally made with beef, but can also be made with other meats such as chicken or lamb.

MAKES ABOUT 170G/6OZ

12 large dried red chillies
1 lemon grass stalk
60ml/4 tbsp chopped shallots
5 garlic cloves, roughly chopped
10ml/2 tsp chopped fresh galangal
5ml/1 tsp cumin seeds
15ml/1 tbsp coriander seeds
2 cloves
6 black peppercorns
5ml/1 tsp shrimp paste,
   prepared
5ml/1 tsp salt
5ml/1 tsp granulated sugar
30ml/2 tbsp oil

1 Remove the seeds from the dried chillies and discard. Soak the chillies in hot water for about 15 minutes.

2 Trim the root end from the lemon grass stalk and slice the lower 5cm/2in of the stalk into small pieces.

3 Place the chopped lemon grass in a dry wok and then add the chopped shallots, garlic and galangal and dry-fry for a moment or two.

4 Stir in the cumin seeds, coriander seeds, cloves and peppercorns and dry-fry over a low heat for 5–6 minutes, stirring constantly. Spoon the mixture into a large mortar.

5 Drain the chillies and add them to the mortar. Grind finely, using the pestle, then add the prepared shrimp paste, salt, sugar and oil and pound again until the mixture forms a rough paste. Use as required, then spoon any leftover paste into a jar, seal tightly and store in the refrigerator for up to 4 months.

COOK'S TIPS
• Preparing a double or larger quantity of paste in a food processor makes the blending of the ingredients much easier and the paste will be smoother.
• For the best results, before you start to process the ingredients, slice them up in the following order: galangal, lemon grass, fresh ginger and turmeric, chillies, nuts, shrimp paste, garlic and shallots. Add some of the oil (or coconut cream if that is to be your frying medium) to the ingredients in the food processor if the mixture is a bit sluggish. If you do this, however, remember to use less oil or coconut cream when you fry the curry paste to eliminate the raw taste of the individual ingredients before adding the meat, poultry, fish or vegetables.
• Shrimp paste is made from fermented shrimps. It can be bought in Asian stores. Unless it is to be fried as part of a recipe, it is always lightly cooked before use. If you have a gas cooker, simply mould the shrimp paste on to the end of a metal skewer and rotate over a low to medium gas flame, or heat under the grill (broiler) of an electric cooker, until the outside begins to look crusty, but not burnt.

COOKING FATS AND OILS

CHINESE: *SHI YOU*

Animal fats and vegetable oils are regarded as essential ingredients the world over, but in Asia they play a particularly important role, largely because so much of the food is fried. Animal fat or lard was historically the medium for frying (and remains so in China), but vegetable oils are valued because they can be heated to much higher temperatures without smoking, something which is essential for quick stir-frying, in which a high degree of heat is absolutely essential. Similarly, most deep-fried food also requires a high temperature in order to achieve the desired crispness.

Oil can be extracted from sources as diverse as radishes and poppies. Rape-seed (canola) oil was a popular cooking medium in China until the Portuguese introduced peanuts during the 16th century.

It was not immediately appreciated that the new crop could be a source of oil, but by the 19th century peanut oil was firmly established throughout Asia, a position it continues to hold despite competition from corn oil. In Japan, sesame oil originally held sway, but Japanese cooks soon appreciated that cooking with a mixture of sesame oil and peanut oil gave better results, especially when cooking their beloved tempura (a deep-fried vegetable and seafood dish introduced by Portuguese missionaries), as the mixed oil could be heated to higher temperatures without smoking.

Coconut and palm oil are common in South-east Asia, although both are less popular than they once were, as they are high in saturated fats.

Aroma and flavour

Fats and oils all have their own distinct aroma and flavour; some are quite strong, others fairly mild. Both lamb and beef fat, for instance are more strongly flavoured than lard (pork fat) or chicken fat, while peanut oil and rape seed oil have more taste than soya, cottonseed or sunflower oils.

Culinary uses

In the East, fats and oils are mainly used as a cooking medium, but are sometimes ingredients in their own right. In some Chinese dishes, for instance, pure lard is often stirred in shortly before serving, much as Western cooks would use cream.

Left: Sunflower oil and groundnut oil

Above: Palm oil

Preparation and cooking techniques

Although many Asian recipes depend for their success on fats and oils, it is not considered appropriate for the flavour of the fat to dominate. A technique frequently employed to neutralize the flavour of an oil is to season it. The method is quite simple. While the oil is being heated, small pieces of aromatic ingredients such as fresh ginger, spring onion (scallion) and garlic are added. When these have flavoured the oil, they are then removed before other ingredients are added to the wok or pan. The technique prevents the finished dish from tasting "oily".

Storage

In normal conditions, fats and oils exposed to the air gradually become rancid due to oxidation. Cooking oil should be stored in a cool, dark place. Oil that has been heated several times in a deep-fryer may acquire an unpleasant flavour. Chinese cooks heat the oil with some fresh ginger after every use to neutralize any off flavours. You may find that you have to discard the oil after using it three or four times.

FLAVOURING OILS

CHINESE: *TIAOWEI YOU*

Several types of flavouring oil are used in Asian cooking for dips and dressings, the most common one being sesame oil, but chilli oil is also popular.

SESAME OIL

MANDARIN: *ZHIMA YOU;* CANTONESE: *MA YOU;* JAPANESE: *GAMA-ABURA*

The type of sesame oil used for flavouring is quite different from the sesame oil used for cooking in India and the Middle East. In both China and Japan, the preferred oil for flavouring is a rich flavoured oil made from processed sesame seeds, which have been roasted or toasted to bring out their flavour.

Right: Toasted sesame oil

Aroma and flavour

Sesame oil from roasted seeds has a wonderfully nutty aroma and taste. It is much stronger than either walnut oil or olive oil. Blended sesame oil has a milder flavour and is much paler in colour.

Culinary uses

Because processed sesame oil smokes easily when heated, it is not really suitable for frying. It is used for salads and dipping sauces, and is added to soups or stir-fries.

Cooking techniques

Heating helps to intensify the aroma of sesame oil, but it should never be heated for too long. It is usual to add a few drops to a soup or stir-fry shortly before serving.

Storage

Always store bottled sesame oil in a cool, dark place, because it will lose its strong aroma if exposed to heat and strong light. It becomes rancid much sooner than ordinary cooking oils, so buy in small quantities.

CHILLI OIL

CHINESE: *LA YOU;* JAPANESE: *YU*

Chilli oil is made by infusing chopped dried red chillies, red chopped onions, garlic and salt in hot vegetable oil for several hours. There is also an "XO chilli oil", which is flavoured with dried

Blended sesame oil (above) and chilli oil

scallops, and is much more expensive. Chilli oil is easy to make at home; simply put about 20 seeded and chopped dried chillies in a heatproof container. Heat 250ml/8fl oz/1 cup groundnut (peanut) or corn oil until it just reaches smoking point, then leave to cool for 5 minutes. Carefully pour the oil into the heatproof container and leave to stand for at least an hour or two. Strain the oil, then use as required.

Aroma and flavour

Chilli oil has a pleasant aroma with a fiery taste that is much stronger than the flavour of either chilli bean paste or chilli sauce.

Culinary uses

Chilli oil is always used as a dipping sauce, never for cooking. In some South-east Asian countries, it is used as a dressing, and it is drizzled on top of the Burmese fish soup, Mohinga. In Thai cooking, it is added to stir-fried prawns (shrimp) just before serving.

Storage

Store bottles of chilli oil in a cool and dark place; the oil will keep for many months in the refrigerator.

VINEGARS

RICE VINEGAR

MANDARIN: *MICU*; CANTONESE: *HUCK TSO*;
JAPANESE: *SU*

Vinegar fermented from rice, or distilled
from rice grains is used extensively in
Asian cooking. The former is dark
amber in colour and is referred to in
China as red or black vinegar; the latter
is clear, so is called white vinegar. The
raw ingredients used for
making rice vinegar
consist of glutinous
rice, long grain
rice, wheat,
barley, and
rice husks. It
is fermented
twice and is
matured for up to
6–7 months. Japan
has a brown rice vinegar
– *gaen mae su* – which is
dark and heady. This vinegar, which has
been likened to balsamic vinegar, is
robust yet wonderfully smooth.

*Above: Rice
vinegar*

Aroma and flavour

Red or black vinegar has a pleasant
fragrant aroma with a mild, sweetish
flavour. The distilled white vinegar is
much stronger. It smells vinegary and
tastes quite tangy and tart. Japanese
brown rice vinegar has a distinctive
sweet and sour flavour.

Using sushi vinegar

The rice that is used to make
sushi is moistened and flavoured
with a mixture of hot rice vinegar,
sugar and salt. The technique is
simple, but it is important to use
Japanese rice and good quality
vinegar. The cooked rice is spread
out in a shallow dish and the hot
vinegar mixture is added. The rice
is turned with a spatula until the
grains are coated, and the mixture
is simultaneously fanned so that
it cools quickly and develops an
attractive sheen. The rice is then
covered until it cools completely
before being moulded.

Culinary uses

There's an old Chinese
saying which goes something like
this: "On rising in the morning, first
check that you have the seven daily
necessities for the kitchen: fuel, rice,
oil, salt, soy sauce, vinegar and tea."
Vinegar has always played a vital role in
Chinese cooking, and in some parts of
the country, particularly in the north, it
is added to almost every dish as a
matter of course, although the amounts
are sometimes so minute as to be
barely detectable. Rice vinegar is an
important ingredient in the world-
renowned sweet and sour sauce, which
originated in northern China, and also
in the popular hot and sour sauce
from Sichuan.

Throughout Asia, rice vinegar also
features in Thai cucumber sauce and
dipping sauces, such as the
Vietnamese vinegar and garlic fish
sauce. It is also widely used in
preserving and pickling.

Thai cooks add rice vinegar
to several dishes, including their
famous hot and sour soup. In
Japan, rice vinegar is famously
used for sushi rice.

Cooking techniques

If rice vinegar is heated for too
long, its fragrance will be lost, the
food will taste extremely tart and
rather unpleasant. In Asian
cooking, therefore, vinegar is
generally the last item to be
stirred into a dish. It is
also important not to use
too much vinegar; in a
good sweet and sour
sauce the key ingredients
should be in perfect
balance, the sour having a
slight edge on the sweet.

Storage

Bottled rice vinegar will keep for a very
long time, provided it is not exposed to
either heat or strong light.

OTHER VINEGARS

Coconut vinegar Made from coconut
nectar or "toddy" tapped from the
flower sheaths of
mature coconut
palms, this amber
vinegar is highly
regarded in the
Philippines.
Pon vinegar This
Japanese vinegar is
made from the juice
of citrus fruit that
resemble limes.

*Coconut vinegar
(right) and pon
vinegar*

SAUCES AND PASTES

SOY SAUCE

MANDARIN: *JIANG YOU*; CANTONESE: *CHI YOU*; JAPANESE: *SHOYU*; INDONESIAN: *KECAP*; *KETJAP*; MALAY: *KICHUP*; *TAUYU*; THAI: *SIEW*

Soy sauce is made from fermented soya beans, and is one of Asia's most important contributions to the global pantry. It is used all over the world, not merely as a condiment in place of salt, but as an ingredient in a host of home-made and manufactured foods.

Making soy sauce involves quite a lengthy process. The soya beans are initially cleaned, soaked until soft and then steamed before being mixed with a yeast culture and wheat flour. The mixture is then fermented for up to two years before being filtered and bottled. There is no short cut to making soy sauce of high quality, and while some modern products may cost less than others, they have inferior flavour and should be avoided.

Aroma and flavour

There are basically three types of Chinese soy sauce on the market. **Light soy sauce** is the initial extraction, like the first pressing of virgin olive oil. It has the most delicate flavour and is light brown in colour with a lovely "beany" fragrance. **Dark soy sauce** is left to mature further, and has caramel added to it, so it is slightly sweeter and has a much darker colour with a powerful aroma. Then there is the regular soy sauce, which is a blend of the two.

There are several different types of Japanese soy sauce too: **Usukuchi soy sauce** is light in colour and tastes less salty than the Chinese light soy. **Tamari** is dark and thick with a strong flavour, and is even less salty than the light type. **Shoyu** is a full-flavoured sauce

Above: Dark (top) and light soy sauces

that is aged for up to 2 years. In between, there is the very popular **Kikkoman**, which is a brand name for the equivalent of the Chinese regular soy sauce – not too weak, nor too strong. It is ideal as a dipping sauce to be used at the table, rather than for cooking.

The Indonesian **kecap manis** is thick and black, with a powerful aroma, but a surprisingly sweet taste. The light variety, **kecap asin,** is quite thin and weak, and is sometimes described as "white soy". Indonesian cooks also use the medium-bodied **kecap sedang,** but this is less popular than kecap manis.

Above: There is a range of Japanese soy sauces, from dark and thick to lighter, less rich types.

small amount of soy sauce. When soy sauce is used in a dressing for a salad or similar cold dish, the dressing should be added only just before the dish is served.

Storage

Naturally fermented soy sauce will not keep for ever; it starts to lose its aroma and flavour as soon as it is exposed to the air for any length of time. Sealed bottles can be stored for a year or two, but once the bottle has been opened, soy sauce will deteriorate fairly rapidly. Try to use it up as fast as you can, certainly before the expiry date on the label. Check the label, too, for advice on storage. Some bottles do not contain preservatives and must be kept in the refrigerator once opened.

Above: Kecap manis (top) and kecap asin are Indonesian soy sauces

Right: Tamari sauce

Culinary uses

As a rule, light soy sauce is used for seafood, white meats, vegetables and soups, while the darker sauce is ideal for red meats, stews, barbecues and gravy. If you are serving soy sauce as a dip, choose the regular variety, or use a blend of three parts light sauce with two parts dark. This proportion also applies to marinades.

Cooking techniques

When soy sauce is used for cooking, it should be stirred in towards the end of the cooking time to avoid dulling the colour of the food, and so that the natural flavour of the principal ingredient is not overwhelmed. This point applies to soups, stews, stir-fries and quick-braised dishes, but not to slow-braised dishes, where the ingredients are simmered for a long time in a sauce that includes only a

Chicken Yakitori

Several classic marinades and sauces have soy sauce as the main ingredient. This Japanese dish uses soy sauce, which is combined with sake and sugar, and thickened with flour, as a marinade for chicken kebabs. If you like, you can make twice the quantity of sauce and reserve half to serve with the cooked kebabs.

SERVES 4

6 boneless chicken thighs, cut into chunks
bunch of spring onions (scallions), cut into short batons
Japanese seven spice powder, to serve

For the yakitori sauce
150ml/¼ pint/⅔ cup soy sauce
90g/3½oz/½ cup caster (superfine) sugar
25ml/5 tsp sake
15ml/1 tbsp plain (all-purpose) flour

1 To make the sauce, place the soy sauce, sugar, sake and flour in a small pan and stir well. Bring to the boil, stirring all the time, then reduce the heat and simmer for 10 minutes, until the sauce in reduced by a third. Set aside.

2 Thread the chicken and spring onion pieces alternately on to 12 bamboo skewers. Grill (broil) for 5–10 minutes until the chicken is cooked through, brushing generously with the sauce once or twice during cooking.

3 Sprinkle the kebabs with Japanese seven spice powder and serve with a little extra yakitori sauce.

FISH SAUCE

Chinese: *yu lu*; Thai: *nam pla*;
Vietnamese: *nuoc mam*

Fish sauce is an essential seasoning
for Thai and Vietnamese cooking, in
much the same way that soy sauce
is important to the Chinese and the
Japanese. In Vietnam it is often made
using shrimps, but in Thailand, the
sauce is more often made using salted,
fermented fish.

Aroma and flavour

All types of fish sauce have a pungent
flavour and aroma and are very salty.
Thai *nam pla* has a slightly stronger
flavour and aroma than the Vietnamese
or Chinese versions. The colour of fish
sauce can vary considerably; lighter-
coloured sauces are considered to be
better than darker versions.

Culinary uses

Fish sauce is used extensively
throughout Asia as a seasoning in all
kinds of savoury dishes. It is also used
to make a dipping sauce, when it is
blended with extra flavourings such as
finely chopped garlic and chillies, and
sugar and lime juice.

Right: Fish
sauce

Storage

Fish sauce
generally
comes in
either glass or
plastic bottles. Once opened it should
be kept in a cool, dark place where it
will keep for up to a year.

OYSTER SAUCE

Mandarin: *haoyou*; Cantonese: *ho yow*

Oyster sauce is a Cantonese speciality.
This thick, brown, soy-based sauce is
flavoured with oyster juice, salt and
caramel, and is thickened with cornflour
(cornstarch). It is thicker
than soy sauce and
fish sauce, but
lighter in
colour.

Aroma and flavour

Oyster sauce has a pleasant, fragrant
aroma, and has a delicious and delicate
flavour that, surprisingly, doesn't taste
of fish at all.

Culinary uses

Oyster sauce is a highly versatile
flavouring and can be used in a wide
variety of dishes. It is especially good
with fairly bland foods, such as chicken
and beancurd, but also works very well
with more strongly flavoured ingredients
such as beef and seafood. It can be
used as a garnish and is often sprinkled
over the top of cooked dishes such as
rice and noodles.

Cooking techniques

The bottled sauce is only used as a
cooking ingredient, and it is never
served as a dip or sauce at the table.
Oyster sauce is best added to dishes
towards the end of the cooking time.

Storage

There are a number of different brands
of this sauce, and the more expensive
versions are usually far superior, and
have a much richer flavour than
cheaper versions. Once opened,
the bottle should be stored in the
refrigerator where the sauce will keep
for a very long time, although it is best
used before the expiry date.

*Above: Oyster
sauce*

*Above:
Dark hoisin
sauce*

*Above:
Light
hoisin sauce*

HOISIN SAUCE

MANDARIN: *HAIXIAN JIANG;* CANTONESE: *HOY SIN JIONG;* VIETNAMESE: *TUONG-DEN*

Another Cantonese speciality, hoisin is also known as barbecue sauce. Its Chinese name literally means "sea-flavour", which is a reflection on just how delicious it is, rather than an indication of its ingredients. Hoisin sauce does not contain so much as a trace of seafood, unlike oyster sauce and fish sauce.

Aroma and flavour

The main components of this very popular sauce are fermented beans, sugar, vinegar, salt, chilli, garlic and sesame oil, but there is no standard formula, so the aroma and flavour of different brands can vary considerably. A good quality product should have a fragrant aroma with a rich, warm, sweet yet salty flavour.

Culinary uses

Hoisin sauce is quite versatile and makes a valuable contribution to the kitchen. Mainly intended as a marinade, it can be used at the table as a dipping sauce, but should not accompany Peking duck as is the practice in some restaurants.

Cooking techniques

When used as a marinade, hoisin can be spooned straight from the jar over spare ribs, chicken or similar foods.

Storage

Hoisin sauce usually comes in glass jars or cans. Once opened, jars should be stored in the refrigerator, where the sauce will keep for several months. Canned hoisin should be decanted into non-metallic containers before being stored in the refrigerator.

CHILLI SAUCE

MANDARIN: *LAJIAO JIANG;* CANTONESE: *LA JYEW JYEUNG;* THAI: *SOD PRIK*

The best known Asian chilli sauce comes from China, although the Vietnamese have a very hot version and there is also a thick, spicy chilli sauce made in Thailand.

Aroma and flavour

This Chinese bottled chilli sauce is quite hot and spicy, with a touch of fruitiness, as it is made from fresh red chillies, salt, vinegar and apples or plums. The Thai version includes both hot and sweet chillies, and adds ginger, spices and vinegar. There is also a thick Chinese sauce which is made exclusively from chillies and salt. This is usually sold in jars and is much hotter than the bottled sauce.

Culinary uses

The bottled sauce is used both for cooking and as a dip, but the thicker sauce is mainly used for cooking as an alternative to chilli bean paste.

Cooking techniques

Use chilli sauce sparingly. It can be quite fiery.

Storage

Once a jar or bottle of chilli sauce has been opened store it in the refrigerator, where it will keep almost indefinitely. Use before the expiry date.

Below: Sweet chilli sauce (top) and chilli sauce

PLUM SAUCE

MANDARIN: *MEIZI JIANG;* CANTONESE: *SHWIN MEI JIONG;* VIETNAMESE: *CUONG NGOT*

Made from plum juice with sugar, salt, vinegar and a thickening agent, plum sauce is a sort of sweet-and-sour sauce. It is generally associated with Chinese food. Thai cooks are partial to plum sauce, but they tend to make their own, using preserved plums and sugar.

Aroma and flavour

There seems to be no standard recipe for the commercially made plum sauce. The various brands all seem to use slightly different seasonings and some even add garlic, ginger or chilli to give it extra tang. Taste before use, as some brands can be quite fiery.

Culinary uses

One of the common uses for plum sauce in the West is to serve it with Peking duck. It is also used as a dip for spring rolls and other dim sum.

Storage

Plum sauce is usually sold in glass jars. One opened, the jar should be kept in the refrigerator.

LEMON SAUCE

MANDARIN: *NINGMENG JIANG;* CANTONESE: *NING MUNG JIONG*

Lemon sauce is one of those condiments that was especially created for the Western market. It probably originated in Hong Kong, like black bean sauce. Thick, smooth and velvety, it has an immediate appeal for the Western palate.

Aroma and flavour

The sauce has a rather piquant citrus aroma with a spicy and tangy sweet flavour. It is another sauce from the sweet-and-sour stable, but with the difference that it is made from fresh lemon juice and rind. Salt and sugar are added, and starch is used for thickening. Most brands have artificial colouring added to give the sauce a bright colour.

Above, from top: oyster, plum and hoisin sauces

Culinary uses

The use of lemon sauce in cooking seems to be limited to a single dish, lemon chicken, which is on the menu of most Cantonese restaurants. Other than that, it can be served with deep-fried food, particularly seafood.

Storage

Once opened, the bottle or jar should be stored in the refrigerator. The fresh flavour of the sauce may be dulled if it is kept for too long, so use it before the expiry date.

Above: Lemon sauce

BLACK BEAN SAUCE

MANDARIN: *CHIZI JIANG;* CANTONESE: *SI JIR JIONG*

A mixture of puréed salted black beans with soy sauce, sugar and spice, this popular sauce is especially manufactured for the convenience of Western cooks, since people in China and South-east Asia generally use only whole fermented beans, and make their own sauce by crushing the beans in the wok while cooking.

Aroma and flavour

Fermented black beans have a powerful "fragrance" and a strong flavour that does not always appeal to the untutored Western palate, but once introduced to its rather earthy taste, many people grow to like it immensely.

Culinary uses

Black bean sauce should not be used cold straight from the jar or bottle, but should always be heated first. It is usually blended with other strongly flavoured seasonings such as spring onions, garlic, ginger and chillies before being added to stews, stir-fries, and braised or steamed dishes. Ready-made black bean sauces seasoned either with garlic or chillies are available too. These should also be heated before being used, to bring out the aroma and flavour.

Storage

Once opened, store the jar in the refrigerator. Black bean sauce keeps very well.

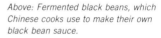

Above: Black bean sauce

YELLOW BEAN SAUCE

MANDARIN: *HUANG JIANG:* CANTONESE: *MO SHIH JIONG;* THAI: *TAO JIEW KAOW*

Also known as brown bean sauce or ground bean sauce, this Chinese favourite consists of crushed fermented soya beans which have been mixed with salt, wheat flour and sugar to make a paste which is not only useful on its own, but is also the basis of numerous more elaborate sauces. hoisin sauce, chu hou sauce, Guilin chilli sauce, Sichuan hot sauce and Peking duck sauce all owe their ancestry to yellow bean sauce.

Aroma and flavour

Regular yellow bean sauce has a wonderfully "beany" aroma with a delectable flavour. It is not as salty as black bean sauce, and cooks in every region of China add

Left: Fermented yellow beans and yellow bean sauce

Above: Fermented black beans, which Chinese cooks use to make their own black bean sauce.

their own spices and seasonings to make individual blends.

Culinary uses

Yellow bean sauce is very versatile in the kitchen. It adds an extra dimension to meat, poultry, fish and even some vegetable dishes, whether in stir-fries, braised dishes or roasts. It is also the ideal basis for a marinade, usually with additional ingredients such as garlic, spring onions (scallions) and rice wine.

Storage

Once a can or jar of yellow bean sauce has been opened, the contents should be transferred to a lidded plastic tub and stored in the refrigerator. Like black bean sauce, it keeps very well.

CHILLI BEAN PASTE

MANDARIN: *DOUBAN JIANG;* CANTONESE: *TOBAN DJAN*

This is a Sichuan speciality. What makes it unique is the fact that the beans used are not soya beans, but a type of broad (fava) bean, hence the name *douban* or *toban* in Chinese. Outside China the sauce is sold under various names, including chilli bean sauce, hot bean sauce or just plain Sichuan sauce.

Aroma and flavour

There are several chilli bean pastes on the market, ranging from mild to hot, but all have a lovely "beany" aroma with a rich flavour. The genuine Pixian paste made in Sichuan is seldom seen in the West, which is a pity, for it is superior in quality to the majority of brands made in Hong Kong, Taiwan or Singapore.

Above: Chilli bean paste

Right: Red bean paste

Miso

This is the collective name for several types of soya bean paste, made from steamed soya beans fermented with various natural yeasts. Some of these starter moulds are based upon rice, others on wheat or barley, and yet more on soya beans themselves. The pastes come in different colours, textures and flavours, depending on the yeast used and the length of the fermentation process. Red or *mugi* miso (*below centre*), the most popular paste, is more strongly flavoured than the sweeter white *kome* miso (*below left*). A third type, *hacho* miso (*below right*), is dark with a strong flavour. Miso is the key ingredient in a soup served at almost every Japanese meal. When mixed with mayonnaise it makes the increasingly popular miso-mayo.

Culinary uses

Chilli bean paste and chilli sauce are not interchangeable; each has its own distinct flavour and consistency. Chilli bean paste is slightly thicker than chilli sauce and is an indispensable seasoning in Sichuan cooking. It is used to add flavour to stir-fries and braised dishes.

Cooking techniques

Chilli bean paste must be thoroughly heated before being used and should never be served cold at the table as a dipping sauce.

Storage

Once opened, the jar should be stored in the refrigerator. Chilli bean paste keeps well, but should be used before the expiry date on the jar.

RED BEAN PASTE

MANDARIN: *DOUSHA;* CANTONESE: *DOW SA*

Made from either red kidney beans or aduki beans, this is a thick, smooth paste, which is sweetened with rock sugar. The paste comes in small cans and is only available from Asian stores.

Aroma and flavour

The paste has a pleasant, mild fragrance with a subtle flavour. Although it is sweetened, the sauce is never cloying, and Asian cooks often add extra sugar to intensify the flavour. Occasionally, other flavourings such as essence of sesame seeds or ground cassia are blended in.

Culinary uses

Red bean paste is mainly used in sweet dishes and is a popular filling for cakes and steamed buns. It is also spread on pancakes, which are then deep-fried.

Storage

Once the can has been opened, the contents should be transferred to a sealed plastic tub and stored in the refrigerator, where the paste will keep for several months. Make a note of the use-by date on the can.

Left: Shrimp paste

SHRIMP PASTE

MALAY: *BLACHAN; BALACHAN;* INDONESIAN: *TERASI; TRASSI;* THAI: *KAPI;* BURMESE: *NGAPI*

Whether you call it *blachan, terasi, kapi* or *ngapi*, shrimp paste is an essential ingredient in scores of savoury dishes throughout South-east Asia. It is made from tiny shrimps which have been salted, dried, pounded and then left to ferment in the hot humid conditions until the aroma is very pungent. The colour of the paste can be anything from oyster pink to purplish brown, depending upon the type of shrimp and the precise process used. It is compressed and sold in block form or packed in tiny tubs or jars.

Aroma and flavour

There's no disguising the origin of this paste. The moment you unwrap it or lift the lid, the smell of rotten fish is quite overwhelming. Do not let this put you off, however. The odour vanishes when the paste is cooked, and this is one of those ingredients that really does make a difference to the food, contributing depth, pungency and a recognizable South-east Asian signature.

Culinary uses

Shrimp paste is good source of protein and vitamin C. It is used to flavour rice dishes, is stirred into satay sauces and gives depth to salad dressings, dipping sauces, curries and braised dishes. It is the key ingredient in the famous *nam prik*, a dipping sauce whose other ingredients include garlic, chillies and fish sauce, and which appears as a condiment at almost every Thai meal. Burmese cooks use it to intensify the flavour of *balachaung*, a spicy dried shrimp mixture forked into rice.

Preparation

Before using shrimp paste in a sambal, dressing or salad, it is necessary to heat it to temper the raw flavour (see right).

Storage

If you buy the paste in block form, store it in a screwtop jar in a cool place. It will keep for several months. Jars of paste should be kept in the refrigerator.

Sesame paste

The sesame paste used in oriental cooking is not the same as tahini, the ingredient that frequently crops up in recipes from the Middle East. Whereas tahini is made from raw sesame seeds, sesame paste is derived from seeds which have been dry-fried or roasted to bring out the rich nutty flavour. Therefore, if an Asian recipe calls for sesame paste, don't be tempted to try tahini. Instead, use peanut butter with a little sesame oil stirred in to approximate the correct flavour.

Preparing shrimp paste

Shrimp paste can be used straight from the packet if it is to be fried with other ingredients, but it needs to be heated to temper its raw taste before using in sambals, dressings and salads.

1 Cut off a small piece of shrimp paste and shape it into a 1cm/½in cube. Mould the paste on to the end of a metal skewer.

2 Hold the end of the skewer in an oven glove and rotate over a low to medium gas flame, or under an electric grill (broiler) until the paste begins to look dry, but not burnt. This method works well, but gives off a strong smell.

3 Alternatively, to avoid the strong smell, wrap the cube of paste in a piece of foil and dry-fry in a frying pan for about 5 minutes, turning it occasionally.

SAMBALS

In the West, sambals have come to mean the side dishes served with a curry, but this is several steps away from the original South-east Asian term, which was, and still is, applied to a number of hot, spicy relishes, sauces and similar accompaniments that are based on chillies. Sambals are particularly popular in Indonesia, and feature strongly in the famous *Rijstafel,* a veritable feast which includes dozens of different dishes, and which was developed in the days when Indonesia was still the Dutch East Indies. Thanks to the connection, *Rijstafel* is also well known and loved in the Netherlands, and bottled sambals are widely available in that country.

In Indonesia, a sambal can also be a main dish. *Sambal goreng,* for instance is a spicy chilli sauce, which may include a variety of foods such as tiny meat balls, cubes of fish, wedges of hard-boiled eggs or vegetables.

Culinary uses

In Malaysia, Singapore and Indonesia *sambal blachan* (chilli and shrimp paste sambal) is a favourite. Fresh red chillies are roughly chopped, then pounded with a little salt and prepared shrimp paste *(blachan).* A little lime or lemon juice is added to the mixture to loosen it slightly. *Sambal blachan* is extremely hot – especially when the seeds have been left in the chillies – so deserves to be served with a health warning! *Sambal oelek* is similar, but a little brown sugar is added to the chopped chillies to bring out the flavours. Sometimes labelled "chopped chilli", this product is now sold in jars in many supermarkets. One teaspoonful (5ml) is equivalent to 1 small chilli. After use, the jar should be closed tightly and kept in the refrigerator.

At a typical Thai meal there may be one or two sambals in addition to the much loved *nam prik,* a combination of dried prawns (shrimp), shrimp paste, garlic, chillies, fish sauce, lemon juice and brown sugar. *Nam prik* complements raw, steamed, fried or boiled vegetables and is often simply stirred into a bowl of plain boiled or steamed Thai rice. Another popular sambal is made from fish sauce, lemon juice, shallots and chillies; a blend that enhances all kinds of fish and seafood dishes.

Sambal oelek

This chilli sambal will keep for about 6 weeks in a sealed jar in the refrigerator, so it is worth making up a reasonable quantity at a time if you frequently cook Indonesian-style dishes. Use a stainless steel or plastic spoon to measure out the sauce as required. This sauce is fiercely hot, and it will irritate the skin, so should you get any on your fingers, immediately wash them well in soapy water.

MAKES ABOUT 350G/12 OZ

450g/1lb fresh red chillies
10ml/2 tsp salt

1 Cut the chillies in half, scrape out the seeds using the point of a sharp knife and discard with the stalks. Plunge the chillies into a pan of boiling water and cook them for 5–8 minutes.

2 Drain the chillies, then place them in the bowl of a food processor or blender and process until finely chopped. The paste should be fairly coarse, so stop processing before it gets too smooth.

3 Spoon the paste into a glass jar, stir in the salt and cover with a piece of greaseproof (waxed) paper or clear film (plastic wrap) before screwing on the lid.

4 Store in the refrigerator. Serve as an accompaniment, or use the sambal as suggested in recipes.

Left: Sambal oelek (left), sambal blachan (front) and nam prik *sauce are very hot chilli sauces.*

Below: Nuoc cham

In Vietnam the salt and pepper of the Western table is replaced by *nuoc cham*. This is a piquant sambal made from, chillies, garlic, sugar, lime juice or rice vinegar, and fish sauce and is the classic combination of hot, sweet, sour and salt flavours that is so typical of Vietnamese cooking.

Sambals and sauces are usually served in small bowls or saucers. At a family meal pieces of cooked meat, fish or vegetables may be dipped into a communal bowl or a tiny spoonful of the sambal may be put on each diner's plate, but on special occasions small individual dishes are used. These little dishes are sold in many Asian stores and supermarkets.

Preparation

For the freshest flavours mix the sambal ingredients just before serving. Use a food processor or blender to blend the wet ingredients and a pestle and mortar to grind the dry ingredients.

Storage

Store any leftovers in a glass jar in the refrigerator. Before putting on the lid, cover the jar with greaseproof (waxed) paper or clear film (plastic wrap) to protect the lid from corrosion.

Nuoc cham

This spicy Vietnamese sambal makes a delicious, if fiery, dipping sauce and is good served with crisp, fried spring rolls.

MAKES ABOUT 105ML/7 TBSP

2 fresh red chillies, seeded
2 garlic cloves, crushed
15ml/1 tbsp sugar
45ml/3 tbsp fish sauce
juice of 1 lime or ½ lemon

1 Place the chillies in a large mortar and pound to a paste using a pestle.

2 Transfer the chillies to a bowl and add the garlic, sugar and fish sauce. Stir in lime or lemon juice to taste.

COOK'S TIP

Be careful, when handling either fresh or dried chillies; they contain capsaicin, an oily substance which can cause intense irritation to sensitive skin, so wash your hands thoroughly after handling them, or wear rubber gloves. And do not touch or rub your eyes.

Sambal kecap

This Indonesian sauce or sambal can be served as a dip for satays instead of the usual peanut sauce, particularly with beef and chicken, and it is also very good with pieces of deep-fried chicken.

MAKES ABOUT 150ML/¼ PINT/⅔ CUP

1 fresh red chilli, seeded and
  finely chopped
2 garlic cloves, crushed
60ml/4 tbsp dark soy sauce
20ml/4 tsp lemon juice or 15ml/
  1 tbsp tamarind juice
30ml/2 tbsp hot water
30ml/2 tbsp deep-fried onion
  slices (optional)

1 Place the chopped chilli, crushed garlic, soy sauce, and lemon juice or tamarind juice in a small bowl with the hot water and mix together well.

2 Stir in the deep-fried onion slices, if using, and leave the sambal to stand at room temperature for about 30 minutes before serving.

Sambal blachan

Serve this hot and pungent sambal as an accompaniment to rice meals.

MAKES ABOUT 30ML/2 TBSP

2–4 fresh red chillies, seeded
salt
1cm/½in cube of shrimp paste
juice of ½ lemon or lime

1 Place the chillies in a mortar, add a little salt and pound them to a paste using a pestle.

2 Cut off a small piece of shrimp paste (blachan) and shape it into a 1cm/½in cube. Mould the paste on to the end of a metal skewer.

3 Holding the end of the skewer in a cloth or oven glove, rotate the paste over a low gas flame, or under an electric grill (broiler) until the outside begins to look dry, but not burnt.

4 Add the shrimp paste to the chillies and pound to mix well. Add lemon or lime juice to taste.

PRESERVED AND PICKLED VEGETABLES

Preserved and pickled food plays an important part in the Asian diet. In the days before refrigeration and rapid transportation, fresh food had to be preserved for the lean months, and so that it could be conveyed to regions that were often a long way from the source of supply.

Preserved and pickled vegetables and, to a lesser extent, fruit are used all over Asia. Some of the more famous examples include *chow chow,* the Chinese sweet mixed pickles that are now an American favourite, and *kimchee,* the tart, garlicky pickle that is served at almost every Korean meal. In Japan, pickled vegetables are hugely popular, as are pickled plums, while Indonesian cooks relish *atjar kuning,* a yellow mixed pickle which is mildly hot.

There are several ways of preserving and pickling food. The most common way is to use salt as a preservative, then dry the food in the sun or by another source of heat. Another age-old method is to partially dry the food, then pickle it in brine or a soy-based solution.

Below: Pickled mustard greens

Below: A selection of Chinese pickles

SICHUAN PRESERVED VEGETABLE

MANDARIN: *ZHACAI;* CANTONESE: *JA CHOI*

This pickle, made from the stems of mustard cabbage, originated in Sichuan province, but is now made in other parts of China. The stems are dried in the sun, then pickled in brine. After being trimmed and cleaned, they are pressed to extract excess liquid (the Mandarin name *zhacai* means "pressed vegetable"), before being blended with chillies and spices, and stored in sealed urns to mature.

Aroma and flavour

Sichuan preserved vegetable has a pungent aroma that may not appeal to the uninitiated. It has a smooth and crunchy texture and tastes quite salty and peppery.

Culinary uses

Unlike most other types of preserved and pickled vegetables, Sichuan preserved vegetable is a very versatile ingredient. It is not merely served raw as a relish, but is also cooked with other foods in stir-fries, soups and steamed dishes.

Preparation and cooking techniques

Because of its strong hot and salty flavour, Sichuan preserved vegetable is often rinsed in water to remove some of the excess salt and chillies before it is finely sliced or shredded for use.

Storage

Sichuan preserved vegetable is normally sold in cans, although you may be able to buy the pickle loose in some Asian stores. Any unused pickle should be transferred to an airtight container and stored in the refrigerator, where it will keep almost indefinitely.

CHINESE PICKLES

There is a wide range of Chinese pickles available in the West. Some appear in packets, some in jars, and some in cans. A pickle may consist of a single ingredient such as ginger, garlic, spring onion bulbs, chillies, cabbage, cucumber, gourd, runner beans, bamboo shoots, carrots or daikon (Chinese radish or mooli) or a mixture. Individual items are generally pickled in a dark soy solution, while mixed vegetables tend to be pickled in clear brine to which sugar, Sichuan

Below: Cucumbers are a popular pickled vegetable in many Asian countries. These are from Korea.

peppercorns, distilled spirit and fresh ginger have been added, with chillies and vinegar as optional ingredients. The cleaned vegetables are pickled in the solution in a sealed earthenware urn. This is left in a cool, dark place for at least a week in summer, or up to a month in winter. The longer the pickling process, the better the taste.

JAPANESE PICKLES

JAPANESE: *TSUKEMONO*

There are many varieties of the Japanese pickles known as *tsukemono*. The vegetables that are used are more or less the same as those used in China, but the method of pickling is somewhat different. To start with, instead of earthenware urns, only

wooden barrels are used in Japan and, instead of being pickled in a brine solution, the vegetables are layered with salt. When the barrel is full, a lid is put on top, and this is weighted down with a large stone or similar weight. The combined effect of the salt and the compression forces the liquid out of the vegetables and they are pickled in their own juices.

Other methods include pickling in sake, miso or rice bran, and the most popular vegetable used are mooli (daikon), bok choy, cucumber, aubergine (eggplant), horseradish and the bulbs of spring onions (scallions). Thinly sliced pink pickled ginger (gari) is traditionally served with sushi and sashimi.

Japanese pickles form an essential part of a meal. They are served as a relish to accompany the cooked food, as well as a dessert or a means of cleansing the palate at the end. They are either served singly or in groups of two or three, always beautifully arranged in small individual dishes.

Umeboshi These small pickled plums (below) are a particular Japanese delicacy. The plums are picked before they are ripe and are pickled in salt, with red shiso leaves to give them their distinctive colour. They have a sharp and salty taste and are often chopped and used as a filling for rice balls.

Pickled bamboo shoots A delicacy in Vietnam, this consists of sliced bamboo shoots in spiced vinegar. The shoots are quite sour and should be soaked in water to remove some of the bitterness. They are mainly used in soups and stocks, and are often served with duck.

Pickled garlic This is a favourite in Thailand. The small bulbs are pickled whole in a sweet and sour brine (below).

Pickled limes Whole limes preserved in brine or a mixture of soy sauce, sugar, salt and vinegar are another Thai speciality.

Below: Chow chow – Chinese sweet mixed pickles

COCONUT MILK AND CREAM

Coconut milk is an essential ingredient in South-east Asian cooking. There is an old saying that "he who plants a coconut palm, plants food and drink, vessels and clothing, a habitation for himself and a heritage for his children". Once mature, the palms will go on producing coconuts for 75–100 years, which helps to explain why they are so highly prized.

The coconut was called the nut of India until the Portuguese, struck by its appearance, changed its name to "coco", meaning clown or monkey. Fresh coconuts are available at certain times of the year in Asian stores and supermarkets. The liquid you can hear sloshing about inside the nut when it is shaken is coconut juice, not coconut milk. As any traveller who has tasted it will attest, the juice makes a refreshing drink, especially when tapped from a fresh green coconut. It can also be made into palm wine, which can be pretty potent.

An average size coconut weighs about 675g/1½lb. If it is fresh, it will be full of liquid, so test by shaking well before buying. To open a coconut, hold

Below: A fresh coconut will break neatly into two pieces if you hit it in just the right place.

Below: Coconut milk

it in the palm of your left hand, with the "eyes" just above your thumb. The fault line runs between the eyes. Hold the coconut over a bowl to catch the juice, then carefully strike the line with the unsharpened side of a cleaver or a hammer. If you have done this correctly, the coconut will break neatly into two pieces. Taste a little of the white flesh to make sure that the coconut is fresh, as on rare occasions the flesh may have become rancid. Slip a palette knife between the outer husk and the flesh and prize out the pieces of fresh

coconut. The thin brown skin on these pieces can be removed with a potato peeler, if you like.

Coconut milk and cream are both made from the grated flesh of the coconut, and in the East, it is possible to buy bags of freshly grated coconut for just this purpose. Warm water is added and the coconut is squeezed repeatedly until the mixture is cloudy and has a wonderful coconut flavour. When strained, this is coconut milk. If the milk is left to stand, coconut cream will float to the surface in much the same way as regular cream does on whole milk.

Coconut milk is now available in cartons and cans, and even in countries with a plentiful supply of coconuts cooks often use these products for convenience and speed. The quality is excellent, and it is even possible to buy a version that is 88 per cent fat free.

Creamed coconut comes in 200g/7oz block. This is a very useful product, as small quantities can be cut off and added to dishes to supply a little richness just before serving. When a very small quantity of coconut milk is called for dissolve 50g/2oz creamed coconut in 100ml/3½fl oz/scant ½ cup hot water.

Above: Creamed coconut block

Coconut cream can be made in the same way, but the amount of creamed coconut should be increased to 75g/3oz. Ready-to-use coconut cream comes in cartons and is a magical ingredient where a rich coconut aroma and flavour are required. In many Thai curries the spices are initially fried in bubbling coconut cream instead of the more usual oil.

Culinary uses

Coconut is widely used in South-east Asian cooking. The milk is used as a cooking medium instead of stock in a variety of dishes, and it is also added at the end of cooking to enrich stews and curries. It can be cooked with rice, to make a savoury accompaniment, or as the basis for rice cakes, and also to make a delicious creamy rice pudding. In Thailand, coconut milk is often used to make aromatic soups.

Making coconut milk

Coconut milk can be made at home, from desiccated (dry unsweetened shredded) coconut. Although the procedure takes a little time, it has plenty of advantages. Desiccated coconut is readily available and is an item that many cooks routinely stock in their store cupboards. You can make as much or as little as you like – although the method is more practical for large quantities – and coconut milk made this way is less expensive than any of the alternatives.

2 Place a sieve (strainer) lined with muslin (cheesecloth) over a large bowl in the sink. Ladle some of the softened coconut into the muslin.

1 Tip 225g/8oz/2⅔ cups desiccated coconut into the bowl of a food processor and pour over 450ml/ ¾ pint/scant 2 cups boiling water. Process for 20–30 seconds and allow to cool a little. If making several batches transfer immediately to a large bowl and repeat.

3 Bring up the ends of the cloth and twist it over the sieve to extract as much of the liquid as possible. Discard the spent coconut. Use the coconut milk as directed in recipes.

Below: Coconut cream

COOK'S TIPS

• When making coconut milk, instead of discarding the spent coconut, it can be re-used to make a second batch of coconut milk. This will be of a poorer quality and should only be used to extend a good quality first quantity of coconut milk.
• Any unused coconut milk or cream can be transferred to a plastic tub and stored in the refrigerator for a day or two, or poured into a freezer container and frozen for use on another occasion.
• Before using newly made coconut milk, leave it to stand for 10 minutes or more, and the coconut cream will float to the top. Skim off the cream using a large spoon if needed, or leave it to enrich the milk.

BEER, WINE AND SPIRITS

The art of making alcoholic beverages is an ancient one. Man has been making alcoholic drinks ever since the discovery that a grain and water mash would ferment if left to stand, producing a sour brew that would intoxicate.

Archaeological finds in northern China provide evidence that the Chinese were using separate drinking cups and bowls for different beverages as long ago as the 22nd century BC. Historians

Below: Leading Japanese beers include Sapporo and Asahi, both of which are widely available in the West.

agree that a considerable length of time must have elapsed from the beginning of the making and drinking of a primitive type of "wine" to the sophistication of using vessels in a variety of shapes for specific purposes, so the Chinese may well have been imbibing some form of alcoholic beverage at the dawn of their civilization more than 5,000 years ago. By the time of the Shang Dynasty (*c.* 1600–1100 BC), a dark wine was being brewed from millet, and was ceremonially served in elaborate bronze drinking vessels.

A new development in the art of brewing was achieved during the early part of the 12th century BC, where textual evidence records that a form of barm or leaven was used in wine-making. With this discovery, the Chinese were able to control both the flavour and alcoholic content of a variety of wines made from different fruits and grains. Wine continues to be an important drink, although its popularity has now been overtaken by beer.

Above: Chinese beers include Five Star beer and the light Pilsener, Tsingtao.

BEER

MANDARIN: *PI JIU*; CANTONESE: *PI CHIEW*

Beer brewing was not introduced into China and Japan until towards the end of the 19th century, but it rapidly became an extremely popular drink. Today, beer is the favourite alcoholic beverage in Asia, and almost every country in the region has breweries producing beers for export as well as for domestic consumption.

The style of beer most favoured by Asian drinkers is a bottom-fermented brew in the style of Pilsener (Pils), a pale, golden-coloured lager with a characteristically well-hopped palate and 4.5–5 per cent alcohol by volume.

Chinese beers

Without doubt, the best known Chinese beer is **Tsingtao**, a light, dry Pilsener-type beer which is brewed from the sweet spring water of Laoshan, using

Chinese barley and hops. It has a refreshing and delicate taste, and enjoys a huge popularity abroad, not just with expatriate Chinese, but among Westerners as well.

In 1898, part of the Shandong Peninsula was ceded to Germany as a colony. Besides the winery in Yantai, the Germans also established a brewery at Tsingtao in 1903, which was called the

Below: Singaporean Tiger beer is popular all over the world.

Anglo-German Brewery Company. Because of the vicissitudes of history, it went through a number of different owners – Britain, Germany and Japan – until after World War II, when it was taken over by the People's Republic of China. Since then a number of breweries have been established all over China, but Tsingtao Brewery remains the largest and most productive brewer in the land.

Other brands that can occasionally be seen in the West are **Beijing Beer**, **Shanghai Beer**, **Snowflake** and **Yu Chuan** ("Jade Spring") **Beer**. These all are Pilsener-type lagers, each with their own individual flavour.

Japanese beers

The huge beer industry of Japan also owes its origins to foreign investment. In 1869, the American firm of Wiegrand and Copeland started an experimental brewery at Yokohama. Soon afterwards, the Japanese Government sent a researcher to Germany to acquire technical know-how, and subsequently the Copeland operation was passed to Japanese management, taking the name Kirin in 1888.

Today, the Kirin Brewery Company has became one of the biggest brewers in the world. It is part of Japan's Mitsubishi conglomerate, and its output even surpasses that of Heineken. Kirin has nine breweries in different parts of Japan, and **Kirin Beer** is exported to almost every country in the world. It used to enjoy 60 per cent of domestic sales, but has recently been pushed down to about 40 per cent, partly owing to the surge of its chief rival **Asahi Beer**, which has rapidly increased its export market in recent years. Other strong contenders for the crown of the

Left: Canned Thai beer

Japanese beer industry are **Sapporo Beer**, which also challenges Kirin's claim of being the oldest brewer; and the newcomer **Suntory Beer**, which only started brewing in 1963.

South-east Asian beers

The world-renowned **Tiger Beer** of Singapore came into being by accident. The breweries were established after Heineken failed to reach an agreement with the Dutch Colonial Government to set up their breweries in Java in 1929, so established the Malayan Breweries in Singapore and later in Kuala Lumpur instead. Tiger Beer is now brewed by Asia Pacific Breweries of Singapore, and has achieved worldwide sales figures envied by all its competitors.

From Thailand, the biggest selling lager is **Singha**, brewed by Boon Rawd Brewery. The name Singha is a reference to the elegant but fearsome lion-like creature of local mythology.

Perhaps not that many people are aware that the Philippines is the home of one of the world's major brewing groups – **San Miguel**. This group has three breweries in the Philippines, one in Hong Kong, and one in Papua New Guinea. Outside of Asia, San Miguel has three breweries in Spain, but ironically these are only offshoots of its headquarters in the Philippines.

Dutch colonial links are still evident in Indonesia, where **Heineken** eventually did establish an associate company in Java to produce a Pilsener-style beer. Elsewhere in Asia, popular beers include the Vietnamese **"33"**; **Taiwan Beer** from Taiwan; and **OB** and **Crown** from Korea, but these are seldom seen in the West.

WINE

MANDARIN: *JIU;* CANTONESE: *CHIEW*

In contrast to their sophisticated approach to food, the Chinese, as a whole, are remarkably indiscriminating when it comes to alcoholic beverages. Unless they are connoisseurs, the Chinese often fail to distinguish between table wine, in which the alcoholic content is low, and distilled spirits, in which it is high. In everyday usage, the Chinese character *jiu* or *chiew* means any alcoholic beverage.

Chinese wines

As can be expected in a country where rice is the staple food, rice wine leads the field. There are hundreds of different varieties of rice wine in China, but only a few of these are exported.

Chinese rice wine is generally known as **huang jiu** (yellow wine) in Chinese, because of its golden amber colour. The best known and best quality rice wine is **Shao Xing**, named after the district where it is made. Shao Xing, or Shao Hsing is situated south of Hangzhou in Zhejiang province, and its wine-making history dates back to 470 BC. The main grains used for making Shao Xing are glutinous rice, millet and ordinary rice, and the water comes from a large lake

Left: Sake

Below: Shao Xing

Above: Glutinous rice wine

which is fed by the fountains and streams that flow down the sandy mountains on one side, and the dense bamboo-forested hills on the other. The water is so clear and the surface so smooth that the lake is known locally as "the mirror".

There are several varieties of Shao Xing wines, ranging in colour from golden amber to dark brown, and in the percentage of alcohol by volume from 14–16 per cent. The aroma is always quite distinctive, smelling subtly fragrant and smoky. Shao Xing should be drunk warm, and always with food. It is also used in cooking, and is added to the food towards the end of the cooking time so that the aroma is retained. One of the most famous Shao Xing wines is **Hua Tiao**, meaning "carved flower". This is a reference to the pretty patterns carved on the urns in which the wine is stored in underground cellars to mature.

As in beer brewing and whisky distilling, what distinguishes Shao Xing rice wine from all its imitators is the water used, which just cannot be replicated elsewhere. So beware of Shao

Xing/Hsing wine made in Taiwan, which pales, literally, by comparison. Read the small print on the label; if it says "made in ROC (Republic of China)" it is a fake.

China also produces some quite good grape wines. Several of these are exported to the West. The names to look for are **Dynasty**, **Great Wall** and **Huadong**. The whites (Riesling and Chardonnay) seem to be more successful than the red Cabernet Sauvignon. China may well become an important wine region in the future.

Mirin

This is a sweet rice wine with a low alcohol content. It is widely used in cooking, and is usually added towards the end, so that the subtle flavour is retained. Mirin is now available in the West. If you cannot locate it, dry sherry can be used instead, but the results will not be the same.

Pears with Chinese White Wine, Star Anise and Ginger

Star anise and ginger complement these sweet, wine-poached pears.

SERVES 4

75g/3oz/6 tbsp caster (superfine) sugar
300ml/ $^{1}/_{2}$ pint/1 $^{1}/_{4}$ cups white wine
thinly pared rind and juice of 1 lemon
7.5cm/3in piece fresh root ginger, bruised
5 star anise
10 cloves
600ml/1 pint/2 $^{1}/_{2}$ cups cold water
6 slightly unripe pears
25g/1oz stem ginger, sliced
natural (plain) yogurt, to serve

1 Place the caster sugar, wine, lemon rind and juice, fresh root ginger, star anise, cloves and water into a large pan. Bring to the boil.

2 Meanwhile, peel the pears. Add them to the wine mixture and ensure that they are covered in liquid, then lower the heat. Cover and simmer for 15 minutes or until the pears are tender.

3 Lift out the pears with a slotted spoon and keep them warm. Boil the wine syrup until reduced by half, then pour over the pears. Cool, then chill. Slice the pears and arrange on serving plates. Remove the root ginger from the sauce and add the stem ginger, then spoon the sauce over the pears.

Japanese wines

It is widely known that **sake** is the national drink of Japan. There are many varieties of this rice-based brew, but only a few are exported to the West. Unlike Chinese rice wine, sake is almost colourless, and it tastes slightly sweeter. It usually has an alcohol content of about 15 per cent. Like Chinese rice wine, sake should be drunk with food. Most types of sake are served warm, with the exception of **Ginjo**, a fine, dry wine which is invariably served chilled.

The traditional way of serving sake is in a porcelain jug, which is immersed in hot water until the wine is judged to be at the right temperature for serving. It is then poured into small cups. The host lifts a cup in both hands and passes it to his guest with a courteous bow. The cup must not be passed in one hand, as this shows disrespect. Having received the cup, also in both hands, the guest bows and downs the warm wine in one swift movement.

Good quality grape wines are also produced in Japan, but the output is quite small, owing to the scarcity of land available for growing vines and the extreme climate, all of which make wine-making difficult.

The three big names are **Suntory**, **Mercian** and **Mann's**. All these companies produce both white and red wines, but very little of the wine output is exported overseas.

SPIRITS

Chinese spirits

The Chinese name for distilled spirit – *bai jiu* – means "white wine" and stems from the fact that it is colourless, as opposed to the "yellow" rice wine. Asking for white wine in China can, therefore, lead to some interesting and potentially disastrous social occasions, as most Chinese spirits have an alcohol content of over 50 per cent.

Most Chinese spirits are distilled from a variety of grains, the commonest of these is sorghum, which is a cross between rice and millet. China has far more distilled spirits than wines, and

Below: Mou-Tai, which is served at state banquets, and Chu Yeh Ching

CHU YEH CHING
CHINESE LIQUEUR

some of the spirits are blended with herbs for use as medicinal tonics.

Mou-Tai is undoubtedly China's top spirit, and it is used for toasts at state banquets and other celebrations. It may be an acquired taste, but it was awarded a medal at the 1915 International Trade Fair in Panama, second only to France's cognac, but ahead of Scotch whisky as the world's top three spirits. Mou-Tai, which means "thatched terrace", is the name of a village in Kweichow in south-west China. The world-renowned spirit is distilled from two grains, wheat and sorghum, with the water taken from the stream running through a nearby gorge. The climate is moist and warm, and the thin layer of mist that hovers permanently over the fast-running stream is supposed to give the spirit its distinctive features.

Traditionally, good rice wines came from south China, while the best spirits were historically produced in the north. Although the distillery in Mou-Tai was established in 1529, the spirit was relatively indifferent until 1704, when a salt merchant from Shanxi in north China visited the area and was so enchanted by the beauty of the village that he decided to settle down there. Seeking new employment, he discovered the local spirit and set about improving it, employing the techniques of distilling the famous Fen Chiew from his native northern province. Mou-tai was the result.

Fen Chiew – the inspiration for Mou-Tai – is one of a small group of Chinese spirits that are available in the West. It comes from the "apricot blossoms village" of Shanxi province in north China, and is distilled from millet and sorghum with the water from a tributary of the Yellow River. Fen Chiew has a history of well over fifteen hundred years, and has afforded inspiration for many of China's greatest poets. This spirit also forms the basis for the famous **Chu Yeh Ching** ("bamboo leaf green"), a medicinal liqueur which is blended with no fewer than twelve different herbs, including bamboo leaves, which give it a lovely, pale green hue. The liqueur tastes quite refreshing despite being 47 per cent alcohol by volume.

Other popular Chinese spirits are **Wu Liang Ye** ("five-grain liqueur") from Sichuan; **Mei Kuei Lu** ("rose dew"); **Wu Chia Pi** ("five-layer skin"); and **Dong Chiew** ("mellow wine"). All of these are quite heady, as they are usually more than 50 per cent proof.

China also produces Western-style brandy, whisky, vodka, rum and gin, but all these drinks are mainly sold for home consumption.

Japanese spirits

Japan has its own spirit distilled from sake called **Shochu** ("burnt wine"). It is quite rough, and is usually diluted with warm water for drinking, even though its alcohol content is only about 25 per cent by volume. Japan produces a

Other Asian spirits

Taiwan produces many of the mainland Chinese drinks as well as the Japanese-inspired **Shokushu** rice spirit. In Korea, look out for **Ginseng Ju**, which comes with what appears to be a parsnip, but is actually a large ginseng root, in every bottle. In the East Indies, the island states in the South China Sea, the local **arrack** or **raki** is crudely distilled from either coconut palm juice or sugar cane molasses. A common practice is to add rice to the fermenting base juice to boost the alcohol content of the spirit. The result is a drink that bears a strong resemblance to rum, and is often sold as such to unwary tourists.

Below: Ginseng Ju

Above: Suntory whisky

Above: Suntory malt whisky

really good quality whisky, however. The first distillery was established in 1923, and in recent years Japanese whisky has attracted considerable attention on the international market. The model for Japan's whiskies is single malt Scotch, but there are equally successful spirits made in the idiom of blended Scotch. Some distilleries blend the home-grown product with imported Scotch malt whisky.

Suntory is the biggest and best-known brand name. Several different labels are marketed worldwide, including **The Whisky, Excellence, Royal, Special Reserve, Old, Kakubin, Gold Label, Gold 1000, White Label, Red Label, Torys Extra** and **Rawhide**, which

has a bourbon flavour. Suntory's rivals in terms of whisky production are Nikka distilleries (**G & G, Super Nikka, Black Nikka** and **Hi Nikka**); Kirin Seagram (**Robert Brown** and **Dunbar**); and Sanraku Ocean (**White Label**). Several other distillers and blenders make Japanese whisky, but they only have a very small output. Perhaps the best known of these is **Godo Shusei**.

Suntory also makes good brandy. The leading brands are **Imperial, XO, VSOP, VSO** and **VO**. Liqueurs include **Midori**, a green, melon-flavoured liqueur; **Ocha**, a green tea liqueur with a delicate tea fragrance; and the **Creme de Kobai**, a pale pink liqueur made from Japanese plums.

EQUIPMENT AND UTENSILS

The equipment in the average Western kitchen will be perfectly adequate for most of the recipes in this book, particularly now that the wok has become an indispensable item in many households. There are some items, however, that will make cooking Asian food easier and more pleasurable. The fact that many of these simple pieces of equipment also look good, and instantly establish you as an adventurous cook in the eyes of your friends is a bonus.

The best way to build up your store of specialist items is to start slowly, with a few basics such as a cleaver, bamboo steamer and wok, then gradually add extra pieces as you experiment with the exciting and different styles of cooking that are explored within these pages. If you enjoy making sushi, for instance, you will need a mat for rolling, and moulds for shaping the rice; if Thai curries are your current favourite, you'll be glad of a rough mortar and a pestle for grinding wet spice mixtures.

Visit an Asian or Chinese store and you'll be amazed at the array of items on sale at very reasonable prices. The design of many utensils has not changed in centuries, and items made from basic materials are often more effective than modern equivalents.

Cleaver

To Western cooks, a cleaver can seem rather intimidating. In reality, cleavers are among the most useful pieces of equipment ever invented. The blade of a heavy cleaver is powerful enough to cut through bone, yet delicate enough in the hands of a master chef to create paper thin slices of raw fish for sushi. The flat of the broad blade is ideal for crushing garlic or ginger, and the same blade can be used to convey the crushed items to the wok or pan.

Cleavers come in several sizes and weights. Number one is the heaviest. The blade is about 23cm/9in long and 10cm/4in wide. It can weigh as much as 1kg/2¼lb and resembles a chopper more than a knife. At the other end of

the scale, number three has a shorter, narrower blade and is only half as heavy as the larger cleaver. It is mainly used for slicing, rather than chopping. Number two is the cook's favourite. This medium-weight cleaver is used for both slicing and chopping. The Chinese name translates

Above: A medium-weight cleaver is a multi-purpose tool.

as "civil and military knife" because the lighter, front half of the blade is used for slicing, shredding, filleting and scoring (civil work), while the heavier rear half is used for chopping with force (military work). The back of the blade is used for pounding and tenderizing, and the flat for crushing and transporting. Even the handle has more than one purpose – the end can be used as a pestle.

Cleavers are made of several types of material. They can be made of carbonized steel with wooden handles, or of stainless steel with metal or wooden handles. Choose the one you are comfortable with. Hold it in your hand and feel the weight; it should be neither too heavy nor too light. One point to remember is that while a stainless steel cleaver may look good, it will require frequent sharpening if it is to stay razor-sharp. To prevent a carbonized steel blade from rusting and getting stained, wipe it dry after every use, then give it a thin coating of vegetable oil. Cleavers should always be sharpened on a fine-grained whetstone, never with a steel sharpener. The cleaver is user-friendly. It is not as

dangerous as it looks, provided you handle it with care. Learn to regard it as just another kitchen knife, and you will be rewarded with a lot of fun and very satisfactory results.

Chopping block

The traditional chopping block in the East is simply a cross-section of a tree trunk, usually hardwood. The ideal size for use in a domestic kitchen is about 30cm/12in in diameter and about 5cm/2in thick, but you will see much larger blocks being used in restaurants.

Season a new block with a liberal dose of vegetable oil on both sides to prevent it from splitting. Let it absorb as much oil as it will take, then clean the block with salt and water and dry it thoroughly. After each use, scrape the surface with the back of your cleaver, then wipe it down with a cloth. Never immerse a wooden block in water.

A large rectangular cutting board of hardwood can be used instead, but make sure it is at least 5cm/2in thick or it may not be able to take a hard blow from a cleaver. Acrylic boards can obviously be used if preferred, but they will not have the same aesthetic appeal as a traditional wooden one.

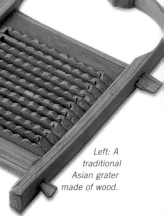

Left: A traditional Asian grater made of wood.

Above: The rough surface of a stone mortar and pestle helps grip the ingredients that are being pounded.

Grater

Traditional graters, used for preparing ginger, galangal and mooli (daikon), are made from wood or bamboo, but a metal cheese grater makes a satisfactory substitute.

Mortar and pestle

Oriental cooks prefer granite or stone mortars and pestles, since these have rough surfaces which help to grip the ingredients that are being chopped or pounded. Bigger, flat-bowled mortars are good for making spice pastes that contain large amounts of fresh spices, onion, herbs and garlic.

Spice mill

If you are going to grind a lot of spices, a spice mill will prove useful. An electric coffee grinder works well for this purpose,

Right: A double-handled wok is useful for all types of cooking; those with a single handle are particularly good for stir-frying.

but it is a good idea to reserve the mill for spices, unless you like to have your coffee flavoured with cardamom or cloves.

Wok

It is not surprising that the wok has become a universal favourite, for it is a remarkably versatile utensil. The rounded bottom was originally designed to fit snugly on a traditional Chinese brazier or stove. It conducts and retains heat evenly and because of its shape, the food always returns to the centre where the heat is most intense. This makes it ideally suited for stir-frying, braising, steaming, boiling and even for deep-frying.

Although the wok might not at first glance appear to be the best utensil for deep-frying, it is actually ideal, requiring far less oil than a flat-bottomed deep-fryer. It has more depth and a greater frying surface, so more food can be cooked more quickly. It is also much safer than a saucepan. As a wok has a larger capacity at the top than at the base, there is plenty of room to

accommodate the oil, even when extra ingredients are added, and it is not likely to overflow and catch fire.

There are two basic types of wok available in the West. The most common type, the double handled wok, is suitable for all types of cooking. The single-handled wok is particularly suitable for quick stir-frying, as it can easily be shaken during cooking. Both types are available with flattened bases for use on electric cookers or gas cookers with burners that would not accommodate a round base.

The best woks are made from lightweight carbonized steel. Cast iron woks are too heavy for all but the strongest cooks to handle, and woks made from other materials, such as stainless steel or aluminium, are not as good for Asian cooking. They also tend to be a great deal more expensive than the standard carbonized steel wok.

A new carbonized steel wok must be seasoned before use. The best way to do this is to place the wok over a high heat until the surface blackens, then wash it in warm, soapy water. Use a stiff brush to get the wok clean, then rinse it well in clean water and place it over a medium heat to dry completely. Finally, wipe the surface with a pad of kitchen paper soaked in vegetable oil. After each use, wash the wok under the hot water tap, but never use detergent as this would remove the "seasoning" and cause the wok to rust. Any food that sticks to the wok should be scraped off with a stiff brush or with a non-metal scourer, and the wok should then be rinsed and dried over a low heat. Before being put away, a little oil should be rubbed in to the surface of the wok.

Below right: A perforated metal scoop and a wire skimmer

Above: Essential wok tools include a dome-shaped lid, wooden or bamboo chopsticks, a long-handled spatula and a large ladle.

Wok tools

Some wok sets come with a spatula and ladle made from cast iron or stainless steel. These are very useful, particularly the ladle. It addition to its obvious purpose as a stirrer, it can be used to measure small quantities of liquid. A standard ladle holds about 175ml/ 6fl oz/¾cup. A dome-shaped lid is also useful, as is a metal draining rack that fits over the wok. Small items such as deep-fried foods can be placed on the rack to keep warm while successive batches are cooked. Other accessories include wooden or bamboo chopsticks. Short ones can be used at the table or in the kitchen – they are ideal for beating eggs – and the long pair are used for deep-frying, as stirrers or tongs. Finally, a wok stand is handy for protecting your table when serving.

Strainers

Several types of strainer are available, but the two most useful are the perforated metal scoop or slotted spoon, and the coarse-mesh, wire skimmer, preferably with a long bamboo handle. Wire skimmers come in a variety of sizes and are useful for removing food from hot oil when deep-frying.

Below: Bamboo steamers come in several sizes.

Steamers

The traditional Chinese steamer is made from bamboo and has a tight-fitting lid. Several sizes are available, and you can stack as many tiers as you like over a wok of boiling water. The modern steamer is free-standing and made of aluminium, but the food cooked in a metal steamer lacks the subtle fragrance that a bamboo steamer imparts. If you do not have a steamer, you can improvise with a wok and a trivet. Having placed the trivet in the wok, fill it one-third full of water

Above: An authentic clay pot can be used in the oven or, with care, on top of the stove.

Asian or Chinese stores. With care, the pots can be used on top of the stove, where they retain an even heat. They are, however, fairly fragile, and are prone to crack easily.

Rice cooker

Electric rice cookers work extremely well and are worth investing in if you cook a lot of rice. However, a good-sized, deep, heavy pan with a tight-fitting lid is just as suitable for this purpose.

Mongolian fire pot

Also known as a Chinese hot pot or steamboat (in Singapore), this is not unlike a fondue pot, in that it allows food to be cooked at the table. The design is different from that of a fondue, however, as it consists of a central funnel, which is filled with burning charcoal, surrounded by a moat in which hot stock is placed. The pot is placed in the centre of the table and guests cook small pieces of meat and vegetables in the hot stock. Once these are all cooked and eaten, the stock is served as a soup. There are several different models available, the most expensive being made of brass, while the cheaper ones are made of aluminium or stainless steel.

Japanese omelette pan

To make the rolled omelettes that are so widely used in Japanese cooking, a rectangular omelette pan or *makiyaki-nabe* is useful, but not essential: a large non-stick, heavy frying pan or a flat, heavy griddle could be used instead.

and bring this to the boil. Place the food in a heatproof bowl on the trivet, cover the wok with the dome-shaped lid and steam the food until it is cooked.

Clay pot

Also known as the sand-pot or Chinese casserole, this earthenware cooking utensil must have preceded the cast iron pot by thousands of years. Several shapes and sizes are available, and most are glazed on the inside only. They are not expensive and can be bought in

Below: A large pan with a tight-fitting lid is ideal for cooking rice.

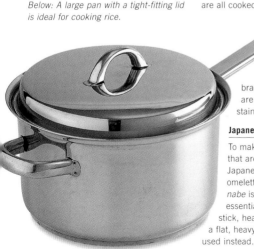

Below: A Mongolian fire pot or steamboat is used for cooking at the table. The central funnel is filled with burning charcoal, and this heats the stock in the surrounding moat.

Sushi equipment

If you are going to make sushi properly, you will need a few simple pieces of equipment. A *makisu*, also known as a *sushimaki sudare*, is essential. This is the bamboo mat (shown below), which is about the size of a table mat, that is used for rolling sheets of nori (seaweed) around vinegared rice and other fillings when making *norimaki*.

Sushi chefs spread the rice on the nori with their fingers, but this is a sticky business and can prove tricky for the uninitiated. A rice paddle or *shamoji* makes the job easier. For pressed sushi, shaped moulds made from wood or plastic are very useful.

CLASSIC COOKING TECHNIQUES

Careful preparation is the foundation of all Asian cooking, from preparing and chopping ingredients to grinding spices and washing and trimming garnishes. Once the ingredients are prepared, then the cooking, which is often relatively quick, can commence.

There are a few classic preparation and cooking techniques upon which Asian cuisine relies. The most important, without a doubt, is the preparation of spices and herbs, which give the dishes their unique flavour and character. Traditional Asian cooks prepare almost everything from scratch (although in the West, there are a number of very good ready-made ingredients such as curry pastes that can be great time–savers).

Spices are roasted and ground into pastes, which form the basis of most dishes. Once the flavouring is prepared, the cooking is usually simple: stewing, steaming, boiling, stir-frying, deep-frying and grilling over hot coals. A few Chinese dishes such as roast duck and pork, are "roasted", but this is not a common Asian cooking method.

GRINDING SPICES

The ideal method for grinding spices is to use a large, rough, Asian-style mortar. The rough sides tend to "grip" the spices, preventing them flying out of the mortar as you pound them. Dry spices are usually dry-roasted in a heavy frying pan before grinding.

1 Spread the dry spices in a single layer and cook over a very high heat for about 1 minute, shaking the pan. Lower the heat and cook for a few more minutes, until they start to colour and emit their aroma.

2 Transfer the toasted spices to the mortar and pound to a fine powder. This releases the essential oils that are vital to the authentic flavour of Asian food.

POUNDING AND PURÉEING

Dry and wet spices, aromatics and herbs are often pounded together to form spice pastes. Other flavouring ingredients such as strong-tasting shrimp paste may also be added.

1 Place the spices, herbs and any other flavouring ingredients in a mortar and pound with a pestle for several minutes to form a smooth paste.

SLOW-COOKING

Stewing is the typical method for preparing soups and curries, and the lengthy cooking time makes sure that meats become very tender. Traditionally, a heavy clay pot, placed over a fire of medium intensity, would have been used.

1 Put all the ingredients in a clay pot and place in an oven preheated to the required temperature. (A heavy, flameproof casserole makes a good alternative if you do not have a clay pot. It can also be placed over a medium heat on the stovetop if you prefer.)

STEAMING

This is an excellent way of preparing delicate foods such as fish and vegetables. Steaming helps to retain the flavour of ingredients and keeps them intact.

1 Place the food in a bamboo steamer. (Some recipes require the steamer to be lined with banana leaves.) Put the steamer on a wok rack over a wok half-filled with boiling water. Steam the food, replenishing the water constantly to prevent it boiling dry.

2 Parcels of food wrapped in banana leaves can also produce steamed results. Place a well-sealed parcel over a barbecue or in a preheated oven. The moisture is trapped within the parcel and steams the food inside.

STIR-FRYING

This is a very quick cooking method and it is usually the preparation of the ingredients that takes time. It is important to prepare all the ingredients before you start to stir-fry. The order in which ingredients are added to the pan is very important.

1 Pour a little oil into a wok and place over a high heat for a few minutes.

2 Add spices and aromatics to the wok and stir-fry for a few moments.

3 Add evenly chopped pieces of meat, poultry, fish or shellfish to the wok and stir-fry for 1 or 2 minutes more, shaking the pan constantly.

4 Add any hardy vegetables such as carrots, green beans or (bell) peppers and stir-fry for 1 minute.

5 Add any delicate vegetables and leaves such as beansprouts, spinach or morning glory and stir-fry for about 1 minute more.

6 Finally add more seasoning and add any fresh herbs such as basil or coriander (cilantro) that should not be cooked for long. Toss to combine and serve immediately.

DEEP-FRYING

This method is used for many dishes such as wontons, spring rolls and prawn crackers. Use an oil that can be heated to a high temperature, such as groundnut (peanut) oil.

1 Pour the oil into a pan or wok (filling it no more than two-thirds full) and heat to about 180°C/350°F. To test the temperature, add a drop of batter or a piece of onion. If it sinks, the oil is not hot enough; if it burns, it is too hot. If it sizzles and rises to the surface, the temperature is perfect.

2 Cook the food in small batches until crisp and lift out with a slotted spoon or wire mesh skimmer when cooked. Drain on a wire rack lined with kitchen paper and serve immediately, or keep warm in the oven until ready to serve.

BOILING

This method is often used to cook delicate meat such as chicken breast portions or duck.

1 Place the meat and any flavourings in a pan and add just enough water to cover. Bring to the boil, then remove from the heat and leave to stand, covered, for 10 minutes, then drain.

COOKING ON THE BARBECUE

Grilling food over glowing coals is very popular. It is widely used by street vendors who cook skewered snacks such as satay or barbecue-cooked chicken or seafood over small open braziers.

1 When using charcoal, light the coals and wait until they are covered with a thin layer of white or pale grey ash before starting to cook. Place the skewers, meat, poultry, fish or shellfish on a rack over the coals and grill, turning occasionally, until browned on all sides and cooked through.

2 If you do not have time to set up a barbecue, cook the food under a preheated grill (broiler).

Wooden and bamboo skewers
If you are using wooden or bamboo skewers, soak them in water for about 30 minutes before using to prevent them from burning.

RECIPES

Some of the world's most exciting dishes come from the Far East and South-east Asia.

Each of the countries in this broad sweep has its own distinct cuisine, but there is a

common emphasis on serving food that is as fresh as posssible. And – particularly in

Japan and Thailand – its presentation is paramount.

SNACKS AND PARTY FOODS

Wander around the streets in any Asian city or town and you

will see vendors standing behind portable cooking carts or

squatting beside burners with battered woks ready to receive

garlic, ginger, chillies and vegetables. The smells are enticing

and those who are tempted to taste are seldom disappointed.

Follow the recipes in this section and treat your party guests

to such delicious snacks as Roasted Coconut Cashew Nuts,

Samosas, Sashimi Moriawase, Ensaimadas or Firecrackers.

COCONUT CHIPS

COCONUT CHIPS ARE A WONDERFULLY TASTY NIBBLE TO SERVE WITH DRINKS. THE CHIPS CAN BE SLICED AHEAD OF TIME AND FROZEN (WITHOUT SALT), ON OPEN TRAYS. WHEN FROZEN, SIMPLY SHAKE INTO PLASTIC BOXES OR BAGS. YOU CAN THEN TAKE OUT AS FEW OR AS MANY AS YOU WISH FOR THE PARTY.

3 Having opened the coconut, use a broad-bladed knife to ease the flesh away from the hard outer shell. Taste a piece of the flesh just to make sure it is fresh. Peel away the brown skin with a potato peeler, if you like.

4 Slice the flesh into wafer-thin shavings, using a food processor, mandoline or sharp knife. Sprinkle these evenly all over one or two baking sheets and sprinkle with salt. Bake for about 25–30 minutes or until crisp, turning them from time to time. Cool and serve. Any leftovers can be stored in airtight containers.

COOK'S TIP

This is the kind of recipe where the slicing blade on a food processor comes into its own. It is worth preparing two or three coconuts at a time, and freezing, surplus chips. The chips can be cooked from frozen, but will need to be spread out well on the baking sheets, before being salted. Allow a little longer for frozen chips to cook.

SERVES EIGHT AS A SNACK

INGREDIENTS
   1 fresh coconut
   salt

1 Preheat the oven to 160°C/325°F/Gas 3. First drain the coconut juice, either by piercing one of the coconut eyes with a sharp instrument or by breaking it carefully.

2 Lay the coconut on a board and hit the centre sharply with a hammer. The shell should break cleanly in two.

ROASTED COCONUT CASHEW NUTS

SERVE THESE HOT AND SWEET CASHEW NUTS IN PAPER OR CELLOPHANE CONES AT PARTIES. NOT ONLY DO THEY LOOK ENTICING AND TASTE TERRIFIC, BUT THE CONES HELP TO KEEP CLOTHES AND HANDS CLEAN AND CAN SIMPLY BE THROWN AWAY AFTERWARDS.

SERVES SIX TO EIGHT

INGREDIENTS
    15ml/1 tbsp groundnut (peanut) oil
    30ml/2 tbsp clear honey
    250g/9oz/2 cups cashew nuts
    115g/4oz/1⅓ cups desiccated (dry
       unsweetened shredded) coconut
    2 small fresh red chillies, seeded and
       finely chopped
    salt and ground black pepper

VARIATIONS
Almonds also work well, or choose
peanuts for a more economical snack.

1 Heat the oil in a wok or large frying
pan and then stir in the honey. After a
few seconds add the nuts and coconut
and stir-fry until both are golden brown.

2 Add the chillies, with salt and pepper
to taste. Toss until all the ingredients
are well mixed. Serve warm or cooled
in paper cones or saucers.

ROLLED OMELETTE

THIS IS A FIRMLY SET, ROLLED OMELETTE, CUT INTO NEAT PIECES AND SERVED COLD. THE TEXTURE SHOULD BE SMOOTH AND SOFT, NOT LEATHERY, AND THE FLAVOUR IS SWEET-SAVOURY. PICKLED GINGER, SOMETIMES CALLED GARI, MAKES AN ATTRACTIVE GARNISH.

SERVES FOUR

INGREDIENTS
8 eggs
60ml/4 tbsp sugar
20ml/4 tsp Japanese soy sauce,
  plus extra, to serve
90ml/6 tbsp sake or dry white wine
vegetable oil, for cooking
wasabi and pickled ginger, to garnish

COOK'S TIP
Wasabi, which can be bought from Asian stores, is a very hot and peppery, bright green paste. Use it sparingly.

1 Put the eggs in a large bowl and stir them together, using a pair of chopsticks and a cutting action.

2 Mix the sugar with the soy sauce and sake or wine in a small bowl. Lightly stir this mixture into the eggs. Pour half the mixture into another bowl.

3 Heat a little oil in a frying pan, then wipe off the excess. Pour a quarter of the mixture from one bowl into the pan, tilting the pan to coat it thinly. When the edge has set, but the middle is moist, roll up the omelette towards you.

4 Moisten some kitchen paper with oil and grease the empty side of the pan. Pour one-third of the remaining egg into the pan. Lift the rolled egg up with your chopsticks and let the raw egg run underneath it. When the edge has set, roll up in the opposite direction, tilting the pan away from you.

5 Slide the roll towards you, grease the pan and pour in half the remaining mixture, letting the egg run under. When set, insert chopsticks in the side of the rolled omelette, then flip over towards the opposite side. Cook the remainder in the same way. Slide the roll so that its join is underneath. Cook for 10 seconds.

6 Slide the roll out on to a bamboo mat and roll up tightly, then press neatly into a rectangular shape. Leave to cool. Cook the second batch in the same way. Slice the cold omelettes into 2.5cm/1in pieces, arrange on a platter and garnish with a little wasabi and with a pickled ginger flower. Serve with soy sauce.

EGG ROLLS

THE TITLE OF THIS RECIPE COULD LEAD TO SOME CONFUSION, ESPECIALLY IN THE UNITED STATES, WHERE EGG ROLLS ARE THE SAME AS SPRING ROLLS. THESE EGG ROLLS, HOWEVER, ARE WEDGES OF A ROLLED THAI-FLAVOURED OMELETTE. THEY ARE FREQUENTLY SERVED AS FINGER FOOD.

SERVES TWO

INGREDIENTS
  3 eggs, beaten
  15ml/1 tbsp soy sauce
  1 bunch garlic chives, thinly sliced
  1–2 small fresh red or green chillies,
    seeded and finely chopped
  small bunch fresh coriander
    (cilantro), chopped
  pinch of granulated sugar
  salt and ground black pepper
  15ml/1 tbsp groundnut (peanut) oil
For the dipping sauce
  60ml/4 tbsp light soy sauce
  fresh lime juice, to taste

COOK'S TIP
Wear gloves while preparing chillies or cut them up with a knife and fork. Wash your hands after in warm, soapy water.

1 Make the dipping sauce. Pour the soy sauce into a bowl. Add a generous squeeze of lime juice. Taste and add more lime juice if needed.

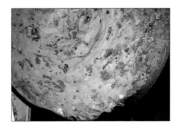

2 Mix the eggs, soy sauce, chives, chillies and coriander. Add the sugar and season to taste. Heat the oil in a large frying pan, pour in the egg mixture and swirl the pan to make an omelette.

3 Cook for 1–2 minutes, until the omelette is just firm and the underside is golden. Slide it out on to a plate and roll up as though it were a pancake. Leave to cool completely.

4 When the omelette is cool, slice it diagonally in 1cm/½in pieces. Arrange the slices on a serving platter and serve with the bowl of dipping sauce.

POTATO, SHALLOT AND GARLIC SAMOSAS WITH GREEN PEAS

MOST SAMOSAS ARE DEEP-FRIED. THESE ARE BAKED, MAKING THEM A HEALTHIER OPTION. THEY ARE PERFECT FOR PARTIES, SINCE THE PASTRIES NEED NO LAST-MINUTE ATTENTION.

MAKES TWENTY-FIVE

INGREDIENTS
1 large potato, about 250g/
    9oz, diced
15ml/1 tbsp groundnut
    (peanut) oil
2 shallots, finely chopped
1 garlic clove, finely chopped
60ml/4 tbsp coconut milk
5ml/1 tsp Thai red or green
    curry paste
75g/3oz/¾ cup peas
juice of ½ lime
25 samosa wrappers or 10 x 5cm/
    4 x 2in strips of filo pastry
salt and ground black pepper
oil, for brushing

1 Preheat the oven to 220°C/425°F/ Gas 7. Bring a small pan of water to the boil, add the diced potato, cover and cook for 10–15 minutes, until tender. Drain and set aside.

2 Meanwhile, heat the groundnut oil in a large frying pan and cook the shallots and garlic over a medium heat, stirring occasionally, for 4–5 minutes, until softened and golden.

3 Add the drained diced potato, coconut milk, red or green curry paste, peas and lime juice to the frying pan. Mash together coarsely with a wooden spoon. Season to taste with salt and pepper and cook over a low heat for 2–3 minutes, then remove the pan from the heat and set aside until the mixture has cooled a little.

4 Lay a samosa wrapper or filo strip flat on the work surface. Brush with a little oil, then place a generous teaspoonful of the mixture in the middle of one end. Turn one corner diagonally over the filling to meet the long edge.

5 Continue folding over the filling, keeping the triangular shape as you work down the strip. Brush with a little more oil if necessary and place on a baking sheet. Prepare all the other samosas in the same way.

6 Bake for 15 minutes, or until the pastry is golden and crisp. Leave to cool slightly before serving.

COOK'S TIP
Many Asian food stores sell what is described as a samosa pad. This is a packet, usually frozen, containing about 50 oblong pieces of samosa pastry. Filo pastry, cut to size, can be used instead.

SAMOSAS

*THESE TASTY SNACKS ARE ENJOYED THE WORLD OVER. THROUGHOUT THE EAST, THEY ARE SOLD BY
STREET VENDORS, AND EATEN AT ANY TIME OF DAY. FILO PASTRY CAN BE USED IF PREFERRED.*

MAKES ABOUT TWENTY

INGREDIENTS
    1 packet 25cm/10in square spring
      roll wrappers, thawed if frozen
    30ml/2 tbsp plain (all-purpose) flour,
      mixed to a paste with water
    vegetable oil, for deep frying
    coriander (cilantro) leaves,
      to garnish
    cucumber, carrot and celery, cut into
      matchsticks, to serve (optional)
For the filling
    25g/1oz/2 tbsp ghee or unsalted
      (sweet) butter
    1 small onion, finely chopped
    1cm/¹/₂in piece fresh root ginger,
      peeled and chopped
    1 garlic clove, crushed
    2.5ml/¹/₂ tsp chilli powder
    1 large potato, about 225g/8oz,
      cooked until just tender and
      finely diced
    50g/2oz/¹/₂ cup cauliflower florets,
      lightly cooked, finely chopped
    50g/2oz/¹/₂ cup frozen peas, thawed
    5–10ml/1–2 tsp garam masala
    15ml/1 tbsp chopped fresh coriander
      (cilantro) leaves and stems
    squeeze of lemon juice
    salt

2 Cut the spring roll wrappers into
three strips (or two for larger samosas).
Brush the edges with a little of the flour
paste. Place a small spoonful of filling
about 2cm/³/₄in in from the edge of
one strip. Fold one corner over the
filling to make a triangle and continue
this folding until the entire strip has
been used and a triangular pastry has
been formed. Seal any open edges
with more flour and water paste, if
necessary adding more water if the
paste is very thick.

3 Heat the oil for deep frying to 190°C/
375°F and fry the samosas, a few at a
time, until golden and crisp. Drain
well on kitchen paper and serve hot
garnished with coriander leaves and
accompanied by cucumber, carrot and
celery matchsticks, if you like.

COOK'S TIP
Prepare samosas in advance by frying
until just cooked through and draining.
Cook in hot oil for a few minutes to
brown and drain again before serving.

1 Heat the ghee or butter in a large wok
and fry the onion, ginger and garlic for
5 minutes until the onion has softened.
Add the chilli powder, cook for 1 minute,
then stir in the potato, cauliflower and
peas. Sprinkle with garam masala and
set aside to cool. Stir in the chopped
coriander, lemon juice and salt.

TUNG TONG

POPULARLY CALLED "GOLD BAGS", THESE CRISP PASTRY PURSES HAVE A CORIANDER-FLAVOURED
FILLING BASED ON WATER CHESTNUTS AND CORN. THEY ARE THE PERFECT VEGETARIAN SNACK.

MAKES EIGHTEEN

INGREDIENTS
    18 spring roll wrappers, about
        8cm/3¼in square, thawed
        if frozen
    oil, for deep-frying
    plum sauce, to serve
For the filling
    4 baby corn cobs
    130g/4½oz can water chestnuts,
        drained and chopped
    1 shallot, coarsely chopped
    1 egg, separated
    30ml/2 tbsp cornflour (cornstarch)
    60ml/4 tbsp water
    small bunch fresh coriander
        (cilantro), chopped
    salt and ground black pepper

1 Make the filling. Place the baby corn, water chestnuts, shallot and egg yolk in a food processor or blender. Process to a coarse paste. Place the egg white in a cup and whisk it lightly with a fork.

2 Put the cornflour in a small pan and stir in the water until smooth. Add the corn mixture and chopped coriander and season with salt and pepper to taste. Cook over a low heat, stirring constantly, until thickened.

3 Leave the filling to cool slightly, then place 5ml/1 tsp in the centre of a spring roll wrapper. Brush the edges with the beaten egg white, then gather up the points and press them firmly together to make a pouch or bag.

4 Repeat with remaining wrappers and filling. Heat the oil in a deep-fryer or wok to 190°C/375°F or until a cube of bread, added to the oil, browns in about 45 seconds. Fry the bags, in batches, for about 5 minutes, until golden brown. Drain on kitchen paper and serve hot, with the plum sauce.

GREEN CURRY PUFFS

*SHRIMP PASTE AND GREEN CURRY SAUCE, USED JUDICIOUSLY, GIVE THESE PUFFS THEIR DISTINCTIVE,
SPICY, SAVOURY FLAVOUR, AND THE ADDITION OF CHILLI STEPS UP THE HEAT.*

MAKES TWENTY-FOUR

INGREDIENTS
    24 small wonton wrappers, about
        8cm/3¼in square, thawed if frozen
    15ml/1 tbsp cornflour (cornstarch),
        mixed to a paste with 30ml/
        2 tbsp water
    oil, for deep-frying
For the filling
    1 small potato, about 115g/4oz,
        boiled and mashed
    25g/1oz/3 tbsp cooked petits pois
        (baby peas)
    25g/1oz/3 tbsp cooked corn
    few sprigs fresh coriander
        (cilantro), chopped
    1 small fresh red chilli, seeded and
        finely chopped
    ½ lemon grass stalk, finely chopped
    15ml/1 tbsp soy sauce
    5ml/1 tsp shrimp paste or fish sauce
    5ml/1 tsp Thai green curry paste

2 Brush a little of the cornflour paste
along two sides of the square. Fold
the other two sides over to meet them,
then press together to make a triangular
pastry and seal in the filling. Make
more pastries in the same way.

3 Heat the oil in a deep-fryer or wok to
190°C/375°F or until a cube of bread,
added to the oil, browns in about
45 seconds. Add the pastries to the oil,
a few at a time, and fry them for about
5 minutes, until golden brown.

4 Remove from the fryer or wok and
drain on kitchen paper. If you intend
serving the puffs hot, place them in a
low oven while cooking successive
batches. The puffs also taste good cold.

COOK'S TIP
Wonton wrappers dry out quickly, so keep
them covered, using clear film (plastic
wrap), until you are ready to use them.

1 Combine the filling ingredients. Lay
out one wonton wrapper and place a
teaspoon of the filling in the centre.

ENSAIMADAS

THESE SWEET BREAD ROLLS ARE A POPULAR SNACK IN THE PHILIPPINES AND COME WITH VARIOUS FILLINGS, SEVERAL OF THEM SAVOURY. THIS VERSION INCLUDES CHEESE.

MAKES TEN TO TWELVE

INGREDIENTS
  30ml/2 tbsp caster (superfine) sugar,
    plus extra for sprinkling
  150ml/¼ pint/⅔ cup warm water
  15ml/1 tbsp dried active yeast
  450g/1lb/4 cups strong white flour
  5ml/1 tsp salt
  115g/4oz/½ cup butter, softened,
    plus 30ml/2 tbsp melted butter for
    the filling
  4 egg yolks
  90–120ml/6–8 tbsp warm milk
  115g/4oz/1 cup grated Cheddar
    cheese (or similar well-flavoured
    hard cheese)

1 Dissolve 5ml/1 tsp of the sugar in the warm water, then sprinkle in the dried yeast. Stir, then set aside for 10 minutes or until frothy. Sift the flour and salt into a large bowl.

2 Cream the softened butter with the remaining sugar in a large bowl. When it is fluffy, beat in the egg yolks and a little of the sifted flour. Gradually stir in the remaining flour with the yeast mixture and enough milk to form a soft but not sticky dough. Transfer to an oiled plastic bag. Close the bag loosely, leaving plenty of room for the dough to rise. Leave in a warm place for about 1 hour, until the dough doubles in bulk.

3 On a lightly floured surface, knock back (punch down) the dough, then roll it out into a large rectangle. Brush with half the melted butter, sprinkle with the cheese, then roll up from a long side like a Swiss roll (jelly roll).

4 Knead the dough thoroughly to distribute the cheese, then divide the dough into 10–12 pieces.

5 Roll each piece of dough into a thin rope, about 38cm/15in long. On greased baking sheets, coil each rope into a loose spiral, spacing them well apart. Tuck the loose ends under to seal. Leave to rise, in a warm place, for about 45 minutes or until doubled in size. Meanwhile, preheat the oven to 220°C/425°F/Gas 7.

6 Bake the ensaimadas in the oven for 15–20 minutes, until golden and cooked through. Remove from the oven, then immediately brush with the remaining melted butter and sprinkle with caster sugar. Serve warm.

THAI TEMPEH CAKES <u>WITH</u> SWEET CHILLI DIPPING SAUCE

MADE FROM SOYA BEANS, TEMPEH IS SIMILAR TO TOFU BUT HAS A NUTTIER TASTE. HERE, IT IS COMBINED WITH A FRAGRANT BLEND OF LEMON GRASS, CORIANDER AND GINGER.

MAKES EIGHT

INGREDIENTS
    1 lemon grass stalk, outer leaves
      removed and inside finely chopped
    2 garlic cloves, chopped
    2 spring onions (scallions),
      finely chopped
    2 shallots, finely chopped
    2 fresh red chillies, seeded and
      finely chopped
    2.5cm/1in piece fresh root ginger,
      finely chopped
    60ml/4 tbsp chopped fresh coriander
      (cilantro), plus extra to garnish
    250g/9oz/2¼ cups tempeh, thawed if
      frozen, sliced
    15ml/1 tbsp fresh lime juice
    5ml/1 tsp granulated sugar
    45ml/3 tbsp plain (all-purpose) flour
    1 large (US extra large) egg,
      lightly beaten
    salt and freshly ground black pepper
    vegetable oil, for frying
For the dipping sauce
    45ml/3 tbsp mirin (see Cook's Tip)
    45ml/3 tbsp white wine vinegar
    2 spring onions (scallions),
      thinly sliced
    15ml/1 tbsp granulated sugar
    2 fresh red chillies, seeded and
      finely chopped
    30ml/2 tbsp chopped fresh
      coriander (cilantro)
    large pinch of salt

1 Make the dipping sauce. Mix together the mirin, vinegar, spring onions, sugar, chillies, coriander and salt in a small bowl. Cover with clear film (plastic wrap) and set aside until ready to serve.

COOK'S TIP
Mirin is a sweet rice wine from Japan. It has quite a delicate flavour and is used for cooking. Rice wine for drinking, called sake, is rather more expensive. Both are available from Asian food stores. If you cannot locate mirin, dry sherry can be used instead, although the results will not be quite the same.

2 Place the lemon grass, garlic, spring onions, shallots, chillies, ginger and coriander in a food processor or blender, then process to a coarse paste. Add the tempeh, lime juice and sugar and process until combined. Add the flour and egg, with salt and pepper to taste. Process again until the mixture forms a coarse, sticky paste.

3 Scrape the paste into a bowl. Take one-eighth of the mixture at a time and form it into rounds with your hands.

4 Heat a little oil in a large frying pan. Fry the tempeh cakes for 5–6 minutes, turning once, until golden. Drain on kitchen paper. Transfer to a platter, garnish and serve with the sauce.

STEAMED FLOWER ROLLS

THESE ATTRACTIVE LITTLE ROLLS ARE TRADITIONALLY SERVED WITH MONGOLIAN FIREPOT.

MAKES SIXTEEN

INGREDIENTS
1 quantity basic dough (below) made
  using only 5ml/1 tsp sugar
15ml/1 tbsp sesame seed oil
chives, to garnish

1 Divide the risen and knocked back
(punched down) dough into two equal
portions. Roll each into a rectangle 30 x
20cm/12 x 8in. Brush the surface of one
with sesame oil and lay the other on top.
Roll up like a Swiss (jelly) roll. Cut into
16 pieces.

COOK'S TIP
When lining the steamer, fold the paper
several times, then cut small holes like a
doily. This lets the steam circulate, yet
prevents the rolls from sticking.

2 Take each dough roll in turn and
press down firmly on the rolled side
with a chopstick. Place the rolls on the
work surface, coiled side uppermost.

3 Pinch the opposite ends of each
roll with the fingers of both hands, then
pull the ends underneath and seal.
The dough should separate into petals.
Place the buns on baking parchment in
a steamer and leave to double in size.
Steam over rapidly boiling water for
30–35 minutes. Serve hot, garnished
with chives.

PORK-STUFFED STEAMED BUNS

THESE TREATS ARE JUST ONE EXAMPLE OF DIM SUM, FEATHERLIGHT STEAMED BUNS WITH A RANGE OF TASTY FILLINGS. THEY ARE NOW A POPULAR SNACK THE WORLD OVER.

MAKES 16

INGREDIENTS
For the basic dough
15ml/1 tbsp sugar
about 300ml/1/2 pint/1 1/4 cups
  warm water
25ml/1 1/2 tbsp dried yeast
450g/1lb/4 cups strong white flour
5ml/1 tsp salt
15g/1/2oz/1 tbsp lard (or white
  cooking fat)
chives, to garnish
For the filling
30ml/2 tbsp oil
1 garlic clove, crushed
225g/8oz roast pork, very finely chopped
2 spring onions (scallions), chopped
10ml/2 tsp yellow bean sauce,
  crushed
10ml/2 tsp sugar
5ml/1 tsp cornflour (cornstarch)
  mixed to a paste with water

1 Make the dough. In a small bowl,
dissolve the sugar in half the water.
Sprinkle in the yeast. Stir well, then
leave for 10–15 minutes until frothy. Sift
the flour and salt into a bowl and rub
in the lard. Stir in the yeast mixture with
enough of the remaining water to make
a soft dough. Knead on a floured
surface for 10 minutes. Transfer to an
oiled bowl and cover. Leave in a warm
place for 1 hour until doubled in bulk.

2 Meanwhile, make the filling. Heat the
oil and fry the garlic until golden. Add
the pork, spring onions, sauce and sugar.
Stir in the cornflour paste and cook,
stirring, until thickened. Leave to cool.

3 Knock back (punch down) the
dough. Knead it for 2 minutes, then
divide into 16 pieces. Roll out each
piece on a floured work surface to a
7.5–10cm/ 3–4in round.

4 Place a spoonful of filling in the
centre of each, gather up the sides and
twist the top to seal. Secure with string.

5 Set the buns on baking parchment
in a large steamer and leave in a warm
place until they have doubled in size.
Steam over rapidly boiling water for
30–35 minutes. Serve hot, garnished
with chives.

CRISPY SHANGHAI SPRING ROLLS

IT IS SAID THAT THESE FAMOUS SNACKS WERE TRADITIONALLY SERVED WITH TEA WHEN VISITORS CAME TO CALL AFTER THE CHINESE NEW YEAR. AS THIS WAS SPRINGTIME, THEY CAME TO BE KNOWN AS SPRING ROLLS. BUY FRESH OR FROZEN SPRING ROLL WRAPPERS FROM ASIAN STORES.

MAKES TWELVE

INGREDIENTS
    12 spring roll wrappers, thawed
      if frozen
    30ml/2 tbsp plain (all-purpose) flour
      mixed to a paste with water
    sunflower oil, for deep frying
For the filling
    6 Chinese dried mushrooms, soaked
      for 30 minutes in warm water
    150g/5oz fresh firm tofu
    30ml/2 tbsp sunflower oil
    225g/8oz finely minced (ground) pork
    225g/8oz peeled cooked prawns
      (shrimp), roughly chopped
    2.5ml/½ tsp cornflour (cornstarch),
      mixed to a paste with 15ml/1 tbsp
      light soy sauce
    75g/3oz each shredded bamboo shoot
      or grated carrot, sliced water
      chestnuts and bean sprouts
    6 spring onions (scallions) or 1 young
      leek, finely chopped
    a little sesame oil
For the dipping sauce
    100ml/3½ fl oz/scant ½ cup
      light soy sauce
    15ml/1 tbsp chilli sauce or finely
      chopped fresh red chilli
    a little sesame oil
    rice vinegar, to taste

1 Make the filling. Drain the mushrooms. Cut off and discard the stems and slice the caps finely. Cut the tofu into slices of a similar size.

2 Heat the oil in a wok and stir-fry the pork for 2–3 minutes or until the colour changes. Add the prawns, cornflour paste and bamboo shoot or carrot. Stir in the water chestnuts.

COOK'S TIP
Thaw frozen spring roll wrappers at room temperature. Separate with a palette knife (metal spatula). Cover with a damp cloth until needed.

3 Increase the heat, add the bean sprouts and spring onions or leek and toss for 1 minute. Stir in the mushrooms and tofu. Off the heat, season, then stir in the sesame oil. Cool quickly on a large platter.

4 Separate the spring roll wrappers (see Cook's Tip). Place a wrapper on the work surface with one corner nearest you. Spoon some of the filling near the centre of the wrapper and fold the nearest corner over the filling. Smear a little of the flour paste on the free sides, turn the sides to the middle and roll up. Repeat this procedure with the remaining wrappers and filling.

5 Deep fry the spring rolls in batches in oil heated to 190°C/375°F until they are crisp and golden. Drain on kitchen paper and serve at once with the dipping sauce, made by mixing all the ingredients in a bowl.

VIETNAMESE RICE PAPER ROLLS

RICE PAPER WRAPPERS COME IN SMALL AND LARGE ROUNDS AND CAN BE BOUGHT FROM ASIAN
SUPERMARKETS. THEY SOFTEN WHEN BRUSHED WITH WARM WATER, BUT THEY ARE VERY BRITTLE SO
MUST BE HANDLED WITH CARE. CASUALTIES CAN BE USED FOR PATCHING OTHER PAPERS.

SERVES EIGHT

INGREDIENTS
    2 litres/3½ pints/8 cups water
    1 small onion, sliced
    a few fresh coriander (cilantro) stems
    30ml/2 tbsp fish sauce
    225g/8oz piece belly pork, boned
        and rind removed
    50g/2oz fine rice vermicelli
    225g/8oz/4 cups beansprouts, rinsed
        and drained
    8 crisp lettuce leaves, halved
    fresh mint and coriander
        (cilantro) leaves
    175g/6oz peeled cooked prawns
        (shrimp), thawed if frozen
    16 large rice papers
    ground black pepper
For the black bean sauce
    15–30ml/1–2 tbsp groundnut
        (peanut) oil
    2 garlic cloves, crushed
    1 fresh red chilli, seeded
        and sliced
    60–75ml/4–5 tbsp canned black
        salted beans
    30ml/2 tbsp fish sauce
    5ml/1 tsp rice vinegar
    10–15ml/2–3 tsp light brown sugar
    15ml/1 tbsp crunchy peanut butter
    15ml/1 tbsp sesame seeds, dry fried
    5ml/1 tsp sesame oil
    90ml/6 tbsp fish, pork or
        chicken stock

1 Mix the water, onion, coriander and fish sauce in a large pan. Bring to the boil. Add the pork and boil for 20–30 minutes, turning the pork from time to time until it is tender when tested with a skewer. Lift the pork from the pan, leave to cool, then slice it into thin strips.

2 Make the sauce. Heat the groundnut oil in a frying pan and fry the garlic and chilli for 1 minute. Stir in all the remaining ingredients, mix well, then transfer to a food processor and process briefly. Pour into a serving bowl and leave to cool.

3 Soak the rice vermicelli in warm water until softened. Drain well, then snip into neat lengths. Bring a pan of water to the boil and add the vermicelli. As soon as the water boils again, after about 1 minute, drain the noodles, rinse them under cold water, then drain them again. Put them in a serving bowl. Put the beansprouts in a separate dish, and arrange the lettuce and herb leaves on a platter. Put the prawns in a bowl.

4 When almost ready to serve place the rice papers two at a time on a dish towel and brush both sides with warm water to soften them.

5 Transfer two rice papers very carefully to each of eight individual serving plates. Each guest places a piece of lettuce on a rice paper wrapper at the end closest to them, topping it with some of the noodles and beansprouts, a few mint or coriander leaves and some strips of pork.

6 Roll up one turn and then place a few prawns on the open part of the wrapper. Continue rolling to make a neat parcel. The roll can be cut in half, if preferred, then it is dipped in the black bean sauce before being eaten. The second wrapper is filled and eaten in the same way.

THAI SPRING ROLLS

CRUNCHY SPRING ROLLS ARE AS POPULAR IN THAILAND AS THEY ARE IN CHINA. THAIS FILL THEIR VERSION WITH A DELICIOUS GARLIC, PORK AND NOODLE MIXTURE.

MAKES ABOUT TWENTY-FOUR

INGREDIENTS
24 × 15cm/6in square spring
   roll wrappers
30ml/2 tbsp plain (all-purpose)
   flour
vegetable oil, for deep frying
Thai sweet chilli dipping sauce,
   to serve (optional)
For the filling
4–6 Chinese dried mushrooms,
   soaked for 30 minutes in warm
   water to cover
50g/2oz cellophane noodles
30ml/2 tbsp vegetable oil
2 garlic cloves, chopped
2 fresh red chillies, seeded
   and chopped
225g/8oz minced (ground) pork
50g/2oz peeled cooked prawns
   (shrimp), thawed if frozen
30ml/2 tbsp nam pla (fish sauce)
5ml/1 tsp sugar
1 carrot, grated
50g/2oz drained canned bamboo
   shoots, chopped
50g/2oz/1 cup beansprouts
2 spring onions, finely chopped
15ml/1 tbsp chopped fresh
   coriander (cilantro)
ground black pepper

1 Drain the mushrooms. Cut off the stems and discard; chop the caps finely.

2 Place the noodles in a large bowl, cover with boiling water and soak for 10 minutes. Drain the noodles and snip them into 5cm/2in lengths.

3 Heat the oil in a wok, add the garlic and chillies and stir-fry for 30 seconds. Transfer to a plate, add the pork and cook, stirring, until it has browned.

4 Add the noodles, mushrooms and prawns. Stir in the nam pla and sugar, then add pepper to taste.

5 Tip the noodle mixture into a bowl and stir in the carrot, bamboo shoots, beansprouts, spring onions and chopped coriander together with the reserved chilli mixture.

6 Unwrap the spring roll wrappers. Cover them with a dampened dishtowel while you are making the rolls, so that they do not dry out. Put the flour in a small bowl and stir in a little water to make a paste. Place a spoonful of filling in the centre of a spring roll wrapper.

7 Turn the bottom edge over to cover the filling, then fold in the left and right sides. Roll the wrapper up almost to the top then brush the top edge with the flour paste and seal. Fill the remaining wrappers in the same way.

8 Heat the oil in a wok or deep-fryer. Fry the spring rolls, a few at a time, until crisp and golden brown. Drain on kitchen paper and keep hot while cooking successive batches. Serve hot with Thai sweet chilli sauce, if you like.

COOK'S TIP
Nam pla is made from anchovies, which are salted, then fermented in wooden barrels. The sauce accentuates the flavour of food, and does not necessarily impart a fishy flavour.

CHA GIO AND NUOC CHAM

CHINESE SPRING ROLL WRAPPERS ARE USED HERE INSTEAD OF THE RICE PAPERS TRADITIONALLY USED IN VIETNAM. CHA GIO IS AN IMMENSELY POPULAR SNACK — THE VEGETABLE CONTENT OF THE FILLING CAN BE VARIED AS LONG AS THE FLAVOURS ARE COMPLEMENTARY.

MAKES FIFTEEN

INGREDIENTS
  25g/1oz cellophane noodles soaked
    for 10 minutes in hot water
    to cover
  6–8 dried wood ears, soaked for
    30 minutes in warm water to cover
  225g/8oz minced (ground) pork
  225g/8oz fresh or canned crab meat
  4 spring onions (scallions), trimmed
    and finely chopped
  5ml/1 tsp fish sauce
  flour and water paste, to seal
  250g/9oz packet spring roll wrappers
  vegetable oil, for deep frying
  salt and ground black pepper
For the *nuoc cham* sauce
  2 fresh red chillies, seeded and
    pounded to a paste
  2 garlic cloves, crushed
  15ml/1 tbsp sugar
  45ml/3 tbsp fish sauce
  juice of 1 lime or 1/2 lemon

1 Make the *nuoc cham* sauce by mixing the chillies, garlic, sugar and fish sauce in a bowl and stirring in lime or lemon juice to taste. Drain the noodles and snip into 2.5cm/1in lengths. Drain the wood ears, trim away any rough stems and slice the wood ears finely.

COOK'S TIP
Serve the rolls Vietnamese-style by wrapping each roll in a lettuce leaf with a few sprigs of fresh mint and coriander (cilantro) and a stick of cucumber.

2 Mix the noodles and the wood ears with the pork and set aside. Remove any cartilage from the crab meat and add to the pork mixture with the spring onions and fish sauce. Season to taste, mixing well.

3 Place a spring roll wrapper in front of you, diamond-fashion. Spoon some mixture just below the centre, fold over the nearest point and roll once.

4 Fold in the sides to enclose, then brush the edges with flour paste and roll up to seal. Repeat with the remaining wrappers and filling.

5 Heat the oil in a wok or deep fryer to 190°C/375°F. Deep fry the rolls in batches for 8–10 minutes or until they are cooked through. Drain them well on kitchen paper and serve hot. To eat, dip the rolls in the *nuoc cham* sauce.

RICE TRIANGLES

PICNICS ARE VERY POPULAR IN JAPAN AND RICE SHAPES — ONIGIRI — ARE IDEAL PICNIC FARE.
YOU CAN PUT ANYTHING YOU LIKE IN THE RICE, SO YOU COULD INVENT YOUR OWN ONIGIRI.

SERVES FOUR

INGREDIENTS
    1 salmon steak
    15ml/1 tbsp salt
    450g/1lb/4 cups freshly cooked
      sushi rice
    4 umeboshi (plum pickles)
    1/2 sheet yaki-nori seaweed, cut into
      four equal strips
    white and black sesame seeds,
      for sprinkling

1 Grill the salmon steak for 4–5
minutes on each side, until the flesh
flakes easily when it is tested with the
tip of a sharp knife. Set aside to cool
while you make other *onigiri*. When the
salmon is cold, flake it, discarding any
skin and bones.

2 Put the salt in a bowl. Spoon a
quarter of the warm cooked rice into
a small rice bowl. Make a hole in the
middle of the rice and put in one
umeboshi. Smooth the rice over to cover.

3 Wet the palms of both hands with
cold water, then rub the salt evenly on
to your palms.

4 Empty the rice and umeboshi from
the bowl on to one hand. Use both
hands to shape the rice into a triangular
shape, using firm but not heavy
pressure. Make three more rice
triangles in the same way.

5 Mix the flaked salmon into the
remaining rice, then shape it into
triangles as before.

6 Wrap a strip of yaki-nori around each
of the umeboshi triangles. Sprinkle
sesame seeds on the salmon triangles.

COOK'S TIP
Always use warm rice for the triangles.
Allow them to cool completely and wrap
each in foil or clear film (plastic wrap).

RICE BALLS <u>WITH</u> FOUR FILLINGS

ONIGIRI, THE JAPANESE NAME FOR THIS DISH, MEANS HAND-MOULDED RICE. JAPANESE RICE IS IDEAL FOR MAKING RICE BALLS, WHICH ARE FILLED HERE WITH SALMON, MACKEREL, UMEBOSHI AND OLIVES. THE NORI COATING MAKES THEM EASY TO PICK UP WITH YOUR FINGERS.

SERVES FOUR

INGREDIENTS

- 50g/2oz salmon fillet, skinned
- 3 umeboshi, 50g/2oz in total weight
- 45ml/3 tbsp sesame seeds
- 2.5ml/½ tsp mirin
- 50g/2oz smoked mackerel fillet
- 2 nori sheets, each cut into
    8 strips
- 6 pitted black olives, wiped and
    finely chopped
- fine salt
- Japanese pickles, to serve

For the rice

- 450g/1lb/2¼ cups Japanese
    short grain rice
- 550ml/18fl oz/2½ cups water

1 To cook the rice, wash it thoroughly with cold water. Drain and put into a heavy pan. Pour in the water and leave for 30 minutes. Put the lid on tightly and bring the pan to the boil. Reduce the heat and simmer for 12 minutes. When you hear a crackling noise remove from the heat and leave to stand, covered, for about 15 minutes.

2 Stir carefully with a dampened rice paddle or wooden spatula to aerate the rice. Leave to cool for 30 minutes while you prepare the fillings. Thoroughly salt the salmon fillet and leave for at least 30 minutes.

3 Stone (pit) the umeboshi. With the back of a fork, mash them slightly. Mix with 15ml/1 tbsp of the sesame seeds and the mirin to make a rough paste.

4 Wash the salt from the salmon. Grill (broil) the salmon and smoked mackerel under a high heat. Using a fork, remove the skin and divide the fish into loose, chunky flakes. Keep the salmon and mackerel pieces separate.

5 Toast the remaining sesame seeds in a dry frying pan over a low heat until they start to pop.

6 Check the temperature of the rice. It should be still quite warm but not hot. To start moulding, you need a teacup and a bowl of cold water to wet your hands. Put the teacup and tablespoons for measuring into the water. Put fine salt into a small dish. Wipe a chopping board with a very wet dishtowel. Wash your hands thoroughly with unperfumed soap and dry.

7 Remove the teacup from the bowl and shake off excess water. Scoop about 30ml/2 tbsp rice into the teacup. With your fingers, make a well in the centre of the rice and put in a quarter of the salmon flakes. Cover the salmon with another 15ml/1 tbsp rice. Press well.

8 Wet your hands and sprinkle them with a pinch of salt. Rub it all over your palms. Turn the rice in the teacup out into one hand and squeeze the rice shape with both hands to make a densely packed flat ball.

9 Wrap the rice ball with a nori strip. Put on to the chopping board. Make three more balls using the remaining salmon, then make four balls using the smoked mackerel and another four balls using the umeboshi paste.

10 Scoop about 45ml/3 tbsp rice into the teacup. Mix in a quarter of the chopped olives. Press the rice with your fingers. Wet your hands with water and rub with a pinch of salt and a quarter of the toasted sesame seeds. Hold the teacup in one hand and shape the rice mixture into a ball as above. The sesame seeds should stick to the rice. This time, do not wrap with nori. Repeat, making three more balls.

11 Serve one of each kind of rice ball on individual plates with a small helping of Japanese pickles.

SIMPLE ROLLED SUSHI

THESE SIMPLE ROLLS, KNOWN AS HOSOMAKI, ARE AN EXCELLENT WAY OF LEARNING THE ART OF ROLLING SUSHI. THEY ARE VERY GOOD FOR PICNICS AND CANAPÉS AND ARE ALWAYS SERVED COLD. YOU WILL NEED A BAMBOO MAT (MAKISU) FOR THE ROLLING PROCESS.

MAKES TWELVE ROLLS

INGREDIENTS

400g/14oz/2 cups sushi rice, soaked
  for 20 minutes in water to cover
55ml/3½ tbsp rice vinegar
15ml/1 tbsp sugar
2.5ml/½ tsp salt
6 sheets yaki-nori seaweed
200g/7oz tuna, in one piece
200g/7oz salmon, in one piece
wasabi paste
½ cucumber, quartered lengthways
  and seeded
pickled ginger, to garnish (optional)
Japanese soy sauce, to serve

1 Drain the rice, then put in a pan with 525ml/18fl oz/2¼ cups water. Bring to the boil, then lower the heat, cover and simmer for 20 minutes, or until all the liquid has been absorbed. Meanwhile, heat the vinegar, sugar and salt, stir well and cool. Add to the hot rice, then remove the pan from the heat and allow to stand (covered) for 20 minutes.

2 Cut the yaki-nori sheets in half lengthways. Cut the tuna and salmon into four long sticks, each about the same length as the long side of the yaki-nori, and about 1cm/½in square if viewed from the side.

3 Place a sheet of yaki-nori, shiny side down, on a bamboo mat. Divide the rice into 12 portions. Spread one portion over the yaki-nori, leaving a 1cm/½ in clear space at the top and bottom.

4 Spread a little wasabi paste in a horizontal line along the middle of the rice and lay one or two sticks of tuna on this.

5 Holding the mat and the edge of the yaki-nori nearest to you, roll up the yaki-nori and rice into a cylinder with the tuna in the middle. Use the mat as a guide – do not roll it into the food. Roll the rice tightly so that it sticks together and encloses the filling firmly.

6 Carefully roll the sushi off the mat. Make 11 more rolls in the same way, four for each filling ingredient, but do not use wasabi with the cucumber. Use a wet knife to cut each roll into six slices and stand them on a platter. Garnish with pickled ginger, if you wish, and serve with soy sauce.

FIRECRACKERS

IT'S EASY TO SEE HOW THESE PASTRY-WRAPPED PRAWN SNACKS GOT THEIR NAME (KRATHAK IN THAI)
— AS WELL AS RESEMBLING FIREWORKS, THEIR CONTENTS EXPLODE WITH FLAVOUR.

3 Place a wonton wrapper on the work surface at an angle so that it forms a diamond shape, then fold the top corner over so that the point is in the centre. Place a prawn, slits down, on the wrapper, with the tail projecting from the folded end, then fold the bottom corner over the other end of the prawn.

4 Fold each side of the wrapper over in turn to make a tightly folded roll. Tie a noodle in a bow around the roll and set it aside. Repeat with the remaining prawns and wrappers.

5 Heat the oil in a deep-fryer or wok to 190°C/375°F or until a cube of bread, added to the oil, browns in 45 seconds. Fry the prawns, a few at a time, for 5–8 minutes, until golden brown and cooked through. Drain well on kitchen paper and keep hot while you cook the remaining batches.

COOK'S TIP
Soak the fine egg noodles used as ties for the prawn rolls in a bowl of boiling water for 2–3 minutes, until softened, then drain, refresh under cold running water and drain well again.

MAKES SIXTEEN

INGREDIENTS
  16 large, raw king prawns (jumbo
    shrimp), heads and shells removed
    but tails left on
  5ml/1 tsp red curry paste
  15ml/1 tbsp Thai fish sauce
  16 small wonton wrappers, about
    8cm/3¼ in square, thawed if frozen
  16 fine egg noodles, soaked
    (see Cook's Tip)
  oil, for deep-frying

1 Place the prawns on their sides and cut two slits through the underbelly of each, one about 1cm/½ in from the head end and the other about 1cm/½ in from the first cut, cutting across the prawn. This will prevent the prawns from curling when they are cooked.

2 Mix the curry paste with the fish sauce in a shallow dish. Add the prawns and turn them in the mixture until they are well coated. Cover and leave to marinate for 10 minutes.

FILIPINO PRAWN FRITTERS

UKOY ARE A FAVOURITE SNACK OR APPETIZER. UNUSUALLY, THEY ARE FIRST SHALLOW FRIED, THEN DEEP FRIED. THEY ARE BEST EATEN FRESH FROM THE PAN, FIRST DIPPED IN THE PIQUANT SAUCE.

4 Peel and grate the sweet potato using the large holes on a grater, and add it to the batter, then stir in the crushed garlic and the drained beansprouts.

5 Pour the oil for shallow frying into a large frying pan. It should be about 5mm/¼in deep. Pour more oil into a wok for deep frying. Heat the oil in the frying pan. Taking a generous spoonful of the batter, drop it carefully into the frying pan so that it forms a fritter, about the size of a large drop scone.

6 Make more fritters in the same way. As soon as the fritters have set, top each one with a single prawn and a few chopped spring onions. Continue to cook over a medium heat for 1 minute, then remove with a fish slice (metal spatula).

SERVES TWO TO FOUR

INGREDIENTS
    16 raw prawns (shrimp) in the shell
    225g/8oz/2 cups plain
      (all-purpose) flour
    5ml/1 tsp baking powder
    2.5ml/½ tsp salt
    1 egg, beaten
    1 small sweet potato
    1 garlic clove, crushed
    115g/4oz/2 cups beansprouts,
      soaked in cold water and
      well drained
    vegetable oil, for shallow and
      deep frying
    4 spring onions (scallions), chopped
For the dipping sauce
    1 garlic clove, sliced
    45ml/3 tbsp rice or wine vinegar
    15–30ml/1–2 tbsp water
    salt, to taste
    6–8 small red chillies

1 Mix together all the ingredients for the dipping sauce and divide between two small bowls.

2 Put the whole prawns in a pan with water to cover. Bring to the boil, then simmer for 4–5 minutes or until the prawns are pink and tender. Lift the prawns from the pan with a slotted spoon. Discard the heads and the body shell, but leave the tails on. Strain and reserve the cooking liquid. Allow to cool.

3 Sift the flour, baking powder and salt into a bowl. Add the beaten egg and about 300ml/½ pint/1¼ cups of the prawn stock to make a batter that has the consistency of thick cream.

VARIATION
Use cooked tiger prawns if you prefer. In this case, make the batter using fish stock or chicken stock.

7 Heat the oil in the wok to 190°C/ 375°F and deep fry the prawn fritters in batches until they are crisp and golden brown. Drain the fritters on absorbent kitchen paper and then arrange on a serving plate or platter. Offer a bowl of the sauce for dipping.

PRAWN AND SESAME TOASTS

THESE ATTRACTIVE LITTLE TOAST TRIANGLES ARE IDEAL FOR SERVING WITH PRE-DINNER DRINKS AND ARE ALWAYS A FAVOURITE HOT SNACK AT PARTIES. THEY ARE SURPRISINGLY EASY TO PREPARE AND YOU CAN COOK THEM IN JUST A FEW MINUTES.

SERVES FOUR

INGREDIENTS

225g/8oz peeled raw prawns (shrimp)
15ml/1 tbsp sherry
15ml/1 tbsp soy sauce
30ml/2 tbsp cornflour (cornstarch)
2 egg whites
4 slices white bread
115g/4oz/½ cup sesame seeds
oil, for deep-frying
sweet chilli sauce,
   to serve

1 Process the prawns, sherry, soy sauce and cornflour in a food processor.

2 In a grease-free bowl, whisk the egg whites until stiff. Fold them into the prawn and cornflour mixture.

3 Cut each slice of bread into four triangular quarters. Spread out the sesame seeds on a large plate. Spread the prawn paste over one side of each bread triangle, then press the coated sides into the sesame seeds so that they stick and cover the prawn paste.

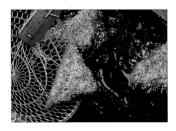

4 Heat the oil in a wok or deep-fryer, to 190°C/375°F or until a cube of bread, added to the oil, browns in about 45 seconds. Add the toasts, a few at a time, prawn side down, and deep-fry for 2–3 minutes, then turn and fry on the other side until golden.

5 Drain on kitchen paper and serve hot with sweet chilli sauce.

SASHIMI MORIAWASE

THE ARRANGEMENT OF A DISH OF SASHIMI IS AS IMPORTANT AS THE FRESHNESS OF THE FISH. CHOOSE TWO TO FIVE KINDS OF FISH FROM EACH GROUP AND ONLY USE THE FRESHEST CATCH OF THE DAY.

SERVES FOUR

INGREDIENTS
500g/1¼lb total of fish from
   the 4 groups
Group A
   skinned fillets, cut lengthways
      if possible
   Maguro akami: lean tuna
   Maguro toro: fatty tuna
   Sake: salmon
   Kajiki: swordfish
   Tai: sea bream or red snapper
   Suzuki: sea bass
   Hamachi: yellowtail
   Katsuo: skipjack tuna
Group B
   skinned fillets
   Hirame: flounder or sole
   Karei: halibut or turbot
Group C
   Ika: squid body, cleaned, boned
      and skinned
   Tako: cooked octopus tentacles
   Hotate-gai: scallop, the coral, black
      stomach and frill removed
Group D
   Aka-ebi: sweet prawns (shrimp),
      peeled, heads can be removed,
      tails intact
   Uni: sea urchin
   Ikura: salted salmon roe
To serve
   1 fresh mooli (daikon), peeled and
      cut into 6cm/2½in lengths
   1 Japanese or salad cucumber
   4 shiso leaves
   2 limes, halved (optional)
   45ml/3 tbsp wasabi paste from
      a tube, or the same amount of
      wasabi powder mixed with 20ml/
      4 tsp water
   1 bottle tamari shoyu

1 Make the tsuma (the mooli strands). Slice the mooli pieces thinly lengthways, then cut the slices into very thin strips lengthways. Rinse under running water, drain and put in the refrigerator.

2 Prepare the cucumber. Trim and cut into 3cm/1¼in lengths, then cut each cucumber cylinder in half lengthways.

3 Place the cucumber on a chopping board, flat-side down. Make very fine cuts across each piece, leaving the slices joined together at one side. Then, gently squeeze the cucumber together between your fingers so that the slices fan out sideways. Set them aside and cover with clear film (plastic wrap).

4 Slice the fish. Group A needs hira giri, a thick cut. Trim the fillet into a long rectangular shape. With the fish skin side up, cut into 1cm/½in thick slices, cutting in the direction of the grain.

5 Group B needs usu zukuri, very thin slices. Place the fillet horizontally to you on its skinned side. Hold the knife almost horizontally to the fillet, shave it very thinly across the grain.

6 Group C fish each require different cutting styles. Slice the cooked octopus diagonally into 5mm/¼in thick ovals. Slice the scallops in half horizontally. If they are thicker than 4cm/1¼in, slice them into three.

7 Cut open the squid body and turn to lie on its skinned side, horizontally to you. Score lines 5mm/¼in apart over the surface, then cut into 5mm/¼in strips. Group D is all ready to arrange.

8 Arrange the sashimi creatively. First, take a handful of mooli and heap up on to the serving plate a large mound or several small mounds. Then, base your design on the following basic rules. Group A and C: Put each slice of fish side by side like domino pieces. You can lay them on a shiso leaf. Group B: Use the thin, soft slices to make a rose shape, or overlap the slices slightly, so that the texture of the plate can be seen through them. Group D: Place the prawns by their tails, 2 or 3 at a time, in a bundle. If the sea urchins come tightly packed in a little box, try to get them out in one piece. The salmon roe can be heaped on thin cucumber slices or scooped into a lime case, made from a half lime, flesh removed. Fill the case with some mooli and place the roe on top.

9 Arrange the cucumber fans, heaped wasabi paste and shiso leaves to perfect your design. Serve immediately. Pour some shoyu into four dishes and mix in the wasabi. As the sauce is quite salty, only dip the edge of the sashimi into it.

HAND-MOULDED SUSHI

IF YOU HAVE ACCESS TO QUALITY SEAFOOD AT THE PEAK OF FRESHNESS, THIS IS A WONDERFUL WAY OF APPRECIATING ITS SUPERB NATURAL FLAVOUR.

SERVES FOUR

INGREDIENTS

400g/14oz/2 cups Japanese short
   grain rice, soaked for 20 minutes
   in water to cover
500ml/18fl oz/2½ cups water
55ml/3½ tbsp rice vinegar, plus
   extra for moulding
30ml/2 tbsp caster (superfine) sugar
10ml/2 tsp salt
4 raw king prawns (jumbo shrimp),
   head and shell removed, tails intact
4 scallops, white muscle only
425g/15oz assorted very fresh fish,
   such as salmon, tuna, sea bass
   and mackerel, skinned, cleaned
   and filleted
45ml/3 tbsp wasabi paste from
   a tube, or the same amount of
   wasabi powder mixed with 15ml/
   1 tbsp water
pickled ginger, to garnish
shoyu (Japanese soy sauce), to serve

1 Drain the rice, then put it in a pan with the measured water. Bring to the boil, then reduce the heat, cover and simmer for 20 minutes, until all the water has been absorbed. Meanwhile, heat the vinegar, sugar and salt in a pan, stir well and cool. Fold into the hot rice, then remove the pan from the heat, cover and leave to stand for 20 minutes.

2 Insert a bamboo skewer or cocktail stick (toothpick) into each prawn lengthways. This stops the prawns curling up when cooked. Boil them in lightly salted water for 2 minutes, or until they turn pink. Drain and cool, then pull out the skewers. Cut open from the belly side but do not slice in two. With the point of a sharp knife, remove the black vein running down the back. Open each prawn out flat and place on a tray.

3 Slice the scallops horizontally in half, but not quite through. Gently open each scallop at this "hinge" to make a butterfly shape. Place on the tray, cut side down. Use a sharp knife to cut all the fish fillets into 7.5 x 4cm/3 x 1½in pieces, 5mm/¼in thick. Place all the raw fish and shellfish on the tray, cover with clear film (plastic wrap), then chill in the refrigerator for at least 1 hour, or up to 4 hours.

4 Spoon the vinegared rice into a bowl. Have ready a small bowl filled with water acidulated with rice vinegar for moulding (see Cook's Tip). Take the tray of seafood from the refrigerator.

5 Wet your hand with the vinegared water and scoop about 25ml/1½ tbsp vinegared rice into your palm. Gently but firmly grip it to make a rectangular block. Do not squash the rice, but ensure that the grains stick together. The size of the blocks must be smaller than the toppings.

6 Put the rice block on a damp chopping board. Taking a piece of salmon topping in your palm, rub a little wasabi paste in the middle of it. Put the rice block on top of the salmon and gently press it. Form your palm into a cup and shape the topped rice to a smooth-surfaced mound. Place it on a serving tray. Work quickly, or the warmth of your hands may cause the salmon to lose its freshness.

7 Repeat this process until all of the rice and toppings are used. Serve immediately with a little shoyu dribbled on individual plates. To eat, pick up a hand-moulded sushi and dip the tip into the shoyu. Eat a little pickled ginger between tasting different sushi to refresh your mouth and prepare yourself for a new flavour sensation.

COOK'S TIP
For moulding the vinegared rice, wet your fingers frequently, by dipping them in a bowl containing a mixture of 150ml/¼ pint/⅔ cup water and 15ml/1 tbsp rice vinegar.

APPETIZERS

Kebabs served with a dipping sauce are popular appetizers

in many Asian countries, including Indonesia, Japan and

Thailand. Other classic Thai appetizers include corn fritters,

rice cakes with spicy dipping sauce, stuffed omelettes, and

fish cakes served with cucumber relish and Thai beer.

All these and more can be tried in your own kitchen.

SON-IN-LAW EGGS

*THE FASCINATING NAME FOR THIS DISH COMES FROM A STORY ABOUT A PROSPECTIVE BRIDEGROOM
WHO VERY MUCH WANTED TO IMPRESS HIS FUTURE MOTHER-IN-LAW AND DEVISED A NEW RECIPE
BASED ON THE ONLY DISH HE KNEW HOW TO MAKE — BOILED EGGS.*

SERVES FOUR TO SIX

INGREDIENTS
   30ml/2 tbsp vegetable oil
   6 shallots, thinly sliced
   6 garlic cloves, thinly sliced
   6 fresh red chillies, sliced
   oil, for deep-frying
   6 hard-boiled eggs, shelled
   salad leaves, to serve
   sprigs of fresh coriander (cilantro),
    to garnish
For the sauce
   75g/3oz/6 tbsp palm sugar or light
    muscovado (brown) sugar
   75ml/5 tbsp Thai fish sauce
   90ml/6 tbsp tamarind juice

COOK'S TIP
The level of heat varies, depending on
which type of chillies are used and
whether you include the seeds.

1 Make the sauce. Put the sugar, fish
sauce and tamarind juice in a pan.
Bring to the boil, stirring until the sugar
dissolves, lower the heat and simmer for
5 minutes. Taste and add more sugar,
fish sauce or tamarind juice, if needed.
Transfer the sauce to a bowl.

2 Heat the vegetable oil in a frying pan
and cook the shallots, garlic and chillies
for 5 minutes. Transfer to a bowl.

3 Heat the oil in a deep-fryer or wok to
190°C/375°F or until a cube of bread,
added to the oil, browns in about
45 seconds. Deep-fry the eggs in the
hot oil for 3–5 minutes, until golden
brown. Remove and drain well on
kitchen paper. Cut the eggs in quarters
and arrange them on a bed of leaves.
Drizzle with the sauce and sprinkle
over the shallot mixture. Garnish with
coriander sprigs and serve immediately.

CORN FRITTERS

*SOMETIMES IT IS THE SIMPLEST DISHES THAT TASTE THE BEST. THESE FRITTERS, PACKED WITH
CRUNCHY CORN, ARE VERY EASY TO PREPARE AND UNDERSTANDABLY POPULAR.*

MAKES TWELVE

INGREDIENTS

3 corn cobs, total weight about
  250g/9oz
1 garlic clove, crushed
small bunch fresh coriander
  (cilantro), chopped
1 small fresh red or green chilli,
  seeded and finely chopped
1 spring onion (scallion),
  finely chopped
15ml/1 tbsp soy sauce
75g/3oz/¾ cup rice flour or plain
  (all-purpose) flour
2 eggs, lightly beaten
60ml/4 tbsp water
oil, for shallow frying
salt and ground black pepper
sweet chilli sauce, to serve

1 Using a sharp knife, slice the kernels
from the cobs and place them in a
large bowl. Add the garlic, chopped
coriander, red or green chilli, spring
onion, soy sauce, flour, beaten eggs and
water and mix well. Season with salt
and pepper to taste and mix again. The
mixture should be firm enough to hold
its shape, but not stiff.

2 Heat the oil in a large frying pan. Add
spoonfuls of the corn mixture, gently
spreading each one out with the back
of the spoon to make a roundish fritter.
Cook for 1–2 minutes on each side.

3 Drain on kitchen paper and keep hot
while frying more fritters in the same
way. Serve hot with sweet chilli sauce.

Chicken and Vegetable Bundles

These delicious dim sum are extremely easy to prepare in your own kitchen and make popular snacks to serve at any time.

3 Remove and discard the mushroom stalks, then cut each cap in half (or in slices if very large). Cut the carrot and courgette into eight batons, each about 5cm/2in long, then mix the mushroom halves and bamboo shoots together.

4 Bring a small pan of water to the boil. Add the leek and blanch until soft. Drain thoroughly, then slit the leek down its length. Separate each layer to give eight long strips.

5 Divide the marinated chicken into eight portions. Do the same with the vegetables. Wrap each strip of leek around a portion of chicken and vegetables to make eight neat bundles. Have ready a pan with about 5cm/2in boiling water and a steamer or a heatproof plate that will fit inside it on a metal trivet.

SERVES FOUR

INGREDIENTS
    4 skinless, boneless chicken thighs
    5ml/1 tsp cornflour (cornstarch)
    10ml/2 tsp dry sherry
    30ml/2 tbsp light soy sauce
    2.5ml/½ tsp salt
    large pinch of ground white pepper
    4 fresh shiitake mushrooms
    50g/2oz/½ cup sliced, drained,
       canned bamboo shoots
    1 small carrot
    1 small courgette (zucchini)
    1 leek, trimmed
    1.5ml/¼ tsp sesame oil

1 Cut each chicken thigh into eight strips. Place the strips in a bowl.

2 Add the cornflour, sherry and half the soy sauce to the chicken. Stir in the salt and pepper and mix well. Cover and marinate for 10 minutes.

6 Place the chicken and vegetable bundles in the steamer or on the plate. Place in the pan, cover and steam over a high heat for 12–15 minutes or until the filling is cooked. Meanwhile, mix the remaining soy sauce with the sesame oil and use as a sauce for the bundles.

MINI PHOENIX ROLLS

THESE ROLLS ARE IDEAL FOR SERVING AS SNACKS OR PARTY FOOD. THEY ARE EQUALLY DELICIOUS WHETHER THEY ARE SERVED HOT OR COLD.

SERVES FOUR

INGREDIENTS
  2 large eggs, plus 1 egg white
  75ml/5 tbsp cold water
  5ml/1 tsp vegetable oil
  175g/6oz lean pork, diced
  75g/3oz/½ cup drained, canned
    water chestnuts
  5cm/2in piece of fresh root ginger,
    grated
  4 dried Chinese mushrooms, soaked
    in hot water until soft
  15ml/1 tbsp dry sherry
  1.5ml/¼ tsp salt
  large pinch of ground white pepper
  30ml/2 tbsp rice vinegar
  2.5ml/½ tsp caster (superfine) sugar
  fresh coriander (cilantro) or flat leaf
    parsley, to garnish

1 Beat the 2 whole eggs with 45ml/ 3 tbsp of the water. Heat a 20cm/8in non-stick omelette pan and brush with a little of the oil. Pour in a quarter of the egg mixture, swirling the pan to coat the base lightly. Cook the omelette until the top is set. Slide it on to a plate and make three more omelettes.

2 Mix the pork and water chestnuts in a food processor. Add 5ml/1 tsp of the root ginger. Drain the mushrooms, chop the caps roughly and add these to the mixture. Process until smooth.

3 Scrape the pork paste into a bowl. Stir in the egg white, sherry, remaining water, salt and pepper. Mix thoroughly, cover and leave in cool place for about 15 minutes.

4 Have ready a pan with about 5cm/2in boiling water and a large heatproof plate that will fit inside it on a metal trivet. Divide the pork mixture among the omelettes and spread into a large square shape in the centre of each of the omelettes.

5 Bring the sides of each omelette over the filling and roll up from the bottom to the top. Arrange the rolls on the plate. Cover the plate tightly with foil and place it in the pan on the trivet. Steam over a high heat for 15 minutes.

6 Make a dipping sauce by mixing the remaining ginger with the rice vinegar and sugar in a small dish. Cut the rolls diagonally in 1cm/½in slices, garnish with the coriander or flat leaf parsley leaves and serve with the sauce.

COOK'S TIP
These rolls can be prepared a day in advance and kept in the refrigerator. They can be steamed before serving.

CHICKEN SATAY WITH PEANUT SAUCE

THESE MINIATURE KEBABS ARE POPULAR ALL OVER SOUTH-EAST ASIA, AND THEY ARE ESPECIALLY DELICIOUS WHEN COOKED ON A BARBECUE. THE PEANUT DIPPING SAUCE IS A PERFECT PARTNER FOR THE MARINATED CHICKEN.

SERVES FOUR

INGREDIENTS
4 skinless, boneless chicken
   breast portions
For the marinade
   2 garlic cloves, crushed
   2.5cm/1in piece fresh root ginger,
      finely grated
   10ml/2 tsp Thai fish sauce
   30ml/2 tbsp light soy sauce
   15ml/1 tbsp clear honey
For the satay sauce
   90ml/6 tbsp crunchy peanut butter
   1 fresh red chilli, seeded and
      finely chopped
   juice of 1 lime
   60ml/4 tbsp coconut milk
   salt

1 First, make the satay sauce. Put all the ingredients in a food processor or blender. Process until smooth, then check the seasoning and add more salt or lime juice if necessary. Spoon the sauce into a bowl, cover with clear film (plastic wrap) and set aside.

2 Using a sharp knife, slice each chicken breast portion into four long strips. Put all the marinade ingredients in a large bowl and mix well, then add the chicken strips and toss together until thoroughly coated. Cover and leave for at least 30 minutes in the refrigerator to marinate. Meanwhile, soak 16 wooden satay sticks or kebab skewers in water, to prevent them from burning during cooking.

3 Preheat the grill (broiler) to high or prepare the barbecue. Drain the satay sticks or skewers. Drain the chicken strips. Thread one strip on to each satay stick or skewer. Grill (broil) for 3 minutes on each side, or until the chicken is golden brown and cooked through. Serve immediately with the satay sauce.

YAKITORI CHICKEN

THESE ARE JAPANESE-STYLE KEBABS. THEY ARE EASY TO EAT AND IDEAL FOR BARBECUES OR PARTIES.
MAKE EXTRA YAKITORI SAUCE IF YOU WOULD LIKE TO SERVE IT WITH THE KEBABS.

SERVES FOUR

INGREDIENTS
6 boneless chicken thighs
bunch of spring onions (scallions)
shichimi (seven-flavour spice),
    to serve (optional)
For the yakitori sauce
150ml/¼ pint/⅔ cup Japanese
    soy sauce
90g/3½oz/scant ½ cup sugar
25ml/1½ tbsp sake or dry
    white wine
15ml/1 tbsp plain (all-purpose)
    flour

3 Cut the spring onions into 3cm/
1¼in pieces. Preheat the grill or light
the barbecue.

4 Thread the chicken and spring
onions alternately on to the drained
skewers. Grill under medium heat
or cook on the barbecue, brushing
generously several times with the sauce.
Allow 5–10 minutes, until the chicken
is cooked but still moist.

5 Serve with a little extra yakitori
sauce, offering shichimi with the kebabs
if available.

COOK'S TIP
Paprika can be used instead of shichimi,
if that is difficult to obtain.

1 Soak 12 bamboo skewers in water
for at least 30 minutes to prevent them
from scorching under the grill (broiler).
Make the sauce. Stir the soy sauce,
sugar and sake or wine into the flour
in a small pan and bring to the boil,
stirring. Lower the heat and simmer the
mixture for 10 minutes, until the sauce
is reduced by one-third. Set aside.

2 Cut each chicken thigh into bitesize
pieces and set aside.

LETTUCE PARCELS

KNOWN AS SANG CHOY IN HONG KONG, THIS IS A POPULAR "ASSEMBLE-IT-YOURSELF" TREAT. THE FILLING — AN IMAGINATIVE BLEND OF TEXTURES AND FLAVOURS — IS SERVED WITH CRISP LETTUCE LEAVES, WHICH ARE USED AS WRAPPERS.

SERVES SIX

INGREDIENTS

2 chicken breast fillets, total weight
  about 350g/12oz
4 Chinese dried mushrooms, soaked
  for 30 minutes in warm water
  to cover
30ml/2 tbsp vegetable oil
2 garlic cloves, crushed
6 drained canned water chestnuts,
  thinly sliced
30ml/2 tbsp light soy sauce
5ml/1 tsp Sichuan peppercorns,
  dry fried and crushed
4 spring onions (scallions),
  finely chopped
5ml/1 tsp sesame oil
vegetable oil, for deep frying
50g/2oz cellophane noodles
salt and ground black pepper
1 crisp lettuce and 60ml/4 tbsp
  hoisin sauce, to serve

1 Remove the skin from the chicken fillets, pat dry and set aside. Chop the chicken into thin strips. Drain the soaked mushrooms. Cut off and discard the mushroom stems; slice the caps finely and set aside.

2 Heat the oil in a wok or large frying pan. Add the garlic, then add the chicken and stir-fry until the pieces are cooked through and no longer pink.

3 Add the sliced mushrooms, water chestnuts, soy sauce and peppercorns. Toss for 2–3 minutes, then season, if needed. Stir in half of the spring onions, then the sesame oil. Remove from the heat and set aside.

4 Heat the oil for deep frying to 190ºC/375ºF. Cut the chicken skin into strips, deep fry until very crisp and drain on kitchen paper. Add the noodles to the hot oil, deep fry until crisp. Transfer to a plate lined with kitchen paper.

5 Crush the noodles and put in a serving dish. Top with the chicken skin, chicken mixture and the remaining spring onions. Wash the lettuce leaves, pat dry and arrange on a large platter.

6 Toss the chicken and noodles to mix. Invite guests to take one or two lettuce leaves, spread the inside with hoisin sauce and add a spoonful of filling, turning in the sides of the leaves and rolling them into a parcel. The parcels are traditionally eaten in the hand.

DRUNKEN CHICKEN

AS THE CHICKEN IS MARINATED FOR SEVERAL DAYS, IT IS IMPORTANT TO USE A VERY FRESH BIRD FROM A REPUTABLE SUPPLIER. "DRUNKEN" FOODS ARE USUALLY SERVED COLD AS PART OF AN APPETIZER, OR CUT INTO NEAT PIECES AND SERVED AS A SNACK WITH COCKTAILS.

SERVES FOUR TO SIX

INGREDIENTS
1 chicken, about 1.4kg/3lb
1cm/¹/₂in piece of fresh root ginger,
    peeled and thinly sliced
2 spring onions (scallions), trimmed
1.75 litres/3 pints/7¹/₂ cups water or
    to cover
15ml/1 tbsp salt
300ml/¹/₂ pint/1¹/₄ cups dry sherry
15–30ml/1–2 tbsp brandy (optional)
spring onions (scallions), shredded,
    and fresh herbs, to garnish

4 Arrange the chicken portions in a shallow dish. Rub salt into the chicken and cover with clear film (plastic wrap). Leave in a cool place for several hours or overnight in the refrigerator.

VARIATION
To serve as a cocktail snack, take the meat off the bones, cut it into bitesize pieces, then spear each piece on a cocktail stick.

5 Later, lift off any fat from the stock. Mix the sherry and brandy, if using, in a jug, add the stock and pour over the chicken. Cover again and leave in the refrigerator to marinate for 2 or 3 days, turning occasionally.

6 When ready to serve, cut the chicken through the bone into chunky pieces and arrange on a serving platter garnished with spring onion shreds and herbs.

1 Rinse and dry the chicken inside and out. Place the ginger and spring onions in the body cavity. Put the chicken in a large pan or flameproof casserole and just cover with water. Bring to the boil, skim and cook for 15 minutes.

2 Turn off the heat, cover the pan or casserole tightly and leave the chicken in the cooking liquid for 3–4 hours, by which time it will be cooked. Drain well. Pour 300ml/¹/₂ pint/1¹/₄ cups of the stock into a jug (pitcher). Freeze the remaining stock for use in the future.

3 Remove the skin from the chicken, joint it neatly. Divide each leg into a drumstick and thigh. Make two more portions from the wings and some of the breast. Finally cut away the remainder of the breast pieces (still on the bone) and divide each breast into two even-size portions.

LAMB SATÉ

THESE TASTY LAMB SKEWERS ARE TRADITIONALLY SERVED WITH DAINTY DIAMOND-SHAPED PIECES OF COMPRESSED RICE, WHICH ARE SURPRISINGLY SIMPLE TO MAKE. OFFER THE REMAINING SAUCE FOR DIPPING.

MAKES TWENTY-FIVE TO THIRTY SKEWERS

INGREDIENTS

  1kg/2¼lb leg of lamb, boned
  3 garlic cloves, crushed
  15–30ml/1–2 tbsp chilli sambal or
    5–10ml/1–2 tsp chilli powder
  90ml/6 tbsp dark soy sauce
  juice of 1 lemon
  salt and ground black pepper
  groundnut (peanut) or sunflower oil,
    for brushing
For the sauce
  6 garlic cloves, crushed
  15ml/1 tbsp chilli sambal or
    2–3 fresh chillies, seeded and
    ground to a paste
  90ml/6 tbsp dark soy sauce
  25ml/1½ tbsp lemon juice
  30ml/2 tbsp boiling water
To serve
  thinly sliced onion
  cucumber wedges (optional)
  compressed-rice shapes (see
    Cook's Tip)

1 Cut the lamb into neat 1cm/½in cubes. Remove any pieces of gristle, but do not trim off any of the fat because this keeps the meat moist during cooking and enhances the flavour. Spread out the lamb cubes in a single layer in a shallow bowl.

2 Put the garlic, chilli sambal or chilli powder, soy sauce and lemon juice in a mortar. Add salt and pepper and grind to a paste. Alternatively, process the mixture using a food processor. Pour over the lamb and mix to coat. Cover and leave in a cool place for at least 1 hour. Soak wooden or bamboo skewers in water to prevent them from scorching during cooking.

3 Prepare the sauce. Put the garlic into a bowl. Add the chilli sambal or fresh chillies, soy sauce, lemon juice and boiling water. Stir well. Preheat the grill. Thread the meat on to the skewers. Brush the skewered meat with oil and grill, turning often. Brush the saté with a little of the sauce and serve hot, with onion, cucumber wedges, if using, rice shapes and the sauce.

COOK'S TIP

Compressed rice shapes are easy to make. Cook two 115g/4oz packets if boil-in-the-bag rice in a large pan of salted, boiling water and simmer for 1¼ hours until the cooked rice fills each bag like a plump cushion. The bags must be covered with water throughout; use a saucer or plate to weigh them down. Let the bags cool completely before slitting them and removing the slabs of cooked rice. With a sharp, wetted knife, cut each rice slab horizontally in half, then into diamond shapes.

RICE CAKES <u>WITH</u> SPICY DIPPING SAUCE

A CLASSIC THAI APPETIZER, THESE RICE CAKES ARE EASY TO MAKE AND WILL KEEP ALMOST INDEFINITELY IN AN AIRTIGHT CONTAINER. START MAKING THEM AT LEAST A DAY BEFORE YOU PLAN TO SERVE THEM, AS THE RICE NEEDS TO DRY OUT OVERNIGHT.

SERVES FOUR TO SIX

INGREDIENTS
    175g/6oz/1 cup Thai jasmine rice
    350ml/12fl oz/1½ cups water
    oil, for deep-frying and greasing
For the spicy dipping sauce
    6–8 dried chillies
    2.5ml/½ tsp salt
    2 shallots, chopped
    2 garlic cloves, chopped
    4 coriander (cilantro) roots
    10 white peppercorns
    250ml/8fl oz/1 cup coconut milk
    5ml/1 tsp shrimp paste
    115g/4oz minced (ground) pork
    115g/4oz cherry tomatoes, chopped
    15ml/1 tbsp Thai fish sauce
    15ml/1 tbsp palm sugar or light
        muscovado (brown) sugar
    30ml/2 tbsp tamarind juice (tamarind
        paste mixed with warm water)
    30ml/2 tbsp coarsely chopped
        roasted peanuts
    2 spring onions (scallions), chopped

1 Make the sauce. Snap off the stems of the chillies, shake out the seeds and soak the chillies in warm water for 20 minutes. Drain and put in a mortar. Sprinkle over the salt and crush. Add the shallots, garlic, coriander and peppercorns. Pound to a coarse paste.

2 Pour the coconut milk into a pan and bring to the boil. When it begins to separate, stir in the pounded chilli paste. Cook for 2–3 minutes, until the mixture is fragrant. Stir in the shrimp paste and cook for 1 minute more.

3 Add the pork, stirring to break up any lumps. Cook for 5–10 minutes, then stir in the tomatoes, fish sauce, palm sugar and tamarind juice. Simmer, stirring occasionally, until the sauce thickens, then stir in the chopped peanuts and spring onions. Remove the sauce from the heat and leave to cool.

4 Preheat the oven to the lowest setting. Grease a baking sheet. Wash the rice in several changes of water. Put it in a pan, add the water and cover tightly. Bring to the boil, reduce the heat and simmer gently for about 15 minutes.

5 Remove the lid and fluff up the rice. Spoon it on to the baking sheet and press it down with the back of a spoon. Leave in the oven to dry out overnight.

6 Break the rice into bitesize pieces. Heat the oil in a wok or deep-fryer. Deep-fry the rice cakes, in batches, for about 1 minute, until they puff up but are not browned. Remove and drain well. Serve with the dipping sauce.

CRISPY PORK BALLS

THESE CRISPY BALLS TAKE A LITTLE TIME TO PREPARE, BUT MAKE A DELICIOUS PARTY FOOD AND LOOK GOOD ON THE TABLE, TOO.

SERVES FOUR TO SIX

INGREDIENTS

4 slices of white bread, crusts removed
5ml/1 tsp olive oil
225g/8oz skinless, boneless pork
  meat, roughly chopped
50g/2oz/⅓ cup drained, canned
  water chestnuts
2 fresh red chillies, seeded and
  roughly chopped
1 egg white
10g/¼oz/¼ cup fresh coriander
  (cilantro) leaves
5ml/1 tsp cornflour (cornstarch)
2.5ml/½ tsp salt
1.5ml/¼ tsp ground white pepper
30ml/2 tbsp light soy sauce
5ml/1 tsp caster (superfine) sugar
30ml/2 tbsp rice vinegar
2.5ml/½ tsp chilli oil
shredded red chillies and fresh
  coriander (cilantro) sprigs

1 Preheat the oven to 120°C/250°F/ Gas ½. Brush the bread slices with olive oil and cut them into 5mm/¼in cubes. Spread over a baking sheet and bake for 15 minutes until dry and crisp.

2 Meanwhile, mix together the pork meat, water chestnuts and chillies in a food processor. Process until a coarse paste is formed.

3 Add the egg white, coriander leaves, cornflour, salt and pepper. Pour in half the soy sauce and process for about 30 seconds. Scrape into a bowl, cover and leave in a cool place for 20 minutes.

4 Remove the toasted bread cubes from the oven and set them aside. Raise the oven temperature to 200°C/400°F/Gas 6. With dampened hands, divide the pork mixture into 12 portions and form into balls.

5 Roughly crush the toasted bread cubes, then transfer to a plate. Roll each ball in turn over the toasted crumbs until coated. Place on a baking sheet and bake for about 20 minutes or until the coating is brown and the pork filling has cooked through.

6 In a small bowl, mix the remaining soy sauce with the caster sugar, rice vinegar and chilli oil. Serve the sauce with the pork balls, garnished with shredded chillies and coriander sprigs.

VARIATION
Chicken can be used instead of pork, with equally delicious results.

STUFFED CHILLIES

*THIS DISH IS NOT AS FIERY AS YOU MIGHT EXPECT, AND WILL LOOK PARTICULARLY PRETTY ON THE
PARTY TABLE. DO GIVE IT A TRY.*

SERVES FOUR TO SIX

INGREDIENTS

    10 fat fresh green chillies
    115g/4oz lean pork, roughly chopped
    75g/3oz raw tiger prawns (shrimp),
      peeled and deveined
    15g/½oz/½ cup fresh coriander
      (cilantro) leaves
    5ml/1 tsp cornflour (cornstarch)
    10ml/2 tsp dry sherry
    10ml/2 tsp soy sauce
    5ml/1 tsp sesame oil
    2.5ml/½ tsp salt
    15ml/1 tbsp cold water
    1 fresh red and 1 fresh green chilli,
      seeded and sliced into rings, and
      cooked peas, to garnish

1 Cut the chillies in half lengthways,
keeping the stalks intact. Scrape out
and discard the seeds and set the
chillies aside.

2 Mix together the pork, prawns and
coriander leaves in a food processor.
Process until smooth. Scrape into a bowl
and mix in the cornflour, sherry, soy
sauce, sesame oil, salt and water. Cover
and leave to marinate for 10 minutes.

3 Fill each half chilli with some of the
meat mixture. Have ready a steamer or
a heatproof plate and a pan with about
5cm/2in boiling water.

4 Place the stuffed chillies in the
steamer or on a plate, meat side up,
and cover with a lid or foil. Steam
steadily for 15 minutes or until the meat
filling is cooked. Serve immediately,
garnished with the chilli rings and peas.

POPIAH

POPIAH ARE THE STRAITS CHINESE OR NONYA VERSION OF THE SPRING ROLL. DO NOT BE PUT OFF BY THE NUMBER OF INGREDIENTS; IT TAKES A LITTLE TIME TO GET EVERYTHING TOGETHER BUT ONCE IT IS ALL ON THE TABLE THE COOK CAN RETIRE AS GUESTS ASSEMBLE THEIR OWN.

MAKES ABOUT TWENTY-FOUR PANCAKES

INGREDIENTS
40g/1½oz/⅓ cup cornflour
  (cornstarch)
215g/7½oz/generous 1¾ cups plain
  (all-purpose) flour
salt
450ml/¾ pint/scant 2 cups
  water
6 eggs, beaten
lard or white cooking fat,
  for frying
For the cooked filling
30ml/2 tbsp vegetable oil
1 onion, finely chopped
2 garlic cloves, crushed
115g/4oz cooked pork, chopped
115g/4oz crab meat or peeled cooked
  prawns (shrimp), thawed if frozen
115g/4oz drained canned bamboo
  shoot, thinly sliced
1 small yam bean, peeled and grated
  or 12 drained canned water
  chestnuts, finely chopped
15–30ml/1–2 tbsp yellow
  salted beans
15ml/1 tbsp light soy sauce
ground black pepper
For the fresh fillings
2 hard-boiled eggs, chopped
2 Chinese sausages, steamed
  and sliced
115g/4oz packet fried tofu, each
  piece halved
225g/8oz/4 cups beansprouts
115g/4oz crab meat or peeled
  cooked prawns (shrimp)
½ cucumber, cut into matchsticks
small bunch of spring onions
  (scallions), finely chopped
20 lettuce leaves, rinsed and dried
fresh coriander (cilantro) sprigs,
  to garnish
selection of sauces, including bottled
  chopped chillies, bottled chopped
  garlic and hoisin sauce, to serve

COOK'S TIP
Yam beans are large tubers with a mild sweet texture similar to water chestnuts.

1 Sift the flours and salt into a bowl. Add the measured water and eggs and mix to a smooth batter.

2 Grease a heavy frying pan with lard. Heat the pan, pouring off any excess lard, then pour in just enough batter to cover the base.

3 As soon as it sets, flip and cook the other side. The pancakes should be quite thin. Repeat with the remaining batter to make 20–24 pancakes in all. Pile the cooked pancakes on top of each other, with a layer of baking parchment between each to prevent them sticking. Wrap in foil and keep warm in a low oven.

4 Make the cooked filling. Heat the oil in a wok and stir-fry the onion and garlic for 5 minutes until softened but not browned. Add the pork, crab meat or prawns, bamboo shoot and grated yam bean or water chestnuts. Stir-fry the mixture over a medium heat for 2–3 minutes.

5 Add the salted yellow beans and soy sauce to the wok, with pepper to taste. Cover and cook gently for 15–20 minutes, adding a little water if the mixture starts to dry out. Spoon into a serving bowl and allow to cool.

6 Meanwhile, arrange the chopped hard-boiled eggs, sliced Chinese sausages, sliced tofu, beansprouts, crab meat or prawns, cucumber, spring onions and lettuce leaves in piles on a large platter or in separate bowls. Spoon the bottled chopped chillies, bottled chopped garlic and hoisin into small bowls.

7 Each person makes up his or her own popiah by spreading a very small amount of chopped chilli, garlic or hoisin sauce on a pancake, adding a lettuce leaf, a little of the cooked filling and a small selection of the fresh ingredients. The pancake wrapper should not be over-filled.

8 The ends can be tucked in and the pancake rolled up in typical spring roll fashion, then eaten in the hand. They also look attractive simply rolled with the filling showing. The popiah can be filled and rolled before guests arrive, in which case, garnish with sprigs of coriander. It is more fun though for everyone to fill and roll their own.

STUFFED THAI OMELETTES

THAI FOOD OFTEN CLEVERLY COMBINES HOT CHILLI WITH SWEET FLAVOURS, AS IN THE FILLING FOR THE OMELETTES. IT MAKES AN INTERESTING CONTRAST TO THE DELICATE FLAVOUR OF THE EGG.

SERVES FOUR

INGREDIENTS
30ml/2 tbsp groundnut
(peanut) oil
2 garlic cloves, finely chopped
1 small onion, finely chopped
225g/8oz minced (ground) pork
30ml/2 tbsp Thai fish sauce
5ml/1 tsp granulated sugar
2 tomatoes, peeled and chopped
15ml/1 tbsp chopped fresh
coriander (cilantro)
ground black pepper
fresh coriander (cilantro)
sprigs and sliced fresh red
chillies, to garnish
For the omelettes
5 eggs
15ml/1 tbsp Thai fish sauce
30ml/2 tbsp groundnut
(peanut) oil

1 Heat the oil in a wok or frying pan, add the garlic and onion, and cook over a medium heat, stirring occasionally, for 3–4 minutes, until soft. Add the pork and cook for about 8 minutes, stirring frequently, until lightly browned.

2 Stir in the Thai fish sauce, sugar and tomatoes, season to taste with pepper and simmer over a low heat until slightly thickened. Mix in the fresh coriander. Remove the wok or frying pan from the heat, cover to keep warm and set aside while you make the omelettes.

3 To make the omelettes, put the eggs and Thai fish sauce in a bowl and beat together lightly with a fork.

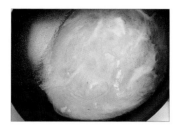

4 Heat 15ml/1 tbsp of the oil in an omelette pan or wok over a medium heat. When the oil is very hot, but not smoking, add half the beaten egg mixture and immediately tilt the pan or wok to spread the egg into a thin, even layer over the base. Cook over a medium heat until the omelette is just set and the underside is golden.

5 Spoon half the filling into the centre of the omelette. Fold into a neat square parcel by bringing the opposite sides of the omelette towards each other. Slide the parcel on to a serving dish, folded side down. Make another omelette parcel in the same way. Garnish with the coriander sprigs and chillies. Cut each omelette in half to serve.

ASSORTED TEMPURA

TEMPURA IS ONE OF JAPAN'S MOST FAMOUS AND DELICIOUS DISHES. FISH, RATHER THAN MEAT, IS TRADITIONALLY USED, BUT CHOOSE ANY VEGETABLE YOU LIKE. THE ESSENCE OF GOOD TEMPURA IS THAT IT SHOULD BE COOKED AND SERVED IMMEDIATELY.

SERVES FOUR TO SIX

INGREDIENTS
   1 small sweet potato, about
     115g/4oz
   8 large tiger prawns (shrimp)
   1 small squid, cleaned
   vegetable oil, for deep frying
   flour, for coating
   1 small carrot, cut into matchsticks
   4 shiitake mushrooms, stems
    removed
   50g/2oz French (green) beans
   1 red (bell) pepper, seeded and
    sliced into 2cm/3⁄4in thick strips
For the dip
   200ml/7fl oz/scant 1 cup water
   45ml/3 tbsp mirin (sweet rice wine)
   10g/1⁄4oz bonito flakes
   45ml/3 tbsp Japanese soy sauce
For the batter
   1 egg
   90ml/6 tbsp iced water
   75g/3oz/3⁄4 cup plain (all-purpose)
    flour
   2.5ml/1⁄2 tsp baking powder

2 Peel the prawns, leaving the tail shells intact, and de-vein. Lay a prawn on its side. Make three or four diagonal slits, about two-thirds of the way in towards the spine, leaving all the pieces attached. Repeat with the rest. Flatten with your fingers. Cut the body of the squid into 3cm/1 1⁄4in thick strips.

3 Put the egg in a large bowl, stir without beating and set half aside. Add the iced water, flour and baking powder. Stir two or three times, leaving some flour unblended.

4 Heat the oil in a deep fryer to 185°C/365°F. Dust the prawns lightly with flour. Holding each in turn by the tail, dip them into the batter, then carefully lower them into the hot oil; cook until golden. Fry the remaining prawns and the squid in the same way. Keep warm.

5 Reduce the temperature of the oil to 170°C/340°F. Drain the sweet potato and pat dry. Dip the vegetables into the batter and deep fry (see Cook's Tip). Drain well, then keep warm. As soon as all the tempura are ready, serve with the dip.

1 Mix the dip ingredients in a pan. Bring to the boil, cool, then strain. Divide among 4–6 bowls. Slice the unpeeled sweet potato thinly. Put in a bowl with cold water to cover.

COOK'S TIP
Batter and deep fry the carrots and beans in small bunches. The mushrooms look best if only the undersides are dipped. Cut a cross in the upper side of the mushroom cap, if you like.

FISH CAKES <u>WITH</u> CUCUMBER RELISH

THESE WONDERFUL SMALL FISH CAKES ARE A VERY FAMILIAR AND POPULAR APPETIZER IN THAILAND AND INCREASINGLY THROUGHOUT SOUTH-EAST ASIA. THEY ARE USUALLY SERVED WITH THAI BEER.

MAKES ABOUT TWELVE

INGREDIENTS
 5 kaffir lime leaves
 300g/11oz cod, cut into chunks
 30ml/2 tbsp red curry paste
 1 egg
 30ml/2 tbsp nam pla (fish sauce)
 5ml/1 tsp sugar
 30ml/2 tbsp cornflour (cornstarch)
 15ml/1 tbsp chopped fresh
  coriander (cilantro)
 50g/2oz green beans, finely sliced
 vegetable oil, for frying
 Chinese mustard cress,
  to garnish
For the cucumber relish
 60ml/4 tbsp coconut or rice vinegar
 50g/2oz/¼ cup sugar
 1 head pickled garlic
 15ml/1 tbsp fresh root ginger
 1 cucumber, cut into matchsticks
 4 shallots, finely sliced

1 Make the cucumber relish. Bring the vinegar and sugar to the boil in a small pan with 60ml/4 tbsp water, stirring until the sugar has dissolved. Remove from the heat and cool.

2 Separate the pickled garlic into cloves. Chop these finely along with the ginger and place in a bowl. Add the cucumber and shallots, pour over the vinegar mixture and mix lightly.

3 Reserve two kaffir lime leaves for garnish and thinly slice the remainder. Put the chunks of fish, curry paste and egg in a food processor and process to a smooth paste. Transfer the mixture to a bowl and stir in the nam pla, sugar, cornflour, sliced kaffir lime leaves, coriander and green beans. Mix well, then shape the mixture into about twelve 5mm/¼in thick cakes, measuring about 5cm/2in in diameter.

4 Heat the oil in a wok or deep-frying pan. Fry the fish cakes, a few at a time, for about 4–5 minutes until cooked and evenly brown.

5 Lift out the fish cakes and drain them on kitchen paper. Keep each batch hot while frying successive batches. Garnish with the reserved kaffir leaves and Chinese mustard cress. Serve with the cucumber relish.

SOFT-SHELL CRABS WITH CHILLI AND SALT

IF FRESH SOFT-SHELL CRABS ARE UNAVAILABLE, YOU CAN BUY FROZEN ONES IN ASIAN SUPERMARKETS.
ALLOW TWO SMALL CRABS PER SERVING, OR ONE IF THEY ARE LARGE. ADJUST THE QUANTITY OF
CHILLI ACCORDING TO YOUR TASTE.

SERVES FOUR

INGREDIENTS
8 small soft-shell crabs, thawed
   if frozen
50g/2oz/½ cup plain
   (all-purpose) flour
60ml/4 tbsp groundnut (peanut) or
   vegetable oil
2 large fresh red chillies, or 1 green
   and 1 red, seeded and thinly sliced
4 spring onions (scallions) or a small
   bunch of garlic chives, chopped
coarse sea salt and ground
   black pepper
To serve
   shredded lettuce, mooli (daikon)
      and carrot
   light soy sauce

1 Pat the crabs dry with kitchen paper.
Season the flour with pepper and coat
the crabs lightly with the mixture.

2 Heat the oil in a shallow pan until
very hot, then put in the crabs (you may
need to do this in two batches). Fry for
2–3 minutes on each side, until the
crabs are golden brown but still juicy
in the middle. Drain the cooked crabs
on kitchen paper and keep hot.

3 Add the sliced chillies and spring
onions or garlic chives to the oil
remaining in the pan and cook gently
for about 2 minutes. Sprinkle over a
generous pinch of salt, then spread
the mixture on to the crabs.

4 Mix the shredded lettuce, mooli and
carrot together. Arrange on plates, top
each portion with two crabs and serve,
with light soy sauce for dipping.

SOUPS

In many Asian countries, for example Japan, soups are served throughout or at the end of a meal, providing the palate with tastes and textures that complement or contrast with those in more dominant dishes. You may choose to serve any of these soups solo, as a light lunch or supper dish, or as a prelude to a dinner party, but however and whenever you place them before your guests, treats such as Cellophane Noodle Soup and Malaysian Prawn Laksa are certain to prove popular.

PUMPKIN AND COCONUT SOUP

THE NATURAL SWEETNESS OF THE PUMPKIN IS HEIGHTENED BY THE ADDITION OF A LITTLE SUGAR IN THIS LOVELY LOOKING SOUP, BUT THIS IS BALANCED BY THE CHILLIES, SHRIMP PASTE AND DRIED SHRIMP. COCONUT CREAM BLURS THE BOUNDARIES BEAUTIFULLY.

SERVES FOUR TO SIX

INGREDIENTS
450g/1lb pumpkin
2 garlic cloves, crushed
4 shallots, finely chopped
2.5ml/½ tsp shrimp paste
1 lemon grass stalk, chopped
2 fresh green chillies, seeded
15ml/1 tbsp dried shrimp soaked
   for 10 minutes in warm water
   to cover
600ml/1 pint/2½ cups
   chicken stock
600ml/1 pint/2½ cups
   coconut cream
30ml/2 tbsp Thai fish sauce
5ml/1 tsp granulated sugar
115g/4oz small cooked shelled
   prawns (shrimp)
salt and ground black pepper
To garnish
2 fresh red chillies, seeded and
   thinly sliced
10–12 fresh basil leaves

1 Peel the pumpkin and cut it into quarters with a sharp knife. Scoop out the seeds with a teaspoon and discard. Cut the flesh into chunks about 2cm/¾in thick and set aside.

2 Put the garlic, shallots, shrimp paste, lemon grass, green chillies and salt to taste in a mortar. Drain the dried shrimp, discarding the soaking liquid, and add them, then use a pestle to grind the mixture into a paste. Alternatively, place all the ingredients in a food processor and process to a paste.

3 Bring the chicken stock to the boil in a large pan. Add the ground paste and stir well to dissolve.

4 Add the pumpkin chunks and bring to a simmer. Simmer for 10–15 minutes, or until the pumpkin is tender.

5 Stir in the coconut cream, then bring the soup back to simmering point. Do not let it boil. Add the fish sauce, sugar and ground black pepper to taste.

6 Add the prawns and cook for a further 2–3 minutes, until they are heated through. Serve in warm soup bowls, garnished with chillies and basil leaves.

COOK'S TIP
Shrimp paste is made from ground shrimp fermented in brine.

OMELETTE SOUP

A VERY SATISFYING SOUP THAT IS QUICK AND EASY TO PREPARE. IT IS VERSATILE, TOO, IN THAT YOU CAN VARY THE VEGETABLES ACCORDING TO WHAT IS AVAILABLE.

SERVES FOUR

INGREDIENTS

  1 egg
  15ml/1 tbsp groundnut (peanut) oil
  900ml/1½ pints/3¾ cups
    vegetable stock
  2 large carrots, finely diced
  4 outer leaves Savoy
    cabbage, shredded
  30ml/2 tbsp soy sauce
  2.5ml/½ tsp granulated sugar
  2.5ml/½ tsp ground black pepper
  fresh coriander (cilantro) leaves,
    to garnish

VARIATION

Use pak choi (bok choy) instead of Savoy cabbage. In Thailand there are about forty different types of pak choi, including miniature versions.

1 Put the egg in a bowl and beat lightly with a fork. Heat the oil in a small frying pan until it is hot, but not smoking. Pour in the egg and swirl the pan so that it coats the base evenly. Cook over a medium heat until the omelette has set and the underside is golden. Slide it out of the pan and roll it up like a pancake. Slice into 5mm/¼in rounds and set aside for the garnish.

2 Put the stock into a large pan. Add the carrots and cabbage and bring to the boil. Reduce the heat and simmer for 5 minutes, then add the soy sauce, granulated sugar and pepper.

3 Stir well, then pour into warmed bowls. Lay a few omelette rounds on the surface of each portion and complete the garnish with the coriander leaves.

BALINESE VEGETABLE SOUP

THE BALINESE BASE THIS POPULAR SOUP ON BEANS, BUT ANY SEASONAL VEGETABLES CAN BE ADDED OR SUBSTITUTED. THE RECIPE ALSO INCLUDES SHRIMP PASTE, WHICH IS KNOWN LOCALLY AS TERASI.

2 Finely grind the chopped garlic, macadamia nuts or almonds, shrimp paste and the coriander seeds to a paste using a pestle and mortar or in a food processor.

SERVES EIGHT

INGREDIENTS
225g/8oz green beans
1.2 litres/2 pints/5 cups lightly
  salted water
1 garlic clove, roughly chopped
2 macadamia nuts or 4 almonds,
  finely chopped
1cm/½ in cube shrimp paste
10–15ml/2–3 tsp coriander seeds,
  dry fried
30ml/2 tbsp vegetable oil
1 onion, finely sliced
400ml/14fl oz can coconut milk
2 bay leaves
225g/8oz/4 cups beansprouts
8 thin lemon wedges
30ml/2 tbsp lemon juice
salt and ground black pepper

1 Trim the beans, then cut them into small pieces. Bring the lightly salted water to the boil, add the beans to the pan and cook for 3–4 minutes. Drain, reserving the cooking water. Set the beans aside.

COOK'S TIP
Dry fry the coriander seeds for about 2 minutes until the aroma is released.

3 Heat the oil in a wok, and fry the onion until transparent. Remove with a slotted spoon. Add the nut paste to the wok and fry it for 2 minutes without allowing it to brown.

4 Pour in the reserved vegetable water. Spoon off 45–60ml/3–4 tbsp of the cream from the top of the coconut milk and set it aside. Add the remaining coconut milk to the wok, bring to the boil and add the bay leaves. Cook, uncovered, for 15–20 minutes.

5 Just before serving, reserve a few beans, fried onions and beansprouts for garnish and stir the rest into the soup. Add the lemon wedges, reserved coconut cream, lemon juice and seasoning; stir well. Pour into individual soup bowls and serve, garnished with reserved beans, onion and beansprouts.

CELLOPHANE NOODLE SOUP

THE NOODLES USED IN THIS SOUP GO BY VARIOUS NAMES: GLASS NOODLES, CELLOPHANE NOODLES,
BEAN THREAD OR TRANSPARENT NOODLES. THEY ARE ESPECIALLY VALUED FOR THEIR BRITTLE TEXTURE.

SERVES FOUR

INGREDIENTS
   4 large dried shiitake mushrooms
   15g/½oz dried lily buds
   ½ cucumber, coarsely chopped
   2 garlic cloves, halved
   90g/3½oz white cabbage, chopped
   1.2 litres/2 pints/5 cups
     boiling water
   115g/4oz cellophane noodles
   30ml/2 tbsp soy sauce
   15ml/1 tbsp palm sugar or light
     muscovado (brown) sugar
   90g/3½oz block silken tofu, diced
   fresh coriander (cilantro) leaves,
     to garnish

1 Soak the shiitake mushrooms in warm water for 30 minutes. In a separate bowl, soak the dried lily buds in warm water, also for 30 minutes.

2 Meanwhile, put the cucumber, garlic and cabbage in a food processor and process to a smooth paste. Scrape the mixture into a large pan and add the measured boiling water.

3 Bring to the boil, then reduce the heat and cook for 2 minutes, stirring occasionally. Strain this stock into another pan, return to a low heat and bring to simmering point.

4 Drain the lily buds, rinse under cold running water, then drain again. Cut off any hard ends. Add the lily buds to the stock with the noodles, soy sauce and sugar and cook for 5 minutes more.

5 Strain the mushroom soaking liquid into the soup. Discard the mushroom stems, then slice the caps. Divide them and the tofu among four bowls. Pour the soup over, garnish and serve.

H O T <u>AND</u> S W E E T   V E G E T A B L E <u>AND</u> T O F U   S O U P

AN INTERESTING COMBINATION OF HOT, SWEET AND SOUR FLAVOURS THAT MAKES FOR A SOOTHING, NUTRITIOUS SOUP. IT TAKES ONLY MINUTES TO MAKE AS THE SPINACH AND SILKEN TOFU ARE SIMPLY PLACED IN BOWLS AND COVERED WITH THE FLAVOURED HOT STOCK.

SERVES FOUR

INGREDIENTS

  1.2 litres/2 pints/5 cups
    vegetable stock
  5–10ml/1–2 tsp Thai red
    curry paste
  2 kaffir lime leaves, torn
  40g/1½oz/3 tbsp palm sugar or light
    muscovado (brown) sugar
  30ml/2 tbsp soy sauce
  juice of 1 lime
  1 carrot, cut into thin batons
  50g/2oz baby spinach leaves, any
    coarse stalks removed
  225g/8oz block silken tofu, diced

1 Heat the stock in a large pan, then add the red curry paste. Stir constantly over a medium heat until the paste has dissolved. Add the lime leaves, sugar and soy sauce and bring to the boil.

2 Add the lime juice and carrot to the pan. Reduce the heat and simmer for 5–10 minutes. Place the spinach and tofu in four individual serving bowls and pour the hot stock on top to serve.

MIXED VEGETABLE SOUP

IN THAILAND, THIS TYPE OF SOUP IS USUALLY MADE IN LARGE QUANTITIES AND THEN REHEATED FOR CONSUMPTION OVER SEVERAL DAYS. IF YOU WOULD LIKE TO DO THE SAME, DOUBLE OR TREBLE THE QUANTITIES. CHILL LEFTOVER SOUP RAPIDLY AND REHEAT THOROUGHLY BEFORE SERVING.

SERVES FOUR

INGREDIENTS

   30ml/2 tbsp groundnut (peanut) oil
   15ml/1 tbsp magic paste (see
     Cook's Tip)
   90g/3½oz Savoy cabbage or
     Chinese leaves (Chinese cabbage),
     finely shredded
   90g/3½oz mooli (daikon),
     finely diced
   1 medium cauliflower,
     coarsely chopped
   4 celery sticks, coarsely chopped
   1.2 litres/2 pints/5 cups
     vegetable stock
   130g/4½oz fried tofu, cut into
     2.5cm/1in cubes
   5ml/1 tsp palm sugar or light
     muscovado (brown) sugar
   45ml/3 tbsp light soy sauce

1 Heat the groundnut oil in a large, heavy pan or wok. Add the magic paste and cook over a low heat, stirring frequently, until it gives off its aroma. Add the shredded Savoy cabbage or Chinese leaves, mooli, cauliflower and celery. Pour in the vegetable stock, increase the heat to medium and bring to the boil, stirring occasionally. Gently stir in the tofu cubes.

2 Add the sugar and soy sauce. Reduce the heat and simmer for 15 minutes, until the vegetables are cooked and tender. Taste and add a little more soy sauce if needed. Serve hot.

COOK'S TIP
Magic paste is a mixture of crushed garlic, white pepper and coriander (cilantro). Look for it at Thai markets.

MISO SOUP

THIS SOUP IS ONE OF THE MOST COMMONLY EATEN DISHES IN JAPAN, AND IT IS USUALLY SERVED WITH EVERY MEAL THAT INCLUDES RICE.

SERVES FOUR

INGREDIENTS
$^{1}/_{2}$ packet silken tofu, drained weight
about 150g/5oz
1 litre/1$^{3}/_{4}$ pints/4 cups freshly made
dashi (kombu and bonito stock) or
instant dashi
10g/$^{1}/_{4}$oz dried wakame seaweed
60ml/4 tbsp white or red miso paste
2 spring onions (scallions), shredded,
to garnish

COOK'S TIP
Reduce the heat when the stock boils, to
retain the delicate flavour of the soup.

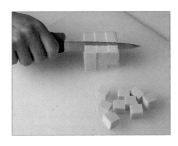

1 Cut the tofu into 1cm/$^{1}/_{2}$in cubes.
Bring the dashi to the boil, lower the
heat and add the wakame seaweed.
Simmer for 1–2 minutes.

2 Pour a little of the soup into a bowl
and add the miso paste, stirring until
it dissolves. Pour the mixture back into
the pan.

3 Add the tofu and heat through for
1 minute. Pour the soup into warmed
serving dishes and serve immediately,
garnished with the shredded spring
onions.

VARIATION
Wakame is a young, dark-coloured
seaweed that can be found dried and in
Japanese supermarkets. Nori seaweed
could be used instead.

SWEET ADUKI BEAN SOUP WITH RICE CAKES

DON'T ASSUME FROM THE WORD SOUP THAT THIS IS A SAVOURY DISH – ZENZAI IS ACTUALLY A CLASSIC AND POPULAR JAPANESE DESSERT, SERVED WITH THE READY-TO-EAT RICE CAKES (MOCHI) THAT ARE SOLD IN JAPANESE SUPERMARKETS. JAPANESE GREEN TEA MAKES A GOOD ACCOMPANIMENT.

SERVES FOUR

INGREDIENTS
165g/5$^{1}/_{2}$ oz/scant 1 cup dried
aduki beans
225g/8oz/1 cup sugar
pinch of salt
4 ready-to-eat rice cakes (mochi)

1 Put the aduki beans in a strainer,
wash them under cold running water,
then drain them and tip them into a
large pan. Add 1 litre/1$^{3}/_{4}$ pints/4 cups
water and bring to the boil. Drain the
aduki beans and return them to the
rinsed out pan.

2 Add a further 1.2 litres/2 pints/
5 cups water to the pan and bring to
the boil, then add a further 1.2 litres/
2 pints/5 cups water and bring to the
boil again. Lower the heat and simmer
for 30 minutes until the beans are soft.

3 Skim the surface of the broth
regularly to remove any scum, if left,
it would give the soup an unpleasant
bitter taste.

4 When the beans are soft enough to
be mashed between your fingers, add
half the sugar and simmer for a further
20 minutes.

5 Add the remaining sugar and the salt
to the pan, stirring until the sugar has
completely dissolved.

6 Heat the grill (broiler), then grill
(broil) both sides of the rice cakes until
softened, but not browned. Add the rice
cakes to the soup and bring to the boil.
Serve the soup immediately in deep
warmed bowls.

CRISPY WONTON SOUP

THE FRESHLY COOKED CRISP WONTONS ARE SUPPOSED TO SIZZLE AND "SING" IN THE HOT SOUP AS THEY ARE TAKEN TO THE TABLE.

2 Place the wonton wrappers under a slightly dampened dishtowel so that they do not dry out. Next, dampen the edges of a wonton wrapper. Place about 5ml/1 tsp of the filling in the centre of the wrapper. Gather it up like a purse and twist the top or roll up as you would a baby spring roll. Fill the remaining wontons in the same way.

3 Make the soup. Drain the wood ears, trim away any rough stems, then slice thinly. Bring the stock to the boil, add the ginger and the spring onions and simmer for 3 minutes. Add the sliced wood ears, shredded spring greens, bamboo shoots and soy sauce. Simmer for 10 minutes, then stir in the sesame oil. Season to taste with salt and pepper, cover and keep hot.

SERVES SIX

INGREDIENTS
  2 wood ears, soaked for 30 minutes
    in warm water to cover
  1.2 litres/2 pints/5 cups
    home-made chicken stock
  2.5cm/1in piece fresh root ginger,
    peeled and grated
  4 spring onions (scallions),
    chopped
  2 rich-green inner spring greens
    (collards) leaves, finely shredded
  50g/2oz drained canned bamboo
    shoots, sliced
  25ml/1½ tbsp dark soy sauce
  2.5ml/½ tsp sesame oil
  salt and ground black pepper
For the filled wontons
  5ml/1 tsp sesame oil
  ½ small onion, finely chopped
  10 drained canned water
    chestnuts, finely chopped
  115g/4oz finely minced (ground) pork
  24 wonton wrappers
  groundnut (peanut) oil, for frying

1 Make the filled wontons. Heat the sesame oil in a small pan, add the onion, water chestnuts and pork and fry, stirring occasionally, until the meat is no longer pink. Tip into a bowl, season to taste and leave to cool.

COOK'S TIP
The wontons can be filled up to two hours ahead. Place them in a single layer on a baking sheet dusted with cornflour (cornstarch) to prevent them from sticking and leave in a cool place.

4 Heat the oil in a wok to 190°C/375°F and fry the wontons, in batches if necessary, for 3–4 minutes or until they are crisp and golden brown all over. Ladle the soup into six warmed soup bowls and share the wontons among them. Serve immediately.

CHIANG MAI NOODLE SOUP

NOWADAYS A SIGNATURE DISH OF THE CITY OF CHIANG MAI, THIS DELICIOUS NOODLE SOUP ORIGINATED IN BURMA, NOW CALLED MYANMAR, WHICH LIES ONLY A LITTLE TO THE NORTH. IT IS ALSO THE THAI EQUIVALENT OF THE FAMOUS MALAYSIAN "LAKSA".

SERVES FOUR TO SIX

INGREDIENTS
    600ml/1 pint/2½ cups coconut milk
    30ml/2 tbsp Thai red curry paste
    5ml/1 tsp ground turmeric
    450g/1lb chicken thighs, boned and
        cut into bitesize chunks
    600ml/1 pint/2½ cups
        chicken stock
    60ml/4 tbsp Thai fish sauce
    15ml/1 tbsp dark soy sauce
    juice of ½–1 lime
    450g/1lb fresh egg noodles, blanched
        briefly in boiling water
    salt and ground black pepper
To garnish
    3 spring onions (scallions), chopped
    4 fresh red chillies, chopped
    4 shallots, chopped
    60ml/4 tbsp sliced pickled mustard
        leaves, rinsed
    30ml/2 tbsp fried sliced garlic
    coriander (cilantro) leaves
    4–6 fried noodle nests (optional)

1 Pour about one-third of the coconut milk into a large, heavy pan or wok. Bring to the boil over a medium heat, stirring frequently with a wooden spoon until the milk separates.

2 Add the curry paste and ground turmeric, stir to mix completely and cook until the mixture is fragrant.

3 Add the chunks of chicken and toss over the heat for about 2 minutes, making sure that all the chunks are thoroughly coated with the paste.

4 Add the remaining coconut milk, the chicken stock, fish sauce and soy sauce. Season with salt and pepper to taste. Bring to simmering point, stirring frequently, then lower the heat and cook gently for 7–10 minutes. Remove from the heat and stir in lime juice to taste.

5 Reheat the fresh egg noodles in boiling water, drain and divide among four to six warmed bowls. Divide the chunks of chicken among the bowls and ladle in the hot soup. Top each serving with spring onions, chillies, shallots, pickled mustard leaves, fried garlic, coriander leaves and a fried noodle nest, if using. Serve immediately.

HOT AND SOUR SOUP

ONE OF CHINA'S MOST POPULAR SOUPS, THIS IS FAMED FOR ITS CLEVER BALANCE OF FLAVOURS. THE "HOT" COMES FROM PEPPER; THE "SOUR" FROM VINEGAR. SIMILAR SOUPS ARE FOUND THROUGHOUT ASIA, SOME RELYING ON CHILLIES AND LIME JUICE TO PROVIDE THE ESSENTIAL FLAVOUR CONTRAST.

SERVES SIX

INGREDIENTS
    4–6 Chinese dried mushrooms
    2–3 small pieces of wood ear
      and a few golden needles (lily
      buds), optional
    115g/4oz pork fillet, cut into
      fine strips
    45ml/3 tbsp cornflour (cornstarch)
    150ml/¼ pint/⅔ cup water
    15–30ml/1–2 tbsp sunflower oil
    1 small onion, finely chopped
    1.5 litres/2½ pints/6¼ cups good
      quality beef or chicken stock, or
      2 × 300g/11oz cans consommé made
      up to the full quantity with water
    150g/5oz drained fresh firm tofu,
      diced
    60ml/4 tbsp rice vinegar
    15ml/1 tbsp light soy sauce
    1 egg, beaten
    5 ml/1 tsp sesame oil
    salt and ground white or black pepper
    2–3 spring onions (scallions),
      shredded, to garnish

1 Place the dried mushrooms in a bowl, with the pieces of wood ear and the golden needles, if using. Add sufficient warm water to cover and leave to soak for about 30 minutes. Drain the mushrooms, reserving the soaking water. Cut off and discard the mushroom stems and slice the caps finely. Trim away any tough stem from the wood ears, then chop them finely. Using kitchen string, tie the golden needles into a bundle.

2 Lightly dust the strips of pork fillet with some of the cornflour; mix the remaining cornflour to a smooth paste with the measured water.

3 Heat the oil in a wok or pan and fry the onion until soft. Increase the heat and fry the pork until it changes colour. Add the stock or consommé, mushrooms, soaking water, and wood ears and golden needles, if using. Bring to the boil, then simmer for 15 minutes.

4 Discard the golden needles, lower the heat and stir in the cornflour paste to thicken. Add the tofu, vinegar, soy sauce, and salt and pepper.

5 Bring the soup to just below boiling point, then drizzle in the beaten egg by letting it drop from a whisk (or to be authentic, the fingertips) so that it forms threads in the soup. Stir in the sesame oil and serve at once, garnished with spring onion shreds.

MISO SOUP ^{WITH} PORK ^{AND} VEGETABLES

THIS IS QUITE A RICH AND FILLING SOUP. ITS JAPANESE NAME, TANUKI JIRU, MEANS RACCOON SOUP FOR HUNTERS, BUT AS RACCOONS ARE NOT EATEN NOWADAYS, PORK IS NOW USED.

SERVES FOUR

INGREDIENTS

200g/7oz lean boneless pork
15cm/6in piece gobo or 1 parsnip
50g/2oz daikon
4 fresh shiitake mushrooms
½ konnyaku or ½ × 225–285g/
  8–10¼oz packet tofu
a little sesame oil, for stir-frying
600ml/1 pint/2½ cups second dashi
  stock, or the same amount of water
  and 10ml/2 tsp dashi-no-moto
70ml/4½ tbsp miso
2 spring onions (scallions), chopped
5ml/1 tsp sesame seeds

1 Press the meat down on a chopping board using the palm of your hand and slice horizontally into very thin long strips, then cut the strips crossways into stamp-size pieces. Set the pork aside.

2 Peel the gobo using a potato peeler, then cut diagonally into 1cm/½in thick slices. Quickly plunge the slices into a bowl of cold water to stop them discolouring. If you are using parsnip, peel, cut it in half lengthways, then cut it into 1cm/½in thick half-moon-shaped slices.

3 Peel and slice the daikon into 1.5cm/⅔in thick discs. Cut the discs into 1.5cm/⅔in cubes. Remove the shiitake stalks and cut the caps into quarters.

4 Place the konnyaku in a pan of boiling water and cook for 1 minute. Drain and cool. Cut in quarters lengthways, then crossways into 3mm/⅛in thick pieces.

5 Heat a little sesame oil in a heavy cast-iron or enamelled pan until purple smoke rises. Stir-fry the pork, then add the tofu, if using, the konnyaku and all the vegetables except for the spring onions. When the colour of the meat has changed, add the stock.

6 Bring to the boil over a medium heat, and skim off the foam until the soup looks fairly clear. Reduce the heat, cover, and simmer for 15 minutes.

7 Put the miso in a small bowl, and mix with 60ml/4 tbsp hot stock to make a smooth paste. Stir one-third of the miso into the soup. Taste and add more miso if required. Add the spring onion and remove from the heat. Serve very hot in individual soup bowls and sprinkle with sesame seeds.

GINGER, CHICKEN AND COCONUT SOUP

THIS AROMATIC SOUP IS RICH WITH COCONUT MILK AND INTENSELY FLAVOURED WITH GALANGAL, LEMON GRASS AND KAFFIR LIME LEAVES.

SERVES FOUR TO SIX

INGREDIENTS

4 lemon grass stalks, roots trimmed
2 × 400ml/14fl oz cans coconut milk
475ml/16fl oz/2 cups chicken stock
2.5cm/1in piece galangal, peeled and
   thinly sliced
10 black peppercorns, crushed
10 kaffir lime leaves, torn
300g/11oz chicken breast fillets,
   cut into thin strips
115g/4oz/1 cup button (white)
   mushrooms
50g/2oz/¹/₂ cup baby corn cobs,
   quartered lengthways
60ml/4 tbsp lime juice
45ml/3 tbsp nam pla (fish sauce)
chopped fresh red chillies, spring
   onions and fresh coriander (cilantro)
   leaves, to garnish

1 Cut off the lower 5cm/2in from each lemon grass stalk and chop it finely. Bruise the remaining pieces of stalk. Bring the coconut milk and chicken stock to the boil in a large pan. Add all the lemon grass, the galangal, peppercorns and half the lime leaves, lower the heat and simmer gently for 10 minutes. Strain into a clean pan.

2 Return the soup to the heat, then add the chicken, mushrooms and corn. Simmer for 5–7 minutes or until the chicken is cooked.

3 Stir in the lime juice and nam pla, then add the remaining lime leaves. Serve hot, garnished with chillies, spring onions and coriander.

HOT-AND-SOUR PRAWN SOUP

THIS IS A CLASSIC THAI SEAFOOD SOUP – TOM YAM KUNG – AND IT IS PROBABLY THE MOST POPULAR AND WELL-KNOWN SOUP FROM THAT COUNTRY.

SERVES FOUR TO SIX

INGREDIENTS

450g/1lb raw king prawns (jumbo
   shrimp), thawed if frozen
1 litre/1³/₄ pints/4 cups chicken
   stock or water
3 lemon grass stalks, root trimmed
10 kaffir lime leaves, torn in half
225g/8oz can straw mushrooms
45ml/3 tbsp nam pla (fish sauce)
60ml/4 tbsp lime juice
30ml/2 tbsp chopped spring onion
   (scallion)
15ml/1 tbsp fresh coriander
   (cilantro) leaves
4 fresh red chillies, seeded
   and thinly sliced
salt and ground black pepper

1 Shell the prawns, putting the shells in a colander. Devein and set aside.

2 Rinse the shells under cold water, then put in a large pan with the stock or water. Bring to the boil.

3 Bruise the lemon grass stalks and add them to the stock with half the lime leaves. Simmer gently for 5–6 minutes, until the stock is fragrant.

4 Strain the stock, return it to the clean pan and reheat. Add the drained mushrooms and the prawns, then cook until the prawns turn pink.

5 Stir in the nam pla, lime juice, spring onion, coriander, chillies and the remaining lime leaves. Taste and adjust the seasoning. The soup should be sour, salty, spicy and hot.

RICE PORRIDGE

ORIGINATING IN CHINA, THIS DISH HAS NOW SPREAD THROUGHOUT THE WHOLE OF SOUTH-EAST ASIA AND IS LOVED FOR ITS COMFORTING BLANDNESS. IT IS INVARIABLY SERVED WITH A FEW STRONGLY FLAVOURED ACCOMPANIMENTS.

2 Pour the stock into a large pan. Bring to the boil and add the rice. Season the minced pork. Add it by taking small teaspoons and tapping the spoon on the side of the pan so that the meat falls into the soup in small lumps.

3 Stir in the fish sauce and pickled garlic and simmer for 10 minutes, until the pork is cooked. Stir in the celery.

4 Serve the rice porridge in individual warmed bowls. Sprinkle the prepared garlic and shallots on top and season with plenty of ground pepper.

COOK'S TIP
Pickled garlic has a distinctive flavour and is available from Asian food stores.

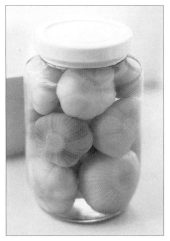

SERVES TWO

INGREDIENTS
   900ml/1½ pints/3¾ cups
    vegetable stock
   200g/7oz/1¾ cups cooked rice
   225g/8oz minced (ground) pork
   15ml/1 tbsp Thai fish sauce
   2 heads pickled garlic,
    finely chopped
   1 celery stick, finely diced
   salt and ground black pepper
To garnish
   30ml/2 tbsp groundnut (peanut) oil
   4 garlic cloves, thinly sliced
   4 small red shallots, finely sliced

1 Make the garnishes by heating the groundnut oil in a frying pan and cooking the garlic and shallots over a low heat until brown. Drain on kitchen paper and reserve for the soup.

Tomato and Beef Soup

Fresh tomatoes and spring onions give this light beef broth a superb flavour. It is quick and easy to make, and ideal as an appetizer or light lunch.

SERVES FOUR

INGREDIENTS

   75g/3oz rump (round) steak
   900ml/1½ pints/3¾ cups beef stock
   30ml/2 tbsp tomato purée (paste)
   6 tomatoes, halved, seeded and
    chopped
   10ml/2 tsp caster (superfine) sugar
   15ml/1 tbsp cornflour (cornstarch)
   15ml/1 tbsp cold water
   1 egg white
   2.5ml/½ tsp sesame oil
   2 spring onions (scallions),
    finely shredded
   salt and ground black pepper

3 Mix the cornflour to a paste with the water. Add the mixture to the soup, stirring constantly until it thickens slightly. Lightly beat the egg white in a cup.

4 Pour the egg white into the soup, stirring. When the egg white changes colour, season, stir and pour the soup into heated bowls. Drizzle with sesame oil and sprinkle with spring onions.

1 Cut the beef into thin strips and place in a pan. Pour over boiling water to cover. Cook for 2 minutes, then drain thoroughly and set aside.

2 Bring the stock to the boil in a clean pan. Stir in the tomato purée, then the tomatoes and sugar. Add the beef strips, allow the stock to boil again, then lower the heat and simmer for 2 minutes.

SEAFOOD WONTON SOUP

*THIS IS A VARIATION ON THE POPULAR WONTON SOUP THAT IS TRADITIONALLY PREPARED USING PORK
RATHER THAN SEAFOOD.*

SERVES FOUR

INGREDIENTS
50g/2oz raw tiger prawns (shrimp)
50g/2oz queen scallops
75g/3oz skinless cod fillet,
    roughly chopped
15ml/1 tbsp finely chopped chives
5ml/1 tsp dry sherry
1 small egg white, lightly beaten
2.5ml/½ tsp sesame oil
1.5ml/¼ tsp salt
large pinch of ground white pepper
900ml/1½ pints/3¾ cups fish stock
20 wonton wrappers
2 cos or romaine lettuce leaves,
    shredded
fresh coriander (cilantro) leaves and
    garlic chives, to garnish

1 Peel and devein the prawns. Rinse
them well, pat them dry on kitchen
paper and cut them into small pieces.

2 Rinse the scallops thoroughly.
Pat them dry, using kitchen paper.
Chop them into small pieces the
same size as the prawns.

3 Place the cod in a food processor and
process until a paste is formed. Scrape
into a bowl and stir in the prawns,
scallops, chives, sherry, egg white,
sesame oil, salt and pepper. Mix
thoroughly, cover and leave in a cool
place to marinate for 20 minutes.

4 Heat the fish stock gently in a pan.
Make the wontons. Place a teaspoonful
of the seafood filling in the centre of a
wonton wrapper, then bring the corners
together to meet at the top. Twist
them together to enclose the filling.
Fill the remaining wonton wrappers
in the same way.

5 Bring a large pan of water to the boil.
Drop in the wontons. When the water
returns to the boil, lower the heat and
simmer gently for 5 minutes or until
the wontons float to the surface.
Drain the wontons and divide them
among four heated soup bowls.

6 Add a portion of lettuce to each bowl.
Bring the fish stock to the boil. Ladle
it into each bowl, garnish each portion
with coriander leaves and garlic chives
and serve immediately.

SMOKED MACKEREL AND TOMATO SOUP

ALL THE INGREDIENTS FOR THIS UNUSUAL SOUP ARE COOKED IN A SINGLE PAN, SO IT IS NOT ONLY QUICK AND EASY TO PREPARE, BUT REDUCES THE CLEARING UP. SMOKED MACKEREL GIVES THE SOUP A ROBUST FLAVOUR, BUT THIS IS TEMPERED BY THE CITRUS TONES IN THE LEMON GRASS AND TAMARIND.

SERVES FOUR

INGREDIENTS

   200g/7oz smoked mackerel fillets
   4 tomatoes
   1 litre/1¾ pints/4 cups
    vegetable stock
   1 lemon grass stalk, finely chopped
   5cm/2in piece fresh galangal,
    finely diced
   4 shallots, finely chopped
   2 garlic cloves, finely chopped
   2.5ml/½ tsp dried chilli flakes
   15ml/1 tbsp Thai fish sauce
   5ml/1 tsp palm sugar or light
    muscovado (brown) sugar
   45ml/3 tbsp thick tamarind juice,
    made by mixing tamarind paste with
    warm water
   small bunch fresh chives or spring
    onions (scallions), to garnish

1 Prepare the smoked mackerel fillets. Remove and discard the skin, if necessary, then chop the flesh into large pieces. Remove any stray bones with your fingers or a pair of tweezers.

2 Cut the tomatoes in half, squeeze out most of the seeds with your fingers, then finely dice the flesh with a sharp knife. Set aside.

3 Pour the stock into a large pan and add the lemon grass, galangal, shallots and garlic. Bring to the boil, reduce the heat and simmer for 15 minutes.

4 Add the fish, tomatoes, chilli flakes, fish sauce, sugar and tamarind juice. Simmer for 4–5 minutes, until the fish and tomatoes are heated through. Serve garnished with chives or spring onions.

THAI FISH BROTH

LEMON GRASS, CHILLIES AND GALANGAL ARE AMONG THE FLAVOURINGS USED IN THIS FRAGRANT SOUP.

SERVES TWO TO THREE

INGREDIENTS

1 litre/1¾ pints/4 cups fish or light
  chicken stock
4 lemon grass stalks
3 limes
2 small fresh hot red chillies, seeded
  and thinly sliced
2cm/¾in piece fresh galangal,
  peeled and thinly sliced
6 fresh coriander (cilantro) stalks
2 kaffir lime leaves, chopped
350g/12oz monkfish fillet, skinned
  and cut into 2.5cm/1in pieces
15ml/1 tbsp rice vinegar
45ml/3 tbsp nam pla (fish sauce)
30ml/2 tbsp chopped coriander
  (cilantro) leaves, to garnish

1 Pour the stock into a pan and bring it to the boil. Meanwhile, slice the bulb end of each lemon grass stalk diagonally into pieces about 3mm/⅛in thick. Peel off four wide strips of lime rind with a potato peeler, taking care to avoid the white pith underneath which would make the soup bitter. Squeeze the limes and reserve the juice.

2 Add the sliced lemon grass, lime rind, chillies, galangal and coriander stalks to the stock, with the kaffir lime leaves. Simmer for 1–2 minutes.

VARIATIONS

Prawns (shrimp), scallops, squid or sole can be substituted for the monkfish. If you use kaffir lime leaves, you will need the juice of only 2 limes.

3 Add the monkfish, rice vinegar and nam pla, with half the reserved lime juice. Simmer for about 3 minutes, until the fish is just cooked. Lift out and discard the coriander stalks, taste the broth and add more lime juice if necessary; the soup should taste quite sour. Sprinkle with the coriander leaves and serve very hot.

NOODLE, PAK CHOI AND SALMON RAMEN

THIS LIGHTLY SPICED JAPANESE NOODLE SOUP IS ENHANCED BY SLICES OF SEARED FRESH SALMON AND CRISP VEGETABLES. THE CONTRASTS IN TEXTURE ARE AS APPEALING AS THE DELICIOUS TASTE.

SERVES FOUR

INGREDIENTS

    1.5 litres/2½ pints/6 cups good
      vegetable stock
    2.5cm/1in piece fresh root ginger,
      finely sliced
    2 garlic cloves, crushed
    6 spring onions (scallions), sliced
    45ml/3 tbsp soy sauce
    45ml/3 tbsp sake
    450g/1lb salmon fillet, skinned
    5ml/1 tsp groundnut (peanut) oil
    350g/12oz ramen or udon noodles
    4 small heads pak choi (bok choy),
      broken into leaves
    1 fresh red chilli, seeded and sliced
    50g/2oz/1 cup beansprouts
    salt and ground black pepper

1 Pour the stock into a large pan and add the ginger, garlic, and a third of the spring onions.

2 Add the soy sauce and sake. Bring to the boil, then reduce the heat and simmer for 30 minutes.

3 Meanwhile, remove any pin bones from the salmon using tweezers, then cut the salmon on the slant into 12 slices, using a very sharp knife.

4 Brush a ridged griddle or frying pan with the oil and heat until very hot. Sear the salmon slices for 1–2 minutes on each side until tender and marked by the ridges of the pan. Set aside.

COOK'S TIP

To obtain the distinctive stripes on the slices of salmon, it is important that the ridged pan or griddle is very hot before they are added. Avoid moving the slices, or the stripes will become blurred.

5 Cook the ramen or udon noodles in a large pan of boiling water for 4–5 minutes or according to the instructions on the packet. Tip into a colander, drain well and refresh under cold running water. Drain again and set aside.

6 Strain the broth into a clean pan and season, then bring to the boil. Add the pak choi. Using a fork, twist the noodles into four nests and put these into deep bowls. Divide the salmon slices, spring onions, chilli and beansprouts among the bowls. Ladle in the broth.

RICE IN GREEN TEA WITH SALMON

THIS IS A COMMON JAPANESE SNACK TO HAVE AFTER DRINKS AND NIBBLES. IN THE KYOTO REGION, OFFERING THIS DISH TO GUESTS USED TO BE A POLITE WAY OF SAYING THE PARTY WAS OVER. THE GUESTS WERE EXPECTED TO DECLINE THE OFFER AND LEAVE IMMEDIATELY.

SERVES FOUR

INGREDIENTS
150g/5oz salmon fillet
¼ sheet nori
250g/9oz/1¼ cups Japanese short
  grain rice cooked as advised on
  the packet, using 350ml/12fl oz/
  1½ cups water
15ml/1 tbsp sencha leaves
600ml/1 pint/2½ cups water
5ml/1 tsp wasabi paste or 5ml/1 tsp
  wasabi powder mixed with 1.5ml/
  ¼ tsp water (optional)
20ml/4 tsp shoyu (Japanese soy sauce)
sea salt

1 Place the salmon fillet in a bowl and cover it with salt. If the fillet is thicker than 2.5cm/1in, slice it in half and salt both halves. Leave for 30 minutes

2 Wipe the salt off the salmon with kitchen paper and grill (broil) the fish under a preheated grill (broiler) for about 5 minutes until cooked through.

3 Using scissors, cut the nori into short, narrow strips about 20 x 5mm/ ¾ x ¼in long, or leave as long narrow strips, if you prefer.

4 Remove the skin and any bones from the salmon, then flake the fish.

5 If the cooked rice is warm, put equal amounts into individual rice bowls or soup bowls. If the rice is cold, put it in a sieve and pour hot water from a kettle over it to warm it up. Drain and pour into the bowls. Place the salmon pieces on top of the rice.

6 Put the sencha leaves in a teapot. Bring the water to the boil, remove from the heat and leave to cool slightly. Pour into the teapot and wait for 45 seconds.

7 Strain the tea gently and evenly over the top of the rice and salmon. Add some nori and wasabi, if using, to the top of each portion of rice, then trickle shoyu over and serve.

COOK'S TIP
Sencha are fine green tea leaves available from Japanese food stores and shops or markets selling specialist teas.

ASPARAGUS AND CRAB SOUP

ASPARAGUS OWES ITS POPULARITY TO THE FRENCH INFLUENCE ON VIETNAMESE COOKING. IT IS OFTEN COMBINED WITH CRAB AND MADE INTO A DELICIOUS SOUP, CAHN CUA.

SERVES FOUR TO SIX

INGREDIENTS

350g/12oz asparagus spears,
  trimmed and halved
900ml/1½ pints/3¾ cups chicken
  stock, preferably home-made
30–45ml/2–3 tbsp sunflower oil
6 shallots, chopped
115g/4oz crab meat, fresh or
  canned, chopped
15ml/1 tbsp cornflour (cornstarch),
  mixed to a paste with water
30ml/2 tbsp fish sauce
1 egg, lightly beaten
chopped chives, plus extra chives
  to garnish
salt and ground black pepper to taste

1 Cook the asparagus spears in the chicken stock for 5–6 minutes until tender. Drain, reserving the stock.

2 Heat the oil and stir-fry the shallots for 2 minutes. Add the asparagus spears, crab meat and chicken stock.

3 Bring the mixture to the boil and cook for 3 minutes, then remove the wok or pan from the heat and spoon some of the liquid into the cornflour mixture. Return this to the wok or pan and stir until the soup begins to thicken slightly.

4 Stir in the fish sauce, with salt and pepper to taste, then pour the beaten egg into the soup, stirring briskly so that the egg forms threads. Finally, stir the chopped chives into the soup and serve immediately, garnished with chives.

COOK'S TIP
If fresh asparagus isn't available, use 350g/12oz can asparagus. Drain and halve the spears.

NORTHERN PRAWN AND SQUASH SOUP

As the title of the recipe suggests, this comes from northern Thailand. It is quite hearty, something of a cross between a soup and a stew. The banana flower isn't essential, but it does add a unique and authentic flavour.

SERVES FOUR

INGREDIENTS
1 butternut squash, about 300g/11oz
1 litre/1¾ pints/4 cups
   vegetable stock
90g/3½oz/scant 1 cup green beans,
   cut into 2.5cm/1in pieces
45g/1¾oz dried banana
   flower (optional)
15ml/1 tbsp Thai fish sauce
225g/8oz raw prawns (shrimp)
small bunch fresh basil
cooked rice, to serve
For the chilli paste
   115g/4oz shallots, sliced
   10 drained bottled green peppercorns
   1 small fresh green chilli, seeded and
      finely chopped
   2.5ml/½ tsp shrimp paste

1 Peel the butternut squash and cut it in half. Scoop out the seeds with a teaspoon and discard, then cut the flesh into neat cubes. Set aside.

2 Make the chilli paste by pounding the shallots, peppercorns, chilli and shrimp paste together using a mortar and pestle or puréeing them in a spice blender.

3 Heat the stock gently in a large pan, then stir in the chilli paste. Add the squash, beans and banana flower, if using. Bring to the boil and cook for 15 minutes.

4 Add the fish sauce, prawns and basil. Bring to simmering point, then simmer for 3 minutes. Serve in warmed bowls, accompanied by rice.

CLEAR SOUP <u>WITH</u> SEAFOOD STICKS

THIS DELICATE SOUP, CALLED O-SUMASHI, WHICH IS OFTEN EATEN WITH SUSHI, IS VERY QUICK TO MAKE IF YOU PREPARE THE FIRST DASHI BEFOREHAND OR IF YOU USE FREEZE-DRIED DASHI-NO-MOTO.

<u>SERVES FOUR</u>

INGREDIENTS
    4 mitsuba sprigs or 4 chives and a
    few sprigs of mustard and cress
    4 seafood sticks
    400ml/14fl oz/1⅔ cups first dashi
    stock, or the same amount of water
    and 5ml/1 tsp dashi-no-moto
    15ml/1 tbsp shoyu
    7.5ml/1½ tsp salt
    grated rind of yuzu (optional),
    to garnish

1 Mitsuba leaves are normally sold with the stems and roots on to retain freshness. Cut off the root, then cut 5cm/2in from the top, retaining both the long straw-like stem and the leaf.

2 Blanch the stems in hot water from the kettle. If you use chives, choose them at least 10cm/4in in length and blanch them, too.

3 Take a seafood stick and carefully tie around the middle with a mitsuba stem or chive, holding it in place with a knot. Do not pull too tightly, as the bow will easily break. Repeat the process to make four tied seafood sticks.

4 Hold one seafood stick in your hand. With your finger, carefully loosen both ends to make it look like a tassel.

5 Place one seafood stick in each soup bowl, then put the four mitsuba leaves or mustard and cress on top.

6 Heat the stock in a pan and bring to the boil. Add shoyu and salt to taste. Pour the stock gently over the mitsuba and seafood stick. Sprinkle with grated yuzu rind, if using.

VARIATION
You can use small prawns (shrimp) instead of seafood sticks. Blanch 12 raw prawns in boiling water until they curl up and form a full circle. Drain. Tie mitsuba stems to make four bows. Arrange three prawns side by side in each bowl and put the mitsuba bows and leaves on top.

LAKSA LEMAK

THIS SPICY SOUP IS NOT A DISH YOU CAN THROW TOGETHER IN 20 MINUTES, BUT IT IS MARVELLOUS PARTY FOOD. GUESTS SPOON NOODLES INTO WIDE SOUP BOWLS, ADD ACCOMPANIMENTS OF THEIR CHOICE, TOP UP WITH SOUP AND THEN TAKE A FEW PRAWN CRACKERS TO NIBBLE.

SERVES SIX

INGREDIENTS
675g/1½lb small clams
2 × 400ml/14fl oz cans coconut milk
50g/2oz ikan bilis (dried anchovies)
900ml/1½ pints/3¾ cups water
115g/4oz shallots, finely chopped
4 garlic cloves, chopped
6 macadamia nuts or blanched
  almonds, chopped
3 lemon grass stalks, root trimmed
90ml/6 tbsp sunflower oil
1cm/½in cube shrimp paste
25g/1oz/¼ cup mild curry powder
a few curry leaves
2–3 aubergines (eggplant), total
  weight about 675g/1½lb, trimmed
675g/1½lb raw peeled prawns
  (shrimp)
10ml/2 tsp sugar
1 head Chinese leaves (Chinese
  cabbage), thinly sliced
115g/4oz/2 cups beansprouts, rinsed
2 spring onions (scallions), chopped
50g/2oz crispy fried onions
115g/4oz fried tofu
675g/1½lb mixed noodles
prawn crackers, to serve

2 Meanwhile, put the shallots, garlic and nuts into a mortar. Cut off the lower 5cm/2in of two of the lemon grass stalks, chop finely and add to the mortar. Pound the mixture to a paste.

3 Heat the oil in a large heavy pan, add the shallot paste and fry until the mixture gives off a rich aroma. Bruise the remaining lemon grass stalk and add to the pan. Toss over the heat to release its flavour. Mix the shrimp paste and curry powder to a paste with a little of the coconut milk, add to the pan and toss the mixture over the heat for 1 minute, stirring all the time, and keeping the heat low. Stir in the remaining coconut milk. Add the curry leaves and leave the mixture to simmer while you prepare the accompaniments.

4 Strain the stock into a pan. Discard the ikan bilis, bring to the boil, then add the aubergines; cook for about 10 minutes or until tender and the skins can be peeled off easily. Lift out of the stock, peel and cut into thick strips.

5 Arrange the aubergines on a serving platter. Sprinkle the prawns with sugar, add to the stock and cook for 2–4 minutes until they turn pink. Remove and place next to the aubergines. Add the Chinese leaves, beansprouts, spring onions and crispy fried onions to the platter, along with the clams.

6 Gradually stir the remaining ikan bilis stock into the pan of soup and bring to the boil. Rinse the fried tofu in boiling water, cool slightly and squeeze to remove excess oil. Cut each piece in half and add to the soup. Lower the heat to a very gentle simmer.

7 Cook the noodles according to the instructions, drain and pile in a dish. Remove the curry leaves and lemon grass from the soup. Place the noodles, soup and the platter of seafood and vegetables on the table, along with a bowl of prawn crackers. Guests can then help themselves.

VARIATION
You could substitute mussels for clams if preferred. Scrub them thoroughly, removing any beards, and cook them in lightly salted water until they open. Like clams, discard any that remain closed.

COOK'S TIP
Dried shrimp or prawn paste, also called blachan, is sold in small blocks and is available from Asian supermarkets.

1 Scrub the clams and then put in a large pan with 1cm/½in water. Bring to the boil, cover and steam for 3–4 minutes until all the clams have opened. Drain. Make up the coconut milk to 1.2 litres/2 pints/5 cups with water. Put the ikan bilis in a pan and add the water. Bring to the boil and simmer for 20 minutes.

COCONUT AND SEAFOOD SOUP

THE LONG LIST OF INGREDIENTS COULD MISLEAD YOU INTO THINKING THAT THIS SOUP IS COMPLICATED AND VERY TIME-CONSUMING TO PREPARE. IN FACT, IT IS EXTREMELY EASY TO PUT TOGETHER AND THE MARRIAGE OF FLAVOURS WORKS BEAUTIFULLY.

SERVES FOUR

INGREDIENTS

600ml/1 pint/2½ cups fish stock
5 thin slices fresh galangal or fresh
   root ginger
2 lemon grass stalks, chopped
3 kaffir lime leaves, shredded
bunch garlic chives, about 25g/1oz
small bunch fresh coriander
   (cilantro), about 15g/½oz
15ml/1 tbsp vegetable oil
4 shallots, chopped
400ml/14fl oz can coconut milk
30–45ml/2–3 tbsp Thai fish sauce
45–60ml/3–4 tbsp Thai green
   curry paste
450g/1lb raw large prawns (shrimp),
   peeled and deveined
450g/1lb prepared squid
a little fresh lime juice (optional)
salt and ground black pepper
60ml/4 tbsp crisp fried shallot
   slices, to serve

2 Reserve a few garlic chives for the garnish, then chop the remainder. Add half the chopped garlic chives to the pan. Strip the coriander leaves from the stalks and set the leaves aside. Add the stalks to the pan. Bring to the boil, reduce the heat to low and cover the pan, then simmer gently for 20 minutes. Strain the stock into a bowl.

3 Rinse and dry the pan. Add the oil and shallots. Cook over a medium heat for 5–10 minutes, until the shallots are just beginning to brown.

4 Stir in the strained stock, coconut milk, the remaining kaffir lime leaves and 30ml/2 tbsp of the fish sauce. Heat gently until simmering and cook over a low heat for 5–10 minutes.

5 Stir in the curry paste and prawns, then cook for 3 minutes. Add the squid and cook for a further 2 minutes. Add the lime juice, if using, and season, adding more fish sauce to taste. Stir in the remaining chives and the reserved coriander leaves. Serve in bowls and sprinkle each portion with fried shallots and whole garlic chives.

1 Pour the fish stock into a large pan and add the slices of galangal or ginger, the lemon grass and half the shredded kaffir lime leaves.

VARIATIONS
• Instead of squid, you could add 400g/
14oz firm white fish, such as monkfish, cut into small pieces.
• You could also replace the squid with mussels. Steam 675g/1½lb live mussels in a tightly covered pan for 3–4 minutes, or until they have opened. Discard any that remain shut, then remove them from their shells and add to the soup.

MALAYSIAN PRAWN LAKSA

THIS SPICY SOUP TASTES JUST AS GOOD WHEN MADE WITH FRESH CRAB MEAT OR ANY FLAKED COOKED FISH. IF YOU ARE SHORT OF TIME OR CAN'T FIND ALL THE SPICY PASTE INGREDIENTS, BUY READY-MADE LAKSA PASTE, WHICH IS AVAILABLE FROM STORES.

SERVES TWO TO THREE

INGREDIENTS
115g/4oz rice vermicelli or stir-fry
  rice noodles
15ml/1 tbsp vegetable or groundnut
  (peanut) oil
600ml/1 pint/2½ cups fish stock
400ml/14fl oz/1⅔ cups thin
  coconut milk
30ml/2 tbsp nam pla (fish sauce)
½ lime
24 cooked peeled prawns (shrimp)
salt and cayenne pepper
60ml/4 tbsp fresh coriander (cilantro)
  sprigs, chopped, to garnish
For the spicy paste
2 lemon grass stalks, finely
  chopped
2 fresh red chillies, seeded
  and chopped
2.5cm/1in piece fresh root ginger,
  peeled and sliced
2.5ml/½ tsp dried shrimp paste
2 garlic cloves, chopped
2.5ml/½ tsp ground turmeric
30ml/2 tbsp tamarind paste

1 Cook the rice vermicelli or noodles in a large pan of boiling salted water according to the instructions on the packet. Tip into a large strainer, then rinse under cold water and drain. Keep warm.

2 To make the spicy paste, place all the prepared ingredients in a mortar and pound with a pestle. Alternatively, put the ingredients in a food processor and whizz until a smooth paste is formed.

3 Heat the vegetable or groundnut oil in a large pan, add the spicy paste and fry, stirring constantly, for a few moments to release all the flavours, but be careful not to let it burn.

4 Add the fish stock and coconut milk and bring to the boil. Stir in the nam pla, then simmer for 5 minutes. Season with salt and cayenne to taste, adding a squeeze of lime. Add the prawns and heat through for a few seconds.

5 Divide the noodles among two or three soup plates. Pour over the soup, making sure that each portion includes an equal number of prawns. Garnish with coriander and serve piping hot.

POULTRY DISHES

The versatility of chicken in Asian cooking is astonishing –
stir-fried with ginger or chillies, roasted with spices, barbecued,
curried, or braised in coconut milk. Duck recipes are largely a
Chinese legacy, but variations appear in Thai and other Asian
cuisines. Some of the dishes in this section, such as Peking Duck
with Pancakes, are familiar favourites, while others offer new
and exciting combinations. Try Japanese Chicken and Mushroom
Donburi or Anita Wong's Duck.

STIR-FRIED CHICKEN WITH BASIL AND CHILLI

THIS QUICK AND EASY CHICKEN DISH IS AN EXCELLENT INTRODUCTION TO THAI CUISINE. THAI BASIL, WHICH IS SOMETIMES KNOWN AS HOLY BASIL, HAS A UNIQUE, PUNGENT FLAVOUR THAT IS BOTH SPICY AND SHARP. DEEP-FRYING THE LEAVES ADDS ANOTHER DIMENSION TO THIS DISH.

2 Add the pieces of chicken to the wok or pan, in batches if necessary, and stir-fry until the chicken changes colour.

3 Stir in the fish sauce, soy sauce and sugar. Continue to stir-fry the mixture for 3–4 minutes, or until the chicken is fully cooked and golden brown.

4 Stir in the fresh Thai basil leaves. Spoon the mixture on to a warm platter, or into individual dishes. Garnish with the chopped chillies and deep-fried Thai basil and serve immediately.

COOK'S TIP
To deep-fry Thai basil leaves, first make sure that the leaves are completely dry or they will splutter when added to the oil. Heat vegetable or groundnut (peanut) oil in a wok or deep-fryer to 190°C/375°F or until a cube of bread, added to the oil, browns in about 45 seconds. Add the leaves and deep-fry them briefly until they are crisp and translucent – this will take only about 30–40 seconds. Lift out the leaves using a slotted spoon or wire basket and leave them to drain on kitchen paper before using.

SERVES FOUR TO SIX

INGREDIENTS
    45ml/3 tbsp vegetable oil
    4 garlic cloves, thinly sliced
    2–4 fresh red chillies, seeded and
      finely chopped
    450g/1lb skinless boneless chicken
      breast portions, cut into
      bitesize pieces
    45ml/3 tbsp Thai fish sauce
    10ml/2 tsp dark soy sauce
    5ml/1 tsp granulated sugar
    10–12 fresh Thai basil leaves
    2 fresh red chillies, seeded and
      finely chopped, and about 20 deep-
      fried Thai basil leaves, to garnish

1 Heat the oil in a wok or large, heavy frying pan. Add the garlic and chillies and stir-fry over a medium heat for 1–2 minutes until the garlic is golden. Take care not to let the garlic burn, otherwise it will taste bitter.

BANG BANG CHICKEN

*WHAT A DESCRIPTIVE NAME THIS SPECIAL DISH FROM SICHUAN HAS! USE TOASTED SESAME PASTE
TO GIVE THE SAUCE AN AUTHENTIC FLAVOUR, ALTHOUGH CRUNCHY PEANUT BUTTER CAN BE USED
INSTEAD. BANG BANG CHICKEN IS PERFECT FOR PARTIES AND IDEAL FOR A BUFFET.*

SERVES FOUR

INGREDIENTS
    3 chicken breast fillets, total weight
    about 450g/1lb
    1 garlic clove, crushed
    2.5ml/1/2 tsp black peppercorns
    1 small onion, halved
    1 large cucumber, peeled, seeded
    and cut into thin strips
    salt and ground black pepper
For the sauce
    45ml/3 tbsp toasted sesame
    paste
    15ml/1 tbsp light soy sauce
    15ml/1 tbsp wine vinegar
    2 spring onions (scallions),
    chopped
    2 garlic cloves, crushed
    5 × 1cm/2 × 1/2in piece fresh
    root ginger, peeled and cut
    into matchsticks
    15ml/1 tbsp Sichuan peppercorns,
    dry fried and crushed
    5ml/1 tsp light brown sugar
For the chilli oil
    60ml/4 tbsp groundnut (peanut) oil
    5ml/1 tsp chilli powder

2 Make the sauce by mixing the
toasted sesame paste with 45ml/3 tbsp
of the chicken stock, saving the rest
for soup. Add the soy sauce, vinegar,
spring onions, garlic, ginger and
crushed peppercorns to the sesame
mixture. Stir in sugar to taste.

3 Make the chilli oil by gently heating
the oil and chilli powder together until
foaming. Simmer for 2 minutes, cool,
then strain off the red-coloured oil and
discard the sediment.

4 Spread out the cucumber batons on
a platter. Cut the chicken fillets into
pieces of about the same size as the
cucumber strips and arrange them on
top. Pour over the sauce, drizzle on the
chilli oil and serve.

VARIATION
Crunchy peanut butter can be used
instead of sesame paste, if you prefer.
Mix it with 30ml/2 tbsp sesame oil and
proceed as in Step 2.

1 Place the chicken in a pan. Just
cover with water, add the garlic,
peppercorns and onion and bring to the
boil. Skim the surface, stir in salt and
pepper to taste, then cover the pan.
Cook for 25 minutes or until the
chicken is just tender. Drain, reserving
the stock.

SICHUAN CHICKEN WITH KUNG PO SAUCE

THIS RECIPE, WHICH HAILS FROM THE SICHUAN REGION OF WESTERN CHINA, HAS BECOME ONE OF THE CLASSIC RECIPES IN THE CHINESE REPERTOIRE.

SERVES THREE

INGREDIENTS

2 chicken breast fillets, total weight
about 350g/12oz
1 egg white
10ml/2 tsp cornflour (cornstarch)
2.5ml/^{1}/$_{2}$ tsp salt
30ml/2 tbsp yellow salted beans
15ml/1 tbsp hoisin sauce
5ml/1 tsp light brown sugar
15ml/1 tbsp rice wine or
medium-dry sherry
15ml/1 tbsp wine vinegar
4 garlic cloves, crushed
150ml/^{1}/$_{4}$ pint/^{2}/$_{3}$ cup chicken stock
45ml/3 tbsp groundnut (peanut) oil
or sunflower oil
2–3 dried chillies, broken into
small pieces
115g/4oz roasted cashew nuts
fresh coriander (cilantro), to garnish

1 Cut the chicken into neat pieces. Lightly whisk the egg white in a dish, whisk in the cornflour and salt, then add the chicken and stir until coated.

COOK'S TIP
Peanuts are the classic ingredient in this dish, but cashew nuts have an even better flavour and have become popular both in home cooking and in restaurants.

2 In a separate bowl, mash the beans with a spoon. Stir in the hoisin sauce, brown sugar, rice wine or sherry, vinegar, garlic and stock.

3 Heat a wok, add the oil and then fry the chicken, turning constantly, for about 2 minutes until tender. Drain over a bowl in order to collect excess oil.

4 Heat the reserved oil and fry the chilli pieces for 1 minute. Return the chicken to the wok and pour in the bean sauce mixture. Bring to the boil and stir in the cashew nuts. Spoon into a heated serving dish and garnish with coriander leaves.

CHICKEN RENDANG

THIS MAKES A MARVELLOUS DISH FOR A BUFFET. SERVE IT WITH PRAWN CRACKERS OR WITH BOILED RICE AND DEEP-FRIED ANCHOVIES, ACAR PICKLE OR SAMBAL NANAS.

3 Add the onions, garlic and ginger to the processor. Cut off the lower 5cm/2in of the lemon grass, chop and add to the processor with the galangal. Process to a fine paste.

4 Heat the oil in a wok or large pan and fry the onion mixture for a few minutes. Reduce the heat, stir in the chilli powder and cook for 2–3 minutes, stirring constantly. Spoon in 120ml/4fl oz/1/2 cup of the coconut milk and add salt to taste.

SERVES FOUR

INGREDIENTS
    1 chicken, about 1.4kg/3lb
    5ml/1 tsp sugar
    75g/3oz/1 cup desiccated (dry unsweetened shredded) coconut
    4 small red or white onions, roughly chopped
    2 garlic cloves, chopped
    2.5cm/1in piece fresh root ginger, peeled and sliced
    1–2 lemon grass stalks, root trimmed
    2.5cm/1in piece fresh galangal, peeled and sliced
    75ml/5 tbsp groundnut (peanut) oil or vegetable oil
    10–15ml/2–3 tsp chilli powder
    400ml/14fl oz can coconut milk
    10ml/2 tsp salt
    fresh chives and deep-fried anchovies, to garnish

1 Joint the chicken into 8 pieces and remove the skin, sprinkle with the sugar and leave to stand for 1 hour.

2 Dry-fry the coconut in a wok or large frying pan over medium to low heat, turning all the time until it is crisp and golden. Transfer the fried coconut to a food processor and process to an oily paste. Transfer to a bowl and reserve.

5 As soon as the mixture bubbles, add the chicken pieces, turning them until they are well coated with the spices. Pour in the coconut milk, stirring constantly to prevent curdling. Bruise the top of the lemon grass stalks and add to the wok or pan. Cover and cook gently for 40–45 minutes until the chicken is tender.

6 Just before serving stir in the coconut paste. Bring to just below boiling point, then simmer for 5 minutes. Transfer to a serving bowl and garnish with fresh chives and deep-fried anchovies.

GREEN CHICKEN CURRY

USE ONE OR TWO FRESH GREEN CHILLIES IN THIS DISH, DEPENDING ON HOW HOT YOU LIKE YOUR CURRY. THE MILD AROMATIC FLAVOUR OF THE RICE IS A GOOD FOIL FOR THE SPICY CHICKEN.

SERVES THREE TO FOUR

INGREDIENTS

4 spring onions (scallions), trimmed
   and coarsely chopped
1–2 fresh green chillies, seeded and
   coarsely chopped
2cm/¾in piece fresh root
   ginger, peeled
2 garlic cloves
5ml/1 tsp Thai fish sauce
large bunch fresh coriander (cilantro)
small handful of fresh parsley
30–45ml/2–3 tbsp water
30ml/2 tbsp sunflower oil
4 skinless, boneless chicken breast
   portions, diced
1 green (bell) pepper, seeded and
   thinly sliced
600ml/1 pint/2½ cups coconut milk
   or 75g/3oz piece of creamed
   coconut dissolved in 400ml/14fl oz/
   1⅔ cups boiling water
salt and ground black pepper
hot coconut rice, to serve

1 Put the spring onions, green chillies, ginger, garlic, fish sauce, coriander and parsley in a food processor or blender. Pour in 30ml/2 tbsp of the water and process to a smooth paste, adding a further 15ml/1 tbsp water if required.

COOK'S TIP

Virtually every Thai cook has their own recipe for curry pastes, which are traditionally made by pounding the ingredients in a mortar with a pestle. Using a food processor or blender simply makes the task less laborious.

2 Heat half the oil in a large frying pan. Cook the diced chicken until evenly browned. Transfer to a plate.

3 Heat the remaining oil in the pan. Add the green pepper and stir-fry for 3–4 minutes, then add the chilli and ginger paste. Stir-fry for 3–4 minutes, until the mixture becomes fairly thick.

4 Return the chicken to the pan and add the coconut liquid. Season with salt and pepper and bring to the boil, then reduce the heat, half cover the pan and simmer for 8–10 minutes.

5 When the chicken is cooked, transfer it, with the green pepper, to a plate. Boil the cooking liquid remaining in the pan for 10–12 minutes, until it is well reduced and fairly thick.

6 Return the chicken and pepper to the green curry sauce, stir well and cook gently for 2–3 minutes to heat through. Spoon the curry over the coconut rice, and serve immediately.

YELLOW CHICKEN CURRY

THE PAIRING OF SLIGHTLY SWEET COCONUT MILK AND FRUIT WITH SAVOURY CHICKEN AND SPICES
IS AT ONCE A COMFORTING, REFRESHING AND EXOTIC COMBINATION.

SERVES FOUR

INGREDIENTS
    300ml/½ pint/1¼ cups
    chicken stock
    30ml/2 tbsp thick tamarind juice,
    made by mixing tamarind paste with
    warm water
    15ml/1 tbsp granulated sugar
    200ml/7fl oz/scant 1 cup
    coconut milk
    1 green papaya, peeled, seeded and
    thinly sliced
    250g/9oz skinless, boneless chicken
    breast portions, diced
    juice of 1 lime
    lime slices, to garnish
For the curry paste
    1 fresh red chilli, seeded and
    coarsely chopped
    4 garlic cloves, coarsely chopped
    3 shallots, coarsely chopped
    2 lemon grass stalks, sliced
    5cm/2in piece fresh turmeric,
    coarsely chopped, or 5ml/1 tsp
    ground turmeric
    5ml/1 tsp shrimp paste
    5ml/1 tsp salt

2 Pour the stock into a wok or medium
pan and bring it to the boil. Stir in the
curry paste. Bring back to the boil
and add the tamarind juice, sugar and
coconut milk. Add the papaya and
chicken and cook over a medium to
high heat for about 15 minutes, stirring
frequently, until the chicken is cooked.

3 Stir in the lime juice, transfer to a
warm dish and serve immediately,
garnished with lime slices.

1 Make the yellow curry paste. Put the
red chilli, garlic, shallots, lemon grass
and turmeric in a mortar or food
processor. Add the shrimp paste and
salt. Pound or process to a paste,
adding a little water if necessary.

COOK'S TIP
Fresh turmeric resembles root ginger in
appearance and is a member of the same
family. When preparing it, wear gloves to
protect your hands from staining.

RED CHICKEN CURRY WITH BAMBOO SHOOTS

BAMBOO SHOOTS HAVE A LOVELY CRUNCHY TEXTURE. IT IS QUITE ACCEPTABLE TO USE CANNED ONES, AS FRESH BAMBOO IS NOT READILY AVAILABLE IN THE WEST. BUY CANNED WHOLE BAMBOO SHOOTS, WHICH ARE CRISPER AND OF BETTER QUALITY THAN SLICED SHOOTS. RINSE BEFORE USING.

SERVES FOUR TO SIX

INGREDIENTS

1 litre/1¾ pints/4 cups coconut milk
450g/1lb chicken breast fillets, cut
　into bitesize pieces
30ml/2 tbsp nam pla (fish sauce)
15ml/1 tbsp sugar
225g/8oz drained canned bamboo
　shoots, rinsed and sliced
5 kaffir lime leaves, torn
salt and ground black pepper
chopped fresh red chillies and
　kaffir lime leaves, to garnish
For the red curry paste
　5ml/1 tsp coriander seeds
　2.5ml/½ tsp cumin seeds
　12–15 fresh red chillies, seeded
　　and roughly chopped
　4 shallots, thinly sliced
　2 garlic cloves, chopped
　15ml/1 tbsp chopped galangal
　2 lemon grass stalks, chopped
　3 kaffir lime leaves, chopped
　4 fresh coriander (cilantro)
　　roots
　10 black peppercorns
　good pinch of ground cinnamon
　5ml/1 tsp ground turmeric
　2.5ml/½ tsp shrimp paste
　5ml/1 tsp salt
　30ml/2 tbsp vegetable oil

2 Add the oil, a little at a time, mixing or processing well after each addition. Transfer to a jar and keep in the refrigerator until ready to use.

3 Pour half of the coconut milk into a large heavy pan. Bring the milk to the boil, stirring constantly until it has separated.

5 Add the chicken pieces, nam pla and sugar to the pan. Stir well, then cook for 5–6 minutes until the chicken changes colour and is cooked through, stirring constantly to prevent the mixture from sticking to the bottom of the pan.

6 Pour the remaining coconut milk into the pan, then add the sliced bamboo shoots and torn kaffir lime leaves. Bring back to the boil over a medium heat, stirring constantly to prevent the mixture sticking, then taste and add salt and pepper if necessary.

7 To serve, spoon the curry into a warmed serving dish and garnish with chopped chillies and kaffir lime leaves.

VARIATION
Instead of, or as well as, bamboo shoots, use straw mushrooms. These are available in cans from Asian stores and supermarkets. Drain well and then stir into the curry at the end of the recipe.

COOK'S TIP
It is essential to use chicken breast fillets, rather than any other cut, for this curry, as it is cooked very quickly. Look out for diced chicken or strips of chicken (which are often labelled "stir-fry chicken") in the supermarket.

1 Make the curry paste. Dry-fry the coriander and cumin seeds for 1–2 minutes, then put in a mortar or food processor with the remaining ingredients except the oil and pound or process to a paste.

4 Stir in 30ml/2 tbsp of the red curry paste and cook the mixture for 2–3 minutes, stirring constantly. Remaining red curry paste can be kept in the refrigerator for up to 3 months.

CHICKEN AND EGG WITH RICE

OYAKO-DON, THE JAPANESE NAME FOR THIS DISH MEANS PARENT (OYA), CHILD (KO) AND BOWL (DON); IT IS SO CALLED BECAUSE IT USES BOTH CHICKEN MEAT AND EGG. A CLASSIC DISH, IT IS EATEN THROUGHOUT THE YEAR.

2 Place the onion, dashi, sugar, soy sauce and mirin (sweet rice wine) in a pan and bring to the boil. Add the chicken and cook over a medium heat for about 5 minutes, or until cooked. Skim off any scum that rises to the surface of the liquid.

3 Ladle a quarter of the chicken and stock mixture into a frying pan and heat until the liquid comes to the boil.

4 Pour a quarter of the beaten egg over the mixture in the frying pan and sprinkle over 15ml/1 tbsp of the peas.

5 Cover and cook over a medium heat until the egg is just set. Slide the egg mixture on to a large plate and keep it warm while cooking the other omelettes in the same way. Transfer to serving dishes and serve with boiled rice.

SERVES FOUR

INGREDIENTS
  300g/11oz chicken breast fillets
  1 large mild onion, thinly sliced
  200ml/7fl oz/scant 1 cup freshly
    made dashi (kombu and bonito
    stock) or instant dashi
  22.5ml/4½ tsp sugar
  60ml/4 tbsp Japanese soy sauce
  30ml/2 tbsp mirin (sweet rice wine)
  4 eggs, beaten
  60ml/4 tbsp frozen peas, thawed
  boiled rice, to serve

1 Slice the chicken fillets diagonally with a sharp knife, then cut the slices into 3cm/1¼ in lengths.

COOK'S TIP
Ideally use either Japanese rice or Thai fragrant rice for this meal and allow 50–75g/2–3oz raw rice per person.

BARBECUE CHICKEN

CHICKEN COOKED ON A BARBECUE IS SERVED ALMOST EVERYWHERE IN THAILAND, FROM ROADSIDE STALLS TO SPORTS STADIA. THIS IS THE PERFECT DISH FOR A SUMMER PARTY, BUT YOU CAN ALSO COOK THIS TASTY CHICKEN IN THE OVEN IF THE WEATHER PROVES DISAPPOINTING.

SERVES FOUR TO SIX

INGREDIENTS
1 chicken, about 1.5kg/3–3½lb,
   cut into 8–10 pieces
lime wedges and fresh red chillies,
   to garnish
For the marinade
2 lemon grass stalks, roots trimmed
2.5cm/1in piece fresh root ginger,
   peeled and thinly sliced
6 garlic cloves, coarsely chopped
4 shallots, coarsely chopped
½ bunch coriander (cilantro)
   roots, chopped
15ml/1 tbsp palm sugar or light
   muscovado (brown) sugar
120ml/4fl oz/½ cup coconut milk
30ml/2 tbsp Thai fish sauce
30ml/2 tbsp light soy sauce

1 Make the marinade. Cut off the lower 5cm/2in of the lemon grass stalks and chop them coarsely. Put into a food processor with the ginger, garlic, shallots, coriander, sugar, coconut milk and sauces and process until smooth.

2 Place the chicken pieces in a dish, pour over the marinade and stir to mix well. Cover the dish and leave in a cool place to marinate for at least 4 hours, or leave it in the refrigerator overnight.

3 Prepare the barbecue or preheat the oven to 200°C/400°F/Gas 6. Drain the chicken, reserving the marinade. If you are cooking in the oven, arrange the chicken pieces in a single layer on a rack set over a roasting pan.

4 Cook the chicken on the barbecue over moderately hot coals or on medium heat for a gas barbecue, or bake in the oven for 20–30 minutes. Turn the pieces and brush with the reserved marinade once or twice during cooking.

5 As soon as the chicken pieces are golden brown and cooked through, transfer them to a serving platter, garnish with the lime wedges and red chillies and serve immediately.

COOK'S TIPS
• Coconut milk is available fresh or in cans or cartons from Asian food stores and most supermarkets and you may also find it in powdered form. Alternatively, use 50g/2oz creamed coconut from a packet and stir it into warm water until completely dissolved.
• Coriander roots are more intensely flavoured than the leaves, but the herb is not always available with the roots intact.

CHICKEN AND MUSHROOM DONBURI

"DONBURI" MEANS A ONE-DISH MEAL THAT IS EATEN FROM A BOWL, AND TAKES ITS NAME FROM THE EPONYMOUS JAPANESE PORCELAIN FOOD BOWL. AS IN MOST JAPANESE DISHES, THE RICE HERE IS COMPLETELY PLAIN BUT IS NEVERTHELESS AN INTEGRAL PART OF THE DISH.

SERVES FOUR

INGREDIENTS
  10ml/2 tsp groundnut (peanut) oil
  50g/2oz/4 tbsp butter
  2 garlic cloves, crushed
  2.5cm/1in piece of fresh root
    ginger, grated
  5 spring onions (scallions), sliced
  1 green fresh chilli, seeded and
    finely sliced
  3 chicken breast fillets, cut into
    thin strips
  150g/5oz tofu, cut into small cubes
  115g/4oz/1¾ shiitake mushrooms,
    stalks discarded and cups sliced
  15ml/1 tbsp Japanese rice wine
  30ml/2 tbsp light soy sauce
  10ml/2 tsp granulated sugar
  400ml/14fl oz/1⅔ cups chicken stock
For the rice
  225–275g/8–10oz/generous
    1–1½ cups Japanese rice or Thai
    fragrant rice

1 Cook the rice by the absorption method or by following the instructions on the packet.

2 While the rice is cooking, heat the oil and half the butter in a large frying pan. Stir-fry the garlic, ginger, spring onions and chilli for 1–2 minutes until slightly softened. Add the strips of chicken and fry, in batches if necessary, until all the pieces are evenly browned.

3 Transfer the chicken mixture to a plate and add the tofu to the pan. Stir-fry for a few minutes, then add the mushrooms. Stir-fry for 2–3 minutes over a medium heat until the mushrooms are tender.

4 Stir in the rice wine, soy sauce and sugar and cook briskly for 1–2 minutes, stirring all the time. Return the chicken to the pan, toss over the heat for about 2 minutes, then pour in the stock. Stir well and cook over a gentle heat for 5–6 minutes until bubbling.

5 Spoon the rice into individual serving bowls and pile the chicken mixture on top, making sure that each portion gets a generous amount of chicken sauce.

COOK'S TIP
Once the rice is cooked, leave it covered until ready to serve. It will stay warm for about 30 minutes. Fork through lightly just before serving.

SOUTHERN CHICKEN CURRY

A MILD COCONUT CURRY FLAVOURED WITH TURMERIC, CORIANDER AND CUMIN SEEDS THAT DEMONSTRATES THE INFLUENCE OF MALAYSIAN COOKING ON THAI CUISINE.

SERVES FOUR

INGREDIENTS

60ml/4 tbsp vegetable oil
1 large garlic clove, crushed
1 chicken, weighing about 1.5kg/
　3–3½lb, chopped into
　12 large pieces
400ml/14fl oz/1⅔ cups
　coconut cream
250ml/8fl oz/1 cup chicken stock
30ml/2 tbsp Thai fish sauce
30ml/2 tbsp sugar
juice of 2 limes

To garnish
2 small fresh red chillies, seeded and
　finely chopped
1 bunch spring onions (scallions),
　thinly sliced

For the curry paste
5ml/1 tsp dried chilli flakes
2.5ml/½ tsp salt
5cm/2in piece fresh turmeric or
　5ml/1 tsp ground turmeric
2.5ml/½ tsp coriander seeds
2.5ml/½ tsp cumin seeds
5ml/1 tsp dried shrimp paste

1 First make the curry paste. Put all the ingredients in a mortar, food processor or spice grinder and pound, process or grind to a smooth paste.

2 Heat the oil in a wok or frying pan and cook the garlic until golden. Add the chicken and cook until golden. Remove the chicken and set aside.

3 Reheat the oil and add the curry paste and then half the coconut cream. Cook for a few minutes until fragrant.

4 Return the chicken to the wok or pan, add the stock, mixing well, then add the remaining coconut cream, the fish sauce, sugar and lime juice. Stir well and bring to the boil, then lower the heat and simmer for 15 minutes.

5 Turn the curry into four warm serving bowls and sprinkle with the chopped fresh chillies and spring onions to garnish. Serve immediately.

COOK'S TIP
Use a large sharp knife or a Chinese cleaver to chop the chicken into pieces. Wash the board, knife and your hands thoroughly afterwards in hot, soapy water as chicken is notorious for harbouring harmful micro-organisms and bacteria.

CASHEW CHICKEN

ALTHOUGH IT IS NOT NATIVE TO SOUTH-EAST ASIA, THE CASHEW TREE IS HIGHLY PRIZED IN THAILAND AND THE CLASSIC PARTNERSHIP OF THESE SLIGHTLY SWEET NUTS WITH CHICKEN IS IMMENSELY POPULAR BOTH IN THAILAND AND ABROAD.

SERVES FOUR TO SIX

INGREDIENTS
 450g/1lb boneless chicken
  breast portions
 1 red (bell) pepper
 2 garlic cloves
 4 dried red chillies
 30ml/2 tbsp vegetable oil
 30ml/2 tbsp oyster sauce
 15ml/1 tbsp soy sauce
 pinch of granulated sugar
 1 bunch spring onions (scallions),
  cut into 5cm/2in lengths
 175g/6oz/1½ cups cashews, roasted
 coriander (cilantro) leaves,
  to garnish

1 Remove and discard the skin from the chicken breasts and trim off any excess fat. With a sharp knife, cut the chicken into bitesize pieces and set aside.

2 Halve the red pepper, scrape out the seeds and membranes and discard, then cut the flesh into 2cm/¾in dice. Peel and thinly slice the garlic and chop the dried red chillies.

3 Preheat a wok and then heat the oil. The best way to do this is to drizzle a "necklace" of oil around the inner rim of the wok, so that it drops down to coat the entire inner surface. Make sure the coating is even by swirling the wok.

4 Add the garlic and dried chillies to the wok and stir-fry over a medium heat until golden. Do not let the garlic burn, otherwise it will taste bitter.

5 Add the chicken to the wok and stir-fry until it is cooked through, then add the red pepper. If the mixture is very dry, add a little water.

6 Stir in the oyster sauce, soy sauce and sugar. Add the spring onions and cashew nuts. Stir-fry for 1–2 minutes more, until heated through. Spoon into a warm dish and serve immediately, garnished with the coriander leaves.

COOK'S TIP
The Thais not only value cashew nuts, but also the "fruit" under which each nut grows. Although they are known as cashew apples, these so-called fruits are actually bulbous portions of the stem. They may be pink, red or yellow in colour and the crisp, sweet flesh can be eaten raw or made into a refreshing drink. They have even been used for making jam. Cashew apples – and undried nuts – are rarely seen outside their growing regions.

CHICKEN AND LEMON GRASS CURRY

THIS FRAGRANT AND TRULY DELICIOUS CURRY IS EXCEPTIONALLY EASY AND TAKES LESS THAN TWENTY MINUTES TO PREPARE AND COOK — A PERFECT MID-WEEK MEAL.

SERVES FOUR

INGREDIENTS
  45ml/3 tbsp vegetable oil
  2 garlic cloves, crushed
  500g/1¼ lb skinless, boneless
    chicken thighs, chopped into
    small pieces
  45ml/3 tbsp Thai fish sauce
  120ml/4fl oz/½ cup
    chicken stock
  5ml/1 tsp granulated sugar
  1 lemon grass stalk, chopped into
    4 sticks and lightly crushed
  5 kaffir lime leaves, rolled into
    cylinders and thinly sliced across,
    plus extra to garnish
  chopped roasted peanuts
    and chopped fresh coriander
    (cilantro), to garnish
For the curry paste
  1 lemon grass stalk,
    coarsely chopped
  2.5cm/1in piece fresh galangal,
    peeled and coarsely chopped
  2 kaffir lime leaves, chopped
  3 shallots, coarsely chopped
  6 coriander (cilantro) roots,
    coarsely chopped
  2 garlic cloves
  2 fresh green chillies, seeded and
    coarsely chopped
  5ml/1 tsp shrimp paste
  5ml/1 tsp ground turmeric

1 Make the curry paste. Place all the ingredients in a large mortar, or food processor and pound with a pestle or process to a smooth paste.

2 Heat the vegetable oil in a wok or large, heavy frying pan, add the garlic and cook over a low heat, stirring frequently, until golden brown. Be careful not to let the garlic burn or it will taste bitter. Add the curry paste and stir-fry with the garlic for about 30 seconds more.

3 Add the chicken pieces to the pan and stir until thoroughly coated with the curry paste. Stir in the Thai fish sauce and chicken stock, with the sugar, and cook, stirring constantly, for 2 minutes more.

4 Add the lemon grass and lime leaves, reduce the heat and simmer for 10 minutes. If the mixture begins to dry out, add a little more stock or water.

5 Remove the lemon grass, if you like. Spoon the curry into four dishes, garnish with the lime leaves, peanuts and coriander and serve immediately.

CHICKEN WITH GINGER AND LEMON GRASS

THIS QUICK AND EASY RECIPE FROM VIETNAM CONTAINS THE UNUSUAL COMBINATION OF GINGER AND LEMON GRASS WITH MANDARIN ORANGE AND CHILLIES. THE DISH IS SERVED TOPPED WITH PEANUTS, WHICH ARE FIRST ROASTED, THEN SKINNED.

SERVES FOUR TO SIX

INGREDIENTS
  3 chicken legs (thighs and drumsticks)
  15ml/1 tbsp vegetable oil
  2cm/¾in piece fresh root ginger,
    finely chopped
  1 garlic clove, crushed
  1 small fresh red chilli, seeded and
    finely chopped
  5cm/2in piece lemon grass, shredded
  150ml/¼ pint/⅔ cup chicken stock
  15ml/1 tbsp fish sauce
  10ml/2 tsp granulated sugar
  2.5ml/½ tsp salt
  juice of ½ lemon
  50g/2oz raw peanuts
  2 spring onions (scallions), shredded
  rind of 1 mandarin or
    satsuma, shredded
  plain boiled rice or rice noodles,
    to serve

1 With the heel of a knife, chop through the narrow end of each of the chicken drumsticks. Remove the jointed parts of the chicken, then remove the skin. Rinse and pat dry with kitchen paper.

COOK'S TIP
To save yourself time and effort, buy ready-roasted peanuts. These are now available with reduced sodium for a low-salt alternative.

2 Heat the oil in a wok or large pan. Add the chicken, ginger, garlic, chilli and lemon grass and cook for 3–4 minutes. Add the chicken stock, fish sauce, sugar, salt and lemon juice. Cover the pan and simmer for 30–35 minutes.

3 To prepare the peanuts, the red skin must be removed. To do this grill (broil) or roast the peanuts under a medium heat until evenly brown, for 2–3 minutes. Turn the nuts out on to a clean cloth and rub briskly to loosen the skins.

4 Transfer the chicken from the pan to a warmed serving dish, and sprinkle with the roasted peanuts, shredded spring onions and the zest of the mandarin or satsuma. Serve hot with plain boiled rice or rice noodles.

CHICKEN WITH LEMON SAUCE

SUCCULENT CHICKEN WITH A REFRESHING LEMONY SAUCE AND JUST A HINT OF LIME IS A SURE
WINNER AS A FAMILY MEAL THAT IS QUICK AND EASY TO PREPARE.

2 Mix together the egg white and cornflour. Add the mixture to the chicken and turn the chicken with tongs until thoroughly coated. Heat the vegetable oil in a non-stick frying pan or wok and fry the chicken fillets for about 15 minutes until they are golden brown on both sides.

3 Meanwhile, make the sauce. Combine all the ingredients in a small pan. Add 1.5ml/¼ tsp salt. Bring to the boil over a low heat, stirring constantly until the sauce is smooth and has thickened.

SERVES FOUR

INGREDIENTS
    4 small skinless chicken breast fillets
    5ml/1 tsp sesame oil
    15ml/1 tbsp dry sherry
    1 egg white, lightly beaten
    30ml/2 tbsp cornflour (cornstarch)
    15ml/1 tbsp vegetable oil
    salt and ground white pepper
    chopped coriander (cilantro) leaves
        and spring onions (scallions) and
        lemon wedges, to garnish
For the sauce
    45ml/3 tbsp fresh lemon juice
    30ml/2 tbsp sweetened lime juice
    45ml/3 tbsp caster (superfine) sugar
    10ml/2 tsp cornflour (cornstarch)
    90ml/6 tbsp cold water

1 Arrange the chicken fillets in a single layer in a bowl. Mix the sesame oil with the sherry and add 2.5ml/½ tsp salt and 1.5ml/¼ tsp pepper. Pour over the chicken, cover and marinate for 15 minutes.

4 Cut the chicken into pieces and place on a warm serving plate. Pour the sauce over, garnish with the coriander leaves, spring onions and lemon wedges.

ROAST LIME CHICKEN WITH SWEET POTATOES

IN THAILAND, THIS CHICKEN WOULD BE SPIT-ROASTED, AS OVENS ARE SELDOM USED. HOWEVER, IT WORKS VERY WELL AS A CONVENTIONAL ROAST. THE SWEET POTATOES ARE AN INSPIRED ADDITION.

SERVES FOUR

INGREDIENTS

4 garlic cloves, 2 finely chopped
  and 2 bruised but left whole
small bunch coriander (cilantro),
  with roots, coarsely chopped
5ml/1 tsp ground turmeric
5cm/2in piece fresh turmeric
1 roasting chicken, about 1.5kg/3¼lb
1 lime, cut in half
4 medium/large sweet potatoes,
  peeled and cut into thick wedges
300ml/½ pint/1¼ cups chicken
  or vegetable stock
30ml/2 tbsp soy sauce
salt and ground black pepper

1 Preheat the oven to 190°C/375°F/ Gas 5. Calculate the cooking time for the chicken, allowing 20 minutes per 500g/1¼lb, plus 20 minutes. Using a mortar and pestle or food processor, grind the chopped garlic, coriander, 10ml/2 tsp salt and turmeric to a paste.

2 Place the chicken in a roasting pan and smear it with the paste. Squeeze the lime juice over and place the lime halves and garlic cloves in the cavity. Cover with foil and roast in the oven.

3 Meanwhile, bring a pan of water to the boil and par-boil the sweet potatoes for 10–15 minutes, until just tender. Drain well and place them around the chicken in the roasting pan. Baste with the cooking juices and sprinkle with salt and pepper. Replace the foil and return the chicken to the oven.

4 About 20 minutes before the end of cooking, remove the foil and baste the chicken. Turn the sweet potatoes over.

5 At the end of the calculated roasting time, check that the chicken is cooked. Lift it out of the roasting pan, tip it so that all the juices collected in the cavity drain into the pan, then place the bird on a carving board. Cover it with tented foil and leave it to rest before carving. Transfer the sweet potatoes to a serving dish and keep them hot in the oven while you make the gravy.

6 Pour away the oil from the roasting pan but keep the juices. Place the roasting pan on top of the stove and heat until the juices are bubbling. Pour in the stock. Bring the mixture to the boil, stirring constantly with a wooden spoon and scraping the base of the pan to incorporate the residue.

7 Stir in the soy sauce and check the seasoning before straining the gravy into a jug (pitcher). Serve it with the carved meat and the sweet potatoes.

COOK'S TIPS

• When the chicken is cooked, the legs should move freely. Insert the tip of a sharp knife or a skewer into the thickest part of one of the thighs. The juices that emerge from the cut should run clear. If there are any traces of pinkness, return the chicken to the oven for a little longer.
• Although originally native to tropical America, sweet potatoes are now a popular food crop throughout South-east Asia. There are many varieties and the flesh ranges in texture from floury to moist and in colour from deep orange through gold to white.

Salt "Baked" Chicken

This is a wonderful way of cooking chicken. All the delicious, succulent juices are sealed inside the salt crust — yet the flavour isn't salty.

SERVES EIGHT

INGREDIENTS

1.5kg/3–3½lb corn-fed chicken
1.5ml/¼ tsp fine sea salt
2.25kg/5lb coarse rock salt
15ml/1 tbsp vegetable oil
2.5cm/1in piece fresh root ginger, finely chopped
4 spring onions (scallions), cut into fine rings
boiled rice, garnished with shredded spring onions (scallions), to serve

1 Rinse the chicken. Pat it dry, both inside and out, with kitchen paper, then rub the inside with the sea salt.

2 Place four pieces of damp kitchen paper on the bottom of a heavy frying pan or wok just large enough to hold the chicken.

3 Sprinkle a layer of rock salt over the kitchen paper, about 1cm/½in thick. Place the chicken on top of the layer of salt.

4 Pour the remaining salt over the chicken until it is completely covered. Dampen six more pieces of kitchen paper and place these around the rim of the pan or wok. Cover with a tight-fitting lid. Put the pan or wok over a high heat for 10 minutes or until it gives off a slightly smoky smell.

5 Immediately reduce the heat to medium and continue to cook the chicken for 30 minutes without lifting the lid. After 30 minutes, turn off the heat and leave for a further 10 minutes before carefully lifting the chicken out of the salt. Brush off any salt still clinging to the chicken and allow the bird to cool for 20 minutes before cutting it into serving-size pieces.

6 Heat the oil in a small pan until very hot. Add the ginger and spring onions and fry for a few seconds, then pour into a heatproof bowl and use as a dipping sauce for the chicken. Serve the chicken with boiled rice, garnished with shredded spring onions.

FRAGRANT CHICKEN CURRY

THIS DISH IS PERFECT FOR A PARTY AS THE CHICKEN AND SAUCE CAN BE PREPARED IN ADVANCE AND COMBINED AND HEATED AT THE LAST MINUTE.

SERVES FOUR

INGREDIENTS
45ml/3 tbsp oil
1 onion, coarsely chopped
2 garlic cloves, crushed
15ml/1 tbsp Thai red curry paste
115g/4oz creamed coconut dissolved
   in 900ml/1½ pints/3¾ cups boiling
   water, or 1 litre/1¾ pints/4 cups
   coconut milk
2 lemon grass stalks,
   coarsely chopped
6 kaffir lime leaves, chopped
150ml/¼ pint/⅔ cup Greek (US
   strained plain) yogurt
30ml/2 tbsp apricot jam
1 cooked chicken, about
   1.5kg/3–3½ lb
30ml/2 tbsp chopped fresh
   coriander (cilantro)
salt and ground black pepper
kaffir lime leaves, shredded, toasted
   coconut and fresh coriander
   (cilantro), to garnish
boiled rice, to serve

COOK'S TIP
If you prefer the sauce to be thicker, stir in a little more creamed coconut after adding the chicken.

1 Heat the oil in a large pan. Add the onion and garlic and cook over a low heat for 5–10 minutes until soft. Stir in the red curry paste. Cook, stirring constantly, for 2–3 minutes. Stir in the diluted creamed coconut or coconut milk, then add the lemon grass, lime leaves, yogurt and apricot jam. Stir well. Cover and simmer for 30 minutes.

2 Remove the pan from the heat and leave to cool slightly. Transfer the sauce to a food processor or blender and process to a smooth purée, then strain it back into the rinsed-out pan, pressing as much of the puréed mixture as possible through the sieve with the back of a wooden spoon. Set aside while you prepare the chicken.

3 Remove the skin from the chicken, slice the meat off the bones and cut it into bitesize pieces. Add to the sauce.

4 Bring the sauce back to simmering point. Stir in the fresh coriander and season with salt and pepper. Garnish with extra lime leaves, shredded coconut and coriander. Serve with rice.

FRAGRANT GRILLED CHICKEN

IF YOU HAVE TIME, PREPARE THE CHICKEN IN ADVANCE AND LEAVE IT TO MARINATE IN THE
REFRIGERATOR FOR SEVERAL HOURS — OR EVEN OVERNIGHT — UNTIL READY TO COOK.

SERVES FOUR

INGREDIENTS
  450g/1lb boneless chicken breast
    portions, with the skin on
  30ml/2 tbsp sesame oil
  2 garlic cloves, crushed
  2 coriander (cilantro) roots,
    finely chopped
  2 small fresh red chillies, seeded
    and finely chopped
  30ml/2 tbsp Thai fish sauce
  5ml/1 tsp sugar
  cooked rice, to serve
  lime wedges, to garnish
For the sauce
  90ml/6 tbsp rice vinegar
  60ml/4 tbsp sugar
  2.5ml/½ tsp salt
  2 garlic cloves, crushed
  1 small fresh red chilli, seeded and
    finely chopped
  115g/4oz/4 cups fresh coriander
    (cilantro), finely chopped

1 Lay the chicken breast portions between two sheets of clear film (plastic wrap), baking parchment or foil and beat with the side of a rolling pin or the flat side of a meat tenderizer until the meat is about half its original thickness. Place in a large, shallow dish or bowl.

2 Mix together the sesame oil, garlic, coriander roots, red chillies, fish sauce and sugar in a jug (pitcher), stirring until the sugar has dissolved. Pour the mixture over the chicken and turn to coat. Cover with clear film and set aside to marinate in a cool place for at least 20 minutes. Meanwhile, make the sauce.

3 Heat the vinegar in a small pan, add the sugar and stir until dissolved. Add the salt and stir until the mixture begins to thicken. Add the remaining sauce ingredients, stir well, then spoon the sauce into a serving bowl.

4 Preheat the grill (broiler) and cook the chicken for 5 minutes. Turn and baste with the marinade, then cook for 5 minutes more, or until cooked through and golden. Serve with rice and the sauce, garnished with lime wedges.

CHICKEN <u>WITH</u> MIXED VEGETABLES

A RIOT OF COLOUR, THIS DELECTABLE DISH HAS PLENTY OF CONTRASTS IN TERMS OF TEXTURE AND TASTE. QUICK AND EASY TO PREPARE, IT'S IDEAL AS A FAMILY MEAL.

SERVES FOUR

INGREDIENTS
350g/12oz chicken breast fillets
20ml/4 tsp vegetable oil
300ml/½ pint/1¼ cups chicken stock
75g/3oz/¾ cup drained, canned
   straw mushrooms
50g/2oz/½ cup sliced, drained,
   canned bamboo shoots
50g/2oz/⅓ cup drained, canned
   water chestnuts, sliced
1 small carrot, sliced
50g/2oz/½ cup mangetouts (snow peas)
15ml/1 tbsp dry sherry
15ml/1 tbsp oyster sauce
5ml/1 tsp caster (superfine) sugar
5ml/1 tsp cornflour (cornstarch)
15ml/1 tbsp cold water
salt and ground white pepper

3 Heat the remaining oil in a non-stick frying pan or wok, add all the vegetables and stir-fry for 2 minutes. Stir in the sherry, oyster sauce, caster sugar and reserved stock. Add the chicken to the pan and cook for 2 minutes more.

4 Mix the cornflour to a paste with the water. Add the mixture to the pan and cook, stirring continuously, until the sauce thickens slightly. Season to taste with salt and pepper and serve immediately.

1 Put the chicken in a bowl. Add 5ml/ 1 tsp of the oil, 1.5ml/¼ tsp salt and a pinch of pepper. Cover and set aside for 10 minutes in a cool place.

2 Bring the stock to the boil in a pan. Add the chicken and cook for 12 minutes, or until tender. Drain and slice, reserving 75ml/5 tbsp of the stock.

Jungle Curry of Guinea Fowl

A TRADITIONAL WILD FOOD COUNTRY CURRY FROM THE NORTH-CENTRAL REGION OF THAILAND, THIS DISH CAN BE MADE USING ANY GAME, FISH OR CHICKEN. GUINEA FOWL IS NOT TYPICAL OF THAI CUISINE, BUT IS A POPULAR AND WIDELY AVAILABLE GAME BIRD IN THE WEST.

SERVES FOUR

INGREDIENTS
    1 guinea fowl or similar game bird
    15ml/1 tbsp vegetable oil
    10ml/2 tsp green curry paste
    15ml/1 tbsp Thai fish sauce
    2.5cm/1in piece fresh galangal,
      peeled and finely chopped
    15ml/1 tbsp fresh green peppercorns
    3 kaffir lime leaves, torn
    15ml/1 tbsp whisky,
      preferably Mekhong
    300ml/½ pint/1¼ cups
      chicken stock
    50g/2oz snake beans or yard-long
      beans, cut into 2.5cm/1in lengths
      (about ½ cup)
    225g/8oz/3¼ cups chestnut
      mushrooms, sliced
    1 piece drained canned bamboo
      shoot, about 50g/2oz, shredded
    5ml/1 tsp dried chilli flakes, to
      garnish (optional)

1 Cut up the guinea fowl, remove and discard the skin, then take all the meat off the bones. Chop the meat into bitesize pieces and set aside.

2 Heat the oil in a wok or frying pan and add the curry paste. Stir-fry over a medium heat for 30 seconds, until the paste gives off its aroma.

3 Add the fish sauce and the guinea fowl meat and stir-fry until the meat is browned all over. Add the galangal, peppercorns, lime leaves and whisky, then pour in the stock.

4 Bring to the boil. Add the vegetables, return to a simmer and cook gently for 2–3 minutes, until they are just cooked. Spoon into a dish, sprinkle with chilli flakes, if you like, and serve.

COOK'S TIPS
• Guinea fowl originated in West Africa and was regarded as a game bird. However, it has been domesticated in Europe for over 500 years. They range in size from 675g/1½ lb to 2kg/4½ lb, but about 1.2kg/2½ lb is average. American readers could substitute two or three Cornish hens, depending on size.
• Fresh green peppercorns are simply unripe berries. They are sold on the stem and look rather like miniature Brussels sprout stalks. Look for them at Thai supermarkets. If unavailable, substitute bottled green peppercorns, but rinse well and drain them first.

DUCK <u>WITH</u> PANCAKES

FOR ANYONE CONSCIOUS OF THEIR CALORIE INTAKE, THIS RECIPE IS CONSIDERABLY LOWER IN FAT THAN TRADITIONAL PEKING DUCK, BUT JUST AS DELICIOUS. GUESTS SPREAD THEIR PANCAKES WITH SAUCE, ADD DUCK AND VEGETABLES, THEN ROLL THEM UP.

SERVES FOUR

INGREDIENTS
  15ml/1 tbsp clear honey
  1.5ml/¼ tsp five spice powder
  1 garlic clove, finely chopped
  15ml/1 tbsp hoisin sauce
  2.5ml/½ tsp salt
  a large pinch of ground white pepper
  2 small skinless duck breast fillets
  ½ cucumber
  10 spring onions (scallions)
  3 Chinese leaves (Chinese cabbage)
  12 Chinese pancakes
For the sauce
  5ml/1 tsp vegetable oil
  2 garlic cloves, chopped
  2 spring onions (scallions), chopped
  1cm/½ in piece of fresh root
    ginger, bruised
  60ml/4 tbsp hoisin sauce
  15ml/1 tbsp dry sherry
  15ml/1 tbsp cold water
  2.5ml/½ tsp sesame oil

1 Mix the honey, five spice powder, garlic, hoisin sauce, salt and pepper in a shallow dish large enough to hold the duck breasts side by side. Add the duck breasts, turning them in the marinade. Cover and leave in a cool place to marinate for 2 hours.

2 Cut the cucumber in half lengthways. Using a teaspoon scrape out and discard the seeds. Cut the flesh into thin batons 5cm/2in long.

3 Cut off and discard the green tops from the spring onions. Finely shred the white parts and place on a serving plate with the cucumber batons.

4 Make the sauce. Heat the oil in a small pan and gently fry the garlic for a few seconds without browning. Add the spring onions, ginger, hoisin sauce, sherry and water. Cook gently for 5 minutes, stirring often, then strain and mix with the sesame oil.

5 Remove the duck from the marinade and drain well. Place the duck on a rack over a grill (broiling) pan. Grill (broil) under a medium to high heat for 8–10 minutes on each side. Allow to cool for 5 minutes before cutting into thin slices. Arrange on a serving platter, cover and keep warm.

6 Line a steamer with the Chinese leaves and place the pancakes on top. Have ready a large pan with 5cm/2in boiling water. Cover the steamer and place on a trivet in the pan. Steam over a high heat for 2 minutes or until the pancakes are hot. Serve at once with the duck, cucumber, spring onions and sauce.

STIR-FRIED CRISPY DUCK

THIS STIR-FRY WOULD BE DELICIOUS WRAPPED IN FLOUR TORTILLAS OR STEAMED CHINESE PANCAKES, WITH A LITTLE EXTRA WARM PLUM SAUCE.

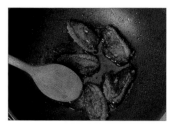

2 Heat the oil in a wok or large frying pan and cook the duck over a high heat until golden and crisp. Keep stirring to prevent the duck from sticking. Remove the duck with a slotted spoon and drain on kitchen paper. You may need to cook the duck in several batches.

3 Add the spring onions to the pan and cook for 2 minutes. Stir in the cabbage and cook for 5 minutes, or until it is softened and golden.

4 Return the duck to the pan with the water chestnuts, cashews and cucumber. Stir-fry for 2 minutes. Add the plum sauce and soy sauce and season to taste, then heat for 2 minutes. Serve garnished with the sliced spring onions.

SERVES TWO

INGREDIENTS
  275–350g/10–12oz boneless
    duck breast fillets
  30ml/2 tbsp plain (all-purpose) flour
  60ml/4 tbsp oil
  1 bunch spring onions (scallions),
    halved lengthwise and cut into
    5cm/2in strips, plus extra to garnish
  275g/10oz/2½ cups finely shredded
    green cabbage
  225g/8oz can water chestnuts,
    drained and sliced
  50g/2oz/½ cup unsalted cashew nuts
  115g/4oz cucumber, cut into strips
  45ml/3 tbsp plum sauce
  15ml/1 tbsp light soy sauce
  salt and ground black pepper

1 Remove any skin from the duck breast, then trim off a little of the fat. Thinly slice the meat into even-size pieces. Season the flour with plenty of salt and pepper and use it to completely coat each piece of duck.

DUCK <u>AND</u> SESAME STIR-FRY

THIS RECIPE COMES FROM NORTHERN THAILAND AND IS INTENDED FOR GAME BIRDS, AS FARMED DUCK WOULD HAVE TOO MUCH FAT. USE WILD DUCK IF YOU CAN GET IT, OR EVEN PARTRIDGE, PHEASANT OR PIGEON. IF YOU DO USE FARMED DUCK, YOU SHOULD REMOVE THE SKIN AND FAT LAYER.

SERVES FOUR

INGREDIENTS

250g/9oz boneless wild duck meat
15ml/1 tbsp sesame oil
15ml/1 tbsp vegetable oil
4 garlic cloves, finely sliced
2.5ml/½ tsp dried chilli flakes
15ml/1 tbsp Thai fish sauce
15ml/1 tbsp light soy sauce
120ml/4fl oz/½ cup water
1 head broccoli, cut into small florets
coriander (cilantro) and 15ml/1 tbsp
   toasted sesame seeds, to garnish

VARIATIONS
Pak choi (bok choy) or Chinese flowering cabbage can be used instead of broccoli.

1 Cut the duck meat into bitesize pieces. Heat the oils in a wok or large, heavy frying pan and stir-fry the garlic over a medium heat until it is golden brown – do not let it burn. Add the duck to the pan and stir-fry for a further 2 minutes, until the meat begins to brown.

2 Stir in the chilli flakes, fish sauce, soy sauce and water. Add the broccoli and continue to stir-fry for about 2 minutes, until the duck is just cooked through.

3 Serve on warmed plates, garnished with coriander and sesame seeds.

CHINESE DUCK CURRY

A RICHLY SPICED CURRY THAT ILLUSTRATES THE POWERFUL CHINESE INFLUENCE ON THAI CUISINE. THE DUCK IS BEST MARINATED FOR AS LONG AS POSSIBLE, ALTHOUGH IT TASTES GOOD EVEN IF YOU ONLY HAVE TIME TO MARINATE IT BRIEFLY.

2 Meanwhile, bring a pan of water to the boil. Add the squash and cook for 10–15 minutes, until just tender. Drain well and set aside.

3 Pour the marinade from the duck into a wok and heat until boiling. Stir in the curry paste and cook for 2–3 minutes, until well blended and fragrant. Add the duck and cook for 3–4 minutes, stirring constantly, until browned on all sides.

4 Add the fish sauce and palm sugar and cook for 2 minutes more. Stir in the coconut milk until the mixture is smooth, then add the cooked squash, with the chillies and lime leaves.

5 Simmer gently, stirring frequently, for 5 minutes, then spoon into a dish, sprinkle with the coriander and serve.

VARIATION
This dish works just as well with skinless, boneless chicken breast portions.

SERVES FOUR

INGREDIENTS
   4 duck breast portions, skin and
     bones removed
   30ml/2 tbsp five-spice powder
   30ml/2 tbsp sesame oil
   grated rind and juice of 1 orange
   1 medium butternut squash, peeled
     and cubed
   10ml/2 tsp Thai red curry paste
   30ml/2 tbsp Thai fish sauce
   15ml/1 tbsp palm sugar or light
     muscovado (brown) sugar
   300ml/½ pint/1¼ cups coconut milk
   2 fresh red chillies, seeded
   4 kaffir lime leaves, torn
   small bunch coriander (cilantro),
     chopped, to garnish

1 Cut the duck meat into bitesize pieces and place in a bowl with the five-spice powder, sesame oil and orange rind and juice. Stir well to mix all the ingredients and coat the duck in the marinade. Cover the bowl with clear film (plastic wrap) and set aside in a cool place to marinate for at least 15 minutes.

STIR-FRIED DUCK <u>WITH</u> PINEAPPLE

*THE FATTY SKIN ON DUCK MAKES IT IDEAL FOR STIR-FRYING: AS SOON AS THE DUCK IS ADDED
TO THE HOT PAN THE FAT IS RELEASED, CREATING DELICIOUS CRISP SKIN AND TENDER FLESH WHEN
COOKED. STIR-FRIED VEGETABLES AND NOODLES MAKE THIS A MEAL IN ITSELF.*

SERVES FOUR

INGREDIENTS
    250g/9oz fresh sesame noodles
    2 duck breast portions, thinly sliced
    3 spring onions (scallions), cut
       into strips
    2 celery sticks, cut into matchsticks
    1 fresh pineapple, peeled, cored and
       cut into strips
    300g/11oz mixed vegetables: carrots,
       (bell) peppers, beansprouts, cabbage,
       shredded or cut into strips
    90ml/6 tbsp plum sauce

1 Cook the noodles in a pan of boiling
water for 3 minutes. Drain.

2 Meanwhile, heat a wok. Add the duck
to the hot wok and stir-fry for about
2 minutes, until crisp. If the duck yields
a lot of fat, drain off all but 30ml/2 tbsp.

3 Add the spring onions and celery to
the wok and stir-fry for 2 minutes more.
Use a draining spoon to remove the
ingredients from the wok and set aside.
Add the pineapple strips and mixed
vegetables, and stir-fry for 2 minutes.

4 Add the cooked noodles and plum
sauce to the wok, then replace the
duck, spring onion and celery mixture.

5 Stir-fry the duck mixture for about
2 minutes more, or until the noodles
and vegetables are hot and the duck is
cooked through. Serve immediately.

COOK'S TIP
Fresh sesame noodles can be bought
from large supermarkets – you'll find
them in the chiller cabinets alongside
fresh pasta. If they aren't available, then
use fresh egg noodles instead and cook
according to the instructions on the
packet. For extra flavour, add a little
sesame oil to the cooking water.

PEKING DUCK <u>WITH</u> MANDARIN PANCAKES

AS THE CHINESE DISCOVERED CENTURIES AGO, THIS IS QUITE THE BEST WAY TO EAT DUCK. THE PREPARATION IS TIME-CONSUMING, BUT IT CAN BE DONE IN EASY STAGES.

SERVES EIGHT

INGREDIENTS
 1 duck, about 2.25kg/5¼lb
 45ml/3 tbsp clear honey
 30ml/2 tbsp water
 5ml/1 tsp salt
 1 bunch spring onions (scallions),
   cut into strips
 ½ cucumber, seeded and cut
   into matchsticks
For the mandarin pancakes
 275g/10oz/2½ cups strong
   white flour
 5ml/1 tsp salt
 45ml/3 tbsp groundnut (peanut)
   or sesame oil
 250ml/8fl oz/1 cup boiling
   water
For the dipping sauces
 120ml/4fl oz/½ cup hoisin
   sauce
 120ml/4fl oz/½ cup plum sauce

1 Place the duck on a trivet in the sink and pour boiling water over the duck to scald and firm up the skin. Carefully lift it out on the trivet and drain thoroughly. Tie kitchen string firmly around the legs of the bird and suspend it from a butcher's hook from a shelf in the kitchen or cellar, whichever is the coolest. Place a bowl underneath to catch the drips and leave overnight.

2 Next day, blend the honey, water and salt and brush half the mixture over the duck skin. Hang up again and leave for 2–3 hours. Repeat and leave to dry completely for a further 3–4 hours.

3 Make the pancakes. Sift the flour and salt into a bowl or food processor. Add 15ml/1 tbsp of the oil, then gradually add enough of the boiling water to form a soft but not sticky dough. Knead for 2–3 minutes by hand or for 30 seconds in the food processor. Allow to rest for 30 minutes.

4 Knead the dough, then divide it into 24 pieces and roll each piece to a 15cm/6in round. Brush the surface of half the rounds with oil, then sandwich the rounds together in pairs.

5 Brush the surface of two heavy frying pans sparingly with oil. Add one pancake pair to each pan and cook gently for 2–3 minutes until cooked but not coloured. Turn over and cook for 2–3 minutes more.

6 Slide the double pancakes out of the pan and pull them apart. Stack on a plate, placing a square of non-stick baking parchment between each while cooking the remainder. Cool, wrap tightly in foil and set aside.

7 Preheat the oven to 230°C/450°F/ Gas 8. When it reaches that temperature, put the duck on a rack in a roasting pan and place it in the oven. Immediately reduce the temperature to 180°C/350°F/ Gas 4 and roast the duck for 1¾ hours without basting. Check that the skin is crisp and, if necessary, increase the oven temperature to the maximum. Roast for 15 minutes more.

8 Meanwhile, place the spring onion strips in iced water to crisp up. Drain. Pat the cucumber pieces dry on kitchen paper. Reheat the prepared pancakes by steaming the foil parcel for 5–10 minutes in a bamboo steamer over a wok or pan of boiling water. Pour the dipping sauces into small dishes to share between the guests.

9 Carve the duck into 4cm/1½in pieces. At the table, each guest smears some of the prepared sauce on a pancake, tops it with a small amount of crisp duck skin and meat and adds cucumber and spring onion strips before enjoying the rolled-up pancake.

COOK'S TIP
Mandarin pancakes can be cooked ahead and frozen. Simply separate the cooked pancakes with squares of freezer paper and wrap them in a plastic bag. They can be heated from frozen as described in the recipe. If time is short, use ready-made pancakes, available from large supermarkets and oriental stores.

ANITA WONG'S DUCK

THE CHINESE ARE PASSIONATELY FOND OF DUCK AND REGARD IT AS ESSENTIAL AT CELEBRATORY MEALS. TO THE CHINESE, DUCK DENOTES MARITAL HARMONY.

SERVES FOUR TO SIX

INGREDIENTS

1 duck with giblets, about
  2.25kg/5lb
60ml/4 tbsp vegetable oil
2 garlic cloves, chopped
2.5cm/1in piece fresh root ginger,
  peeled and thinly sliced
45ml/3 tbsp bean paste
30ml/2 tbsp light soy sauce
15ml/1 tbsp dark soy sauce
15ml/1 tbsp sugar
2.5ml/½ tsp five-spice powder
3 star anise points
450ml/¾ pint/scant 2 cups duck
  stock (see Cook's Tip)
salt
shredded spring onions (scallions),
  to garnish

1 Make the stock, strain into a bowl and blot with kitchen paper to remove excess fat. Measure 450ml/¾ pint/ scant 2 cups into a jug (pitcher).

2 Heat the oil in a large pan. Fry the garlic without browning, then add the duck. Turn frequently until the outside is slightly brown. Transfer to a plate.

3 Add the ginger to the pan, then stir in the bean paste. Cook for 1 minute, then add both soy sauces, the sugar and the five-spice powder. Return the duck to the pan and fry until the outside is coated. Add the star anise and stock, and season. Cover tightly; simmer for 2–2½ hours or until tender. Skim off the fat. Leave the duck in the sauce to cool.

4 Cut the duck into serving portions and pour over the sauce. Garnish with spring onion curls and serve cold.

COOK'S TIP
To make stock, put the duck giblets in a pan with a small onion and a piece of bruised ginger. Cover with 600ml/1 pint/ 2½ cups water, bring to the boil and then simmer, covered, for 20 minutes.

DUCK <u>WITH</u> PINEAPPLE <u>AND</u> GINGER

USE THE BONELESS DUCK BREAST FILLETS THAT ARE WIDELY AVAILABLE OR ALTERNATIVELY DO AS THE CHINESE AND USE A WHOLE BIRD, SAVING THE LEGS FOR ANOTHER MEAL AND USING THE CARCASS TO MAKE STOCK FOR SOUP. MUCH MORE IN LINE WITH CHINESE FRUGALITY!

SERVES TWO TO THREE

INGREDIENTS
    2 duck breast fillets
    4 spring onions (scallions), chopped
    15ml/1 tbsp light soy sauce
    225g/8oz can pineapple rings
    75ml/5 tbsp water
    4 pieces drained Chinese stem ginger
      in syrup, plus 45ml/3 tbsp syrup
      from the jar
    30ml/2 tbsp cornflour (cornstarch)
      mixed to a paste with a little water
    1/4 each red and green (bell) pepper,
      seeded and cut into thin strips
    salt and ground black pepper
    cooked thin egg noodles, baby
      spinach and green beans, blanched,
      to serve

1 Strip the skin from the duck. Select a shallow bowl that will fit into your steamer and that will accommodate the duck fillets side by side. Spread out the chopped spring onions in the bowl, arrange the duck on top and cover with baking parchment. Set the steamer over boiling water and cook the duck for about 1 hour or until tender. Remove the duck from the steamer and leave to cool slightly.

2 Cut the duck fillets into thin slices. Place on a plate and moisten them with a little of the cooking juices from the steaming bowl. Strain the remaining juices into a small pan and set aside. Cover the duck slices with the baking parchment or foil and keep warm.

3 Drain the canned pineapple rings, reserving 75ml/5 tbsp of the juice. Add this to the reserved cooking juices in the pan, together with the measured water. Stir in the ginger syrup, then stir in the cornflour paste and cook, stirring until thickened. Season to taste.

4 Cut the pineapple and ginger into attractive shapes. Put the cooked noodles, baby spinach and green beans on a plate, add slices of duck and top with the pineapple, ginger and pepper strips. Pour over the sauce and serve.

MEAT DISHES

Meat curries are traditional in many Asian countries. They are based on wet pastes, rather than dry spice mixtures, with chillies, garlic, shallots, ginger or galangal the predominant flavourings. Fresh lemon grass and coriander are often included, and coconut milk is what marries the various ingredients together. Stir-frying is another popular way of cooking meat, a technique that has the advantage of speed. Try some of these delicious recipes for a quick tasty supper.

ADOBO

FOUR INGREDIENTS ARE ESSENTIAL IN AN ADOBO, ONE OF THE BEST-LOVED RECIPES IN THE FILIPINO REPERTOIRE. THEY ARE VINEGAR, GARLIC, PEPPERCORNS AND BAY LEAVES.

SERVES FOUR

INGREDIENTS

1 chicken, about 1.4kg/3lb, or
  4 chicken quarters
350g/12oz pork leg steaks
  (with fat)
10ml/2 tsp sugar
60ml/4 tbsp sunflower oil
75ml/5 tbsp wine or cider vinegar
4 plump garlic cloves, crushed
1/2 tsp black peppercorns,
  crushed lightly
15ml/1 tbsp light soy sauce
4 bay leaves
2.5ml/1/2 tsp annatto seeds, soaked
  in 30ml /2 tbsp boiling water, or
  2.5ml/1/2 tsp ground turmeric
salt
For the plantain chips
  1–2 large plantains and/or
  1 sweet potato
  vegetable oil, for deep frying

1 Wipe the chicken and cut into eight even-size pieces, or halve the chicken quarters, if using. Cut the pork into neat pieces. Spread out all the meat on a board, sprinkle lightly with sugar and set aside.

2 Heat the oil in a wok or large frying pan and fry the chicken and pork pieces, in batches if necessary, until they are golden on both sides.

3 Add the vinegar, garlic, peppercorns, soy sauce and bay leaves and stir well.

4 Strain the annatto seed liquid and stir it into the pan or stir in the turmeric. Add salt to taste. Bring to the boil, cover, lower the heat and simmer for 30–35 minutes. Remove the lid and simmer for 10 minutes more.

5 Meanwhile, prepare the plantain chips. Heat the oil in a deep fryer to 195°C/390°F. Peel the plantains or sweet potato (or both), if you like, and slice them into rounds or chips. Deep fry them, in batches if necessary, until cooked but not brown. Drain on kitchen paper. When ready to serve, reheat the oil and fry the plantains or sweet potato until crisp – it will only take a few seconds. Drain. Spoon the adobo into a serving dish and serve with the chips.

COOK'S TIP
Sprinkling the chicken lightly with sugar turns the skin beautifully brown when fried, but do not have the oil too hot to begin with or they will over-brown.

LION'S HEAD MEAT BALLS

THESE LARGER-THAN-USUAL PORK MEAT BALLS ARE FIRST FRIED, THEN SIMMERED IN STOCK. THEY ARE TRADITIONALLY SERVED WITH A FRINGE OF GREENS SUCH AS PAK CHOI TO REPRESENT THE LION'S MANE.

SERVES TWO TO THREE

INGREDIENTS
    450g/1lb lean pork, minced (ground)
      finely with a little fat
    4–6 drained canned water chestnuts,
      finely chopped
    5ml/1 tsp finely chopped fresh
      root ginger
    1 small onion, finely chopped
    30ml/2 tbsp dark soy sauce
    beaten egg, to bind
    30ml/2 tbsp cornflour (cornstarch),
      seasoned with salt and black pepper
    30ml/2 tbsp groundnut (peanut) oil
    300ml/1/2 pint/1 1/4 cups
      chicken stock
    2.5ml/1/2 tsp sugar
    115g/4oz pak choi (bok choy), stalks
      trimmed and the leaves rinsed
    salt and ground black pepper

1 Mix the pork, water chestnuts, ginger and onion with 15ml/1 tbsp of the soy sauce in a bowl. Add salt and pepper to taste, stir in enough beaten egg to bind, then form into eight or nine balls. Toss a little of the cornflour into the bowl and make a paste with the remaining cornflour and water.

VARIATION
Crab meat or prawns (shrimp) can be used instead of some of the pork in this recipe. Alternatively, you could try substituting minced (ground) lamb or beef for the pork used here.

2 Heat the oil in a large frying pan and brown the meat balls all over. Using a slotted spoon, transfer the meat balls to a wok or deep frying pan.

3 Add the stock, sugar and the remaining soy sauce to the oil that is left in the pan. Heat gently, stirring to incorporate the sediment on the bottom of the pan. Pour over the meat balls, cover and simmer for 20–25 minutes.

4 Increase the heat and add the pak choi. Continue to cook for 2–3 minutes or until the leaves are just wilted.

5 Lift out the greens and arrange on a serving platter. Top with the meat balls and keep hot. Stir the cornflour paste into the sauce. Bring to the boil, stirring, until it thickens. Pour over the meat balls and serve at once.

SWEET AND SOUR PORK, THAI-STYLE

IT WAS THE CHINESE WHO ORIGINALLY CREATED SWEET AND SOUR COOKING, BUT THE THAIS ALSO DO IT VERY WELL. THIS VERSION HAS A FRESHER AND CLEANER FLAVOUR THAN THE ORIGINAL. IT MAKES A GOOD ONE-DISH MEAL WHEN SERVED OVER RICE.

SERVES FOUR

INGREDIENTS
  350g/12oz lean pork
  30ml/2 tbsp vegetable oil
  4 garlic cloves, thinly sliced
  1 small red onion, sliced
  30ml/2 tbsp Thai fish sauce
  15ml/1 tbsp granulated sugar
  1 red (bell) pepper, seeded and diced
  ½ cucumber, seeded and sliced
  2 plum tomatoes, cut into wedges
  115g/4oz piece of fresh pineapple,
    cut into small chunks
  2 spring onions (scallions), cut into
    short lengths
  ground black pepper
To garnish
  coriander (cilantro) leaves
  spring onions (scallions), shredded

1 Place the pork in the freezer for 30–40 minutes, until firm. Using a sharp knife, cut it into thin strips.

2 Heat the oil in a wok or large frying pan. Add the garlic. Cook over a medium heat until golden, then add the pork and stir-fry for 4–5 minutes. Add the onion slices and toss to mix.

3 Add the fish sauce, sugar and ground black pepper to taste. Toss the mixture over the heat for 3–4 minutes more.

4 Stir in the red pepper, cucumber, tomatoes, pineapple and spring onions. Stir-fry for 3–4 minutes more, then spoon into a bowl. Garnish with the coriander and spring onions and serve.

LEMON GRASS PORK

CHILLIES AND LEMON GRASS FLAVOUR THIS SIMPLE STIR-FRY, WHILE PEANUTS ADD AN INTERESTING CONTRAST IN TEXTURE. LOOK FOR JARS OF CHOPPED LEMON GRASS, WHICH ARE HANDY WHEN THE FRESH VEGETABLE ISN'T AVAILABLE.

SERVES FOUR

INGREDIENTS
  675g/1½lb boneless
    pork loin
  2 lemon grass stalks,
    finely chopped
  4 spring onions (scallions),
    thinly sliced
  5ml/1 tsp salt
  12 black peppercorns,
    coarsely crushed
  30ml/2 tbsp groundnut
    (peanut) oil
  2 garlic cloves, chopped
  2 fresh red chillies, seeded
    and chopped
  5ml/1 tsp soft light brown sugar
  30ml/2 tbsp Thai fish sauce
  25g/1oz/¼ cup roasted unsalted
    peanuts, chopped
  ground black pepper
  cooked rice noodles, to serve
  coarsely torn coriander (cilantro)
    leaves, to garnish

1 Trim any excess fat from the pork. Cut the meat across into 5mm/¼in thick slices, then cut each slice into 5mm/¼in strips. Put the pork into a bowl with the lemon grass, spring onions, salt and crushed peppercorns; mix well. Cover with clear film (plastic wrap) and leave to marinate in a cool place for 30 minutes.

2 Preheat a wok, add the oil and swirl it around. Add the pork mixture and stir-fry over a medium heat for about 3 minutes, until browned all over.

3 Add the garlic and red chillies and stir-fry for a further 5–8 minutes over a medium heat, until the pork is cooked through and tender.

4 Add the sugar, fish sauce and chopped peanuts and toss to mix, then season to taste with black pepper. Serve immediately on a bed of rice noodles, garnished with the coarsely torn coriander leaves.

COOK'S TIP
The heat in chillies is not in the seeds, but in the membranes surrounding them, which are removed along with the seeds.

PORK AND PINEAPPLE COCONUT CURRY

THE HEAT OF THIS CURRY BALANCES OUT ITS SWEETNESS TO MAKE A SMOOTH AND FRAGRANT DISH.
IT TAKES VERY LITTLE TIME TO COOK, SO IS IDEAL FOR A QUICK SUPPER BEFORE GOING OUT OR FOR
A MID-WEEK FAMILY MEAL ON A BUSY EVENING.

SERVES FOUR

INGREDIENTS
400ml/14fl oz can or carton
   coconut milk
10ml/2 tsp Thai red
   curry paste
400g/14oz pork loin steaks,
   trimmed and thinly sliced
15ml/1 tbsp Thai fish sauce
5ml/1 tsp palm sugar or light
   muscovado (brown) sugar
15ml/1 tbsp tamarind juice, made
   by mixing tamarind paste with
   warm water
2 kaffir lime leaves, torn
½ medium pineapple, peeled
   and chopped
1 fresh red chilli, seeded and
   finely chopped

1 Pour the coconut milk into a bowl and let it settle, so that the cream rises to the surface. Scoop the cream into a measuring jug (cup). You should have about 250ml/8fl oz/1 cup. If necessary, add a little of the coconut milk.

2 Pour the coconut cream into a large pan and bring it to the boil.

3 Cook the coconut cream for about 10 minutes, until the cream separates, stirring frequently to prevent it from sticking to the base of the pan and scorching. Add the red curry paste and stir until well mixed. Cook, stirring occasionally, for about 4 minutes, until the paste is fragrant.

4 Add the sliced pork and stir in the fish sauce, sugar and tamarind juice. Cook, stirring constantly, for 1–2 minutes, until the sugar has dissolved and the pork is no longer pink.

5 Add the remaining coconut milk and the lime leaves. Bring to the boil, then stir in the pineapple. Reduce the heat and simmer gently for 3 minutes, or until the pork is fully cooked. Sprinkle over the chilli and serve.

CHA SHAO

THIS DISH IS OFTEN KNOWN AS BARBECUE PORK AND IS VERY POPULAR IN SOUTHERN CHINA AND MALAYSIA AS WELL AS SINGAPORE. IF YOU LIKE, THE MARINADE CAN BE HEATED THOROUGHLY, THEN SERVED WITH THE MEAT AS A SAUCE.

SERVES SIX

INGREDIENTS
    900g/2lb pork fillet, trimmed
    15ml/1 tbsp clear honey
    45ml/3 tbsp rice wine or
      medium-dry sherry
    spring onion (scallion) curls,
      to garnish
For the marinade
    150ml/1/4 pint/2/3 cup dark
      soy sauce
    90ml/6 tbsp rice wine or
      medium-dry sherry
    150ml/1/4 pint/2/3 cup well-flavoured
      chicken stock
    15ml/1 tbsp soft brown sugar
    1cm/1/2in piece fresh root ginger,
      peeled and finely sliced
    40ml/2 1/2 tbsp chopped onion

1 Mix all the marinade ingredients in a pan and stir over a medium heat until the mixture boils. Lower the heat and simmer gently for 15 minutes, stirring from time to time. Leave to cool.

2 Put the pork fillets in a shallow dish that is large enough to hold them side by side. Pour over 250ml/8fl oz/1 cup of the marinade, cover and chill for at least 8 hours, turning the meat over several times.

COOK'S TIP
You will have extra marinade when making this dish. Chill or freeze this and use to baste other grilled (broiled) dishes or meats, such as spare ribs.

3 Preheat the oven to 200°C/400°F/ Gas 6. Drain the pork fillets, reserving the marinade in the dish. Place the meat on a rack over a roasting pan and pour water into the pan to a depth of 1cm/1/2in. Place the pan in the oven and roast for 20 minutes.

4 Stir the honey and rice wine or sherry into the marinade. Remove the meat from the oven and place in the marinade, turning to coat. Put back on the rack and roast for 20–30 minutes or until cooked. Serve hot or cold, in slices, garnished with spring onion curls.

CURRIED PORK WITH PICKLED GARLIC

This very rich curry is best accompanied by lots of plain rice and perhaps a light vegetable dish. It could serve four if served with a vegetable curry. Asian stores sell pickled garlic. It is well worth investing in a jar, as the taste is sweet and delicious.

SERVES TWO

INGREDIENTS

130g/4½oz lean pork steaks
30ml/2 tbsp vegetable oil
1 garlic clove, crushed
15ml/1 tbsp Thai red curry paste
130ml/4½fl oz/generous ½ cup
  coconut cream
2.5cm/1in piece fresh root ginger,
  finely chopped
30ml/2 tbsp vegetable or
  chicken stock
30ml/2 tbsp Thai fish sauce
5ml/1 tsp granulated sugar
2.5ml/½ tsp ground turmeric
10ml/2 tsp lemon juice
4 pickled garlic cloves,
  finely chopped
strips of lemon and lime rind,
  to garnish

1 Place the pork steaks in the freezer for 30–40 minutes, until firm, then, using a sharp knife, cut the meat into fine slivers, trimming off any excess fat.

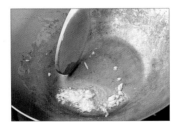

2 Heat the oil in a wok or large, heavy frying pan and cook the garlic over a low to medium heat until golden brown. Do not let it burn. Add the curry paste and stir it in well.

3 Add the coconut cream and stir until the liquid begins to reduce and thicken. Stir in the pork. Cook for 2 minutes more, until the pork is cooked through.

4 Add the ginger, stock, fish sauce, sugar and turmeric, stirring constantly, then add the lemon juice and pickled garlic. Spoon into bowls, garnish with strips of rind, and serve.

PORK CHOPS <u>WITH</u> FIELD MUSHROOMS

IN THAILAND, MEAT IS FREQUENTLY COOKED OVER A BRAZIER OR OPEN FIRE, SO IT ISN'T SURPRISING THAT MANY TASTY BARBECUE-STYLE DISHES COME FROM THERE. THESE FABULOUS PORK CHOPS ARE GREAT FAVOURITES WITH EVERYONE AND ARE DELICIOUS SERVED WITH NOODLES OR RICE.

SERVES FOUR

INGREDIENTS
    4 pork chops
    4 large field (portabello) mushrooms
    45ml/3 tbsp vegetable oil
    4 fresh red chillies, seeded and
      thinly sliced
    45ml/3 tbsp Thai fish sauce
    90ml/6 tbsp fresh lime juice
    4 shallots, chopped
    5ml/1 tsp roasted ground rice
    30ml/2 tbsp spring onions
      (scallions), chopped, plus shredded
      spring onions to garnish
    coriander (cilantro) leaves, to garnish
For the marinade
    2 garlic cloves, chopped
    15ml/1 tbsp granulated sugar
    15ml/1 tbsp Thai fish sauce
    30ml/2 tbsp soy sauce
    15ml/1 tbsp sesame oil
    15ml/1 tbsp whisky or dry sherry
    2 lemon grass stalks, finely chopped
    2 spring onions (scallions), chopped

1 Make the marinade. Combine the garlic, sugar, sauces, oil and whisky or sherry in a large, shallow dish. Stir in the lemon grass and spring onions.

2 Add the pork chops, turning to coat them in the marinade. Cover and leave to marinate for 1–2 hours.

3 Lift the chops out of the marinade and place them on a barbecue grid over hot coals or on a grill (broiler) rack. Add the mushrooms and brush them with 15ml/1 tbsp of the oil. Cook the pork chops for 5–7 minutes on each side and the mushrooms for about 2 minutes. Brush both with the marinade while cooking.

4 Heat the remaining oil in a wok or small frying pan, then remove the pan from the heat and stir in the chillies, fish sauce, lime juice, shallots, ground rice and chopped spring onions. Put the pork chops and mushrooms on a large serving plate and spoon over the sauce. Garnish with the coriander leaves and shredded spring onion.

SWEET-AND-SOUR PORK STIR-FRY

THIS IS A GREAT IDEA FOR A QUICK FAMILY SUPPER. REMEMBER TO CUT THE CARROTS INTO THIN MATCHSTICK STRIPS SO THAT THEY COOK IN TIME.

SERVES FOUR

INGREDIENTS
    450g/1lb pork fillet (tenderloin)
    30ml/2 tbsp plain (all-purpose) flour
    45ml/3 tbsp oil
    1 onion, roughly chopped
    1 garlic clove, crushed
    1 green (bell) pepper, seeded
      and sliced
    350g/12oz carrots, cut into thin
      strips
    225g/8oz can bamboo shoots, drained
    15ml/1 tbsp white wine vinegar
    15ml/1 tbsp soft brown sugar
    10ml/2 tsp tomato purée (paste)
    30ml/2 tbsp light soy sauce
    salt and ground black pepper

1 Thinly slice the pork. Season the flour and toss the pork in it to coat.

2 Heat the oil and cook the pork for 5 minutes, until golden. Remove the pork and drain on kitchen paper. You may need to do this in several batches.

3 Add the onion and garlic to the pan and cook for 3 minutes. Stir in the pepper and carrots and stir-fry over a high heat for 6–8 minutes, or until beginning to soften slightly.

4 Return the meat to the pan with the bamboo shoots. Add the remaining ingredients with 120ml/4fl oz/½ cup water and bring to the boil. Simmer gently for 2–3 minutes, or until piping hot. Adjust the seasoning, if necessary, and serve immediately.

VARIATION
Finely sliced strips of skinless chicken breast fillet can be used in this recipe instead of the pork.

STIR-FRIED PORK WITH DRIED SHRIMP

YOU MIGHT EXPECT THE DRIED SHRIMP TO GIVE THIS DISH A FISHY FLAVOUR, BUT INSTEAD IT SIMPLY IMPARTS A DELICIOUS SAVOURY TASTE.

SERVES FOUR

INGREDIENTS

250g/9oz pork fillet
(tenderloin), sliced
30ml/2 tbsp vegetable oil
2 garlic cloves, finely chopped
45ml/3 tbsp dried shrimp
10ml/2 tsp dried shrimp paste or
5mm/¼ in piece from block of
shrimp paste
30ml/2 tbsp soy sauce
juice of 1 lime
15ml/1 tbsp palm sugar or light
muscovado (brown) sugar
1 small fresh red or green chilli,
seeded and finely chopped
4 pak choi (bok choy) or 450g/1lb
spring greens (collards), shredded

1 Place the pork in the freezer for about 30 minutes, until firm. Using a sharp knife, cut it into thin slices.

2 Heat the oil in a wok or frying pan and cook the garlic until golden brown. Add the pork and stir-fry for about 4 minutes, until just cooked through.

3 Add the dried shrimp, then stir in the shrimp paste, with the soy sauce, lime juice and sugar. Add the chilli and pak choi or spring greens and toss over the heat until the vegetables are just wilted.

4 Transfer the stir-fry to warm individual bowls and serve immediately.

PORK BELLY <u>WITH</u> FIVE SPICES

THE CHINESE INFLUENCE ON THAI CUISINE STEMS FROM THE EARLY YEARS OF ITS HISTORY, WHEN COLONISTS FROM SOUTHERN CHINA SETTLED IN THE COUNTRY, BRINGING WITH THEM DISHES LIKE THIS, ALTHOUGH THAI COOKS HAVE PROVIDED THEIR OWN UNIQUE IMPRINT.

SERVES FOUR

INGREDIENTS
    1 large bunch fresh coriander
      (cilantro) with roots
    30ml/2 tbsp vegetable oil
    1 garlic clove, crushed
    30ml/2 tbsp five-spice powder
    500g/1¼lb pork belly, cut into
      2.5cm/1in pieces
    400g/14oz can chopped tomatoes
    150ml/¼ pint/⅔ cup hot water
    30ml/2 tbsp dark soy sauce
    45ml/3 tbsp Thai fish sauce
    30ml/2 tbsp granulated sugar
    1 lime, halved

COOK'S TIP
Make sure that you buy Chinese five-spice powder, as the Indian variety is made up from quite different spices.

1 Cut off the coriander roots. Chop five of them finely and freeze the remainder for another occasion. Chop the coriander stalks and leaves and set them aside. Keep the roots separate.

2 Heat the oil in a large pan and cook the garlic until golden brown. Stirring constantly, add the chopped coriander roots and then the five-spice powder.

3 Add the pork and stir-fry until the meat is thoroughly coated in spices and has browned. Stir in the tomatoes and hot water. Bring to the boil, then stir in the soy sauce, fish sauce and sugar.

4 Reduce the heat, cover the pan and simmer for 30 minutes. Stir in the chopped coriander stalks and leaves, squeeze over the lime juice and serve.

PUCHERO

A FILIPINO POT-AU-FEU WITH SPANISH CONNECTIONS. SOMETIMES IT IS SERVED AS TWO COURSES, FIRST SOUP, THEN MEAT AND VEGETABLES WITH RICE, BUT IT CAN HAPPILY BE SERVED AS IS, ON RICE IN A WIDE SOUP BOWL. EITHER WAY IT IS VERY SATISFYING AND A SIESTA AFTERWARDS IS RECOMMENDED.

SERVES SIX TO EIGHT

INGREDIENTS

   225g/8oz/generous 1 cup chickpeas,
     soaked overnight in water to cover
   1.4kg/3lb chicken, cut into 8 pieces
   350g/12oz belly of pork, rinded,
     or pork fillet, cubed
   2 chorizo sausages, thickly sliced
   2 onions, chopped
   2.5 litres/4 pints/10 cups water
   60ml/4 tbsp vegetable oil
   2 garlic cloves, crushed
   3 large tomatoes, peeled, seeded
     and chopped
   15ml/1 tbsp tomato purée
     (paste)
   1–2 sweet potatoes, cut into
     1cm/½in cubes
   2 plantains, sliced (optional)
   salt and ground black pepper
   chives or chopped spring onions
     (scallions), to garnish
   ½ head Chinese leaves (Chinese
     cabbage), shredded, and boiled
     rice, to serve
For the sauce
   1 large aubergine (eggplant)
   3 garlic cloves, crushed
   60–90ml/4–6 tbsp wine or
     cider vinegar

1 Drain the chickpeas and put in a large pan. Cover with water, bring to the boil and boil rapidly for 10 minutes. Reduce the heat and simmer for 30 minutes until half tender. Drain.

2 Put the chicken pieces, pork, sausage and half of the onions in a large pan. Add the chickpeas and pour in the water. Bring to the boil and lower the heat, cover and simmer for 1 hour or until the meat is just tender when tested with a skewer.

3 Meanwhile, make the aubergine sauce. Preheat the oven to 200°C/ 400°F/Gas 6. Prick the aubergine in several places, then place it on a baking sheet and bake for 30 minutes or until very soft.

4 Cool slightly, then peel away the aubergine skin and scrape the flesh into a bowl. Mash the flesh with the crushed garlic, season to taste and add enough vinegar to sharpen the sauce, which should be quite piquant. Set aside.

5 Heat the oil in a frying pan and fry the remaining onion and garlic for 5 minutes, until soft but not brown. Stir in the tomatoes and tomato purée and cook for 2 minutes, then add this mixture to a large pan with the diced sweet potato. Add the plantains, if using. Cook over a gentle heat for about 20 minutes until the sweet potato is thoroughly cooked. Add the Chinese leaves for the last minute or two.

6 Spoon the thick meat soup into a soup tureen, and put the vegetables in a separate serving bowl. Garnish both with whole or chopped chives or spring onions and serve with boiled rice and the aubergine sauce.

PORK ON LEMON GRASS STICKS

THIS SIMPLE RECIPE MAKES A SUBSTANTIAL SNACK, AND THE LEMON GRASS STICKS NOT ONLY ADD A SUBTLE FLAVOUR BUT ALSO MAKE A GOOD TALKING POINT.

SERVES FOUR

INGREDIENTS
  300g/11oz minced (ground) pork
  4 garlic cloves, crushed
  4 fresh coriander (cilantro) roots,
    finely chopped
  2.5ml/½ tsp granulated sugar
  15ml/1 tbsp soy sauce
  salt and ground black pepper
  8 x 10cm/4in lengths of lemon
    grass stalk
  sweet chilli sauce,
    to serve

VARIATION
Slimmer versions of these pork sticks are perfect for parties. The mixture will be enough for 12 lemon grass sticks if you use it sparingly.

1 Place the minced pork, crushed garlic, chopped coriander root, sugar and soy sauce in a large bowl. Season with salt and pepper to taste and mix well.

2 Divide into eight portions and mould each one into a ball. It may help to dampen your hands before shaping the mixture to prevent it from sticking.

3 Stick a length of lemon grass halfway into each ball, then press the meat mixture around the lemon grass to make a shape like a chicken leg.

4 Cook the pork sticks under a hot grill (broiler) for 3–4 minutes on each side, until golden and cooked through. Serve with the chilli sauce for dipping.

BRAISED BEEF IN A RICH PEANUT SAUCE

LIKE MANY DISHES BROUGHT TO THE PHILIPPINES BY SPANISH SETTLERS, THIS SLOW-COOKING ESTOFADO, RENAMED KARI KARI, RETAINS MUCH OF ITS ORIGINAL CHARM. RICE AND PEANUTS ARE USED TO THICKEN THE JUICES, YIELDING A RICH GLOSSY SAUCE.

SERVES FOUR TO SIX

INGREDIENTS

900g/2lb stewing beef, chuck, shin
  or blade steak
30ml/2 tbsp vegetable oil
15ml/1 tbsp annatto seeds, or
  5ml/1 tsp paprika and a pinch
  of ground turmeric
2 onions, chopped
2 garlic cloves, crushed
275g/10oz celeriac or swede (rutabaga),
  peeled and roughly chopped
425ml/15fl oz/1¾ cups beef stock
350g/12oz new potatoes, peeled and
  cut into large dice
15ml/1 tbsp fish sauce
30ml/2 tbsp tamarind sauce
10ml/2 tsp granulated sugar
1 bay leaf
1 sprig thyme
45ml/3 tbsp long grain rice
50g/2oz/⅓ cup peanuts or 30ml/
  2 tbsp peanut butter
15ml/1 tbsp white wine vinegar
salt and ground black pepper

1 Cut the beef into 2.5cm/1in cubes and set aside.

2 Heat the vegetable oil in a wok or large pan. Add the annatto seeds, if using, and stir to colour the oil a dark red. Remove the seeds with a slotted spoon and discard. If you are not using annatto seeds, paprika and turmeric can be added later.

3 Soften the onions, garlic and the celeriac or swede in the oil without letting them colour. Add the beef cubes and fry over a high heat to seal. If you are not using annatto seeds to redden the sauce, stir in the paprika and ground turmeric with the beef.

4 Add the beef stock, potatoes, fish sauce and tamarind sauce, granulated sugar, bay leaf and thyme. Bring to a simmer and allow to cook on the top of the stove for about 2 hours.

5 Cover the rice with cold water and leave to stand for 30 minutes. Roast the peanuts under a hot grill (broiler), if using, then rub the skins off in a clean cloth. Drain the rice and grind with the peanuts or peanut butter, using a mortar and pestle, or food processor.

6 When the beef is tender, add 60ml/ 4 tbsp of the cooking liquid to the ground rice and nuts. Blend smoothly and stir into the contents of the pan. Simmer gently on the stove to thicken, for about 15–20 minutes. To finish, stir in the wine vinegar and season well.

SLICED SEARED BEEF

JAPANESE CHEFS USE A COOKING TECHNIQUE CALLED TATAKI TO COOK RARE STEAK. THEY NORMALLY USE A COAL FIRE AND SEAR A CHUNK OF BEEF ON LONG SKEWERS, THEN PLUNGE IT INTO COLD WATER TO STOP IT COOKING FURTHER. USE A WIRE MESH GRILL OVER THE HEAT SOURCE TO COOK THIS WAY.

SERVES FOUR

INGREDIENTS
   500g/1¼lb chunk of beef thigh
     (a long, thin chunk looks better
     than a thick, round chunk)
   generous pinch of salt
   10ml/2 tsp vegetable oil
For the marinade
   200ml/7fl oz/scant 1 cup rice
     vinegar
   70ml/4½ tbsp sake
   135ml/4½fl oz/scant ⅔ cup shoyu
   15ml/1 tbsp caster
     (superfine) sugar
   1 garlic clove, thinly sliced
   1 small onion, thinly sliced
   sansho
For the garnish
   6 shiso leaves and shiso flowers
     (if available)
   about 15cm/6in Japanese or ordinary
     salad cucumber
   ½ lemon, thinly sliced
   1 garlic clove, finely grated (optional)

1 Mix the marinade ingredients in a small pan and warm through until the sugar has dissolved. Remove from the heat and leave to cool.

COOK'S TIPS
• If you don't have a mesh grill or griddle, heat 15ml/1 tbsp vegetable oil in a hot frying pan to sear the beef. Wash all the oil from the meat and wipe off any excess with a kitchen paper.
• If preparing this dish ahead of time, spear the beef rolls with a cocktail stick (toothpick) to secure.

2 Generously sprinkle the beef with the salt and rub well into the meat. Leave for 2–3 minutes, then rub the oil in evenly with your fingers.

3 Fill a large mixing bowl with plenty of cold water. Put a mesh grill tray over the heat on the top of the stove, or heat a griddle to a high temperature. Sear the beef, turning frequently until about 5mm/¼in of the flesh in from the surface is cooked. Try not to burn grid marks on the meat. Immediately plunge the meat into the bowl of cold water for a few seconds to stop it from cooking further.

4 Wipe the meat with kitchen paper or a dishtowel and immerse fully in the marinade for 1 day.

5 Next day, prepare the garnish. Chop the shiso leaves in half lengthways, then cut into very thin strips crossways. Slice the cucumber diagonally into 5mm/¼in thick oval shapes, then cut each oval into 5mm/¼in matchsticks. Scoop out the watery seed part first if using an ordinary salad cucumber.

6 Remove the meat from the marinade. Strain the remaining marinade through a sieve, reserving both the liquid and the marinated onion and garlic.

7 Using a sharp knife, cut the beef thinly into slices of about 5mm/¼in thick.

8 Heap the cucumber sticks on a large serving plate and put the marinated onion and garlic on top. Arrange the beef slices as you would sashimi, leaning alongside or on the bed of cucumber and other vegetables. You can also either make a fan shape with the beef slices, or, if the slices are large enough, you could roll them.

9 Fluff the shiso strips and put on top of the beef. Decorate with some shiso flowers, if using. Lightly sprinkle with the lemon rings, and serve with the reserved marinade in individual bowls.

10 To eat, take a few beef slices on to individual plates. Roll a slice with your choice of garnish, then dip it into the marinade. Add a little grated garlic, if you like.

SPICY SHREDDED BEEF

THE ESSENCE OF THIS RECIPE IS THAT THE BEEF IS CUT INTO VERY FINE STRIPS. THIS IS EASIER TO ACHIEVE IF THE PIECE OF BEEF IS PLACED IN THE FREEZER FOR 30 MINUTES UNTIL IT IS VERY FIRM BEFORE BEING SLICED WITH A SHARP KNIFE.

SERVES TWO

INGREDIENTS
225g/8oz rump or fillet (tenderloin) of beef
15ml/1 tbsp each light and dark soy sauce
15ml/1 tbsp rice wine or medium-dry sherry
5ml/1 tsp soft dark brown sugar or golden granulated sugar
90ml/6 tbsp vegetable oil
1 large onion, thinly sliced
2.5cm/1in piece fresh root ginger, peeled and grated
1–2 carrots, cut into matchsticks
2–3 fresh or dried chillies, halved, seeded (optional) and chopped
salt and ground black pepper
fresh chives, to garnish

1 With a sharp knife, slice the beef very thinly, then cut each slice into fine strips or shreds.

2 Mix together the light and dark soy sauces with the rice wine or sherry and sugar in a bowl. Add the strips of beef and stir well to ensure they are evenly coated with the marinade.

3 Heat a wok and add half the oil. When it is hot, stir-fry the onion and ginger for 3–4 minutes, then transfer to a plate. Add the carrot, stir-fry for 3–4 minutes until slightly softened, then transfer to a plate and keep warm.

4 Heat the remaining oil in the wok, then quickly add the beef, with the marinade, followed by the chillies. Cook over high heat for 2 minutes, stirring all the time.

5 Return the fried onion and ginger to the wok and stir-fry for 1 minute more. Season with salt and pepper to taste, cover and cook for 30 seconds. Spoon the meat into two warmed bowls and add the strips of carrots. Garnish with fresh chives and serve.

COOK'S TIP
Remove and discard the seeds from the chillies before you chop them – unless, of course, you like really fiery food. In which case, you could add some or all of the seeds with the chopped chillies.

MARINATED BEEF STEAKS

BULGOGI IS A VERY POPULAR DISH FOR OUTDOOR ENTERTAINING. TRADITIONALLY IT WOULD HAVE BEEN COOKED ON A GENGHIS KHAN GRILL, WHICH IS SHAPED LIKE THE CROWN OF A HAT, BUT A RIDGED HEAVY FRYING PAN OR WOK WORKS ALMOST AS WELL.

SERVES THREE TO FOUR

INGREDIENTS
    450g/1lb fillet of beef or rump
      (round) steak, in the piece
    sesame oil, for frying
For the marinade
    150ml/¼ pint/⅔ cup dark soy sauce
    30ml/2 tbsp sesame oil
    30ml/2 tbsp sake or dry white wine
    1 garlic clove, cut into thin slivers
    15ml/1 tbsp sugar
    30ml/2 tbsp crushed roasted
      sesame seeds
    4 spring onions (scallions), cut into
      long lengths
    salt and ground black pepper

1 Put the meat into the freezer until it is firm enough to slice very thinly and evenly. Arrange the slices of beef in a shallow glass dish.

2 Make the marinade. Mix the soy sauce, oil, sake or wine, garlic, sugar and sesame seeds in a bowl and add the spring onions. Season to taste.

3 Pour the marinade over the slices of beef and mix well. Cover the dish and transfer to the refrigerator. Chill for at least 3 hours or overnight.

4 Heat the merest slick of oil in a ridged heavy frying pan or wok. Drain the beef slices and fry over a high heat for a few seconds, turning once. Serve at once.

SIZZLING STEAK

THIS WAS ORIGINALLY A SPECIALITY OF THE COLISEUM RESTAURANT IN THE BATU ROAD IN KUALA LUMPUR. THE STEAKS WERE BROUGHT TO THE TABLE ON INDIVIDUAL HOT METAL PLATTERS, EACH SET ON A THICK WOODEN BOARD. THIS RECIPE COMES CLOSE TO RECREATING THIS WONDERFUL DISH.

SERVES TWO

INGREDIENTS

  2 rump (round) or sirloin steaks
    (450g/1lb)
  15–30ml/1–2 tbsp vegetable oil
  shredded spring onion (scallion)
For the marinade and sauce
  15ml/1 tbsp brandy
  15ml/1 tbsp rich brown sauce
  30ml/2 tbsp groundnut (peanut) oil
    or sunflower oil
  a few drops of sesame oil
  2 garlic cloves, halved or crushed
  150ml/1/4 pint/2/3 cup beef stock
  30ml/2 tbsp tomato ketchup
  15ml/1 tbsp oyster sauce
  15ml/1 tbsp Worcestershire
    sauce
  salt and sugar

1 Put the steaks side by side in a bowl. Mix the brandy, brown sauce, groundnut or sunflower oil, sesame oil and garlic in a jug (pitcher) and pour this marinade over the steaks. Cover loosely with clear film (plastic wrap) and leave for 1 hour, turning once. Drain the meat well, reserving the marinade.

2 Heat the oil in a heavy, ridged frying pan and fry the steaks for 3–5 minutes on each side, depending on how well done you like them. Transfer to a plate and keep warm while preparing the sauce: this allows the meat to relax, making it more tender.

3 Pour the marinade into the frying pan, if liked, discarding any large pieces of garlic.

4 Stir in the beef stock, ketchup, oyster sauce and Worcestershire sauce, with salt and sugar to taste. Bring to the boil, boil rapidly to reduce by half, then taste again for seasoning.

5 Serve each cooked steak on a very hot plate, pouring the sauce over each portion just before serving. Garnish with the shredded spring onion.

COOK'S TIP

If you don't have a ridged frying pan, simply substitute a large, heavy frying pan instead.

THICK BEEF CURRY IN SWEET PEANUT SAUCE

THIS CURRY IS DELICIOUSLY RICH AND THICKER THAN MOST OTHER THAI CURRIES. SERVE IT WITH BOILED JASMINE RICE AND SALTED DUCK'S EGGS, IF YOU LIKE.

SERVES FOUR TO SIX

INGREDIENTS
    600ml/1 pint/2½ cups coconut milk
    45ml/3 tbsp Thai red curry paste
    45ml/3 tbsp Thai fish sauce
    30ml/2 tbsp palm sugar or light
        muscovado (brown) sugar
    2 lemon grass stalks, bruised
    450g/1lb rump (round) steak,
        cut into thin strips
    75g/3oz/¾ cup roasted
        peanuts, ground
    2 fresh red chillies, sliced
    5 kaffir lime leaves, torn
    salt and ground black pepper
    2 salted eggs, cut in wedges, and
        10–15 Thai basil leaves, to garnish

1 Pour half the coconut milk into a large, heavy pan. Place over a medium heat and bring to the boil, stirring constantly until the milk separates.

2 Stir in the red curry paste and cook for 2–3 minutes until the mixture is fragrant and thoroughly blended. Add the fish sauce, sugar and bruised lemon grass stalks. Mix well.

3 Continue to cook until the colour deepens. Gradually add the remaining coconut milk, stirring constantly. Bring back to the boil.

COOK'S TIP
If you don't have the time to make your own red curry paste, you can buy a ready-made Thai curry paste. There is a wide range available in most Asian stores and large supermarkets.

4 Add the beef and peanuts. Cook, stirring constantly, for 8–10 minutes, or until most of the liquid has evaporated. Add the chillies and lime leaves. Season to taste and serve, garnished with wedges of salted eggs and Thai basil leaves.

SPICY MEAT BALLS

SERVE THESE SPICY LITTLE PATTIES – PERGEDEL DJAWA – WITH EGG NOODLES AND CHILLI SAMBAL.

SERVES FOUR TO SIX

INGREDIENTS

1cm/1/2in cube shrimp paste
1 large onion, roughly chopped
1–2 fresh red chillies, seeded
  and chopped
2 garlic cloves, crushed
15ml/1 tbsp coriander seeds
5ml/1 tsp cumin seeds
450g/1lb lean minced (ground) beef
10ml/2 tsp dark soy sauce
5ml/1 tsp dark brown sugar
juice of 1 1/2 lemons
a little beaten egg
vegetable oil, for shallow frying
salt and ground black pepper
chilli sambal, to serve
1 green and 2 fresh red chillies,
  to garnish

1 Wrap the shrimp paste in a piece of foil and warm in a frying pan for 5 minutes, turning a few times. Unwrap and put in a food processor.

COOK'S TIP
When processing the shrimp paste, onion, chillies and garlic, do not process for too long, otherwise the onion will become too wet and spoil the consistency of the meat balls.

2 Add the onion, chillies and garlic to the food processor and process until finely chopped. Set aside. Dry-fry the coriander and cumin seeds in a hot frying pan for 1 minute, to release the aroma. Tip the seeds into a mortar and grind with a pestle.

3 Put the meat in a large bowl. Stir in the onion mixture. Add the ground spices, soy sauce, brown sugar, lemon juice and beaten egg. Season to taste.

4 Shape the meat mixture into small, even-size balls, and chill these for 5–10 minutes to firm them up.

5 Heat the oil in a wok or large frying pan and fry the meat balls for 4–5 minutes, turning often, until cooked through and browned. You may have to do this in batches.

6 Drain the meat balls on kitchen paper, and then pile them on to a warm serving platter or into a large serving bowl. Finely slice the green chilli and one of the red chillies and sprinkle over the meat balls. Garnish with the remaining red chilli, if you like. Serve with the Chilli Sambal (see below) handed round separately.

VARIATION
Minced (ground) beef is traditionally used for this dish, but pork, lamb – or even turkey – would also be good.

CHILLI SAMBAL

THIS FIERCE CONDIMENT IS BOTTLED AS SAMBAL OELEK, BUT IT IS EASY TO PREPARE AND WILL KEEP FOR SEVERAL WEEKS IN A WELL-SEALED JAR IN THE REFRIGERATOR. USE A STAINLESS-STEEL OR PLASTIC SPOON TO MEASURE; IF SAUCE DRIPS ON YOUR FINGERS, WASH WELL IN SOAPY WATER IMMEDIATELY.

MAKES 450G/1LB

INGREDIENTS
450g/1lb fresh red chillies,
  seeded
10ml/2 tsp salt

1 Bring a pan of water to the boil, add the seeded chillies and cook them for 5–8 minutes.

2 Drain the chillies and then grind them in a food processor, without making the paste too smooth.

3 Scrape into a screw-topped glass jar, stir in the salt and cover with a piece of baking parchment or clear film (plastic wrap). Screw on the lid and store in the refrigerator. Spoon into small dishes, to serve as an accompaniment, or to use in recipes as suggested.

GREEN BEEF CURRY <u>WITH</u> THAI AUBERGINES

THIS IS A VERY QUICK CURRY SO BE SURE TO USE GOOD QUALITY MEAT. SIRLOIN IS RECOMMENDED, BUT TENDER RUMP (ROUND) STEAK COULD BE USED INSTEAD.

SERVES FOUR TO SIX

INGREDIENTS
  450g/1lb beef sirloin
  15ml/1 tbsp vegetable oil
  45ml/3 tbsp Thai green curry paste
  600ml/1 pint/2½ cups coconut milk
  4 kaffir lime leaves, torn
  15–30ml/1–2 tbsp Thai fish sauce
  5ml/1 tsp palm sugar or light
    muscovado (brown) sugar
  150g/5oz small Thai aubergines
    (eggplant), halved
  a small handful of fresh Thai basil
  2 fresh green chillies, to garnish

1 Trim off any excess fat from the beef. Using a sharp knife, cut it into long, thin strips. This is easiest to do if it is well chilled. Set it aside.

2 Heat the oil in a large, heavy pan or wok. Add the curry paste and cook for 1–2 minutes, until it is fragrant.

3 Stir in half the coconut milk, a little at a time. Cook, stirring frequently, for about 5–6 minutes, until an oily sheen appears on the surface of the liquid.

4 Add the beef to the pan with the kaffir lime leaves, Thai fish sauce, sugar and aubergine halves. Cook for 2–3 minutes, then stir in the remaining coconut milk.

5 Bring back to a simmer and cook until the meat and aubergines are tender. Stir in the Thai basil just before serving. Finely shred the green chillies and use to garnish the curry.

COOK'S TIP
To make the green curry paste, put 15 fresh green chillies, 2 chopped lemon grass stalks, 3 sliced shallots, 2 garlic cloves, 15ml/1 tbsp chopped galangal, 4 chopped kaffir lime leaves, 2.5ml/ ½ tsp grated kaffir lime rind, 5ml/1 tsp chopped coriander root, 6 black peppercorns, 5ml/1 tsp each roasted coriander and cumin seeds, 15ml/1 tbsp granulated sugar, 5ml/1 tsp salt and 5ml/1 tsp shrimp paste into a food processor and process until smooth. Gradually add 30ml/2 tbsp vegetable oil, processing after each addition.

STIR-FRIED BEEF IN OYSTER SAUCE

ANOTHER SIMPLE BUT DELICIOUS RECIPE. IN THAILAND THIS IS OFTEN MADE WITH JUST STRAW MUSHROOMS, WHICH ARE READILY AVAILABLE FRESH, BUT OYSTER MUSHROOMS MAKE A GOOD SUBSTITUTE AND USING A MIXTURE MAKES THE DISH EXTRA INTERESTING.

SERVES FOUR TO SIX

INGREDIENTS
    450g/1lb rump (round) steak
    30ml/2 tbsp soy sauce
    15ml/1 tbsp cornflour (cornstarch)
    45ml/3 tbsp vegetable oil
    15ml/1 tbsp chopped garlic
    15ml/1 tbsp chopped fresh
      root ginger
    225g/8oz/3¼ cups mixed mushrooms
      such as shiitake, oyster and straw
    30ml/2 tbsp oyster sauce
    5ml/1 tsp granulated sugar
    4 spring onions (scallions), cut into
      short lengths
    ground black pepper
    2 fresh red chillies, seeded and cut
      into strips, to garnish

1 Place the steak in the freezer for 30–40 minutes, until firm, then, using a sharp knife, slice it on the diagonal into long thin strips.

2 Mix together the soy sauce and cornflour in a large bowl. Add the steak, turning to coat well, cover with clear film (plastic wrap) and leave to marinate at room temperature for 1–2 hours.

3 Heat half the oil in a wok or large, heavy frying pan. Add the garlic and ginger and cook for 1–2 minutes, until fragrant. Drain the steak, add it to the wok or pan and stir well to separate the strips. Cook, stirring frequently, for a further 1–2 minutes, until the steak is browned all over and tender. Remove from the wok or pan and set aside.

4 Heat the remaining oil in the wok or pan. Add the shiitake, oyster and straw mushrooms. Stir-fry over a medium heat until golden brown.

5 Return the steak to the wok and mix it with the mushrooms. Spoon in the oyster sauce and sugar, mix well, then add ground black pepper to taste. Toss over the heat until all the ingredients are thoroughly combined.

6 Stir in the spring onions. Tip the mixture on to a serving platter, garnish with the strips of red chilli and serve.

BEEF RENDANG

IN INDONESIA, THIS SPICY DISH IS USUALLY SERVED WITH THE MEAT QUITE DRY; IF YOU PREFER MORE SAUCE, SIMPLY ADD MORE WATER WHEN STIRRING IN THE POTATOES.

SERVES SIX TO EIGHT

INGREDIENTS
2 onions or 5–6 shallots, chopped
4 garlic cloves, chopped
2.5cm/1in piece fresh galangal,
   peeled and sliced, or 15ml/1 tbsp
   galangal paste
2.5cm/1in piece fresh root ginger,
   peeled and sliced
4–6 fresh red chillies, seeded
   and roughly chopped
lower part only of 1 lemon grass
   stem, sliced
2.5cm/1in piece fresh turmeric,
   peeled and sliced, or 5ml/1 tsp
   ground turmeric
1kg/2¼lb prime beef in one piece
5ml/1 tsp coriander seeds, dry fried
5ml/1 tsp cumin seeds, dry fried
2 kaffir lime leaves, torn into pieces
2 x 400ml/14fl oz cans coconut milk
300ml/½ pint/1¼ cups water
30ml/2 tbsp dark soy sauce
5ml/1 tsp tamarind pulp, soaked in
   60ml/4 tbsp warm water
8–10 small new potatoes, scrubbed
salt and ground black pepper
deep-fried onions (see below),
   sliced fresh red chillies and spring
   onions, to garnish

1 Put the onions or shallots in a food processor. Add the garlic, galangal, ginger, chillies, sliced lemon grass and fresh or ground turmeric. Process to a fine paste or grind in a mortar, using a pestle.

2 Cut the meat into cubes using a large sharp knife, then place the cubes in a bowl.

3 Grind the dry-fried coriander and cumin seeds, then add to the meat with the onion, chilli paste and kaffir lime leaves; stir well. Cover and leave in a cool place to marinate while you prepare the other ingredients.

COOK'S TIP
This dish is even better if you can cook it a day or two in advance of serving, which allows the flavours to mellow beautifully. Add the potatoes on reheating and simmer until tender.

4 Pour the coconut milk and water into a wok, then stir in the spiced meat and the soy sauce. Strain the tamarind water and add to the wok. Stir over medium heat until the liquid boils, then simmer gently, half-covered, for 1½ hours.

5 Add the potatoes and simmer for 20–25 minutes, or until meat and potatoes are tender. Add water if liked. Season and serve, garnished with deep-fried onions, chillies and spring onions.

DEEP-FRIED ONIONS

KNOWN AS BAWANG GORENG, THESE ARE A TRADITIONAL GARNISH AND ACCOMPANY MANY INDONESIAN DISHES. ASIAN STORES SELL THEM READY-PREPARED, BUT IT IS EASY TO MAKE THEM. THE SMALL RED ONIONS SOLD IN THE SAME OUTLETS ARE EXCELLENT AS THEY CONTAIN LESS WATER.

MAKES 450G/1LB

INGREDIENTS
450g/1lb onions
vegetable oil, for deep frying

1 Thinly slice the onions with a sharp knife or in a food processor. Spread the slices out in a single layer on kitchen paper and leave them to dry, in an airy place, for 30 minutes–2 hours.

2 Heat the oil in a deep fryer or wok to 190°C/375°F. Fry the onions in batches, until crisp and golden, turning all the time. Drain well on kitchen paper, cool and store in an airtight container, unless using immediately.

MUSSAMAN CURRY

THIS DISH IS TRADITIONALLY BASED ON BEEF, BUT CHICKEN, LAMB OR TOFU CAN BE USED INSTEAD.
IT HAS A RICH, SWEET AND SPICY FLAVOUR AND IS BEST SERVED WITH BOILED RICE. MUSSAMAN
CURRY PASTE IS AVAILABLE FROM SPECIALIST STORES.

4 Return the coconut cream and curry paste mixture to the pan with the beef and stir until thoroughly blended. Simmer for a further 4–5 minutes, stirring occasionally.

5 Stir the fish sauce, sugar, tamarind juice, cardamom pods, cinnamon stick, potato chunks and onion wedges into the beef curry. Continue to simmer for a further 15–20 minutes, or until the potato is cooked and tender.

6 Add the roasted peanuts to the pan and mix well to combine. Cook for about 5 minutes more, then transfer to warmed individual serving bowls and serve immediately.

COOK'S TIP

To make Mussaman curry paste, halve 12 large dried chillies and discard the seeds, then soak the chillies in hot water for about 15 minutes. Remove the chillies from the water and chop finely. Place the chopped chillies in a mortar or food processor and pound or process with 60ml/4 tbsp chopped shallots, 5 garlic cloves, the base of 1 lemon grass stalk and 30ml/2 tbsp chopped fresh galangal. Dry-fry 5ml/1 tsp cumin seeds, 15ml/1 tbsp coriander seeds, 2 cloves and 6 black peppercorns over a low heat for 1–2 minutes. Grind the toasted spices to a powder, then combine with 5ml/1 tsp shrimp paste, 5ml/1 tsp salt, 5ml/1 tsp granulated sugar and 30ml/2 tbsp vegetable oil. Add the shallot mixture to the spice mixture and stir well to make a paste.

SERVES FOUR TO SIX

INGREDIENTS
675g/1½lb stewing steak
600ml/1 pint/2½ cups coconut milk
250ml/8fl oz/1 cup coconut cream
45ml/3 tbsp Mussaman curry paste
30ml/2 tbsp Thai fish sauce
15ml/1 tbsp palm sugar or light
  muscovado (brown) sugar
60ml/4 tbsp tamarind juice (tamarind
  paste mixed with warm water)
6 green cardamom pods
1 cinnamon stick
1 large potato, about 225g/8oz,
  cut into even chunks
1 onion, cut into wedges
50g/2oz/½ cup roasted peanuts

1 Trim off any excess fat from the stewing steak, then, using a sharp knife, cut it into 2.5cm/1in chunks.

2 Pour the coconut milk into a large, heavy pan and bring to the boil over a medium heat. Add the chunks of beef, reduce the heat to low, partially cover the pan and simmer gently for about 40 minutes, or until tender.

3 Transfer the coconut cream to a separate pan. Cook over a medium heat, stirring constantly, for about 5 minutes, or until it separates. Stir in the Mussaman curry paste and cook rapidly for 2–3 minutes, until fragrant and thoroughly blended.

D R Y   B E E F   C U R R Y   <u>W I T H</u>   P E A N U T   <u>A N D</u>   L I M E

ORIGINATING FROM THE MOUNTAINOUS NORTHERN REGIONS OF THAILAND, DRY CURRIES ARE NOW POPULAR THROUGHOUT THE COUNTRY. THIS DRY BEEF CURRY IS USUALLY SERVED WITH A MOIST DISH SUCH AS NORTHERN FISH CURRY WITH SHALLOTS AND LEMON GRASS.

<u>SERVES FOUR TO SIX</u>

INGREDIENTS
400g/14oz can coconut milk
900g/2lb stewing steak,
   finely chopped
300ml/½ pint/1¼ cups beef stock
30ml/2 tbsp crunchy peanut butter
juice of 2 limes
lime slices, shredded coriander
   (cilantro) and fresh red chilli slices,
   to garnish
For the red curry paste
30ml/2 tbsp coriander seeds
5ml/1 tsp cumin seeds
seeds from 6 green cardamom pods
2.5ml/½ tsp grated or ground nutmeg
1.5ml/¼ tsp ground cloves
2.5ml/½ tsp ground cinnamon
20ml/4 tsp paprika
pared rind of 1 mandarin orange,
   finely chopped
4–5 small fresh red chillies, seeded
   and finely chopped
25ml/5 tsp granulated sugar
2.5ml/½ tsp salt
1 piece lemon grass, about 10cm/4in
   long, shredded
3 garlic cloves, crushed
2cm/¾in piece fresh galangal,
   peeled and finely chopped
4 red shallots, finely chopped
1 piece shrimp paste,
   2cm/¾in square
50g/2oz coriander (cilantro) root or
   stem, chopped
juice of ½ lime
30ml/2 tbsp vegetable oil

1 Strain the coconut milk into a bowl, retaining the thicker coconut milk in the strainer or sieve.

2 Pour the thin coconut milk from the bowl into a large, heavy pan, then scrape in half the residue from the sieve. Reserve the remaining thick coconut milk. Add the chopped steak. Pour in the beef stock and bring to the boil. Reduce the heat, cover the pan and simmer gently for 50 minutes.

3 Make the curry paste. Dry-fry all the seeds for 1–2 minutes. Tip into a bowl and add the nutmeg, cloves, cinnamon, paprika and orange rind. Pound the chillies with the sugar and salt. Add the spice mixture, lemon grass, garlic, galangal, shallots and shrimp paste and pound to a paste. Work in the coriander, lime juice and oil.

4 Strain the beef, reserving the cooking liquid, and place a cupful of liquid in a wok. Stir in 30–45ml/2–3 tbsp of the curry paste, according to taste. Boil rapidly until all the liquid has evaporated. Stir in the reserved thick coconut milk, the peanut butter and the beef. Simmer, uncovered, for 15–20 minutes, adding a little more cooking liquid if the mixture starts to stick to the pan, but keep the curry dry.

5 Just before serving, stir in the lime juice. Serve in warmed bowls, garnished with the lime slices, shredded coriander and sliced red chillies.

VARIATION
The curry is equally delicious made with lean leg or shoulder of lamb.

CITRUS BEEF CURRY

THIS SUPERBLY AROMATIC THAI-STYLE CURRY IS NOT TOO HOT BUT FULL OF FLAVOUR. FOR A SPECIAL MEAL, IT GOES PERFECTLY WITH FRIED NOODLES.

SERVES FOUR

INGREDIENTS
   450g/1lb rump (round) steak
   30ml/2 tbsp sunflower oil
   30ml/2 tbsp medium curry paste
   2 bay leaves
   400ml/14fl oz/1⅔ cups coconut milk
   300ml/½ pint/1¼ cups beef stock
   30ml/2 tbsp lemon juice
   45ml/3 tbsp nam pla (fish sauce)
   15ml/1 tbsp sugar
   115g/4oz baby (pearl) onions, peeled
      but left whole
   225g/8oz new potatoes, halved
   115g/4oz/1 cup unsalted roasted
      peanuts, roughly chopped
   115g/4oz fine green beans, halved
   1 red (bell) pepper, seeded and
      thinly sliced
   unsalted roasted peanuts, to garnish

1 Trim any fat off the beef and cut the beef into 5cm/2in strips.

2 Heat the sunflower oil in a large, heavy pan, add the curry paste and cook over a medium heat for 30 seconds, stirring constantly.

3 Add the beef and cook, stirring, for 2 minutes until it is beginning to brown and is thoroughly coated with the spices.

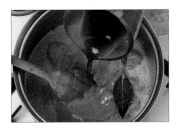

4 Stir in the bay leaves, coconut milk, stock, lemon juice, nam pla and sugar, and bring to the boil, stirring.

5 Add the onions and potatoes, then bring back to the boil, reduce the heat and simmer, uncovered, for 5 minutes.

6 Stir in the peanuts, beans and pepper and simmer for a further 10 minutes, or until the beef and potatoes are tender. Serve in shallow bowls, with a spoon and fork, to enjoy all the rich and creamy juices. Sprinkle with extra unsalted roasted peanuts.

BEEF IN OYSTER SAUCE

THE OYSTER SAUCE GIVES THE BEEF EXTRA RICHNESS AND DEPTH OF FLAVOUR. TO COMPLETE THE
DISH, ALL YOU NEED IS PLAIN BOILED RICE OR NOODLES.

SERVES FOUR

INGREDIENTS
    350g/12 oz rump (round) steak
    15ml/1 tbsp vegetable oil
    300ml/½ pint/1¼ cups beef stock
    2 garlic cloves, finely chopped
    1 small carrot, thinly sliced
    3 celery sticks, sliced
    15ml/1 tbsp dry sherry
    5ml/1 tsp caster (superfine) sugar
    45ml/3 tbsp oyster sauce
    5ml/1 tsp cornflour (cornstarch)
    15ml/1 tbsp cold water
    4 spring onions (scallions), chopped
    ground white pepper
    rice or noodles, to serve

1 Slice the steak thinly. Place the
slices in a bowl, add 5ml/1 tsp of
the vegetable oil and stir to coat.

2 Bring the stock to the boil in a large
pan. Add the beef and cook, stirring, for
2 minutes. Drain, reserving 45ml/3 tbsp
of the stock, and set aside.

3 Heat the remaining oil and stir-fry the
garlic for a few seconds, then add the
carrot and celery and stir-fry for 2 minutes.

4 Stir in the sherry, caster sugar, oyster
sauce and a large pinch of pepper. Add
the steak to the pan with the reserved
stock. Simmer for 2 minutes.

5 Mix the cornflour to a paste with the
water. Add the mixture to the pan and
cook, stirring, until thickened.

6 Stir in the spring onions, mixing well,
then serve at once, with rice or noodles.

VARIATION
To increase the number of servings,
add more vegetables, such as peppers,
mangetouts (snow peas), water chestnuts,
baby corn on the cob and mushrooms.

BEEF STEW <u>WITH</u> STAR ANISE

*NOT A WESTERN IDEA OF A STEW, BUT MORE OF A FRAGRANT SOUP WITH TENDER MORSELS OF BEEF.
THE BEANSPROUTS, SPRING ONION AND CORIANDER ARE ADDED AT THE END OF COOKING FOR A
DELIGHTFUL CONTRAST IN TASTE AND TEXTURE.*

<u>SERVES FOUR</u>

INGREDIENTS
1 litre/1¾ pints/4 cups vegetable or
  chicken stock
450g/1lb beef steak, cut into slivers
3 garlic cloves, finely chopped
3 coriander (cilantro) roots,
  finely chopped
2 cinnamon sticks
4 star anise
30ml/2 tbsp light soy sauce
30ml/2 tbsp Thai fish sauce
5ml/1 tsp granulated sugar
115g/4oz/1⅓ cups beansprouts
1 spring onion (scallion),
  finely chopped
small bunch fresh coriander
  (cilantro), coarsely chopped

1 Pour the stock into a large, heavy
pan. Add the beef, garlic, chopped
coriander roots, cinnamon sticks, star
anise, soy sauce, fish sauce and sugar.
Bring to the boil, then reduce the heat
to low and simmer for 30 minutes. Skim
off any foam that rises to the surface of
the liquid with a slotted spoon.

2 Meanwhile, divide the beansprouts
among four individual serving bowls.
Remove and discard the cinnamon
sticks and star anise from the stew
with a slotted spoon. Ladle the stew
over the beansprouts, garnish with the
chopped spring onion and chopped
fresh coriander and serve immediately.

MINTED LAMB STIR-FRY

LAMB AND MINT ARE A LONG-ESTABLISHED PARTNERSHIP THAT WORKS PARTICULARLY WELL IN THIS FULL-FLAVOURED STIR-FRY. SERVE WITH PLENTY OF FRESH CRUSTY BREAD.

SERVES TWO

INGREDIENTS
    275g/10oz lamb neck (US shoulder
      or breast) fillet or boneless
      leg steaks
    30ml/2 tbsp sunflower oil
    10ml/2 tsp sesame oil
    1 onion, roughly chopped
    2 garlic cloves, crushed
    1 red chilli, seeded and
      finely chopped
    75g/3oz fine green beans, halved
    225g/8oz fresh spinach, shredded
    30ml/2 tbsp oyster sauce
    30ml/2 tbsp nam pla (fish sauce)
    15ml/1 tbsp lemon juice
    5ml/1 tsp sugar
    45ml/3 tbsp chopped fresh mint
    salt and ground black pepper
    mint sprigs, to garnish
    noodles or rice, to serve

1 Trim the lamb of any excess fat and cut into thin slices. Heat the sunflower and sesame oils in a wok or large frying pan and cook the lamb over a high heat until browned. Remove with a slotted spoon and drain on kitchen paper.

2 Add the onion, garlic and chilli to the wok, cook for 2–3 minutes, then add the beans and stir-fry for 3 minutes.

3 Stir in the shredded spinach with the browned lamb meat, oyster sauce, nam pla, lemon juice and sugar. Stir-fry for a further 3–4 minutes, stirring constantly, until the lamb is cooked through.

4 Sprinkle in the chopped mint and toss lightly, then adjust the seasoning. Serve piping hot, garnished with mint sprigs and accompanied by noodles or rice.

MONGOLIAN FIREPOT

THIS MODE OF COOKING WAS INTRODUCED TO CHINA BY THE MONGOL HORDES WHO INVADED IN THE 13TH CENTURY. IT CALLS FOR PLENTY OF PARTICIPATION ON THE PART OF THE GUESTS, WHO COOK THE ASSEMBLED INGREDIENTS AT THE TABLE, DIPPING THE MEATS IN A VARIETY OF DIFFERENT SAUCES.

SERVES SIX TO EIGHT

INGREDIENTS
900g/2lb boned leg of lamb,
  preferably bought thinly sliced
225g/8oz lamb's liver and/or kidneys
900ml/1½ pints/3¾ cups lamb
  stock (see Cook's Tip)
900ml/1½ pints/3¾ cups
  chicken stock
1cm/½in piece fresh root ginger,
  peeled and thinly sliced
45ml/3 tbsp rice wine or
  medium-dry sherry
½ head Chinese leaves (Chinese
  cabbage), rinsed and shredded
few young spinach leaves
250g/9oz fresh firm tofu, diced
  (optional)
115g/4oz cellophane noodles
salt and ground black pepper
For the dipping sauce
50ml/2fl oz/¼ cup red wine vinegar
7.5ml/½ tbsp dark soy sauce
1cm/½in piece fresh root ginger,
  peeled and finely shredded
1 spring onion (scallion), shredded
To serve
steamed flower rolls
bowls of tomato sauce, sweet chilli
  sauce, mustard oil and sesame oil
dry-fried coriander seeds, crushed

COOK'S TIP
When buying the lamb, ask the butcher for the bones and make your own lamb stock. Rinse the bones and place them in a large pan with water to cover. Bring to the boil and skim the surface well. Add 1 peeled onion, 2 peeled carrots, 1cm/½in piece of peeled and bruised ginger, 5ml/1 tsp salt and ground black pepper to taste. Bring back to the boil, then simmer for about an hour until the stock is full of flavour. Strain, leave to cool, then skim and use.

1 When buying the lamb, ask your butcher to slice it thinly on a slicing machine, if possible. If you have had to buy the lamb in the piece, however, put it in the freezer for about an hour, so that it is easier to slice thinly.

2 Trim the liver and remove the skin and core from the kidneys, if using. Place them in the freezer too. If you managed to buy sliced lamb, keep it in the refrigerator until needed.

3 Mix both types of stock in a large pan. Add the sliced ginger and rice wine or sherry, with salt and pepper to taste. Heat to simmering point; simmer for 15 minutes.

4 Slice all the meats thinly and arrange them attractively on a large platter.

5 Place the shredded Chinese leaves, spinach leaves and the diced tofu on a separate platter. Soak the noodles in warm or hot water, following the instructions on the packet.

6 Make the dipping sauce by mixing all the ingredients in a small bowl. The other sauces and the crushed coriander seeds should be spooned into separate small dishes and placed on a serving tray. Have ready a basket of freshly steamed flower rolls.

7 Fill the moat of the hotpot with the simmering stock. Alternatively, fill a fondue pot and place it over a burner. Each guest selects a portion of meat from the platter and cooks it in the hot stock, using chopsticks or a fondue fork. The meat is then dipped in one of the sauces and coated with the coriander seeds (if you like) before being eaten with a steamed flower roll.

8 When all or most of the meat has been eaten, top up the stock if necessary, then add the vegetables, tofu and drained noodles. Cook for a minute or two, until the noodles are tender and the vegetables retain a little crispness. Serve the soup in warmed bowls, with any remaining steamed flower rolls.

FISH
DISHES

*Fish is a main source of protein in the Asian diet, which is
hardly surprising considering the vast lengths of coastline.
The fish is steamed, stir-fried, baked, grilled with local spices
or herbs, and served in curries and sauces. Serving a fish whole,
rather than cutting it into portions, has great appeal in Asia, as
the fish is aesthetically pleasing and the juices are retained.
Impress your guests with Steamed Fish with Five Willow Sauce,
or Baked Sea Bass with Lemon Grass and Red Onions.*

FISH MOOLIE

THIS IS A VERY POPULAR SOUTH-EAST ASIAN FISH CURRY IN A COCONUT SAUCE, WHICH IS TRULY
DELICIOUS. CHOOSE A FIRM-TEXTURED FISH SO THAT THE PIECES STAY INTACT DURING THE BRIEF
COOKING PROCESS. HALIBUT AND COD WORK EQUALLY WELL.

5 Heat the oil in a wok. Add the onion mixture and cook for a few minutes without browning. Stir in the coconut milk and bring to the boil, stirring constantly to prevent curdling.

SERVES FOUR

INGREDIENTS
   500g/1¼lb monkfish or other
      firm-textured fish fillets, skinned
      and cut into 2.5cm/1in cubes
   2.5ml/½ tsp salt
   50g/2oz/⅔ cup desiccated (dry
      unsweetened shredded) coconut
   6 shallots or small onions, chopped
   6 blanched almonds
   2–3 garlic cloves, roughly chopped
   2.5cm/1in piece fresh root ginger,
      peeled and sliced
   2 lemon grass stalks, trimmed
   10ml/2 tsp ground turmeric
   45ml/3 tbsp vegetable oil
   2 × 400ml/14fl oz cans coconut milk
   1–3 fresh chillies, seeded and sliced
   salt and ground black pepper
   fresh chives, to garnish
   boiled rice, to serve

1 Spread out the pieces of fish in a shallow dish and sprinkle them with the salt. Dry fry the coconut in a wok or large frying pan over medium to low heat, turning all the time until it is crisp and golden (see Cook's Tip).

2 Transfer the coconut to a food processor and process to an oily paste. Scrape into a bowl and reserve.

3 Add the shallots or onions, almonds, garlic and ginger to the food processor. Cut off the lower 5cm/2in of the lemon grass stalks, chop them roughly and add to the processor. Process the mixture to a paste.

4 Add the turmeric to the mixture in the processor and process briefly to mix. Bruise the remaining lemon grass and set the stalks aside.

6 Add the cubes of fish, most of the sliced chilli and the bruised lemon grass stalks. Cook for 3–4 minutes. Stir in the coconut paste (moistened with some of the sauce if necessary) and cook for a further 2–3 minutes only. Do not overcook the fish. Taste and adjust the seasoning.

7 Remove the lemon grass. Transfer to a hot serving dish and sprinkle with the remaining slices of chilli. Garnish with chopped and whole chives and serve with boiled rice.

COOK'S TIP
Dry frying is a feature of Malay cooking. When dry frying do not be distracted. The coconut must be constantly on the move so that it becomes crisp and of a uniform golden colour.

GREEN FISH CURRY

ANY FIRM-FLESHED FISH CAN BE USED FOR THIS DELICIOUS CURRY, WHICH GAINS ITS RICH COLOUR FROM A MIXTURE OF FRESH HERBS; TRY EXOTICS SUCH AS MAHI MAHI, HOKI OR SWORDFISH OR HUMBLER FISH SUCH AS COLEY. SERVE IT WITH BASMATI OR THAI FRAGRANT RICE AND LIME WEDGES.

SERVES FOUR

INGREDIENTS
4 garlic cloves, roughly chopped
5cm/2in piece fresh root ginger,
  peeled and roughly chopped
2 fresh green chillies, seeded and
  roughly chopped
grated rind and juice of 1 lime
5–10ml/1–2 tsp shrimp
  paste (optional)
5ml/1 tsp coriander seeds
5ml/1 tsp five-spice powder
75ml/5 tbsp sesame oil
2 red onions, finely chopped
900g/2lb hoki fillets, skinned
400ml/14fl oz/1⅔ cups coconut milk
45ml/3 tbsp nam pla (fish sauce)
50g/2oz fresh coriander (cilantro)
50g/2oz fresh mint leaves
50g/2oz fresh basil leaves
6 spring onions, chopped
150ml/¼ pint/⅔ cup sunflower or
  groundnut (peanut) oil
sliced fresh green chilli and chopped
  fresh coriander (cilantro), to garnish
cooked Basmati or Thai fragrant rice
  and lime wedges, to serve

2 Heat a wok or large shallow pan, and pour in the remaining sesame oil. When it is hot, stir-fry the red onions over a high heat for 2 minutes. Add the fish and stir-fry for 1–2 minutes to seal the fillets on all sides.

3 Lift out the red onions and fish and put them on a plate. Add the curry paste to the wok or pan and fry for 1 minute, stirring. Return the hoki fillets and red onions to the wok or pan, pour in the coconut milk and bring to the boil. Lower the heat, add the nam pla and simmer for 5–7 minutes, until the fish is cooked through.

4 Meanwhile, process the herbs, spring onions, lime rind and oil in a food processor to a coarse paste. Stir into the fish curry. Garnish with chilli and coriander and serve with rice and lime wedges.

1 First make the curry paste. Combine the garlic, fresh root ginger, green chillies, the lime juice and shrimp paste (if using) in a food processor. Add the coriander seeds and five-spice powder, with half the sesame oil. Whizz to a fine paste, then set aside until required.

HOKI STIR-FRY

ANY FIRM WHITE FISH, SUCH AS MONKFISH, HAKE OR COD, CAN BE USED FOR THIS ATTRACTIVE STIR-FRY. VARY THE VEGETABLES ACCORDING TO WHAT IS AVAILABLE, BUT TRY TO INCLUDE AT LEAST THREE DIFFERENT COLOURS. SHRIMP-FRIED RICE WOULD BE THE PERFECT ACCOMPANIMENT.

SERVES FOUR TO SIX

INGREDIENTS

  675g/1½lb hoki fillet, skinned
  salt, pepper and five-spice powder
  2 carrots
  115g/4oz/1 cup small mangetouts
    (snow peas)
  115g/4oz asparagus spears
  4 spring onions (scallions)
  45ml/3 tbsp groundnut (peanut) oil
  2.5cm/1in piece fresh root ginger,
    peeled and cut into thin slivers
  2 garlic cloves, finely chopped
  300g/11oz beansprouts
  8–12 small baby corn cobs
  15–30ml/1–2 tbsp light soy sauce

3 Heat a wok, then pour in the oil. As soon as it is hot, add the ginger and garlic. Stir-fry for 1 minute, then add the white parts of the spring onions and cook for 1 minute more.

COOK'S TIP
When adding the oil to the hot wok, drizzle it around the inner rim like a necklace. The oil will run down to coat the entire surface of the wok. Swirl the wok to make sure the coating is even.

4 Add the hoki strips and stir-fry for 2–3 minutes, until all the pieces of fish are opaque. Add the beansprouts. Toss them around to coat them in the oil, then put in the carrots, mangetouts, asparagus and corn. Continue to stir-fry for 3–4 minutes, by which time the fish should be cooked, but all the vegetables will still be crunchy. Add soy sauce to taste, toss everything quickly together, then stir in the green parts of the spring onions. Serve immediately.

1 Cut the hoki into finger-size strips and season with salt, pepper and five-spice powder. Cut the carrots diagonally into slices as thin as the mangetouts.

2 Top and tail the mangetouts. Trim the asparagus spears and cut in half crossways. Trim the spring onions and cut them diagonally into 2cm/¾in pieces, keeping the white and green parts separate. Set aside.

STEAMED FISH WITH CHILLI SAUCE

STEAMING IS ONE OF THE BEST METHODS OF COOKING FISH. BY LEAVING THE FISH WHOLE AND ON THE BONE, MAXIMUM FLAVOUR IS RETAINED AND THE FLESH REMAINS BEAUTIFULLY MOIST. THE BANANA LEAF IS BOTH AUTHENTIC AND ATTRACTIVE, BUT YOU CAN USE BAKING PARCHMENT.

SERVES FOUR

INGREDIENTS
    1 large or 2 medium firm fish such
      as sea bass or grouper, scaled
      and cleaned
    30ml/2 tbsp rice wine
    3 fresh red chillies, seeded and
      thinly sliced
    2 garlic cloves, finely chopped
    2cm/¾in piece fresh root ginger,
      peeled and finely shredded
    2 lemon grass stalks, crushed and
      finely chopped
    2 spring onions
      (scallions), chopped
    30ml/2 tbsp Thai fish sauce
    juice of 1 lime
    1 fresh banana leaf
For the chilli sauce
    10 fresh red chillies, seeded
      and chopped
    4 garlic cloves, chopped
    60ml/4 tbsp Thai fish sauce
    15ml/1 tbsp granulated sugar
    75ml/5 tbsp fresh lime juice

1 Thoroughly rinse the fish under cold running water. Pat it dry with kitchen paper. With a sharp knife, slash the skin of the fish a few times on both sides.

2 Mix together the rice wine, chillies, garlic, shredded ginger, lemon grass and spring onions in a non-metallic bowl. Add the fish sauce and lime juice and mix to a paste. Place the fish on the banana leaf and spread the spice paste evenly over it, rubbing it in well where the skin has been slashed.

3 Put a rack or a small upturned plate in the base of a wok. Pour in boiling water to a depth of 5cm/2in. Lift the banana leaf, together with the fish, and place it on the rack or plate. Cover with a lid and steam for 10–15 minutes, or until the fish is cooked.

4 Meanwhile, make the sauce. Place all the ingredients in a food processor and process until smooth. If the mixture seems to be too thick, add a little cold water. Scrape into a serving bowl.

5 Serve the fish hot, on the banana leaf if you like, with the sweet chilli sauce to spoon over the top.

STEAMED FISH WITH FIVE WILLOW SAUCE

A FISH KETTLE WILL COME IN USEFUL FOR THIS RECIPE. CARP IS TRADITIONALLY USED, BUT ANY CHUNKY FISH THAT CAN BE COOKED WHOLE SUCH AS SALMON OR SEA BREAM CAN BE GIVEN THIS TREATMENT. MAKE SURE YOU HAVE A SUITABLE LARGE PLATTER FOR SERVING THIS SPECTACULAR DISH.

SERVES FOUR

INGREDIENTS
    1–2 carp or similar whole fish,
      total weight about 1kg/2¼ lb,
      cleaned and scaled
    2.5cm/1in piece fresh root ginger,
      peeled and thinly sliced
    4 spring onions (scallions), sliced
    2.5ml/½ tsp salt
For the five willow sauce
    375g/13oz jar chow chow (Chinese
      sweet mixed pickles)
    300ml/½ pint/1¼ cups water
    30ml/2 tbsp rice vinegar
    25ml/1½ tbsp sugar
    25ml/1½ tbsp cornflour (cornstarch)
    15ml/1 tbsp light soy sauce
    15ml/1 tbsp rice wine or
      medium-dry sherry
    1 small green (bell) pepper, seeded
      and diced
    1 carrot, peeled and cut into
      matchsticks
    1 tomato, peeled, seeded
      and diced

2 Fold up one or two pieces of foil to make a long wide strip. You will need one for each fish. Place the fish on the foil and then lift the fish on to the trivet. Lower the trivet into the fish kettle and tuck the ends of the foil over the fish.

3 Pour boiling water into the fish kettle to a depth of 2.5cm/1in. Bring to a full rolling boil, then lower the heat and cook the fish until the flesh flakes, topping up the kettle with boiling water as necessary. See Cook's Tip for cooking times.

5 In a small bowl, mix the cornflour to a paste with the remaining water. Stir in the soy sauce and rice wine or sherry.

6 Add the mixture to the sauce and bring to the boil, stirring until it thickens and becomes glossy. Add all the vegetables, the chopped pickles and the pickle liquid and cook over a gentle heat for 2 minutes.

7 Using the foil strips as a support, carefully transfer the cooked fish to a platter, then ease the foil away. Spoon the warm sauce over the fish and serve.

COOK'S TIP
If using one large fish that is too long to fit in a fish kettle, cut it in half and cook it on a rack placed over a large roasting tin. Pour in a similar quantity of boiling water as for the fish kettle, cover with foil and cook on top of the stove. Allow about 20–25 minutes for a 1kg/2¼ lb fish; 15–20 minutes for a 675g/1½ lb fish. Reassemble the halved fish before coating it with the sauce.

1 Rinse the fish inside and out. Dry with kitchen paper. Create a support for each fish by placing a broad strip of oiled foil on the work surface. Place the fish on the foil. Mix the ginger, spring onions and salt, then tuck the mixture into the body cavity.

4 Meanwhile, prepare the sauce. Tip the chow chow (Chinese sweet mixed pickles) into a strainer placed over a bowl and reserve the liquid. Cut each of the pickles in half. Pour 250ml/8fl oz/1 cup of the water into a pan and bring to the boil. Add the vinegar and sugar and stir until dissolved.

SEA BASS WITH GINGER AND LEEKS

YOU CAN USE WHOLE FISH OR THICK FILLETS FOR THIS RECIPE, WHICH IS ALSO EXCELLENT MADE WITH BREAM, SNAPPER, POMFRET AND TREVALLY. SERVE THE FISH WITH FRIED RICE AND STIR-FRIED CHINESE GREEN VEGETABLES SUCH AS BOK CHOY, IF YOU LIKE.

SERVES FOUR

INGREDIENTS

  1 sea bass, about 1.4–1.5kg/
    3–3½lb, scaled and cleaned
  8 spring onions (scallions)
  60ml/4 tbsp teriyaki marinade or
    dark soy sauce
  30ml/2 tbsp cornflour (cornstarch)
  juice of 1 lemon
  30ml/2 tbsp rice wine vinegar
  5ml/1 tsp ground ginger
  60ml/4 tbsp groundnut (peanut) oil
  2 leeks, shredded
  2.5cm/1in piece fresh root ginger,
    peeled and grated
  105ml/7 tbsp chicken or fish stock
  30ml/2 tbsp rice wine or dry sherry
  5ml/1 tsp caster (superfine) sugar
  salt and ground black pepper

1 Make several diagonal slashes on either side of the sea bass so it can absorb the flavours, then season the fish inside and out with salt and ground black pepper. Trim the spring onions, cut them in half lengthways, then slice them diagonally into 2cm/¾in lengths. Put half of the spring onions in the cavity of the fish and reserve the rest for later use.

2 In a shallow dish, mix together the teriyaki marinade or dark soy sauce, the cornflour, lemon juice, rice wine vinegar and ground ginger to make a smooth, runny paste. Turn the fish in the marinade to coat it thoroughly, working it into the slashes, then leave it to marinate for 20–30 minutes, turning it several times.

3 Heat a wok or frying pan that is large enough to hold the sea bass comfortably. Add the oil, then the leeks and grated ginger. Fry gently for about 5 minutes, until the leeks are tender. Remove the leeks and ginger with a slotted spoon, and drain on kitchen paper leaving the oil in the wok or pan.

4 Lift the sea bass out of the marinade and lower it carefully into the hot oil. Fry over a medium heat for 2–3 minutes on each side. Stir the stock, rice wine or sherry and sugar into the marinade, with salt and pepper to taste. Pour the mixture over the fish. Return the leeks and ginger to the wok, together with the reserved spring onions. Cover and simmer for about 15 minutes, until the fish is cooked through. Serve at once.

BAKED SEA BASS WITH LEMON GRASS AND RED ONIONS

MOIST, TENDER SEA BASS IS FLAVOURED WITH A COMBINATION OF TRADITIONAL THAI INGREDIENTS IN THIS SIMPLE BUT MOUTHWATERING CLAY-POT DISH.

SERVES TWO TO THREE

INGREDIENTS

   1 sea bass, about 675g/1½lb,
     cleaned and scaled
   30ml/2 tbsp olive oil
   2 lemon grass stalks, finely sliced
   1 red onion, finely shredded
   1 chilli, seeded and finely chopped
   5cm/2in piece fresh root ginger,
     finely shredded
   45ml/3 tbsp chopped fresh
     coriander (cilantro)
   rind and juice of 2 limes
   30ml/2 tbsp light soy sauce
   salt and ground black pepper

COOK'S TIP
This recipe will taste delicious using fish such as red or grey mullet, red snapper, salmon or tilapia. Depending on the weight of the fish, you may need to use two smaller fish rather than a whole one.

1 Soak a fish clay pot in cold water for 20 minutes, then drain. Make four to five diagonal slashes on both sides of the fish. Repeat the slashes on one side in the opposite direction to give an attractive cross-hatched effect. Rub the sea bass inside and out with salt, pepper and 15ml/1 tbsp of the olive oil.

2 Mix together the Thai ingredients – the lemon grass, red onion, chilli, ginger, coriander and lime rind.

3 Place a little of the lemon grass and red onion mixture in the base of the clay pot, then lay the fish on top. Sprinkle the remaining mixture over the fish, then sprinkle over the lime juice, soy sauce and the remaining olive oil. Cover and place in an unheated oven.

4 Set the oven to 220°C/425°F/Gas 7 and cook the fish for 30–40 minutes, or until the flesh flakes easily when tested with a knife. Serve immediately.

MOHINGHA

BURMESE HOUSEWIVES BUY THIS WELL-KNOWN AND DELICIOUS ONE-COURSE MEAL FROM HAWKERS, RECOGNIZED BY A BAMBOO POLE CARRIED ACROSS THEIR SHOULDERS. AT ONE END IS A CONTAINER WITH A CHARCOAL FIRE AND AT THE OTHER END IS EVERYTHING ELSE THEY NEED TO MAKE THE MEAL.

SERVES EIGHT

INGREDIENTS
 675g/1¹/₂lb huss, cod or mackerel,
  cleaned but left on the bone
 3 lemon grass stalks
 2.5cm/1in piece fresh root
  ginger, peeled
 30ml/2 tbsp fish sauce
 3 onions, roughly chopped
 4 garlic cloves, roughly chopped
 2–3 fresh red chillies, seeded
  and chopped
 5ml/1 tsp ground turmeric
 75ml/5 tbsp groundnut (peanut) oil
 400ml/14fl oz can coconut milk
 25g/1oz/3 tbsp rice flour
 25g/1oz/3 tbsp chickpea flour
  (besan)
 pieces of banana trunk, or heart, if
  available, or 540g/1lb 5oz drained
  canned bamboo shoot, sliced
 salt and ground black pepper
 wedges of hard-boiled egg, thinly
  sliced red onions, finely chopped
  spring onions (scallions), a few deep
  fried prawns (shrimp) and fried
  chillies (see Cook's Tip), to garnish
 450g/1lb dried or fresh rice noodles,
  cooked according to the instructions
  on the packet, to serve

1 Place the fish in a large pan and pour in cold water to cover. Bruise two lemon grass stalks and half the ginger and add to the pan. Bring to the boil, add the fish sauce and cook for 10 minutes. Lift out the fish and allow to cool while straining the stock into a large bowl. Discard any skin and bones from the fish and break the flesh into small pieces.

COOK'S TIP
To make fried chillies, dry roast 8–10 dried red chillies in a heavy frying pan, then pound them, fry in 30ml/2 tbsp peanut oil and stir in 25g/1oz dried shrimps, pounded.

2 Cut off the lower 5cm/2in of the remaining lemon grass stalk and discard; roughly chop the remaining lemon grass. Put it in a food processor with the remaining ginger, the onions, garlic, chillies and turmeric. Process to a smooth paste. Heat the oil in a frying pan and fry the paste until it gives off a rich aroma. Remove from the heat and add the fish.

3 Stir the coconut milk into the reserved fish stock, then add enough water to make up to 2.5 litres/4 pints/ 10 cups and pour into a large pan. In a jug, mix the rice flour and chickpea flour to a thin cream with some of the stock. Stir this into the coconut and stock mixture and bring to the boil, stirring all the time.

4 Add the banana trunk or heart or bamboo shoots and cook for 10 minutes until just tender. Stir in the fish mixture and season. Cook until hot. Guests pour soup over the noodles and add hard-boiled egg, onions, spring onions, prawns and fried chillies as a garnish.

ESCABECHE

THIS PICKLED FISH DISH IS EATEN WHEREVER THERE ARE — OR HAVE BEEN — SPANISH SETTLERS. HERE IT HAS BEEN MODIFIED IN ORDER TO REFLECT THE CHINESE INFLUENCE ON FILIPINO CUISINE.

SERVES SIX

INGREDIENTS
675–900g/1½–2lb white fish fillets,
  such as sole or plaice
45–60ml/3–4 tbsp seasoned flour
vegetable oil, for shallow frying
For the sauce
2.5cm/1in piece fresh root ginger,
  peeled and thinly sliced
2–3 garlic cloves, crushed
1 onion, cut into thin rings
30ml/2 tbsp vegetable oil
½ large green (bell) pepper,
  seeded and cut in small neat
  squares
½ large red (bell) pepper, seeded
  and cut in small neat squares
1 carrot, cut into matchsticks
25ml/1½ tbsp cornflour (cornstarch)
450ml/¾ pint/scant 2 cups water
45–60ml/3–4 tbsp herb or
  cider vinegar
15ml/1 tbsp light soft brown sugar
5–10ml/1–2 tsp fish sauce
salt and ground black pepper
1 small chilli, seeded and sliced
  and spring onions (scallions), finely
  shredded, to garnish (optional)
boiled rice, to serve

1 Wipe the fish fillets and leave them whole, or cut into serving portions, if you like. Pat dry on kitchen paper then dust lightly with seasoned flour.

2 Heat oil for shallow frying in a frying pan and fry the fish in batches until golden and almost cooked. Transfer to an ovenproof dish and keep warm.

3 Make the sauce in a wok or large frying pan. Fry the ginger, garlic and onion in the oil for 5 minutes or until the onion is softened but not browned.

4 Add the pepper squares and carrot strips and stir-fry for 1 minute.

5 Put the cornflour in a small bowl and add a little of the water to make a paste. Stir in the remaining water, the vinegar and the sugar. Pour the cornflour mixture over the vegetables in the wok and stir until the sauce boils and thickens a little. Season with fish sauce and salt and pepper if needed.

6 Add the fish to the sauce and reheat briefly without stirring. Transfer to a warmed serving platter and garnish with chilli and spring onions, if liked. Serve with boiled rice.

COOK'S TIP
Red snapper or small sea bass could be used for this recipe, in which case ask your fishmonger to cut them into fillets.

SWEET AND SOUR FISH

*WHEN FISH SUCH AS RED MULLET OR SNAPPER IS COOKED IN THIS WAY THE SKIN BECOMES CRISP,
WHILE THE FLESH INSIDE REMAINS MOIST AND JUICY. THE SWEET AND SOUR SAUCE, WITH ITS
COLOURFUL CHERRY TOMATOES, COMPLEMENTS THE FISH BEAUTIFULLY.*

SERVES FOUR TO SIX

INGREDIENTS
    1 large or 2 medium fish, such as
      snapper or mullet, heads removed
    20ml/4 tsp cornflour (cornstarch)
    120ml/4fl oz/½ cup vegetable oil
    15ml/1 tbsp chopped garlic
    15ml/1 tbsp chopped fresh
      root ginger
    30ml/2 tbsp chopped shallots
    225g/8oz cherry tomatoes
    30ml/2 tbsp red wine vinegar
    30ml/2 tbsp granulated sugar
    30ml/2 tbsp tomato ketchup
    15ml/1 tbsp Thai fish sauce
    45ml/3 tbsp water
    salt and ground black pepper
    coriander (cilantro) leaves and
      shredded spring onions
      (scallions), to garnish

1 Rinse and dry the fish. Score the skin
diagonally on both sides, then coat the
fish lightly all over with 15ml/1 tbsp of
the cornflour. Shake off any excess.

2 Heat the oil in a wok or large frying
pan. Add the fish and cook over a
medium heat for 6–7 minutes. Turn
the fish over and cook for 6–7 minutes
more, until it is crisp and brown.

3 Remove the fish with a metal spatula
or fish slice and place on a large platter.
Pour off all but 30ml/2 tbsp of the oil
from the wok or pan and reheat. Add
the garlic, ginger and shallots and cook
over a medium heat, stirring occasionally,
for 3–4 minutes, until golden.

4 Add the cherry tomatoes and cook
until they burst open. Stir in the vinegar,
sugar, tomato ketchup and fish sauce.
Lower the heat and simmer gently for
1–2 minutes, then taste and adjust the
seasoning, adding more vinegar, sugar
and/or fish sauce, if necessary.

5 In a cup, mix the remaining 5ml/1 tsp
cornflour to a paste with the water. Stir
into the sauce. Heat, stirring, until it
thickens. Pour the sauce over the fish,
garnish with coriander leaves and
shredded spring onions and serve.

P A P E R - W R A P P E D ᴬᴺᴰ S T E A M E D R E D S N A P P E R

ORIGINALLY, THIS ELEGANT DISH FEATURED A WHOLE RED SNAPPER WRAPPED IN LAYERED JAPANESE HAND-MADE PAPER SOAKED IN SAKE AND TIED WITH RIBBONS. THIS VERSION IS A LITTLE EASIER.

4 At each end, fold the top corners down diagonally, then fold the bottom corners up to meet the opposite folded edge to make a triangle. Press flat with your palm. Repeat the process to make four parcels.

5 Cut 2.5cm/1in from the tip of the asparagus, and slice in half lengthways. Slice the asparagus stems and spring onions diagonally into thin ovals. Par-boil the tips for 1 minute in lightly salted water and drain. Set aside.

6 Open the parcels. Place the asparagus slices and the spring onions inside. Sprinkle with salt and place the fish on top. Add more salt and some sake, then sprinkle in the lime rind. Refold the parcels.

7 Pour hot water from a kettle into a deep roasting pan fitted with a wire rack to 1cm/½in below the rack. Place the parcels on the rack. Cook in the centre of the preheated oven for 20 minutes. Check by carefully unfolding a parcel from one triangular side. The fish should have changed from translucent to white.

8 Transfer the parcels on to individual plates. Unfold both triangular ends on the plate and lift open the middle a little. Insert a thin slice of lime and place two asparagus tips on top. Serve immediately, asking the guests to open their own parcels. Add a little shoyu, if you like.

SERVES FOUR

INGREDIENTS
  4 small red snapper fillets, no greater
    than 18 × 6cm/7 × 2½ in, or whole
    snapper, 20cm/8in long, gutted but
    head, tail and fins intact
  8 asparagus spears, hard
    ends discarded
  4 spring onions (scallions)
  60ml/4 tbsp sake
  grated rind of ½ lime
  ½ lime, thinly sliced
  5ml/1 tsp shoyu (optional)
  salt

1 Sprinkle the red snapper fillets with salt on both sides and leave in the refrigerator for 20 minutes. Preheat the oven to 180°C/350°F/Gas 4.

2 To make the parcels, lay greaseproof (waxed) paper measuring 38 × 30cm/ 15 × 12in on a work surface. Use two pieces for extra thickness. Fold up one-third of the paper and turn back 1cm/½in from one end to make a flap.

3 Fold 1cm/½in in from the other end to make another flap. Fold the top edge down to fold over the first flap. Interlock the two flaps to form a long rectangle.

MARINATED AND GRILLED SWORDFISH

IN MEDIEVAL TIMES, SAIKYO (THE WESTERN CAPITAL OF ANCIENT JAPAN) HAD A VERY SOPHISTICATED CULTURE. ARISTOCRATS COMPETED WITH EACH OTHER AS TO THEIR CHEF'S SKILLS, AND MANY OF THE CLASSIC RECIPES OF TODAY ARE FROM THIS PERIOD. KAJIKI SAIKYO YAKI IS ONE SUCH EXAMPLE.

SERVES FOUR

INGREDIENTS
    4 × 175g/6oz swordfish steaks
    2.5ml/½ tsp salt
    300g/11oz saikyo or shiro miso
    45ml/3 tbsp sake
For the asparagus
    25ml/1½ tbsp shoyu
    25ml/1½ tbsp sake
    8 asparagus spears, the hard ends
        discarded, each spear cut
        into three

1 Place the swordfish in a shallow container. Sprinkle with the salt on both sides and leave for 2 hours. Drain and wipe the fish with kitchen paper.

2 Mix the miso and sake, then spread half across the bottom of the cleaned container. Cover with a sheet of muslin (cheesecloth) the size of a dishtowel, folded in half, then open the fold. Place the swordfish, side by side, on top, and cover with the muslin. Spread the rest of the miso mixture on the muslin. Make sure the muslin is touching the fish. Marinate for 2 days in the coolest part of the refrigerator.

3 Preheat the grill (broiler) to medium. Oil the wire rack and grill (broil) the fish slowly for about 8 minutes on each side, turning every 2 minutes. If the steaks are thin, check every time you turn the fish to see if they are ready.

4 Mix the shoyu and sake in a bowl. Grill the asparagus for 2 minutes on each side, then dip into the bowl. Return to the grill for 2 minutes more on each side. Dip into the sauce again and set aside.

5 Serve the steak hot on four individual serving plates. Garnish with the drained, grilled asparagus.

GREY MULLET <u>WITH</u> PORK

THIS UNUSUAL COMBINATION OF FISH AND MEAT MAKES A SPECTACULAR MAIN DISH AND IT REQUIRES SURPRISINGLY LITTLE EFFORT TO PREPARE.

SERVES FOUR

INGREDIENTS

  1 grey mullet or snapper, about
    900g/2lb, gutted and cleaned
  50g/2oz lean pork
  3 dried Chinese mushrooms, soaked
    in hot water until soft
  2.5ml/½ tsp cornflour (cornstarch)
  30ml/2 tbsp light soy sauce
  15ml/1 tbsp vegetable oil
  15ml/1 tbsp finely shredded fresh
    root ginger
  15ml/1 tbsp shredded spring onion
    (scallion)
  salt and ground black pepper
  rice, to serve
  sliced spring onion (scallion),
    to garnish

1 Make four diagonal cuts on either side of the fish and rub with a little salt; place the fish on a heatproof serving dish.

2 Cut the pork into thin strips. Place in a bowl. Drain the soaked mushrooms, remove and discard the stalks and slice the caps thinly. Add the mushrooms to the pork, with the cornflour and half the soy sauce. Stir in 5ml/1 tsp of the oil and black pepper. Arrange the pork mixture along the length of the fish. Sprinkle the ginger shreds over the top.

3 Cover the fish loosely with foil. Have ready a large pan or roasting pan with about 5cm/2in boiling water, which is big enough to fit the heatproof dish inside it on a metal trivet. Place the dish in the pan or roasting pan, cover and steam over a high heat for 15 minutes.

4 Test the fish by pressing the flesh gently. If it comes away from the bone with a slight resistance, the fish is cooked. Carefully pour away any excess liquid from the dish.

5 Heat the remaining oil in a small pan. When it is hot, fry the shredded spring onion for a few seconds, then pour it over the fish, taking great care as it will splatter. Drizzle with the remaining soy sauce, garnish with sliced spring onion and serve immediately with rice.

HOT AND FRAGRANT TROUT

THIS WICKEDLY HOT SPICE PASTE COULD BE USED AS A MARINADE FOR ANY FISH OR MEAT. IT ALSO MAKES A WONDERFUL SPICY DIP FOR GRILLED MEAT.

SERVES FOUR

INGREDIENTS
    2 large fresh green chillies, seeded
        and coarsely chopped
    5 shallots, peeled
    5 garlic cloves, peeled
    30ml/2 tbsp fresh lime juice
    30ml/2 tbsp Thai fish sauce
    15ml/1 tbsp palm sugar or light
        muscovado (brown) sugar
    4 kaffir lime leaves, rolled
        into cylinders and
        thinly sliced
    2 trout or similar firm-fleshed
        fish, about 350g/12oz
        each, cleaned
    fresh garlic chives, to garnish
    boiled rice, to serve

1 Wrap the chillies, shallots and garlic in a foil package. Place under a hot grill (broiler) for 10 minutes, until softened.

2 When the package is cool enough to handle, tip the contents into a mortar or food processor and pound with a pestle or process to a paste.

3 Add the lime juice, fish sauce, sugar and lime leaves and mix well. With a teaspoon, stuff this paste inside the fish. Smear a little on the skin too. Grill (broil) the fish for about 5 minutes on each side, until just cooked through. Lift the fish on to a platter, garnish with garlic chives and serve with rice.

TROUT WITH TAMARIND AND CHILLI SAUCE

SOMETIMES TROUT CAN TASTE RATHER BLAND, BUT THIS SPICY SAUCE REALLY GIVES IT A ZING.
IF YOU LIKE YOUR FOOD VERY SPICY, ADD AN EXTRA CHILLI.

SERVES FOUR

INGREDIENTS

    4 trout, cleaned
    6 spring onions (scallions), sliced
    60ml/4 tbsp soy sauce
    15ml/1 tbsp vegetable oil
    30ml/2 tbsp chopped fresh coriander
    (cilantro) and strips of fresh red
    chilli, to garnish
For the sauce
    50g/2oz tamarind pulp
    105ml/7 tbsp boiling water
    2 shallots, coarsely chopped
    1 fresh red chilli, seeded and chopped
    1cm/½ in piece fresh root ginger,
    peeled and chopped
    5ml/1 tsp soft light brown sugar
    45ml/3 tbsp Thai fish sauce

3 Make the sauce. Put the tamarind pulp in a small bowl and pour on the boiling water. Mash well with a fork until softened. Tip the tamarind mixture into a food processor or blender, and add the shallots, fresh chilli, ginger, sugar and fish sauce. Process to a coarse pulp. Scrape into a bowl.

4 Heat the oil in a large frying pan or wok and cook the trout, one at a time if necessary, for about 5 minutes on each side, until the skin is crisp and browned and the flesh cooked. Put on warmed plates and spoon over some of the sauce. Sprinkle with the coriander and chilli and serve with the remaining sauce.

1 Slash the trout diagonally four or five times on each side. Place them in a shallow dish that is large enough to hold them all in a single layer.

2 Fill the cavities with spring onions and douse each fish with soy sauce. Carefully turn the fish over to coat both sides with the sauce. Sprinkle any remaining spring onions over the top.

TROUT WITH BLACK RICE

PINK TROUT FILLETS COOKED WITH GINGER, GARLIC AND CHILLI MAKE A STUNNING CONTRAST TO
THE NUTTY BLACK RICE. AN IDEAL CHOICE FOR A ROMANTIC DINNER FOR TWO.

SERVES TWO

INGREDIENTS

   2.5cm/1in piece fresh root ginger,
     peeled and grated
   1 garlic clove, crushed
   1 fresh red chilli, seeded and
     finely chopped
   30ml/2 tbsp soy sauce
   2 trout fillets, each about 200g/7oz
   oil, for greasing
For the rice
   15ml/1 tbsp sesame oil
   50g/2oz/¾ cup fresh shiitake
     mushrooms, sliced
   8 spring onions (scallions), finely
     chopped
   150g/5oz/¾ cup black rice
   4 slices fresh root ginger
   900ml/1½ pints/3¾ cups
     boiling water

1 Make the rice. Heat the sesame oil in a pan and fry the mushrooms with half the spring onions for 2–3 minutes.

2 Add the rice and sliced ginger to the pan and stir well. Cover with the boiling water and bring to the boil. Reduce the heat, cover and simmer for 25–30 minutes or until the rice is tender. Drain well and cover to keep warm.

3 While the rice is cooking, preheat the oven to 200°C/400°F/Gas 6. In a small bowl mix together the grated ginger, garlic, chilli and soy sauce.

4 Place the fish, skin side up, in a lightly oiled shallow baking dish. Using a sharp knife, make several slits in the skin of the fish, then spread the ginger paste all over the fillets.

5 Cover the dish tightly with foil and cook in the oven for 20–25 minutes or until the trout fillets are cooked through.

6 Divide the rice between two warmed serving plates. Remove the ginger. Lay the fish on top and sprinkle over the reserved spring onions, to garnish.

THAI-STYLE TROUT

THE COMBINATION OF CLASSIC THAI AROMATIC INGREDIENTS – GINGER, LEMON GRASS, COCONUT MILK AND LIME – GIVES THIS SIMPLE DISH A FABULOUS FLAVOUR. SERVE WITH PLENTY OF STEAMED THAI FRAGRANT RICE TO SOAK UP THE DELICIOUS SAUCE.

SERVES FOUR

INGREDIENTS
    200g/7oz spinach leaves
    1 lemon grass stalk, finely chopped
    2.5cm/1in piece fresh root ginger,
      peeled and finely grated
    2 garlic cloves, crushed
    200ml/7fl oz/scant 1 cup coconut milk
    30ml/2 tbsp freshly squeezed
      lime juice
    15ml/1 tbsp soft light brown sugar
    4 trout fillets, each about 200g/7oz
    salt and ground black pepper
    steamed Thai fragrant rice, to serve

COOK'S TIP
To steam Thai fragrant rice, cook it in a pan of salted boiling water for three-quarters of the time noted on the packet. Transfer it to a colander lined with muslin or cheesecloth and steam over simmering water for 5–10 minutes until just tender.

1 Preheat the oven to 200°C/400°F/ Gas 6. Place the spinach in a pan, with just the water that adheres to the leaves after washing. Cover with a lid and cook gently for 3–4 minutes until the leaves have just wilted. Drain the spinach in a colander and press it with the back of a spoon to remove any excess moisture.

2 Transfer the spinach to a mixing bowl and stir in the chopped lemon grass, grated ginger and garlic.

3 Combine the coconut milk, lime juice, sugar and seasoning in a jug (pitcher). Place the trout fillets side by side in a shallow baking dish and pour the coconut milk mixture over.

4 Bake the trout for 20–25 minutes until cooked. Place on individual serving plates, on top of the steamed Thai fragrant rice. Toss the spinach mixture in the juices remaining in the dish, spoon on top of the fish and serve.

CHINESE-STYLE STEAMED TROUT

IF YOU THINK STEAMED TROUT SOUNDS DULL, THINK AGAIN. THIS FISH, MARINATED IN A BLACK BEAN, GINGER AND GARLIC MIXTURE BEFORE BEING MOISTENED WITH RICE WINE AND SOY SAUCE, IS SUPERB.

3 Place a little ginger and garlic inside the cavity of each fish, then lay them on a plate or dish that will fit inside a large steamer. Rub the bean mixture into the fish, working it into the slashes, then sprinkle the remaining ginger and garlic over the top. Cover with clear film (plastic wrap) and place the fish in the refrigerator for at least 30 minutes.

4 Remove the fish from the refrigerator and place the steamer over a pan of boiling water. Sprinkle the rice wine or sherry and half the soy sauce over the fish and place the plate of fish inside the steamer. Steam for 15–20 minutes, or until the fish is cooked and the flesh flakes easily when tested with a fork.

SERVES SIX

INGREDIENTS

2 trout, each about 675–800g/
  1½–1¾lb
25ml/1½ tbsp salted black beans
2.5ml/½ tsp granulated sugar
30ml/2 tbsp finely shredded fresh
  root ginger
4 garlic cloves, thinly sliced
30ml/2 tbsp Chinese rice wine or
  dry sherry
30ml/2 tbsp light soy sauce
4–6 spring onions (scallions), finely
  shredded or sliced diagonally
45ml/3 tbsp groundnut (peanut) oil
10ml/2 tsp sesame oil

1 Wash the fish inside and out under cold running water, then pat dry on kitchen paper. Using a sharp knife, slash 3–4 deep crosses on either side of each fish.

2 Place half the black beans and the sugar in a small bowl and mash together with the back of a fork. When the beans are thoroughly mashed, stir in the remaining whole beans.

5 Using a fish slice (metal spatula), carefully lift the fish on to a warmed serving dish. Sprinkle the fish with the remaining soy sauce, then sprinkle with the shredded or sliced spring onions.

6 In a small pan, heat the groundnut oil until very hot and smoking, then trickle it over the spring onions and fish. Lightly sprinkle the sesame oil over the fish and serve immediately.

THAI MARINATED SEA TROUT

*SEA TROUT HAS A SUPERB TEXTURE AND A FLAVOUR LIKE THAT OF WILD SALMON. IT IS BEST
SERVED WITH STRONG BUT COMPLEMENTARY FLAVOURS, SUCH AS CHILLIES AND LIME, THAT CUT
THE RICHNESS OF ITS FLESH.*

SERVES SIX

INGREDIENTS

6 sea trout cutlets, each about
  115g/4oz, or wild or farmed salmon
2 garlic cloves, chopped
1 fresh long red chilli, seeded
  and chopped
45ml/3 tbsp chopped Thai basil
15ml/1 tbsp palm sugar or
  granulated sugar
3 limes
400ml/14fl oz/1⅔ cups
  coconut milk
15ml/1 tbsp Thai fish sauce

1 Place the sea trout cutlets side by
side in a shallow dish. Using a pestle,
pound the garlic and chilli in a large
mortar to break both up roughly. Add
30ml/2 tbsp of the Thai basil with
the sugar and continue to pound to
a rough paste.

2 Grate the rind from 1 lime and
squeeze it. Mix the rind and juice into
the chilli paste, with the coconut milk.
Pour the mixture over the cutlets. Cover
and chill for about 1 hour. Cut the
remaining limes into wedges.

3 Take the fish out of the refrigerator so
that it can return to room temperature.
Remove the cutlets from the marinade
and place them in an oiled hinged wire
fish basket or directly on the lightly
oiled grill. Cook the fish for 4 minutes
on each side, trying not to move them.
They may stick to the grill rack if not
seared first.

4 Strain the remaining marinade into
a pan, reserving the contents of the
sieve. Bring the marinade to the boil,
then simmer gently for 5 minutes,
stirring. Stir in the contents of the sieve
and continue to simmer for 1 minute
more. Add the Thai fish sauce and the
remaining Thai basil.

5 Lift each fish cutlet on to a plate,
pour over the sauce and serve with
the lime wedges.

COOK'S TIP
Sea trout is best cooked when the
barbecue is cool to medium hot, and the
coals have a medium to thick coating
of ash. Always remember to oil the
barbecue rack or hinged grill lightly and
take care when cooking any fish in a
marinade, as the residue can cause
flare-ups if it drips on to the coals.

THAI FISH ᴇɴ PAPILLOTE

*THE AROMATIC SMELL THAT WAFTS OUT OF THESE FISH PARCELS AS YOU OPEN THEM IS DELICIOUSLY
TEMPTING. INSTEAD OF SALMON FILLETS, YOU COULD USE THICK FILLETS OF HAKE, HALIBUT, OR
HOKI, OR FRESH OR UNDYED SMOKED HADDOCK.*

SERVES FOUR

INGREDIENTS
  2 carrots
  2 courgettes (zucchini)
  6 spring onions (scallions)
  2.5cm/1in piece fresh root
    ginger, peeled
  1 lime
  2 garlic cloves, thinly sliced
  30ml/2 tbsp teriyaki marinade or
    nam pla (fish sauce)
  5–10ml/1–2 tsp clear sesame oil
  4 salmon fillets, weighing about
    200g/7oz each
  ground black pepper
  rice, to serve

1 Cut the carrots, courgettes and spring onions into matchsticks and set them aside. Cut the ginger into matchsticks and put these in a small bowl. Using a zester, pare the lime thinly. Add the pared rind to the ginger, with the garlic. Squeeze the lime juice.

2 Place the teriyaki marinade or nam pla into a bowl and stir in the lime juice and sesame oil.

3 Preheat the oven to 220°C/425°F/ Gas 7. Cut out four rounds of baking parchment, each with a diameter of 40cm/16in. Season the salmon with pepper. Lay a fillet on one side of each paper round, about 3cm/1¼in off centre. Sprinkle a quarter of the ginger mixture over each and pile a quarter of the vegetable matchsticks on top. Spoon a quarter of the teriyaki or nam pla mixture over the top.

4 Fold the bare side of the baking parchment over the salmon and roll the edges of the parchment over to seal each parcel very tightly.

5 Place the salmon parcels on a baking sheet and cook in the oven for about 10–12 minutes, depending on the thickness of the fillets. Put the parcels on plates and serve with rice.

SALMON MARINATED ^{WITH} THAI SPICES

THIS RECIPE IS AN ASIAN INTERPRETATION OF GRAVADLAX, A SCANDINAVIAN SPECIALITY. USE VERY FRESH SALMON. THE RAW FISH IS MARINATED FOR SEVERAL DAYS IN A BRINE FLAVOURED WITH THAI SPICES, WHICH EFFECTIVELY "COOKS" IT.

SERVES FOUR TO SIX

INGREDIENTS
  tail piece of 1 salmon, weighing
    about 675g/1½lb, cleaned,
    scaled and filleted
    (see Cook's Tip)
  20ml/4 tsp coarse sea salt
  20ml/4 tsp granulated sugar
  2.5cm/1in piece fresh root ginger,
    peeled and grated
  2 lemon grass stalks, coarse outer
    leaves removed, thinly sliced
  4 kaffir lime leaves, finely chopped
    or shredded
  grated rind of 1 lime
  1 fresh red chilli, seeded and
    finely chopped
  5ml/1 tsp black peppercorns,
    coarsely crushed
  30ml/2 tbsp chopped fresh
    coriander (cilantro)
  fresh coriander (cilantro) sprigs and
    quartered kaffir limes, to garnish
For the dressing
  150ml/¼ pint/⅔ cup mayonnaise
  juice of ½ lime
  10ml/2 tsp chopped fresh
    coriander (cilantro)

1 Remove any remaining bones from the salmon – a pair of tweezers is the best tool for doing this, as they are likely to be both tiny and slippery.

2 Put the coarse sea salt, sugar, ginger, lemon grass, lime leaves, lime rind, chopped chilli, crushed black peppercorns and chopped coriander in a bowl and mix together.

3 Place one-quarter of the spice mixture in a shallow dish. Place one salmon fillet, skin down, on top. Spread two-thirds of the remaining mixture over the flesh, then place the remaining fillet on top, flesh side down. Sprinkle the rest of the spice mixture over the fish.

4 Cover with foil, then place a board on top. Add some weights, such as clean cans of fruit. Chill for 2–5 days, turning the fish daily in the spicy brine.

5 Make the dressing by mixing the mayonnaise, lime juice and chopped coriander in a bowl.

6 Scrape the spices off the fish. Slice it as thinly as possible. Garnish with the coriander and kaffir limes, and serve with the lime dressing.

COOK'S TIP
Ask your fishmonger to scale the fish, split it lengthways and remove it from the backbone in two matching fillets.

NORTHERN FISH CURRY <u>WITH</u> SHALLOTS AND LEMON GRASS

THIS IS A THIN, SOUPY CURRY WITH WONDERFULLY STRONG FLAVOURS. SERVE IT IN BOWLS WITH LOTS OF STICKY RICE TO SOAK UP THE DELICIOUS JUICES.

SERVES FOUR

INGREDIENTS
450g/1lb salmon fillet
500ml/17fl oz/2¼ cups
  vegetable stock
4 shallots, finely chopped
2 garlic cloves, finely chopped
2.5cm/1in piece fresh galangal,
  finely chopped
1 lemon grass stalk, finely chopped
2.5ml/½ tsp dried chilli flakes
15ml/1 tbsp Thai fish sauce
5ml/1 tsp palm sugar or light
  muscovado (brown) sugar

1 Place the salmon in the freezer for 30–40 minutes to firm up the flesh slightly. Remove and discard the skin, then use a sharp knife to cut the fish into 2.5cm/1in cubes, removing any stray bones with your fingers or with tweezers as you do so.

2 Pour the stock into a large, heavy pan and bring it to the boil over a medium heat. Add the shallots, garlic, galangal, lemon grass, chilli flakes, fish sauce and sugar. Bring back to the boil, stir well, then reduce the heat and simmer gently for 15 minutes.

3 Add the fish, bring back to the boil, then turn off the heat. Leave the curry to stand for 10–15 minutes until the fish is cooked through, then serve.

ASIAN SEARED SALMON

SALMON FILLETS ONLY TAKE A FEW MINUTES TO COOK, BUT MAKE SURE YOU ALLOW ENOUGH TIME FOR THE FISH TO SOAK UP ALL THE FLAVOURS OF THE MARINADE BEFORE YOU START COOKING.

SERVES FOUR

INGREDIENTS
 grated rind and juice of 1 lime
 15ml/1 tbsp soy sauce
 2 spring onions (scallions), sliced
 1 fresh red chilli, seeded and
  finely chopped
 2.5cm/1in piece fresh root ginger,
  peeled and grated
 1 lemon grass stalk, finely chopped
 4 salmon fillets, each about
  175g/6oz
 30ml/2 tbsp olive oil
 salt and ground black pepper
 45ml/3 tbsp fresh coriander
  (cilantro), to garnish
For the noodles
 250g/9oz medium egg noodles
 30ml/2 tbsp olive oil
 1 carrot, cut into fine strips
 1 red (bell) pepper, seeded and cut
  into fine strips
 1 yellow (bell) pepper, seeded and
  cut into fine strips
 115g/4oz mangetouts
  (snow peas)
 15ml/1 tbsp sesame oil

1 Put the grated lime rind in a jug (pitcher) and pour in the lime juice. Add the soy sauce, spring onions, chilli, ginger and lemon grass. Season with pepper and stir well. Place the salmon in a shallow non-metallic dish and pour the lime mixture over. Cover and marinate in the refrigerator for at least 30 minutes.

2 Bring a large pan of lightly salted water to the boil and cook the noodles according to the instructions on the packet. Drain well and set aside.

COOK'S TIP
Fresh root ginger is a wonderful ingredient. Thin slices can be added to boiling water to make a refreshing tea, and grated ginger makes a great addition to curries and stir-fries. Ginger freezes successfully and can be shaved or grated from frozen.

3 Brush a griddle pan with 15ml/1 tbsp of the olive oil and heat until hot. Remove the fish from the marinade, pat dry and add to the griddle pan. Cook the salmon fillets for 6 minutes, turning once.

4 When the salmon is almost cooked, add to the remaining marinade in a separate pan and heat through.

5 While the fish is cooking, heat the remaining oil in a wok or large frying pan. Add the carrot and stir-fry for 3 minutes. Add the drained noodles, pepper strips and mangetouts and toss over the heat for 2 minutes more. Drizzle the sesame oil over and season well.

6 Serve the salmon on a bed of noodles and vegetables. Garnish with coriander.

MOOLI LAYERED <u>WITH</u> SMOKED SALMON

THIS TRADITIONAL JAPANESE RECIPE ORIGINALLY CALLED FOR SALTED SLICED SALMON AND MOOLI TO BE PICKLED IN A WOODEN BARREL FOR A LONG TIME. THIS VERSION IS LESS SALTY AND FAR QUICKER.

1 Slice the mooli very thinly into rounds. Put in a shallow container, sprinkle with salt and vinegar, and add the chopped dashi-konbu. Mix and rub gently with your hands. Cover and leave in the refrigerator for 1 hour.

2 Drain in a sieve and squeeze out the excess liquid. If necessary, rinse with running water for 30 seconds, then drain and squeeze out again.

3 Cut the smoked salmon slices into 4cm/1½in squares. Take one slice of mooli, top with a salmon slice, then cover with another mooli slice. Repeat until all the salmon is used. Place in a shallow container, cover with clear film (plastic wrap), then leave to pickle at room temperature for up to 1 day.

4 Arrange the mooli rounds on a serving plate and put a pinch of poppy seeds in the centre.

SERVES FOUR

INGREDIENTS
  10cm/4in mooli (daikon), about
    6cm/2½in in diameter, peeled
  10ml/2 tsp salt
  5ml/1 tsp rice vinegar
  5cm/2in square dashi-konbu
    (dried kelp seaweed), chopped
    into 1cm/½in strips
  50g/2oz smoked salmon, thinly sliced
  2.5ml/½ tsp white poppy seeds

COOK'S TIPS
• Use a good quality smoked salmon for this recipe as the flavour of cheaper varieties is often obscured, if not lost altogether, by the smoking process. The salmon must also be absolutely fresh.
• Nowadays mooli is available from most large supermarkets, but look in Japanese food stores and markets if you have difficulty finding it.
• You can use a mandoline, a food cutter or a vegetable slicer to make paper-thin slices of mooli.
• Taste the mooli after salting and squeezing to check whether it needs to be rinsed. The degree of saltiness will depend on its original water content.

SALMON TERIYAKI

SAKE TERIYAKI IS A WELL-KNOWN JAPANESE DISH, WHICH USES A SWEET AND SHINY SAUCE FOR MARINATING AS WELL AS FOR GLAZING THE INGREDIENTS.

SERVES FOUR

INGREDIENTS
    4 small salmon fillets with skin on,
      each weighing about 150g/5oz
    50g/2oz/1 cup beansprouts, washed
    50g/2oz mangetouts (snow peas)
    20g/¾oz carrot, cut into thin strips
    salt
For the teriyaki sauce
    45ml/3 tbsp shoyu (Japanese
      soy sauce)
    45ml/3 tbsp sake
    45ml/3 tbsp mirin or sweet sherry
    15ml/1 tbsp plus 10ml/2 tsp caster
      (superfine) sugar

1 Make the teriyaki sauce. Mix the shoyu, sake, mirin and 15ml/1 tbsp caster sugar in a pan. Heat, stirring, to dissolve the sugar. Cool for 1 hour.

2 Place the salmon fillets, skin side down, in a shallow glass or china dish. Pour over the teriyaki sauce. Leave to marinate for 30 minutes.

3 Meanwhile, bring a pan of lightly salted water to the boil. Add the beansprouts, then after 1 minute, the mangetouts. Leave for 1 minute then add the thin carrot strips. Remove the pan from the heat after 1 minute, then drain the vegetables and keep warm.

4 Preheat the grill (broiler) to medium. Take the salmon fillet out of the sauce and pat dry with kitchen paper. Reserve the sauce. Lightly oil a grilling (broiling) tray. Grill (broil) the salmon for about 6 minutes, turning once, until golden.

5 Meanwhile, pour the remaining teriyaki sauce into a small pan, add the remaining sugar and heat until dissolved. Brush the salmon with the sauce.

6 Continue to grill the salmon until the surface of the fish bubbles. Turn over and repeat on the other side.

7 Heap the vegetables on to serving plates. Place the salmon on top and spoon over the rest of the sauce.

COOK'S TIP
To save time, you could use ready-made teriyaki sauce for the marinade. This useful ingredient comes in bottles and is handy for marinating chicken before cooking it on the barbecue. Add a splash of sake, if you have some.

SHELLFISH DISHES

*Asian cooks have access to a wonderful assortment of fresh
shellfish, not only from the ocean, but also from freshwater
lakes, rivers and canals. Favoured cooking methods are
steaming, deep-frying and stir-frying, and they are also used
in stews and soups, and made into curries. In Asia, shellfish
are cooked when really fresh, but the Western cook may have to
resort to good-quality frozen shellfish. If you haven't tried
cooking with shellfish before, try some of these exotic recipes.*

SINIGANG

MANY FILIPINOS WOULD CONSIDER THIS SOURED SOUP-LIKE STEW TO BE THEIR NATIONAL DISH. IT IS ALWAYS SERVED WITH NOODLES OR RICE. IN ADDITION, FISH — IN THE FORM OF EITHER PRAWNS OR THIN SLIVERS OF FISH FILLET — IS OFTEN ADDED FOR GOOD MEASURE.

3 Pour the prepared fish stock into a large pan and add the diced mooli. Cook the mooli for 5 minutes, then add the beans and continue to cook for 3–5 minutes more.

SERVES FOUR TO SIX

INGREDIENTS
15ml/1 tbsp tamarind pulp
150ml/¼ pint/⅔ cup warm water
2 tomatoes
115g/4oz spinach or Chinese leaves (Chinese cabbage)
115g/4oz peeled cooked large prawns (shrimp), thawed if frozen
1.2 litres/2 pints/5 cups prepared fish stock (see Cook's Tip)
½ mooli (daikon), peeled and diced
115g/4oz green beans, cut into 1cm/½in lengths
225g/8oz piece of cod or haddock fillet, skinned and cut into strips
fish sauce, to taste
squeeze of lemon juice, to taste
salt and ground black pepper
boiled rice or noodles, to serve

1 Put the tamarind pulp in a bowl and pour over the warm water. Set aside while you peel and chop the tomatoes, discarding the seeds. Strip the spinach or Chinese leaves from the stems and tear into small pieces.

2 Remove the heads and shells from the prawns, leaving the tails intact.

4 Add the fish strips, tomato and spinach. Strain in the tamarind juice and cook for 2 minutes. Stir in the prawns and cook for 1–2 minutes to heat. Season with salt and pepper and add a little fish sauce and lemon juice to taste. Transfer to individual serving bowls and serve immediately, with rice or noodles.

COOK'S TIP
A good fish stock is essential for Sinigang. Ask your fishmonger for about 675g/1½lb fish bones. Wash them, then place in a large pan with 2 litres/3½ pints/8 cups water. Add half a peeled onion, a piece of bruised peeled ginger, and a little salt and pepper. Bring to the boil, skim, then simmer for 20 minutes. Cool slightly, then strain. Freeze unused fish stock.

STIR-FRIED PRAWNS WITH NOODLES

ONE OF THE MOST APPEALING ASPECTS OF THAI FOOD IS ITS APPEARANCE. INGREDIENTS ARE
CAREFULLY CHOSEN SO THAT EACH DISH, EVEN A SIMPLE STIR-FRY LIKE THIS ONE, IS BALANCED IN
TERMS OF COLOUR, TEXTURE AND FLAVOUR.

SERVES FOUR

INGREDIENTS
130g/4½oz rice noodles
30ml/2 tbsp groundnut (peanut) oil
1 large garlic clove, crushed
150g/5oz large prawns (shrimp),
  peeled and deveined
15g/½oz dried shrimp
1 piece mooli (daikon), about
  75g/3oz, grated
15ml/1 tbsp Thai fish sauce
30ml/2 tbsp soy sauce
30ml/2 tbsp palm sugar or light
  muscovado (brown) sugar
30ml/2 tbsp fresh lime juice
90g/3½oz/1¾ cups beansprouts
40g/1½oz/⅓ cup peanuts, chopped
15ml/1 tbsp sesame oil
chopped coriander (cilantro),
  5ml/1 tsp dried chilli flakes and
  2 shallots, finely chopped, to garnish

1 Soak the noodles in a bowl of boiling water for 5 minutes, or according to the packet instructions. Heat the oil in a wok or large frying pan. Add the garlic, and stir-fry over a medium heat for 2–3 minutes, until golden brown.

2 Add the prawns, dried shrimp and grated mooli and stir-fry for a further 2 minutes. Stir in the fish sauce, soy sauce, sugar and lime juice.

3 Drain the noodles thoroughly, then snip them into smaller lengths with scissors. Add to the wok or pan with the beansprouts, peanuts and sesame oil. Toss to mix, then stir-fry for 2 minutes. Serve immediately, garnished with the coriander, chilli flakes and shallots.

COOK'S TIP
Some cooks salt the mooli and leave it to drain, then rinse and dry before use.

STIR-FRIED PRAWNS <u>WITH</u> TAMARIND

THE SOUR, TANGY FLAVOUR THAT IS CHARACTERISTIC OF MANY THAI DISHES COMES FROM TAMARIND. FRESH TAMARIND PODS FROM THE TAMARIND TREE CAN SOMETIMES BE BOUGHT, BUT PREPARING THEM FOR COOKING IS A LABORIOUS PROCESS. IT IS MUCH EASIER TO USE A BLOCK OF TAMARIND PASTE.

SERVES FOUR TO SIX

INGREDIENTS

6 dried red chillies
30ml/2 tbsp vegetable oil
30ml/2 tbsp chopped onion
30ml/2 tbsp palm sugar or light
  muscovado (brown) sugar
30ml/2 tbsp chicken stock or water
15ml/1 tbsp Thai fish sauce
90ml/6 tbsp tamarind juice, made
  by mixing tamarind paste with
  warm water
450g/1lb raw prawns
  (shrimp), peeled
15ml/1 tbsp fried chopped garlic
30ml/2 tbsp fried sliced shallots
2 spring onions (scallions), chopped,
  to garnish

1 Heat a wok or large frying pan, but do not add any oil at this stage. Add the dried chillies and dry-fry them by pressing them against the surface of the wok or pan with a spatula, turning them occasionally. Do not let them burn. Set them aside to cool slightly.

2 Add the oil to the wok or pan and reheat. Add the chopped onion and cook over a medium heat, stirring occasionally, for 2–3 minutes, until softened and golden brown.

3 Add the sugar, stock or water, fish sauce, dry-fried red chillies and the tamarind juice, stirring constantly until the sugar has dissolved. Bring to the boil, then lower the heat slightly.

4 Add the prawns, garlic and shallots. Toss over the heat for 3–4 minutes, until the prawns are cooked. Garnish with the spring onions and serve.

COOK'S TIP
Leave a few prawns (shrimp) in their shells for a garnish, if you like.

SALT AND PEPPER PRAWNS

THESE SUCCULENT SHELLFISH BEG TO BE EATEN WITH THE FINGERS, SO PROVIDE FINGER BOWLS OR HOT CLOTHS FOR YOUR GUESTS.

SERVES THREE TO FOUR

INGREDIENTS
   15–18 large raw prawns (shrimp),
      in the shell, about 450g/1lb
   vegetable oil, for deep frying
   3 shallots or 1 small onion, very
      finely chopped
   2 garlic cloves, crushed
   1cm/½in piece fresh root ginger,
      peeled and very finely grated
   1–2 fresh red chillies, seeded and
      finely sliced
   2.5ml/½ tsp sugar or to taste
   3–4 spring onions (scallions),
      shredded, to garnish

For the fried salt
   10ml/2 tsp salt
   5ml/1 tsp Sichuan peppercorns

1 Make the fried salt by dry frying the salt and peppercorns in a heavy frying pan over medium heat until the peppercorns begin to release their aroma. Cool the mixture, then tip into a mortar and crush with a pestle.

COOK'S TIP
"Fried salt" is also known as "Cantonese salt" or simply "salt and pepper mix". It is widely used as a table condiment or as a dip for deep fried or roasted food, but can also be an ingredient, as here. Black or white peppercorns can be substituted for the Sichuan peppercorns. It really is best made when required.

2 Carefully remove the heads and legs from the raw prawns and discard. Leave the body shells and the tails in place. Pat the prepared prawns dry with sheets of kitchen paper.

3 Heat the oil for deep frying to 190°C/375°F. Fry the prawns for 1 minute, then lift them out and drain thoroughly on kitchen paper. Spoon 30ml/2 tbsp of the hot oil into a large frying pan, leaving the rest of the oil to one side to cool.

4 Heat the oil in the frying pan. Add the fried salt, with the shallots or onion, garlic, ginger, chillies and sugar. Toss together for 1 minute, then add the prawns and toss them over the heat for 1 minute more until they are coated and the shells are impregnated with the seasonings. Serve at once, garnished with the spring onions.

SATAY PRAWNS

THIS DELICIOUS DISH IS INSPIRED BY THE CLASSIC INDONESIAN SATAY. THE COMBINATION OF MILD PEANUTS, AROMATIC SPICES, SWEET COCONUT MILK AND ZESTY LEMON JUICE IN THE SPICY DIP IS PERFECT AND IS GUARANTEED TO HAVE GUESTS COMING BACK FOR MORE.

SERVES FOUR TO SIX

INGREDIENTS
  450g/1lb king prawns (jumbo shrimp)
  25ml/1½ tbsp vegetable oil
For the peanut sauce
  25ml/1½ tbsp vegetable oil
  15ml/1 tbsp chopped garlic
  1 small onion, chopped
  3–4 fresh red chillies, seeded
    and chopped
  3 kaffir lime leaves, torn
  1 lemon grass stalk, bruised
    and chopped
  5ml/1 tsp medium curry paste
  250ml/8fl oz/1 cup coconut milk
  1cm/½in piece cinnamon stick
  75g/3oz/⅓ cup crunchy
    peanut butter
  45ml/3 tbsp tamarind juice, made
    by mixing tamarind paste with
    warm water
  30ml/2 tbsp Thai fish sauce
  30ml/2 tbsp palm sugar or light
    muscovado (brown) sugar
  juice of ½ lemon
For the garnish
  ½ bunch fresh coriander
    (cilantro) leaves (optional)
  4 fresh red chillies, finely sliced
    (optional)
  spring onions (scallions),
    cut diagonally

1 Remove the heads from the prawns and peel, leaving the tail ends intact. Slit each prawn along the back with a small, sharp knife and remove the black vein. Rinse under cold running water, pat completely dry on kitchen paper and set the prawns aside.

2 Make the peanut sauce. Heat half the oil in a wok or large, heavy frying pan. Add the garlic and onion and cook over a medium heat, stirring occasionally, for 3–4 minutes, until the mixture has softened but not browned.

3 Add the chillies, kaffir lime leaves, lemon grass and curry paste. Stir well and cook for a further 2–3 minutes, then stir in the coconut milk, cinnamon stick, peanut butter, tamarind juice, fish sauce, sugar and lemon juice. Cook, stirring constantly, until well blended.

4 Bring to the boil, then reduce the heat to low and simmer gently for 15–20 minutes, until the sauce thickens. Stir occasionally with a wooden spoon to prevent the sauce from sticking to the base of the wok or frying pan.

5 Thread the prawns on to skewers and brush with a little oil. Cook under a preheated grill (broiler) for 2 minutes on each side until they turn pink and are firm to the touch. Alternatively, pan-fry the prawns, then thread on to skewers.

6 Remove the cinnamon stick from the sauce and discard. Arrange the skewered prawns on a warmed platter, garnish with spring onions and coriander leaves and sliced red chillies, if liked, and serve with the sauce.

VARIATIONS
• For a curry-style dish, heat the oil in a wok or large frying pan. Add the prawns (shrimp) and stir-fry for 3–4 minutes, or until pink. Mix the prawns with the sauce and serve with jasmine rice.
• You can use this basic sauce for satay pork or chicken, too. With a sharp knife, cut pork fillet (tenderloin) or skinless, boneless chicken breast portions into long thin strips and stir-fry in hot oil until golden brown all over and cooked through. Then stir into the sauce instead of the king prawns (jumbo shrimp).
• You could use Thai red or green curry paste for this recipe. Make your own or buy a good-quality product from an Asian food store. Once opened, jars of curry paste should be kept in the refrigerator and used within 2 months.
• You can make the satay sauce in advance and leave it to cool. Transfer to a bowl, cover with clear film (plastic wrap) and store in the refrigerator. Reheat gently, stirring occasionally, before stir-frying the prawns (shrimp).

SAMBAL GORENG <u>WITH</u> PRAWNS

SAMBAL GORENG *IS AN IMMENSELY USEFUL AND ADAPTABLE SAUCE. HERE IT IS COMBINED WITH PRAWNS AND GREEN PEPPER, BUT YOU COULD ADD FINE STRIPS OF CALF'S LIVER, CHICKEN LIVERS, TOMATOES, GREEN BEANS OR HARD-BOILED EGGS.*

SERVES FOUR TO SIX

INGREDIENTS

    350g/12oz peeled cooked prawns
      (shrimp)
    1 green (bell) pepper, seeded
      and sliced
    60ml/4 tbsp tamarind juice
    pinch of sugar
    45ml/3 tbsp coconut milk or cream
    boiled rice, to serve
    lime rind and red onion, to garnish
For the sambal goreng
    2.5cm/1in cube shrimp paste
    2 onions, roughly chopped
    2 garlic cloves, roughly chopped
    2.5cm/1in piece fresh galangal,
      peeled and sliced
    10ml/2 tsp chilli sambal
    1.5ml/¼ tsp salt
    30ml/2 tbsp vegetable oil
    45ml/3 tbsp tomato purée (paste)
    600ml/1 pint/2½ cups vegetable
      stock or water

1 Make the sambal goreng. Grind the shrimp paste with the onions and garlic using a mortar and pestle. Alternatively put in a food processor and process to a paste. Add the galangal, chilli sambal and salt. Process or pound to a fine paste.

COOK'S TIP
Store the remaining sauce in the refrigerator for up to 3 days or freeze it for up to 3 months.

2 Heat the oil in a wok or frying pan and fry the paste for 1–2 minutes, without browning, until the mixture gives off a rich aroma. Stir in the tomato purée and the stock or water and cook for 10 minutes. Ladle half the sauce into a bowl and leave to cool. This leftover sauce can be used in another recipe (see Cook's Tip).

3 Add the prawns and green pepper to the remaining sauce. Cook over a medium heat for 3–4 minutes, then stir in the tamarind juice, sugar and coconut milk or cream. Spoon into warmed serving bowls and garnish with strips of lime rind and sliced red onion. Serve at once with boiled rice.

VARIATIONS
To make tomato sambal goreng, add 450g/1lb peeled coarsely chopped tomatoes to the sauce mixture, before stirring in the stock or water.
To make egg sambal goreng, add 3 or 4 chopped hard-boiled eggs, and 2 peeled chopped tomatoes to the sauce.

FRIED PRAWN BALLS

WHEN THE MOON WAXES IN SEPTEMBER, THE JAPANESE CELEBRATE THE ARRIVAL OF AUTUMN BY MAKING AN OFFERING TO THE MOON, AND HAVE A FEAST. THE DISHES OFFERED, SUCH AS TINY RICE DUMPLINGS, SWEET CHESTNUTS AND THESE SHINJYO, SHOULD ALL BE ROUND IN SHAPE.

MAKES ABOUT FOURTEEN

INGREDIENTS
    150g/5oz raw prawns (shrimp),
      peeled
    75ml/5 tbsp second dashi stock
      or the same amount of water and
      2.5ml/½ tsp dashi-no-moto
    1 large (US extra large) egg white,
      well beaten
    30ml/2 tbsp sake
    15ml/1 tbsp cornflour (cornstarch)
    1.5ml/¼ tsp salt
    vegetable oil, for deep-frying
To serve
    25ml/1½ tbsp ground sea salt
    2.5ml/½ tsp sansho
    ½ lemon, cut into 4 wedges

1 Mix the prawns, dashi stock, beaten egg white, sake, cornflour and salt in a food processor or blender, and process until smooth. Scrape from the sides and transfer to a small mixing bowl.

2 In a wok or small pan, heat the vegetable oil to 175°C/347°F.

3 Take two dessertspoons and wet them with a little vegetable oil. Scoop about 30ml/2 tbsp prawn-ball paste into the spoons and form a small ball. Carefully plunge the ball into the hot oil and deep-fry until lightly browned. Drain on a wire rack. Repeat this process, one at a time, until all the prawn-ball paste is used.

4 Mix the salt and sansho on a small plate. Serve the fried prawn balls on a large serving platter or on four serving plates. Garnish with lemon wedges and serve hot with the sansho salt.

COOK'S TIP
Serve the salt and sansho in separate mounds on each plate, if you like.

GREEN PRAWN CURRY

GREEN CURRY HAS BECOME A FIRM FAVOURITE IN THE WEST, AND THIS PRAWN DISH IS JUST ONE OF A RANGE OF DELICIOUS GREEN CURRY RECIPES. HOME-MADE GREEN CURRY PASTE HAS THE BEST FLAVOUR, BUT YOU CAN ALSO BUY IT READY-MADE FROM GOOD SUPERMARKETS.

2 Add the prawns, kaffir lime leaves and chopped lemon grass. Fry for 2 minutes, until the prawns are pink.

3 Stir in the coconut milk and bring to a gentle boil. Simmer, stirring for about 5 minutes or until the prawns are tender.

4 Stir in the fish sauce, cucumber batons and whole basil leaves, then top with the green chillies and serve from the pan.

SERVES FOUR TO SIX

INGREDIENTS

30ml/2 tbsp vegetable oil
30ml/2 tbsp green curry paste
450g/1lb raw king prawns (jumbo shrimp), peeled and deveined
4 kaffir lime leaves, torn
1 lemon grass stalk, bruised and chopped
250ml/8fl oz/1 cup coconut milk
30ml/2 tbsp fish sauce
½ cucumber, seeded and cut into thin batons
10–15 basil leaves
4 fresh green chillies, sliced, to garnish

1 Heat the oil in a wok or large pan. Add the green curry paste and fry gently until bubbling and fragrant.

VARIATION
Strips of skinless chicken breast fillet can be used in place of the prawns if you prefer. Add them to the pan in step 2 and fry until browned on all sides.

PRAWNS <u>WITH</u> YELLOW CURRY PASTE

*FISH AND SHELLFISH, SUCH AS PRAWNS, AND COCONUT MILK, WERE MADE FOR EACH OTHER. THIS IS
A VERY QUICK RECIPE IF YOU MAKE THE YELLOW CURRY PASTE IN ADVANCE, OR BUY IT READY-MADE.
IT KEEPS WELL IN A SCREW-TOP JAR IN THE REFRIGERATOR FOR UP TO FOUR WEEKS.*

SERVES FOUR TO SIX

INGREDIENTS
600ml/1 pint/2½ cups coconut milk
30ml/2 tbsp yellow curry paste
15ml/1 tbsp fish sauce
2.5ml/½ tsp salt
5ml/1 tsp granulated sugar
450g/1lb raw king prawns (jumbo
　shrimp), thawed if frozen, peeled
　and deveined
225g/8oz cherry tomatoes
juice of ½ lime
red (bell) peppers, seeded and
　cut into thin strips, and fresh
　coriander (cilantro) leaves,
　to garnish

1 Put half the coconut milk in a wok
or large pan and bring to the boil. Add
the yellow curry paste and stir until it
disperses. Lower the heat and simmer
gently for about 10 minutes.

2 Add the fish sauce, salt, sugar and
remaining coconut milk to the sauce.
Simmer for 5 minutes more.

3 Add the prawns and cherry tomatoes.
Simmer very gently for about 5 minutes
until the prawns are pink and tender.

4 Spoon into a serving dish, sprinkle
with lime juice and garnish with strips
of pepper and coriander.

COOK'S TIPS
• Unused coconut milk can be stored in
the refrigerator for 1–2 days, or poured
into a freezer container and frozen.
• If making your own coconut milk,
instead of discarding the spent coconut,
it can be reused to make a second batch
of coconut milk. This will be of a poorer
quality and should only be used to
extend a good quality first quantity
of milk.
• Leave newly made coconut milk to
stand for 10 minutes. The coconut
cream will float to the top – skim off
with a spoon.

CURRIED SEAFOOD WITH COCONUT MILK

THIS CURRY IS BASED ON A THAI CLASSIC. THE LOVELY GREEN COLOUR IS IMPARTED BY THE FINELY CHOPPED CHILLI AND FRESH HERBS ADDED DURING THE LAST FEW MOMENTS OF COOKING.

SERVES FOUR

INGREDIENTS

  225g/8oz small ready-prepared squid
  225g/8oz raw tiger prawns
    (jumbo shrimp)
  400ml/14fl oz/1⅔ cups coconut milk
  2 kaffir lime leaves, finely shredded
  30ml/2 tbsp Thai fish sauce
  450g/1lb firm white fish fillets,
    skinned, boned and cut into chunks
  2 fresh green chillies, seeded and
    finely chopped
  30ml/2 tbsp torn fresh basil or
    coriander (cilantro) leaves
  squeeze of fresh lime juice
  cooked Thai jasmine rice,
    to serve
For the curry paste
  6 spring onions (scallions),
    coarsely chopped
  4 fresh coriander (cilantro) stems,
    coarsely chopped, plus 45ml/3 tbsp
    chopped fresh coriander (cilantro)
  4 kaffir lime leaves, shredded
  8 fresh green chillies, seeded and
    coarsely chopped
  1 lemon grass stalk,
    coarsely chopped
  2.5cm/1in piece fresh root ginger,
    peeled and coarsely chopped
  45ml/3 tbsp chopped fresh basil
  15ml/1 tbsp vegetable oil

1 Make the curry paste. Put all the ingredients, except the oil, in a food processor and process to a paste. Alternatively, pound together in a mortar with a pestle. Stir in the oil.

2 Rinse the squid and pat dry with kitchen paper. Cut the bodies into rings and halve the tentacles, if necessary.

3 Heat a wok until hot, add the prawns and stir-fry, without any oil, for about 4 minutes, until they turn pink.

4 Remove the prawns from the wok and leave to cool slightly, then peel off the shells, saving a few with shells on for the garnish. Make a slit along the back of each one and remove the black vein.

5 Pour the coconut milk into the wok, then bring to the boil over a medium heat, stirring constantly. Add 30ml/ 2 tbsp of curry paste, the shredded lime leaves and fish sauce and stir well to mix. Reduce the heat to low and simmer gently for about 10 minutes.

6 Add the squid, prawns and chunks of fish and cook for about 2 minutes, until the seafood is tender. Take care not to overcook the squid as it will become tough very quickly.

7 Just before serving, stir in the chillies and basil or coriander. Taste and adjust the flavour with a squeeze of lime juice. Garnish with prawns in their shells, and serve with Thai jasmine rice.

VARIATIONS
• You can use any firm-fleshed white fish for this curry, such as monkfish, cod, haddock or John Dory.
• If you prefer, you could substitute shelled scallops for the squid. Slice them in half horizontally and add them with the prawns (shrimp). As with the squid, be careful not to overcook them.

CHINESE-STYLE SCALLOPS AND PRAWNS

SERVE THIS LIGHT, DELICATE DISH FOR LUNCH OR SUPPER ACCOMPANIED BY AROMATIC STEAMED RICE OR FINE RICE NOODLES AND STIR-FRIED PAK CHOI.

SERVES FOUR

INGREDIENTS

15ml/1 tbsp stir-fry or
  sunflower oil
500g/1¼lb raw tiger prawns
  (shrimp), peeled
1 star anise
225g/8oz scallops, halved if large
2.5cm/1in piece fresh root ginger,
  peeled and grated
2 garlic cloves, thinly sliced
1 red (bell) pepper, seeded and cut
  into thin strips
115g/4oz/1¾ cups shiitake or button
  (white) mushrooms, thinly sliced
juice of 1 lemon
5ml/1 tsp cornflour (cornstarch)
30ml/2 tbsp light soy sauce
chopped fresh chives,
  to garnish
salt and ground black pepper

1 Heat the oil in a wok until very hot. Put in the prawns and star anise and stir-fry over a high heat for 2 minutes. Add the scallops, ginger and garlic and stir-fry for 1 minute more, by which time the prawns should have turned pink and the scallops should be opaque. Season with a little salt and plenty of pepper and then remove from the wok using a slotted spoon. Discard the star anise.

2 Add the red pepper and mushrooms to the wok and stir-fry for 1–2 minutes.

3 Make a cornflour paste by combining the cornflour with 30ml/2 tbsp cold water. Stir until smooth.

4 Pour the lemon juice, cornflour paste and soy sauce into the wok, bring to the boil and bubble for 1–2 minutes, stirring all the time, until the sauce is smooth and slightly thickened.

VARIATIONS
Other types of shellfish can be used in this dish. Try it with thinly sliced rings of squid, or use mussels or clams. You could even substitute bitesize chunks of firm white fish, such as monkfish, cod or haddock, for the scallops. These can be added to the dish in step 1, as with the scallops.

SOTONG SAMBAL

SQUID IS READILY AVAILABLE THESE DAYS, AND IT NOW COMES CLEANED, WHICH IS A DEFINITE BONUS.
WASH THOROUGHLY INSIDE THE POCKET TO MAKE SURE THAT ALL THE QUILL HAS BEEN REMOVED.

SERVES TWO

INGREDIENTS
  8 small squid, each about 10cm/
     4in long, total weight about
     350g/12oz
  lime juice (optional)
  salt
  boiled rice, to serve
For the stuffing
  175g/6oz white fish fillets, such as
     sole or plaice, skinned
  2.5cm/1in piece fresh root ginger,
     peeled and finely sliced
  2 spring onions (scallions),
     chopped
  50g/2oz peeled cooked prawns
     (shrimp), roughly chopped
For the sambal sauce
  4 macadamia nuts or
     blanched almonds
  1cm/½in piece fresh galangal,
     peeled, or 5ml/1 tsp drained
     bottled galangal
  2 lemon grass stalks, root
     trimmed
  1cm/½in cube shrimp paste
  4 fresh red chillies, or to taste,
     seeded and roughly chopped
  175g/6oz small onions, roughly
     chopped
  60–90ml/4–6 tbsp vegetable oil
  400ml/14fl oz can coconut milk

1 Clean the squid, leaving them whole.
Set aside with the tentacles. Put the
white fish, ginger and spring onions
in a mortar. Add a little salt and pound
to a paste with a pestle. Use a food
processor, if preferred.

2 Transfer the fish mixture to a bowl
and stir in the prawns.

3 Divide the filling among the squid,
using a spoon or a forcing bag fitted
with a plain tube. Tuck the tentacles
into the stuffing and secure the top of
each squid with a cocktail stick.

4 Make the sauce. Put the macadamia
nuts or almonds and galangal in a food
processor. Cut off the lower 5cm/2in
from the lemon grass stalks, chop them
roughly and add them to the processor
with the shrimp paste, chillies and
onions. Process to a paste.

5 Heat the oil in a wok and fry the
mixture to bring out the full flavours.
Bruise the remaining lemon grass and
add it to the wok with the coconut milk.
Stir constantly until the sauce comes to
the boil, then lower the heat and
simmer the sauce for 5 minutes.

6 Arrange the squid in the sauce,
and cook for 15–20 minutes. Taste and
season with salt and lime juice, if you
like. Serve with boiled rice.

STIR-FRIED SQUID WITH GINGER

THE ABUNDANCE OF FISH AROUND THE GULF OF THAILAND SUSTAINS THRIVING MARKETS FOR THE RESTAURANT AND HOTEL TRADE, AND EVERY MARKET NATURALLY FEATURES STALLS WHERE DELICIOUS, FRESHLY-CAUGHT SEAFOOD IS COOKED AND SERVED. THIS RECIPE IS POPULAR AMONG STREET TRADERS.

SERVES TWO

INGREDIENTS

   4 ready-prepared baby squid,
     total weight about 250g/9oz
   15ml/1 tbsp vegetable oil
   2 garlic cloves, finely chopped
   30ml/2 tbsp soy sauce
   2.5cm/1in piece fresh root ginger,
     peeled and finely chopped
   juice of ½ lemon
   5ml/1 tsp granulated sugar
   2 spring onions (scallions), chopped

VARIATIONS

This dish is often prepared with fresh galangal rather than ginger and works well with most kinds of seafood, including prawns (shrimp) and scallops.

1 Rinse the squid well and pat dry with kitchen paper. Cut the bodies into rings and halve the tentacles, if necessary.

2 Heat the oil in a wok or frying pan and cook the garlic until golden brown, but do not let it burn. Add the squid and stir-fry for 30 seconds over a high heat.

3 Add the soy sauce, ginger, lemon juice, sugar and spring onions. Stir-fry a further 30 seconds, then serve.

COOK'S TIP

Squid has an undeserved reputation for being rubbery in texture. This is always a result of overcooking it.

SQUID <u>IN</u> CLOVE SAUCE

THE ISLAND OF MADURA, BETWEEN BALI AND JAVA, MAKES USE OF VARIOUS SPICES THAT WERE ORIGINALLY INTRODUCED TO INDONESIA BY INDIAN AND ARAB TRADERS. THIS RECIPE WITH CLOVES AND NUTMEG, ALONG WITH TOMATO AND SOY SAUCE, IS KNOWN AS CUMI CUMI SMOOR.

SERVES THREE TO FOUR

INGREDIENTS

675g/1½lb ready-cleaned squid
45ml/3 tbsp groundnut (peanut) oil
1 onion, finely chopped
2 garlic cloves, crushed
1 beefsteak tomato, skinned
  and chopped
15ml/1 tbsp dark soy sauce
2.5ml/½ tsp grated nutmeg
6 whole cloves
150ml/¼ pint/⅔ cup water
juice of ½ lemon or lime
salt and ground black pepper,
  to taste
shredded spring onions (scallions)
  and fresh coriander (cilantro) sprigs,
  to garnish
plain boiled rice, to serve

3 Heat the oil in a clean pan and fry the onion and garlic, until soft and beginning to brown. Add the tomato, soy sauce, nutmeg, cloves, water and lemon or lime juice. Bring to the boil and then reduce the heat and add the squid, with seasoning to taste.

4 Cook the squid in the sauce for 3–5 minutes, uncovered, over a gentle heat, stirring from time to time. Take care not to overcook the squid. Serve hot or warm, with plain rice, or as part of a buffet spread. Garnish with shredded spring onions and fresh coriander.

1 Wash the squid and pat dry on kitchen paper. Use a sharp kitchen knife to cut the squid into long, thin ribbons. Carefully remove the "bone" from each tentacle, and discard.

2 Heat a wok, toss in the squid and stir constantly for 2–3 minutes, when the squid will have curled into attractive shapes or into firm rings. Lift out and set aside in a warm place.

VARIATION
Instead of squid try using 450g/1lb cooked and peeled tiger prawns (shrimp) in this recipe. Add them to the pan for the final 1–2 minutes.

DEEP-FRIED SMALL PRAWNS <u>AND</u> CORN

THIS DISH IS CALLED KAKIAGÉ, *AN INEXPENSIVE AND INFORMAL STYLE OF TEMPURA. THIS IS ONLY ONE OF MANY VERSIONS AND IT IS A GOOD WAY OF USING UP SMALL QUANTITIES OF VEGETABLES.*

SERVES FOUR

INGREDIENTS
200g/7oz small cooked, peeled
   prawns (shrimp)
4–5 button (white) mushrooms
4 spring onions (scallions)
75g/3oz/½ cup canned, drained or
   frozen sweetcorn, thawed
30ml/2 tbsp frozen peas, thawed
vegetable oil, for deep-frying
chives, to garnish
For the tempura batter
300ml/½ pint/1¼ cups ice-cold water
2 eggs, beaten
150g/5oz/1¼ cups plain
   (all-purpose) flour
1.5ml/¼ tsp baking powder
For the dipping sauce
400ml/14fl oz/1⅔ cups second dashi
   stock, or the same amount of water
   and 5ml/1 tsp dashi-no-moto
100ml/3fl oz/scant ½ cup shoyu
100ml/3fl oz/scant ½ cup mirin
15ml/1 tbsp chopped chives

1 Roughly chop half the prawns. Cut the mushrooms into small cubes. Slice the white part from the spring onions and chop this roughly.

2 To make the tempura batter, in a medium mixing bowl, mix the cold water and eggs. Add the flour and baking powder, and very roughly fold in with a pair of chopsticks or a fork. Do not beat. The batter should still be quite lumpy. Heat plenty of oil in a wok or a deep-fryer to 170°C/338°F.

3 Mix the prawns and vegetables into the batter. Pour a quarter of the batter into a small bowl, then drop gently into the oil. Using wooden spoons, carefully gather the scattered batter to form a fist-size ball. Deep-fry until golden. Drain on kitchen paper.

4 In a small pan, mix all the liquid dipping-sauce ingredients together and bring to the boil, then immediately turn off the heat. Sprinkle with chives.

5 Garnish the *kakiage* with chives, and serve with the dipping sauce.

CHILLI CRABS

EAT THESE CRABS SINGAPOREAN STYLE, WITH THE FINGERS. GIVE GUESTS CRAB CRACKERS FOR THE CLAWS AND HAVE SOME FINGER BOWLS OR NAPKINS.

SERVES FOUR

INGREDIENTS

2 cooked crabs, each about
  675g/1½lb
90ml/6 tbsp sunflower oil
2.5cm/1in piece fresh root ginger,
  peeled and chopped
2–3 garlic cloves, crushed
1–2 red chillies, seeded and pounded
  to a paste
175ml/6fl oz/¾ cup tomato ketchup
30ml/2 tbsp soft brown sugar
15ml/1 tbsp light soy sauce
salt
120ml/4fl oz/½ cup boiling water
hot toast and cucumber chunks,
  to serve

COOK'S TIP
Ready-cooked whole crabs are available
from supermarkets and fish stores.

1 To prepare the crabs twist off the large claws, then turn the crab on its back with its mouth and eyes facing away from you. Using both of your thumbs, push the body, with the small legs attached, upwards from beneath the flap, separating the body from the main shell in the process. Discard the stomach sac and grey spongy lungs known as "dead men's fingers".

2 Using a teaspoon, scrape the brown creamy meat from the large shell into a small bowl. Twist the legs from the body. Cut the body section in half. Pick out the white meat. If you prefer, pick out the meat from the legs, or leave for guests to remove at the table.

3 Heat the oil in a wok and gently fry the ginger, garlic and fresh chilli paste for 1–2 minutes without browning. Stir in the ketchup, sugar and soy sauce, with salt to taste and heat gently.

4 Stir in the crab meat together with the claws and crab legs, if these were reserved. Pour in the boiling water, stir well and cook over a high heat until heated through. Pile the crab and crab claws mixture on serving plates with the chunks of cucumber and serve with pieces of toast.

CRAB <u>AND</u> TOFU STIR-FRY

FOR A YEAR-ROUND LIGHT MEAL, THIS SPEEDY STIR-FRY IS THE IDEAL CHOICE. AS YOU NEED ONLY A LITTLE CRAB MEAT — AND YOU COULD USE THE CANNED VARIETY — THIS IS A VERY ECONOMICAL DISH.

<u>SERVES TWO</u>

INGREDIENTS

250g/9oz silken tofu
60ml/4 tbsp vegetable oil
2 garlic cloves, finely chopped
115g/4oz white crab meat
130g/4½oz/generous 1 cup baby
   corn, halved lengthways
2 spring onions (scallions), chopped
1 fresh red chilli, seeded and
   finely chopped
30ml/2 tbsp soy sauce
15ml/1 tbsp Thai fish sauce
5ml/1 tsp palm sugar or light
   muscovado (brown) sugar
juice of 1 lime
small bunch fresh coriander
   (cilantro), chopped, to garnish

1 Using a sharp knife, cut the silken tofu into 1cm/½in cubes.

2 Heat the oil in a wok or large, heavy frying pan. Add the tofu cubes and stir-fry until golden all over, taking care not to break them up. Remove the tofu with a slotted spoon and set aside.

3 Add the garlic to the wok or pan and stir-fry until golden. Add the crab meat, tofu, corn, spring onions, chilli, soy sauce, fish sauce and sugar. Cook, stirring constantly, until the vegetables are just tender. Stir in the lime juice, transfer to warmed bowls, sprinkle with the coriander and serve immediately.

CRISP-FRIED CRAB CLAWS

CRAB CLAWS ARE READILY AVAILABLE IN THE FREEZER CABINET IN MANY ASIAN STORES AND
SUPERMARKETS. THAW OUT THOROUGHLY AND DRY ON KITCHEN PAPER BEFORE DIPPING IN THE BATTER.

SERVES FOUR

INGREDIENTS
    50g/2oz/$^1/_3$ cup rice flour
    15ml/1 tbsp cornflour (cornstarch)
    2.5ml/$^1/_2$ tsp sugar
    1 egg
    60ml/4 tbsp cold water
    1 lemon grass stalk, root trimmed
    2 garlic cloves, finely chopped
    15ml/1 tbsp chopped fresh
      coriander (cilantro)
    1–2 fresh red chillies, seeded
      and finely chopped
    5ml/1 tsp nam pla (fish sauce)
    vegetable oil, for frying
    12 half-shelled crab claws
    ground black pepper
For the chilli vinegar dip
    45ml/3 tbsp sugar
    120ml/4fl oz/$^1/_2$ cup water
    120ml/4fl oz/$^1/_2$ cup red wine
      vinegar
    15ml/1 tbsp nam pla (fish sauce)
    2–4 fresh red chillies, seeded
      and chopped

1 Make the chilli dip. Mix the sugar
and water in a pan, stirring until the
sugar has dissolved. Bring to the boil,
lower the heat and simmer for 5–7
minutes. Add the remaining ingredients.

2 Combine the rice flour, cornflour and
sugar in a bowl. Beat the egg with the
cold water, then stir the egg and water
mixture into the flour mixture and mix
well until it forms a light batter.

3 Cut off the lower 5cm/2in of the
lemon grass stalk and chop it finely. Add
the lemon grass to the batter, with the
garlic, coriander, red chillies and nam
pla. Stir in pepper to taste.

4 Heat the oil in a wok or deep-fryer.
Pat the crab claws dry and dip into the
batter. Drop the battered claws into
the hot oil, a few at a time. Fry until
golden brown. Drain on kitchen paper
and keep hot. Pour the dip into a serving
bowl and serve with the crab claws.

CRAB MEAT ᴵᴺ VINEGAR

A REFRESHING SUMMER TSUMAMI (A DISH THAT ACCOMPANIES ALCOHOLIC DRINKS). FOR THE DRESSING, USE A JAPANESE OR GREEK CUCUMBER, IF POSSIBLE — THEY ARE ABOUT ONE-THIRD OF THE SIZE OF ORDINARY SALAD CUCUMBERS AND CONTAIN LESS WATER.

SERVES FOUR

INGREDIENTS

½ red (bell) pepper, seeded
pinch of salt
275g/10oz cooked white crab meat,
  or 2 × 165g/5½oz canned white
  crab meat, drained
about 300g/11oz Japanese or
  salad cucumber
For the vinegar mixture
  15ml/1 tbsp rice vinegar
  10ml/2 tsp caster (superfine) sugar
  10ml/2 tsp awakuchi shoyu

1 Slice the red pepper into thin strips lengthways. Sprinkle with a little salt and leave for about 15 minutes. Rinse well and drain.

2 For the vinegar mixture, combine the rice vinegar, sugar and awakuchi shoyu in a small bowl.

3 Loosen the crab meat with cooking chopsticks and mix it with the sliced red pepper in a mixing bowl. Divide among four small bowls.

4 If you use salad cucumber, scoop out the seeds. Finely grate the cucumber with a fine-toothed grater or use a food processor. Drain in a fine-meshed sieve.

5 Mix the cucumber with the vinegar mixture, and pour a quarter on to the crab meat mixture in each bowl. Serve cold immediately, before the cucumber loses its colour.

VARIATIONS
• The vinegar mixture is best made using awakuchi shoyu, but ordinary shoyu can be used instead. It will make a darker dressing, however.
• This dressing can be made into a low-fat substitute for vinaigrette: reduce the sugar by half and add a few drops of oil.

CLAMS <u>AND</u> SPRING ONIONS <u>WITH</u> MISO <u>AND</u> MUSTARD SAUCE

THE JAPANESE ARE REALLY FOND OF SHELLFISH, AND CLAMS ARE AMONG THE MOST POPULAR. IN SEASON, THEY BECOME SWEET AND JUICY, AND ARE EXCELLENT WITH THIS SWEET-AND-SOUR DRESSING.

SERVES FOUR

INGREDIENTS
   900g/2lb carpet shell clams or
      cockles, or 300g/11oz can baby
      clams in brine, or 130g/4½oz
      cooked and shelled cockles
   15ml/1 tbsp sake
   8 spring onions (scallions), green and
      white parts separated, then chopped
      in half
   10g/¼oz dried wakame
For the *nuta* dressing
   60ml/4 tbsp shiro miso
   20ml/4 tsp caster (superfine) sugar
   30ml/2 tbsp sake
   15ml/1 tbsp rice vinegar
   about 1.5ml/¼ tsp salt
   7.5ml/1½ tsp English (hot) mustard
   sprinkling of dashi-no-moto (if using
      canned shellfish)

1 If using fresh clams or cockles, wash the shells under running water. Discard any that remain open when tapped.

2 Pour 1cm/½in water into a small pan and add the clams or cockles. Sprinkle with the sake, cover, then bring to the boil. Cook over a vigorous heat for 5 minutes after the water reaches boiling point. Remove from the heat and leave to stand for 2 minutes. Discard any shells which remain closed.

3 Drain the shells and keep the liquid in a small bowl. Wait until the shells have cooled slightly, then remove the meat from most of the shells.

4 Cook the white part of the spring onions in a pan of rapidly boiling water, then add the remaining green parts after 2 minutes. Cook for 4 minutes altogether. Drain well.

5 Mix the shiro miso, sugar, sake, rice vinegar and salt for the *nuta* dressing, in a small pan. Stir in 45ml/3 tbsp of the reserved clam liquid, or the same amount of water and dashi-no-moto, if using canned shellfish.

6 Put the pan on a medium heat and stir constantly. When the sugar has dissolved, add the mustard. Check the seasoning and add a little more salt if desired. Remove from the heat and leave to cool.

7 Soak the wakame in a bowl of water for 10 minutes. Drain and squeeze out excess moisture by hand.

8 Mix together the clams or cockles, onions, wakame and dressing in a bowl. Heap up in a large bowl or divide among four small bowls and serve cold.

PAN-STEAMED MUSSELS <u>WITH</u> THAI HERBS

LIKE SO MANY THAI DISHES, THIS IS VERY EASY TO PREPARE. THE LEMON GRASS AND KAFFIR LIME
LEAVES ADD A REFRESHING TANG TO THE MUSSELS.

SERVES FOUR TO SIX

INGREDIENTS

  1kg/2¼lb fresh mussels
  2 lemon grass stalks, finely chopped
  4 shallots, chopped
  4 kaffir lime leaves, coarsely torn
  2 fresh red chillies, sliced
  15ml/1 tbsp Thai fish sauce
  30ml/2 tbsp fresh lime juice
  thinly sliced spring onions (scallions)
    and coriander (cilantro) leaves,
    to garnish

1 Clean the mussels by pulling off the
beards, scrubbing the shells well and
removing any barnacles. Discard any
mussels that are broken or which do
not close when tapped sharply.

2 Place the mussels in a large, heavy
pan and add the lemon grass, shallots,
kaffir lime leaves, chillies, fish sauce
and lime juice. Mix well. Cover the
pan tightly and steam the mussels
over a high heat, shaking the pan
occasionally, for 5–7 minutes, until
the shells have opened.

3 Using a slotted spoon, transfer the
cooked mussels to a warmed serving
dish or individual bowls. Discard any
mussels that have failed to open.

4 Garnish the mussels with the thinly
sliced spring onions and coriander
leaves. Serve immediately.

MUSSELS AND CLAMS WITH LEMON GRASS AND COCONUT CREAM

LEMON GRASS HAS AN INCOMPARABLE AROMATIC FLAVOUR AND IS WIDELY USED WITH ALL KINDS OF SEAFOOD IN THAILAND AS THE FLAVOURS MARRY SO PERFECTLY.

SERVES SIX

INGREDIENTS
  1.8kg/4lb fresh mussels
  450g/1lb baby clams
  120ml/4fl oz/½ cup dry white wine
  1 bunch spring onions
    (scallions), chopped
  2 lemon grass stalks, chopped
  6 kaffir lime leaves, chopped
  10ml/2 tsp Thai green curry paste
  200ml/7fl oz/scant 1 cup
    coconut cream
  30ml/2 tbsp chopped fresh
    coriander (cilantro)
  salt and ground black pepper
  garlic chives, to garnish

1 Clean the mussels by pulling off the beards, scrubbing the shells well and scraping off any barnacles with the blade of a knife. Scrub the clams. Discard any mussels or clams that are damaged or broken or which do not close immediately when tapped sharply.

2 Put the wine in a large pan with the spring onions, lemon grass and lime leaves. Stir in the curry paste. Simmer until the wine has almost evaporated.

COOK'S TIPS
• In these days of marine pollution, it is unwise to gather fresh shellfish yourself. Those available from fish stores have either been farmed or have undergone a purging process to clean them.
• Depending on where you live, you may have difficulty obtaining clams. If so, use a few extra mussels instead.

3 Add the mussels and clams to the pan and increase the heat to high. Cover tightly and steam the shellfish for 5–6 minutes, until they open.

4 Using a slotted spoon, transfer the mussels and clams to a heated serving bowl, cover and keep hot. Discard any shellfish that remain closed. Strain the cooking liquid into a clean pan through a sieve lined with muslin (cheesecloth) and simmer briefly to reduce to about 250ml/8fl oz/1 cup.

5 Stir the coconut cream and chopped coriander into the sauce and season with salt and pepper to taste. Heat through. Pour the sauce over the mussels and clams, garnish with the garlic chives and serve immediately.

VEGETABLE
MAIN DISHES

To talk of main dishes is somewhat inappropriate, since in Asia all dishes are traditionally served together. However, the term provides a useful way of distinguishing more substantial dishes, composed of a relatively large number of ingredients, from what Westerners might term side dishes. Delicious vegetable curries, unusual stir-fries, stuffed vegetables and a tasty tempura are included here. Most are very quick and easy to make, with the majority of time required for preparation, rather than cooking.

THAI VEGETABLE CURRY WITH LEMON GRASS RICE

FRAGRANT JASMINE RICE, SUBTLY FLAVOURED WITH LEMON GRASS AND CARDAMOM, IS THE PERFECT ACCOMPANIMENT FOR THIS RICHLY SPICED VEGETABLE CURRY.

SERVES FOUR

INGREDIENTS

10ml/2 tsp vegetable oil
400ml/14fl oz/1⅔ cups coconut milk
300ml/½ pint/1¼ cups
   vegetable stock
225g/8oz new potatoes, halved or
   quartered, if large
8 baby corn cobs
5ml/1 tsp golden caster
   (superfine) sugar
185g/6½oz/1¼ cups broccoli florets
1 red (bell) pepper, seeded and
   sliced lengthways
115g/4oz spinach, tough stalks
   removed, leaves shredded
30ml/2 tbsp chopped fresh
   coriander (cilantro)
salt and ground black pepper
For the spice paste
1 fresh red chilli, seeded
   and chopped
3 fresh green chillies, seeded
   and chopped
1 lemon grass stalk, outer leaves
   removed and lower 5cm/2in
   finely chopped
2 shallots, chopped
finely grated rind of 1 lime
2 garlic cloves, chopped
5ml/1 tsp ground coriander
2.5ml/½ tsp ground cumin
1cm/½in piece fresh galangal,
   finely chopped, or 2.5ml/½ tsp
   dried galangal (optional)
30ml/2 tbsp chopped fresh
   coriander (cilantro)
15ml/1 tbsp chopped fresh
   coriander (cilantro) roots and
   stems (optional)
For the rice
225g/8oz/1¼ cups jasmine
   rice, rinsed
6 cardamom pods, bruised
1 lemon grass stalk, outer leaves
   removed, cut into 3 pieces
475ml/16fl oz/2 cups water

1 Make the spice paste. Place all the ingredients in a food processor and process to a coarse paste. Heat the oil in a large, heavy pan. Add the paste and stir-fry over a medium heat for 1–2 minutes, until fragrant.

2 Pour in the coconut milk and stock and bring to the boil. Reduce the heat, add the potatoes and simmer gently for about 15 minutes, until almost tender.

3 Meanwhile, put the rice into a large pan with the cardamoms and lemon grass. Pour in the water. Bring to the boil, reduce the heat, cover, and cook for 10–15 minutes, until the water has been absorbed and the rice is tender.

4 When the rice is cooked and slightly sticky, season to taste with salt, then replace the lid and leave to stand for about 10 minutes.

5 Add the baby corn to the potatoes, season with salt and pepper to taste, then cook for 2 minutes. Stir in the sugar, broccoli and red pepper, and cook for 2 minutes more, or until the vegetables are tender.

6 Stir the shredded spinach and half the fresh coriander into the vegetable mixture. Cook for 2 minutes, then spoon the curry into a warmed serving dish.

7 Remove and discard the cardamom pods and lemon grass from the rice and fluff up the grains with a fork. Garnish the curry with the remaining fresh coriander and serve with the rice.

COOK'S TIP
Cardamom pods may be dark brown, cream, or pale green. The brown pods are usually larger, coarser and do not have such a good flavour as the others. Always remove them before serving.

VEGETABLE FOREST CURRY

THIS IS A THIN, SOUPY CURRY WITH LOTS OF FRESH GREEN VEGETABLES AND ROBUST FLAVOURS.
IN THE FORESTED REGIONS OF THAILAND, WHERE IT ORIGINATED, IT WOULD BE MADE USING EDIBLE
WILD LEAVES AND ROOTS. SERVE IT WITH RICE OR NOODLES FOR A SIMPLE LUNCH OR SUPPER.

SERVES TWO

INGREDIENTS

600ml/1 pint/2½ cups water
5ml/1 tsp Thai red curry paste
5cm/2in piece fresh galangal or fresh
  root ginger
90g/3½oz/scant 1 cup green beans
2 kaffir lime leaves, torn
8 baby corn cobs,
  halved widthways
2 heads Chinese broccoli, chopped
90g/3½oz/generous
  3 cups beansprouts
15ml/1 tbsp drained bottled green
  peppercorns, crushed
10ml/2 tsp granulated sugar
5ml/1 tsp salt

1 Heat the water in a large pan. Add the red curry paste and stir until it has dissolved completely. Bring to the boil.

2 Meanwhile, using a sharp knife, peel and finely chop the fresh galangal or root ginger.

3 Add the galangal or ginger, green beans, lime leaves, baby corn cobs, broccoli and beansprouts to the pan. Stir in the crushed peppercorns, sugar and salt. Bring back to the boil, then reduce the heat to low and simmer for 2 minutes. Serve immediately.

BRAISED AUBERGINE AND COURGETTES

FRESH VEGETABLES AND RED CHILLIES FORM THE BASIS OF A DISH THAT IS SIMPLE, SPICY AND LOOKS QUITE SENSATIONAL. SERVE IT AS AN ACCOMPANIMENT, OR WITH RICE OR NOODLES AS A MAIN VEGETARIAN MEAL.

SERVES FOUR

INGREDIENTS

    1 aubergine (eggplant), about
       350g/12oz
    2 small courgettes (zucchini)
    15ml/1 tbsp vegetable oil
    2 garlic cloves, finely chopped
    2 fresh red chillies, seeded and
      finely chopped
    1 small onion, diced
    15ml/1 tbsp black bean sauce
    15ml/1 tbsp dark soy sauce
    45ml/3 tbsp cold water
    salt
    chilli flowers (optional), to garnish

1 Trim the aubergine and slice it in half lengthways, then across into 1cm/½in thick slices. Layer the slices in a colander, sprinkling each layer with salt. Leave the aubergine to stand for about 20 minutes.

2 Roll cut the courgettes by slicing off one end diagonally, then rolling the courgette through 180 degrees and taking off another diagonal slice, which will form a triangular wedge. Make more wedges of courgette in the same way.

COOK'S TIP
Chilli flowers make a pretty garnish. Using small scissors, slit a fresh red chilli from the tip to within 1cm/½in of the stem end. Repeat this at regular intervals so that you have slender "petals" attached at the stem. Rinse the chilli to remove the seeds, then place it in a bowl of iced water for 4 hours until the "petals" curl.

3 Rinse the aubergine slices well, drain and dry thoroughly on kitchen paper.

4 Heat the oil in a wok or non-stick frying pan. Stir-fry the garlic, chillies and onion with the black bean sauce for a few seconds.

5 Add the aubergine slices and stir-fry for 2 minutes, sprinkling over a little water to prevent them from burning.

6 Stir in the courgettes, soy sauce and measured water. Cook, stirring occasionally, for 5 minutes. Serve hot, garnished with chilli flowers.

BRAISED TOFU <u>WITH</u> MUSHROOMS

THE SHIITAKE, OYSTER, STRAW AND BUTTON MUSHROOMS FLAVOUR THE TOFU BEAUTIFULLY TO MAKE THIS THE PERFECT VEGETARIAN MAIN COURSE.

SERVES FOUR

INGREDIENTS
  350g/12oz tofu
  2.5ml/½ tsp sesame oil
  10ml/2 tsp light soy sauce
  15ml/1 tbsp vegetable oil
  2 garlic cloves, finely chopped
  2.5ml/½ tsp grated fresh root ginger
  115g/4oz/1 cup fresh shiitake
  mushrooms, stalks removed
  175g/6oz/1½ cups fresh
  oyster mushrooms
  115g/4oz/1 cup drained, canned
  straw mushrooms
  115g/4oz/1 cup button (white)
  mushrooms, cut in half
  15ml/1 tbsp dry sherry
  15ml/1 tbsp dark soy sauce
  90ml/6 tbsp vegetable stock
  5ml/1 tsp cornflour (cornstarch)
  15ml/1 tbsp cold water
  salt and ground white pepper
  2 spring onions (scallions), shredded

1 Put the tofu in a dish and sprinkle with the sesame oil, light soy sauce and a large pinch of pepper. Leave to marinate for 10 minutes, then drain and cut into 2.5 x 1cm/1 x ½in pieces.

2 Heat the vegetable oil in a non-stick frying pan or wok. When it is very hot, fry the garlic and ginger for a few seconds. Add all the mushrooms and stir-fry for 2 minutes.

3 Stir in the sherry, soy sauce and stock, with salt, if needed, and pepper. Simmer for 4 minutes.

4 Mix the cornflour to a paste with the water. Stir the mixture into the pan or wok and cook, stirring, until thickened.

5 Carefully add the pieces of tofu, toss gently to coat thoroughly and simmer for 2 minutes.

6 Sprinkle the shredded spring onions over the top of the mixture, transfer to a serving dish and serve immediately.

TOFU AND GREEN BEAN RED CURRY

THIS IS ONE OF THOSE VERSATILE RECIPES THAT SHOULD BE IN EVERY COOK'S REPERTOIRE. THIS VERSION USES GREEN BEANS, BUT OTHER TYPES OF VEGETABLE WORK EQUALLY WELL. THE TOFU TAKES ON THE FLAVOUR OF THE SPICE PASTE AND ALSO BOOSTS THE NUTRITIONAL VALUE.

SERVES FOUR TO SIX

INGREDIENTS
   600ml/1 pint/2½ cups canned
     coconut milk
   15ml/1 tbsp Thai red curry paste
   45ml/3 tbsp Thai fish sauce
   10ml/2 tsp palm sugar or light
     muscovado (brown) sugar
   225g/8oz/3¼ cups button
     (white) mushrooms
   115g/4oz/scant 1 cup green
     beans, trimmed
   175g/6oz firm tofu, rinsed, drained
     and cut in 2cm/¾in cubes
   4 kaffir lime leaves, torn
   2 fresh red chillies, seeded
     and sliced
   fresh coriander (cilantro) leaves,
     to garnish

1 Pour about one-third of the coconut milk into a wok or pan. Cook until it starts to separate and an oily sheen appears on the surface.

2 Add the red curry paste, fish sauce and sugar to the coconut milk. Mix thoroughly, then add the mushrooms. Stir and cook for 1 minute.

3 Stir in the remaining coconut milk. Bring back to the boil, then add the green beans and tofu cubes. Simmer gently for 4–5 minutes more.

4 Stir in the kaffir lime leaves and sliced red chillies. Spoon the curry into a serving dish, garnish with the coriander leaves and serve immediately.

AUBERGINE AND SWEET POTATO STEW WITH COCONUT MILK

SCENTED WITH FRAGRANT LEMON GRASS, GINGER AND LOTS OF GARLIC, THIS IS A PARTICULARLY GOOD COMBINATION OF FLAVOURS. AUBERGINES AND SWEET POTATOES GO WELL TOGETHER AND THE COCONUT MILK ADDS A MELLOW NOTE.

SERVES SIX

INGREDIENTS

400g/14oz baby aubergines
    (eggplant) or 2 standard aubergines
60ml/4 tbsp groundnut (peanut) oil
225g/8oz Thai red shallots or other
    small shallots or pickling onions
5ml/1 tsp fennel seeds,
    lightly crushed
4–5 garlic cloves, thinly sliced
25ml/1½ tbsp finely chopped fresh
    root ginger
475ml/16fl oz/2 cups vegetable stock
2 lemon grass stalks, outer layers
    discarded, finely chopped or minced
15g/½oz/⅔ cup fresh coriander
    (cilantro), stalks and leaves
    chopped separately
3 kaffir lime leaves, lightly bruised
2–3 small fresh red chillies
45–60ml/3–4 tbsp Thai green
    curry paste
675g/1½lb sweet potatoes, peeled
    and cut into thick chunks
400ml/14fl oz/1⅔ cups coconut milk
2.5–5ml/½–1 tsp palm sugar or light
    muscovado (brown) sugar
250g/9oz/3½ cups mushrooms,
    thickly sliced
juice of 1 lime, to taste
salt and ground black pepper
boiled rice and 18 fresh Thai basil
    or ordinary basil leaves, to serve

2 Heat half the oil in a wide pan or deep, lidded frying pan. Add the aubergines and cook (uncovered) over a medium heat, stirring occasionally, until lightly browned on all sides. Remove from the pan and set aside.

3 Slice 4–5 of the shallots. Cook the whole shallots in the oil remaining in the pan, adding a little more oil if necessary, until lightly browned. Set aside with the aubergines. Add the remaining oil to the pan and cook the sliced shallots, fennel seeds, garlic and ginger over a low heat for 5 minutes.

4 Pour in the vegetable stock, then add the lemon grass, chopped coriander stalks and any roots, lime leaves and whole chillies. Cover and simmer over a low heat for 5 minutes.

5 Stir in 30ml/2 tbsp of the curry paste and the sweet potatoes. Simmer gently for about 10 minutes, then return the aubergines and browned shallots to the pan and cook for a further 5 minutes.

6 Stir in the coconut milk and the sugar. Season to taste with salt and pepper, then stir in the mushrooms and simmer gently for 5 minutes, or until all the vegetables are cooked and tender.

7 Stir in more curry paste and lime juice to taste, followed by the chopped coriander leaves. Adjust the seasoning, if necessary, and ladle the vegetables into warmed bowls. Sprinkle basil leaves over the stew and serve with rice.

COOK'S TIP
Although this is called a stew, green curry paste is an important ingredient, as it is in most of these recipes. The quantity given is only a guide, however, so use less if you prefer.

1 Trim the aubergines. Slice baby aubergines in half lengthways. Cut standard aubergines into chunks.

SWEET PUMPKIN AND PEANUT CURRY

A HEARTY, SOOTHING CURRY PERFECT FOR AUTUMN OR WINTER EVENINGS. ITS CHEERFUL COLOUR ALONE WILL BRIGHTEN YOU UP — AND IT TASTES TERRIFIC.

SERVES FOUR

INGREDIENTS
  30ml/2 tbsp vegetable oil
  4 garlic cloves, crushed
  4 shallots, finely chopped
  30ml/2 tbsp yellow curry paste
  600ml/1 pint/2½ cups
    vegetable stock
  2 kaffir lime leaves, torn
  15ml/1 tbsp chopped fresh galangal
  450g/1lb pumpkin, peeled, seeded
    and diced
  225g/8oz sweet potatoes, diced
  90g/3½oz/scant 1 cup peanuts,
    roasted and chopped
  300ml/½ pint/1¼ cups coconut milk
  90g/3½oz/1½ cups chestnut
    mushrooms, sliced
  15ml/1 tbsp soy sauce
  30ml/2 tbsp Thai fish sauce
  50g/2oz/⅓ cup pumpkin
    seeds, toasted, and fresh green
    chilli flowers, to garnish

1 Heat the oil in a large pan. Add the garlic and shallots and cook over a medium heat, stirring occasionally, for 10 minutes, until softened and golden. Do not let them burn.

2 Add the yellow curry paste and stir-fry over a medium heat for 30 seconds, until fragrant, then add the stock, lime leaves, galangal, pumpkin and sweet potatoes. Bring to the boil, stirring frequently, then reduce the heat to low and simmer gently for 15 minutes.

3 Add the peanuts, coconut milk and mushrooms. Stir in the soy sauce and fish sauce and simmer for 5 minutes more. Spoon into warmed individual serving bowls, garnish with the pumpkin seeds and chillies and serve.

COOK'S TIP
The well-drained vegetables from any of these curries would make a very tasty filling for a pastry or pie. This may not be a Thai tradition, but it is a good example of fusion food.

CORN AND CASHEW NUT CURRY

A SUBSTANTIAL CURRY, THIS COMBINES ALL THE ESSENTIAL FLAVOURS OF SOUTHERN THAILAND. IT IS
DELICIOUSLY AROMATIC, BUT THE FLAVOUR IS FAIRLY MILD.

SERVES FOUR

INGREDIENTS
    30ml/2 tbsp vegetable oil
    4 shallots, chopped
    90g/3½oz/scant 1 cup cashew nuts
    5ml/1 tsp Thai red curry paste
    400g/14oz potatoes, peeled and cut
        into chunks
    1 lemon grass stalk, finely chopped
    200g/7oz can chopped tomatoes
    600ml/1 pint/2½ cups boiling water
    200g/7oz/generous 1 cup drained
        canned whole kernel corn
    4 celery sticks, sliced
    2 kaffir lime leaves, rolled into
        cylinders and thinly sliced
    15ml/1 tbsp tomato ketchup
    15ml/1 tbsp light soy sauce
    5ml/1 tsp palm sugar or light
        muscovado (brown) sugar
    5ml/1 tsp Thai fish sauce
    4 spring onions (scallions),
        thinly sliced
    small bunch fresh basil, chopped

COOK'S TIP
Rolling the lime leaves into cylinders
before slicing produces very fine strips
– a technique known as cutting *en
chiffonnade*. Remove the central rib
from the leaves before cutting them.

1 Heat the oil in a large, heavy pan or
wok. Add the shallots and stir-fry over
a medium heat for 2–3 minutes, until
softened. Add the cashew nuts and
stir-fry for a few minutes until golden.

2 Stir in the red curry paste. Stir-fry for
1 minute, then add the potatoes, lemon
grass, tomatoes and boiling water.

3 Bring back to the boil, then reduce
the heat to low, cover and simmer
gently for 15–20 minutes, or until the
potatoes are tender.

4 Stir the corn, celery, lime leaves,
tomato ketchup, soy sauce, sugar and
fish sauce into the pan or wok. Simmer
for a further 5 minutes, until heated
through, then spoon into warmed
serving bowls. Sprinkle with the sliced
spring onions and basil and serve.

TOFU AND VEGETABLE THAI CURRY

*TRADITIONAL THAI INGREDIENTS — CHILLIES, GALANGAL, LEMON GRASS AND KAFFIR LIME LEAVES —
GIVE THIS CURRY A WONDERFULLY FRAGRANT AROMA. THE TOFU NEEDS TO MARINATE FOR AT LEAST
2 HOURS, SO BEAR THIS IN MIND WHEN TIMING YOUR MEAL.*

SERVES FOUR

INGREDIENTS
175g/6oz firm tofu
45ml/3 tbsp dark soy sauce
15ml/1 tbsp sesame oil
5ml/1 tsp chilli sauce
2.5cm/1in piece fresh root ginger,
  peeled and finely grated
1 head broccoli, about 225g/8oz
½ head cauliflower, about 225g/8oz
30ml/2 tbsp vegetable oil
1 onion, sliced
400ml/14fl oz/1⅔ cups coconut milk
150ml/¼ pint/⅔ cup water
1 red (bell) pepper, seeded
  and chopped
175g/6oz/generous 1 cup green
  beans, halved
115g/4oz/1½ cups shiitake or button
  (white) mushrooms, halved
shredded spring onions (scallions),
  to garnish
boiled jasmine rice or noodles,
  to serve
For the curry paste
  2 fresh red or green chillies, seeded
    and chopped
  1 lemon grass stalk, chopped
  2.5cm/1in piece fresh
    galangal, chopped
  2 kaffir lime leaves
  10ml/2 tsp ground coriander
  a few fresh coriander (cilantro)
    sprigs, including the stalks
  45ml/3 tbsp water

1 Rinse and drain the tofu. Using a
sharp knife, cut it into 2.5cm/1in cubes.
Place the cubes in an ovenproof dish
that is large enough to hold them all in
a single layer.

2 Mix together the soy sauce, sesame
oil, chilli sauce and grated ginger in a
jug (pitcher) and pour over the tofu.
Toss gently to coat all the cubes evenly,
cover with clear film (plastic wrap) and
leave to marinate for at least 2 hours
or overnight if possible, turning and
basting the tofu occasionally.

3 Make the curry paste. Place the
chillies, lemon grass, galangal, lime
leaves, ground coriander and fresh
coriander in a food processor and
process until well blended. Add the
water and process to a thick paste.

4 Preheat the oven to 190°C/375°F/
Gas 5. Cut the broccoli and cauliflower
into small florets. Cut any stalks into
thin slices.

5 Heat the vegetable oil in a frying pan
and add the sliced onion. Cook over a
low heat for about 8 minutes, until soft
and lightly browned. Stir in the curry
paste and the coconut milk. Add the
water and bring to the boil.

6 Stir in the red pepper, green beans,
broccoli and cauliflower. Transfer to
a Chinese sand pot or earthenware
casserole. Cover and place towards the
bottom of the oven.

7 Stir the tofu and marinade, then place
the dish on a shelf near the top of the
oven. Cook for 30 minutes. Remove both
the dish and the sand pot or casserole
from the oven. Add the tofu, with any
remaining marinade, to the curry, with
the mushrooms, and stir well.

8 Return the sand pot or casserole to
the oven, reduce the temperature to
180°C/350°F/Gas 4 and cook for about
15 minutes, or until the vegetables are
tender. Garnish with the spring onions
and serve with the rice or noodles.

COOK'S TIP
Tofu or beancurd is made from soya
beans and is sold in blocks. It is a
creamy white colour and has a solid
gel-like texture. Tofu has a bland flavour
and its absorbent nature means that it
takes on the flavours of marinades or
other foods with which it is cooked.

SNAKE BEANS WITH TOFU

ANOTHER NAME FOR SNAKE BEANS IS YARD-LONG BEANS. THIS IS SOMETHING OF AN EXAGGERATION BUT THEY DO GROW TO LENGTHS OF 35CM/14IN AND MORE. LOOK FOR THEM IN ASIAN STORES AND MARKETS, BUT IF YOU CAN'T FIND ANY, SUBSTITUTE OTHER GREEN BEANS.

SERVES FOUR

INGREDIENTS
500g/1¼lb long beans, thinly sliced
200g/7oz silken tofu, cut into cubes
2 shallots, thinly sliced
200ml/7fl oz/scant 1 cup
  coconut milk
115g/4oz/1 cup roasted
  peanuts, chopped
juice of 1 lime
10ml/2 tsp palm sugar or light
  muscovado (brown) sugar
60ml/4 tbsp soy sauce
5ml/1 tsp dried chilli flakes

VARIATIONS
The sauce also works very well with mangetouts (snow peas). Alternatively, stir in sliced yellow or red (bell) pepper.

1 Bring a pan of lightly salted water to the boil. Add the beans and blanch them for 30 seconds.

2 Drain the beans immediately, then refresh under cold water and drain again, shaking well to remove as much water as possible. Place in a serving bowl and set aside.

3 Put the tofu and shallots in a pan with the coconut milk. Heat gently, stirring, until the tofu begins to crumble.

4 Add the peanuts, lime juice, sugar, soy sauce and chilli flakes. Heat, stirring, until the sugar has dissolved. Pour the sauce over the beans, toss to combine and serve immediately.

MUSHROOMS WITH GARLIC AND CHILLI SAUCE

WHEN YOU ARE PLANNING A BARBECUE FOR FRIENDS AND FAMILY, IT CAN BE TRICKY FINDING SOMETHING REALLY SPECIAL FOR THE VEGETARIANS IN THE PARTY. THESE TASTY MUSHROOM KEBABS ARE IDEAL BECAUSE THEY LOOK, SMELL AND TASTE WONDERFUL.

SERVES FOUR

INGREDIENTS

12 large field (portabello), chestnut or oyster mushrooms or a mixture, cut in half
4 garlic cloves, coarsely chopped
6 coriander (cilantro) roots, coarsely chopped
15ml/1 tbsp granulated sugar
30ml/2 tbsp light soy sauce
ground black pepper
For the dipping sauce
15ml/1 tbsp granulated sugar
90ml/6 tbsp rice vinegar
5ml/1 tsp salt
1 garlic clove, crushed
1 small fresh red chilli, seeded and finely chopped

1 If using wooden skewers, soak eight of them in cold water for at least 30 minutes to prevent them burning over the barbecue or under the grill.

2 Make the dipping sauce by heating the sugar, rice vinegar and salt in a small pan, stirring occasionally until the sugar and salt have dissolved. Add the garlic and chilli, pour into a serving dish and keep warm.

3 Thread three mushroom halves on to each skewer. Lay the filled skewers side by side in a shallow dish.

4 In a mortar or spice grinder pound or blend the garlic and coriander roots. Scrape into a bowl and mix with the sugar, soy sauce and a little pepper.

5 Brush the soy sauce mixture over the mushrooms and leave to marinate for 15 minutes. Prepare the barbecue or preheat the grill (broiler) and cook the mushrooms for 2–3 minutes on each side. Serve with the dipping sauce.

AUBERGINE ᴬᴺᴰ PEPPER TEMPURA
ᵂᴵᵀᴴ SWEET CHILLI DIP

THESE CRUNCHY VEGETABLES IN A BEAUTIFULLY LIGHT BATTER ARE QUICK AND EASY TO MAKE AND TASTE VERY GOOD WITH THE PIQUANT DIP. ALTHOUGH TEMPURA IS A SIGNATURE DISH OF JAPANESE CUISINE, IT HAS NOW BECOME POPULAR THROUGHOUT ASIA, WITH EACH COUNTRY ADDING ITS OWN CHARACTERISTIC TOUCH — IN THE CASE OF THAILAND, THIS CHILLI-FLAVOURED SAUCE.

SERVES FOUR

INGREDIENTS
    2 aubergines (eggplant)
    2 red (bell) peppers
    vegetable oil, for deep-frying
For the tempura batter
    250g/9oz/2¼ cups plain
       (all-purpose) flour
    2 egg yolks
    500ml/17fl oz/2¼ cups iced water
    5ml/1 tsp salt
For the dip
    150ml/¼ pint/⅔ cup water
    10ml/2 tsp granulated sugar
    1 fresh red chilli, seeded and
       finely chopped
    1 garlic clove, crushed
    juice of ½ lime
    5ml/1 tsp rice vinegar
    35ml/2½ tbsp Thai fish sauce
    ½ small carrot, finely grated

1 Using a sharp knife or a mandolin, slice the aubergines into thin batons. Halve, seed and slice the red peppers thinly.

2 Make the dip. Mix together all the ingredients in a bowl and stir until the sugar has dissolved. Cover with clear film (plastic wrap) and set aside.

VARIATIONS
Tempura batter is also good with pieces of fish or whole shellfish, such as large prawns (jumbo shrimp) or baby squid, as well as with a variety of vegetables.

3 Make the tempura batter. Set aside 30ml/2 tbsp of the flour. Put the egg yolks in a large bowl and beat in the iced water. Tip in the remaining flour with the salt and stir briefly together – the mixture should resemble thick pancake batter but be lumpy and not properly mixed. If it is too thick, add a little more iced water. Do not leave the batter to stand; use it immediately.

4 Pour the oil for deep-frying into a wok or deep-fryer and heat to 190°C/ 375°F or until a cube of bread, added to the oil, browns in about 30 seconds.

5 Pick up a small, haphazard handful of aubergine batons and pepper slices, dust it with the reserved flour, then dip it into the batter. Immediately drop the batter-coated vegetables into the hot oil, taking care as the oil will froth up furiously. Repeat to make two or three more fritters, but do not cook any more than this at one time, or the oil may overflow.

6 Cook the fritters for 3–4 minutes, until they are golden and crisp all over, then lift them out with a metal basket or slotted spoon. Drain thoroughly on kitchen paper and keep hot.

7 Repeat until all the vegetables have been coated in batter and cooked. Serve immediately, with the dip.

STUFFED SWEET PEPPERS

THIS IS AN UNUSUAL RECIPE IN THAT THE STUFFED PEPPERS ARE STEAMED RATHER THAN BAKED, BUT THE RESULT IS BEAUTIFULLY LIGHT AND TENDER. THE FILLING INCORPORATES TYPICAL THAI INGREDIENTS SUCH AS RED CURRY PASTE AND FISH SAUCE.

SERVES FOUR

INGREDIENTS
3 garlic cloves, finely chopped
2 coriander (cilantro) roots,
  finely chopped
400g/14oz/3 cups
  mushrooms, quartered
5ml/1 tsp Thai red curry paste
1 egg, lightly beaten
15ml/1 tbsp Thai fish sauce
15ml/1 tbsp light soy sauce
2.5ml/½ tsp granulated sugar
3 kaffir lime leaves, finely chopped
4 yellow (bell) peppers, halved
  lengthways and seeded

VARIATIONS
Use red or orange (bell) peppers if you
prefer, or a combination of the two.

1 In a mortar or spice grinder pound
or blend the garlic with the coriander
roots. Scrape into a bowl.

2 Put the mushrooms in a food
processor and pulse briefly until they
are finely chopped. Add to the garlic
mixture, then stir in the curry paste,
egg, sauces, sugar and lime leaves.

3 Place the pepper halves in a single
layer in a steamer basket. Spoon the
mixture loosely into the pepper halves.
Do not pack the mixture down tightly
or the filling will dry out too much.
Bring the water in the steamer to the
boil, then lower the heat to a simmer.
Steam the peppers for 15 minutes, or
until the flesh is tender. Serve hot.

SWEET AND SOUR VEGETABLES WITH TOFU

BIG, BOLD AND BEAUTIFUL, THIS IS A HEARTY STIR-FRY THAT WILL SATISFY THE HUNGRIEST GUESTS. STIR-FRIES ARE ALWAYS A GOOD CHOICE WHEN ENTERTAINING AS YOU CAN PREPARE THE INGREDIENTS AHEAD OF TIME AND THEN THEY TAKE SUCH A SHORT TIME TO COOK.

SERVES FOUR

INGREDIENTS
  4 shallots
  3 garlic cloves
  30ml/2 tbsp groundnut (peanut) oil
  250g/9oz Chinese leaves (Chinese
    cabbage), shredded
  8 baby corn cobs, sliced on
    the diagonal
  2 red (bell) peppers, seeded and
    thinly sliced
  200g/7oz/1¾ cups mangetouts
    (snow peas), trimmed and sliced
  250g/9oz tofu, rinsed, drained and
    cut in 1cm/½ in cubes
  60ml/4 tbsp vegetable stock
  30ml/2 tbsp light soy sauce
  15ml/1 tbsp granulated sugar
  30ml/2 tbsp rice vinegar
  2.5ml/½ tsp dried chilli flakes
  small bunch coriander
    (cilantro), chopped

1 Slice the shallots thinly using a sharp knife. Finely chop the garlic.

2 Heat the oil in a wok or large frying pan and cook the shallots and garlic for 2–3 minutes over a medium heat, until golden. Do not let the garlic burn or it will taste bitter.

3 Add the shredded cabbage, toss over the heat for 30 seconds, then add the corn cobs and repeat the process.

4 Add the red peppers, mangetouts and tofu in the same way, each time adding a single ingredient and tossing it over the heat for about 30 seconds before adding the next ingredient.

5 Pour in the stock and soy sauce. Mix together the sugar and vinegar in a small bowl, stirring until the sugar has dissolved, then add to the wok or pan. Sprinkle over the chilli flakes and coriander, toss to mix well and serve.

STIR-FRIED CRISPY TOFU

THE ASPARAGUS GROWN IN ASIA TENDS TO HAVE SLENDER STALKS. LOOK FOR IT IN THAI MARKETS OR SUBSTITUTE THE THIN ASPARAGUS POPULARLY KNOWN AS SPRUE.

SERVES TWO

INGREDIENTS

250g/9oz fried tofu cubes
30ml/2 tbsp groundnut (peanut) oil
15ml/1 tbsp Thai green curry paste
30ml/2 tbsp light soy sauce
2 kaffir lime leaves, rolled into
  cylinders and thinly sliced
30ml/2 tbsp granulated sugar
150ml/¼ pint/⅔ cup vegetable stock
250g/9oz Asian asparagus, trimmed
  and sliced into 5cm/2in lengths
30ml/2 tbsp roasted peanuts,
  finely chopped

VARIATION
Substitute slim carrot sticks or broccoli florets for the asparagus.

1 Preheat the grill (broiler) to medium. Place the tofu cubes in a grill pan and grill (broil) for 2–3 minutes, then turn them over and continue to cook until they are crisp and golden brown all over. Watch them carefully; they must not be allowed to burn.

2 Heat the oil in a wok or heavy frying pan. Add the green curry paste and cook over a medium heat, stirring constantly, for 1–2 minutes, until it gives off its aroma.

3 Stir the soy sauce, lime leaves, sugar and vegetable stock into the wok or pan and mix well. Bring to the boil, then reduce the heat to low so that the mixture is just simmering.

4 Add the asparagus and simmer gently for 5 minutes. Meanwhile, chop each piece of tofu into four, then add to the pan with the peanuts.

5 Toss to coat all the ingredients in the sauce, then spoon into a warmed dish and serve immediately.

STIR-FRIED SEEDS AND VEGETABLES

THE CONTRAST BETWEEN THE CRUNCHY SEEDS AND VEGETABLES AND THE RICH, SAVOURY SAUCE IS WHAT MAKES THIS DISH SO DELICIOUS. SERVE IT SOLO, OR WITH RICE OR NOODLES.

SERVES FOUR

INGREDIENTS
    30ml/2 tbsp vegetable oil
    30ml/2 tbsp sesame seeds
    30ml/2 tbsp sunflower seeds
    30ml/2 tbsp pumpkin seeds
    2 garlic cloves, finely chopped
    2.5cm/1in piece fresh root ginger,
      peeled and finely chopped
    2 large carrots, cut into batons
    2 large courgettes (zucchini), cut
      into batons
    90g/3½oz/1½ cups oyster
      mushrooms, torn in pieces
    150g/5oz watercress or spinach
      leaves, coarsely chopped
    small bunch fresh mint or
      coriander (cilantro), leaves and
      stems chopped
    60ml/4 tbsp black bean sauce
    30ml/2 tbsp light soy sauce
    15ml/1 tbsp palm sugar or light
      muscovado (brown) sugar
    30ml/2 tbsp rice vinegar

1 Heat the oil in a wok or large frying pan. Add the seeds. Toss over a medium heat for 1 minute, then add the garlic and ginger and continue to stir-fry until the ginger is aromatic and the garlic is golden. Do not let the garlic burn or it will taste bitter.

2 Add the carrot and courgette batons and the sliced mushrooms to the wok or pan and stir-fry over a medium heat for a further 5 minutes, or until all the vegetables are crisp-tender and are golden at the edges.

3 Add the watercress or spinach with the fresh herbs. Toss over the heat for 1 minute, then stir in the black bean sauce, soy sauce, sugar and vinegar. Stir-fry for 1–2 minutes, until combined and hot. Serve immediately.

COOK'S TIP
Oyster mushrooms have acquired their name because of their texture, rather than flavour, which is quite superb. They are delicate, so it is usually better to tear them into pieces along the lines of the gills, rather than slice them with a knife.

RICE DISHES

It is impossible to think of Asian cuisine without rice. It is served in one form or another at every meal, and is a staple food in all Asian countries. Thailand is one of the world's major producers of both long grain and glutinous rice. Thai fragrant rice, also known as jasmine rice, is valued the world over for its subtle fragrance. The grains are slightly sticky when cooked, although not so sticky as those of glutinous rice. It goes well with both savoury and sweet dishes.

COCONUT RICE

THIS RICH DISH IS USUALLY SERVED WITH A TANGY PAPAYA SALAD TO BALANCE THE SWEETNESS OF THE COCONUT MILK AND SUGAR. IT IS ONE OF THOSE COMFORTING TREATS THAT EVERYONE ENJOYS.

SERVES FOUR TO SIX

INGREDIENTS

250ml/8fl oz/1 cup water
475ml/16fl oz/2 cups coconut milk
2.5ml/½ tsp salt
30ml/2 tbsp granulated sugar
450g/1lb/2⅔ cups jasmine rice

COOK'S TIP

For a special occasion serve in a halved papaya and garnish with thin shreds of fresh coconut. Use a vegetable peeler to pare the coconut finely, as you would when making curls of Parmesan cheese.

1 Place the measured water, coconut milk, salt and sugar in a heavy pan. Wash the rice in several changes of cold water until it runs clear.

2 Add the jasmine rice, cover tightly with a lid and bring to the boil over a medium heat. Reduce the heat to low and simmer gently, without lifting the lid unnecessarily, for 15–20 minutes, until the rice is tender and cooked through. Test it by biting a grain.

3 Turn off the heat and leave the rice to rest in the pan, still covered with the lid, for a further 5–10 minutes.

4 Gently fluff up the rice grains with chopsticks or a fork before transferring it to a warmed dish and serving.

INDONESIAN COCONUT RICE

THIS WAY OF COOKING RICE IS VERY POPULAR THROUGHOUT THE WHOLE OF SOUTH-EAST ASIA.
COCONUT RICE GOES PARTICULARLY WELL WITH FISH, CHICKEN AND PORK.

SERVES FOUR TO SIX

INGREDIENTS
  350g/12oz/1¾ cups Thai fragrant rice
  400ml/14fl oz can coconut milk
  300ml/½ pint/1¼ cups water
  2.5ml/½ tsp ground coriander
  5cm/2in cinnamon stick
  1 lemon grass stalk, bruised
  1 bay leaf
  salt
  deep-fried onions, to garnish

1 Put the rice in a strainer and rinse thoroughly under cold water. Drain well, then put in a pan. Pour in the coconut milk and water. Add the coriander, cinnamon stick, lemon grass and bay leaf. Season with salt. Bring to the boil, then lower the heat, cover and simmer for 8–10 minutes.

2 Lift the lid and check that all the liquid has been absorbed, then fork the rice through carefully, removing the cinnamon stick, lemon grass and bay leaf.

3 Cover the pan with a tight-fitting lid and continue to cook over the lowest possible heat for 3–5 minutes more.

4 Pile the rice on to a warm serving dish and serve garnished with the crisp deep-fried onions.

COOK'S TIP
When bringing the rice to the boil, stir it frequently to prevent it from settling on the bottom of the pan. Once the rice is nearly tender, continue to cook over a very low heat or just leave to stand for 5 minutes. The important thing is to cover the pan tightly.

FESTIVE RICE

*THIS PRETTY THAI DISH IS TRADITIONALLY SHAPED INTO A CONE AND SURROUNDED BY A VARIETY OF
ACCOMPANIMENTS BEFORE BEING SERVED.*

2 Heat the oil in a frying pan with a lid.
Cook the garlic, onions and turmeric
over a low heat for 2–3 minutes, until
the onions have softened. Add the rice
and stir well to coat in oil.

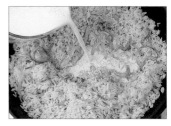

3 Pour in the water and coconut milk
and add the lemon grass. Bring to the
boil, stirring. Cover the pan and cook
gently for 12 minutes, or until all the
liquid has been absorbed by the rice.

SERVES EIGHT

INGREDIENTS
  450g/1lb/2⅔ cups jasmine rice
  60ml/4 tbsp oil
  2 garlic cloves, crushed
  2 onions, thinly sliced
  2.5ml/½ tsp ground turmeric
  750ml/1¼ pints/3 cups water
  400ml/14fl oz can coconut milk
  1–2 lemon grass stalks, bruised
For the accompaniments
  omelette strips
  2 fresh red chillies, seeded
    and shredded
  cucumber chunks
  tomato wedges
  deep-fried onions
  prawn (shrimp) crackers

1 Put the jasmine rice in a large strainer
and rinse it thoroughly under cold
water. Drain well.

COOK'S TIP
Jasmine rice is widely available in most
supermarkets and Asian stores. It is also
known as Thai fragrant rice.

4 Remove the pan from the heat and lift
the lid. Cover with a clean dishtowel,
replace the lid and leave to stand in a
warm place for 15 minutes. Remove the
lemon grass, mound the rice mixture in
a cone on a serving platter and garnish
with the accompaniments, then serve.

INDONESIAN PINEAPPLE FRIED RICE

WHEN BUYING A PINEAPPLE, LOOK FOR A SWEET-SMELLING FRUIT WITH AN EVEN BROWNISH-YELLOW SKIN. TO TEST FOR RIPENESS, TAP THE BASE — A DULL SOUND INDICATES THAT THE FRUIT IS RIPE. THE FLESH SHOULD ALSO GIVE SLIGHTLY WHEN PRESSED.

SERVES FOUR TO SIX

INGREDIENTS
 1 pineapple
 30ml/2 tbsp vegetable oil
 1 small onion, finely chopped
 2 fresh green chillies, seeded
  and chopped
 225g/8oz lean pork, cut into strips
 115g/4oz cooked, peeled
  prawns (shrimp)
 675–900g/1½–2lb/3–4 cups plain
  boiled rice, cooked and completely
  cold
 50g/2oz/⅓ cup roasted cashew nuts
 2 spring onions (scallions), chopped
 30ml/2 tbsp fish sauce
 15ml/1 tbsp soy sauce
 2 fresh red chillies, sliced, and
  10–12 fresh mint leaves (optional),
  to garnish

4 Stir in the prawns and rice and toss well together. Continue to stir-fry until the rice is thoroughly heated.

5 Add the chopped pineapple, cashew nuts and spring onions. Season to taste with fish sauce and soy sauce.

6 Spoon into the pineapple skin shells. Garnish with sliced red chillies, and with shredded mint leaves, if you like.

COOK'S TIP
This dish is ideal to prepare for a special occasion meal. Served in the pineapple skin shells, it is sure to be the talking point of the dinner.

1 Using a sharp knife, cut the pineapple into quarters. Remove the flesh from both halves by cutting around inside the skin. Reserve the pineapple skin shells for serving the rice.

2 Slice the pineapple flesh and chop it into small even-size cubes. You will need about 115g/4oz of pineapple in total. Any remaining fruit can be reserved for use in a dessert.

3 Heat the oil in a wok or large pan. Add the onion and chillies and fry for about 3–5 minutes until softened. Add the strips of pork and cook until they have browned on all sides.

CHICKEN AND BASIL COCONUT RICE

FOR THIS DISH, THE RICE IS PARTIALLY BOILED BEFORE BEING SIMMERED WITH COCONUT SO THAT IT FULLY ABSORBS THE FLAVOUR OF THE CHILLIES, BASIL AND SPICES.

SERVES FOUR

INGREDIENTS
    350g/12oz/1¾ cups Thai fragrant
        rice, rinsed
    30–45ml/2–3 tbsp groundnut
        (peanut) oil
    1 large onion, finely sliced into rings
    1 garlic clove, crushed
    1 fresh red chilli, seeded and
        finely sliced
    1 fresh green chilli, seeded and
        finely sliced
    generous handful of basil leaves
    3 skinless chicken breast fillets,
        about 350g/12oz, finely sliced
    5mm/¼in piece of lemon grass,
        pounded or finely chopped
    600ml/1 pint/2½ cups
        coconut cream
    salt and ground black pepper

1 Bring a pan of lightly salted water to the boil. Add the rice to the pan and boil for about 6 minutes, until partially cooked. Drain and set aside.

2 Heat the oil in a frying pan and fry the onion rings for 5–10 minutes until golden and crisp. Lift out, drain on kitchen paper and set aside.

3 Fry the garlic and chillies in the oil remaining in the pan for 2–3 minutes, then add the basil leaves and fry briefly until they begin to wilt.

4 Remove a few basil leaves and set them aside for the garnish, then add the chicken slices with the lemon grass and fry for 2–3 minutes until golden.

5 Add the rice. Stir-fry for a few minutes to coat the grains, then pour in the coconut cream. Cook for 4–5 minutes or until the rice is tender, adding a little more water if necessary. Adjust the seasoning.

6 Pile the rice into a warmed serving dish, sprinkle with the fried onion rings and basil leaves, and serve immediately.

SAVOURY FRIED RICE

THIS IS TYPICAL THAI STREET FOOD, EATEN AT ALL TIMES OF THE DAY. THE RECIPE CAN BE ADAPTED TO USE WHATEVER VEGETABLES YOU HAVE AVAILABLE AND YOU COULD ALSO ADD MEAT OR SHELLFISH.

SERVES TWO

INGREDIENTS
  30ml/2 tbsp vegetable oil
  2 garlic cloves, finely chopped
  1 small fresh red chilli, seeded and
    finely chopped
  50g/2oz/½ cup cashew nuts, toasted
  50g/2oz/⅔ cup desiccated
    (dry unsweetened shredded)
    coconut, toasted
  2.5ml/½ tsp palm sugar or light
    muscovado (brown) sugar
  30ml/2 tbsp light soy sauce
  15ml/1 tbsp rice vinegar
  1 egg
  115g/4oz/1 cup green beans, sliced
  ½ spring cabbage or 115g/4oz spring
    greens (collards) or pak choi (bok
    choy), shredded
  90g/3½oz jasmine rice, cooked
  lime wedges, to serve

1 Heat the oil in a wok or large, heavy frying pan. Add the garlic and cook over a medium to high heat until golden. Do not let it burn or it will taste bitter.

2 Add the red chilli, cashew nuts and toasted coconut to the wok or pan and stir-fry briefly, taking care to prevent the coconut from scorching. Stir in the sugar, soy sauce and rice vinegar. Toss over the heat for 1–2 minutes.

3 Push the stir-fry to one side of the wok or pan and break the egg into the empty side. When the egg is almost set stir it into the garlic and chilli mixture with a wooden spatula or spoon.

4 Add the green beans, greens and cooked rice. Stir over the heat until the greens have just wilted, then spoon into a dish to serve. Offer the lime wedges separately, for squeezing over the rice.

RICE OMELETTE

RICE OMELETTES MAKE A GREAT SUPPER DISH. IN JAPAN, THEY ARE A FAVOURITE WITH CHILDREN, WHO USUALLY TOP THEM WITH A LIBERAL HELPING OF TOMATO KETCHUP.

SERVES FOUR

INGREDIENTS

    1 skinless, boneless chicken thigh,
      about 115g/4oz, cubed
    40ml/8 tsp butter
    1 small onion, chopped
    ½ carrot, diced
    2 shiitake mushrooms, stems
      removed and chopped
    15ml/1 tbsp finely chopped
      fresh parsley
    225g/8oz/2 cups cooked long grain
      white rice
    30ml/2 tbsp tomato ketchup
    6 eggs, lightly beaten
    60ml/4 tbsp milk
    5ml/1 tsp salt, plus extra to season
    freshly ground black pepper
    tomato ketchup, to serve

1 Season the chicken with salt and pepper. Melt 10ml/2 tsp butter in a frying pan. Fry the onion for 1 minute, then add the chicken and fry until the cubes are white and cooked. Add the carrot and mushrooms, stir-fry over a medium heat until soft, then add the parsley. Set this mixture aside. Wipe the frying pan with kitchen paper.

2 Melt a further 10ml/2 tsp butter in the frying pan, add the rice and stir well. Mix in the fried ingredients, ketchup and pepper. Stir well, adding salt to taste, if necessary. Keep the mixture warm. Beat the eggs with the milk in a bowl. Stir in the measured salt and add pepper to taste.

3 Melt 5ml/1 tsp of the remaining butter in an omelette pan. Pour in a quarter of the egg mixture and stir it briefly with a fork, then allow it to set for 1 minute. Top with a quarter of the rice mixture.

4 Fold the omelette over the rice and slide it to the edge of the pan to shape it into a curve. Slide it on to a warmed plate, cover with kitchen paper and press neatly into a rectangular shape. Keep hot while cooking three more omelettes from the remaining ingredients. Serve immediately, with tomato ketchup.

CURRIED CHICKEN AND RICE

THIS SIMPLE ONE-POT MEAL IS PERFECT FOR CASUAL ENTERTAINING. IT CAN BE MADE USING VIRTUALLY ANY MEAT OR VEGETABLES THAT YOU HAVE TO HAND.

SERVES FOUR

INGREDIENTS
    60ml/4 tbsp vegetable oil
    4 garlic cloves, finely chopped
    1 chicken (about 1.5kg/3–3½lb)
      or chicken pieces, skin and bones
      removed and meat cut into
      bitesize pieces
    5ml/1 tsp garam masala
    450g/1lb/2⅔ cups jasmine rice,
      rinsed and drained
    10ml/2 tsp salt
    1 litre/1¾ pints/4 cups
      chicken stock
    small bunch fresh coriander
      (cilantro), chopped, to garnish

COOK'S TIP
You will probably need to brown the chicken in batches, so don't be tempted to add too much chicken at once.

1 Heat the oil in a wok or flameproof casserole, which has a lid. Add the garlic and cook over a low to medium heat until golden brown. Add the chicken, increase the heat and brown the pieces on all sides (see Cook's Tip).

2 Add the garam masala, stir well to coat the chicken all over in the spice, then tip in the drained rice. Add the salt and stir to mix.

3 Pour in the stock, stir well, then cover the wok or casserole and bring to the boil. Reduce the heat to low and simmer gently for 10 minutes, until the rice is cooked and tender.

4 Lift the wok or casserole off the heat, leaving the lid on, and leave for 10 minutes. Fluff up the rice grains with a fork and spoon on to a platter. Sprinkle with the coriander and serve immediately.

THAI FRIED RICE

THIS SUBSTANTIAL AND TASTY DISH IS BASED ON JASMINE RICE. DICED CHICKEN, RED PEPPER AND CORN KERNELS ADD COLOUR AND EXTRA FLAVOUR.

SERVES FOUR

INGREDIENTS
  475ml/16fl oz/2 cups water
  50g/2oz/½ cup coconut milk powder
  350g/12oz/1¾ cups jasmine
    rice, rinsed
  30ml/2 tbsp groundnut (peanut) oil
  2 garlic cloves, chopped
  1 small onion, finely chopped
  2.5cm/1in piece of fresh root ginger,
    peeled and grated
  225g/8oz skinless, boneless chicken
    breast portions, cut into
    1cm/½in dice
  1 red (bell) pepper, seeded
    and sliced
  115g/4oz/1 cup drained canned
    whole kernel corn
  5ml/1 tsp chilli oil
  5ml/1 tsp hot curry powder
  2 eggs, beaten
  salt
  spring onion (scallion) shreds,
    to garnish

3 Push the onion mixture to the sides of the wok, add the chicken to the centre and stir-fry for 2 minutes. Add the rice and toss well. Stir-fry over a high heat for about 3 minutes more, until the chicken is cooked through.

4 Stir in the sliced red pepper, corn, chilli oil and curry powder, with salt to taste. Toss over the heat for 1 minute. Stir in the beaten eggs and cook for 1 minute more. Garnish with the spring onion shreds and serve.

1 Pour the water into a pan and whisk in the coconut milk powder. Add the rice and bring to the boil. Reduce the heat, cover and cook for 12 minutes, or until the rice is tender and the liquid has been absorbed. Spread the rice on a baking sheet and leave until cold.

2 Heat the oil in a wok, add the garlic, onion and ginger and stir-fry over a medium heat for 2 minutes.

COOK'S TIP
It is important that the rice is completely cold before being fried.

FRIED RICE <u>WITH</u> PORK

THIS CLASSIC RICE DISH LOOKS PARTICULARLY PRETTY GARNISHED WITH STRIPS OF OMELETTE, AS IN
THE RECIPE FOR FRIED JASMINE RICE WITH PRAWNS AND THAI BASIL.

SERVES FOUR TO SIX

INGREDIENTS
 45ml/3 tbsp vegetable oil
 1 onion, chopped
 15ml/1 tbsp chopped garlic
 115g/4oz pork, cut into small cubes
 2 eggs, beaten
 1kg/2¼lb/4 cups cooked rice
 30ml/2 tbsp Thai fish sauce
 15ml/1 tbsp dark soy sauce
 2.5ml/½ tsp caster (superfine) sugar
 4 spring onions (scallions),
   finely sliced, to garnish
 2 red chillies, sliced, to garnish
 1 lime, cut into wedges, to garnish

COOK'S TIP
To make 1kg/2¼lb/4 cups cooked rice,
you will need approximately 400g/14oz/
2 cups uncooked rice.

1 Heat the oil in a wok or large frying
pan. Add the onion and garlic and cook
for about 2 minutes until softened.

2 Add the pork to the softened onion
and garlic. Stir-fry until the pork
changes colour and is cooked.

3 Add the eggs and cook until
scrambled into small lumps.

4 Add the rice and continue to stir and
toss, to coat it with the oil and prevent
it from sticking.

5 Add the fish sauce, soy sauce and
sugar and mix well. Continue to fry until
the rice is thoroughly heated. Spoon
into warmed individual bowls and serve,
garnished with sliced spring onions,
chillies and lime wedges.

CONGEE <u>WITH</u> CHINESE SAUSAGE

CONGEE — SOFT RICE — IS COMFORT FOOD. GENTLE ON THE STOMACH, IT IS FREQUENTLY EATEN FOR BREAKFAST OR SERVED TO INVALIDS. THROUGHOUT THE EAST, PEOPLE WILL FREQUENTLY HAVE JUST A CUP OF TEA ON RISING; LATER THEY WILL SETTLE DOWN TO A BOWL OF CONGEE OR ITS REGIONAL EQUIVALENT.

SERVES TWO TO THREE

INGREDIENTS

115g/4oz/generous 1/2 cup
   long-grain rice
25g/1oz/3 tbsp glutinous rice
1.2 litres/2 pints/5 cups water
about 2.5ml/1/2 tsp salt
5ml/1 tsp sesame oil
thin slice of fresh root ginger,
   peeled and bruised
2 Chinese sausages
1 egg, lightly beaten (optional)
2.5ml/1/2 tsp light soy sauce
roasted peanuts, chopped, and thin
   shreds of spring onion (scallion),
   to garnish

1 Wash both rices thoroughly. Drain and place in a large pan. Add the water, bring to the boil and immediately reduce to the lowest heat, using a heat diffuser if you have one.

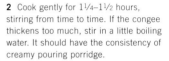

2 Cook gently for 1 1/4–1 1/2 hours, stirring from time to time. If the congee thickens too much, stir in a little boiling water. It should have the consistency of creamy pouring porridge.

3 About 15 minutes before serving, add salt to taste and the sesame oil, together with the piece of ginger.

4 Steam the Chinese sausages for about 10 minutes, then slice and stir into the congee. Cook for 5 minutes.

5 Just before serving, remove the ginger and stir in the lightly beaten egg, if using. Serve hot, garnished with the peanuts and spring onions and topped with a drizzle of soy sauce.

VARIATION
If you prefer, use roast duck instead of Chinese sausages. Cut the cooked duck into bitesize pieces and add once the rice is cooked. Congee is also popular with tea eggs.

FRIED RICE WITH BEEF

ONE OF THE JOYS OF THAI COOKING IS THE EASE AND SPEED WITH WHICH A REALLY GOOD MEAL CAN BE PREPARED. THIS ONE CAN BE ON THE TABLE IN 15 MINUTES.

SERVES FOUR

INGREDIENTS

  200g/7oz beef steak
  15ml/1 tbsp vegetable oil
  2 garlic cloves,
    finely chopped
  1 egg
  250g/9oz/2¼ cups cooked
    jasmine rice
  ½ medium head broccoli,
    coarsely chopped
  30ml/2 tbsp dark soy sauce
  15ml/1 tbsp light soy sauce
  5ml/1 tsp palm sugar or light
    muscovado (brown) sugar
  15ml/1 tbsp Thai fish sauce
  ground black pepper
  chilli sauce, to serve

1 Trim the steak and cut into very thin strips with a sharp knife.

2 Heat the oil in a wok or frying pan and cook the garlic over a low to medium heat until golden. Do not let it burn. Increase the heat to high, add the steak and stir-fry for 2 minutes.

3 Move the pieces of beef to the edges of the wok or pan and break the egg into the centre. When the egg starts to set, stir-fry it with the meat.

4 Add the rice and toss all the contents of the wok together, scraping up any residue on the base, then add the broccoli, soy sauces, sugar and fish sauce and stir-fry for 2 minutes more. Season to taste with pepper and serve immediately with chilli sauce.

COOK'S TIP
Soy sauce is made from fermented soya beans. The first extraction is sold as light soy sauce and has a delicate, "beany" fragrance. Dark soy sauce has been allowed to mature for longer.

NASI GORENG

ONE OF THE MOST FAMOUS INDONESIAN DISHES, THIS IS A MARVELLOUS WAY TO USE UP LEFTOVER RICE, CHICKEN AND MEATS. IT IS IMPORTANT THAT THE RICE BE QUITE COLD AND THE GRAINS SEPARATE BEFORE THE OTHER INGREDIENTS ARE ADDED, SO COOK THE RICE THE DAY BEFORE IF POSSIBLE.

SERVES FOUR TO SIX

INGREDIENTS

2 eggs
30ml/2 tbsp water
105ml/7 tbsp oil
225g/8oz pork fillet or fillet
   (tenderloin) of beef, cut into neat
   strips
115g/4oz peeled cooked prawns
   (shrimp), thawed if frozen
175–225g/6–8oz cooked chicken,
   finely chopped
2 fresh red chillies, halved
   and seeded
1cm/½in cube shrimp paste
2 garlic cloves, crushed
1 onion, roughly chopped
675g/1½lb/6 cups cold cooked
   long grain rice, preferably
   basmati (about 350g/12oz/1¾ cups
   raw rice)
30ml/2 tbsp dark soy sauce or
   45–60ml/3–4 tbsp tomato ketchup
salt and ground black pepper
deep-fried onions, celery leaves
   and fresh coriander (cilantro) sprigs,
   to garnish

1 Put the eggs in a bowl and beat in the water, with salt and pepper to taste. Using a non-stick frying pan make two or three omelettes using as little oil as possible for greasing. Roll up each omelette and cut in strips when cold. Set aside. Place the strips of pork or beef in a bowl. Put the prawns and chopped chicken in separate bowls. Shred one of the chillies and reserve it.

2 Put the shrimp paste in a food processor. Add the remaining chilli, the garlic and the onion. Process to a fine paste. Alternatively, pound the mixture in a mortar, using a pestle.

3 Heat the remaining oil in a wok and fry the paste, without browning, until it gives off a rich, spicy aroma. Add the pork or beef and toss over the heat to seal in the juices, then cook for 2 minutes more, stirring constantly.

4 Add the prawns and stir-fry for 2 minutes. Finally, stir in the chicken, cold rice, dark soy sauce or ketchup and seasoning to taste. Reheat the rice fully, stirring all the time to keep the rice light and fluffy and prevent it from sticking to the base of the pan.

5 Spoon into individual dishes and arrange the omelette strips and reserved chilli on top. Garnish with the deep-fried onions and coriander sprigs.

FRAGRANT HARBOUR FRIED RICE

FRAGRANT HARBOUR IS THE CHINESE NAME FOR HONG KONG, THE CROSSROADS FOR SO MANY STYLES OF COOKING. FRIED RICE IS EVER POPULAR AS YET ANOTHER WAY OF USING UP LITTLE BITS OF THIS AND THAT TO MAKE A VERITABLE FEAST. COOK THE RICE THE DAY BEFORE IF POSSIBLE.

SERVES FOUR

INGREDIENTS
    225g/8oz/generous 1 cup long
        grain rice
    about 90ml/6 tbsp vegetable oil
    2 eggs, beaten
    4 Chinese dried mushrooms, soaked
        for 30 minutes in warm water to cover
    8 shallots or 2 small onions, sliced
    115g/4oz peeled cooked prawns
        (shrimp), thawed if frozen
    3 garlic cloves, crushed
    115g/4oz cooked pork, cut into
        thin strips
    115g/4oz Chinese sausage
    30ml/2 tbsp light soy sauce
    115g/4oz/1 cup frozen peas, thawed
    2 spring onions (scallions), shredded
    1–2 fresh or dried red chillies,
        seeded (optional)
    salt and ground black pepper
    fresh coriander (cilantro) leaves,
        to garnish

1 Bring a large pan of lightly salted water to the boil. Add the rice and cook for 12–15 minutes until just tender. Drain and leave to go cold. Ideally use the next day.

2 Heat about 15ml/1 tbsp of the oil in a large frying pan over a medium heat, pour in the beaten eggs and allow to set without stirring. Slide the omelette on to a plate, roll it up and cut into fine strips. Set aside.

3 Drain the mushrooms, cut off and discard the stems and slice the caps finely. Heat a wok, add 15ml/1 tbsp of the remaining oil and, when hot, stir-fry the shallots or onions until crisp and golden brown. Remove with a slotted spoon and set aside.

4 Add the prawns and garlic to the wok, with a little more oil if needed, and fry for 1 minute. Remove the prawns and garlic and set aside. Add 15ml/1 tbsp more oil to the wok.

5 Stir-fry the shredded pork and mushrooms for 2 minutes; lift out and reserve. Steam the Chinese sausage in a colander for 5 minutes or until it plumps up. Trim and slice at an angle.

6 Wipe the wok, reheat with the remaining oil and stir-fry the rice, adding more oil if needed so the grains are coated. Stir in the soy sauce, salt and pepper, plus half the cooked ingredients.

7 Add the peas and half the spring onions and toss over the heat until the peas are cooked. Pile the fried rice on a heated platter and arrange the remaining cooked ingredients on top, with the remaining spring onions. Add the chilli, if using, and the coriander leaves, to garnish.

COOK'S TIP
There are many theories on the best way to cook rice. This gives excellent results every time: Put 225g/8oz/generous 1 cup long grain rice in a sieve and rinse thoroughly in cold water. Place in a large bowl, add salt to taste and pour in just under 600ml/1 pint/2½ cups boiling water. Cover with microwave film, leaving a gap and cook in a 675 watt microwave on full power for 10 minutes. Leave to stand for 5 minutes more. Cool, then stir with a chopstick.

CHINESE JEWELLED RICE

ANOTHER FRIED RICE MEDLEY, THIS TIME WITH CRAB MEAT AND WATER CHESTNUTS, PROVIDING CONTRASTING TEXTURES AND FLAVOURS.

SERVES FOUR

INGREDIENTS

350g/12oz/1¾ cups white long
  grain rice
45ml/3 tbsp vegetable oil
1 onion, roughly chopped
4 dried black Chinese mushrooms,
  soaked for 10 minutes in warm
  water to cover
115g/4oz cooked ham, diced
175g/6oz drained canned white
  crab meat
75g/3oz/½ cup drained canned
  water chestnuts
115g/4oz/1 cup peas, thawed
  if frozen
30ml/2 tbsp oyster sauce
5ml/1 tsp granulated sugar
salt

1 Rinse the rice, then cook for about 10–12 minutes in a pan of lightly salted boiling water. Drain, refresh under cold water, drain again and allow to cool. Heat half the oil in a wok. When very hot, stir-fry the rice for 3 minutes. Transfer the cooked rice to a bowl and set aside.

2 Heat the remaining oil in the wok and cook the onion until softened but not coloured. Drain the mushrooms, cut off and discard the stems, then chop the caps.

3 Add the chopped mushrooms to the wok, with all the remaining ingredients except the rice. Stir-fry for 2 minutes, then add the rice and stir-fry for about 3 minutes more. Serve at once.

COOK'S TIP
When adding the oil to the hot wok, drizzle it in a "necklace" just below the rim. As it runs down, it will coat the inner surface as it heats.

CHINESE FRIED RICE

THIS DISH, A VARIATION ON SPECIAL FRIED RICE, IS MORE ELABORATE THAN THE MORE FAMILIAR
EGG FRIED RICE, AND IS ALMOST A MEAL IN ITSELF.

SERVES FOUR

INGREDIENTS
50g/2oz cooked ham
50g/2oz cooked prawns (shrimp),
  peeled
3 eggs
5ml/1 tsp salt
2 spring onions (scallions), chopped
60ml/4 tbsp vegetable oil
115g/4oz/1 cup green peas, thawed
15ml/1 tbsp light soy sauce
15ml/1 tbsp Chinese rice wine or
  dry sherry
450g/1lb/4 cups cooked white long
  grain rice

1 Dice the cooked ham finely. Pat the cooked prawns dry on kitchen paper.

2 In a bowl, beat the eggs with a pinch of salt and a few spring onion pieces.

VARIATIONS
This is a versatile recipe and is ideal for using up leftovers. Use cooked chicken or turkey instead of the ham, doubling the quantity if you omit the prawns.

3 Heat about half the oil in a wok, stir-fry the peas, prawns and ham for 1 minute, then add the soy sauce and rice wine or sherry. Transfer to a bowl and keep hot.

4 Heat the remaining oil in the wok and scramble the eggs lightly. Add the rice and stir to make sure that the grains are separate. Add the remaining salt, the remaining spring onions and the prawn mixture. Toss over the heat to mix. Serve hot or cold.

FRIED JASMINE RICE WITH PRAWNS AND THAI BASIL

THAI BASIL (BAI GRAPAO), ALSO KNOWN AS HOLY BASIL, HAS A UNIQUE, PUNGENT FLAVOUR THAT IS BOTH SPICY AND SHARP. IT CAN BE FOUND IN MOST ASIAN FOOD MARKETS.

SERVES FOUR TO SIX

INGREDIENTS
    45ml/3 tbsp vegetable oil
    1 egg, beaten
    1 onion, chopped
    15ml/1 tbsp chopped garlic
    15ml/1 tbsp shrimp paste
    1kg/2¼lb/4 cups cooked jasmine rice
    350g/12oz cooked shelled prawns
      (shrimp)
    50g/2oz thawed frozen peas
    oyster sauce, to taste
    2 spring onions (scallions), chopped
    15–20 Thai basil leaves, roughly
      snipped, plus an extra sprig,
      to garnish

1 Heat 15ml/1 tbsp of the oil in a wok or frying pan. Add the beaten egg and swirl it around to set like a thin pancake.

2 Cook the pancake (on one side only) over a gentle heat until golden. Slide the pancake on to a board, roll up and cut into thin strips. Set aside.

3 Heat the remaining oil in the wok or pan, add the onion and garlic and stir-fry for 2–3 minutes. Stir in the shrimp paste and mix well until thoroughly combined.

4 Add the rice, prawns and peas and toss and stir together, until everything is heated through.

5 Season with oyster sauce to taste, taking great care as the shrimp paste is salty. Mix in the spring onions and basil leaves. Transfer to a serving dish and top with the strips of egg pancake. Serve, garnished with a sprig of basil.

MALACCA FRIED RICE

THERE ARE MANY VERSIONS OF THIS DISH THROUGHOUT ASIA, ALL BASED UPON LEFTOVER COOKED RICE. INGREDIENTS VARY ACCORDING TO WHAT IS AVAILABLE, BUT PRAWNS ARE A POPULAR ADDITION.

SERVES FOUR TO SIX

INGREDIENTS
    2 eggs
    45ml/3 tbsp vegetable oil
    4 shallots or 1 onion, finely chopped
    5ml/1 tsp chopped fresh root ginger
    1 garlic clove, crushed
    225g/8oz raw prawns (shrimp),
      peeled and deveined
    5ml/1 tsp chilli sauce (optional)
    3 spring onions (scallions), green
      part only, roughly chopped
    225g/8oz/2 cups frozen peas
    225g/8oz thickly sliced roast
      pork, diced
    45ml/3 tbsp light soy sauce
    350g/12oz/3 cups cooked white long
      grain rice, cooled
    salt and freshly ground black pepper

1 In a bowl, beat the eggs well with salt and freshly ground black pepper to taste. Heat 15ml/1 tbsp of the oil in a large, non-stick frying pan, pour in the eggs and cook until set, without stirring. This will take less than a minute. Roll up the pancake, slide it on to a plate, cut into thin strips and set aside.

COOK'S TIP
You don't have to wait until the day after you've served a Sunday roast to try this. Most delicatessens sell sliced roast pork.

2 Heat the remaining vegetable oil in a preheated wok, add the shallots or onion, ginger, garlic and prawns, and cook for 1–2 minutes, taking care that the garlic does not burn.

3 Add the chilli sauce, if using, the spring onions, peas, pork and soy sauce. Stir to heat through, then add the rice. Fry over a medium heat for 6–8 minutes. Spoon into a dish, decorate with the pancake strips and serve immediately.

NOODLE DISHES

In Asia, you are never very far from a noodle seller. This popular food is bought from breakfast to bedtime, from special restaurants and kiosks, floating barges or streetside stalls. Most of the noodles on sale are made from rice, although you will also find mung bean noodles, whose almost glassy appearance makes them a popular choice for stir-fries. Their bland taste means that they are a good vehicle for other flavours, and they are often served simply, with a selection of condiments or dips.

MEE GORENG

THIS IS A TRULY INTERNATIONAL DISH COMBINING INDIAN, CHINESE AND WESTERN INGREDIENTS.
IT IS A DELICIOUS TREAT FOR LUNCH OR SUPPER AND IN SINGAPORE AND MALAYSIA CAN BE BOUGHT
IN MANY STREETS FROM ONE OF THE MANY HAWKERS' STALLS.

2 If using fried tofu, cut each cube in half, refresh it in a pan of boiling water, then drain well. Heat 30ml/2 tbsp of the oil in a large frying pan. If using plain tofu, cut into cubes and fry until brown, then lift it out with a slotted spoon and set aside.

3 Beat the eggs with the water and seasoning. Add to the oil in the frying pan and cook without stirring until set. Flip over, cook the other side, then slide it out of the pan, roll up and slice thinly.

SERVES FOUR TO SIX

INGREDIENTS
   450g/1lb fresh yellow egg noodles
   60–90ml/4–6 tbsp vegetable oil
   115g/4oz fried tofu or 150g/5oz
      firm tofu
   2 eggs
   30ml/2 tbsp water
   1 onion, sliced
   1 garlic clove, crushed
   15ml/1 tbsp light soy sauce
   30–45ml/2–3 tbsp tomato ketchup
   15ml/1 tbsp chilli sauce (or to taste)
   1 large cooked potato, diced
   4 spring onions (scallions), shredded
   1–2 fresh green chillies, seeded
      and finely sliced (optional)

1 Bring a large pan of water to the boil, add the fresh egg noodles and cook for just 2 minutes. Drain the noodles and immediately rinse them under cold water to halt cooking. Drain again and set aside.

4 Heat the remaining oil in a wok and fry the onion and garlic for 2–3 minutes. Add the drained noodles, soy sauce, ketchup and chilli sauce. Toss well over medium heat for 2 minutes, then add the diced potato. Reserve a few spring onions for garnish and stir the rest into the noodles with the chilli, if using, and the tofu.

5 When hot, stir in the omelette. Serve on a hot platter garnished with the remaining spring onion.

PLAIN NOODLES <u>WITH</u> FOUR FLAVOURS

A WONDERFULLY SIMPLE WAY OF SERVING NOODLES, THIS DISH ALLOWS EACH INDIVIDUAL DINER TO SEASON THEIR OWN, SPRINKLING OVER THE FOUR FLAVOURS AS THEY LIKE. FLAVOURINGS ARE ALWAYS PUT OUT IN LITTLE BOWLS WHENEVER NOODLES ARE SERVED.

<u>SERVES FOUR</u>

INGREDIENTS
  4 small fresh red or green chillies
  60ml/4 tbsp Thai fish sauce
  60ml/4 tbsp rice vinegar
  granulated sugar
  mild or hot chilli powder
  350g/12oz fresh or dried noodles

1 Prepare the four flavours. For the first, finely chop 2 small red or green chillies, discarding the seeds or leaving them in, depending on how hot you like your flavouring. Place them in a small bowl and add the Thai fish sauce.

2 For the second flavour, chop the remaining chillies finely and mix them with the rice vinegar in a small bowl. Put the sugar and chilli powder in separate small bowls.

3 Cook the noodles until tender, following the instructions on the packet. Drain well, tip into a large bowl and serve immediately with the four flavours handed separately.

SWEET AND HOT VEGETABLE NOODLES

THIS NOODLE DISH HAS THE COLOUR OF FIRE, BUT ONLY THE MILDEST SUGGESTION OF HEAT. GINGER AND PLUM SAUCE GIVE IT ITS FRUITY FLAVOUR, WHILE LIME ADDS A DELICIOUS TANG.

SERVES FOUR

INGREDIENTS
130g/4½oz dried rice noodles
30ml/2 tbsp groundnut (peanut) oil
2.5cm/1in piece fresh root ginger,
  sliced into thin batons
1 garlic clove, crushed
130g/4½oz drained canned bamboo
  shoots, sliced into thin batons
2 medium carrots, sliced into batons
130g/4½oz/1½ cups beansprouts
1 small white cabbage, shredded
30ml/2 tbsp Thai fish sauce
30ml/2 tbsp soy sauce
30ml/2 tbsp plum sauce
10ml/2 tsp sesame oil
15ml/1 tbsp palm sugar or light
  muscovado (brown) sugar
juice of ½ lime
90g/3½oz mooli (daikon), sliced into
  thin batons
small bunch fresh coriander
  (cilantro), chopped
60ml/4 tbsp sesame seeds, toasted

1 Cook the noodles in a large pan of boiling water, following the instructions on the packet. Meanwhile, heat the oil in a wok or large frying pan and stir-fry the ginger and garlic for 2–3 minutes over a medium heat, until golden.

2 Drain the noodles and set them aside. Add the bamboo shoots to the wok, increase the heat to high and stir-fry for 5 minutes. Add the carrots, beansprouts and cabbage and stir-fry for a further 5 minutes, until they are beginning to char on the edges.

3 Stir in the sauces, sesame oil, sugar and lime juice. Add the mooli and coriander, toss to mix, then spoon into a warmed bowl, sprinkle with toasted sesame seeds and serve immediately.

COOK'S TIP
Use a large, sharp knife for shredding cabbage. Remove any tough outer leaves, if necessary, then cut the cabbage into quarters. Cut off and discard the hard core from each quarter, place flat side down, then slice the cabbage very thinly to make fine shreds.

SICHUAN NOODLES WITH SESAME SAUCE

THIS TASTY VEGETARIAN DISH RESEMBLES THAMIN LETHOK, A BURMESE DISH, WHICH ALSO CONSISTS OF FLAVOURED NOODLES SERVED WITH SEPARATE VEGETABLES THAT ARE TOSSED AT THE TABLE. THIS ILLUSTRATES NEATLY HOW RECIPES MIGRATE FROM ONE COUNTRY TO ANOTHER.

SERVES THREE TO FOUR

INGREDIENTS

450g/1lb fresh or 225g/8oz dried
  egg noodles
1/2 cucumber, sliced lengthways,
  seeded and diced
4–6 spring onions (scallions)
a bunch of radishes, about 115g/4oz
225g/8oz mooli (daikon), peeled
115g/4oz/2 cups beansprouts, rinsed
  then left in iced water and drained
60ml/4 tbsp groundnut (peanut) oil
  or sunflower oil
2 garlic cloves, crushed
45ml/3 tbsp toasted sesame paste
15ml/1 tbsp sesame oil
15ml/1 tbsp light soy sauce
5–10ml/1–2 tsp chilli sauce, to taste
15ml/1 tbsp rice vinegar
120ml/4fl oz/1/2 cup chicken stock
  or water
5ml/1 tsp sugar, or to taste
salt and ground black pepper
roasted peanuts or cashew nuts,
  to garnish

1 If using fresh noodles, cook them in boiling water for 1 minute then drain well. Rinse the noodles in fresh water and drain again. Cook dried noodles according to the instructions on the packet, draining and rinsing them as for fresh noodles.

2 Sprinkle the cucumber with salt, leave for 15 minutes, rinse well, then drain and pat dry on kitchen paper. Place in a large salad bowl.

3 Cut the spring onions into fine shreds. Cut the radishes in half and slice finely. Coarsely grate the mooli using a mandolin or a food processor. Add all the vegetables to the cucumber and toss gently.

4 Heat half the oil in a wok or frying pan and stir-fry the noodles for about 1 minute. Using a slotted spoon, transfer the noodles to a large serving bowl and keep warm.

5 Add the remaining oil to the wok. When it is hot, fry the garlic to flavour the oil. Remove from the heat and stir in the sesame paste, with the sesame oil, soy and chilli sauces, vinegar and stock or water. Add a little sugar and season to taste. Warm through over a gentle heat. Do not overheat or the sauce will thicken too much. Pour the sauce over the noodles and toss well. Garnish with peanuts or cashew nuts and serve with the vegetables.

MEE KROB

*THE NAME OF THIS DISH MEANS "DEEP-FRIED NOODLES" AND IT IS VERY POPULAR IN THAILAND.
THE TASTE IS A STUNNING COMBINATION OF SWEET AND HOT, SALTY AND SOUR, WHILE THE TEXTURE
CONTRIVES TO BE BOTH CRISP AND CHEWY. TO SOME WESTERN PALATES, IT MAY SEEM RATHER
UNUSUAL, BUT THIS DELICIOUS DISH IS WELL WORTH MAKING.*

SERVES ONE

INGREDIENTS
   vegetable oil, for deep-frying
   130g/4½oz rice vermicelli noodles
For the sauce
   30ml/2 tbsp vegetable oil
   130g/4½oz fried tofu, cut into
     thin strips
   2 garlic cloves, finely chopped
   2 small shallots, finely chopped
   15ml/1 tbsp light soy sauce
   30ml/2 tbsp palm sugar or light
     muscovado (brown) sugar
   60ml/4 tbsp vegetable stock
   juice of 1 lime
   2.5ml/½ tsp dried chilli flakes
For the garnish
   15ml/1 tbsp vegetable oil
   1 egg, lightly beaten with
     15ml/1 tbsp cold water
   25g/1oz/⅓ cup beansprouts
   1 spring onion (scallion),
     thinly shredded
   1 fresh red chilli, seeded and
     finely chopped
   1 whole head pickled garlic, sliced
     across the bulb so each slice looks
     like a flower

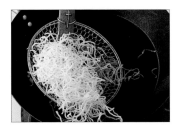

1 Heat the oil for deep-frying in a wok or large pan to 190°C/375°F or until a cube of bread, added to the oil, browns in about 45 seconds. Add the noodles and deep-fry until golden and crisp. Drain on kitchen paper and set aside.

2 Make the sauce. Heat the oil in a wok, add the fried tofu and cook over a medium heat until crisp. Using a slotted spoon, transfer it to a plate.

3 Add the garlic and shallots to the wok and cook until golden brown. Stir in the soy sauce, sugar, stock, lime juice and chilli flakes. Cook, stirring, until the mixture begins to caramelize.

4 Add the reserved tofu and stir until it has soaked up some of the liquid. Remove the wok from the heat and set aside.

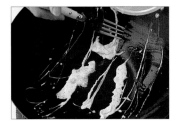

5 Prepare the egg garnish. Heat the oil in a wok or frying pan. Pour in the egg in a thin stream to form trails. As soon as it sets, lift it out with a fish slice or metal spatula and place on a plate.

6 Crumble the noodles into the tofu sauce, mix well, then spoon into warmed serving bowls. Sprinkle with the beansprouts, spring onion, fried egg strips, chilli and pickled garlic "flowers" and serve immediately.

COOK'S TIP
Successful deep-frying depends, to a large extent, on the type of oil used and the temperature to which it is heated. A bland-tasting oil, such as sunflower, will not alter the flavour of the food. All fats have a "smoke point" – the temperature at which they begin to decompose. Most vegetable oils have a high smoke point, with groundnut (peanut) oil the highest of all and so also the safest.

NOODLES AND VEGETABLES IN COCONUT SAUCE

WHEN EVERYDAY VEGETABLES ARE GIVEN THE THAI TREATMENT, THE RESULT IS A DELECTABLE DISH WHICH EVERYONE WILL ENJOY. NOODLES ADD BULK AND A WELCOME CONTRAST IN TEXTURE.

3 Increase the heat to medium, stir in the coconut milk and vegetable stock and bring to the boil. Add the broccoli florets and the noodles, lower the heat and simmer gently for 20 minutes.

4 Meanwhile, make the garnish. Split the lemon grass stalks lengthways through the root. Gather the coriander into a small bouquet and lay it on a platter, following the curve of the rim.

5 Tuck the lemon grass halves into the coriander bouquet and add the chillies to resemble flowers.

6 Stir the fish sauce, soy sauce and chopped coriander into the noodle mixture. Spoon on to the platter, taking care not to disturb the herb bouquet, and serve immediately.

SERVES FOUR TO SIX

INGREDIENTS
  30ml/2 tbsp sunflower oil
  1 lemon grass stalk, finely chopped
  15ml/1 tbsp Thai red curry paste
  1 onion, thickly sliced
  3 courgettes (zucchini), thickly sliced
  115g/4oz Savoy cabbage,
   thickly sliced
  2 carrots, thickly sliced
  150g/5oz broccoli, stem thickly
   sliced and head separated
   into florets
  2 × 400ml/14fl oz cans coconut milk
  475ml/16fl oz/2 cups vegetable stock
  150g/5oz dried egg noodles
  15ml/1 tbsp Thai fish sauce
  30ml/2 tbsp soy sauce
  60ml/4 tbsp chopped fresh
   coriander (cilantro)
For the garnish
  2 lemon grass stalks
  1 bunch fresh coriander (cilantro)
  8–10 small fresh red chillies

1 Heat the oil in a large pan or wok. Add the lemon grass and red curry paste and stir-fry for 2–3 seconds. Add the onion and cook over a medium heat, stirring occasionally, for about 5–10 minutes, until the onion has softened but not browned.

2 Add the courgettes, cabbage, carrots and slices of broccoli stem. Using two spoons, toss the vegetables with the onion mixture. Reduce the heat to low and cook gently, stirring occasionally, for a further 5 minutes.

SOUTHERN CURRIED NOODLES

CHICKEN OR PORK CAN BE USED TO PROVIDE THE PROTEIN IN THIS TASTY DISH. IT IS SO QUICK AND EASY TO PREPARE AND COOK, IT MAKES THE PERFECT SNACK FOR BUSY PEOPLE.

SERVES TWO

INGREDIENTS
    30ml/2 tbsp vegetable oil
    10ml/2 tsp magic paste
    1 lemon grass stalk, finely chopped
    5ml/1 tsp Thai red curry paste
    90g/3½oz skinless, boneless chicken
      breast portion or pork fillet
      (tenderloin), sliced into slivers
    30ml/2 tbsp light soy sauce
    400ml/14fl oz/1⅔ cups coconut milk
    2 kaffir lime leaves, rolled into
      cylinders and thinly sliced
    250g/9oz dried medium egg noodles
    90g/3½oz Chinese leaves (Chinese
      cabbage), shredded
    90g/3½oz spinach or watercress
      (leaves), shredded
    juice of 1 lime
    small bunch fresh coriander
      (cilantro), chopped

1 Heat the oil in a wok or large, heavy frying pan. Add the magic paste and lemon grass and stir-fry over a low to medium heat for 4–5 seconds, until they give off their aroma.

2 Stir in the curry paste, then add the chicken or pork. Stir-fry over a medium to high heat for 2 minutes, until the chicken or pork is coated in the paste and seared on all sides.

3 Add the soy sauce, coconut milk and sliced lime leaves. Bring to a simmer, then add the noodles. Simmer gently for 4 minutes, tossing the mixture occasionally to make sure that the noodles cook evenly.

4 Add the Chinese leaves and watercress. Stir well, then add the lime juice. Spoon into a warmed bowl, sprinkle with the coriander and serve.

CHIANG MAI NOODLES

AN INTERESTING NOODLE DISH THAT COMBINES SOFT, BOILED NOODLES WITH CRISP DEEP-FRIED ONES AND ADDS THE USUAL PANOPLY OF THAI SWEET, HOT AND SOUR FLAVOURS.

SERVES FOUR

INGREDIENTS

250ml/8fl oz/1 cup coconut cream
15ml/1 tbsp magic paste
5ml/1 tsp Thai red curry paste
450g/1lb chicken thigh meat,
   chopped into small pieces
30ml/2 tbsp dark soy sauce
2 red (bell) peppers, seeded and
   finely diced
600ml/1 pint/2½ cups chicken or
   vegetable stock
90g/3½oz fresh or dried rice noodles
For the garnishes
   vegetable oil, for deep-frying
   90g/3½oz fine dried rice noodles
   2 pickled garlic cloves, chopped
   small bunch fresh coriander
      (cilantro), chopped
   2 limes, cut into wedges

1 Pour the coconut cream into a large wok or frying pan and bring to the boil over a medium heat. Continue to boil, stirring frequently, for 8–10 minutes, until the milk separates and an oily sheen appears on the surface.

2 Add the magic paste and red curry paste and cook, stirring constantly, for 3–5 seconds, until fragrant.

3 Add the chicken and toss over the heat until sealed on all sides. Stir in the soy sauce and the diced peppers and stir-fry for 3–4 minutes. Pour in the stock. Bring to the boil, then lower the heat and simmer for 10–15 minutes, until the chicken is fully cooked.

4 Meanwhile, make the noodle garnish. Heat the oil in a pan or deep-fryer to 190°C/375°F or until a cube of bread, added to the oil, browns in 45 seconds. Break all the noodles in half, then divide them into four portions. Add one portion at a time to the hot oil. They will puff up on contact. As soon as they are crisp, lift the noodles out with a slotted spoon and drain on kitchen paper.

5 Bring a large pan of water to the boil and cook the fresh or dried noodles until tender, following the instructions on the packet. Drain well, divide among four warmed individual dishes, then spoon the curry sauce over them. Top each portion with a cluster of fried noodles. Sprinkle the chopped pickled garlic and coriander over the top and serve immediately, offering lime wedges for squeezing.

COOK'S TIP
If you are planning to serve this dish to guests, you can save on preparation time by making the noodle garnish in advance. Deep-fry the noodles a few hours before you need them and drain well on kitchen paper. Transfer the crispy noodles to a wire rack lined with fresh sheets of kitchen paper and set aside until ready to use.

THAI NOODLES WITH CHINESE CHIVES

THIS RECIPE REQUIRES A LITTLE TIME FOR PREPARATION, BUT THE COOKING TIME IS VERY FAST.
EVERYTHING IS COOKED IN A HOT WOK AND SHOULD BE EATEN IMMEDIATELY. THIS IS A FILLING
AND TASTY VEGETARIAN DISH, IDEAL FOR A WEEKEND LUNCH.

SERVES FOUR

INGREDIENTS
   350g/12oz dried rice noodles
   1cm/½in piece fresh root ginger,
     peeled and grated
   30ml/2 tbsp light soy sauce
   45ml/3 tbsp vegetable oil
   225g/8oz Quorn (mycoprotein),
     cut into small cubes
   2 garlic cloves, crushed
   1 large onion, cut into thin wedges
   115g/4oz fried tofu, thinly sliced
   1 fresh green chilli, seeded and
     thinly sliced
   175g/6oz/2 cups beansprouts
   2 large bunches garlic chives, total
     weight about 115g/4oz, cut into
     5cm/2in lengths
   50g/2oz/½ cup roasted
     peanuts, ground
   30ml/2 tbsp dark soy sauce
   30ml/2 tbsp chopped fresh coriander
     (cilantro), and 1 lemon, cut into
     wedges, to garnish

1 Place the noodles in a bowl, cover with warm water and leave to soak for 30 minutes. Drain and set aside.

2 Mix the ginger, light soy sauce and 15ml/1 tbsp of the oil in a bowl. Add the Quorn, then set aside for 10 minutes. Drain, reserving the marinade.

3 Heat 15ml/1 tbsp of the remaining oil in a frying pan and cook the garlic for a few seconds. Add the Quorn and stir-fry for 3–4 minutes. Using a slotted spoon, transfer to a plate and set aside.

4 Heat the remaining oil in the pan and stir-fry the onion for 3–4 minutes, until softened and tinged with brown. Add the tofu and chilli, stir-fry briefly and then add the noodles. Stir-fry over a medium heat for 4–5 minutes.

5 Stir in the beansprouts, garlic chives and most of the ground peanuts, reserving a little for the garnish. Stir well, then add the Quorn, the dark soy sauce and the reserved marinade.

6 When hot, spoon on to serving plates and garnish with the remaining ground peanuts, the coriander and lemon.

BAMIE GORENG

THIS FRIED NOODLE DISH IS WONDERFULLY ACCOMMODATING. YOU CAN ADD OTHER VEGETABLES,
SUCH AS MUSHROOMS, TINY PIECES OF CHAYOTE, BROCCOLI, LEEKS OR BEANSPROUTS. USE WHATEVER
IS TO HAND, BEARING IN MIND THE NEED FOR A BALANCE OF COLOURS, FLAVOURS AND TEXTURES.

SERVES SIX TO EIGHT

INGREDIENTS
    450g/1lb dried egg noodles
    2 eggs
    25g/1oz/2 tbsp butter
    90ml/6 tbsp vegetable oil
    1 chicken breast fillet, sliced
    115g/4oz pork fillet, sliced
    115g/4oz calf's liver, sliced (optional)
    2 garlic cloves, crushed
    115g/4oz peeled cooked prawns
        (shrimp)
    115g/4oz pak choi (bok choy)
    2 celery sticks, finely sliced
    4 spring onions (scallions), shredded
    about 60ml/4 tbsp chicken stock
    dark soy sauce and light soy sauce
    salt and ground black pepper
    deep-fried onions and shredded
        spring onions (scallions),
        to garnish

1 Bring a pan of lightly salted water to
the boil, add the noodles and cook them
for 3–4 minutes. Drain, rinse under cold
water and drain again. Set aside.

2 Put the eggs in a bowl, beat and add
salt and pepper to taste. Heat the butter
with 5ml/1 tsp oil in a small pan, add
the eggs and stir over a low heat until
scrambled but still quite moist. Set aside.

3 Heat the remaining oil in a wok and
fry the chicken, pork and liver (if using)
with the garlic for 2–3 minutes, until the
meat has changed colour. Add the
prawns, pak choi, sliced celery and
shredded spring onions and toss to mix.

4 Add the noodles and toss over the
heat until the prawns and noodles are
heated through and the greens are
lightly cooked. Add enough stock just to
moisten and season with dark and light
soy sauce to taste. Finally, add the
scrambled eggs and toss to mix. Spoon
on to a warmed serving platter or into
individual dishes and serve at once,
garnished with onions.

COOK'S TIP
Pak choi is similar to Swiss chard and
is available from Asian stores and large
supermarkets.

NOODLES WITH CHICKEN, PRAWNS AND HAM

THE CUISINE OF THE PHILIPPINES IS A HARMONIOUS BLEND OF MALAY, CHINESE AND SPANISH INFLUENCES. THIS RECIPE HAS CHINESE ORIGINS, AND IS KNOWN IN MALAYSIA AS PANSIT GUISADO. ANY KIND OF MEAT CAN BE COOKED WITH THE PRAWNS.

SERVES FOUR TO SIX

INGREDIENTS
285g/10oz dried egg noodles
15ml/1 tbsp vegetable oil
1 onion, chopped
1 garlic clove, crushed
2.5cm/1in piece fresh root ginger,
    peeled and grated
50g/2oz canned water chestnuts,
    drained and sliced
15ml/1 tbsp light soy sauce
30ml/2 tbsp fish sauce or chicken stock
175g/6oz cooked chicken breast, sliced
150g/5oz cooked ham, thickly sliced
225g/8oz peeled, cooked prawn
    (shrimp) tails
175g/6oz/¾ cup beansprouts
200g/7oz canned baby corn, drained
2 limes, cut into wedges, and
    shredded fresh coriander (cilantro)

1 Soak the egg noodles in a large bowl of water, and cook them according to the instructions on the packet. Drain the noodles and set aside.

2 Meanwhile, in a wok or large pan, fry the onion, garlic and ginger until soft. Add the water chestnuts, soy sauce and fish sauce or chicken stock, and the chicken and ham and prawn tails.

3 Add the noodles, beansprouts and corn. Stir-fry for 6–8 minutes. Garnish with the lime wedges and shredded coriander. Serve immediately.

COOK'S TIP
Egg noodles can be prepared in advance. Cook them up to 24 hours before they are needed, and keep them in a large bowl of cold water.

SPECIAL CHOW MEIN

ANOTHER EXAMPLE OF THE CHINESE INFLUENCE IN THAI COOKING. LAP CHEONG IS A SPECIAL AIR-DRIED CHINESE SAUSAGE AND IS AVAILABLE FROM MOST CHINESE SUPERMARKETS.

SERVES FOUR TO SIX

INGREDIENTS
  450g/1lb egg noodles
  45ml/3 tbsp vegetable oil
  2 garlic cloves, sliced
  5ml/1 tsp chopped fresh root ginger
  2 fresh red chillies, seeded
    and chopped
  2 lap cheong, total weight
    about 75g/3oz, rinsed and
    sliced (optional)
  1 chicken breast fillet, thinly
    sliced
  16 uncooked tiger prawns (jumbo
    shrimp), peeled, tails left intact,
    and deveined
  115g/4oz/2 cups green beans
  225g/8oz/2½ cups beansprouts
  small bunch garlic chives,
    about 50g/2oz
  30ml/2 tbsp soy sauce
  15ml/1 tbsp oyster sauce
  15ml/1 tbsp sesame oil
  salt and ground black pepper
  2 shredded spring onions (scallions)
    and fresh coriander (cilantro)
    leaves, to garnish

1 Cook the noodles in a large pan of boiling water, according to the instructions on the packet. Drain well.

2 Heat 15ml/1 tbsp of the oil in a wok or large frying pan and stir-fry the garlic, ginger and chillies for 2 minutes. Add the lap cheong, if using, chicken, prawns and beans. Stir-fry over a high heat for 2 minutes more, or until the chicken and prawns are cooked. Transfer the mixture to a bowl and set aside.

3 Heat the rest of the oil in the wok. Add the beansprouts and garlic chives and stir-fry for 1–2 minutes.

4 Add the drained noodles and toss over the heat to mix. Season with the soy sauce, oyster sauce and salt and pepper to taste. Return the prawn mixture to the wok. Mix well with the noodles and toss until heated through.

5 Stir the sesame oil into the noodles. Spoon into a warmed bowl and serve immediately, garnished with the spring onions and coriander leaves.

LAMB AND GINGER STIR-FRY WITH EGG NOODLES

FRESH ROOT GINGER ADDS A BRIGHT TANG TO THIS LAMB AND NOODLE DISH, GIVING IT A SIMULTANEOUSLY HOT AND YET REFRESHING TASTE.

SERVES FOUR

INGREDIENTS

45ml/3 tbsp sesame oil
3 spring onions (scallions), sliced
2 garlic cloves, crushed
2.5cm/1in piece fresh root ginger,
  peeled and finely sliced
1 red chilli, seeded and finely sliced
1 red (bell) pepper, seeded and sliced
450g/1lb lean boneless lamb, cut
  into fine strips
115g/4oz/1½ cups fresh shiitake
  mushrooms, sliced
2 carrots, cut into matchstick strips
300g/11oz fresh Chinese egg noodles
300g/11oz pak choi (bok choy),
  shredded
soy sauce, to serve

1 Heat half the oil in a wok or large frying pan. Stir-fry the spring onions and garlic for about 5 minutes, or until golden. Add the ginger, chilli and red pepper and continue stir-frying for 5 minutes, until the chilli and pepper start to soften. Use a draining spoon to remove the vegetables and set aside.

2 Add the remaining oil and stir-fry the lamb in batches until golden. Add the mushrooms and carrots and stir-fry for 2–3 minutes. Remove from the wok and set aside with the red pepper mixture. Add the noodles and pak choi to the wok and stir-fry for 5 minutes.

3 Finally, replace all the cooked ingredients and stir-fry for a couple of minutes or until the mixture is heated through. Serve at once, offering soy sauce to season at the table.

COOK'S TIP
If fresh egg noodles are not available, use the dried type. Cook them according to the packet instructions, drain and rinse under cold water, then drain well.

CELLOPHANE NOODLES <u>WITH</u> PORK

SIMPLE, SPEEDY AND SATISFYING, THIS IS AN EXCELLENT WAY OF USING MUNG BEAN NOODLES. THE DISH IS POPULAR ALL OVER THAILAND.

SERVES TWO

INGREDIENTS

200g/7oz cellophane noodles
30ml/2 tbsp vegetable oil
15ml/1 tbsp magic paste
200g/7oz minced (ground) pork
1 fresh green or red chilli, seeded
    and finely chopped
300g/11oz/3½ cups beansprouts
bunch spring onions (scallions),
    finely chopped
30ml/2 tbsp soy sauce
30ml/2 tbsp Thai fish sauce
30ml/2 tbsp sweet chilli sauce
15ml/1 tbsp palm sugar or light
    muscovado (brown) sugar
30ml/2 tbsp rice vinegar
30ml/2 tbsp roasted peanuts,
    chopped, to garnish
small bunch fresh coriander
    (cilantro), chopped, to garnish

1 Place the noodles in a large bowl, cover with boiling water and soak for 10 minutes. Drain the noodles and set aside until ready to use.

2 Heat the oil in a wok or large, heavy frying pan. Add the magic paste and stir-fry for 2–3 seconds, then add the pork. Stir-fry the meat, breaking it up with a wooden spatula, for 2–3 minutes, until browned all over.

3 Add the chopped chilli to the meat and stir-fry for 3–4 seconds, then add the beansprouts and chopped spring onions, stir-frying for a few seconds after each addition.

4 Snip the noodles into 5cm/2in lengths and add to the wok, with the soy sauce, Thai fish sauce, sweet chilli sauce, sugar and rice vinegar.

5 Toss the ingredients together over the heat until well combined and the noodles have warmed through. Pile on to a platter or into a large bowl. Sprinkle over the peanuts and coriander and serve immediately.

VARIATION

This dish is also very good made with chicken. Replace the pork with the same quantity of minced (ground) chicken.

RICE NOODLES WITH PORK

RICE NOODLES HAVE LITTLE FLAVOUR THEMSELVES BUT THEY HAVE A WONDERFUL ABILITY TO TAKE ON THE FLAVOUR OF OTHER INGREDIENTS.

SERVES FOUR TO SIX

INGREDIENTS
  450g/1lb pork fillet
  225g/8oz dried rice noodles
  115g/4oz/1 cup broccoli florets
  1 red (bell) pepper, quartered
    and seeded
  45ml/3 tbsp groundnut (peanut) oil
  2 garlic cloves, crushed
  10 spring onions (scallions), trimmed
    and cut into 5cm/2in slices
  1 lemon grass stalk, finely chopped
  1–2 fresh red chillies, seeded and
    finely chopped
  300ml/½ pint/1¼ cups coconut milk
  15ml/1 tbsp tomato purée (paste)
  3 kaffir lime leaves (optional)
For the marinade
  45ml/3 tbsp light soy sauce
  15ml/1 tbsp rice wine
  30ml/2 tbsp groundnut (peanut) oil
  2.5cm/1in piece of fresh root ginger

1 Cut the pork into strips about 2.5cm/1in long and 1cm/½in wide. Mix all the marinade ingredients in a bowl, add the pork, stir to coat and marinate for 1 hour.

2 Spread out the noodles in a shallow dish, pour over hot water to cover and soak for 20 minutes until soft. Drain. Blanch the broccoli in a small pan of boiling water for 2 minutes, then drain and refresh under cold water. Set aside.

3 Place the pepper pieces under a hot grill (broiler) for a few minutes until the skin blackens and blisters. Put in a plastic bag for about 10 minutes and then, when cool enough to handle, peel away the skin and slice the flesh thinly.

4 Drain the pork, reserving the marinade. Heat 30ml/2 tbsp of the oil in a large frying pan. Stir-fry the pork, in batches if necessary, for 3–4 minutes until the meat is tender. Transfer to a plate and keep warm.

5 Add a little more oil to the pan if necessary and fry the garlic, spring onions, lemon grass and chillies over a low to medium heat for 2–3 minutes. Add the broccoli and pepper and stir-fry for a few minutes more.

6 Stir in the reserved marinade, coconut milk and tomato purée, with the kaffir lime leaves, if using. Simmer gently until the broccoli is nearly tender, then add the pork and noodles. Toss over the heat, for 3–4 minutes until completely heated through.

CANTONESE FRIED NOODLES

Chow mein is hugely popular with the thrifty Chinese who believe in turning leftovers into tasty dishes. For this delicious dish, boiled noodles are fried to form a crispy crust, which is topped with a savoury sauce containing whatever tastes good and needs eating up.

SERVES TWO TO THREE

INGREDIENTS
225g/8oz lean beef steak or
  pork fillet (tenderloin)
225g/8oz can bamboo shoots, drained
1 leek, trimmed
25g/1oz Chinese dried mushrooms,
  soaked for 30 minutes in 120ml/
  4fl oz/¹⁄₂ cup warm water
150g/5oz Chinese leaves
  (Chinese cabbage)
450g/1lb cooked egg noodles
  (255g/8oz dried), drained well
90ml/6 tbsp vegetable oil
30ml/2 tbsp dark soy sauce
15ml/1 tbsp cornflour (cornstarch)
15ml/1 tbsp rice wine or dry sherry
5ml/1 tsp sesame oil
5ml/1 tsp caster (superfine) sugar
salt and ground black pepper

1 Slice the beef or pork, bamboo shoots and leek into matchsticks. Drain the mushrooms, reserving 90ml/6 tbsp of the soaking water. Cut off and discard the stems, then slice the caps finely. Cut the Chinese leaves into 2.5cm/1in diamond-shaped pieces and sprinkle with salt. Pat the noodles dry with kitchen paper.

2 Heat a third of the oil in a large wok or frying pan and sauté the noodles. After turning them over once, press the noodles evenly against the bottom of the pan with a wooden spatula until they form a flat, even cake. Cook over medium heat for about 4 minutes or until the noodles at the bottom have become crisp.

3 Turn the noodle cake over with a fish slice (metal spatula) or invert on to a large plate and slide back into the wok. Cook for 3 minutes more, then slide on to a heated plate. Keep warm.

4 Heat 30ml/2 tbsp of the remaining oil in the wok. Add the strips of leek, then the meat strips and stir-fry for 10–15 seconds. Sprinkle over half the soy sauce and then add the bamboo shoots and mushrooms, with salt and pepper to taste. Toss over the heat for 1 minute, then transfer this mixture to a plate and set aside.

5 Heat the remaining oil in the wok and sauté the Chinese leaves for 1 minute. Return the meat and vegetable mixture to the wok and sauté with the leaves for 30 seconds, stirring constantly.

6 Mix the cornflour with the reserved mushroom water. Stir into the wok along with the rice wine or sherry, sesame oil, sugar and remaining soy sauce. Cook for 15 seconds to thicken. Divide the noodles among 2–3 serving dishes and pile the meat and vegetables on top.

SPICY FRIED NOODLES

THIS IS A WONDERFULLY VERSATILE DISH AS YOU CAN ADAPT IT TO INCLUDE YOUR FAVOURITE
INGREDIENTS — JUST AS LONG AS YOU KEEP A BALANCE OF FLAVOURS, TEXTURES AND COLOURS.

SERVES FOUR

INGREDIENTS
    225g/8oz egg thread noodles
    60ml/4 tbsp vegetable oil
    2 garlic cloves, finely chopped
    175g/6oz pork fillet (tenderloin),
      sliced into thin strips
    1 skinless, boneless chicken breast
      portion (about 175g/6oz), sliced
      into thin strips
    115g/4oz/1 cup cooked peeled
      prawns (shrimp), rinsed if canned
    45ml/3 tbsp fresh lemon juice
    45ml/3 tbsp Thai fish sauce
    30ml/2 tbsp soft light brown sugar
    2 eggs, beaten
    ½ fresh red chilli, seeded and
      finely chopped
    50g/2oz/⅔ cup beansprouts
    60ml/4 tbsp roasted
      peanuts, chopped
    3 spring onions (scallions), cut into
      5cm/2in lengths and shredded
    45ml/3 tbsp chopped fresh
      coriander (cilantro)

1 Bring a large pan of water to the boil.
Add the noodles, remove the pan from
the heat and leave for 5 minutes.

2 Meanwhile, heat 45ml/3 tbsp of the
oil in a wok or large frying pan, add the
garlic and cook for 30 seconds. Add
the pork and chicken and stir-fry until
lightly browned, then add the prawns
and stir-fry for 2 minutes.

3 Stir in the lemon juice, then add
the fish sauce and sugar. Stir-fry
until the sugar has dissolved.

4 Drain the noodles and add to the wok
or pan with the remaining 15ml/1 tbsp
oil. Toss all the ingredients together.

5 Pour the beaten eggs over the
noodles and stir-fry until almost set,
then add the chilli and beansprouts.

6 Divide the roasted peanuts, spring
onions and coriander leaves into two
equal portions, add one portion to the
pan and stir-fry for about 2 minutes.

7 Tip the noodles on to a serving platter.
Sprinkle on the remaining roasted
peanuts, spring onions and chopped
coriander and serve immediately.

COOK'S TIP
Store beansprouts in the refrigerator and
use within a day of purchase, as they
tend to lose their crispness and become
slimy and unpleasant quite quickly. The
most commonly used beansprouts are
sprouted mung beans, but you could use
other types of beansprouts instead.

CHAP CHAE

*A KOREAN STIR-FRY OF MIXED VEGETABLES AND NOODLES GARNISHED ATTRACTIVELY WITH THE
YELLOW AND WHITE EGG SHAPES THAT ARE SO TYPICALLY KOREAN.*

SERVES FOUR

INGREDIENTS

225g/8oz rump (round) or
   sirloin steak
115g/4oz cellophane noodles, soaked
   for 20 minutes in hot water to cover
4 Chinese dried mushrooms, soaked
   for 30 minutes in warm water
groundnut (peanut) oil, for stir-frying
2 eggs, separated
1 carrot, cut into matchsticks
1 onion, sliced
2 courgettes (zucchini) or ½
   cucumber, cut into sticks
½ red (bell) pepper, seeded and cut
   into strips
4 button mushrooms, sliced
75g/3oz/1½ cups beansprouts,
   washed and drained
15ml/1 tbsp light soy sauce
salt and ground black pepper
sliced spring onions (scallions) and
   sesame seeds, to garnish

1 Put the steak in the freezer until it is
firm enough to cut into 5cm/2in strips.

2 Mix the ingredients for the marinade
in a shallow dish (see Cook's Tip) and
stir in the steak strips. Drain the noodles
and cook them in boiling water for 5
minutes. Drain again, then snip into
short lengths. Drain the mushrooms, cut
off and discard the stems; slice the caps.

3 Prepare the garnish. Heat the oil in
a small frying pan. Beat the egg yolks
together and pour into the pan. When
set, slide them on to a plate. Add the
egg whites to the pan and cook until
set. Cut both yolks and whites into
diamond shapes and set aside.

COOK'S TIP
To make the marinade, blend together
15ml/1 tbsp sugar, 30ml/2 tbsp light soy
sauce, 45ml/3 tbsp sesame oil, 4 finely
chopped spring onions, 1 crushed garlic
clove and 10ml/2 tsp crushed toasted
sesame seeds.

4 Drain the beef. Heat the oil in a wok
or large frying pan and stir-fry the beef
until it changes colour. Add the carrot
and onion and stir-fry for 2 minutes,
then add the other vegetables, tossing
them until just cooked.

5 Add the noodles and season with
soy sauce, salt and pepper. Cook for
1 minute. Spoon into a serving dish
and garnish with egg, spring onions
and sesame seeds.

SUKIYAKI

YOU WILL NEED A SPECIAL CAST-IRON SUKIYAKI PAN (SUKIYAKI-NABE) AND BURNER OR A SIMILAR TABLE-TOP COOKER FOR THIS DISH. IT IS GREAT FUN BECAUSE GUESTS CAN COOK THEIR OWN DINNER IN FRONT OF THEM, AND THEN HELP THEMSELVES TO THE DELICIOUS MORSELS OF FOOD.

SERVES FOUR

INGREDIENTS
  1kg/2¼lb beef topside (pot roast),
    thinly sliced
  lard or white cooking fat,
    for cooking
  4 leeks or spring onions (scallions),
    sliced into 1cm/½in pieces
  bunch of shungiku leaves, stems
    removed, chopped (optional)
  bunch of enoki mushrooms, brown
    roots cut off (optional)
  8 shiitake mushrooms,
    stems removed
  300g/11oz shirataki noodles, boiled
    for 2 minutes, drained and halved
  2 pieces grilled (broiled) tofu, about
    10 × 7cm/4 × 2¾in, cut into
    3cm/1¼in cubes
  4 fresh eggs, to serve
For the sukiyaki stock
  100ml/3½fl oz/scant ½ cup mirin
    (sweet rice wine)
  45ml/3 tbsp sugar
  105ml/7 tbsp Japanese soy sauce
For the seasoning mix
  200ml/7fl oz/scant 1 cup dashi
    (kombu and bonito stock) or
    instant dashi
  100ml/3½fl oz/scant ½ cup sake
    or dry white wine
  15ml/1 tbsp Japanese soy sauce

1 Make the sukiyaki stock. Pour the mirin into a pan and bring to the boil. Stir in the sugar and soy sauce, bring to the boil, then remove from the heat and set aside.

2 To make the seasoning mix, heat the dashi, sake or wine and soy sauce in a small pan. As soon as the mixture boils, remove from the heat and set aside.

3 Fan out the beef slices on a large serving plate. Put the lard for cooking on the same plate. Arrange all the remaining ingredients, except the eggs, on one or more large plates.

4 Stand the portable cooker on a suitably heavy mat to protect the dining table and ensure that it can be heated safely. Melt the lard, add three or four slices of beef and some leeks or spring onions, and then pour in the sukiyaki stock. Gradually add the remaining ingredients, except the eggs.

5 Place each egg in a ramekin and beat lightly with chopsticks. Place one before each diner. When the beef and vegetables are cooked, diners help themselves to whatever they fancy, dipping their chosen piece of meat, vegetable or grilled tofu in the raw egg before eating.

6 When the stock has thickened, gradually stir in the seasoning mix and carry on cooking until all the ingredients have been eaten.

THAI CRISPY NOODLES WITH BEEF

RICE VERMICELLI IS DEEP-FRIED BEFORE BEING ADDED TO THIS DISH, AND IN THE PROCESS THE
VERMICELLI EXPANDS TO AT LEAST FOUR TIMES ITS ORIGINAL SIZE.

SERVES FOUR

INGREDIENTS
  450g/1lb rump (round) steak
  teriyaki sauce, for brushing
  175g/6oz rice vermicelli
  groundnut (peanut) oil, for deep-
    frying and stir-frying
  8 spring onions (scallions),
    diagonally sliced
  2 garlic cloves, crushed
  4–5 carrots, cut into julienne strips
  1–2 fresh red chillies, seeded and
    finely sliced
  2 small courgettes (zucchini),
    diagonally sliced
  5ml/1 tsp grated fresh root ginger
  60ml/4 tbsp rice vinegar
  90ml/6 tbsp light soy sauce
  about 475ml/16fl oz/2 cups
    spicy stock

1 Beat the steak to about 2.5cm/1in
thick. Place in a shallow dish, brush
generously with the teriyaki sauce and
set aside for 2–4 hours to marinate.

2 Separate the rice vermicelli into
manageable loops. Pour oil into a large
wok to a depth of about 5cm/2in, and
heat until a strand of vermicelli cooks
as soon as it is lowered into the oil.

3 Carefully add a loop of vermicelli to
the oil. Almost immediately, turn to cook
on the other side, then remove and
drain on kitchen paper. Repeat with the
remaining loops. Transfer the cooked
noodles to a separate wok or deep
serving bowl and keep them warm while
you cook the steak and vegetables.

4 Strain the oil from the wok into a
heatproof bowl and set it aside. Heat
15ml/1 tbsp groundnut oil in the clean
wok. When it sizzles, fry the steak for
about 30 seconds on each side, until
browned. Transfer to a board and cut
into thick slices. The meat should be
well browned on the outside but still
pink inside. Set aside.

5 Add a little extra oil to the wok, add
the spring onions, garlic and carrots
and stir-fry over a medium heat for
5–6 minutes, until the carrots are
slightly soft and have a glazed
appearance. Add the chillies, courgettes
and ginger and stir-fry for 1–2 minutes.

6 Stir in the rice vinegar, soy sauce and
stock. Cook for 4 minutes, or until the
sauce has thickened slightly. Return the
slices of steak to the wok and cook for
a further 1–2 minutes.

7 Spoon the steak, vegetables and
sauce over the noodles and toss lightly
and carefully to mix. Serve immediately.

COOK'S TIP
As soon as you add the meat mixture to
the noodles, they will begin to soften
in the sauce. If you wish to keep a few
crispy noodles, leave some on the
surface so that they do not come into
contact with the hot liquid.

MIXED MEAT FRIED NOODLES WITH PRAWNS

THIS FRIED NOODLE DISH, KNOWN AS BAMIE GORENG, IS WONDERFULLY ACCOMMODATING. TO THE BASIC RECIPE YOU CAN ADD OTHER VEGETABLES, SUCH AS MUSHROOMS, TINY PIECES OF CHAYOTE, BROCCOLI, LEEKS OR BEANSPROUTS. AS WITH FRIED RICE, YOU CAN USE WHATEVER YOU HAVE TO HAND.

SERVES SIX TO EIGHT

INGREDIENTS
450g/1lb dried egg noodles
115g/4oz skinless chicken
  breast fillets
115g/4oz pork fillet (tenderloin)
115g/4oz calf's liver (optional)
2 eggs, beaten
90ml/6 tbsp vegetable oil
25g/1oz butter or margarine
2 garlic cloves, crushed
115g/4oz peeled, cooked
  prawns (shrimp)
115g/4oz spinach or Chinese leaves
  (Chinese cabbage)
2 celery sticks, finely sliced
4 spring onions (scallions), shredded
60ml/4 tbsp chicken stock
dark soy sauce and light soy sauce
salt and ground black pepper
Deep-fried Onions and celery leaves,
  to garnish (optional)

1 Cook the noodles in salted, boiling water for 3–4 minutes. Drain, rinse with cold water and drain again. Set aside until required.

2 Finely slice the chicken, pork fillet and calf's liver, if using. Season the eggs. Heat 5ml/1 tsp oil with the butter or margarine in a small pan until melted and then stir in the eggs and keep stirring until scrambled. Set them aside.

3 Heat the remaining oil in a wok or large pan and fry the garlic with the chicken, pork and liver, if using, for 2–3 minutes, until they change colour. Add the prawns, spinach or Chinese leaves, celery and spring onions, tossing them together well.

4 Add the cooked, drained noodles and toss well again so that all the ingredients are well mixed. Add enough stock just to moisten, and dark and light soy sauce to taste. Stir in the beaten eggs. Garnish the dish with Deep-fried Onions and celery leaves.

COOK'S TIP
When choosing ingredients for this dish, bear in mind the need to achieve a balance of colour, flavour and texture.

CRISPY FRIED RICE VERMICELLI

THIS VERSION OF THE POPULAR CELEBRATORY DISH MEE KROB CONTAINS PORK AND PRAWNS. THE CRISP TANGLE OF FRIED RICE VERMICELLI IS TOSSED IN A PIQUANT GARLIC, SWEET AND SOUR SAUCE.

SERVES FOUR TO SIX

INGREDIENTS
  vegetable oil, for deep frying
  175g/6oz rice vermicelli
  15ml/1 tbsp chopped garlic
  4–6 small dried red chillies
  30ml/2 tbsp chopped shallots
  15ml/1 tbsp dried shrimps, rinsed
  115g/4oz minced (ground) pork
  115g/4oz raw peeled prawns
    (shrimp), thawed if frozen,
    chopped
  30ml/2 tbsp brown bean sauce
  30ml/2 tbsp rice wine vinegar
  45ml/3 tbsp nam pla (fish sauce)
  75g/3oz palm sugar
  30ml/2 tbsp tamarind or lime juice
  115g/4oz/2 cups beansprouts
For the garnish
  2 spring onions (scallions), shredded
  30ml/2 tbsp fresh coriander
    (cilantro) leaves
  2-egg omelette, rolled and sliced
  2 fresh red chillies, seeded and cut
    into thin strips

1 Heat the oil in a wok. Cut or break the rice vermicelli into small handfuls about 7.5cm/3in long. Deep fry these for a few seconds in the hot oil until they puff up. Lift out with a slotted spoon and drain on kitchen paper.

VARIATION

Pickled garlic can also be used as one of the garnish ingredients. Thai garlic is smaller than European garlic; the heads are pickled whole, in sweet and sour brine.

2 Ladle off all but 30ml/2 tbsp of the oil, pouring it into a pan and setting aside to cool. Reheat the oil in the wok and fry the garlic, chillies, shallots and shrimps for about 1 minute.

3 Add the pork and stir-fry for 3–4 minutes, until no longer pink. Add the prawns and fry for 2 minutes. Spoon into a bowl and set aside.

4 Add the brown bean sauce, vinegar, nam pla and sugar. Heat gently, stirring in any sediment. Bring to a gentle boil, stir to dissolve the sugar and cook until thick and syrupy.

5 Add the tamarind or lime juice to the sauce and adjust the seasoning as necessary. The sauce should be sweet, sour and salty. Lower the heat, then return the pork and prawn mixture to the wok, add the beansprouts and stir them into the sauce.

6 Add the fried rice noodles to the wok and toss gently to coat them with the sauce without breaking them up too much. Transfer the mixture to a large, warm serving platter or individual serving dishes. Garnish with the shredded spring onions, coriander leaves, omelette strips and fresh red chillies and serve immediately.

COOK'S TIP

Always deep fry rice vermicelli in small quantities, as it puffs up to two or three times its original volume. It cooks in seconds, so be ready to remove from the wok using a slotted spoon or wire basket as soon as it is puffy and before it takes on any colour.

STIR-FRIED NOODLES IN SEAFOOD SAUCE

THE CHINESE WOULD HAVE US BELIEVE THAT IT WAS THEY WHO INVENTED PASTA, SO IT SEEMS APPROPRIATE TO INCLUDE A CHINESE-STYLE PASTA DISH.

SERVES SIX TO EIGHT

INGREDIENTS

225g/8oz Chinese egg noodles
8 spring onions (scallions), trimmed
8 asparagus spears, plus extra
   steamed asparagus spears, to
   serve (optional)
30ml/2 tbsp stir-fry oil
5cm/2in piece fresh root ginger,
   peeled and cut into very fine
   matchsticks
3 garlic cloves, chopped
60ml/4 tbsp oyster sauce
450g/1lb cooked crab meat (all
   white, or two-thirds white and
   one-third brown)
30ml/2 tbsp rice wine vinegar
15–30ml/1–2 tbsp light
   soy sauce

1 Put the noodles in a large pan or wok, cover with lightly salted boiling water, place a lid on top and leave for 3–4 minutes, or for the time suggested on the packet. Drain and set aside.

2 Cut off the green spring onion tops and slice them thinly. Set aside. Cut the white parts into 2cm/¾in lengths and quarter them lengthways. Cut the asparagus spears on the diagonal into 2cm/¾in pieces.

3 Heat the stir-fry oil in a pan or wok until very hot, then add the ginger, garlic and white spring onion batons. Stir-fry over a high heat for 1 minute. Add the oyster sauce, crab meat, rice wine vinegar and soy sauce to taste. Stir-fry for about 2 minutes, until the crab and sauce are hot. Add the noodles and toss until heated through. At the last moment, toss in the spring onion tops and serve with a few extra asparagus spears, if you like.

STIR-FRIED NOODLES WITH SOY SALMON

TERIYAKI SAUCE FORMS THE MARINADE FOR THE SALMON IN THIS RECIPE. SERVED WITH SOFT-FRIED NOODLES, IT MAKES A STUNNING DISH.

SERVES FOUR

INGREDIENTS
- 350g/12oz salmon fillet, skinned
- 30ml/2 tbsp shoyu (Japanese soy sauce)
- 30ml/2 tbsp sake
- 60ml/4 tbsp mirin or sweet sherry
- 5ml/1 tsp soft light brown sugar
- 10ml/2 tsp grated fresh root ginger
- 3 garlic cloves, 1 crushed, and 2 sliced into rounds
- 30ml/2 tbsp groundnut (peanut) oil
- 225g/8oz dried egg noodles, cooked and drained
- 50g/2oz/1 cup alfalfa sprouts
- 30ml/2 tbsp sesame seeds, lightly toasted

1 Using a sharp cook's knife, slice the salmon thinly. Spread out the slices in a large, shallow dish, keeping them in a single layer if possible.

2 In a bowl, mix together the soy sauce, sake, mirin or sherry, sugar, ginger and crushed garlic. Pour over the salmon, cover and leave for 30 minutes.

3 Preheat the grill (broiler). Drain the salmon, reserving the marinade. Place the salmon in a layer on a baking sheet. Cook under the grill for 2–3 minutes.

4 Meanwhile, heat a wok until hot, add the oil and swirl it around. Add the garlic rounds and cook until golden brown. Remove the garlic and discard.

5 Add the cooked noodles and reserved marinade to the wok and stir-fry for 3–4 minutes until the marinade has reduced to a syrupy glaze and coats the noodles.

6 Toss in the alfalfa sprouts. Transfer immediately to warmed serving plates and top with the salmon. Sprinkle over the toasted sesame seeds. Serve at once.

THAI FRIED NOODLES

PHAT THAI HAS A FASCINATING FLAVOUR AND TEXTURE. IT IS MADE WITH RICE NOODLES AND IS CONSIDERED ONE OF THE NATIONAL DISHES OF THAILAND.

SERVES FOUR TO SIX

INGREDIENTS
  16 raw tiger prawns
    (jumbo shrimp)
  350g/12oz rice noodles
  45ml/3 tbsp vegetable oil
  15ml/1 tbsp chopped garlic
  2 eggs, lightly beaten
  15ml/1 tbsp dried
    shrimp, rinsed
  30ml/2 tbsp pickled
    mooli (daikon)
  50g/2oz fried tofu, cut into
    small slivers
  2.5ml/½ tsp dried chilli flakes
  1 large bunch garlic chives,
    about 115g/4oz, cut into
    5cm/2in lengths
  225g/8oz/2½ cups beansprouts
  50g/2oz/½ cup roasted peanuts,
    coarsely ground
  5ml/1 tsp granulated sugar
  15ml/1 tbsp dark soy sauce
  30ml/2 tbsp Thai fish sauce
  30ml/2 tbsp tamarind juice, made
    by mixing tamarind paste with
    warm water
To garnish
  fresh coriander (cilantro) leaves
  lime wedges

1 Peel the prawns, leaving the tails intact. Carefully cut along the back of each prawn and remove the dark vein.

2 Place the rice noodles in a large bowl, add warm water to cover and leave to soak for 20–30 minutes, then drain thoroughly and set aside.

3 Heat 15ml/1 tbsp of the oil in a wok. Stir-fry the garlic until golden. Stir in the prawns and cook for 1–2 minutes, until pink. Remove and set aside.

4 Heat 15ml/1 tbsp of the remaining oil in the wok. Add the eggs and tilt the wok to make a thin layer. Stir to scramble and break up. Remove from the wok and set aside with the prawns.

5 Heat the remaining oil in the same wok. Add the dried shrimp, pickled mooli, tofu slivers and dried chilli flakes. Stir briefly. Add the noodles and stir-fry for about 5 minutes.

6 Add the garlic chives, half the beansprouts and half the peanuts. Add the granulated sugar, then season with soy sauce, fish sauce and tamarind juice. Mix well and cook until the noodles are heated through.

7 Return the prawn and egg mixture to the wok and mix with the noodles. Serve topped with the remaining beansprouts and peanuts, and garnished with the coriander leaves and lime wedges.

COOK'S TIP
There are numerous species of prawns (shrimp) and they range in colour from black to white, although most turn pink when cooked. Genuine Indo-Pacific tiger prawns, of which there are several types, have a fine flavour and a good texture. They grow up to 28cm/11in in length. However, not all large, warm water varieties are so succulent, and even farmed prawns tend to be quite expensive.

SIDE DISHES AND ACCOMPANIMENTS

Strictly speaking, a traditional Asian meal consists of several

dishes, rather than a main dish served with side dishes.

However, to make menu-planning easier, this chapter contains

a selection of vegetable dishes that go particularly well with

the meat, poultry, fish and vegetable dishes. Their classic

combinations of crisp textures and sweet, sharp, spicy and

aromatic flavours provide a refreshing complement and perfect

balance to the curries and main dishes included in this book.

BROCCOLI <u>WITH</u> SOY SAUCE

A WONDERFULLY SIMPLE DISH THAT YOU WILL WANT TO MAKE AGAIN AND AGAIN. THE BROCCOLI COOKS IN NEXT TO NO TIME, SO DON'T START COOKING UNTIL YOU ARE ALMOST READY TO EAT.

2 Bring a pan of lightly salted water to the boil. Add the broccoli and cook for 3–4 minutes until tender but still crisp.

3 Drain the broccoli thoroughly and arrange in a heated serving dish.

SERVES FOUR

INGREDIENTS
   450g/1lb broccoli
   15ml/1 tbsp vegetable oil
   2 garlic cloves, crushed
   30ml/2 tbsp light soy sauce
   salt
   fried garlic slices, to garnish

VARIATION
Most leafy vegetables taste delicious prepared this way. Try blanched cos or romaine lettuce and you may be surprised at how crisp and clean the taste is.

1 Trim the thick stems of the broccoli; cut the head into large florets.

4 Heat the oil in a small pan. Fry the garlic for 2 minutes to release the flavour, then remove it with a slotted spoon. Pour the oil carefully over the broccoli, taking care as it will splatter. Drizzle the soy sauce over the broccoli, sprinkle over the fried garlic and serve.

STIR-FRIED BEANSPROUTS

THIS FRESH, CRUNCHY VEGETABLE, WHICH IS SYNONYMOUS WITH CHINESE RESTAURANTS, TASTES MUCH BETTER WHEN STIR-FRIED AT HOME.

SERVES FOUR

INGREDIENTS

15ml/1 tbsp vegetable oil
1 garlic clove, finely chopped
5ml/1 tsp grated fresh root ginger
1 small carrot, cut into matchsticks
50g/2oz/½ cup drained, canned
  bamboo shoots, cut into matchsticks
450g/1lb/8 cups beansprouts
2.5ml/½ tsp salt
large pinch of ground white pepper
15ml/1 tbsp dry sherry
15ml/1 tbsp light soy sauce
2.5ml/½ tsp sesame oil

3 Add the beansprouts to the pan or wok with the salt and pepper. Drizzle over the sherry and toss the beansprouts over the heat for 3 minutes until hot.

4 Sprinkle over the soy sauce and sesame oil, toss to mix thoroughly, then serve immediately.

1 Heat the vegetable oil in a non-stick frying pan or wok. Add the chopped garlic and grated ginger and stir-fry for a few minutes.

2 Add the carrot and bamboo shoot matchsticks to the pan or wok and stir-fry for a few minutes.

COOK'S TIP
Beansprouts keep best when stored in the refrigerator or other cool place in a bowl of cold water, but you must remember to change the water daily.

STIR-FRIED CHINESE LEAVES

THIS SIMPLE WAY OF COOKING CHINESE LEAVES PRESERVES THEIR DELICATE FLAVOUR AND IS VERY QUICK TO PREPARE.

SERVES FOUR

INGREDIENTS
    675g/1½ lb Chinese leaves
    (Chinese cabbage)
    15ml/1 tbsp vegetable oil
    2 garlic cloves, finely chopped
    2.5 m/1in piece of fresh root ginger,
    finely chopped
    2.5ml/½ tsp salt
    15ml/1 tbsp oyster sauce
    4 spring onions (scallions), cut into
    2.5cm/1in lengths

1 Stack the Chinese leaves together and cut them into 2.5cm/1in slices.

2 Heat the oil in a wok or large deep pan. Stir-fry the garlic and ginger for 1 minute.

3 Add the Chinese leaves to the wok or pan and stir-fry for 2 minutes. Sprinkle the salt over and drizzle with the oyster sauce. Toss the leaves over the heat for 2 minutes more.

4 Stir in the spring onions. Toss the mixture well, transfer it to a heated serving plate and serve.

COOK'S TIP
For guests who are vegetarian, substitute 15 ml/1 tbsp light soy sauce and 5 ml/ 1 tsp of caster (superfine) sugar for the oyster sauce.

SAUTÉED GREEN BEANS

THE SMOKY FLAVOUR OF THE DRIED SHRIMPS USED IN THIS RECIPE ADDS AN EXTRA DIMENSION TO GREEN BEANS COOKED IN THIS WAY.

SERVES FOUR

INGREDIENTS
    450g/1lb green beans
    15ml/1 tbsp vegetable oil
    3 garlic cloves, finely chopped
    5 spring onions (scallions), cut into
      2.5cm/1in lengths
    25g/1oz dried shrimps, soaked in
      warm water and drained
    15ml/1 tbsp light soy sauce
    salt

1 Trim the green beans. Cut each green bean in half.

2 Bring a pan of lightly salted water to the boil and cook the beans for 3–4 minutes until tender but still crisp. Drain, refresh under cold water and drain again.

COOK'S TIP
Don't be tempted to use too many dried shrimps. Their flavour is very strong and could overwhelm the more delicate taste of the beans.

3 Heat the oil in a non-stick frying pan or wok until very hot. Stir-fry the garlic and spring onions for 30 seconds, then add the shrimps. Mix lightly.

4 Add the green beans and soy sauce. Toss the mixture over the heat until the beans are hot. Serve immediately.

SICHUAN SPICED AUBERGINE

THIS STRAIGHTFORWARD YET VERSATILE VEGETARIAN DISH CAN BE SERVED HOT, WARM OR COLD, AS THE OCCASION DEMANDS. TOPPED WITH A SPRINKLING OF TOASTED SESAME SEEDS, IT IS EASY TO PREPARE AND TASTES ABSOLUTELY DELICIOUS.

SERVES FOUR TO SIX

INGREDIENTS
    2 aubergines (eggplant), total
      weight about 600g/1lb 6oz, cut
      into large chunks
    15ml/1 tbsp salt
    5ml/1 tsp chilli powder or to taste
    75–90ml/5–6 tbsp sunflower oil
    15ml/1 tbsp rice wine or
      medium-dry sherry
    100ml/3½fl oz/scant ½ cup water
    75ml/5 tbsp chilli bean sauce
      (see Cook's Tip)
    salt and ground black pepper
    a few toasted sesame seeds,
      to garnish

1 Place the aubergine chunks on a plate, sprinkle them with the salt and leave to stand for 15–20 minutes. Rinse well, drain and dry thoroughly on kitchen paper. Toss the aubergine cubes in the chilli powder.

2 Heat a wok and add the oil. When the oil is hot, add the aubergine chunks, with the rice wine or sherry. Stir constantly until the aubergine chunks start to turn a little brown. Stir in the water, cover the wok and steam for 2–3 minutes. Add the chilli bean sauce and cook for 2 minutes. Season to taste, then spoon on to a serving dish, scatter with sesame seeds and serve.

COOK'S TIP
If you can't get hold of chilli bean sauce, use 15–30ml/1–2 tbsp chilli paste mixed with 2 crushed garlic cloves, 15ml/1 tbsp each of dark soy sauce and rice vinegar, and 10ml/2 tsp light soy sauce.

KAN SHAO GREEN BEANS

A PARTICULAR STYLE OF COOKING FROM SICHUAN, KAN SHAO MEANS "DRY-COOKED" – IN OTHER WORDS USING NO STOCK OR WATER. THE SLIM GREEN BEANS AVAILABLE ALL THE YEAR ROUND FROM SUPERMARKETS ARE IDEAL FOR USE IN THIS QUICK AND TASTY RECIPE.

SERVES SIX

INGREDIENTS
    175ml/6fl oz/¾ cup sunflower oil
    450/1lb fresh green beans, topped,
      tailed and cut in half
    5 × 1cm/2 × ½in piece fresh
      root ginger, peeled and cut
      into matchsticks
    5ml/1 tsp sugar
    10ml/2 tsp light soy sauce
    salt and ground black pepper

VARIATION
This simple recipe works just as well with other fresh green vegetables such as baby asparagus spears and okra.

1 Heat the oil in a wok. When the oil is just beginning to smoke, carefully add the beans and stir-fry them for 1–2 minutes until just tender.

2 Lift out the green beans on to a plate lined with kitchen paper. Using a ladle carefully remove all but 30ml/2 tbsp oil from the wok.

3 Reheat the remaining oil, add the ginger and stir-fry for a minute or two to flavour the oil.

4 Return the green beans to the wok, stir in the sugar, soy sauce and salt and pepper, and toss together quickly to ensure the beans are well coated. Serve the beans at once.

FRAGRANT MUSHROOMS IN LETTUCE LEAVES

THIS QUICK AND EASY VEGETABLE DISH IS SERVED ON LETTUCE LEAF "SAUCERS" SO CAN BE EATEN WITH THE FINGERS — A GREAT TREAT FOR CHILDREN.

SERVES TWO

INGREDIENTS

30ml/2 tbsp vegetable oil
2 garlic cloves, finely chopped
2 baby cos or romaine lettuces,
   or 2 Little Gem (Bibb) lettuces
1 lemon grass stalk, finely chopped
2 kaffir lime leaves, rolled in
   cylinders and thinly sliced
200g/7oz/3 cups oyster or chestnut
   mushrooms, sliced
1 small fresh red chilli, seeded
   and finely chopped
juice of ½ lemon
30ml/2 tbsp light soy sauce
5ml/1 tsp palm sugar or light
   muscovado (brown) sugar
small bunch fresh mint, leaves
   removed from the stalks

1 Heat the oil in a wok or frying pan. Add the garlic and cook over a medium heat, stirring occasionally, until golden. Do not let it burn or it will taste bitter.

2 Meanwhile, separate the individual lettuce leaves and set aside.

3 Increase the heat under the wok or pan and add the lemon grass, lime leaves and sliced mushrooms. Stir-fry for about 2 minutes.

4 Add the chilli, lemon juice, soy sauce and sugar to the wok or pan. Toss the mixture over the heat to combine the ingredients together, then stir-fry for a further 2 minutes.

5 Arrange the lettuce leaves on a large plate. Spoon a small amount of the mushroom mixture on to each leaf, top with a mint leaf and serve.

THAI ASPARAGUS

THIS IS AN EXCITINGLY DIFFERENT WAY OF COOKING ASPARAGUS. THE CRUNCHY TEXTURE IS RETAINED AND THE FLAVOUR IS COMPLEMENTED BY THE ADDITION OF GALANGAL AND CHILLI.

<u>SERVES FOUR</u>

INGREDIENTS

   350g/12oz asparagus stalks
   30ml/2 tbsp vegetable oil
   1 garlic clove, crushed
   15ml/1 tbsp sesame seeds, toasted
   2.5cm/1in piece fresh galangal,
     finely shredded
   1 fresh red chilli, seeded and
     finely chopped
   15ml/1 tbsp Thai fish sauce
   15ml/1 tbsp light soy sauce
   45ml/3 tbsp water
   5ml/1 tsp palm sugar or light
     muscovado (brown) sugar

VARIATIONS
Try this with broccoli or pak choi (bok choy). The sauce also works very well with green beans.

1 Snap the asparagus stalks. They will break naturally at the junction between the woody base and the more tender portion of the stalk. Discard the woody parts of the stems.

2 Heat the oil in a wok and stir-fry the garlic, sesame seeds and galangal for 3–4 seconds, until the garlic is just beginning to turn golden.

3 Add the asparagus stalks and chilli, toss to mix, then add the fish sauce, soy sauce, water and sugar. Using two spoons, toss over the heat for a further 2 minutes, or until the asparagus just begins to soften and the liquid is reduced by half.

4 Carefully transfer to a warmed platter and serve immediately.

PAK CHOI WITH LIME DRESSING

THE COCONUT DRESSING FOR THIS THAI SPECIALITY IS TRADITIONALLY MADE USING FISH SAUCE, BUT VEGETARIANS COULD USE MUSHROOM SAUCE INSTEAD. BEWARE, THIS IS A FIERY DISH!

SERVES FOUR

INGREDIENTS
  30ml/2 tbsp oil
  3 fresh red chillies, cut into
    thin strips
  4 garlic cloves, thinly sliced
  6 spring onions (scallions),
    sliced diagonally
  2 pak choi (bok choy), shredded
  15ml/1 tbsp crushed peanuts
For the dressing
  30ml/2 tbsp fresh lime juice
  15–30ml/1–2 tbsp Thai fish sauce
  250ml/8fl oz/1 cup coconut milk

1 Make the dressing. Put the lime juice and fish sauce in a bowl and mix well together, then gradually whisk in the coconut milk until combined.

2 Heat the oil in a wok and stir-fry the chillies for 2–3 minutes, until crisp. Transfer to a plate using a slotted spoon. Add the garlic to the wok and stir-fry for 30–60 seconds, until golden brown. Transfer to the plate.

3 Stir-fry the white parts of the spring onions for about 2–3 minutes, then add the green parts and stir-fry for 1 minute more. Transfer to the plate.

4 Bring a large pan of lightly salted water to the boil and add the pak choi. Stir twice, then drain immediately.

5 Place the pak choi in a large bowl, add the dressing and toss to mix. Spoon into a large serving bowl and sprinkle with the crushed peanuts and the stir-fried chilli mixture. Serve warm or cold.

VARIATION
If you don't like particularly spicy food, substitute red (bell) pepper strips for some or all of the chillies.

STEAMED MORNING GLORY <u>WITH</u> FRIED GARLIC <u>AND</u> SHALLOTS

MORNING GLORY GOES BY VARIOUS NAMES, INCLUDING WATER SPINACH, WATER CONVOLVULUS AND SWAMP CABBAGE. IT IS A GREEN LEAFY VEGETABLE WITH LONG JOINTED STEMS AND ARROW-SHAPED LEAVES. THE STEMS REMAIN CRUNCHY WHILE THE LEAVES WILT LIKE SPINACH WHEN COOKED.

SERVES FOUR

INGREDIENTS
   2 bunches morning glory, total weight
      about 250g/9oz, trimmed and
      coarsely chopped into 2.5cm/
      1in lengths
   30ml/2 tbsp vegetable oil
   4 shallots, thinly sliced
   6 large garlic cloves, thinly sliced
   sea salt
   1.5ml/¼ tsp dried chilli flakes

VARIATIONS
Use spinach instead of morning glory, or
substitute young spring greens (collards),
sprouting broccoli or Swiss chard.

1 Place the morning glory in a steamer
and steam over a pan of boiling water
for 30 seconds, until just wilted. If
necessary, cook it in batches. Place the
leaves in a bowl or spread them out on
a large serving plate.

2 Heat the oil in a wok and stir-fry the
shallots and garlic over a medium to
high heat until golden. Spoon the
mixture over the morning glory, sprinkle
with a little sea salt and the chilli flakes
and serve immediately.

STIR-FRIED PINEAPPLE WITH GINGER

THIS DISH MAKES AN INTERESTING ACCOMPANIMENT TO GRILLED MEAT OR STRONGLY-FLAVOURED FISH SUCH AS TUNA OR SWORDFISH. IF THE IDEA SEEMS STRANGE, THINK OF IT AS RESEMBLING A FRESH MANGO CHUTNEY, BUT WITH PINEAPPLE AS THE PRINCIPAL INGREDIENT.

SERVES FOUR

INGREDIENTS

1 pineapple
15ml/1 tbsp vegetable oil
2 garlic cloves, finely chopped
2 shallots, finely chopped
5cm/2in piece fresh root ginger,
   peeled and finely shredded
30ml/2 tbsp light soy sauce
juice of ½ lime
1 large fresh red chilli, seeded and
   finely shredded

VARIATION

This also tastes excellent if peaches or nectarines are substituted for the diced pineapple. Use three or four, depending on their size.

1 Trim and peel the pineapple. Cut out the core and dice the flesh.

2 Heat the oil in a wok or frying pan. Stir-fry the garlic and shallots over a medium heat for 2–3 minutes, until golden. Do not let the garlic burn or the dish will taste bitter.

3 Add the pineapple. Stir-fry for about 2 minutes, or until the pineapple cubes start to turn golden on the edges.

4 Add the ginger, soy sauce, lime juice and chopped chilli. Toss together until well mixed. Cook over a low heat for a further 2 minutes, then serve.

SOUTHERN-STYLE YAM

THE FOOD OF THE SOUTHERN REGION IS NOTORIOUSLY HOT AND BECAUSE OF THE PROXIMITY TO THE BORDERS WITH MALAYSIA, THAILAND'S MUSLIM MINORITY ARE MOSTLY TO BE FOUND IN THIS AREA. THEY HAVE INTRODUCED RICHER CURRY FLAVOURS REMINISCENT OF INDIAN FOOD.

SERVES FOUR

INGREDIENTS
   90g/3½oz Chinese leaves (Chinese
      cabbage), shredded
   90g/3½oz/generous 1 cup
      beansprouts
   90g/3½oz/scant 1 cup green
      beans, trimmed
   90g/3½oz broccoli, preferably the
      purple sprouting variety, divided
      into florets
   15ml/1 tbsp sesame seeds, toasted
For the yam
   60ml/4 tbsp coconut cream
   5ml/1 tsp Thai red curry paste
   90g/3½oz/1¼ cups oyster
      mushrooms or field
      (portabello) mushrooms, sliced
   60ml/4 tbsp coconut milk
   5ml/1 tsp ground turmeric
   5ml/1 tsp thick tamarind juice, made
      by mixing tamarind paste with
      warm water
   juice of ½ lemon
   60ml/4 tbsp light soy sauce
   5ml/1 tsp palm sugar or light
      muscovado (brown) sugar

1 Steam the shredded Chinese leaves, beansprouts, green beans and broccoli separately or blanch them in boiling water for 1 minute per batch. Drain, place in a serving bowl and leave to cool.

2 Make the yam. Pour the coconut cream into a wok or frying pan and heat gently for 2–3 minutes, until it separates. Stir in the red curry paste. Cook over a low heat for 30 seconds, until the mixture is fragrant.

3 Increase the heat to high and add the mushrooms to the wok or pan. Cook for a further 2–3 minutes.

4 Pour in the coconut milk and add the ground turmeric, tamarind juice, lemon juice, soy sauce and sugar to the wok or pan. Mix thoroughly.

5 Pour the mixture over the prepared vegetables and toss well to combine. Sprinkle with the toasted sesame seeds and serve immediately.

COOK'S TIPS
• There's no need to buy coconut cream especially for this dish. Use a carton or can of coconut milk. Skim the cream off the top and cook 60ml/4 tbsp of it before adding the curry paste. Add the measured coconut milk later, as described in the recipe.
• Oyster mushrooms may have fawn, peacock-blue or yellow caps, depending on the variety.

FRIED VEGETABLES <u>WITH</u> NAM PRIK

NAM PRIK IS THE UNIVERSAL THAI SAUCE. IT CAN BE SERVED AS A CONDIMENT, BUT IT IS MORE OFTEN USED AS A DIP FOR FRESH OR COOKED VEGETABLES.

<u>SERVES FOUR</u>

INGREDIENTS

3 large (US extra large) eggs
1 aubergine (eggplant), halved
  lengthways and cut into long,
  thin slices
½ small butternut squash,
  peeled, seeded and cut into
  long, thin slices
2 courgettes (zucchini),
  trimmed and cut into long,
  thin slices
105ml/7 tbsp vegetable or
  sunflower oil
salt and ground black pepper
nam prik or sweet chilli sauce,
  to serve (see Cook's Tip)

1 Beat the eggs in a large bowl. Add the aubergine, butternut squash and courgette slices. Toss the vegetables until coated all over in the egg, then season with salt and pepper.

2 Heat the oil in a wok. When it is hot, add the vegetables, one strip at a time, making sure that each strip has plenty of egg clinging to it. Do not cook more than eight strips at a time or the oil will cool down too much.

COOK'S TIP
Nam prik is quite a complex sauce, numbering dried shrimp, tiny aubergines (eggplant), shrimp paste and lime or lemon juice among its ingredients.

3 As each strip turns golden and is cooked, lift it out, using a wire basket or slotted spoon, and drain on kitchen paper. Keep hot while cooking the remaining vegetables. Transfer to a warmed dish and serve with the nam prik or sweet chilli sauce as a dip.

STEAMED VEGETABLES <u>WITH</u> CHIANG MAI SPICY DIP

IN THAILAND, STEAMED VEGETABLES ARE OFTEN PARTNERED WITH RAW ONES TO CREATE THE CONTRASTING TEXTURES THAT ARE SUCH A FEATURE OF THE NATIONAL CUISINE. BY HAPPY COINCIDENCE, IT IS AN EXTREMELY HEALTHY WAY TO SERVE THEM.

SERVES FOUR

INGREDIENTS
 1 head broccoli, divided
  into florets
 130g/4½oz 1 cup green
  beans, trimmed
 130g/4½oz asparagus, trimmed
 ½ head cauliflower, divided
  into florets
 8 baby corn cobs
 130g/4½oz mangetouts (snow peas)
  or sugar snap peas
 salt
For the dip
 1 fresh green chilli, seeded
 4 garlic cloves, peeled
 4 shallots, peeled
 2 tomatoes, halved
 5 pea aubergines (eggplant)
 30ml/2 tbsp lemon juice
 30ml/2 tbsp soy sauce
 2.5ml/½ tsp salt
 5ml/1 tsp granulated sugar

COOK'S TIP
Cauliflower varieties with pale green curds have a more delicate flavour than those with white curds.

1 Place the broccoli, green beans, asparagus and cauliflower in a steamer and steam over boiling water for about 4 minutes, until just tender but still with a "bite". Transfer them to a bowl and add the corn cobs and mangetouts or sugar snap peas. Season to taste with a little salt. Toss to mix, then set aside.

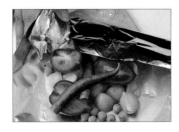

2 Make the dip. Preheat the grill (broiler). Wrap the chilli, garlic cloves, shallots, tomatoes and aubergines in a foil package. Grill (broil) for 10 minutes, until the vegetables have softened, turning the package over once or twice.

3 Unwrap the foil and tip its contents into a mortar or food processor. Add the lemon juice, soy sauce, salt and sugar. Pound with a pestle or process to a fairly liquid paste.

4 Scrape the dip into a serving bowl or four individual bowls. Serve, surrounded by the steamed and raw vegetables.

VARIATIONS
You can use a combination of other vegetables if you like. Use pak choi (bok choy) instead of the cauliflower or substitute raw baby carrots for the corn cobs and mushrooms in place of the mangetouts (snow peas).

SINGAPORE RICE VERMICELLI

SIMPLE AND SPEEDILY PREPARED, THIS LIGHTLY CURRIED RICE NOODLE DISH WITH VEGETABLES AND PRAWNS IS ALMOST A COMPLETE MEAL IN A BOWL.

SERVES FOUR

INGREDIENTS
- 225g/8oz/2 cups dried rice vermicelli
- 15ml/1 tbsp vegetable oil
- 1 egg, lightly beaten
- 2 garlic cloves, finely chopped
- 1 large fresh red or green chilli, seeded and finely chopped
- 15ml/1 tbsp medium curry powder
- 1 red (bell) pepper, thinly sliced
- 1 green (bell) pepper, thinly sliced
- 1 carrot, cut into matchsticks
- 1.5ml/¼ tsp salt
- 60ml/4 tbsp vegetable stock
- 115g/4oz cooked peeled prawns (shrimp), thawed if frozen
- 75g/3oz lean ham, cut into cubes
- 15ml/1 tbsp light soy sauce

1 Soak the rice vermicelli in a bowl of boiling water for 4 minutes, or according to the instructions on the packet, then drain thoroughly and set aside.

2 Heat 5ml/1 tsp of the oil in a non-stick frying pan or wok. Add the egg and scramble until set. Remove with a slotted spoon and set aside.

3 Heat the remaining oil in the clean pan. Stir-fry the garlic and chilli for a few seconds, then stir in the curry powder. Cook for 1 minute, stirring, then stir in the peppers, carrot sticks, salt and stock.

4 Bring to the boil. Add the prawns, ham, scrambled egg, rice vermicelli and soy sauce. Mix well. Cook, stirring, until all the liquid has been absorbed and the mixture is hot. Serve immediately.

BROWN RICE WITH LIME AND LEMON GRASS

It is unusual to find brown rice given the Thai treatment, but the nutty flavour of the grains is enhanced by the fragrance of limes and lemon grass in this delicious dish.

SERVES FOUR

INGREDIENTS
2 limes
1 lemon grass stalk
225g/8oz/generous 1 cup brown
   long grain rice
15ml/1 tbsp olive oil
1 onion, chopped
2.5cm/1in piece fresh root ginger,
   peeled and finely chopped
7.5ml/1½ tsp coriander seeds
7.5ml/1½ tsp cumin seeds
750ml/1¼ pints/3 cups
   vegetable stock
60ml/4 tbsp chopped fresh
   coriander (cilantro)
spring onion (scallion) green and
   toasted coconut strips, to garnish
lime wedges, to serve

1 Pare the limes, using a cannelle knife (zester) or fine grater, taking care to avoid cutting the bitter pith. Set the rind aside. Finely chop the lower portion of the lemon grass stalk and set it aside.

2 Rinse the rice in plenty of cold water until the water runs clear. Tip it into a sieve and drain thoroughly.

3 Heat the oil in a large pan. Add the onion, ginger, coriander and cumin seeds, lemon grass and lime rind and cook over a low heat for 2–3 minutes.

4 Add the rice to the pan and cook, stirring constantly, for 1 minute, then pour in the stock and bring to the boil. Reduce the heat to very low and cover the pan. Cook gently for 30 minutes, then check the rice. If it is still crunchy, cover the pan and cook for 3–5 minutes more. Remove from the heat.

5 Stir in the fresh coriander, fluff up the rice grains with a fork, cover the pan and leave to stand for 10 minutes. Transfer to a warmed dish, garnish with spring onion green and toasted coconut strips, and serve with lime wedges.

KIMCHI

NO SELF-RESPECTING KOREAN MOVES FAR WITHOUT THE BELOVED KIMCHI. IN THE PAST, LARGE STONE POTS WERE FILLED WITH THIS PICKLED CABBAGE, AND BURIED IN THE GROUND FOR THE WINTER.

SERVES SIX TO EIGHT

INGREDIENTS

675g/1½lb Chinese leaves (Chinese cabbage), shredded
1 large or 2 medium yam beans, total weight about 675g/1½lb or 2 hard pears, peeled and thinly sliced
60ml/4 tbsp salt
200ml/7fl oz/scant 1 cup water
4 spring onions (scallions), chopped
4 garlic cloves, crushed
2.5cm/1in piece fresh root ginger, peeled and finely chopped
10–15ml/2–3 tsp chilli powder

1 Place the Chinese leaves and yam beans or pears in a bowl and sprinkle evenly with salt. Mix well, then press down into the bowl.

2 Pour the water over the vegetables, then cover the bowl and leave overnight in a cool place. Next day, drain off the brine from the vegetables and set it aside. Mix the brined vegetables with the spring onions, garlic, ginger and chilli powder. Pack the mixture into a 900g/2lb jar or two smaller ones. Pour over the reserved brine.

3 Cover with clear film (plastic wrap) and place on a sunny windowsill or in a warm place for 2–3 days. Store in the refrigerator, where the mixture can be kept for several weeks.

HOT THAI PICKLED SHALLOTS

PICKLING THAI SHALLOTS IN THIS WAY DEMANDS SOME PATIENCE, WHILE THE VINEGAR AND SPICES WORK THEIR MAGIC, BUT THE RESULTS ARE DEFINITELY WORTH THE WAIT. THINLY SLICED, THE SHALLOTS ARE OFTEN USED AS A CONDIMENT WITH SOUTH-EAST ASIAN MEALS.

MAKES TWO TO THREE JARS

INGREDIENTS
 5–6 small red or green bird's
  eye chillies
 500g/1¼lb Thai pink
  shallots, peeled
 2 large garlic cloves, peeled, halved
  and green shoots removed
For the vinegar
 40g/1½oz/3 tbsp granulated sugar
 10ml/2 tsp salt
 5cm/2in piece fresh root ginger,
  peeled and sliced
 15ml/1 tbsp coriander seeds
 2 lemon grass stalks, cut in
  half lengthways
 4 kaffir lime leaves or pared strips of
  lime rind
 600ml/1 pint/2½ cups cider vinegar
 15ml/1 tbsp chopped fresh
  coriander (cilantro)

1 The chillies can be left whole or halved and seeded. The pickle will be hotter if you leave the seeds in. If leaving the chillies whole, prick them several times with a cocktail stick (toothpick). Bring a large pan of water to the boil. Add the chillies, shallots and garlic. Blanch for 1–2 minutes, then drain. Rinse all the vegetables under cold water, then drain again.

2 Prepare the vinegar. Put the sugar, salt, ginger, coriander seeds, lemon grass and lime leaves or lime rind in a pan, pour in the vinegar and bring to the boil. Reduce the heat to low and simmer for 3–4 minutes. Leave to cool.

3 Remove and discard the ginger, then bring the vinegar back to the boil. Add the fresh coriander, garlic and chillies and cook for 1 minute.

4 Pack the shallots into sterilized jars, distributing the lemon grass, lime leaves, chillies and garlic among them. Pour over the hot vinegar. Cool, then seal and store in a cool, dark place for 2 months before eating.

COOK'S TIPS
• Always be careful when making pickles to be sure that bowls and pans used for vinegar are non-reactive, that is, they are not chemically affected by the acid of the vinegar. China and glass bowls and stainless steel pans are suitable. Kilner and Mason jars are ideal containers.
• When packing pickles, make sure that metal lids will not come in contact with the pickle. The acid in the vinegar will corrode the metal. Use plastic-coated or glass lids with rubber rings. Alternatively, cover the top of the jar with a circle of cellophane or waxed paper to prevent direct contact when using metal lids.
• Take care when handling hot jars. Let them cool slightly after sterilizing and before filling to avoid burning yourself. However, do not let them cool down completely, or they may crack when the hot vinegar is poured in.

SAMBAL NANAS

SAMBALS ARE THE LITTLE SIDE DISHES SERVED AT ALMOST EVERY MALAY MEAL. IN POORER SOCIETIES,
A MAIN MEAL MAY SIMPLY BE A BOWL OF RICE AND A SAMBAL MADE FROM POUNDED SHRIMP PASTE,
CHILLIES AND LIME JUICE. THIS SAMBAL INCLUDES CUCUMBER AND PINEAPPLE.

SERVES TEN AS AN ACCOMPANIMENT

INGREDIENTS

1 small or ½ large fresh
  ripe pineapple
½ cucumber, halved lengthways
50g/2oz dried shrimps
1 large fresh red chilli, seeded
1cm/½in cube shrimp paste,
  prepared (see Cook's Tip)
juice of 1 large lemon or lime
light brown sugar, to taste (optional)

1 Cut off both ends of the pineapple. Stand it upright on a board, then slice off the skin from top to bottom, cutting out the spines. Slice the pineapple, removing the central core. Cut into thin slices and set aside.

2 Trim the ends from the cucumber and slice thinly. Sprinkle with salt and set aside. Place the dried shrimps in a food processor and chop fairly finely. Add the chilli, prepared shrimp paste and lemon or lime juice and process again to a paste.

3 Rinse the cucumber, drain and dry on kitchen paper. Mix with the pineapple and chill. Just before serving, spoon in the spice mixture with sugar to taste. Mix well and serve.

COOK'S TIP

The pungent shrimp paste, also called blachan, is popular in many South-east Asian countries, and is available in Asian supermarkets. Since it can taste a bit raw in a sambal, dry fry it by wrapping in foil and heating in a frying pan over a low heat for 5 minutes, turning from time to time. If the shrimp paste is to be fried with other spices, this preliminary cooking can be eliminated.

COCONUT AND PEANUT RELISH AND HOT CHILLI AND GARLIC DIPPING SAUCE

THIS PAIR OF FLAVOURSOME ACCOMPANIMENTS CAN BE SERVED WITH MANY INDONESIAN DISHES.

MAKES 120ML/4FL OZ/½ CUP OF EACH

INGREDIENTS

For the coconut and peanut relish
  115g/4oz fresh coconut, grated,
    or desiccated (dry unsweetened
    shredded) coconut
  175g/6oz/1 cup salted peanuts
  5mm/¼in cube shrimp paste
  1 small onion, quartered
  2–3 garlic cloves, crushed
  45ml/3 tbsp vegetable oil
  2.5ml/½ tsp tamarind pulp, soaked
    in 30ml/2 tbsp warm water
  5ml/1 tsp coriander seeds, roasted
    and ground
  2.5ml/½ tsp cumin seeds, roasted
    and ground
  5ml/1 tsp dark brown sugar

For the hot chilli and garlic
dipping sauce
  1 garlic clove
  2 fresh Thai red chillies, seeded
    and roughly chopped
  10ml/2 tsp granulated sugar
  5ml/1 tsp tamarind juice
  60ml/4 tbsp soy sauce
  juice of ½ lime

1 First make the coconut and peanut relish. Dry-fry the coconut in a wok or large pan over a medium heat, stirring the coconut constantly until crisp and golden in colour. Allow to cool and add half to the peanuts in a bowl. Toss together to mix.

2 Process the shrimp paste, the onion and garlic in a food processor or with a pestle and mortar to form a paste. Fry the paste in hot oil, without browning.

3 Strain the tamarind and reserve the juice. Add the coriander, cumin, tamarind juice and brown sugar to the fried paste in the pan. Cook for 3 minutes, stirring.

4 Stir in the remaining toasted coconut and leave to cool. When cold, mix with the peanut and coconut mixture. Leave the relish to stand for 30 minutes before serving.

5 To make the hot chilli and garlic dipping sauce, process the garlic, chillies and sugar in a food processor or with a pestle and mortar to create a smooth paste.

6 Add the tamarind juice, soy sauce and lime juice, and mix together. Leave the dipping sauce to stand for 30 minutes before serving.

SALADS

Asia has a fine repertoire of salads and cold dishes.
These aren't salads in the Western sense, but rather
combinations of fresh and cooked vegetables, often with a little
chicken, beef or seafood. Dressings are seldom oil-based.
Instead, they tend to be tart and spicy mixtures, made by
adding Thai fish sauce to lime juice, tamarind juice or a little
rice vinegar. Noodles often feature and it is not uncommon
for fruit, such as papaya or mango, to be included.

FRUIT AND RAW VEGETABLE GADO-GADO

*A BANANA LEAF, WHICH CAN BE BOUGHT FROM ASIAN STORES, CAN BE USED INSTEAD OF THE MIXED
SALAD LEAVES TO LINE THE PLATTER FOR A SPECIAL OCCASION.*

SERVES SIX

INGREDIENTS

 ¹/₂ cucumber
 2 pears (not too ripe) or 175g/6oz
  wedge of yam bean
 1–2 eating apples
 juice of ¹/₂ lemon
 mixed salad leaves
 6 small tomatoes, cut in wedges
 3 slices fresh pineapple, cored and
  cut in wedges
 3 eggs, hard-boiled and shelled
 175g/6oz egg noodles, cooked,
  cooled and chopped
 deep-fried onions, to garnish
For the peanut sauce
 2–4 fresh red chillies, seeded
  and ground, or 15ml/1 tbsp
  chilli sambal
 300ml/¹/₂ pint/1¹/₄ cups
  coconut milk
 350g/12oz/1¹/₄ cups crunchy
  peanut butter
 15ml/1 tbsp dark soy sauce or
  dark brown sugar
 5ml/1 tsp tamarind pulp, soaked in
  45ml/3 tbsp warm water
 coarsely crushed peanuts
 salt

2 Simmer gently until the sauce
thickens, then stir in the soy sauce or
sugar. Strain in the tamarind juice, add
salt to taste and stir well. Spoon into a
bowl and sprinkle with a few coarsely
crushed peanuts.

VARIATION
Quail's eggs can be used instead of
normal eggs and look very attractive in
this dish. Hard boil for 3 minutes and
halve or leave whole.

3 To make the salad, core the
cucumber and peel the pears or yam
bean. Cut them into matchsticks. Finely
shred the apples and sprinkle them with
the lemon juice. Spread a bed of lettuce
leaves on a flat platter, then pile the
fruit and vegetables on top.

4 Add the sliced or quartered hard-
boiled eggs, the chopped noodles and
the deep-fried onions. Serve at once,
with the sauce.

1 Make the peanut sauce. Put the
ground chillies or chilli sambal in a pan.
Pour in the coconut milk, then stir in
the peanut butter. Heat gently, stirring,
until well blended.

EXOTIC FRUIT AND VEGETABLE SALAD

THIS IS A VARIATION ON THE FAMOUS INDONESIAN SALAD KNOWN AS GADO-GADO. CHOOSE SOME OR ALL OF THE SUGGESTED FRUITS AND VEGETABLES TO MAKE AN ATTRACTIVE CENTREPIECE FOR AN INDONESIAN OR THAI MEAL.

SERVES SIX TO EIGHT

INGREDIENTS
    115g/4oz green beans, trimmed
    2 carrots, cut into batons
    115g/4oz/2 cups bean sprouts
    ¼ head Chinese leaves (Chinese
      cabbage), shredded
    ½ small cucumber, cut into thin strips
    8 spring onions (scallions), sliced
      diagonally
    6 cherry tomatoes, halved
    12–16 cooked tiger prawns (shrimp)
    1 small mango
    1 small papaya
    1 quantity Lontong (compressed rice)
    4 hard-boiled eggs, quartered
    fresh coriander (cilantro)
For the peanut dressing
    120ml/8 tbsp crunchy or smooth
      peanut butter, preferably unsalted
    1 garlic clove, crushed
    300ml/½ pint/1¼ cups coconut milk
    15ml/1 tbsp tamarind water (see
      Cook's Tip) or juice of ½ lemon
    15–30ml/1–2 tbsp light soy sauce
    hot chilli sauce, to taste

1 First, make the peanut dressing. Place all the ingredients except the chilli sauce in a pan and heat the mixture, stirring all the time, until it is very hot and smooth. Stir in chilli sauce to taste. Keep the dressing warm, or allow to cool and reheat before serving.

2 Cook the beans and carrots in boiling water for 3–4 minutes until just tender but still firm. Drain, then refresh under cold water and drain again. Cook the bean sprouts in boiling water for 2 minutes, then drain and refresh.

3 Arrange the carrots, beans and bean sprouts on a large, attractive platter, with the shredded Chinese leaves, cucumber strips, spring onions, tomatoes, and prawns.

4 Peel the mango and cut the flesh into cubes. Quarter the papaya, remove the skin and seeds, then slice the flesh. Add to the salad platter, with the lontong. Garnish with the egg quarters and fresh coriander.

5 Reheat the peanut dressing, if necessary. As soon as it is warm, pour it into a serving bowl. Place the bowl in the centre of the salad and serve. Guests help themselves to the salad, adding as much dressing as they like.

COOK'S TIP
To make tamarind water, break off a 2.5cm/1in cube of tamarind and put it in a bowl. Pour in 150ml/¼ pint/⅔ cup warm water. Using your fingers, squeeze the tamarind so that the juices dissolve into the water. Strain, discarding the solid tamarind, and use as directed in the recipe. Any unused tamarind water can be kept in a container in the refrigerator for up to 1 week.

GREEN PAPAYA SALAD

THIS SALAD APPEARS IN MANY GUISES IN SOUTH-EAST ASIA. AS GREEN PAPAYA IS NOT EASY TO GET HOLD OF, FINELY GRATED CARROTS, CUCUMBER OR EVEN CRISP GREEN APPLE CAN BE USED INSTEAD. ALTERNATIVELY, USE VERY THINLY SLICED WHITE CABBAGE.

SERVES FOUR

INGREDIENTS

1 green papaya
4 garlic cloves, coarsely chopped
15ml/1 tbsp chopped shallots
3–4 fresh red chillies, seeded
  and sliced
2.5ml/½ tsp salt
2–3 snake beans or 6 green beans,
  cut into 2cm/¾ in lengths
2 tomatoes, cut into thin wedges
45ml/3 tbsp Thai fish sauce
15ml/1 tbsp caster (superfine) sugar
juice of 1 lime
30ml/2 tbsp crushed roasted peanuts
sliced fresh red chillies, to garnish

1 Cut the papaya in half lengthways. Scrape out the seeds with a spoon and discard, then peel, using a swivel vegetable peeler or a small sharp knife. Shred the flesh finely in a food processor or using a grater.

2 Put the garlic, shallots, red chillies and salt in a large mortar and grind to a paste with a pestle. Add the shredded papaya, a small amount at a time, pounding with the pestle until it becomes slightly limp and soft.

3 Add the sliced snake or green beans and wedges of tomato to the mortar and crush them lightly with the pestle until they are incorporated.

4 Season the mixture with the fish sauce, sugar and lime juice. Transfer the salad to a serving dish and sprinkle with the crushed roasted peanuts. Garnish with the sliced red chillies and serve the salad immediately.

THAI FRUIT AND VEGETABLE SALAD

THIS FRUIT SALAD IS TRADITIONALLY PRESENTED WITH THE MAIN COURSE AND SERVES AS A COOLER TO COUNTERACT THE HEAT OF THE CHILLIES THAT WILL INEVITABLY BE PRESENT IN THE OTHER DISHES. IT IS A TYPICALLY HARMONIOUS BALANCE OF FLAVOURS.

SERVES FOUR TO SIX

INGREDIENTS
    1 small pineapple
    1 small mango, peeled and sliced
    1 green apple, cored and sliced
    6 rambutans or lychees, peeled and
      stoned (pitted)
    115g/4oz/1 cup green beans,
      trimmed and halved
    1 red onion, sliced
    1 small cucumber, cut into
      short sticks
    115g/4oz/1⅓ cups beansprouts
    2 spring onions (scallions), sliced
    1 ripe tomato, quartered
    225g/8oz cos, romaine or iceberg
      lettuce leaves
For the coconut dipping sauce
    30ml/2 tbsp coconut cream
    30ml/2 tbsp granulated sugar
    75ml/5 tbsp boiling water
    1.5ml/¼ tsp chilli sauce
    15ml/1 tbsp Thai fish sauce
    juice of 1 lime

1 Make the coconut dipping sauce. Spoon the coconut cream, sugar and boiling water into a screw-top jar. Add the chilli and fish sauces and lime juice, close tightly and shake to mix.

2 Trim both ends of the pineapple with a serrated knife, then cut away the outer skin. Remove the central core with an apple corer. Alternatively, quarter the pineapple lengthways and remove the portion of core from each wedge with a knife. Chop the pineapple and set aside with the other fruits.

3 Bring a small pan of lightly salted water to the boil over a medium heat. Add the green beans and cook for 3–4 minutes, until just tender but still retaining some "bite". Drain, refresh under cold running water, drain well again and set aside.

4 To serve, arrange all the fruits and vegetables in small heaps on a platter or in a shallow bowl. Pour the coconut sauce into a small serving bowl and serve separately as a dip.

SWEET AND SOUR SALAD

ACAR BENING MAKES A PERFECT ACCOMPANIMENT TO A VARIETY OF SPICY DISHES AND CURRIES, WITH ITS CLEAN TASTE AND BRIGHT, JEWEL-LIKE COLOURS, AND POMEGRANATE SEEDS, THOUGH NOT TRADITIONAL, MAKE A BEAUTIFUL GARNISH. THIS IS AN ESSENTIAL DISH FOR A BUFFET PARTY.

SERVES EIGHT

INGREDIENTS

1 small cucumber
1 onion, thinly sliced
1 small, ripe pineapple or 425g/
   15oz can pineapple rings
1 green (bell) pepper, seeded and
   thinly sliced
3 firm tomatoes, chopped
30ml/2 tbsp golden granulated sugar
45–60ml/3–4 tbsp white wine vinegar
120ml/4fl oz/$^1/_2$ cup water
salt
seeds of 1–2 pomegranates,
   to garnish

1 Halve the cucumber lengthways, remove the seeds, slice and spread on a plate with the onion. Sprinkle with salt. After 10 minutes, rinse and dry.

2 If using a fresh pineapple, peel and core it, removing all the eyes, then cut it into bitesize pieces. If using canned pineapple, drain the rings and cut them into small wedges. Place the pineapple in a bowl with the cucumber, onion, green pepper and tomatoes.

3 Heat the sugar, vinegar and measured water in a pan, stirring until the sugar has dissolved. Remove the pan from the heat and leave to cool. When cold, add a little salt to taste and pour over the fruit and vegetables. Cover and chill until required. Serve in small bowls, garnished with pomegranate seeds.

VARIATION
To make an Indonesian-style cucumber salad, salt a salad cucumber as described in the recipe. Make half the dressing and pour it over the cucumber. Add a few chopped spring onions (scallions). Cover and chill. Serve sprinkled with toasted sesame seeds.

Hot and Sour Noodle Salad

NOODLES MAKE THE PERFECT BASIS FOR A SALAD, ABSORBING THE DRESSING AND PROVIDING A CONTRAST IN TEXTURE TO THE CRISP VEGETABLES.

SERVES TWO

INGREDIENTS

   200g/7oz thin rice noodles
   small bunch fresh coriander (cilantro)
   2 tomatoes, seeded and sliced
   130g/4½oz baby corn cobs, sliced
   4 spring onions (scallions),
     thinly sliced
   1 red (bell) pepper, seeded and
     finely chopped
   juice of 2 limes
   2 small fresh green chillies, seeded
     and finely chopped
   10ml/2 tsp granulated sugar
   115g/4oz/1 cup peanuts, toasted
     and chopped
   30ml/2 tbsp soy sauce
   salt

1 Bring a large pan of lightly salted water to the boil. Snap the noodles into short lengths, add to the pan and cook for 3–4 minutes. Drain, then rinse under cold water and drain again.

2 Set aside a few coriander leaves for the garnish. Chop the remaining leaves and place them in a large serving bowl.

3 Add the noodles to the bowl, with the tomato slices, corn cobs, spring onions, red pepper, lime juice, chillies, sugar and toasted peanuts. Season with the soy sauce, then taste and add a little salt if you think the mixture needs it. Toss the salad lightly but thoroughly, then garnish with the reserved coriander leaves and serve immediately.

BAMBOO SHOOT SALAD

THIS HOT, SHARP-FLAVOURED SALAD ORIGINATED IN NORTH-EASTERN THAILAND. USE CANNED WHOLE BAMBOO SHOOTS, IF YOU CAN FIND THEM — THEY HAVE MORE FLAVOUR THAN SLICED ONES.

SERVES FOUR

INGREDIENTS

   400g/14oz canned bamboo shoots,
     in large pieces
   25g/1oz/about 3 tbsp glutinous rice
   30ml/2 tbsp chopped shallots
   15ml/1 tbsp chopped garlic
   45ml/3 tbsp chopped spring
     onions (scallions)
   30ml/2 tbsp Thai fish sauce
   30ml/2 tbsp fresh lime juice
   5ml/1 tsp granulated sugar
   2.5ml/½ tsp dried chilli flakes
   20–25 small fresh mint leaves
   15ml/1 tbsp toasted sesame seeds

COOK'S TIP

Glutinous rice does not, in fact, contain any gluten – it's just sticky.

1 Rinse the bamboo shoots under cold running water, then drain them and pat them thoroughly dry with kitchen paper and set them aside.

2 Dry-roast the rice in a frying pan until it is golden brown. Leave to cool slightly, then tip into a mortar and grind to fine crumbs with a pestle.

3 Transfer the rice to a bowl and add the shallots, garlic, spring onions, fish sauce, lime juice, sugar, chillies and half the mint leaves. Mix well.

4 Add the bamboo shoots to the bowl and toss to mix. Serve sprinkled with the toasted sesame seeds and the remaining mint leaves.

CABBAGE SALAD

THIS IS A SIMPLE AND DELICIOUS WAY OF SERVING A SOMEWHAT MUNDANE VEGETABLE. CLASSIC THAI FLAVOURS PERMEATE THIS COLOURFUL WARM SALAD.

SERVES FOUR TO SIX

INGREDIENTS
  30ml/2 tbsp vegetable oil
  2 large fresh red chillies, seeded
    and cut into thin strips
  6 garlic cloves, thinly sliced
  6 shallots, thinly sliced
  1 small cabbage, shredded
  30ml/2 tbsp coarsely chopped
    roasted peanuts, to garnish
For the dressing
  30ml/2 tbsp Thai fish sauce
  grated rind of 1 lime
  30ml/2 tbsp fresh lime juice
  120ml/4fl oz/½ cup coconut milk

VARIATION
Other vegetables, such as cauliflower, broccoli and Chinese leaves (Chinese cabbage), can be cooked in this way.

1 Make the dressing by mixing the fish sauce, lime rind and juice and coconut milk in a bowl. Whisk until thoroughly combined, then set aside.

2 Heat the oil in a wok. Stir-fry the chillies, garlic and shallots over a medium heat for 3–4 minutes, until the shallots are brown and crisp. Remove with a slotted spoon and set aside.

3 Bring a large pan of lightly salted water to the boil. Add the cabbage and blanch for 2–3 minutes. Tip it into a colander, drain well and put into a bowl.

4 Whisk the dressing again, add it to the warm cabbage and toss to mix. Transfer the salad to a serving dish. Sprinkle with the fried shallot mixture and the peanuts. Serve immediately.

FRIED EGG SALAD

CHILLIES AND EGGS MAY SEEM UNLIKELY PARTNERS, BUT ACTUALLY WORK VERY WELL TOGETHER. THE PEPPERY FLAVOUR OF THE WATERCRESS MAKES IT THE PERFECT FOUNDATION FOR THIS TASTY SALAD.

SERVES TWO

INGREDIENTS

- 15ml/1 tbsp groundnut (peanut) oil
- 1 garlic clove, thinly sliced
- 4 eggs
- 2 shallots, thinly sliced
- 2 small fresh red chillies, seeded and thinly sliced
- ½ small cucumber, finely diced
- 1cm/½in piece fresh root ginger, peeled and grated
- juice of 2 limes
- 30ml/2 tbsp soy sauce
- 5ml/1 tsp caster (superfine) sugar
- small bunch coriander (cilantro)
- bunch watercress, coarsely chopped

1 Heat the oil in a frying pan. Add the garlic and cook over a low heat until it starts to turn golden. Crack in the eggs. Break the yolks with a wooden spatula, then fry until the yolks are almost firm. Remove from the pan and set aside.

2 Mix the shallots, chillies, cucumber and ginger in a bowl. In a separate bowl, whisk the lime juice with the soy sauce and sugar. Pour this dressing over the vegetables and toss lightly.

3 Set aside a few coriander sprigs for the garnish. Chop the rest and add them to the salad. Toss it again.

4 Reserve a few watercress sprigs and arrange the remainder on two serving plates. Cut the fried eggs into slices and divide them between the watercress mounds. Spoon the shallot mixture over them and serve, garnished with the reserved coriander and watercress.

TANGY CHICKEN SALAD

THIS FRESH AND LIVELY DISH TYPIFIES THE CHARACTER OF THAI CUISINE. IT IS IDEAL FOR A LIGHT LUNCH ON A HOT AND LAZY SUMMER'S DAY.

SERVES FOUR TO SIX

INGREDIENTS

  4 skinless, boneless chicken
    breast portions
  2 garlic cloves, crushed
  30ml/2 tbsp soy sauce
  30ml/2 tbsp vegetable oil
  120ml/4fl oz/½ cup coconut
    cream
  30ml/2 tbsp Thai fish sauce
  juice of 1 lime
  30ml/2 tbsp palm sugar or light
    muscovado (brown) sugar
  115g/4oz/½ cup water
    chestnuts, sliced
  50g/2oz/½ cup cashew nuts, roasted
    and coarsely chopped
  4 shallots, thinly sliced
  4 kaffir lime leaves, thinly sliced
  1 lemon grass stalk, thinly sliced
  5ml/1 tsp chopped fresh galangal
  1 large fresh red chilli, seeded and
    finely chopped
  2 spring onions (scallions),
    thinly sliced
  10–12 fresh mint leaves, torn
  1 lettuce, separated into leaves,
    to serve
  2 fresh red chillies, seeded and
    sliced, to garnish

1 Place the chicken in a large dish. Rub with the garlic, soy sauce and 15ml/ 1 tbsp of the oil. Cover and leave to marinate for 1–2 hours.

2 Heat the remaining oil in a wok or frying pan and stir-fry the chicken for 3–4 minutes on each side, or until cooked. Remove and set aside to cool.

3 In a pan, heat the coconut cream, fish sauce, lime juice and sugar. Stir until the sugar has dissolved; set aside.

4 Tear the cooked chicken into strips and put it in a bowl. Add the water chestnuts, cashew nuts, shallots, kaffir lime leaves, lemon grass, galangal, red chilli, spring onions and mint leaves.

5 Pour the coconut dressing over the mixture and toss well. Serve the chicken on a bed of lettuce leaves and garnish with sliced red chillies.

SAENG WA OF GRILLED PORK

PORK FILLET IS CUT IN STRIPS BEFORE BEING GRILLED. SHREDDED AND THEN TOSSED WITH A DELICIOUS SWEET-SOUR SAUCE, IT MAKES A MARVELLOUS WARM SALAD.

3 Transfer the cooked pork strips to a board. Slice the meat across the grain, then shred it with a fork. Place in a large bowl and add the shallot slices, lemon grass, kaffir lime leaves, ginger, chilli and chopped coriander.

4 Make the dressing. Place the sugar, fish sauce, lime juice and tamarind juice in a bowl. Whisk until the sugar has completely dissolved. Pour the dressing over the pork mixture and toss well to mix, then serve.

VARIATION

If you want to extend this dish a little, add cooked rice or noodles. Thin strips of red or yellow (bell) pepper could also be added. For a colour contrast, add lightly cooked green beans, sugar snap peas or mangetouts (snow peas).

SERVES FOUR

INGREDIENTS
    30ml/2 tbsp dark soy sauce
    15ml/1 tbsp clear honey
    400g/14oz pork fillet (tenderloin)
    6 shallots, very thinly
      sliced lengthways
    1 lemon grass stalk, thinly sliced
    5 kaffir lime leaves, thinly sliced
    5cm/2in piece fresh root ginger,
      peeled and sliced into
      fine shreds
    ½ fresh long red chilli, seeded and
      sliced into fine shreds
    small bunch fresh coriander
      (cilantro), chopped
For the dressing
    30ml/2 tbsp palm sugar or light
      muscovado (brown) sugar
    30ml/2 tbsp Thai fish sauce
    juice of 2 limes
    20ml/4 tsp thick tamarind juice,
      made by mixing tamarind paste
      with warm water

1 Preheat the grill (broiler) to medium. Mix the soy sauce with the honey in a small bowl or jug (pitcher) and stir until the honey has completely dissolved.

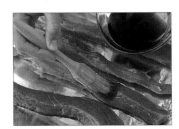

2 Using a sharp knife, cut the pork fillet lengthways into quarters to make four long, thick strips. Place the pork strips in a grill pan. Brush generously with the soy sauce and honey mixture, then grill (broil) for about 10–15 minutes, until cooked through and tender. Turn the strips over frequently and baste with the soy sauce and honey mixture.

BEEF AND MUSHROOM SALAD

ALL THE INGREDIENTS FOR THIS TRADITIONAL THAI DISH — KNOWN AS YAM NUA YANG *— ARE
WIDELY AVAILABLE IN LARGER SUPERMARKETS.*

SERVES FOUR

INGREDIENTS
675g/1½lb fillet (tenderloin) or
    rump (round) steak
30ml/2 tbsp olive oil
2 small mild red chillies, seeded
    and sliced
225g/8oz/3¼ cups fresh shiitake
    mushrooms, stems removed and
    caps sliced
For the dressing
3 spring onions (scallions),
    finely chopped
2 garlic cloves, finely chopped
juice of 1 lime
15–30ml/1–2 tbsp Thai fish sauce
5ml/1 tsp soft light brown sugar
30ml/2 tbsp chopped fresh
    coriander (cilantro)
To serve
1 cos or romaine lettuce, torn
    into strips
175g/6oz cherry tomatoes, halved
5cm/2in piece cucumber, peeled,
    halved and thinly sliced
45ml/3 tbsp toasted sesame seeds

VARIATION
If you can find them, yellow chillies
make a colourful addition to this dish.

1 Preheat the grill (broiler) to medium,
then cook the steak for 2–4 minutes on
each side, depending on how well done
you like it. (In Thailand, the beef is
traditionally served quite rare.) Leave
to cool for at least 15 minutes.

2 Slice the meat as thinly as possible
and place the slices in a bowl.

3 Heat the olive oil in a small frying
pan. Add the seeded and sliced red
chillies and the sliced shiitake
mushroom caps. Cook for 5 minutes,
stirring occasionally. Turn off the heat
and add the steak slices to the pan.
Stir well to coat the beef slices in the
chilli and mushroom mixture.

4 Make the dressing by mixing all the
ingredients in a bowl, then pour it over
the meat mixture and toss gently.

5 Arrange the lettuce, tomatoes and
cucumber on a serving plate. Spoon the
steak mixture in the centre and sprinkle
the sesame seeds over. Serve at once.

LARP <u>OF</u> CHIANG MAI

CHIANG MAI IS A CITY IN THE NORTH-EAST OF THAILAND. THE CITY IS CULTURALLY VERY CLOSE TO LAOS AND FAMOUS FOR ITS CHICKEN SALAD, WHICH WAS ORIGINALLY CALLED "LAAP" OR "LARP". DUCK, BEEF OR PORK CAN BE USED INSTEAD OF CHICKEN.

SERVES FOUR TO SIX

INGREDIENTS

450g/1lb minced (ground) chicken
1 lemon grass stalk, root trimmed
3 kaffir lime leaves, finely chopped
4 fresh red chillies, seeded
  and chopped
60ml/4 tbsp lime juice
30ml/2 tbsp nam pla (fish sauce)
15ml/1 tbsp roasted ground rice (see
  Cook's Tip)
2 spring onions (scallions), chopped
30ml/2 tbsp fresh coriander
  (cilantro) leaves
thinly sliced kaffir lime leaves, mixed
  salad leaves and fresh mint sprigs,
  to garnish

1 Heat a large non-stick frying pan. Add the minced chicken and moisten with a little water. Stir constantly over a medium heat for 7–10 minutes until it is cooked. Meanwhile, cut off the lower 5cm/2in of the lemon grass stalk and chop finely.

2 Transfer the cooked chicken to a bowl and add the chopped lemon grass, lime leaves, chillies, lime juice, nam pla, ground rice, spring onions and coriander. Mix thoroughly.

3 Spoon the chicken mixture into a salad bowl. Sprinkle sliced kaffir lime leaves over the top and garnish with salad leaves and sprigs of mint.

COOK'S TIP
Use glutinous rice for the roasted ground rice. Put the rice in a frying pan and dry-roast it until golden brown. Remove and grind to a powder, using a pestle and mortar or a food processor. When the rice is cold, store it in a glass jar in a cool and dry place.

THAI BEEF SALAD

A HEARTY MAIN MEAL SALAD, THIS COMBINES TENDER STRIPS OF STEAK WITH A WONDERFUL CHILLI AND LIME DRESSING.

SERVES FOUR

INGREDIENTS

2 sirloin steaks, each about 225g/8oz
1 lemon grass stalk, root trimmed
1 red onion, finely sliced
1/2 cucumber, cut into strips
30ml/2 tbsp chopped spring
  onion (scallion)
juice of 2 limes
15–30ml/1–2 tbsp nam pla
  (fish sauce)
Chinese mustard cress or salad cress,
  to garnish

COOK'S TIP
Look out for gui chai leaves in Thai groceries. These look like very thin spring onions and are often used as a substitute for the more familiar vegetable.

1 Pan-fry or grill (broil) the steaks for 6–8 minutes for medium-rare. Allow to rest for 10–15 minutes. Meanwhile, cut off the lower 5cm/2in from the lemon grass stalk and chop it finely.

2 When the meat is cool, slice it thinly and put the slices in a large bowl.

3 Add the sliced onion, cucumber, lemon grass and chopped spring onion to the meat slices.

4 Toss the salad and season with the lime juice and nam pla. Transfer to a serving bowl or plate and serve at room temperature or chilled, garnished with Chinese mustard cress or salad cress.

AUBERGINE SALAD

AN APPETIZING AND UNUSUAL SALAD THAT YOU WILL FIND YOURSELF MAKING OVER AND OVER AGAIN.
ROASTING THE AUBERGINES REALLY BRINGS OUT THEIR FLAVOUR.

SERVES FOUR TO SIX

INGREDIENTS
2 aubergines (eggplant)
15ml/1 tbsp vegetable oil
30ml/2 tbsp dried shrimp, soaked in
   warm water for 10 minutes
15ml/1 tbsp coarsely chopped garlic
1 hard-boiled egg, chopped
4 shallots, thinly sliced
   into rings
fresh coriander (cilantro) leaves and
   2 fresh red chillies, seeded and
   sliced, to garnish
For the dressing
30ml/2 tbsp fresh lime juice
5ml/1 tsp palm sugar or light
   muscovado (brown) sugar
30ml/2 tbsp Thai fish sauce

1 Preheat the grill (broiler) to medium
or preheat the oven to 180°C/350°F/
Gas 4. Prick the aubergines several
times with a skewer, then arrange on a
baking sheet. Cook them under the grill
for 30–40 minutes, or until they are
charred and tender. Alternatively, roast
them by placing them directly on the
shelf of the oven for about 1 hour,
turning them at least twice. Remove the
aubergines and set aside until they are
cool enough to handle.

2 Meanwhile, make the dressing. Put
the lime juice, palm or muscovado
sugar and fish sauce into a small bowl.
Whisk well with a fork or balloon whisk.
Cover with clear film (plastic wrap) and
set aside until required.

3 When the aubergines are cool enough
to handle, peel off the skin and cut the
flesh into medium slices.

4 Heat the oil in a small frying pan.
Drain the dried shrimp thoroughly and
add them to the pan with the garlic.
Cook over a medium heat for about
3 minutes, until golden. Remove from
the pan and set aside.

5 Arrange the aubergine slices on a
serving dish. Top with the hard-boiled
egg, shallots and dried shrimp mixture.
Drizzle over the dressing and garnish
with the coriander and red chillies.

VARIATION
For a special occasion, use salted duck's
or quail's eggs, cut in half, instead of
chopped hen's eggs.

RICE SALAD

*THE SKY'S THE LIMIT WITH THIS RECIPE. USE WHATEVER FRUIT, VEGETABLES AND EVEN LEFTOVER
MEAT THAT YOU MIGHT HAVE, MIX WITH COOKED RICE AND POUR OVER THE FRAGRANT DRESSING.*

SERVES FOUR TO SIX

INGREDIENTS
    350g/12oz/3 cups cooked rice
    1 Asian pear, cored and diced
    50g/2oz dried shrimp, chopped
    1 avocado, peeled, stoned (pitted)
      and diced
    ½ medium cucumber, finely diced
    2 lemon grass stalks, finely chopped
    30ml/2 tbsp sweet chilli sauce
    1 fresh green or red chilli, seeded
      and finely sliced
    115g/4oz/1 cup flaked (sliced)
      almonds, toasted
    small bunch fresh coriander
      (cilantro), chopped
    fresh Thai sweet basil leaves,
      to garnish
For the dressing
    300ml/½ pint/1¼ cups water
    10ml/2 tsp shrimp paste
    15ml/1 tbsp palm sugar or light
      muscovado (brown) sugar
    2 kaffir lime leaves, torn into
      small pieces
    ½ lemon grass stalk, sliced

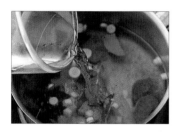

1 Make the dressing. Put the measured
water in a small pan with the shrimp
paste, sugar, kaffir lime leaves and lemon
grass. Heat gently, stirring, until the
sugar dissolves, then bring to boiling
point and simmer for 5 minutes. Strain
into a bowl and set aside until cold.

2 Put the cooked rice in a large salad
bowl and fluff up the grains with a fork.
Add the Asian pear, dried shrimp,
avocado, cucumber, lemon grass and
sweet chilli sauce. Mix well.

3 Add the diced chilli, almonds and
coriander to the bowl and toss well.
Garnish with Thai basil leaves and serve
with the bowl of dressing to spoon over
the top of individual portions.

SCENTED FISH SALAD

FOR A TROPICAL TASTE OF THE FAR EAST, TRY THIS DELICIOUS FISH SALAD SCENTED WITH COCONUT, FRUIT AND WARM THAI SPICES. DO TRY TO LOCATE THE PITAYA OR DRAGON FRUIT. THE FLESH OF THESE FUCHSIA-PINK OR YELLOW EXOTICS IS SWEET AND REFRESHING, WITH A SLIGHTLY ACIDIC MELON-LIKE FLAVOUR THAT GOES PARTICULARLY WELL WITH FISH.

SERVES FOUR

INGREDIENTS
350g/12oz fillet of red mullet, sea
　bream or snapper
1 cos or romaine lettuce
1 papaya or mango, peeled
　and sliced
1 pitaya, peeled and sliced
1 large ripe tomato, cut into wedges
½ cucumber, peeled and cut
　into batons
3 spring onions (scallions), sliced
salt
For the marinade
　5ml/1 tsp coriander seeds
　5ml/1 tsp fennel seeds
　2.5ml/½ tsp cumin seeds
　5ml/1 tsp caster (superfine) sugar
　2.5ml/½ tsp hot chilli sauce
　30ml/2 tbsp garlic oil
For the dressing
　15ml/1 tbsp creamed coconut
　　(coconut cream)
　45ml/3 tbsp boiling water
　60ml/4 tbsp groundnut (peanut) oil
　finely grated rind and juice of 1 lime
　1 fresh red chilli, seeded and
　　finely chopped
　5ml/1 tsp granulated sugar
　45ml/3 tbsp chopped fresh
　　coriander (cilantro)

1 Cut the fish into even strips, removing any stray bones. Place it on a plate.

2 Make the marinade. Put the coriander, fennel and cumin seeds in a mortar. Add the sugar and crush with a pestle. Stir in the chilli sauce, garlic oil, and salt to taste and mix to a paste.

3 Spread the paste over the fish, cover and leave to marinate in a cool place for at least 20 minutes.

4 Make the dressing. Place the coconut and salt in a screw-top jar. Stir in the water. Add the oil, lime rind and juice, chilli, sugar and coriander. Shake well.

5 Wash and dry the lettuce leaves. Place in a bowl and add the papaya or mango, pitaya, tomato, cucumber and spring onions. Pour in the dressing and toss well to coat.

6 Heat a large non-stick frying-pan, add the fish and cook for 5 minutes, turning once. Add the cooked fish to the salad, toss lightly and serve immediately.

COOK'S TIPS
• If planning ahead, you can leave the fish in its marinade for up to 8 hours in the refrigerator. The dressing can also be made in advance, but do not add the fresh coriander (cilantro) until the last minute and shake vigorously again before pouring it over the salad.
• To make garlic oil, heat 120ml/4fl oz/ ½ cup bland-flavoured oil, such as sunflower, in a small pan. Add 30ml/ 2 tbsp crushed garlic and cook gently for 5 minutes, until the garlic is pale gold. Do not let it burn or the oil will taste bitter. Cool, strain into a clean screw-top jar and use as required.

SEAFOOD SALAD WITH FRUITY DRESSING

WHITE FISH IS BRIEFLY SEARED, THEN SERVED WITH PRAWNS AND SALAD TOSSED IN AN OIL-FREE
APRICOT AND APPLE DRESSING. THE FRUIT FLAVOURS MAKE A DELICATE ACCOMPANIMENT TO THE FISH.

SERVES FOUR

INGREDIENTS
  1 baby onion, sliced lengthways
  lemon juice
  400g/14oz very fresh sea bream or
    sea bass, filleted
  30ml/2 tbsp sake
  4 large king prawns (jumbo shrimp),
    heads and shells removed
  about 400g/14oz mixed salad leaves
For the fruity dressing
  2 ripe apricots, skinned and
    stoned (pitted)
  ¼ apple, peeled and cored
  60ml/4 tbsp second dashi stock or
    the same amount of water and
    5ml/1 tsp dashi-no-moto
  10ml/2 tsp shoyu
  salt and ground white pepper

1 Soak the onion slices in ice-cold water for 30 minutes. Drain well.

2 Bring a pan half-full of water to the boil. Add a dash of lemon juice and plunge the fish fillet into it. Remove after 30 seconds, and cool immediately under cold running water for 30 seconds to stop the cooking. Cut into 8mm/⅓in thick slices crossways.

3 Pour the sake into a small pan, bring to the boil, then add the prawns. Cook for 1 minute, or until their colour has completely changed to pink.

4 Cool immediately under cold running water for 30 seconds to again stop the cooking. Cut the prawns into 1cm/½in thick slices crossways.

5 Slice one apricot very thinly, then set aside. Purée the remaining dressing ingredients in a food processor. Add salt, if required, and pepper. Chill.

6 Lay a small amount of mixed leaves on four plates. Mix the fish, prawn, apricot and onion slices in a bowl. Add the remaining leaves, then pour on the dressing and toss well. Heap up on the plates and serve immediately.

COOK'S TIP
You can use a knife and fork to eat these salads, of course; however, marinated fish definitely tastes better with wooden rather than metal cutlery.

TURBOT SASHIMI SALAD WITH WASABI

EATING SASHIMI, OR RAW FISH, WITH TRADITIONAL SAUCES DISAPPEARED WHEN SHOYU BECAME
POPULAR IN THE 17TH CENTURY. THE USE OF SAUCES RETURNED WITH THE WESTERN-INSPIRED SALAD.

SERVES FOUR

INGREDIENTS
  ice cubes
  400g/14oz very fresh thick turbot,
    skinned and filleted
  300g/11oz mixed salad leaves
  8 radishes, thinly sliced
For the wasabi dressing
  25g/1oz rocket (arugula) leaves
  50g/2oz cucumber, chopped
  90ml/6 tbsp rice vinegar (use brown
    if available)
  75ml/5 tbsp olive oil
  5ml/1 tsp salt
  15ml/1 tbsp wasabi paste from a
    tube, or the same amount of
    wasabi powder mixed with 7.5ml/
    1½ tsp water

1 First make the dressing. Roughly tear the rocket leaves and process with the cucumber and rice vinegar in a food processor or blender. Pour into a small bowl and add the rest of the dressing ingredients, except for the wasabi. Check the seasoning and add more salt, if required. Chill until needed.

2 Chill the serving plates while you prepare the fish, if you like.

3 Prepare a bowl of cold water with a few ice cubes. Cut the turbot fillet in half lengthways, then cut into 5mm/¼in thick slices crossways. Plunge these into the ice-cold water as you slice. After 2 minutes or so, they will start to curl and become firm. Take out and drain on kitchen paper.

4 In a large bowl, mix the fish, salad leaves and radishes. Mix the wasabi into the dressing and toss well with the salad. Serve immediately.

POMELO SALAD

TYPICALLY, A THAI MEAL INCLUDES A SELECTION OF ABOUT FIVE DISHES, ONE OF WHICH IS OFTEN A REFRESHING AND PALATE-CLEANSING SALAD THAT FEATURES TROPICAL FRUIT.

SERVES FOUR TO SIX

INGREDIENTS
    30ml/2 tbsp vegetable oil
    4 shallots, finely sliced
    2 garlic cloves, finely sliced
    1 large pomelo
    15ml/1 tbsp roasted peanuts
    115g/4oz cooked peeled
        prawns (shrimp)
    115g/4oz cooked crab meat
    10–12 small fresh mint leaves
For the dressing
    30ml/2 tbsp Thai fish sauce
    15ml/1 tbsp palm sugar or light
        muscovado (brown) sugar
    30ml/2 tbsp fresh lime juice
For the garnish
    2 spring onions (scallions),
        thinly sliced
    2 fresh red chillies, seeded and
        thinly sliced
    fresh coriander (cilantro) leaves
    shredded fresh coconut (optional)

1 Make the dressing. Mix the fish sauce, sugar and lime juice in a bowl. Whisk well, then cover with clear film (plastic wrap) and set aside.

2 Heat the oil in a small frying pan, add the shallots and garlic and cook over a medium heat until they are golden. Remove from the pan and set aside.

3 Peel the pomelo and break the flesh into small pieces, taking care to remove any membranes.

4 Grind the peanuts coarsely and put them in a salad bowl. Add the pomelo flesh, prawns, crab meat, mint leaves and the shallot mixture. Pour over the dressing, toss lightly and sprinkle with the spring onions, chillies and coriander leaves. Add the shredded coconut, if using. Serve immediately.

COOK'S TIP
The pomelo is a large citrus fruit that looks rather like a grapefruit, although it is not, as is sometimes thought, a hybrid. It is slightly pear-shaped with thick, yellow, dimpled skin and pinkish-yellow flesh that is both sturdier and drier than that of a grapefruit. It also has a sharper taste. Pomelos are sometimes known as "shaddocks" after the sea captain who brought them from their native Polynesia to the Caribbean.

PIQUANT PRAWN SALAD

THE FISH SAUCE DRESSING ADDS A SUPERB FLAVOUR TO THE NOODLES AND PRAWNS. THIS DELICIOUS SALAD CAN BE ENJOYED WARM OR COLD, AND WILL SERVE SIX AS AN APPETIZER.

SERVES FOUR

INGREDIENTS

    200g/7oz rice vermicelli
    8 baby corn cobs, halved
    150g/5oz mangetouts (snow peas)
    15ml/1 tbsp vegetable oil
    2 garlic cloves, finely chopped
    2.5cm/1in piece fresh root ginger,
      peeled and finely chopped
    1 fresh red or green chilli, seeded
      and finely chopped
    450g/1lb raw peeled tiger prawns
      (jumbo shrimp)
    4 spring onions (scallions), very
      thinly sliced
    15ml/1 tbsp sesame seeds, toasted
    1 lemon grass stalk, thinly shredded
For the dressing
    15ml/1 tbsp chopped fresh chives
    15ml/1 tbsp Thai fish sauce
    5ml/1 tsp soy sauce
    45ml/3 tbsp groundnut (peanut) oil
    5ml/1 tsp sesame oil
    30ml/2 tbsp rice vinegar

1 Put the rice vermicelli in a wide heatproof bowl, pour over boiling water and leave to soak for 10 minutes. Drain, refresh under cold water and drain well again. Tip into a large serving bowl and set aside until required.

2 Boil or steam the corn cobs and mangetouts for about 3 minutes, until tender but still crunchy. Refresh under cold running water and drain. Make the dressing by mixing all the ingredients in a screw-top jar. Close tightly and shake vigorously to combine.

3 Heat the oil in a large frying pan or wok. Add the garlic, ginger and red or green chilli and cook for 1 minute. Add the tiger prawns and toss over the heat for about 3 minutes, until they have just turned pink. Stir in the spring onions, corn cobs, mangetouts and sesame seeds, and toss lightly to mix.

4 Tip the contents of the pan or wok over the rice vermicelli. Pour the dressing on top and toss well. Sprinkle with lemon grass and serve, or chill for 1 hour before serving.

THAI PRAWN SALAD WITH GARLIC DRESSING AND FRIZZLED SHALLOTS

IN THIS INTENSELY FLAVOURED SALAD, SWEET PRAWNS AND MANGO ARE PARTNERED WITH A SWEET-SOUR GARLIC DRESSING HEIGHTENED WITH THE HOT TASTE OF CHILLI. THE CRISP FRIZZLED SHALLOTS ARE A TRADITIONAL ADDITION TO THAI SALADS.

SERVES FOUR TO SIX

INGREDIENTS

675g/1½lb medium raw prawns
    (shrimp), peeled and deveined, with
    tails intact
finely shredded rind of 1 lime
½ fresh red chilli, seeded and
    finely chopped
30ml/2 tbsp olive oil, plus extra
    for brushing
1 ripe but firm mango
2 carrots, cut into long thin shreds
10cm/4in piece cucumber, sliced
1 small red onion, halved and
    thinly sliced
a few fresh mint sprigs
a few fresh coriander (cilantro) sprigs
45ml/3 tbsp roasted peanuts,
    coarsely chopped
4 large shallots, thinly sliced and
    fried until crisp in 30ml/2 tbsp
    groundnut (peanut) oil
salt and ground black pepper
For the dressing
1 large garlic clove, chopped
10–15ml/2–3 tsp caster
    (superfine) sugar
juice of 2 limes
15–30ml/1–2 tbsp Thai fish sauce
1 fresh red chilli, seeded and
    finely chopped
5–10ml/1–2 tsp light rice vinegar

2 Make the dressing. Place the garlic in a mortar with 10ml/2 tsp of the caster sugar. Pound with a pestle until smooth, then work in about three-quarters of the lime juice, followed by 15ml/1 tbsp of the Thai fish sauce.

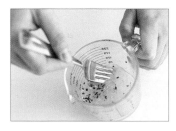

3 Transfer the dressing to a jug (pitcher). Stir in half the chopped red chilli. Taste the dressing and add more sugar, lime juice and/or fish sauce, if you think they are necessary, and stir in light rice vinegar to taste.

4 Peel and stone (pit) the mango. The best way to do this is to cut either side of the large central stone (pit), as close to it as possible, with a sharp knife. Cut the flesh into very fine strips and cut off any flesh still adhering to the stone.

5 Place the strips of mango in a bowl and add the carrots, cucumber slices and red onion. Pour over about half the dressing and toss thoroughly. Arrange the salad on four to six individual serving plates or in bowls.

6 Heat a ridged, cast-iron griddle pan or heavy frying pan until very hot. Brush with a little oil, then sear the marinated prawns for 2–3 minutes on each side, until they turn pink and are patched with brown on the outside. Arrange the prawns on the salads.

7 Sprinkle the remaining dressing over the salads and garnish with the mint and coriander sprigs. Sprinkle over the remaining chilli with the peanuts and crisp-fried shallots. Serve immediately.

COOK'S TIP
To devein the prawns (shrimp), make a shallow cut down the back of each prawn, using a small, sharp knife. Using the tip of the knife, lift out the thin, black vein, then rinse the prawn thoroughly under cold, running water, drain it and pat it dry with kitchen paper.

1 Place the prawns in a glass dish with the lime rind, chilli, oil and seasoning. Toss to mix and leave to marinate at room temperature for 30–40 minutes.

DESSERTS

After a spicy meal, it is customary to serve a platter of fresh
fruits, often carved into the most beautiful shapes, to cleanse
the palate. Ices are popular too, especially when based on
watermelon or fresh lime juice. However, Asians also love
sticky sweetmeats, and will often pick up their favourite treats
from a stall at a night market, where they will be presented
prettily on palm leaves or with a decoration of tiny flowers.
Fried bananas and pineapple are also widely enjoyed.

FRIED BANANAS

THESE DELICIOUSLY SWEET TREATS ARE A FAVOURITE WITH CHILDREN AND ADULTS ALIKE.
IN THAILAND, YOU WILL FIND THEM ON SALE FROM PORTABLE ROADSIDE STALLS AND MARKETS
AT ALMOST EVERY HOUR OF THE DAY AND NIGHT.

SERVES FOUR

INGREDIENTS

   115g/4oz/1 cup plain (all-purpose)
     flour
   2.5ml/½ tsp bicarbonate of soda
     (baking soda)
   pinch of salt
   30ml/2 tbsp granulated sugar
   1 egg, beaten
   90ml/6 tbsp water
   30ml/2 tbsp shredded coconut or
     15ml/1 tbsp sesame seeds
   4 firm bananas
   vegetable oil, for deep-frying
   fresh mint sprigs, to decorate
   30ml/2 tbsp clear honey, to
     serve (optional)

1 Sift the flour, bicarbonate of soda
and salt into a large bowl. Stir in the
granulated sugar and the egg, and
whisk in just enough of the water to
make quite a thin batter.

2 Whisk the shredded coconut or
sesame seeds into the batter so that
they are evenly distributed.

3 Peel the bananas. Carefully cut each
one in half lengthways, then in half
crossways to make 16 pieces of about
the same size. Don't do this until you
are ready to cook them because, once
peeled, bananas quickly discolour.

VARIATIONS
This recipe works just as well with many
other types of fruit, such as pineapple
rings or apple wedges.

4 Heat the oil in a wok or deep-fryer to
a temperature of 190°C/375°F or until
a cube of bread, dropped in the oil,
browns in about 45 seconds. Dip the
banana pieces in the batter, then gently
drop a few into the oil. Deep-fry until
golden brown, then lift out and drain
well on kitchen paper.

5 Cook the remaining banana pieces
in the same way. Serve immediately
with honey, if using, and decorated with
sprigs of fresh mint.

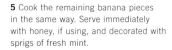

COCONUT PANCAKES

THESE LIGHT AND SWEET PANCAKES ARE OFTEN SERVED AS STREET FOOD BY THE HAWKERS IN
BANGKOK AND THEY MAKE A DELIGHTFUL DESSERT.

MAKES EIGHT

INGREDIENTS
    75g/3oz/¾ cup plain (all-purpose)
      flour, sifted
    60ml/4 tbsp rice flour
    45ml/3 tbsp caster (superfine) sugar
    50g/2oz/⅔ cup desiccated (dry
      unsweetened shredded) coconut
    1 egg
    275ml/9fl oz/generous 1 cup
      coconut milk
    vegetable oil, for frying
    lime wedges and maple syrup,
      to serve

1 Place the plain flour, rice flour, sugar
and coconut in a bowl, stir to mix and
then make a small well in the centre.
Break the egg into the well and pour in
the coconut milk.

2 With a whisk or fork, beat the egg
into the coconut milk and then
gradually incorporate the surrounding
dry ingredients, whisking constantly
until the mixture forms a batter. The
mixture will not be entirely smooth,
because of the coconut, but there
shouldn't be any large lumps.

COOK'S TIP
Maple syrup is not, of course, indigenous
to Thailand, but then nor are chillies. It
is an international favourite for serving
with pancakes. Make sure that you buy
the pure syrup for the best flavour.

VARIATION
Serve with honey instead of maple syrup,
if you like.

3 Heat a little oil in a 13cm/5in non-
stick frying pan. Pour in about 45ml/
3 tbsp of the mixture and quickly
spread to a thin layer with the back of a
spoon. Cook over a high heat for about
30–60 seconds, until bubbles appear
on the surface of the pancake, then
turn it over with a spatula and cook the
other side until golden.

4 Slide the pancake on to a plate and
keep it warm in a very low oven. Make
more pancakes in the same way. Serve
warm with lime wedges for squeezing
and maple syrup for drizzling.

BANANA FRITTERS

KNOWN AS PISANG GORENG, THESE DELICIOUS DEEP-FRIED BANANAS SHOULD BE COOKED AT THE LAST MINUTE, SO THAT THE BATTER IS CRISP AND THE BANANA INSIDE IS SOFT AND WARM.

SERVES EIGHT

INGREDIENTS
115g/4oz/1 cup self-raising (self-rising) flour
40g/1½ oz/¼ cup rice flour
2.5ml/½ tsp salt
200ml/7fl oz/scant 1 cup water
finely grated lime rind (optional)
8 baby bananas
vegetable oil, for deep frying
strips of lime rind, to garnish
caster (superfine) sugar and lime wedges, to serve

COOK'S TIP
Tiny bananas are available from some Asian stores and many larger supermarkets, alternatively use small bananas and cut in half lengthways and then in half again.

1 Sift together the self-raising flour, rice flour and salt into a bowl. Add just enough water to make a smooth, coating batter. Mix well, then add the lime rind, if using.

VARIATION
Instead of lime, add finely grated orange rind to the batter.

2 Heat the oil in a deep fryer or wok to 190°C/375°F. Meanwhile, peel the bananas. Dip them into the batter two or three times until well coated, then deep fry until crisp and golden. Drain on kitchen paper. Serve hot, dredged with caster sugar and garnished with strips of lime. Offer the lime wedges for squeezing over the bananas.

BLACK GLUTINOUS RICE PUDDING

THIS VERY UNUSUAL RICE PUDDING, KNOWN AS BUBOR PULOT HITAM, IS FLAVOURED WITH BRUISED FRESH ROOT GINGER AND IS QUITE DELICIOUS SERVED WITH COCONUT MILK OR CREAM. WHEN COOKED, BLACK RICE STILL RETAINS ITS HUSK AND HAS A LOVELY NUTTY TEXTURE.

SERVES SIX

INGREDIENTS
115g/4oz/⅔ cup black glutinous rice
475ml/16fl oz/2 cups water
1cm/½in piece fresh root ginger, peeled and bruised
50g/2oz/⅓ cup dark brown sugar
50g/2oz/¼ cup caster (superfine) sugar
300ml/½ pint/1¼ cups coconut milk, to serve

COOK'S TIP
To make coconut milk, blend 225g/8oz/2⅔ cups desiccated (dry unsweetened shredded) coconut with 450ml/¾ pint/1¾ cups boiling water in a food processor for 30 seconds. Tip into a sieve lined with muslin (cheesecloth) and twist the muslin to extract the liquid.

1 Put the black glutinous rice in a sieve and rinse it well under plenty of cold running water. Drain the rice and put it in a large pan, along with the water. Bring the water to the boil and stir it as it heats, in order to prevent the rice from settling on the base of the pan. Cover the pan and cook over a very low heat for about 30 minutes.

2 Add the ginger and both types of sugar to the pan. Cook for 15 minutes more, adding a little more water if necessary, until the rice is cooked and porridge-like.

3 Remove the ginger and pour into individual bowls. Serve warm, topped with coconut milk or coconut cream.

THAI FRIED PINEAPPLE

A VERY SIMPLE AND QUICK THAI DESSERT — PINEAPPLE FRIED IN BUTTER, BROWN SUGAR AND LIME JUICE, AND SPRINKLED WITH TOASTED COCONUT. THE SLIGHTLY SHARP TASTE OF THE FRUIT MAKES THIS A VERY REFRESHING TREAT AT THE END OF A MEAL.

3 Meanwhile, dry-fry the coconut in a small frying pan until lightly browned. Remove from the heat and set aside.

4 Sprinkle the sugar into the pan with the pineapple, add the lime juice and cook, stirring constantly, until the sugar has dissolved. Divide the pineapple wedges among four bowls, sprinkle with the coconut, decorate with the lime slices and serve with the yogurt.

SERVES FOUR

INGREDIENTS
  1 pineapple
  40g/1½oz/3 tbsp butter
  15ml/1 tbsp desiccated (dry
    unsweetened shredded) coconut
  60ml/4 tbsp soft light brown sugar
  60ml/4 tbsp fresh lime juice
  lime slices, to decorate
  thick and creamy natural (plain)
    yogurt, to serve

1 Using a sharp knife, cut the top off the pineapple and peel off the skin, taking care to remove the eyes. Cut the pineapple in half and remove and discard the woody core. Cut the flesh lengthways into 1cm/½in wedges.

2 Heat the butter in a large, heavy frying pan or wok. When it has melted, add the pineapple wedges and cook over a medium heat for 1–2 minutes on each side, or until they have turned pale golden in colour.

COCONUT RICE PUDDING

A DELICIOUS ADAPTATION OF THE CLASSIC CREAMY RICE PUDDING, THIS DESSERT IS FLAVOURED WITH COCONUT MILK AND FINISHED WITH A COCONUT CRUST.

SERVES FOUR

INGREDIENTS

  75g/3oz/scant ½ cup short grain
    pudding rice
  40g/1½oz/3 tbsp caster
    (superfine) sugar
  2.5ml/½ tsp vanilla essence (extract)
  300ml/½ pint/1¼ cups milk
  400ml/14fl oz/1⅔ cups coconut milk
  105ml/7 tbsp single (light) cream
  30ml/2 tbsp desiccated (dry
    unsweetened shredded) coconut
    or slivers of fresh coconut

VARIATION
If preferred, this pudding can be made
with extra full cream (whole) milk instead
of the single cream.

1 Soak a small clay pot in cold water for 15 minutes, then drain. Add the rice, sugar, vanilla essence, milk, coconut milk and cream.

2 Cover the clay pot and place in a cold oven. Set the oven to 180°C/350°F/Gas 4 and cook for 1 hour.

3 Remove the lid from the clay pot, stir the pudding gently, then re-cover and cook for a further 30–45 minutes, or until the rice is tender.

4 Remove the lid, stir the pudding, then sprinkle with coconut and bake uncovered for 10–15 minutes.

TROPICAL FRUIT GRATIN

THIS OUT-OF-THE-ORDINARY GRATIN IS STRICTLY FOR GROWN-UPS. A COLOURFUL COMBINATION OF FRUIT IS TOPPED WITH A SIMPLE SABAYON BEFORE BEING FLASHED UNDER THE GRILL.

SERVES FOUR

INGREDIENTS
2 tamarillos
½ sweet pineapple
1 ripe mango
175g/6oz/1½ cups blackberries
120ml/4fl oz/½ cup sparkling
   white wine
115g/4oz/½ cup caster
   (superfine) sugar
6 egg yolks

VARIATION
Boiling drives off the alcohol in the wine, but children do not always appreciate the flavour. Substitute orange juice if making the gratin for them. White grape juice or pineapple juice would also work well.

1 Cut each tamarillo in half lengthways, then into thick slices. Cut the rind and core from the pineapple and take spiral slices off the outside to remove the eyes. Cut the flesh into chunks. Peel the mango, cut it in half and cut the flesh from the stone (pit) in slices.

2 Divide all the fruit, including the blackberries, among four 14cm/5½in gratin dishes set on a baking sheet and set aside. Heat the wine and sugar in a pan until the sugar has dissolved. Bring to the boil and cook for 5 minutes.

3 Put the egg yolks in a large heatproof bowl. Place the bowl over a pan of simmering water and whisk until pale. Slowly pour on the hot sugar syrup, whisking all the time, until the mixture thickens. Preheat the grill (broiler).

4 Spoon the mixture over the fruit. Place the baking sheet holding the dishes on a low shelf under the hot grill until the topping is golden. Serve the gratin hot.

GRILLED PINEAPPLE ᵂᴵᵀᴴ PAPAYA SAUCE

PINEAPPLE COOKED THIS WAY TAKES ON A SUPERB FLAVOUR AND IS SENSATIONAL WHEN SERVED WITH THE PAPAYA SAUCE.

SERVES SIX

INGREDIENTS
1 sweet pineapple
melted butter, for greasing
   and brushing
2 pieces drained stem ginger in
   syrup, cut into fine matchsticks,
   plus 30ml/2 tbsp of the syrup
   from the jar
30ml/2 tbsp demerara (raw) sugar
pinch of ground cinnamon
fresh mint sprigs, to decorate
For the sauce
1 ripe papaya, peeled and seeded
175ml/6fl oz/¾ cup apple juice

1 Peel the pineapple and take spiral slices off the outside to remove the eyes. Cut it crossways into six slices, each 2.5cm/1in thick. Line a baking sheet with a sheet of foil, rolling up the sides to make a rim. Grease the foil with melted butter. Preheat the grill (broiler).

2 Arrange the pineapple slices on the lined baking sheet. Brush with butter, then top with the ginger matchsticks, sugar and cinnamon. Drizzle over the stem ginger syrup. Grill (broil) for 5–7 minutes or until the slices are golden and lightly charred on top.

3 Meanwhile, make the sauce. Cut a few slices from the papaya and set aside, then purée the rest with the apple juice in a blender or food processor.

4 Press the purée through a sieve placed over a bowl, then stir in any juices from cooking the pineapple. Serve the pineapple slices with a little sauce drizzled around each plate. Decorate with the reserved papaya slices and the mint sprigs.

COOK'S TIP
Try the papaya sauce with savoury dishes, too. It tastes great with grilled chicken and game birds as well as pork and lamb.

TAPIOCA PUDDING

THIS PUDDING, MADE FROM LARGE PEARL TAPIOCA AND COCONUT MILK AND SERVED WARM, IS MUCH LIGHTER THAN THE WESTERN-STYLE VERSION. YOU CAN ADJUST THE SWEETNESS TO YOUR TASTE. SERVE WITH LYCHEES OR THE SMALLER, SIMILAR-TASTING LONGANS — ALSO KNOWN AS "DRAGON'S EYES".

SERVES FOUR

INGREDIENTS

115g/4oz/⅔ cup tapioca
475ml/16fl oz/2 cups water
175g/6oz/¾ cup granulated sugar
pinch of salt
250ml/8fl oz/1 cup coconut milk
250g/9oz prepared tropical fruits
finely shredded lime rind
  and shaved fresh coconut (optional),
  to decorate

1 Put the tapioca in a bowl and pour over warm water to cover. Leave to soak for 1 hour so the grains swell. Drain.

2 Pour the measured water in a large pan and bring to the boil over a medium heat. Add the sugar and salt and stir until dissolved.

3 Add the tapioca and coconut milk, reduce the heat to low and simmer gently for 10 minutes, or until the tapioca becomes transparent.

4 Spoon into one large or four individual bowls and serve warm with the tropical fruits. Decorate with the lime rind and coconut shavings, if using.

BAKED RICE PUDDING, THAI-STYLE

BLACK GLUTINOUS RICE, ALSO KNOWN AS BLACK STICKY RICE, HAS LONG DARK GRAINS AND A NUTTY TASTE REMINISCENT OF WILD RICE. THIS BAKED PUDDING HAS A DISTINCT CHARACTER AND FLAVOUR ALL OF ITS OWN, AS WELL AS AN INTRIGUING APPEARANCE.

SERVES FOUR TO SIX

INGREDIENTS
   175g/6oz/1 cup white or black
     glutinous rice
   30ml/2 tbsp soft light brown sugar
   475ml/16fl oz/2 cups coconut milk
   250ml/8fl oz/1 cup water
   3 eggs
   30ml/2 tbsp granulated sugar

1 Combine the glutinous rice and brown sugar in a pan. Pour in half the coconut milk and the water.

2 Bring to the boil, reduce the heat to low and simmer, stirring occasionally, for 15–20 minutes, or until the rice has absorbed most of the liquid. Preheat the oven to 150°C/300°F/Gas 2.

3 Spoon the rice mixture into a single large ovenproof dish or divide it among individual ramekins. Beat the eggs with the remaining coconut milk and sugar in a bowl.

4 Strain the egg mixture into a jug (pitcher), then pour it evenly over the par-cooked rice in the dish or ramekins.

5 Place the dish or ramekins in a roasting pan. Carefully pour in enough hot water to come halfway up the sides of the dish or ramekins.

6 Cover with foil and bake for about 35–60 minutes, or until the custard has set. Serve warm or cold.

COOK'S TIP
Throughout South-east Asia, black glutinous rice is usually used for sweet dishes, while its white counterpart is more often used in savoury recipes.

STEWED PUMPKIN IN COCONUT CREAM

FRUIT STEWED IN COCONUT MILK IS A POPULAR DESSERT IN THAILAND. PUMPKINS, BANANAS AND MELONS CAN ALL BE PREPARED IN THIS SIMPLE BUT TASTY WAY.

SERVES FOUR TO SIX

INGREDIENTS

1kg/2¼ lb kabocha pumpkin
750ml/1¼ pints/3 cups coconut milk
175g/6oz/¾ cup granulated sugar
pinch of salt
4–6 fresh mint sprigs, to decorate

COOK'S TIP
To make the decoration, wash the pumpkin seeds to remove any fibres, then pat them dry on kitchen paper. Roast them in a dry frying pan, or spread them out on a baking sheet and grill (broil) until golden brown, tossing them frequently to prevent them from burning.

1 Cut the pumpkin in half using a large, sharp knife, then cut away and discard the skin. Scoop out the seed cluster. Reserve a few seeds and throw away the rest. Using a sharp knife, cut the pumpkin flesh into pieces that are about 5cm/2in long and 2cm/¾in thick.

2 Pour the coconut milk into a pan. Add the sugar and salt and bring to the boil. Add the pumpkin and simmer for about 10–15 minutes, until it is tender. Serve warm, in individual dishes. Decorate each serving with a mint sprig and toasted pumpkin seeds (see Cook's Tip).

MANGOES WITH STICKY RICE

STICKY RICE IS JUST AS GOOD IN DESSERTS AS IN SAVOURY DISHES, AND MANGOES, WITH THEIR DELICATE FRAGRANCE AND VELVETY FLESH, COMPLEMENT IT ESPECIALLY WELL. YOU NEED TO START PREPARING THIS DISH THE DAY BEFORE YOU INTEND TO SERVE IT.

SERVES FOUR

INGREDIENTS

115g/4oz/⅔ cup white
   glutinous rice
175ml/6fl oz/¾ cup thick
   coconut milk
45ml/3 tbsp granulated sugar
pinch of salt
2 ripe mangoes
strips of pared lime rind,
   to decorate

1 Rinse the glutinous rice thoroughly in several changes of cold water, then leave to soak overnight in a bowl of fresh cold water.

COOK'S TIP
Like cream, the thickest and richest part of coconut milk always rises to the top. Whenever you open a can or carton, spoon off this top layer and use it with fruit or to enrich a spicy savoury dish just before serving.

2 Drain the rice well and spread it out evenly in a steamer lined with muslin or cheesecloth. Cover and steam over a pan of simmering water for about 20 minutes, or until the rice is tender.

3 Reserve 45ml/3 tbsp of the cream from the top of the coconut milk. Pour the remainder into a pan and add the sugar and salt. Heat, stirring constantly, until the sugar has dissolved, then bring to the boil. Remove the pan from the heat, pour the coconut milk into a bowl and leave to cool.

4 Tip the cooked rice into a bowl and pour over the cooled coconut milk mixture. Stir well, then leave the rice mixture to stand for 10–15 minutes.

5 Meanwhile, peel the mangoes, cut the flesh away from the central stones (pits) and cut into slices.

6 Spoon the rice on to individual serving plates. Arrange the mango slices on one side, then drizzle with the reserved coconut cream. Decorate with strips of lime rind and serve.

EXOTIC FRUIT SUSHI

THIS IDEA CAN BE ADAPTED TO INCORPORATE A WIDE VARIETY OF FRUITS, BUT TO KEEP TO THE EXOTIC THEME TAKE YOUR INSPIRATION FROM THE TROPICS. THE SUSHI NEEDS TO CHILL OVERNIGHT TO ENSURE THE RICE MIXTURE FIRMS PROPERLY, SO BE SURE YOU START THIS IN GOOD TIME.

SERVES FOUR

INGREDIENTS
  150g/5oz/⅔ cup short grain
    pudding rice
  350ml/12fl oz/1½ cups water
  400ml/14fl oz/1⅔ cups
    coconut milk
  75g/3oz/⅓ cup caster (superfine)
    sugar
  a selection of exotic fruit, such as
    1 mango, 1 kiwi fruit, 2 figs and
    1 star fruit, thinly sliced
  30ml/2 tbsp apricot jam, sieved
For the raspberry sauce
  225g/8oz/2 cups raspberries
  25g/1oz/¼ cup icing
    (confectioner's) sugar

1 Rinse the rice well under cold running water, drain and place in a pan with 300ml/½ pint/1¼ cups of the water. Pour in 175ml/6fl oz/¾ cup of the coconut milk. Cook over a very low heat for 25 minutes, stirring often and gradually adding the remaining coconut milk, until the rice has absorbed all the liquid and is tender.

2 Grease a 18cm/7in square tin (pan) and line it with clear film (plastic wrap). Stir 30ml/2 tbsp of the caster sugar into the rice mixture and pour it into the tin. Cool, then chill overnight.

3 Cut the rice mixture into 16 small bars, shape into ovals and flatten the tops. Place on a baking sheet lined with baking parchment. Arrange the sliced fruit on top, using one type of fruit only for each sushi.

4 Place the remaining sugar in a small pan with the remaining 50ml/4 tbsp water. Bring to the boil, then lower the heat and simmer until thick and syrupy. Stir in the jam and cool slightly.

5 To make the sauce, purée the raspberries with the icing sugar in a food processor or blender. Press through a sieve, then divide among four small bowls. Arrange a few different fruit sushi on each plate and spoon over a little of the cool apricot syrup. Serve with the sauce.

PAPAYA BAKED <u>WITH</u> GINGER

*GINGER ENHANCES THE FLAVOUR OF PAPAYA IN THIS RECIPE, WHICH TAKES NO MORE THAN
TEN MINUTES TO PREPARE! DON'T OVERCOOK PAPAYA OR THE FLESH WILL BECOME VERY WATERY.*

SERVES FOUR

INGREDIENTS

2 ripe papayas
2 pieces stem ginger in syrup,
    drained, plus 15ml/1 tbsp syrup
    from the jar
8 amaretti or other dessert biscuits
    (cookies), coarsely crushed
45ml/3 tbsp raisins
shredded, finely pared rind and juice
    of 1 lime
25g/1oz/¼ cup pistachio
    nuts, chopped
15ml/1 tbsp light muscovado sugar
60ml/4 tbsp double (heavy) cream,
    plus extra to serve

VARIATION
Use Greek yogurt and almonds instead
of cream and pistachios.

1 Preheat the oven to 200°C/400°F/
Gas 6. Cut the papayas in half and
scoop out their seeds. Place the halves
in a baking dish and set aside. Cut the
stem ginger into fine matchsticks.

2 Make the filling. Combine the
crushed amaretti biscuits, stem ginger
matchsticks and raisins in a bowl.

3 Stir in the lime rind and juice, two
thirds of the nuts, then add the sugar
and cream. Mix well.

4 Fill the papaya halves and drizzle
with the ginger syrup. Sprinkle with
the remaining nuts. Bake for about
25 minutes or until tender. Serve with
extra cream.

LEMON GRASS SKEWERS WITH LIME CHEESE

GRILLED FRUITS MAKE A FINE FINALE TO A BARBECUE, WHETHER THEY ARE COOKED OVER THE COALS OR UNDER A HOT GRILL. THE LEMON GRASS SKEWERS GIVE THE FRUIT A SUBTLE LEMON TANG. THE FRUITS USED HERE MAKE AN IDEAL EXOTIC MIX, BUT ALMOST ANY SOFT FRUIT CAN BE SUBSTITUTED.

SERVES FOUR

INGREDIENTS
  4 long fresh lemon grass stalks
  1 mango, peeled, stoned (pitted)
   and sliced
  1 papaya, peeled, seeded and diced
  1 star fruit, cut into slices and halved
  8 fresh bay leaves
  a nutmeg
  60ml/4 tbsp maple syrup
  50g/2oz/⅓ cup demerara (raw) sugar
For the lime cheese
  150g/5oz/⅔ cup curd cheese or low-
   fat soft cheese
  120ml/4fl oz/½ cup double (heavy)
   cream
  grated rind and juice of ½ lime
  30ml/2 tbsp icing (confectioner's)
   sugar

1 Prepare the barbecue or preheat the grill (broiler). Cut the top of each lemon grass stalk into a point with a sharp knife. Discard the outer leaves, then use the back of the knife to bruise the length of each stalk to release the oils. Thread each stalk, skewer-style, with the fruit pieces and bay leaves.

2 Support a piece of foil on a baking sheet and roll up the edges to make a rim. Grease the foil, lay the kebabs on top and grate a little nutmeg over each. Drizzle the maple syrup over and dust liberally with the sugar. Grill (broil) for 5 minutes, until lightly charred.

3 Meanwhile, make the lime cheese. Mix together the cheese, cream, grated lime rind and juice and icing sugar in a bowl. Serve at once with the lightly charred fruit kebabs.

COOK'S TIP
Only fresh lemon grass will work as skewers for this recipe. It is now possible to buy lemon grass stalks in jars. These are handy for curries and similar dishes, but are too soft to use as skewers.

COCONUT JELLY WITH STAR ANISE FRUITS

SERVE THIS DESSERT AFTER ANY ASIAN-STYLE MEAL WITH PLENTY OF REFRESHING EXOTIC FRUIT.

SERVES FOUR

INGREDIENTS
  250ml/8fl oz/1 cup cold water
  75g/3oz/⅓ cup caster (superfine)
   sugar
  15ml/1 tbsp powdered gelatine
  400ml/14fl oz/1⅔ cups coconut milk
For the syrup and fruit
  250ml/8fl oz/1 cup water
  3 star anise
  50g/2oz/¼ cup caster (superfine) sugar
  1 star fruit, sliced
  12 lychees, peeled and stoned (pitted)
  115g/4oz/1 cup blackberries

1 Pour the water into a pan and add the sugar. Heat gently until the sugar has dissolved. Sprinkle over the gelatine and continue to heat gently, stirring, until the gelatine has dissolved. Stir in the coconut milk, remove from the heat and set aside to cool.

2 Grease an 18cm/7in square tin (pan). Line with clear film (plastic wrap). Pour in the milk mixture and chill until set.

3 To make the syrup, combine the water, star anise and sugar in a pan. Bring to the boil, stirring, then lower the heat and simmer for 10–12 minutes until syrupy. Place the fruit in a heatproof bowl and pour over the hot syrup. Cool, then chill.

4 To serve, cut the coconut jelly into diamonds and remove from the tin. Arrange the coconut jelly on individual plates, adding a few of the fruits and their syrup to each portion.

COOK'S TIP
Coconut milk is available in cans or as a powder. If using the powder, reconstitute it with cold water according to the packet instructions.

CHURROS

THESE IRRESISTIBLE FRITTERS, SERVED AT EVERY OPPORTUNITY WITH HOT CHOCOLATE OR COFFEE,
CAME TO THE PHILIPPINES WITH THE SPANISH WHO WERE KEEN TO KEEP MEMORIES OF HOME ALIVE.

MAKES ABOUT TWENTY-FOUR

INGREDIENTS
    450ml/15fl oz/scant 2 cups water
    15ml/1 tbsp olive oil
    15ml/1 tbsp sugar, plus extra
        for sprinkling
    2.5ml/$\frac{1}{2}$ tsp salt
    150g/5oz/1$\frac{1}{4}$ cups plain
        (all-purpose) flour
    1 large (US extra large) egg
    sunflower oil, for deep-frying
    caster (superfine) sugar,
        for sprinkling

COOK'S TIP
If you don't have a piping (pastry) bag,
you could fry teaspoons of mixture in
the same way. Don't try to fry too many
churros at a time as they swell a little
during cooking.

1 Mix the water, oil, sugar and salt in a
large pan and bring to the boil. Remove
from the heat, and then sift in the
flour. Beat well with a wooden spoon
until smooth.

2 Beat in the egg to make a smooth,
glossy mixture with a piping consistency.
Spoon into a piping (pastry) bag fitted
with a large star nozzle.

3 Heat the oil in a wok or deep fryer to
190°C/375°F. Pipe loops of the mixture,
two at a time, into the hot oil. Cook
the loops for 3–4 minutes until they
are golden.

4 Lift out the churros with a wire
skimmer or slotted spoon and drain
them on kitchen paper. Dredge them
with caster sugar and serve warm.

LECHE FLAN

SERVE THIS DESSERT HOT OR COLD WITH WHIPPED CREAM. THE USE OF EVAPORATED MILK REFLECTS
THE 50 YEARS OF AMERICAN PRESENCE IN THE PHILIPPINES.

SERVES EIGHT

INGREDIENTS
    5 large eggs
    30ml/2 tbsp caster (superfine)
        sugar
    few drops vanilla essence (extract)
    410g/14$\frac{1}{2}$oz can evaporated
        (unsweetened condensed) milk
    300ml/$\frac{1}{2}$ pint/1$\frac{1}{4}$ cups milk
    5ml/1 tsp finely grated lime rind
    strips of lime rind, to decorate
For the caramel
    225g/8oz/1 cup sugar
    120ml/4fl oz/$\frac{1}{2}$ cup water

1 Make the caramel. Put the sugar and
water in a heavy pan. Stir to dissolve
the sugar, then boil without stirring
until golden. Pour into eight ramekins,
rotating to coat the sides.

2 Preheat the oven to 150°C/300°F/
Gas 2. Beat the eggs, sugar and vanilla
essence in a bowl. Mix the evaporated
milk and fresh milk in a pan. Heat to
just below boiling point, then pour on
to the egg mixture, stirring all the time.
Strain the custard mixture into a jug,
add the grated lime rind and cool. Pour
into the caramel-coated ramekins.

3 Place the ramekins in a roasting pan
and pour in enough warm water to come
halfway up the sides of the dishes.

4 Transfer the roasting pan to the oven
and cook the custards for 35–45
minutes or until they just shimmer when
the ramekins are gently shaken.

5 Serve the custards in their ramekin
dishes or by inverting on to serving
plates, in which case break the caramel
and use as decoration. The custards
can be served warm or cold, decorated
with strips of lime rind.

COOK'S TIP
Make extra caramel, if you like, for a
garnish. Pour on to lightly oiled foil and
leave to set, then crush with a rolling pin.

COCONUT CUSTARD

THIS TRADITIONAL DESSERT CAN BE BAKED OR STEAMED AND IS OFTEN SERVED WITH SWEET STICKY RICE AND A SELECTION OF FRESH FRUIT. MANGOES AND TAMARILLOS GO PARTICULARLY WELL WITH THE CUSTARD AND RICE.

2 Strain the mixture into a jug (pitcher), then pour it into four individual heatproof glasses, ramekins or an ovenproof dish.

3 Stand the glasses, ramekins or dish in a roasting pan. Fill the pan with hot water to reach halfway up the sides of the ramekins or dish.

4 Bake for about 35–40 minutes, or until the custards are set. Test with a fine skewer or cocktail stick (toothpick).

5 Remove the roasting pan from the oven, lift out the ramekins or dish and leave to cool.

6 If you like, turn out the custards on to serving plate(s). Decorate with the mint leaves and a dusting of icing sugar, and serve with sliced fruit.

SERVES FOUR

INGREDIENTS
 4 eggs
 75g/3oz/6 tbsp soft light brown sugar
 250ml/8fl oz/1 cup coconut milk
 5ml/1 tsp vanilla, rose or
  jasmine extract
 fresh mint leaves and icing
  (confectioners') sugar, to decorate
 sliced fruit, to serve

1 Preheat the oven to 150°C/300°F/ Gas 2. Whisk the eggs and sugar in a bowl until smooth. Add the coconut milk and extract and whisk well.

COCONUT CREAM DIAMONDS

DESSERTS LIKE THESE ARE SERVED IN COUNTRIES ALL OVER THE FAR EAST, OFTEN WITH MANGOES, PINEAPPLE OR GUAVAS. ALTHOUGH COMMERCIALLY GROUND RICE CAN BE USED FOR THIS DISH, GRINDING JASMINE RICE YOURSELF — IN A FOOD PROCESSOR — GIVES A MUCH BETTER RESULT.

SERVES FOUR TO SIX

INGREDIENTS

    75g/3oz/scant ½ cup jasmine rice,
      soaked overnight in 175ml/6fl oz/
      ¾ cup water
    350ml/12fl oz/1½ cups
      coconut milk
    150ml/¼ pint/⅔ cup single
      (light) cream
    50g/2oz/¼ cup caster
      (superfine) sugar
    raspberries and fresh mint leaves,
      to decorate
For the coulis
    75g/3oz/¾ cup blackcurrants,
      stalks removed
    30ml/2 tbsp caster (superfine) sugar
    75g/3oz/½ cup fresh or
      frozen raspberries

4 Line a rectangular tin (pan) with non-stick baking parchment. Pour the coconut rice mixture into the pan, cool, then chill in the refrigerator until the dessert is set and firm.

5 Meanwhile, make the coulis. Put the blackcurrants in a bowl and sprinkle with the sugar. Set aside for about 30 minutes. Tip the blackcurrants and raspberries into a wire sieve set over a bowl. Using a spoon, press the fruit against the sides of the sieve so that the juices collect in the bowl. Taste the coulis and add more sugar if necessary.

6 Carefully cut the coconut cream into diamonds. Spoon a little of the coulis on to each dessert plate, arrange the coconut cream diamonds on top and decorate with the fresh raspberries and mint leaves. Serve immediately.

1 Put the rice and its soaking water into a food processor and process for a few minutes until the mixture is soupy.

2 Heat the coconut milk and cream in a non-stick pan. When the mixture is on the point of boiling, stir in the rice mixture. Cook over a very gentle heat for 10 minutes, stirring constantly.

3 Stir the sugar into the coconut rice mixture and continue cooking for a further 10–15 minutes, or until the mixture is thick and creamy.

VARIATION
You could use other soft fruit in the coulis, such as blackberries or redcurrants.

PAPAYAS IN JASMINE FLOWER SYRUP

THE FRAGRANT SYRUP CAN BE PREPARED IN ADVANCE, USING FRESH JASMINE FLOWERS FROM A HOUSE PLANT OR THE GARDEN. IT TASTES FABULOUS WITH PAPAYAS, BUT IT IS ALSO GOOD WITH ALL SORTS OF DESSERTS. TRY IT WITH ICE CREAM OR SPOONED OVER LYCHEES OR MANGOES.

SERVES TWO

INGREDIENTS

105ml/7 tbsp water
45ml/3 tbsp palm sugar or light
 muscovado (brown) sugar
20–30 jasmine flowers, plus a
 few extra, to decorate (optional)
2 ripe papayas
juice of 1 lime

COOK'S TIP

Although scented white jasmine flowers are perfectly safe to eat, it is important to be sure that they have not been sprayed with pesticides or other harmful chemicals. Washing them may not remove all the residue.

1 Place the water and sugar in a small pan. Heat gently, stirring occasionally, until the sugar has dissolved, then simmer, without stirring, over a low heat for 4 minutes.

2 Pour into a bowl, leave to cool slightly, then add the jasmine flowers. Leave to steep for at least 20 minutes.

3 Peel the papayas and slice in half lengthways. Scoop out and discard the seeds. Place the papayas on serving plates and squeeze over the lime.

4 Strain the syrup into a clean bowl, discarding the flowers. Spoon the syrup over the papayas. If you like, decorate with a few fresh jasmine flowers.

STEAMED CUSTARD ᴵᴺ NECTARINES

*STEAMING NECTARINES OR PEACHES BRINGS OUT THEIR NATURAL COLOUR AND SWEETNESS, SO THIS IS
A GOOD WAY OF MAKING THE MOST OF UNDERRIPE OR LESS FLAVOURFUL FRUIT.*

SERVES FOUR TO SIX

INGREDIENTS
   6 nectarines
   1 large (US extra large) egg
   45ml/3 tbsp palm sugar or light
      muscovado (brown) sugar
   30ml/2 tbsp coconut milk

COOK'S TIP
Palm sugar, also known as jaggery, is
made from the sap of certain Asian palm
trees, such as coconut and palmyrah. It
is available from Asian food stores. If you
buy it as a cake or large lump, grate it
before use.

1 Cut the nectarines in half. Using a
teaspoon, scoop out the stones (pits)
and a little of the surrounding flesh.

2 Lightly beat the egg, then add the
sugar and the coconut milk. Beat until
the sugar has dissolved.

3 Transfer the nectarines to a steamer
and carefully fill the cavities three-
quarters full with the custard mixture.
Steam over a pan of simmering water
for 5–10 minutes. Remove from the
heat and leave to cool completely before
transferring to plates and serving.

GREEN AND YELLOW LAYERED CAKES

THIS COLOURFUL TWO-TONE DESSERT IS MADE BY MOULDING CONTRASTING MIXTURES IN A SMALL POUCH. ITS JAPANESE NAME, CHAKIN-SHIBORI, IS DERIVED FROM THE PREPARATION TECHNIQUE, IN WHICH CHAKIN MEANS A POUCH SHAPE AND SHIBORI MEANS A MOULDING ACTION.

MAKES SIX

INGREDIENTS
For the yolk mixture (kimi-an)
   6 small hard-boiled eggs
   50g/2oz/¼ cup sugar
For the pea mixture (endo-an)
   200g/7oz/1¾ cups frozen peas
   40g/1½oz/3 tbsp sugar

1 Make the yolk mixture. Shell the eggs, cut them in half and scoop the yolks into a sieve placed over a bowl. Using a wooden spoon, press the yolks through the sieve. Add the sugar and mix well.

2 To make the pea mixture, cook the peas in lightly salted boiling water for about 3–4 minutes, until softened. Drain and place in a mortar, then crush with a pestle. Transfer the paste to a pan. Add the sugar and cook over a low heat until thick. Stir constantly so that the mixture does not burn.

3 Spread out the pea paste in a shallow dish so that it cools as quickly as possible. Divide both mixtures into six portions.

COOK'S TIP
Use a food processor instead of a mortar and pestle if you prefer. Process for a few seconds to make a coarse paste.

4 Wet a piece of muslin (cheesecloth) or thin cotton and wring it out well. Place a portion of the pea mixture on the cloth and put a similar amount of the yolk mixture on top. Wrap the mixture up and twist the top of the cloth to join the mixtures together and mark a spiral pattern on the top. Unwrap and place on a plate. Make five more cakes in the same way. Serve cold.

THAI RICE CAKE

*NOT A DRY SNACK FROM THE HEALTH FOOD STORE, BUT A SUMPTUOUS CELEBRATION GATEAU, MADE
FROM THAI FRAGRANT RICE, TANGY CREAM AND WITH A FRESH FRUIT TOPPING.*

SERVES EIGHT TO TEN

INGREDIENTS
   225g/8oz/generous 1 cup Thai
     fragrant rice, rinsed
   1 litre/1¾ pints/4 cups milk
   115g/4oz/scant ½ cup caster
     (superfine) sugar
   6 green cardamom pods, crushed
   2 bay leaves
   300ml/½ pint/1¼ cups whipping cream
   6 eggs, separated
   red and white currants, sliced star
     fruit and kiwi fruit, to decorate
For the topping
   250ml/8fl oz/1 cup double
     (heavy) cream
   150g/5oz/⅔ cup low-fat soft cheese
   5ml/1 tsp vanilla essence (extract)
   grated rind of 1 lemon
   40g/1½oz/3 tbsp caster sugar

1 Grease and line a 25cm/10in round,
deep cake tin (pan). Cook the rice in a
pan of boiling unsalted water for 3
minutes, then drain, return to the pan
and pour in the milk. Stir in the caster
sugar, cardamoms and bay leaves.
Bring to the boil, then lower the heat
and simmer the rice for 20 minutes,
stirring occasionally. Allow the mixture
to cool, then remove the bay leaves and
cardamom husks.

2 Preheat the oven to 180°C/350°F/
Gas 4. Spoon the rice mixture into a
bowl. Beat in the cream and then the
egg yolks. Whisk the egg whites until
they form soft peaks, then fold them
into the rice mixture.

3 Spoon into the prepared tin and bake
for 45–50 minutes until risen and golden
brown. Chill overnight in the tin. Turn
the cake out on to a large serving plate.

4 Whip the cream until stiff, then
gently fold in the soft cheese, vanilla
essence, lemon rind and sugar.

5 Cover the top of the cake with the
cream mixture, swirling it attractively.
Decorate with red and white currants,
sliced star fruit and kiwi fruit.

COOK'S TIP
Do not worry if the centre of the cake is
slightly wobbly when you take it out of
the oven. It will firm up as the cake
starts to cool.

COLD MANGO SOUFFLÉS TOPPED WITH TOASTED COCONUT

FRAGRANT, FRESH MANGO IS ONE OF THE MOST DELICIOUS EXOTIC FRUITS AROUND, WHETHER IT IS SIMPLY SERVED IN SLICES OR USED AS THE BASIS FOR AN ICE CREAM OR SOUFFLÉ.

MAKES FOUR

INGREDIENTS

4 small mangoes, peeled, stoned
(pitted) and chopped
30ml/2 tbsp water
15ml/1 tbsp powdered gelatine
2 egg yolks
115g/4oz/½ cup caster
(superfine) sugar
120ml/4fl oz/½ cup milk
grated rind of 1 orange
300ml/½ pint/1¼ cups double
(heavy) cream
toasted flaked or coarsely shredded
coconut, to decorate

1 Place a few pieces of mango in the base of each of four 150ml/¼ pint/⅔ cup ramekins. Wrap a greased collar of baking parchment around the outside of each dish, extending well above the rim. Secure with adhesive tape, then tie tightly with string.

2 Pour the water into a small heatproof bowl and sprinkle the gelatine over the surface. Leave for 5 minutes or until spongy. Place the bowl in a pan of hot water, stirring occasionally, until the gelatine has dissolved.

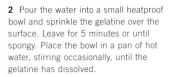

3 Meanwhile, whisk the egg yolks with the caster sugar and milk in another heatproof bowl. Place the bowl over a pan of simmering water and continue to whisk until the mixture is thick and frothy. Remove from the heat and continue whisking until the mixture cools. Whisk in the liquid gelatine.

4 Purée the remaining mango pieces in a food processor or blender, then fold the purée into the egg yolk mixture with the orange rind. Set the mixture aside until starting to thicken.

5 Whip the double cream to soft peaks. Reserve 60ml/4 tbsp and fold the rest into the mango mixture. Spoon into the ramekins until the mixture is 2.5cm/1in above the rim of each dish. Chill for 3–4 hours or until set.

6 Carefully remove the paper collars from the soufflés. Spoon a little of the reserved cream on top of each soufflé and decorate with some toasted flaked or coarsely shredded coconut.

MANGO AND LIME FOOL

CANNED MANGOES ARE USED HERE FOR CONVENIENCE, BUT THE DISH TASTES EVEN BETTER IF MADE WITH FRESH ONES. CHOOSE A VARIETY LIKE THE VOLUPTUOUS ALPHONSO MANGO, WHICH IS WONDERFULLY FRAGRANT AND TASTES INDESCRIBABLY DELICIOUS.

SERVES FOUR

INGREDIENTS
   400g/14oz can sliced mango
   grated rind of 1 lime
   juice of ½ lime
   150ml/¼ pint/⅔ cup double
      (heavy) cream
   90ml/6 tbsp Greek (US strained
      plain) yogurt
   fresh mango slices, to decorate
      (optional)

COOK'S TIP
When mixing the cream and yogurt mixture with the mango purée, whisk just enough to combine, so as not to lose the lightness of the whipped cream mixture. If you prefer, fold the mixtures together lightly, so that the fool is rippled.

1 Drain the canned mango slices and put them in the bowl of a food processor. Add the grated lime rind and the lime juice. Process until the mixture forms a smooth purée. Alternatively, mash the mango slices with a potato masher, then press through a sieve into a bowl with the back of a wooden spoon. Stir in the lime rind and juice.

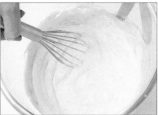

2 Pour the cream into a bowl and add the yogurt. Whisk until the mixture is thick and then quickly whisk in the mango mixture.

3 Spoon into four tall cups or glasses and chill for 1–2 hours. Just before serving, decorate each glass with fresh mango slices, if you like.

EXOTIC FRUIT SALAD <u>WITH</u> PASSION FRUIT DRESSING

PASSION FRUIT MAKES A SUPERB DRESSING FOR ANY FRUIT, BUT REALLY BRINGS OUT THE FLAVOUR OF EXOTIC VARIETIES. YOU CAN EASILY DOUBLE THE RECIPE, THEN SERVE THE REST FOR BREAKFAST.

SERVES SIX

INGREDIENTS
 1 mango
 1 papaya
 2 kiwi fruit
 coconut or vanilla ice cream, to serve
For the dressing
 3 passion fruit
 thinly pared rind and juice of 1 lime
 5ml/1 tsp hazelnut or walnut oil
 15ml/1 tbsp clear honey

COOK'S TIP
A clear golden honey scented with orange blossom or acacia blossom would be perfect for the dressing.

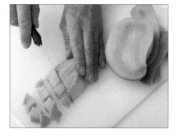

1 Peel the mango, cut it into three slices, then cut the flesh into chunks and place it in a large bowl. Peel the papaya and cut it in half. Scoop out the seeds, then chop the flesh.

2 Cut both ends off each kiwi fruit, then stand them on a board. Using a small sharp knife, cut off the skin from top to bottom. Cut each kiwi fruit in half lengthways, then cut into thick slices. Combine all the fruit in a large bowl.

3 Make the dressing. Cut each passion fruit in half and scoop the seeds out into a sieve set over a small bowl. Press the seeds well to extract all their juices. Lightly whisk the remaining dressing ingredients into the passion fruit juice, then pour the dressing over the fruit. Mix gently to combine. Leave to chill for 1 hour before serving with scoops of coconut or vanilla ice cream.

WATERMELON ICE

AFTER A HOT AND SPICY THAI MEAL, THE ONLY THING MORE REFRESHING THAN ICE-COLD
WATERMELON IS THIS WATERMELON ICE. MAKING IT IS SIMPLICITY ITSELF.

3 Spoon the watermelon into a food processor. Process to a slush, then mix with the sugar syrup. Chill the mixture in the refrigerator for 3–4 hours.

4 Strain the mixture into a freezerproof container. Freeze for 2 hours, then remove from the freezer and beat with a fork to break up the ice crystals. Return the mixture to the freezer and freeze for 3 hours more, beating the mixture at half-hourly intervals. Freeze until firm.

5 Alternatively, use an ice-cream maker. Pour the chilled mixture into the machine and churn until it is firm enough to scoop. Serve immediately, or scrape into a freezerproof container and store in the freezer.

6 About 30 minutes before serving, transfer the ice to the refrigerator so that it softens slightly. This allows the full flavour of the watermelon to be enjoyed and makes it easier to scoop.

SERVES FOUR TO SIX

INGREDIENTS
    90ml/6 tbsp caster
      (superfine) sugar
    105ml/7 tbsp water
    4 kaffir lime leaves, torn into
      small pieces
    500g/1¼lb watermelon

1 Put the sugar, water and lime leaves in a pan. Heat gently until the sugar has dissolved. Pour into a large bowl and set aside to cool.

2 Cut the watermelon into wedges with a large knife. Cut the flesh from the rind, remove the seeds and chop.

ICED FRUIT MOUNTAIN

THIS DRAMATIC DISPLAY OF FRUIT ARRANGED ON A "MOUNTAIN" OF ICE CUBES IS BOUND TO DELIGHT YOUR GUESTS. CUT THE PIECES OF FRUIT LARGER THAN FOR A FRUIT SALAD AND SUPPLY COCKTAIL STICKS FOR SPEARING.

SERVES SIX TO EIGHT

INGREDIENTS
1 star fruit
4 kumquats
6 physalis
225g/8oz seedless black grapes
225g/8oz large strawberries
1 apple and/or 1 Asian pear
2 large oranges, peeled
8 fresh lychees, peeled (optional)
1 Charentais melon and/or
    1/2 watermelon
caster (superfine) sugar, for dipping
wedges of kaffir lime, to decorate

COOK'S TIP
The list of fruits is just a suggestion.
Use any colourful seasonal fruits.

1 Slice the star fruit and halve the kumquats. Leave the hulls on the strawberries. Cut the apple and/or Asian pear into wedges, and the oranges into segments. Use a melon baller for the melon or, alternatively, cut the melon into neat wedges. Chill all the fruit.

2 Prepare the ice cube "mountain". Choose a wide, shallow bowl that, when turned upside down, will fit neatly on a serving platter. Fill the bowl with crushed ice cubes. Put it in the freezer, with the serving platter. Leave in the freezer for at least 1 hour.

3 Remove the serving platter, ice cubes and bowl from the freezer. Invert the serving platter on top of the bowl of ice, then turn platter and bowl over. Lift off the bowl and arrange the pieces of fruit on the "mountain".

4 Decorate the mountain with the kaffir lime wedges, and serve the fruit at once, handing round a bowl of sugar separately for guests with a sweet tooth.

CHINESE HONEYED APPLES

THESE SCRUMPTIOUS TREATS ARE BEST PREPARED FOR A SELECT NUMBER AS THEY REQUIRE THE COOK'S COMPLETE ATTENTION. THE HONEY COATING CRISPENS WHEN THE FRITTERS ARE DIPPED IN ICED WATER.

SERVES FOUR TO FIVE

INGREDIENTS
4 crisp eating apples
juice of 1/2 lemon
25g/1oz/1/4 cup cornflour (cornstarch)
sunflower oil, for deep-frying
toasted sesame seeds, for sprinkling
For the fritter batter
115g/4oz/1 cup plain (all-purpose)
    flour
generous pinch of salt
120–150ml/4–5fl oz/
    1/2–2/3 cup water
30ml/2 tbsp sunflower oil
2 egg whites
For the sauce
250ml/8fl oz/1 cup clear honey
120ml/4fl oz/1/2 cup sunflower oil
5ml/1 tsp white wine vinegar

1 Peel, core and cut the apples into eighths, brush each piece lightly with lemon juice then dust with cornflour. Make the sauce. Heat the honey and oil in a pan, stirring until blended. Remove from the heat and stir in the vinegar.

2 Sift the flour and salt into a bowl, then stir in the water and oil. Whisk the egg whites until stiff; fold into the batter.

3 Spear each piece of apple in turn on a skewer, dip in the batter and fry in hot oil until golden. Drain on kitchen paper, place in a dish and pour the sauce over.

4 Transfer the fritters to a lightly oiled serving dish. Sprinkle with sesame seeds. Serve immediately, offering bowls of iced water for dipping.

MALAYSIAN COCONUT ICE CREAM

THIS ICE CREAM IS DELECTABLE AND VERY EASY TO MAKE IN AN ICE-CREAM MAKER, ESPECIALLY IF YOU USE THE TYPE WITH A BOWL THAT IS PLACED IN THE FREEZER TO CHILL BEFORE THE ICE-CREAM MIXTURE IS ADDED. THE ICE CREAM IS THEN CHURNED BY A MOTORIZED LID WITH A PADDLE.

2 Pour the mixture into the frozen freezer bowl of an ice-cream maker (or follow the appliance instructions) and churn till the mixture has thickened. (This will take 30–40 minutes.)

3 Transfer the mixture to a lidded plastic tub, cover and freeze until the consistency is right for scooping. If you do not have an ice-cream maker, pour the mixture into a shallow container and freeze on the coldest setting.

4 When ice crystals form around the sides of the ice cream, beat the mixture, then return it to the freezer. Do this at least twice. The more you do it, the creamier the mixture will be.

5 Make the sauce. Mix the sugar, measured water and ginger in a pan. Stir over medium heat until the sugar has dissolved, then bring the liquid to the boil. Add the pandan leaf, if using, tying it into a knot so that it can easily be removed with the ginger before serving. Lower the heat and simmer for 3–4 minutes. Set aside till required.

6 Serve the ice cream in coconut shells or in a bowl. Sprinkle with the strips of coconut and serve with the gula melaka sauce, which can be hot, warm or cold.

SERVES SIX

INGREDIENTS
    400ml/14fl oz can coconut milk
    400ml/14fl oz can condensed milk
    2.5ml/½ tsp salt
For the gula melaka sauce
    150g/5oz/¾ cup palm sugar or
        muscovado (molasses) sugar
    150ml/¼ pint/⅔ cup water
    1cm/½in slice fresh root
      ginger, bruised
    1 pandan leaf (if available)
    coconut shells (optional) and thinly
        pared strips of coconut, to serve

1 Chill the cans of coconut and condensed milk very thoroughly. In a bowl, mix the coconut milk with the condensed milk. Gently whisk together with the salt.

COOK'S TIP
Coconut milk takes longer to freeze than double (heavy) cream, so allow plenty of time for the process.

COCONUT AND LEMON GRASS ICE CREAM

THE COMBINATION OF CREAM AND COCONUT MILK MAKES FOR A WONDERFULLY RICH ICE CREAM.
THE LEMON GRASS FLAVOURING IS VERY SUBTLE, BUT QUITE DELICIOUS.

SERVES FOUR

INGREDIENTS
   2 lemon grass stalks
   475ml/16fl oz/2 cups double
   (heavy) cream
   120ml/4fl oz/½ cup coconut milk
   4 large (US extra large) eggs
   105ml/7 tbsp caster
   (superfine) sugar
   5ml/1 tsp vanilla essence (extract)

1 Cut the lemon grass stalks in half lengthways. Use a mallet or rolling pin to mash the pieces, breaking up the fibres so that all the flavour is released.

2 Pour the cream and coconut milk into a pan. Add the lemon grass stalks and heat gently, stirring frequently, until the mixture starts to simmer.

3 Put the eggs, sugar and vanilla essence in a large bowl. Using an electric whisk, whisk until the mixture is very light and fluffy.

4 Strain the cream mixture into a heatproof bowl that will fit over a pan of simmering water. Whisk in the egg mixture, then place the bowl over the pan and continue to whisk until the mixture thickens. Remove it from the heat and leave to cool. Chill the coconut custard in the refrigerator for 3–4 hours.

5 Pour the mixture into a plastic tub or similar freezerproof container. Freeze for 4 hours, beating two or three times at hourly intervals with a fork to break up the ice crystals.

6 Alternatively, use an ice-cream maker. Pour the chilled mixture into the machine and churn until it is firm enough to scoop. Serve immediately, or scrape into a freezerproof container and place in the freezer.

7 About 30 minutes before serving, transfer the container to the refrigerator so that the ice cream softens slightly. Serve in scoops.

VARIATION
To make Coconut and Mango Ice Cream, purée the contents of two 400g/14oz cans of mangoes in syrup and add to the coconut custard before chilling it in the refrigerator. An ice cream made in this way will serve six.

NUTRITIONAL INFORMATION

The nutritional analysis below is per portion (i.e. serving or item), unless otherwise stated. Measurements for sodium do not include salt added to taste.

p132 Coconut chips Energy 167Kcal/690kJ; Protein 1.5g; Carbohydrate 1.8g, of which sugars 1.8g; Fat 17.2g, of which saturates 14.8g; Cholesterol 0mg; Calcium 6mg; Fibre 0g; Sodium 8mg.

p133 Roasted Coconut Cashew Nuts Energy 436Kcal/1810kJ; Protein 9.7g; Carbohydrate 22.1g, of which sugars 16.6g; Fat 34.9g, of which saturates 14.8g; Cholesterol 0mg; Calcium 20mg; Fibre 4g; Sodium 128mg.

p134 Rolled Omelette Energy 273Kcal/1139kJ; Protein 14.7g; Carbohydrate 13.2g, of which sugars 13.1g; Fat 16.6g, of which saturates 4.1g; Cholesterol 441mg; Calcium 70mg; Fibre 0g; Sodium 520mg.

p135 Egg Rolls Energy 189Kcal/780kJ; Protein 11.5g; Carbohydrate 1g, of which sugars 0.9g; Fat 15.3g, of which saturates 3.9g; Cholesterol 331mg; Calcium 76mg; Fibre 0.7g; Sodium 660mg.

p136 Potato, Shallot and Garlic Samosas Energy 36Kcal/151kJ; Protein 1g; Carbohydrate 6.8g, of which sugars 0.4g; Fat 0.7g, of which saturates 0.1g; Cholesterol 0mg; Calcium 11mg; Fibre 0.4g; Sodium 4mg.

p137 Samosas Energy 56Kcal/235kJ; Protein 1.4g; Carbohydrate 10.4g, of which sugars 0.6g; Fat 1.3g, of which saturates 0.7g; Cholesterol 3mg; Calcium 17mg; Fibre 0.6g; Sodium 9mg.

p138 Tung Tong Energy 113Kcal/471kJ; Protein 1.6g; Carbohydrate 13.4g, of which sugars 0.7g; Fat 6.2g, of which saturates 0.9g; Cholesterol 11mg; Calcium 21mg; Fibre 0.7g; Sodium 55mg.

p139 Green Curry Puffs Energy 75Kcal/314kJ; Protein 1.1g; Carbohydrate 8.4g, of which sugars 0.6g; Fat 4.3g, of which saturates 0.6g; Cholesterol 0mg; Calcium 12mg; Fibre 0.4g; Sodium 70mg.

p140 Ensaimadas Energy 340Kcal/1423kJ; Protein 8.7g; Carbohydrate 38g, of which sugars 3.7g; Fat 17.8g, of which saturates 10.3g; Cholesterol 121mg; Calcium 171mg; Fibre 1.4g; Sodium 370mg.

p141 Thai Tempeh Cakes with Sweet Chilli Dipping Sauce Energy 148Kcal/611kJ; Protein 4.2g; Carbohydrate 5.4g, of which sugars 1g; Fat 12.3g, of which saturates 1.6g; Cholesterol 30mg; Calcium 174mg; Fibre 0.3g; Sodium 13mg.

p142 Steamed Flower Rolls
Energy 108Kcal/458kJ; Protein 2.6g; Carbohydrate 22.8g, of which sugars 1.4g; Fat 1.3g, of which saturates 0.4g; Cholesterol 1mg; Calcium 40mg; Fibre 0.9g; Sodium 122mg.

p142 Pork-stuffed Steamed Buns Energy 150Kcal/633kJ; Protein 7g; Carbohydrate 23.7g, of which sugars 2g; Fat 3.6g, of which saturates 1g; Cholesterol 16mg; Calcium 41mg; Fibre 0.9g; Sodium 157mg.

p144 Crispy Shanghai Spring Rolls Energy 103Kcal/432kJ; Protein 8.9g; Carbohydrate 7.3g, of which sugars 0.9g; Fat 4.4g, of which saturates 1g; Cholesterol 49mg; Calcium 95mg; Fibre 0.5g; Sodium 140mg.

p145 Vietnamese Rice Paper Rolls Energy 186Kcal/778kJ; Protein 10.8g; Carbohydrate 12.8g, of which sugars 1.6g; Fat 10.6g, of which saturates 3.8g; Cholesterol 63mg; Calcium 46mg; Fibre 0.9g; Sodium 288mg.

p146 Thai Spring Rolls Energy 135Kcal/562kJ; Protein 3.1g; Carbohydrate 7.8g, of which sugars 0.5g; Fat 10.3g, of which saturates 1.4g; Cholesterol 10mg; Calcium 15mg; Fibre 0.4g; Sodium 41mg.

p148 Cha Gio and Nuoc Cham Energy 153Kcal/636kJ; Protein 6.7g; Carbohydrate 10.8g, of which sugars 0.1g; Fat 9.8g, of which saturates 1.4g; Cholesterol 21mg; Calcium 5mg; Fibre 0.3g; Sodium 98mg.

p149 Rice Triangles Energy 152Kcal/638kJ; Protein 10.8g; Carbohydrate 16.6g, of which sugars 0g; Fat 5.2g, of which saturates 0.8g; Cholesterol 22mg; Calcium 13mg; Fibre 0g; Sodium 1495mg.

p150 Rice Balls with Four Fillings Energy 196Kcal/817kJ; Protein 8.9g; Carbohydrate 16.7g, of which sugars 0.1g; Fat 10.7g, of which saturates 1.7g; Cholesterol 13mg; Calcium 85mg; Fibre 1g; Sodium 101mg.

p152 Simple Rolled Sushi Energy 178Kcal/746kJ; Protein 10.2g; Carbohydrate 26.4g, of which sugars

1.4g; Fat 3.1g, of which saturates 0.5g; Cholesterol 13mg; Calcium 13mg; Fibre 0.1g; Sodium 17mg.

p153 Firecrackers Energy 110Kcal/457kJ; Protein 4.5g; Carbohydrate 7.6g, of which sugars 0g; Fat 6.8g, of which saturates 0.8g; Cholesterol 43mg; Calcium 20mg; Fibre 0.2g; Sodium 87mg.

p154 Filipino Prawn Fritters Energy 696Kcal/2939kJ; Protein 32.9g; Carbohydrate 109.9g, of which sugars 8.5g; Fat 16.9g, of which saturates 2.7g; Cholesterol 281mg; Calcium 312mg; Fibre 6.8g; Sodium 1036mg.

p155 Prawn and Sesame Toasts Energy 433Kcal/1806kJ; Protein 19.1g; Carbohydrate 27.7g, of which sugars 1.2g; Fat 27.6g, of which saturates 3.6g; Cholesterol 110mg; Calcium 271mg; Fibre 2.7g; Sodium 559mg.

p156 Sashimi Moriawase Energy 130Kcal/545kJ; Protein 24.5g; Carbohydrate 0.6g, of which sugars 0.6g; Fat 3.2g, of which saturates 0.5g; Cholesterol 100mg; Calcium 181mg; Fibre 0.5g; Sodium 109mg.

p158 Hand-moulded Sushi Energy 532Kcal/2233kJ; Protein 36.5g; Carbohydrate 83.6g, of which sugars 7.9g; Fat 4.7g, of which saturates 0.5g; Cholesterol 116mg; Calcium 170mg; Fibre 0g; Sodium 1123mg.

p162 Son-in-law Eggs Energy 243Kcal/1018kJ; Protein 10.1g; Carbohydrate 21.4g, of which sugars 21.3g; Fat 13.6g, of which saturates 3g; Cholesterol 289mg; Calcium 51mg; Fibre 0.2g; Sodium 1176mg.

p163 Corn Fritters Energy 76Kcal/315kJ; Protein 2.1g; Carbohydrate 7.6g, of which sugars 0.5g; Fat 4.1g, of which saturates 0.6g; Cholesterol 32mg; Calcium 12mg; Fibre 0.5g; Sodium 102mg.

p164 Chicken and Vegetable Bundles Energy 110Kcal/459kJ; Protein 13.2g; Carbohydrate 3.2g, of which sugars 2.6g; Fat 4.6g, of which saturates 1.2g; Cholesterol 59mg; Calcium 24mg; Fibre 1.4g; Sodium 558mg.

p165 Mini Phoenix Rolls Energy 119Kcal/495kJ; Protein 14.4g; Carbohydrate 0.8g, of which sugars 0.5g; Fat 5.9g, of which saturates 1.7g; Cholesterol 142mg; Calcium 25mg; Fibre 0.3g; Sodium 237mg.

p166 Chicken Satay with Peanut Sauce Energy 375Kcal/1564kJ; Protein 42.9g; Carbohydrate 3.9g, of which sugars 2.4g; Fat 20.9g, of which saturates 5.6g; Cholesterol 149mg; Calcium 27mg; Fibre 1.3g; Sodium 249mg.

p167 Yakitori Chicken Energy 126Kcal/

528kJ; Protein 17.6g; Carbohydrate 0.5g, of which sugars 0.5g; Fat 5.9g, of which saturates 1.7g; Cholesterol 88mg; Calcium 16mg; Fibre 0.3g; Sodium 28mg.

p168 Lettuce Parcels Energy 310Kcal/1288kJ; Protein 19.9g; Carbohydrate 8.4g, of which sugars 1.4g; Fat 21.8g, of which saturates 2.7g; Cholesterol 55mg; Calcium 17mg; Fibre 0.5g; Sodium 296mg.

p169 Drunken Chicken Energy 293Kcal/1228kJ; Protein 38.8g; Carbohydrate 0.5g, of which sugars 0.5g; Fat 10.5g, of which saturates 2.8g; Cholesterol 142mg; Calcium 14mg; Fibre 0g; Sodium 102mg.

p170 Lamb Saté Energy 72Kcal/300kJ; Protein 4.2g; Carbohydrate 0.4g, of which sugars 0.3g; Fat 6g, of which saturates 1.2g; Cholesterol 15mg; Calcium 3mg; Fibre 0g; Sodium 342mg.

p171 Rice Cakes with Spicy Dipping Sauce Energy 361Kcal/1508kJ; Protein 11.7g; Carbohydrate 42g, of which sugars 8.8g; Fat 16g, of which saturates 2.9g; Cholesterol 19mg; Calcium 38mg; Fibre 0.8g; Sodium 359mg.

p172 Crispy Pork Balls Energy 162Kcal/682kJ; Protein 14.9g; Carbohydrate 15.7g, of which sugars 2.7g; Fat 3.1g, of which saturates 1.6g; Cholesterol 39mg; Calcium 37mg; Fibre 0.5g; Sodium 978mg.

p173 Stuffed Chillies Energy 70Kcal/292kJ; Protein 10g; Carbohydrate 1.9g, of which sugars 1.7g; Fat 2.2g, of which saturates 0.6g; Cholesterol 55mg; Calcium 23mg; Fibre 1g; Sodium 482mg.

p174 Popiah Energy 110Kcal/463kJ; Protein 7.6g; Carbohydrate 10.2g, of which sugars 1g; Fat 4.6g, of which saturates 1.2g; Cholesterol 92mg; Calcium 88mg; Fibre 0.7g; Sodium 135mg.

p176 Stuffed Thai Omelettes Energy 303Kcal/1258kJ; Protein 19.8g; Carbohydrate 1.4g, of which sugars 1g; Fat 24.3g, of which saturates 6.4g; Cholesterol 303mg; Calcium 48mg; Fibre 0.2g; Sodium 314mg.

p177 Assorted Tempura Energy 220Kcal/925kJ; Protein 7.2g; Carbohydrate 32.2g, of which sugars 6.2g; Fat 7.8g, of which saturates 1.7g; Cholesterol 80mg; Calcium 66mg; Fibre 2.6g; Sodium 246mg.

p178 Fish Cakes with Cucumber Relish Energy 144Kcal/600kJ; Protein 5.4g; Carbohydrate 9.7g, of which sugars 5.1g; Fat 9.5g, of which saturates 1.4g; Cholesterol 30mg; Calcium 10mg;

Fibre 0.2g; Sodium 25mg.

p179 Soft-shell Crabs with Chilli and Salt Energy 207Kcal/866kJ; Protein 10.5g; Carbohydrate 16.2g, of which sugars 0.7g; Fat 11.6g, of which saturates 2.1g; Cholesterol 35mg; Calcium 36mg; Fibre 0.7g; Sodium 632mg.

p182 Pumpkin and Coconut Soup Energy 77Kcal/328kJ; Protein 6.8g; Carbohydrate 10.9g, of which sugars 10.2g; Fat 1g, of which saturates 0.5g; Cholesterol 56mg; Calcium 104mg; Fibre 1.3g; Sodium 877mg.

p183 Omelette Soup Energy 68Kcal/283kJ; Protein 2.7g; Carbohydrate 3.9g, of which sugars 3.6g; Fat 4.7g, of which saturates 1g; Cholesterol 55mg; Calcium 28mg; Fibre 1.1g; Sodium 772mg.

p184 Balinese Vegetable Soup Energy 63Kcal/262kJ; Protein 1.9g; Carbohydrate 5.4g, of which sugars 4.4g; Fat 3.9g, of which saturates 0.5g; Cholesterol 0mg; Calcium 36mg; Fibre 1.3g; Sodium 57mg.

p185 Cellophane Noodle Soup Energy 143Kcal/598kJ; Protein 4.1g; Carbohydrate 28.3g, of which sugars 4.7g; Fat 1.2g, of which saturates 0.1g; Cholesterol 0mg; Calcium 135mg; Fibre 0.9g; Sodium 8mg.

p186 Hot and Sweet Vegetable and Tofu Soup Energy 103Kcal/434kJ; Protein 5.5g; Carbohydrate 13.3g, of which sugars 12.8g; Fat 3.5g, of which saturates 0.4g; Cholesterol 0mg; Calcium 320mg; Fibre 0.7g; Sodium 769mg.

p187 Mixed Vegetable Soup Energy 134Kcal/554kJ; Protein 7.7g; Carbohydrate 7.5g, of which sugars 6.6g; Fat 8.2g, of which saturates 1.5g; Cholesterol 0mg; Calcium 220mg; Fibre 3g; Sodium 1044mg.

p188 Miso Soup Energy 34Kcal/141kJ; Protein 3.4g; Carbohydrate 1g, of which sugars 0.7g; Fat 1.8g, of which saturates 0.2g; Cholesterol 0mg; Calcium 193mg; Fibre 0g; Sodium 746mg.

p188 Sweet Aduki Bean Soup with Rice Cakes Energy 352Kcal/1501kJ; Protein 8.7g; Carbohydrate 83.8g, of which sugars 59.6g; Fat 0.4g, of which saturates 0.1g; Cholesterol 0mg; Calcium 40mg; Fibre 4.6g; Sodium 5mg.

p190 Crispy Wonton Soup Energy 169Kcal/704kJ; Protein 5.8g; Carbohydrate 16.8g, of which sugars 2.6g; Fat 8.8g, of which saturates 1.9g; Cholesterol 13mg; Calcium 32mg; Fibre 1.5g; Sodium 449mg.

p191 Chiang Mai Noodle Soup Energy 606Kcal/2569kJ; Protein 39.5g; Carbohydrate 88.7g, of which sugars

10.1g; Fat 12.9g, of which saturates 3.7g; Cholesterol 135mg; Calcium 84mg; Fibre 3.3g; Sodium 1111mg.

p192 Hot and Sour Soup Energy 98Kcal/409kJ; Protein 7.8g; Carbohydrate 5.9g, of which sugars 0.9g; Fat 4.9g, of which saturates 0.9g; Cholesterol 49mg; Calcium 139mg; Fibre 0.2g; Sodium 349mg.

p193 Miso Soup with Pork and Vegetables Energy 104Kcal/435kJ; Protein 14.2g; Carbohydrate 2.3g, of which sugars 1.2g; Fat 4.3g, of which saturates 1g; Cholesterol 32mg; Calcium 178mg; Fibre 0.8g; Sodium 474mg.

p194 Ginger, Chicken and Coconut Soup Energy 134Kcal/571kJ; Protein 19.8g; Carbohydrate 10.7g, of which sugars 10.4g; Fat 1.7g, of which saturates 0.7g; Cholesterol 53mg; Calcium 66mg; Fibre 0.5g; Sodium 887mg.

p194 Hot-and-sour Prawn Soup Energy 103Kcal/434kJ; Protein 21.5g; Carbohydrate 1.1g, of which sugars 0.7g; Fat 1.4g, of which saturates 0.2g; Cholesterol 219mg; Calcium 100mg; Fibre 0.8g; Sodium 892mg.

p196 Rice Porridge Energy 331Kcal/1393kJ; Protein 24.7g; Carbohydrate 31.6g, of which sugars 0.4g; Fat 12.7g, of which saturates 4.4g; Cholesterol 74mg; Calcium 34mg; Fibre 0.3g; Sodium 683mg.

p197 Tomato and Beef Soup Energy 94Kcal/398kJ; Protein 6.6g; Carbohydrate 12.1g, of which sugars 5.2g; Fat 2.7g, of which saturates 1g; Cholesterol 11mg; Calcium 17mg; Fibre 1.6g; Sodium 243mg.

p198 Seafood Wonton Soup Energy 89Kcal/376kJ; Protein 10.2g; Carbohydrate 10.5g, of which sugars 0g; Fat 0.6g, of which saturates 0.1g; Cholesterol 39mg; Calcium 19mg; Fibre 0.3g; Sodium 330mg.

p199 Smoked Mackerel and Tomato Soup Energy 209Kcal/868kJ; Protein 10.3g; Carbohydrate 6.6g, of which sugars 6.5g; Fat 15.9g, of which saturates 3.2g; Cholesterol 53mg; Calcium 19mg; Fibre 0.8g; Sodium 681mg.

p200 Thai Fish Broth Energy 125Kcal/534kJ; Protein 28.1g; Carbohydrate 0.9g, of which sugars 0.6g; Fat 1.2g, of which saturates 0.2g; Cholesterol 25mg; Calcium 17mg; Fibre 0g; Sodium 986mg.

p201 Noodle, Pak Choi and Salmon Ramen Energy 543Kcal/2267kJ; Protein 28.4g; Carbohydrate 73.5g, of which sugars 1.6g; Fat 13.8g, of which saturates 2.3g; Cholesterol 56mg; Calcium 46mg; Fibre 0.4g; Sodium 1284mg.

p202 Rice in Green Tea with Salmon Energy 294Kcal/1229kJ; Protein 13g; Carbohydrate 47.2g, of which sugars 0.4g; Fat 5.1g, of which saturates 0.7g; Cholesterol 19mg; Calcium 19mg; Fibre 0g; Sodium 375mg.

p203 Asparagus and Crab Soup Energy 131Kcal/547kJ; Protein 9g; Carbohydrate 9.5g, of which sugars 2.4g; Fat 6.6g, of which saturates 0.8g; Cholesterol 21mg; Calcium 66mg; Fibre 1.8g; Sodium 455mg.

p204 Northern Prawn and Squash Soup Energy 67Kcal/284kJ; Protein 11.5g; Carbohydrate 3.6g, of which sugars 2.9g; Fat 0.9g, of which saturates 0.2g; Cholesterol 110mg; Calcium 82mg; Fibre 1.7g; Sodium 409mg.

p205 Clear Soup with Seafood Sticks Energy 10Kcal/44kJ; Protein 1.2g; Carbohydrate 1.1g, of which sugars 0.3g; Fat 0.2g, of which saturates 0g; Cholesterol 4mg; Calcium 3mg; Fibre 0g; Sodium 1200mg.

p206 Laksa Lemak Energy 869Kcal/3664kJ; Protein 60.8g; Carbohydrate 103.1g, of which sugars 16.9g; Fat 26.5g, of which saturates 2.4g; Cholesterol 300mg; Calcium 589mg; Fibre 7.1g; Sodium 2051mg.

p208 Coconut and Seafood Soup Energy 253Kcal/1068kJ; Protein 37.8g; Carbohydrate 6.9g, of which sugars 5.5g; Fat 8.5g, of which saturates 1.6g; Cholesterol 473mg; Calcium 135mg; Fibre 0.1g; Sodium 930mg.

p209 Malaysian Prawn Laska Energy 385Kcal/1616kJ; Protein 14.9g; Carbohydrate 65.3g, of which sugars 18.2g; Fat 6.8g, of which saturates 1.5g; Cholesterol 122mg; Calcium 120mg; Fibre 2g; Sodium 1132mg.

p212 Stir-fried Chicken with Basil and Chilli Energy 200Kcal/836kJ; Protein 27.2g; Carbohydrate 1.5g, of which sugars 1.4g; Fat 9.5g, of which saturates 1.3g; Cholesterol 79mg; Calcium 7mg; Fibre 0g; Sodium 424mg.

p213 Bang Bang Chicken Energy 304Kcal/1269kJ; Protein 30.2g;

Carbohydrate 4.5g, of which sugars 3.3g; Fat 18.5g, of which saturates 4g; Cholesterol 79mg; Calcium 20mg; Fibre 1.1g; Sodium 289mg.

p214 Sichuan Chicken with Kung Po Sauce Energy 504Kcal/2103kJ; Protein 37.1g; Carbohydrate 18.2g, of which sugars 3.9g; Fat 31.9g, of which saturates 6.3g; Cholesterol 82mg; Calcium 23mg; Fibre 1.2g; Sodium 617mg.

p215 Chicken Rendang Energy 495Kcal/2060kJ; Protein 31.7g; Carbohydrate 10.9g, of which sugars 9.5g; Fat 36.5g, of which saturates 16.2g; Cholesterol 118mg; Calcium 60mg; Fibre 3.4g; Sodium 1210mg.

p216 Green Chicken Curry Energy 334Kcal/1413kJ; Protein 49.4g; Carbohydrate 11.9g, of which sugars 11.7g; Fat 10.4g, of which saturates 2g; Cholesterol 140mg; Calcium 78mg; Fibre 1.1g; Sodium 462mg.

p217 Yellow Chicken Curry Energy 125Kcal/533kJ; Protein 15.7g; Carbohydrate 14.2g, of which sugars 14.1g; Fat 1.1g, of which saturates 0.3g; Cholesterol 44mg; Calcium 41mg; Fibre 1.9g; Sodium 956mg.

p218 Red Chicken Curry with Bamboo Shoots Energy 255Kcal/1077kJ; Protein 29.5g; Carbohydrate 18g, of which sugars 16.9g; Fat 7.8g, of which saturates 1.5g; Cholesterol 79mg; Calcium 92mg; Fibre 0.9g; Sodium 1104mg.

p220 Chicken and Egg with Rice Energy 226Kcal/950kJ; Protein 26.5g; Carbohydrate 13.7g, of which sugars 10.8g; Fat 6.7g, of which saturates 1.9g; Cholesterol 243mg; Calcium 57mg; Fibre 1.6g; Sodium 1186mg.

p221 Barbecue Chicken Energy 248Kcal/1041kJ; Protein 31.1g; Carbohydrate 6.2g, of which sugars 6.1g; Fat 11.2g, of which saturates 3.2g; Cholesterol 126mg; Calcium 21mg; Fibre 0g; Sodium 841mg.

p222 Chicken and Mushroom Donburi Energy 461Kcal/1941kJ; Protein 36g; Carbohydrate 66.6g, of which sugars 24.1g; Fat 5.6g, of which saturates 0.9g; Cholesterol 79mg; Calcium 227mg; Fibre 0.5g; Sodium 771mg.

p223 Southern Chicken Curry Energy 612Kcal/2541kJ; Protein 38.5g; Carbohydrate 9g, of which sugars 8.9g; Fat 47.1g, of which saturates 26.4g; Cholesterol 139mg; Calcium 22mg; Fibre 0g; Sodium 447mg.

p224 Cashew Chicken Energy 458Kcal/1909kJ; Protein 37.1g; Carbohydrate 12.2g, of which sugars 6.2g; Fat 29.3g, of which saturates 5.5g; Cholesterol 79mg; Calcium 35mg; Fibre 2.5g; Sodium 554mg.

p225 Chicken and Lemon Grass Curry
Energy 212Kcal/890kJ; Protein 30.1g;
Carbohydrate 1.4g, of which sugars
1.3g; Fat 9.6g, of which saturates 1.4g;
Cholesterol 88mg; Calcium 8mg;
Fibre 0g; Sodium 342mg.

**p226 Chicken with Ginger and Lemon
Grass** Energy 359Kcal/1491kJ; Protein
27.3g; Carbohydrate 4.1g, of which
sugars 3.3g; Fat 26g, of which saturates
6.1g; Cholesterol 144mg; Calcium
20mg; Fibre 0.9g; Sodium 351mg.

p227 Chicken with Lemon Sauce
Energy 233Kcal/990kJ; Protein 24.9g;
Carbohydrate 29.7g, of which sugars
11.3g; Fat 2g, of which saturates 0.4g;
Cholesterol 70mg; Calcium 14mg;
Fibre 0g; Sodium 90mg.

**p228 Roast Lime Chicken with Sweet
Potatoes** Energy 529Kcal/2201kJ;
Protein 47.3g; Carbohydrate 8.7g,
of which sugars 2.7g; Fat 34g, of
which saturates 9.4g; Cholesterol
248mg; Calcium 26mg; Fibre 0.9g;
Sodium 840mg.

p230 Salt "Baked" Chicken Energy
259Kcal/1076kJ; Protein 23.4g;
Carbohydrate 0.2g, of which sugars
0.1g; Fat 18.3g, of which saturates
4.9g; Cholesterol 124mg; Calcium
10mg; Fibre 0.1g; Sodium 2295mg.

p231 Fragrant Chicken Curry Energy
837Kcal/3472kJ; Protein 50.2g;
Carbohydrate 14.2g, of which sugars
13.7g; Fat 64.6g, of which saturates
29.2g; Cholesterol 253mg; Calcium
85mg; Fibre 0.3g; Sodium 240mg.

p232 Fragrant Grilled Chicken
Energy 243Kcal/1022kJ; Protein 28g;
Carbohydrate 17.7g, of which sugars
17.6g; Fat 7.1g, of which saturates
1.2g; Cholesterol 79mg; Calcium 73mg;
Fibre 1.5g; Sodium 502mg.

p233 Chicken with Mixed Vegetables
Energy 159Kcal/669kJ; Protein 22.9g;
Carbohydrate 6.4g, of which sugars
3.3g; Fat 4.4g, of which saturates 0.7g;
Cholesterol 61mg; Calcium 22mg;
Fibre 1.2g; Sodium 449mg.

p234 Jungle Curry of Guinea Fowl
Energy 368Kcal/1540kJ; Protein 56.8g;
Carbohydrate 1.4g, of which sugars
0.9g; Fat 14g, of which saturates 3.2g;
Cholesterol 0mg; Calcium 82mg;
Fibre 1.1g; Sodium 454mg.

p235 Duck with Pancakes Energy
226Kcal/947kJ; Protein 17.8g;
Carbohydrate 14.2g, of which sugars
8g; Fat 10.9g, of which saturates 1.7g;
Cholesterol 83mg; Calcium 74mg;
Fibre 1.3g; Sodium 378mg.

p236 Stir-fried Crispy Duck Energy
701Kcal/2923kJ; Protein 40.8g;
Carbohydrate 34.9g, of which sugars
13.3g; Fat 45.2g, of which saturates
8.2g; Cholesterol 151mg; Calcium
169mg; Fibre 7.1g; Sodium 862mg.

p237 Duck and Sesame Stir-fry
Energy 152Kcal/634kJ; Protein 14.4g;
Carbohydrate 1.3g, of which sugars
1.1g; Fat 10g, of which saturates 2.1g;
Cholesterol 69mg; Calcium 33mg;
Fibre 1.1g; Sodium 517mg.

p238 Chinese Duck Curry Energy
297Kcal/1245kJ; Protein 30.3g;
Carbohydrate 9.4g, of which sugars
9.1g; Fat 15.7g, of which saturates
4.1g; Cholesterol 165mg; Calcium
67mg; Fibre 0.6g; Sodium 275mg.

p239 Stir-fried Duck with Pineapple
Energy 260Kcal/1103kJ; Protein 18.2g;
Carbohydrate 35.9g, of which sugars
26.9g; Fat 5.9g, of which saturates
1.6g; Cholesterol 83mg; Calcium 66mg;
Fibre 4.3g; Sodium 188mg.

**p240 Peking Duck with Mandarin
Pancakes** Energy 330Kcal/1386kJ;
Protein 19.2g; Carbohydrate 34.3g, of
which sugars 8.1g; Fat 13.8g, of which
saturates 3g; Cholesterol 84mg; Calcium
67mg; Fibre 1.4g; Sodium 582mg.

p242 Anita Wong's Duck Energy
331Kcal/1385kJ; Protein 31.4g;
Carbohydrate 4.1g, of which sugars 4g;
Fat 21.2g, of which saturates 4.7g;
Cholesterol 169mg; Calcium 21mg;
Fibre 0g; Sodium 1098mg.

p243 Duck with Pineapple and Ginger
Energy 492Kcal/2080kJ; Protein 31.2g;
Carbohydrate 73.4g, of which sugars
45.6g; Fat 10.2g, of which saturates
3.1g; Cholesterol 165mg; Calcium
50mg; Fibre 1.5g; Sodium 816mg.

p246 Adobo Energy 672Kcal/2795kJ;
Protein 63.1g; Carbohydrate 2.4g, of
which sugars 2.4g; Fat 45.5g, of which
saturates 11.1g; Cholesterol 285mg;
Calcium 21mg; Fibre 0g; Sodium
477mg.

p247 Lion's Head Meat Balls Energy
611Kcal/2553kJ; Protein 45.3g;

Carbohydrate 34.2g, of which sugars
5.6g; Fat 33.5g, of which saturates
10.2g; Cholesterol 149mg; Calcium
61mg; Fibre 1.7g; Sodium 1482mg.

p248 Sweet and Sour Pork, Thai-style
Energy 214Kcal/894kJ; Protein 20.3g;
Carbohydrate 12.5g, of which sugars
11.9g; Fat 9.5g, of which saturates 2g;
Cholesterol 55mg; Calcium 34mg;
Fibre 2g; Sodium 337mg.

p249 Lemon Grass Pork Energy 12Kcal/
49kJ; Protein 1.5g; Carbohydrate 0.1g,
of which sugars 0.1g; Fat 0.6g, of
which saturates 0.2g; Cholesterol 4mg;
Calcium 1mg; Fibre 0g; Sodium 34mg.

p250 Pork and Pineapple Coconut Curry
Energy 191Kcal/807kJ; Protein 22.2g;
Carbohydrate 16.4g, of which sugars
16.3g; Fat 4.5g, of which saturates
1.6g; Cholesterol 63mg; Calcium 55mg;
Fibre 1.2g; Sodium 449mg.

p251 Cha Shao Energy 203Kcal/853kJ;
Protein 32.1g; Carbohydrate 3.5g, of
which sugars 3.5g; Fat 6g, of which
saturates 1.2g; Cholesterol 95mg; Calcium
11mg; Fibre 0g; Sodium 108mg.

p252 Curried Pork with Pickled Garlic
Energy 214Kcal/891kJ; Protein 14.6g;
Carbohydrate 8g, of which sugars 7.9g;
Fat 13.9g, of which saturates 2.4g;
Cholesterol 41mg; Calcium 37mg; Fibre
0g; Sodium 1046mg.

p253 Pork Chops with Field Mushrooms
Energy 339Kcal/1418kJ; Protein 39.7g;
Carbohydrate 2.3g, of which sugars 1g;
Fat 19.1g, of which saturates 4.1g;
Cholesterol 90mg; Calcium 26mg;
Fibre 1g; Sodium 618mg.

p254 Sweet-and-sour Pork Stir-fry
Energy 322Kcal/1348kJ; Protein 28g;
Carbohydrate 23.4g, of which sugars
13.7g; Fat 13.6g, of which saturates
2.7g; Cholesterol 71mg; Calcium 64mg;
Fibre 4g; Sodium 637mg.

p255 Stir-fried Pork with Dried Shrimp
Energy 202Kcal/843kJ; Protein 23.1g;
Carbohydrate 6.6g, of which sugars
6.2g; Fat 9.4g, of which saturates 1.7g;
Cholesterol 96mg; Calcium 377mg;
Fibre 3.8g; Sodium 554mg.

p256 Pork Belly with Five Spices
Energy 426Kcal/1774kJ; Protein 26.1g;
Carbohydrate 11g, of which sugars
10.6g; Fat 31.2g, of which saturates
9.8g; Cholesterol 89mg; Calcium 82mg;
Fibre 2.2g; Sodium 936mg.

p257 Puchero Energy 813Kcal/3393kJ;
Protein 53.4g; Carbohydrate 37.4g, of
which sugars 7.7g; Fat 51g, of which
saturates 14.3g; Cholesterol 89mg;
Calcium 82mg; Fibre 2.2g; Sodium
936mg.

p258 Pork on Lemon Grass Sticks
Energy 129Kcal/538kJ; Protein 14.5g;
Carbohydrate 1.4g, of which sugars
1.3g; Fat 7.3g, of which saturates 2.7g;
Cholesterol 50mg; Calcium 7mg;
Fibre 0g; Sodium 317mg.

**p259 Braised Beef in a Rich Peanut
Sauce** Energy 549Kcal/2307kJ; Protein
57.3g; Carbohydrate 36.9g, of which
sugars 11.7g; Fat 20.3g, of which
saturates 5.4g; Cholesterol 151mg;
Calcium 83mg; Fibre 3.9g; Sodium 505mg.

p260 Sliced Seared Beef Energy
216Kcal/904kJ; Protein 28.8g;
Carbohydrate 2.2g, of which sugars
1.8g; Fat 5.9g, of which saturates 1.9g;
Cholesterol 84mg; Calcium 12mg;
Fibre 0.2g; Sodium 977mg.

p262 Spicy Shredded Beef Energy
538Kcal/2229kJ; Protein 26.1g;
Carbohydrate 17.2g, of which saturates
14.1g; Fat 40.2g, of which saturates
7.1g; Cholesterol 69mg; Calcium 51mg;
Fibre 2.9g; Sodium 1136mg.

p263 Marinated Beef Steaks Energy
249Kcal/1039kJ; Protein 32.2g;
Carbohydrate 1.1g, of which sugars 1g;
Fat 12.8g, of which saturates 4.7g;
Cholesterol 92mg; Calcium 9mg;
Fibre 0g; Sodium 1015mg.

p264 Sizzling Steak Energy 518Kcal/
2157kJ; Protein 48.5g; Carbohydrate
8.9g, of which sugars 8.4g; Fat 30.4g,
of which saturates 9.1g; Cholesterol
137mg; Calcium 33mg; Fibre 0.4g;
Sodium 695mg.

**p265 Thick Beef Curry in Sweet Peanut
Sauce** Energy 310Kcal/1296kJ; Protein
29.1g; Carbohydrate 9.7g, of which
sugars 8.5g; Fat 17.4g, of which saturates
5.3g; Cholesterol 69mg; Calcium 59mg;
Fibre 1.2g; Sodium 215mg.

p266 Spicy Meat Balls Energy 343Kcal/
1423kJ; Protein 25.1g; Carbohydrate
6g, of which sugars 4.6g; Fat 24.4g, of
which saturates 8.5g; Cholesterol
86mg; Calcium 71mg; Fibre 0.9g;
Sodium 432mg.

p268 Chilli Sambal Energy 90Kcal/
374kJ; Protein 13.1g; Carbohydrate
3.1g, of which sugars 3.1g; Fat 2.7g, of
which saturates 0g; Cholesterol 0mg;
Calcium 136mg; Fibre 0g; Sodium
3962mg.

**p268 Green Beef Curry with Thai
Aubergines** Energy 226Kcal/949kJ;
Protein 24.7g; Carbohydrate 9.4g, of
which sugars 9.3g; Fat 10.2g, of which
saturates 3.8g; Cholesterol 69mg; Calcium
53mg; Fibre 0.8g; Sodium 393mg.

p269 Stir-fried Beef in Oyster Sauce
Energy 282Kcal/1177kJ; Protein 25.4g;

Carbohydrate 10.7g, of which sugars 3.4g; Fat 15.5g, of which saturates 4.2g; Cholesterol 69mg; Calcium 16mg; Fibre 0.8g; Sodium 697mg.

p270 Beef Rendang Energy 322Kcal/ 1356kJ; Protein 37.4g; Carbohydrate 20.1g, of which sugars 9.5g; Fat 10.8g, of which saturates 5g; Cholesterol 102mg; Calcium 58mg; Fibre 1.1g; Sodium 584mg.

p270 Deep-fried Onions Energy 738Kcal/3078kJ; Protein 10.4g; Carbohydrate 63.5g, of which saturates 45g; Fat 50.4g, of which saturates 4.5g; Cholesterol 0mg; Calcium 212mg; Fibre 13.9g; Sodium 18mg.

p272 Mussaman Curry Energy 500Kcal/ 2095kJ; Protein 44.3g; Carbohydrate 24.4g, of which sugars 14.7g; Fat 25.7g, of which saturates 15g; Cholesterol 113mg; Calcium 75mg; Fibre 1.7g; Sodium 749mg.

p273 Dry Beef Curry with Peanut and Lime Energy 406Kcal/1705kJ; Protein 55.4g; Carbohydrate 6.4g, of which sugars 5.9g; Fat 18g, of which saturates 5.1g; Cholesterol 170mg; Calcium 92mg; Fibre 0.6g; Sodium 812mg.

p274 Citrus Beef Curry Energy 452Kcal/1891kJ; Protein 35.4g; Carbohydrate 26.7g, of which sugars 15.5g; Fat 23.4g, of which saturates 5.1g; Cholesterol 75mg; Calcium 78mg; Fibre 4.1g; Sodium 270mg.

p275 Beef in Oyster Sauce Energy 171Kcal/717kJ; Protein 20g; Carbohydrate 8.3g, of which sugars 5.6g; Fat 6.6g, of which saturates 1.9g; Cholesterol 52mg; Calcium 28mg; Fibre 1.1g; Sodium 343mg.

p276 Beef Stew with Star Anise Energy 179Kcal/750kJ; Protein 26g; Carbohydrate 3.1g, of which sugars 2.4g; Fat 7g, of which saturates 2.7g; Cholesterol 71mg; Calcium 17mg; Fibre 0.5g; Sodium 1015mg.

p277 Minted Lamb Stir-fry Energy 487Kcal/2018kJ; Protein 31.8g; Carbohydrate 12.8g, of which sugars

10.5g; Fat 34.4g, of which saturates 10.7g; Cholesterol 103mg; Calcium 245mg; Fibre 3.9g; Sodium 991mg.

p278 Mongolian Firepot Energy 444Kcal/1852kJ; Protein 40.7g; Carbohydrate 17.2g, of which sugars 1.4g; Fat 22.6g, of which saturates 8.9g; Cholesterol 278mg; Calcium 236mg; Fibre 0.3g; Sodium 194mg.

p282 Fish Moolie Energy 287Kcal/ 1204kJ; Protein 21.3g; Carbohydrate 13g, of which sugars 12.3g; Fat 17.2g, of which saturates 8.2g; Cholesterol 18mg; Calcium 79mg; Fibre 2.1g; Sodium 493mg.

p283 Green Fish Curry Energy 584Kcal/ 2424kJ; Protein 40.7g; Carbohydrate 7.8g, of which sugars 4.3g; Fat 43.4g, of which saturates 7.7g; Cholesterol 0mg; Calcium 136mg; Fibre 1.1g; Sodium 736mg.

p284 Hoki Stir-fry Energy 276Kcal/ 1153kJ; Protein 33.8g; Carbohydrate 7.9g, of which sugars 5.9g; Fat 12.3g, of which saturates 2.3g; Cholesterol 0mg; Calcium 74mg; Fibre 3.4g; Sodium 709mg.

p285 Steamed Fish with Chilli Sauce Energy 123Kcal/519kJ; Protein 23.3g; Carbohydrate 0.8g, of which sugars 0.7g; Fat 3g, of which saturates 0.5g; Cholesterol 95mg; Calcium 158mg; Fibre 0.1g; Sodium 616mg.

p286 Steamed Fish with Five Willow Sauce Energy 321Kcal/1350kJ; Protein 45.3g; Carbohydrate 8.1g, of which sugars 6.6g; Fat 12.2g, of which saturates 2.4g; Cholesterol 168mg; Calcium 150mg; Fibre 2.6g; Sodium 784mg.

p288 Sea Bass with Ginger and Leeks Energy 297Kcal/1240kJ; Protein 35g; Carbohydrate 3g, of which sugars 2.7g; Fat 15.7g, of which saturates 3g; Cholesterol 140mg; Calcium 247mg; Fibre 1.3g; Sodium 196mg.

p289 Baked Sea Bass with Lemon Grass and Red Onions Energy 323Kcal/ 1347kJ; Protein 39.6g; Carbohydrate 5g, of which sugars 3.8g; Fat 16.1g, of which saturates 2.4g; Cholesterol 160mg; Calcium 275mg; Fibre 0.7g; Sodium 1208mg.

p290 Mohingha Energy 517Kcal/ 2156kJ; Protein 21.9g; Carbohydrate 58.7g, of which sugars 5.9g; Fat 20.9g, of which saturates 4.3g; Cholesterol 45mg; Calcium 54mg; Fibre 1.6g; Sodium 382mg.

p291 Escabeche Energy 268Kcal/ 1120kJ; Protein 22g; Carbohydrate 18.9g, of which sugars 4g; Fat 12.1g, of which saturates 1.5g; Cholesterol

52mg; Calcium 33mg; Fibre 0.9g; Sodium 253mg.

p292 Sweet and Sour Fish Energy 444Kcal/1856kJ; Protein 17.2g; Carbohydrate 39.7g, of which sugars 11.6g; Fat 25.2g, of which saturates 2.6g; Cholesterol 0mg; Calcium 78mg; Fibre 0.9g; Sodium 269mg.

p293 Paper-wrapped and Steamed Red Snapper Energy 161Kcal/676kJ; Protein 26.2g; Carbohydrate 1.3g, of which sugars 1.2g; Fat 2g, of which saturates 0.4g; Cholesterol 46mg; Calcium 68mg; Fibre 1g; Sodium 98mg.

p294 Marinated and Grilled Swordfish Energy 214Kcal/899kJ; Protein 34g; Carbohydrate 2.4g, of which sugars 2.3g; Fat 7.6g, of which saturates 1.7g; Cholesterol 72mg; Calcium 29mg; Fibre 1.3g; Sodium 1275mg.

p295 Grey Mullet with Pork Energy 229Kcal/962kJ; Protein 34.7g; Carbohydrate 0.7g, of which sugars 0.7g; Fat 9.8g, of which saturates 2.3g; Cholesterol 62mg; Calcium 46mg; Fibre 0.1g; Sodium 647mg.

p296 Hot and Fragrant Trout Energy 193Kcal/814kJ; Protein 28g; Carbohydrate 5.1g, of which sugars 5g; Fat 6.9g, of which saturates 1.4g; Cholesterol 89mg; Calcium 35mg; Fibre 0.4g; Sodium 340mg.

p297 Trout with Tamarind and Chilli Sauce Energy 193Kcal/813kJ; Protein 28.3g; Carbohydrate 2.8g, of which sugars 2.7g; Fat 7.7g, of which saturates 1.5g; Cholesterol 89mg; Calcium 38mg; Fibre 0.4g; Sodium 873mg.

p298 Trout with Black Rice Energy 584Kcal/2446kJ; Protein 46.5g; Carbohydrate 59.6g, of which sugars 2.3g; Fat 17.4g, of which saturates 3.1g; Cholesterol 134mg; Calcium 70mg; Fibre 0.9g; Sodium 1164mg.

p299 Thai-style Trout Energy 285Kcal/ 1202kJ; Protein 40.8g; Carbohydrate 6.4g, of which sugars 6.3g; Fat 11g, of which saturates 2.4g; Cholesterol 134mg; Calcium 137mg; Fibre 1.1g; Sodium 215mg.

p300 Chinese-style Steamed Trout Energy 282Kcal/1182kJ; Protein 34.4g; Carbohydrate 1.1g, of which sugars 1g; Fat 15g, of which saturates 3g; Cholesterol 111mg; Calcium 37mg; Fibre 0.1g; Sodium 444mg.

p301 Thai Marinated Sea Trout Energy 139Kcal/587kJ; Protein 21.3g; Carbohydrate 4.1g, of which sugars 4.1g; Fat 4.3g, of which saturates 0.1g; Cholesterol 0mg; Calcium 30mg; Fibre 0g; Sodium 253mg.

p302 Thai Fish en Papillote Energy 381Kcal/1588kJ; Protein 41.2g; Carbohydrate 2.5g, of which sugars 2.3g; Fat 23g, of which saturates 4g; Cholesterol 100mg; Calcium 58mg; Fibre 0.9g; Sodium 274mg.

p303 Salmon Marinated with Thai Spices Energy 484Kcal/2004kJ; Protein 25.7g; Carbohydrate 0.6g, of which sugars 0.5g; Fat 42.1g, of which saturates 6.7g; Cholesterol 91mg; Calcium 30mg; Fibre 0g; Sodium 716mg.

p304 Northern Fish Curry with Shallots and Lemon Grass Energy 212Kcal/882kJ; Protein 23.1g; Carbohydrate 1.7g, of which sugars 1.6g; Fat 12.5g, of which saturates 2.2g; Cholesterol 56mg; Calcium 28mg; Fibre 0.2g; Sodium 267mg.

p305 Asian Seared Salmon Energy 629Kcal/2633kJ; Protein 39g; Carbohydrate 51.6g, of which sugars 7.6g; Fat 31g, of which saturates 5.7g; Cholesterol 94mg; Calcium 61mg; Fibre 3.6g; Sodium 187mg.

p306 Mooli Layered with Smoked Salmon Energy 22Kcal/91kJ; Protein 3.7g; Carbohydrate 0.3g, of which sugars 0.3g; Fat 0.7g, of which saturates 0.1g; Cholesterol 5mg; Calcium 11mg; Fibre 0.1g; Sodium 1232mg.

p307 Salmon Teriyaki Energy 314Kcal/1308kJ; Protein 31.5g; Carbohydrate 2.4g, of which sugars 2g; Fat 16.6g, of which saturates 2.9g; Cholesterol 75mg; Calcium 43mg; Fibre 0.6g; Sodium 871mg.

p310 Sinigang Energy 94Kcal/396kJ; Protein 17.7g; Carbohydrate 3.1g, of which sugars 2.7g; Fat 1.3g, of which saturates 0.2g; Cholesterol 76mg; Calcium 96mg; Fibre 1.8g; Sodium 348mg.

p311 Stir-fried Prawns with Noodles Energy 312Kcal/1299kJ; Protein 11.8g; Carbohydrate 35.8g, of which sugars 8.2g; Fat 13.3g, of which saturates 2.4g; Cholesterol 73mg; Calcium 52mg; Fibre 1.1g; Sodium 524mg.

p312 Stir-fried Prawns with Tamarind Energy 185Kcal/776kJ; Protein 20.6g; Carbohydrate 9.7g, of which sugars 8.4g; Fat 7.4g, of which saturates 0.9g; Cholesterol 219mg; Calcium 102mg; Fibre 0.7g; Sodium 393mg.

p313 Salt and Pepper Prawns Energy 253Kcal/1054kJ; Protein 26.6g; Carbohydrate 1.6g, of which sugars 1.1g; Fat 15.6g, of which saturates 1.9g; Cholesterol 293mg; Calcium 124mg; Fibre 0.3g; Sodium 1596mg.

p314 Satay Prawns Energy 321Kcal/1340kJ; Protein 24.6g;

Carbohydrate 13.5g, of which sugars 11.9g; Fat 19.1g, of which saturates 3.6g; Cholesterol 219mg; Calcium 122mg; Fibre 1.2g; Sodium 794mg.

p316 Sambal Goreng with Prawns Energy 144Kcal/605kJ; Protein 16.7g; Carbohydrate 5.7g, of which sugars 4.9g; Fat 6.3g, of which saturates 0.8g; Cholesterol 171mg; Calcium 87mg; Fibre 1.4g; Sodium 356mg.

p317 Fried Prawn Balls Energy 71Kcal/ 293kJ; Protein 2.1g; Carbohydrate 2.0g, of which sugars 0g; Fat 5.6g, of which saturates 0.7g; Cholesterol 21mg; Calcium 9mg; Fibre 0g; Sodium 60mg.

p318 Green Prawn Curry Energy 152Kcal/636kJ; Protein 20.2g; Carbohydrate 3.6g, of which sugars 3.5g; Fat 6.4g, of which saturates 0.9g; Cholesterol 219mg; Calcium 110mg; Fibre 0.1g; Sodium 550mg.

p319 Prawns with Yellow Curry Paste Energy 173Kcal/728kJ; Protein 20.3g; Carbohydrate 8.6g, of which sugars 8.6g; Fat 6.6g, of which saturates 1.1g; Cholesterol 219mg; Calcium 134mg; Fibre 0g; Sodium 877mg.

p320 Curried Seafood with Coconut Milk Energy 230Kcal/971kJ; Protein 39.9g; Carbohydrate 6.3g, of which sugars 5.6g; Fat 5.2g, of which saturates 0.9g; Cholesterol 288mg; Calcium 97mg; Fibre 0.2g; Sodium 614mg.

p322 Chinese-style Scallops and Prawns Energy 194Kcal/818kJ; Protein 36.3g; Carbohydrate 7.8g, of which sugars 3.3g; Fat 2.1g, of which saturates 0.5g; Cholesterol 270mg; Calcium 122mg; Fibre 1g; Sodium 877mg.

p323 Sotong Sambal Energy 543Kcal/ 2274kJ; Protein 50.5g; Carbohydrate 19.6g, of which sugars 15.3g; Fat 29.9g, of which saturates 4.1g; Cholesterol 483mg; Calcium 149mg; Fibre 1.8g; Sodium 517mg.

p324 Stir-fried Squid with Ginger Energy 168Kcal/704kJ; Protein 19.9g; Carbohydrate 5.1g, of which sugars 3.5g; Fat 7.7g, of which saturates 1.2g; Cholesterol 281mg; Calcium 24mg; Fibre 0.2g; Sodium 1207mg.

p325 Squid in Clove Sauce Energy 303Kcal/1271kJ; Protein 35.5g; Carbohydrate 7g, of which sugars 3.6g; Fat 15g, of which saturates 3g; Cholesterol 506mg; Calcium 41mg; Fibre 0.9g; Sodium 609mg.

p326 Deep-fried Small Prawns and Corn Energy 412Kcal/1721kJ; Protein 17.4g; Carbohydrate 35.3g, of which sugars 2.8g; Fat 23.3g, of which saturates

3.3g; Cholesterol 211mg; Calcium 1160mg; Fibre 2g; Sodium 190mg.

p327 Chilli Crabs Energy 308Kcal/ 1286kJ; Protein 14.4g; Carbohydrate 19.1g, of which sugars 18.6g; Fat 19.9g, of which saturates 2.3g; Cholesterol 37mg; Calcium 30mg; Fibre 0.4g; Sodium 1227mg.

p328 Crab and Tofu Stir-fry Energy 370Kcal/1532kJ; Protein 23.3g; Carbohydrate 6.2g, of which sugars 5.1g; Fat 28.1g, of which saturates 3.3g; Cholesterol 41mg; Calcium 720mg; Fibre 1.2g; Sodium 2487mg.

p329 Crisp-fried Crab Claws Energy 360Kcal/1500kJ; Protein 13.7g; Carbohydrate 26.7g, of which sugars 9.8g; Fat 22.3g, of which saturates 2.9g; Cholesterol 98mg; Calcium 90mg; Fibre 0.3g; Sodium 711mg.

p330 Crab Meat in Vinegar Energy 79Kcal/331kJ; Protein 13.3g; Carbohydrate 4.8g, of which sugars 4.6g; Fat 0.8g, of which saturates 0.1g; Cholesterol 50mg; Calcium 99mg; Fibre 0.8g; Sodium 559mg.

p331 Clams and Spring Onions with Miso and Mustard Sauce Energy 81Kcal/344kJ; Protein 12.6g; Carbohydrate 6.9g, of which sugars 5.3g; Fat 0.6g, of which saturates 0.2g; Cholesterol 50mg; Calcium 65mg; Fibre 0.3g; Sodium 1583mg.

p332 Pan-steamed Mussels with Thai Herbs Energy 66Kcal/282kJ; Protein 13.1g; Carbohydrate 0.2g, of which sugars 0.2g; Fat 1.5g, of which saturates 0.3g; Cholesterol 30mg; Calcium 148mg; Fibre 0g; Sodium 336mg.

p333 Mussels and Clams with Lemon Grass and Coconut Cream Energy 177Kcal/745kJ; Protein 21.8g; Carbohydrate 1.9g, of which sugars 1.2g; Fat 7.8g, of which saturates 5.3g; Cholesterol 58mg; Calcium 212mg; Fibre 0.3g; Sodium 594mg.

p336 Thai Vegetable Curry with Lemon Grass Rice Energy 441Kcal/1867kJ; Protein 11.2g; Carbohydrate 91g, of

which sugars 33g; Fat 6.1g, of which saturates 1.4g; Cholesterol 58mg; Calcium 212mg; Fibre 0.3g; Sodium 594mg.

p338 Vegetable Forest Curry Energy 107Kcal/448kJ; Protein 11g; Carbohydrate 11.3g, of which sugars 9.4g; Fat 2.2g, of which saturates 0.5g; Cholesterol 0mg; Calcium 129mg; Fibre 6.8g; Sodium 1427mg.

p339 Braised Aubergine and Courgettes Energy 49Kcal/206kJ; Protein 1.5g; Carbohydrate 4g, of which sugars 3.4g; Fat 3.2g, of which saturates 0.4g; Cholesterol 0mg; Calcium 18mg; Fibre 2.1g; Sodium 448mg.

p340 Braised Tofu with Mushrooms Energy 116Kcal/483kJ; Protein 9.6g; Carbohydrate 1.7g, of which sugars 1g; Fat 7.5g, of which saturates 1g; Cholesterol 0mg; Calcium 456mg; Fibre 1.4g; Sodium 456mg.

p341 Tofu and Green Bean Red Curry Energy 110Kcal/460kJ; Protein 5.7g; Carbohydrate 10.2g, of which sugars 9.6g; Fat 5.5g, of which saturates 0.9g; Cholesterol 0mg; Calcium 282mg; Fibre 1.3g; Sodium 437mg.

p342 Aubergine and Sweet Potato Stew with Coconut Milk Energy 236Kcal/ 992kJ; Protein 3.5g; Carbohydrate 30.2g, of which sugars 12.4g; Fat 12.2g, of which saturates 2.2g; Cholesterol 0mg; Calcium 65mg; Fibre 5g; Sodium 210mg.

p344 Sweet Pumpkin and Peanut Curry Energy 292Kcal/1218kJ; Protein 8.4g; Carbohydrate 22.2g, of which sugars 11.2g; Fat 19.5g, of which saturates 3.3g; Cholesterol 0mg; Calcium 87mg; Fibre 4.3g; Sodium 768mg.

p345 Corn and Cashew Nut Curry Energy 342Kcal/1431kJ; Protein 8.7g; Carbohydrate 38.4g, of which sugars 12g; Fat 18.1g, of which saturates 3.2g; Cholesterol 0mg; Calcium 37mg; Fibre 3.5g; Sodium 564mg.

p346 Tofu and Vegetable Thai Curry Energy 210Kcal/873kJ; Protein 11g; Carbohydrate 15.1g, of which sugars 13.3g; Fat 12g, of which saturates 1.8g; Cholesterol 0mg; Calcium 328mg; Fibre 5g; Sodium 927mg.

p348 Snake Beans with Tofu Energy 263Kcal/1091kJ; Protein 14.5g; Carbohydrate 13.3g, of which sugars 10g; Fat 17.2g, of which saturates 3g; Cholesterol 0mg; Calcium 335mg; Fibre 4.7g; Sodium 1353mg.

p349 Mushrooms with Garlic and Chilli Sauce Energy 40Kcal/167kJ; Protein 3.6g; Carbohydrate 4.5g, of which sugars 4.1g; Fat 1g, of which saturates

0.2g; Cholesterol 0mg; Calcium 14mg; Fibre 2.1g; Sodium 1035mg.

p350 Aubergine and Pepper Tempura with Sweet Chilli Dip Energy 442Kcal/1856kJ; Protein 9.5g; Carbohydrate 57.7g, of which sugars 9.6g; Fat 20.9g, of which saturates 3.1g; Cholesterol 101mg; Calcium 122mg; Fibre 6.2g; Sodium 859mg.

p352 Stuffed Sweet Peppers Energy 100Kcal/417kJ; Protein 5.5g; Carbohydrate 12g, of which sugars 11.3g; Fat 3.6g, of which saturates 0.8g; Cholesterol 55mg; Calcium 29mg; Fibre 3.9g; Sodium 388mg.

p353 Sweet and Sour Vegetables with Tofu Energy 177Kcal/736kJ; Protein 10.5g; Carbohydrate 13.7g, of which sugars 12.5g; Fat 9.2g, of which saturates 1.5g; Cholesterol 0mg; Calcium 461mg; Fibre 4.3g; Sodium 844mg.

p354 Stir-fried Crispy Tofu Energy 510Kcal/2122kJ; Protein 33.5g; Carbohydrate 18.8g, of which sugars 17.2g; Fat 33.9g, of which saturates 2.2g; Cholesterol 0mg; Calcium 1893mg; Fibre 2.2g; Sodium 1085mg.

p355 Stir-fried Seeds and Vegetables Energy 248Kcal/1030kJ; Protein 7.6g; Carbohydrate 12g, of which sugars 9.2g; Fat 19.1g, of which saturates 2.5g; Cholesterol 0mg; Calcium 238mg; Fibre 3.2g; Sodium 743mg.

p358 Coconut Rice Energy 457Kcal/ 1947kJ; Protein 8.6g; Carbohydrate 102.4g, of which sugars 5.8g; Fat 4.4g, of which saturates 1.3g; Cholesterol 0mg; Calcium 92mg; Fibre 0.5g; Sodium 381mg.

p359 Indonesian Coconut Rice Energy 357Kcal/1521kJ; Protein 6.7g; Carbohydrate 80g, of which sugars 4.9g; Fat 3.5g, of which saturates 0.2g; Cholesterol 0mg; Calcium 74mg; Fibre 0.4g; Sodium 114mg.

p360 Festive Rice Energy 285Kcal/ 1204kJ; Protein 4.6g; Carbohydrate 52.6g, of which sugars 3.8g; Fat 7.7g, of which saturates 0.7g; Cholesterol 0mg; Calcium 49mg; Fibre 0.6g; Sodium 58mg.

p361 Indonesian Pineapple Fried Rice Energy 954Kcal/4042kJ; Protein 33.3g; Carbohydrate 169.2g, of which sugars 22.3g; Fat 20.8g, of which saturates 2.7g; Cholesterol 92mg; Calcium 160mg; Fibre 3.8g; Sodium 587mg.

p362 Chicken and Basil Coconut Rice Energy 583Kcal/2458kJ; Protein 28.9g; Carbohydrate 80.7g, of which sugars 4.2g; Fat 18.3g, of which saturates 8.7g; Cholesterol 61mg; Calcium 67mg; Fibre 1.2g; Sodium 62mg.

p363 Savoury Fried Rice Energy 548Kcal/2271kJ; Protein 14.6g; Carbohydrate 25.1g, of which sugars 7g; Fat 43.9g, of which saturates 18.2g; Cholesterol 110mg; Calcium 183mg; Fibre 7.5g; Sodium 1200mg.

p364 Rice Omelette Energy 336Kcal/1403kJ; Protein 19.3g; Carbohydrate 21.5g, of which sugars 3.7g; Fat 19.7g, of which saturates 8.4g; Cholesterol 383mg; Calcium 87mg; Fibre 0.4g; Sodium 829mg.

p365 Curried Chicken and Rice Energy 1024Kcal/4293kJ; Protein 54.9g; Carbohydrate 96.7g, of which sugars 0g; Fat 49g, of which saturates 10.7g; Cholesterol 248mg; Calcium 74mg; Fibre 0.5g; Sodium 1360mg.

p366 Thai Fried Rice Energy 573Kcal/2423kJ; Protein 25.4g; Carbohydrate 91.6g, of which sugars 11.2g; Fat 14.2g, of which saturates 2.5g; Cholesterol 154mg; Calcium 102mg; Fibre 1.7g; Sodium 269mg.

p367 Fried Rice with Pork Energy 513Kcal/2165kJ; Protein 17.1g; Carbohydrate 80g, of which sugars 2.1g; Fat 16.1g, of which saturates 2.3g; Cholesterol 132mg; Calcium 75mg; Fibre 0.7g; Sodium 511mg.

p368 Congee with Chinese Sausage Energy 427Kcal/1796kJ; Protein 12.7g; Carbohydrate 55.2g, of which sugars 0.9g; Fat 18.9g, of which saturates 6.7g; Cholesterol 130mg; Calcium 70mg; Fibre 0.5g; Sodium 939mg.

p369 Fried Rice with Beef Energy 250Kcal/1048kJ; Protein 17.9g; Carbohydrate 22.4g, of which sugars 2.8g; Fat 10.4g, of which saturates 3g; Cholesterol 84mg; Calcium 60mg; Fibre 1.7g; Sodium 859mg.

p370 Nasi Goreng Energy 602Kcal/2523kJ; Protein 36.2g; Carbohydrate 55.3g, of which sugars 2.4g; Fat 27.6g, of which saturates 4.6g; Cholesterol 232mg; Calcium 85mg; Fibre 0.6g; Sodium 698mg.

p371 Fragrant Harbour Fried Rice Energy 587Kcal/2457kJ; Protein 25g; Carbohydrate 57.2g, of which sugars 3.5g; Fat 30.2g, of which saturates 6.5g; Cholesterol 199mg; Calcium 105mg; Fibre 2.3g; Sodium 936mg.

p372 Chinese Jewelled Rice Energy 522Kcal/2208kJ; Protein 22.4g; Carbohydrate 83.8g, of which sugars 5.5g; Fat 13.2g, of which saturates 2.2g; Cholesterol 48mg; Calcium 123mg; Fibre 2.7g; Sodium 714mg.

p373 Chinese Fried Rice Energy 367Kcal/1536kJ; Protein 14.9g;

Carbohydrate 38g, of which sugars 1.2g; Fat 18.2g, of which saturates 3.3g; Cholesterol 203mg; Calcium 68mg; Fibre 1.6g; Sodium 997mg.

p374 Fried Jasmine Rice with Prawns and Thai Basil Energy 567Kcal/2394kJ; Protein 31.5g; Carbohydrate 81.6g, of which sugars 2.4g; Fat 15g, of which saturates 2.6g; Cholesterol 143mg; Calcium 243mg; Fibre 1.4g; Sodium 1577mg.

p375 Malacca Fried Rice Energy 443Kcal/1856kJ; Protein 37.6g; Carbohydrate 35.5g, of which sugars 3g; Fat 17.8g, of which saturates 3.7g; Cholesterol 286mg; Calcium 100mg; Fibre 3g; Sodium 996mg.

p378 Mee Goreng Energy 643Kcal/2702kJ; Protein 21.2g; Carbohydrate 88.1g, of which sugars 6.2g; Fat 25.2g, of which saturates 5g; Cholesterol 148mg; Calcium 249mg; Fibre 3.9g; Sodium 637mg.

p379 Plain Noodles with Four Flavours Energy 55Kcal/236kJ; Protein 2g; Carbohydrate 11.6g, of which sugars 0.4g; Fat 0.5g, of which saturates 0.1g; Cholesterol 5mg; Calcium 5mg; Fibre 0.5g; Sodium 191mg.

p380 Sweet and Hot Vegetable Noodles Energy 249Kcal/1040kJ; Protein 5g; Carbohydrate 43.3g, of which sugars 15.3g; Fat 6.1g, of which saturates 1.2g; Cholesterol 0mg; Calcium 58mg; Fibre 2.9g; Sodium 943mg.

p381 Sichuan Noodles with Sesame Sauce Energy 546Kcal/2283kJ; Protein 14.1g; Carbohydrate 58.5g, of which sugars 5.3g; Fat 30g, of which saturates 4.9g; Cholesterol 23mg; Calcium 158mg; Fibre 5.2g; Sodium 509mg.

p382 Mee Krob Energy 1293Kcal/5362kJ; Protein 28.8g; Carbohydrate 109.1g, of which sugars 2g; Fat 80.5g, of which saturates 10.6g; Cholesterol 509mg; Calcium 733mg; Fibre 0.4g; Sodium 1180mg.

p384 Noodles and Vegetables in Coconut Sauce Energy 293Kcal/1235kJ; Protein 8.9g; Carbohydrate 44.7g, of which sugars 17.3g; Fat 10g, of which saturates 2.1g; Cholesterol 11mg; Calcium 131mg; Fibre 4.2g; Sodium 1007mg.

p385 Southern Curried Noodles Energy 709Kcal/2989kJ; Protein 29.5g; Carbohydrate 102.1g, of which sugars 14.6g; Fat 23.1g, of which saturates 4.8g; Cholesterol 69mg; Calcium 251mg; Fibre 5.5g; Sodium 1666mg.

p386 Chiang Mai Noodles Energy 360Kcal/1501kJ; Protein 26.8g; Carbohydrate 25.4g, of which sugars

6.7g; Fat 16.6g, of which saturates 12.1g; Cholesterol 118mg; Calcium 22mg; Fibre 1.4g; Sodium 281mg.

p387 Thai Noodles with Chinese Chives Energy 551Kcal/2299kJ; Protein 23.3g; Carbohydrate 82.3g, of which sugars 7.1g; Fat 13.1g, of which saturates 1.5g; Cholesterol 0mg; Calcium 470mg; Fibre 5g; Sodium 1221mg.

p388 Bamie Goreng Energy 542Kcal/2277kJ; Protein 29.2g; Carbohydrate 54.2g, of which sugars 1.8g; Fat 24.8g, of which saturates 6.4g; Cholesterol 245mg; Calcium 89mg; Fibre 2.7g; Sodium 300mg.

p389 Noodles with Chicken, Prawns and Ham Energy 474Kcal/2001kJ; Protein 39.1g; Carbohydrate 57.8g, of which sugars 5.9g; Fat 11.2g, of which saturates 2.6g; Cholesterol 179mg; Calcium 92mg; Fibre 4.2g; Sodium 1548mg.

p390 Special Chow Mein Energy 624Kcal/2631kJ; Protein 29.3g; Carbohydrate 84.5g, of which sugars 4.6g; Fat 21.2g, of which saturates 4.2g; Cholesterol 107mg; Calcium 76mg; Fibre 4.8g; Sodium 808mg.

p391 Lamb and Ginger Stir-fry with Egg Noodles Energy 367Kcal/1532kJ; Protein 26.9g; Carbohydrate 15.9g, of which sugars 5.9g; Fat 22.2g, of which saturates 7.3g; Cholesterol 90mg; Calcium 153mg; Fibre 3.7g; Sodium 223mg.

p392 Cellophane Noodles with Pork Energy 720Kcal/3009kJ; Protein 29.4g; Carbohydrate 99.9g, of which sugars 15.4g; Fat 21.6g, of which saturates 5.1g; Cholesterol 66mg; Calcium 58mg; Fibre 2.4g; Sodium 1933mg.

p393 Stir-fried Pork with Mushrooms Energy 264Kcal/1106kJ; Protein 26.8g; Carbohydrate 14.3g, of which sugars 13g; Fat 10.6g, of which saturates 2.5g; Cholesterol 71mg; Calcium 67mg; Fibre 3g; Sodium 86mg.

p394 Pork Chow Mein Energy 407Kcal/1709kJ; Protein 26.7g; Carbohydrate 38.4g, of which sugars 6.8g; Fat 16g,

of which saturates 3.5g; Cholesterol 68mg; Calcium 44mg; Fibre 3.6g; Sodium 682mg.

p395 Steamboat Energy 365Kcal/1528kJ; Protein 39.3g; Carbohydrate 23.3g, of which sugars 0.2g; Fat 12.2g, of which saturates 2.6g; Cholesterol 364mg; Calcium 283mg; Fibre 0g; Sodium 416mg.

p396 Five-flavour Noodles Energy 231Kcal/975kJ; Protein 16.5g; Carbohydrate 29.2g, of which sugars 12.2g; Fat 6.2g, of which saturates 1.2g; Cholesterol 32mg; Calcium 79mg; Fibre 3.9g; Sodium 737mg.

p397 Rice Noodles with Pork Energy 464Kcal/1941kJ; Protein 29.6g; Carbohydrate 54.4g, of which sugars 8.3g; Fat 13.6g, of which saturates 3.4g; Cholesterol 71mg; Calcium 68mg; Fibre 1.9g; Sodium 450mg.

p398 Cantonese Fried Noodles Energy 719Kcal/3004kJ; Protein 36.3g; Carbohydrate 52.5g, of which sugars 7.1g; Fat 41.8g, of which saturates 6.2g; Cholesterol 84mg; Calcium 195mg; Fibre 6.6g; Sodium 1301mg.

p399 Spicy Fried Noodles Energy 570Kcal/2391kJ; Protein 38.5g; Carbohydrate 48.9g, of which sugars 8.7g; Fat 25.9g, of which saturates 5.1g; Cholesterol 241mg; Calcium 73mg; Fibre 2.5g; Sodium 700mg.

p400 Chap Chae Energy 302Kcal/1262kJ; Protein 19.3g; Carbohydrate 30.1g, of which sugars 5.3g; Fat 11.5g, of which saturates 3g; Cholesterol 144mg; Calcium 47mg; Fibre 1.7g; Sodium 351mg.

p401 Sukiyaki Energy 465Kcal/1965kJ; Protein 67.7g; Carbohydrate 23.1g, of which sugars 12.7g; Fat 12.1g, of which saturates 3.9g; Cholesterol 235mg; Calcium 248mg; Fibre 1.7g; Sodium 2106mg.

p402 Thai Crispy Noodles with Beef Energy 493Kcal/2052kJ; Protein 29.5g; Carbohydrate 43.4g, of which sugars 7.2g; Fat 21.9g, of which saturates 5.7g; Cholesterol 65mg; Calcium 43mg; Fibre 2g; Sodium 1697mg.

p403 Mixed Meat Fried Noodles with Prawns Energy 515Kcal/2163kJ; Protein 24.2g; Carbohydrate 54.2g, of which sugars 1.8g; Fat 24g, of which saturates 6.2g; Cholesterol 168mg; Calcium 87mg; Fibre 2.7g; Sodium 282mg.

p404 Crispy Fried Rice Vermicelli Energy 494Kcal/2063kJ; Protein 14g; Carbohydrate 59.2g, of which sugars 22.8g; Fat 22.4g, of which saturates 3.4g; Cholesterol 75mg; Calcium 48mg; Fibre 0.5g; Sodium 738mg.

p406 Stir-fried Noodles in Seafood Sauce Energy 263Kcal/1109kJ; Protein 19.5g; Carbohydrate 30.8g, of which sugars 4.5g; Fat 7.7g, of which saturates 1.4g; Cholesterol 65mg; Calcium 116mg; Fibre 2g; Sodium 644mg.

p407 Stir-fried Noodles with Soy Salmon Energy 569Kcal/2380kJ; Protein 31.8g; Carbohydrate 41.9g, of which sugars 2.5g; Fat 29g, of which saturates 5.4g; Cholesterol 73mg; Calcium 118mg; Fibre 2.5g; Sodium 690mg.

p408 Thai Fried Noodles Energy 580Kcal/2416kJ; Protein 21.2g; Carbohydrate 76g, of which sugars 2.7g; Fat 20g, of which saturates 3.1g; Cholesterol 169mg; Calcium 256mg; Fibre 1.6g; Sodium 647mg.

p412 Broccoli with Soy Sauce Energy 47Kcal/197kJ; Protein 5.2g; Carbohydrate 2.7g, of which sugars 2.2g; Fat 1.8g, of which saturates 0.3g; Cholesterol 0mg; Calcium 64mg; Fibre 2.9g; Sodium 543mg.

p413 Stir-fried Beansprouts Energy 77Kcal/322kJ; Protein 3.8g; Carbohydrate 6.4g, of which sugars 4g; Fat 3.8g, of which saturates 0.5g; Cholesterol 0mg; Calcium 29mg; Fibre 2.2g; Sodium 523mg.

p414 Stir-fried Chinese Leaves Energy 71Kcal/294kJ; Protein 4.8g; Carbohydrate 3.8g, of which sugars 3.6g; Fat 4.1g, of which saturates 0.5g; Cholesterol 0mg; Calcium 288mg; Fibre 3.6g; Sodium 543mg.

p415 Sautéed Green Beans Energy 56Kcal/232kJ; Protein 2.5g; Carbohydrate 4.3g, of which sugars 3.2g; Fat 3.4g, of which saturates 0.5g; Cholesterol 0mg; Calcium 46mg; Fibre 2.7g; Sodium 268mg.

p416 Sichuan Spiced Aubergine Energy 149Kcal/616kJ; Protein 1.6g; Carbohydrate 3.8g, of which sugars 3.5g; Fat 14.3g, of which saturates 1.8g; Cholesterol 0mg; Calcium 16mg; Fibre 3g; Sodium 939mg.

p416 Kan Shao Green Beans Energy 179Kcal/735kJ; Protein 1.5g; Carbohydrate 3.2g, of which sugars 2.6g; Fat 17.9g, of which saturates 2.2g; Cholesterol 0mg; Calcium 28mg; Fibre 1.7g; Sodium 119mg.

p418 Fragrant Mushrooms in Lettuce Leaves Energy 133Kcal/548kJ; Protein 3.1g; Carbohydrate 3.4g, of which sugars 3g; Fat 12g, of which saturates 1.5g; Cholesterol 0mg; Calcium 37mg; Fibre 2g; Sodium 1076mg.

p419 Thai Asparagus Energy 120Kcal/492kJ; Protein 4.1g; Carbohydrate 2.4g, of which sugars 2.3g; Fat 10.4g, of which saturates 1.4g; Cholesterol 0mg; Calcium 75mg; Fibre 2.1g; Sodium 537mg.

p420 Pak Choi with Lime Dressing Energy 79Kcal/329kJ; Protein 1.8g; Carbohydrate 4.5g, of which sugars 4.4g; Fat 6.1g, of which saturates 0.8g; Cholesterol 0mg; Calcium 99mg; Fibre 1.2g; Sodium 398mg.

p421 Steamed Morning Glory with Fried Garlic and Shallots Energy 64Kcal/263kJ; Protein 1.3g; Carbohydrate 1.4g, of which sugars 1.2g; Fat 5.9g, of which saturates 0.7g; Cholesterol 0mg; Calcium 92mg; Fibre 1.5g; Sodium 9mg.

p422 Stir-fried Pineapple with Ginger Energy 110Kcal/467kJ; Protein 1g; Carbohydrate 20.8g, of which sugars 20.8g; Fat 3.2g, of which saturates 0.3g; Cholesterol 0mg; Calcium 37mg; Fibre 2.4g; Sodium 538mg.

p423 Southern-style Yam Energy 89Kcal/368kJ; Protein 4.2g; Carbohydrate 4.1g, of which sugars 3.4g; Fat 6.3g, of which saturates 3.4g; Cholesterol 0mg; Calcium 90mg; Fibre 2g; Sodium 1122mg.

p424 Fried Vegetables with Nam Prik Energy 90Kcal/378kJ; Protein 10.1g; Carbohydrate 8.4g, of which sugars 7.1g; Fat 2g, of which saturates 0.4g; Cholesterol 0mg; Calcium 111mg; Fibre 6.3g; Sodium 1010mg.

p425 Steamed Vegetables with Chiang Mai Spicy Dip Energy 70Kcal/295kJ; Protein 6.8g; Carbohydrate 8.1g, of which sugars 7.2g; Fat 1.4g, of which saturates 0.3g; Cholesterol 0mg; Calcium 73mg; Fibre 4.7g; Sodium 1005mg.

p426 Singapore Rice Vermicelli Energy 317Kcal/1327kJ; Protein 14.1g; Carbohydrate 51.3g, of which sugars 5.1g; Fat 5.6g, of which saturates 1.1g; Cholesterol 122mg; Calcium 50mg; Fibre 1.7g; Sodium 728mg.

p427 Brown Rice with Lime and Lemon Grass Energy 241Kcal/1021kJ; Protein 4.4g; Carbohydrate 48.7g, of which sugars 2.7g; Fat 4.6g, of which saturates 0.8g; Cholesterol 0mg; Calcium 15mg; Fibre 1.6g; Sodium 213mg.

p428 Kimchi Energy 55Kcal/229kJ; Protein 3.4g; Carbohydrate 8.5g, of which sugars 8.4g; Fat 1g, of which saturates 0.1g; Cholesterol 0mg; Calcium 199mg; Fibre 3.8g; Sodium 1732mg.

p429 Hot Thai Pickled Shallots Energy 129Kcal/551kJ; Protein 3.9g; Carbohydrate 29.2g, of which sugars 29.2g; Fat 0.5g, of which saturates 0g; Cholesterol 0mg; Calcium 71mg; Fibre 3.5g; Sodium 1991mg.

p430 Sambal Nanas Energy 29Kcal/125kJ; Protein 3g; Carbohydrate 4.2g, of which sugars 4.1g; Fat 0.2g, of which saturates 0g; Cholesterol 25mg; Calcium 69mg; Fibre 0.5g; Sodium 218mg.

p431 Coconut and Peanut Relish and Hot Chilli and Garlic Dipping Sauce Energy 2139Kcal/8846kJ; Protein 51.9g; Carbohydrate 42g, of which sugars 34.3g; Fat 197.1g, of which saturates 81.9g; Cholesterol 0mg; Calcium 123mg; Fibre 27.1g; Sodium 5007mg.

p434 Fruit and Raw Vegetable Gado-gado Energy 490Kcal/2043kJ; Protein 18.9g; Carbohydrate 28.5g, of which sugars 21g; Fat 34.3g, of which saturates 8.6g; Cholesterol 116mg; Calcium 80mg; Fibre 6.2g; Sodium 493mg.

p435 Exotic Fruit and Vegetable Salad Energy 288Kcal/1204kJ; Protein 15.4g; Carbohydrate 18.5g, of which sugars 13.6g; Fat 17.5g, of which saturates 4.5g; Cholesterol 161mg; Calcium 118mg; Fibre 4.5g; Sodium 431mg.

p436 Green Papaya Salad Energy 63Kcal/263kJ; Protein 2.5g; Carbohydrate 6.2g, of which sugars 5.6g; Fat 3.3g, of which saturates 0.6g; Cholesterol 0mg; Calcium 19mg; Fibre 1.8g; Sodium 835mg.

p437 Thai Fruit and Vegetable Salad Energy 159Kcal/673kJ; Protein 3.5g; Carbohydrate 32.2g, of which sugars 31g; Fat 2.7g, of which saturates 1.7g; Cholesterol 0mg; Calcium 69mg; Fibre 4.7g; Sodium 188mg.

p438 Sweet and Sour Salad Energy 43Kcal/186kJ; Protein 0.7g; Carbohydrate 10.2g, of which sugars 10g; Fat 0.3g, of which saturates 0.1g; Cholesterol 0mg; Calcium 18mg; Fibre 1.4g; Sodium 5mg.

p439 Hot and Sour Noodle Salad Energy 761Kcal/3173kJ; Protein 24.1g; Carbohydrate 101.6g, of which sugars 15.6g; Fat 27.7g, of which saturates 5.2g; Cholesterol 0mg; Calcium 117mg; Fibre 7.9g; Sodium 1840mg.

p440 Bamboo Shoot Salad Energy 80Kcal/336kJ; Protein 4.5g; Carbohydrate 9.4g, of which sugars 2.9g; Fat 2.8g, of which saturates 0.4g; Cholesterol 0mg; Calcium 51mg; Fibre 2g; Sodium 185mg.

p441 Cabbage Salad Energy 124Kcal/513kJ; Protein 3.4g; Carbohydrate 7.1g, of which sugars 6.5g; Fat 9.2g, of which saturates 1.4g; Cholesterol 0mg; Calcium 57mg; Fibre 2.3g; Sodium 306mg.

p442 Fried Egg Salad Energy 215Kcal/894kJ; Protein 14.2g; Carbohydrate 2.4g, of which sugars 2.2g; Fat 16.9g, of which saturates 4.2g; Cholesterol 381mg; Calcium 112mg; Fibre 0.8g; Sodium 1223mg.

p443 Tangy Chicken Salad Energy 404Kcal/1691kJ; Protein 40.4g; Carbohydrate 11.3g, of which sugars 9g; Fat 22.3g, of which saturates 9.8g; Cholesterol 105mg; Calcium 25mg; Fibre 0.8g; Sodium 666mg.

p444 Saeng Wa of Grilled Pork Energy 170Kcal/718kJ; Protein 22g; Carbohydrate 12.2g, of which sugars 12.1g; Fat 4g, of which saturates 1.4g; Cholesterol 63mg; Calcium 16mg; Fibre 0.2g; Sodium 873mg.

p445 Beef and Mushroom Salad Energy 381Kcal/1588kJ; Protein 39.7g; Carbohydrate 4g, of which sugars 3.8g; Fat 23g, of which saturates 6.6g; Cholesterol 103mg; Calcium 105mg; Fibre 2.4g; Sodium 352mg.

p446 Larp of Chiang Mai Energy 135Kcal/572kJ; Protein 27.4g; Carbohydrate 3.4g, of which sugars 0.4g; Fat 1.3g, of which saturates 0.4g; Cholesterol 79mg; Calcium 8mg; Fibre 0.1g; Sodium 424mg.

p446 Thai Beef Salad Energy 161Kcal/674kJ; Protein 26.9g; Carbohydrate 1.8g, of which sugars 1.4g; Fat 5.1g, of which saturates 2.3g; Cholesterol 57mg; Calcium 14mg; Fibre 0.3g; Sodium 347mg.

p448 Aubergine Salad Energy 90Kcal/376kJ; Protein 7.2g; Carbohydrate 4.7g, of which sugars 4.3g; Fat 4.9g, of which saturates 0.9g; Cholesterol 86mg; Calcium 113mg; Fibre 3g; Sodium 612mg.

p449 Rice Salad Energy 404Kcal/1689kJ; Protein 16.1g; Carbohydrate

36.7g, of which sugars 8.5g; Fat 22.4g, of which saturates 2.6g; Cholesterol 63mg; Calcium 247mg; Fibre 4g; Sodium 550mg.

p450 Scented Fish Salad Energy 304Kcal/1269kJ; Protein 17.6g; Carbohydrate 11.7g, of which sugars 11.6g; Fat 21.1g, of which saturates 3.6g; Cholesterol 0mg; Calcium 89mg; Fibre 2.6g; Sodium 88mg.

p452 Seafood Salad with Fruity Dressing Energy 135Kcal/568kJ; Protein 22.3g; Carbohydrate 4.6g, of which sugars 4.3g; Fat 3.1g, of which saturates 0.5g; Cholesterol 100mg; Calcium 173mg; Fibre 1.5g; Sodium 359mg.

p452 Turbot Sashimi Salad with Wasabi Energy 231Kcal/960kJ; Protein 18.4g; Carbohydrate 1.6g, of which sugars 1.6g; Fat 16.9g, of which saturates 2.8g; Cholesterol 0mg; Calcium 73mg; Fibre 0.8g; Sodium 563mg.

p454 Pomelo Salad Energy 159Kcal/ 665kJ; Protein 13.4g; Carbohydrate 8.4g, of which sugars 8.1g; Fat 8.2g, of which saturates 1.1g; Cholesterol 44mg; Calcium 107mg; Fibre 1.1g; Sodium 1004mg.

p455 Piquant Prawn Salad Energy 412Kcal/1717kJ; Protein 25g; Carbohydrate 43.1g, of which sugars 1.8g; Fat 14.8g, of which saturates 2.4g; Cholesterol 219mg; Calcium 139mg; Fibre 1.5g; Sodium 702mg.

p456 Thai Prawn Salad with Garlic Dressing and Frizzled Shallots Energy 292Kcal/1222kJ; Protein 33.5g; Carbohydrate 13.4g, of which sugars 11.8g; Fat 11.9g, of which saturates 2g; Cholesterol 329mg; Calcium 160mg; Fibre 2.7g; Sodium 596mg.

p460 Fried Bananas Energy 462Kcal/ 1930kJ; Protein 6.2g; Carbohydrate 53.4g, of which sugars 29.2g; Fat 26.2g, of which saturates 3.4g; Cholesterol 48mg; Calcium 83mg; Fibre 2.3g; Sodium 21mg.

p461 Coconut Pancakes Energy 183Kcal/763kJ; Protein 2.9g; Carbohydrate 23.1g, of which sugars 6.9g; Fat 9g, of which saturates 4.1g; Cholesterol 24mg; Calcium 33mg; Fibre 1.4g; Sodium 49mg.

p462 Banana Fritters Energy 236Kcal/ 988kJ; Protein 2.5g; Carbohydrate 32.3g, of which sugars 15.9g; Fat 11.4g, of which saturates 1.4g; Cholesterol 0mg; Calcium 56mg; Fibre 1.4g; Sodium 176mg.

p462 Black Glutinous Rice Pudding Energy 135Kcal/568kJ; Protein 1.7g; Carbohydrate 31.8g, of which sugars

17.4g; Fat 0.3g, of which saturates 0g; Cholesterol 0mg; Calcium 12mg; Fibre 0g; Sodium 2mg.

p464 Thai Fried Pineapple Energy 228Kcal/960kJ; Protein 1.1g; Carbohydrate 33.7g, of which sugars 33.7g; Fat 10.9g, of which saturates 7.2g; Cholesterol 21mg; Calcium 42mg; Fibre 2.6g; Sodium 66mg.

p465 Coconut Rice Pudding Energy 257Kcal/1077kJ; Protein 5.4g; Carbohydrate 34.5g, of which sugars 19.9g; Fat 11.5g, of which saturates 8.2g; Cholesterol 19mg; Calcium 153mg; Fibre 1g; Sodium 153mg.

p466 Tropical Fruit Gratin Energy 331Kcal/1399kJ; Protein 6.2g; Carbohydrate 56.7g, of which sugars 56.6g; Fat 8.7g, of which saturates 2.4g; Cholesterol 302mg; Calcium 117mg; Fibre 4.7g; Sodium 23mg.

p466 Grilled Pinapple with Papaya Sauce Energy 148Kcal/626kJ; Protein 0.8g; Carbohydrate 29.6g, of which sugars 29.6g; Fat 3.7g, of which saturates 2.2g; Cholesterol 9mg; Calcium 39mg; Fibre 2.5g; Sodium 53mg.

p468 Tapioca Pudding Energy 325Kcal/ 1388kJ; Protein 1g; Carbohydrate 84.9g, of which sugars 57.4g; Fat 0.4g, of which saturates 0.2g; Cholesterol 0mg; Calcium 51mg; Fibre 1.8g; Sodium 74mg.

p469 Baked Rice Pudding, Thai-style Energy 292Kcal/1226kJ; Protein 8.8g; Carbohydrate 52.7g, of which sugars 19.9g; Fat 5.2g, of which saturates 1.4g; Cholesterol 143mg; Calcium 70mg; Fibre 0g; Sodium 185mg.

p470 Stewed Pumpkin in Coconut Cream Energy 246Kcal/1051kJ; Protein 2.5g; Carbohydrate 60.4g, of which sugars 59.2g; Fat 1.1g, of which saturates 0.6g; Cholesterol 0mg; Calcium 150mg; Fibre 2.5g; Sodium 209mg.

p470 Mangoes with Sticky Rice Energy 200Kcal/846kJ; Protein 3.1g; Carbohydrate 46g, of which sugars 24.3g; Fat 0.8g, of which saturates 0.2g; Cholesterol 0mg; Calcium 32mg; Fibre 2g; Sodium 51mg.

p472 Exotic Fruit Sushi Energy 347Kcal/ 1483kJ; Protein 4.5g; Carbohydrate 83.3g, of which sugars 50.9g; Fat 2g, of which saturates 0.7g; Cholesterol 0mg; Calcium 82mg; Fibre 3.5g; Sodium 121mg.

p473 Papaya Baked with Ginger Energy 360Kcal/1505kJ; Protein 3.4g; Carbohydrate 41.7g, of which sugars 37.2g; Fat 21.1g, of which saturates

11.1g; Cholesterol 41mg; Calcium 82mg; Fibre 4.3g; Sodium 94mg.

p474 Lemon Grass Skewers with Lime Cheese Energy 400Kcal/1674kJ; Protein 7g; Carbohydrate 44.7g, of which sugars 44.6g; Fat 23.3g, of which saturates 14.5g; Cholesterol 60mg; Calcium 94mg; Fibre 2.6g; Sodium 239mg.

p474 Coconut Jelly with Star Anise Fruits Energy 178Kcal/759kJ; Protein 1.1g; Carbohydrate 45.3g, of which sugars 45.3g; Fat 0.4g, of which saturates 0.2g; Cholesterol 0mg; Calcium 60mg; Fibre 1.2g; Sodium 113mg.

p476 Churros Energy 73Kcal/302kJ; Protein 0.9g; Carbohydrate 5.4g, of which sugars 0.6g; Fat 5.4g, of which saturates 0.7g; Cholesterol 10mg; Calcium 10mg; Fibre 0.2g; Sodium 45mg.

p476 Leche Flan Energy 275Kcal/ 1161kJ; Protein 10.4g; Carbohydrate 39.4g, of which sugars 39.4g; Fat 9.6g, of which saturates 4.6g; Cholesterol 162mg; Calcium 232mg; Fibre 0g; Sodium 163mg.

p478 Coconut Custard Energy 161Kcal/ 681kJ; Protein 6.5g; Carbohydrate 22.7g, of which sugars 22.7g; Fat 5.7g, of which saturates 1.7g; Cholesterol 190mg; Calcium 57mg; Fibre 0g; Sodium 140mg.

p479 Coconut Cream Diamonds Energy 252Kcal/1067kJ; Protein 3.4g; Carbohydrate 44.2g, of which sugars 28.1g; Fat 8.2g, of which saturates 4.9g; Cholesterol 21mg; Calcium 95mg; Fibre 1.2g; Sodium 110mg.

p480 Papayas in Jasmine Flower Syrup Energy 215Kcal/914kJ; Protein 1.9g; Carbohydrate 54.3g, of which sugars 54.3g; Fat 0.4g, of which saturates 0g; Cholesterol 0mg; Calcium 93mg; Fibre 7.7g; Sodium 19mg.

p481 Steamed Custard in Nectarines Energy 150Kcal/637kJ; Protein 5g; Carbohydrate 29.7g, of which sugars 29.7g; Fat 2.2g, of which saturates 0.6g; Cholesterol 67mg; Calcium 32mg; Fibre 2.4g; Sodium 36mg.

p482 Green and Yellow Layered Cakes Energy 160Kcal/673kJ; Protein 8.6g; Carbohydrate 19.5g, of which sugars 16.4g; Fat 5.9g, of which saturates 1.7g; Cholesterol 193mg; Calcium 44mg; Fibre 1.6g; Sodium 71mg.

p483 Thai Rice Cake Energy 595Kcal/ 2483kJ; Protein 12.3g; Carbohydrate 51.8g, of which sugars 27.7g; Fat 39.2g, of which saturates 22.7g; Cholesterol 232mg; Calcium 233mg; Fibre 0.1g; Sodium 125mg.

p484 Cold Mango Soufflés Topped with Toasted Coconut Energy 612Kcal/ 2552kJ; Protein 4.7g; Carbohydrate 53.9g, of which sugars 53.4g; Fat 43.5g, of which saturates 26.2g; Cholesterol 194mg; Calcium 117mg; Fibre 3.9g; Sodium 38mg.

p485 Mango and Lime Fool Energy 269Kcal/1118kJ; Protein 2.8g; Carbohydrate 15.2g, of which sugars 14.9g; Fat 22.6g, of which saturates 13.8g; Cholesterol 51mg; Calcium 64mg; Fibre 2.6g; Sodium 26mg.

p486 Exotic Fruit Salad with Passion Fruit Dressing Energy 61Kcal/258kJ; Protein 0.9g; Carbohydrate 13.5g, of which sugars 13.4g; Fat 0.7g, of which saturates 0.1g; Cholesterol 0mg; Calcium 21mg; Fibre 2.4g; Sodium 6mg.

p487 Watermelon Ice Energy 128Kcal/ 545kJ; Protein 0.8g; Carbohydrate 32.4g, of which sugars 32.4g; Fat 0.4g, of which saturates 0.1g; Cholesterol 0mg; Calcium 21mg; Fibre 0.1g; Sodium 4mg.

p488 Iced Fruit Mountain Energy 109Kcal/464kJ; Protein 2.1g; Carbohydrate 25.8g, of which sugars 25.8g; Fat 0.5g, of which saturates 0.1g; Cholesterol 0mg; Calcium 61mg; Fibre 2.6g; Sodium 10mg.

p488 Chinese Honeyed Apples Energy 674Kcal/2824kJ; Protein 4.8g; Carbohydrate 87.7g, of which sugars 60g; Fat 36.2g, of which saturates 4.4g; Cholesterol 0mg; Calcium 49mg; Fibre 2.7g; Sodium 45mg.

p490 Malaysian Coconut Ice Cream Energy 335Kcal/1421kJ; Protein 6g; Carbohydrate 66.4g, of which sugars 66.4g; Fat 6.9g, of which saturates 4.3g; Cholesterol 24mg; Calcium 226mg; Fibre 0g; Sodium 332mg.

p491 Coconut and Lemon Grass Ice Cream Energy 787Kcal/3261kJ; Protein 9.6g; Carbohydrate 30.9g, of which sugars 30.9g; Fat 70.5g, of which saturates 41.6g; Cholesterol 391mg; Calcium 115mg; Fibre 0g; Sodium 145mg.

FOOD AND SHOPPING

AUSTRALIA

Asian Supermarkets Pty Ltd
116 Charters Towers Road
Townsville, QLD 4810
Tel: (07) 4772 3997
Fax: (07) 4771 3919

Burlington Supermarkets
Chinatown Mall
Fortitude Valley, QLD 4006
Tel: (07) 3216 1828

Duc Hung Long Asian Foodstore
95 The Crescent
Fairfield, NSW 2165
Tel: (02) 9728 1092

Exotic Asian Groceries
  Q Supercentre
Cnr Market and Bermuda
  Streets
Mermaid Waters, QLD 4218
Tel: (07) 5572 8188

Harris Farm Markets
Sydney Markets
Flemongton, NSW 2140
Tel: (02) 9746 2055

Kongs Trading Pty Ltd
8 Kingscote Street
Kewdale, WA 6105
Tel: (08) 9353 3380
Fax: (08) 9353 3390

PK Supermarkets Pty Ltd
369 Victoria Avenue
Chatswood, NSW 2067
Tel: (02) 9419 8822

Saigon Asian Food Retail
  and Wholesale
6 Cape Street
Dickson, ACT 2602
Tel: (02) 6247 4251

The Spice and Herb
  Asian Shop
200 Old Cleveland Road
Capalaba, QLD 4157
Tel: (07) 3245 5300

Sydney Fish Market Pty Ltd
Cnr Pyrmont Bridge Road and
  Bank Street
Pyrmont, NSW 2009
Tel: (02) 9660 1611

UNITED KINGDOM

Arigato
48–50 Brewer Street
London W1R 3HM
Tel: 020 7287 1722

Golden Gate Cake Shop
13 Macclesfield Street
London W1V 7LH
Tel: 020 7287 9862

Golden Gate Supermarket
16 Newport Place
London WC2H 7JS
Tel: 020 7437 6266

Golden Gate Hong Kong Ltd
14 Lisle Street
London WC2 7BE
Tel: 020 7437 0014

Good Harvest Fish Market
14 Newport Place
London WC2H 7PR
Tel: 020 7437 0712

Hong Kong Supermarket
62 High Street
London SW4 7UL
Tel: 020 7720 2069

Hopewell Emporium
2f Dyne Road
London NW6 7XB
Tel: 020 7624 5473

Loon Fung Supermarket
42–44 Gerrard Street
London W1V 7LP
Tel: 020 7437 7332

Manila Supermarket
11–12 Hogarth Place
London SW5 0QT
Tel: 020 7373 8305

Miah, A. and Co
20 Magdalen Street
Norwich NR3 1HE
Tel: 01603 615395

Miura Japanese Foods
44 Coombe Road
Nr Kingston KT2 7AF
Tel: 020 8549 8076

also at
5 Limpsfield Road
Sanderstead
Surrey CR2 9LA
Tel: 020 8651 4498

Natural House
Japan Centre
212 Piccadilly
London W1V 9LD
Tel: 020 7434 4218

New Peking Supermarket
59 Westbourne Grove
London W2 4UA
Tel: 020 7928 8770

Newport Supermarket
28–29 Newport Court
London WC2H 7PQ
Tel: 020 7437 2386

Oriental City
399 Edgware Road
London NW9 0JJ
Tel: 020 8200 0009

Rum Wong Supermarket
London Road
Guildford
Surrey GU1 2AF
Tel: 01483 451 568

S. W. Trading Ltd
Horn Lane
Greenwich
London SE10 0RT
Tel: 020 8293 9393

Sri Thai
56 Shepherd's Bush Road
London W6 7PH
Tel: 020 7602 0621

Talad Thai Ltd
320 Upper Richmond Road
London SW15 6TL
Tel: 020 8789 8084

Tawana
18–20 Chepstow Road
London W2 5BD
Tel: 020 7221 6316

Wang Thai Supermarket
101 Kew Road
Richmond, Surrey TW9 2PN
Tel: 020 8332 2959

The Wing On Department
  Store (Hong Kong) Ltd
37–38 Margaret Street
London W1N 7FA
Tel: 020 7580 3677

Wing Tai
11a Aylesham Centre
Rye Lane, London SE15 5EW
Tel: 020 7635 0714

Wing Yip
395 Edgware Road
London NW2 6LN
Tel: 020 7450 0422

also at
Oldham Road
Ancoats
Manchester M4 5HU
Tel: 0161 832 3215

T.K. Trading
Unit 6/7
The Chase Centre
Chase Road
London NW10 6QD
Tel: 020 8453 1001

UNITED STATES

Ai Hoa
860 North Hill Street
Los Angeles, CA 90026
Tel (213) 482-48

Asian Food Market
6450 Market Street
Upper Darby, PA 19082
Tel: (610) 352-4433

Asian Foods, Etc.
1375 Prince Avenue
Atlanta, GA 30341
Tel: (404) 543-8624

Asian Foods Ltd.
260-280 West Lehigh
   Avenue
Philadelphia, PA 19133
Tel: (215) 291-9500

Asian Market
2513 Stewart Avenue
Las Vegas, NV 89101
Tel: (702) 387-3373

Asian Market
18815 Eureka Road
South Gate, MI 48195
Fax: (734) 246-4795
www.asianmarket.qpg.com

Augusta Market Oriental Foods
2117 Martin Luther King Jr.
   Boulevard
Altanta, GA 30901
Tel: (706) 722-4988

Bachri's Chili & Spice Gourmet
5617 Villa Haven
Pittsburgh, PA 15236
Tel: (412) 831-1131
Fax: (412) 831-2542

Bangkok Market
4757 Melrose Avenue
Los Angeles, CA 90029
Tel: (203) 662-7990

Bharati Food & Spice Center
6163 Reynolds Road Suite G
Morrow, GA 30340
Tel: (770) 961-9007

First Asian Food Center
3420 East Ponce De Leon
   Avenue
Scottsdale, GA 30079
Tel: (404) 292-6508

The House of Rice Store
3221 North Hayden Road
Scottsdale, AZ 85251
Tel: (480) 947-6698

Han Me Oriental Food & Gifts
2 E. Derenne Avenue
Savannah, GA 31405
Tel: (912) 355-6411

Hong Tan Oriental Food
2802 Capitol Street
Savannah, GA 31404
Tel: (404) 233-9184

Huy Fong Foods Inc.
5001 Earle Avenue
Rosemead, CA 91770
Tel: (626) 286-8328
Fax: (626) 286-8522

Khanh Tam Oriental Market
4051 Buford Highway NE
Atlanta, GA 30345
Tel: (404) 728-0393

May's American Oriental Market
422 West University Avenue
Saint Paul, MN 55103
Tel: (651) 293-1118

Modern Thai Incorporated
135 Yacht Club Way #210
Hypuluxo, FL 33462
Tel: (888) THAI-8888

Norcross Oriental Market
6062 Norcross-Tucker Road
Chamblee, GA 30341
Tel: (770) 496-1656

Oriental Grocery
11827 Del Amo Boulevard
Cerritos, CA 90701
Tel: (310) 924-1029

Oriental Market
670 Central Park Avenue
Yonkers, NY 10013
(212) 349-1979

The Oriental Pantry
423 Great Road
Acton, MA 01720
Tel: (978) 264-4576

Saigon Asian Market
10090 Central Avenue
Biloxi, MS 39532
Tel: (228) 392-8044
Fax: (228) 392-8039
www.saigonor.qpg.com

Siam Market
27266 East Baseline Street
Highland, CA 92346
Tel: (909) 862-8060

Thai Market
3297 Las Vegas Boulevard
Las Vegas, NV 89030
Tel: (702) 643-8080

Thai Market
916 Harrelson Street
Fort Walton Beach, FL 32547
Tel: (904) 863-2013

Thai Number One Market
5927 Cherry Avenue
Long Beach, CA 90805
Tel: (310) 422-6915

Thai-Lao Market
1721 West La Palma
   Avenue
Anaheim, CA 92801
Tel: (714) 535-2656

Unimart American and Asian
   Groceries
1201 Howard Street
San Francisco, CA 94103
Tel: (415) 431-0362

INDEX

Author Acknowledgements
Sallie Morris would like to thank her family:
Johnnie, Alex and James for their support;
Beryl Castles for her help in typing the
manuscript; Beth Ware for advice on recipes
from the Philippines; Rupert Welchman
for his advice on Japanese recipes; John
Phengsiri at the Wang Thai Supermarket in
Richmond; Bart's Spices Ltd; Cherry Valley
Farms (Tel: 01472 371 271), who supplied
ducklings for recipe testing; Ken the Fishman
from Grimsby (Tel: 0860 240 213), and
Magimix (Tel: 01483 427 411) for supplying
a food processor, ice-cream maker and
electric steamer for recipe testing.

Deh-Ta Hsiung would like to thank Sallie
Morris and Emi Kazuko for their advice
and help in writing about South-east
Asian and Japanese foods.

Thanks also to the following people and
organizations for their invaluable help in

researching this book: Charles Bradley,
Pat Checkley (Tourist Authority of Thailand),
Jonathan Hart, Chris Lee, Alissra Sinclair-
Knopp (Language and Culture Consultant,
The Thai Consulting Group), The Tourist
Authority of Thailand, The Thai Embassy
and a special thank you to Prisana Smith of
the Tam Nak Thai Restaurant, 50–54 Westow
Hill, London, SE19 1RX who has been an
invaluable source of advice and information.
Special thanks also to Clare Spurrell for
her assistance with research and her
editorial contribution.

Picture Acknowledgements
All photographs are by Nicki Dowey and
Janine Hosegood, except the following:
Tony Stone p8t (Glen Allison), 12 (Ron
Dahlquist); Cephas Picture Library p8b,
9t (Alain Proust), 9b (Nigel Blythe),
10b, 11t, 11b; Japanese Information
and Cultural Centre, Embassy of Japan,
London p10t.